American Corporate Identity
2007

American Corporate Identity 2007

David E. Carter

COLLINS | DESIGN
An Imprint of HarperCollins*Publishers*

AMERICAN CORPORATE IDENTITY 2007

HarperCollins books may be purchased for educational, business, or sales promotional use. For information, please write: Special Markets Department, HarperCollins Publishers Inc., 10 East 53rd Street, New York, NY 10022.

First Edition

First published in 2006 by:
Collins Design
An Imprint of HarperCollins*Publishers*
10 East 53rd Street
New York, NY 10022
Tel: (212) 207-7000
Fax: (212) 207-7654
collinsdesign@harpercollins.com
www.harpercollins.com

Distributed throughout the world by:
HarperCollinsPublishers
10 East 53rd Street
New York, NY 10022
Fax: (212) 207-7654

Book and competition design by
Designs on You!

Library of Congress Control Number: 2006925217

ISBN-10: 0-06-113742-1
ISBN-13: 978-0-06-113742-6

Printed in China by Everbest Printing Company through Crescent Hill Books, Louisville, Kentucky.

First Printing, 2006

Table of Contents

Complete Corporate Identity Systems

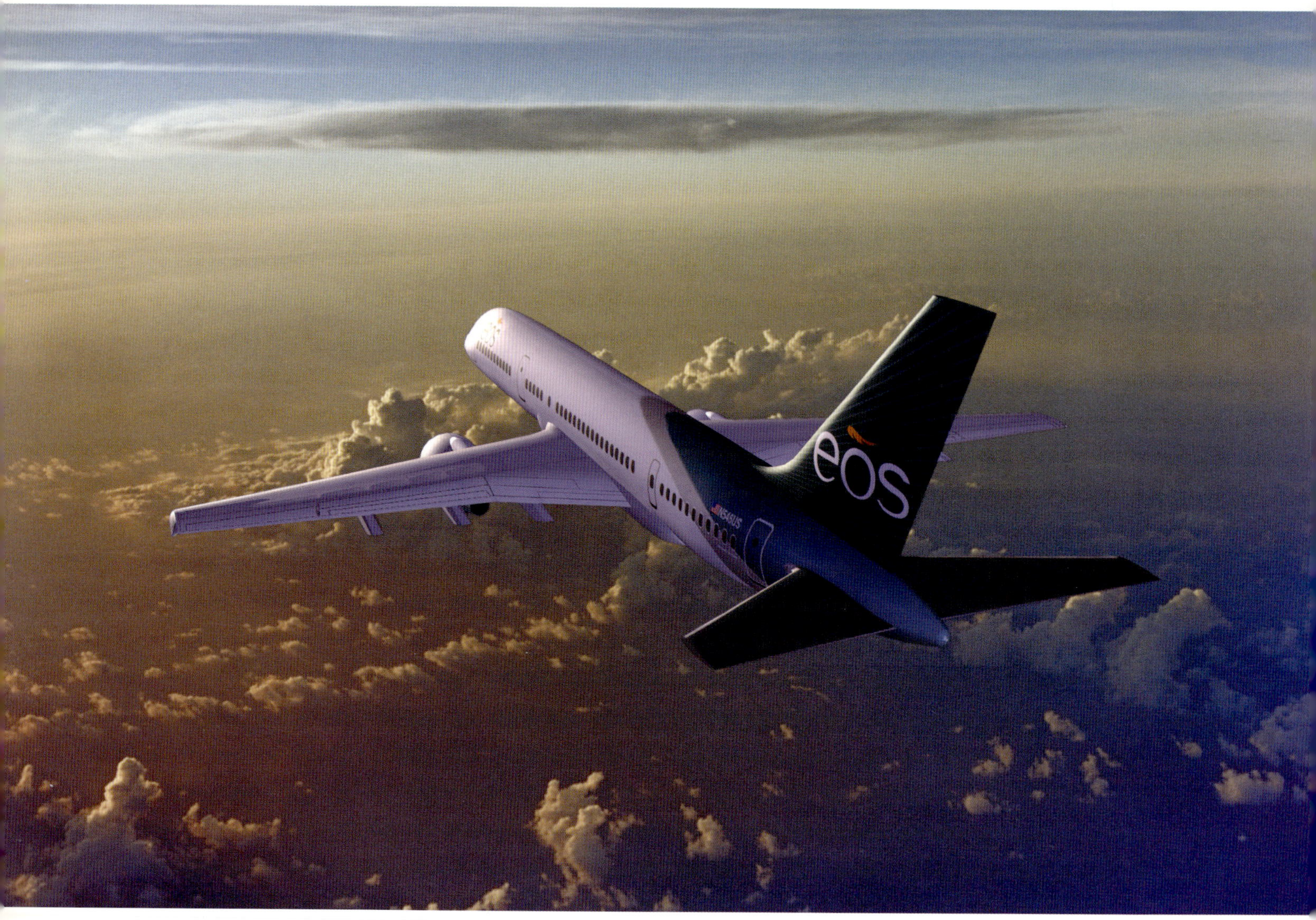
eos

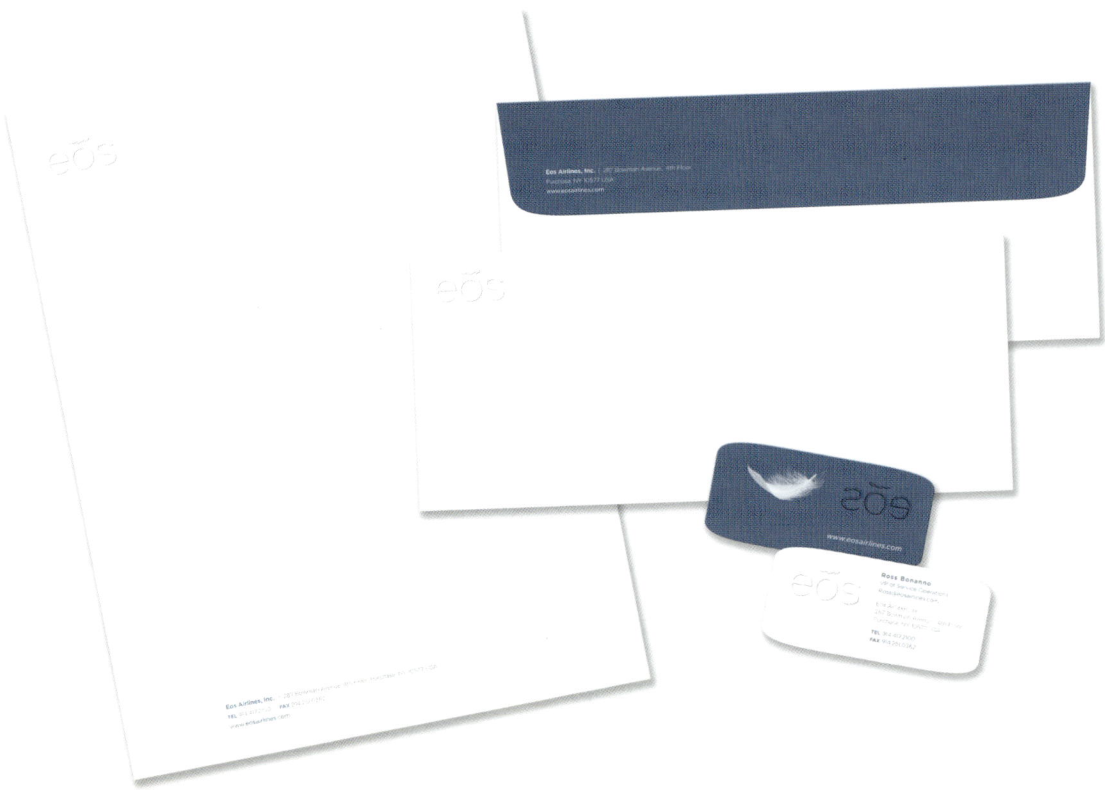

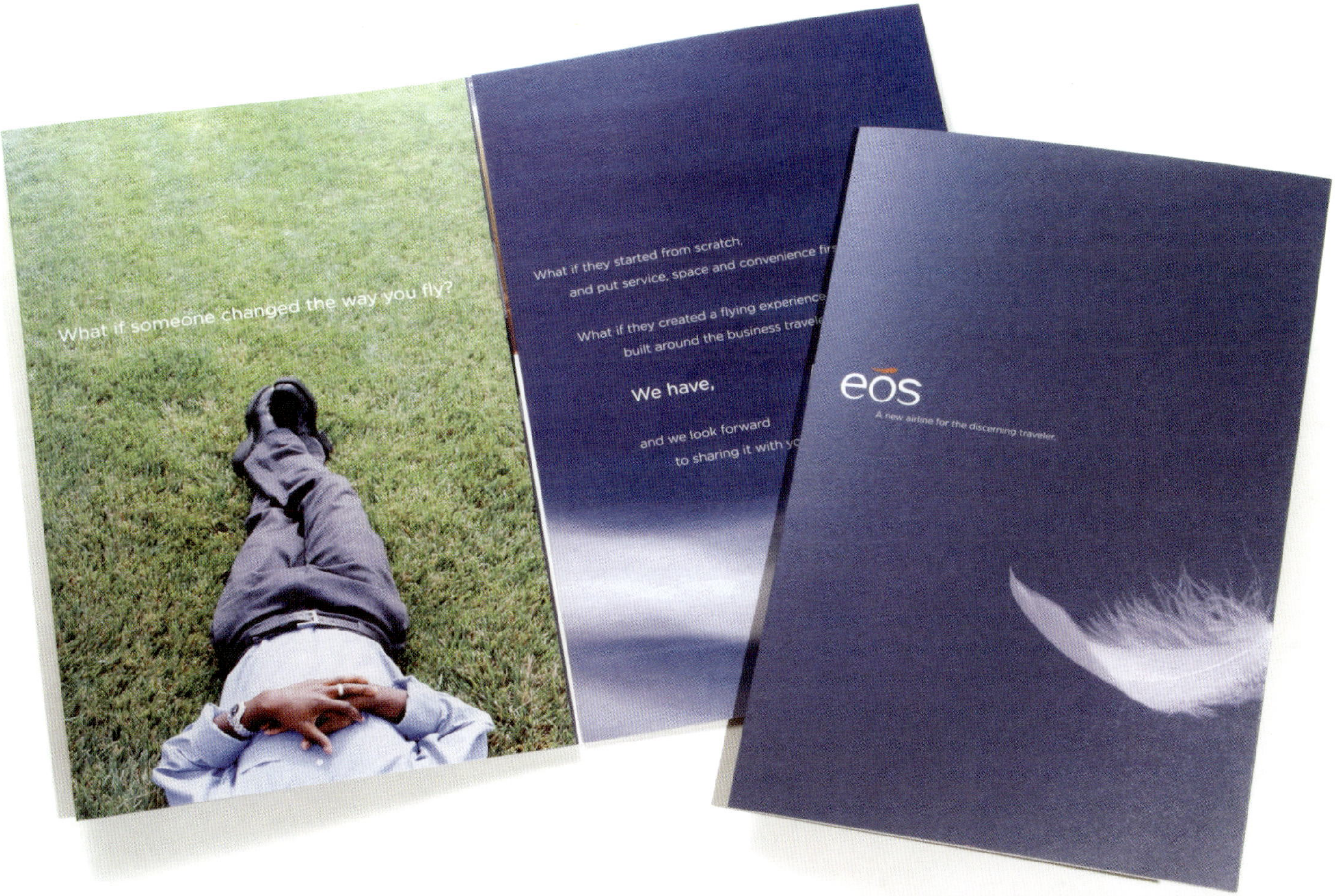

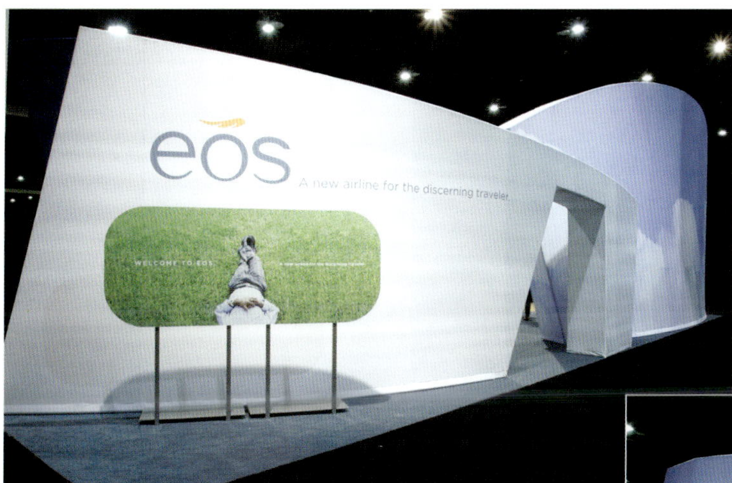

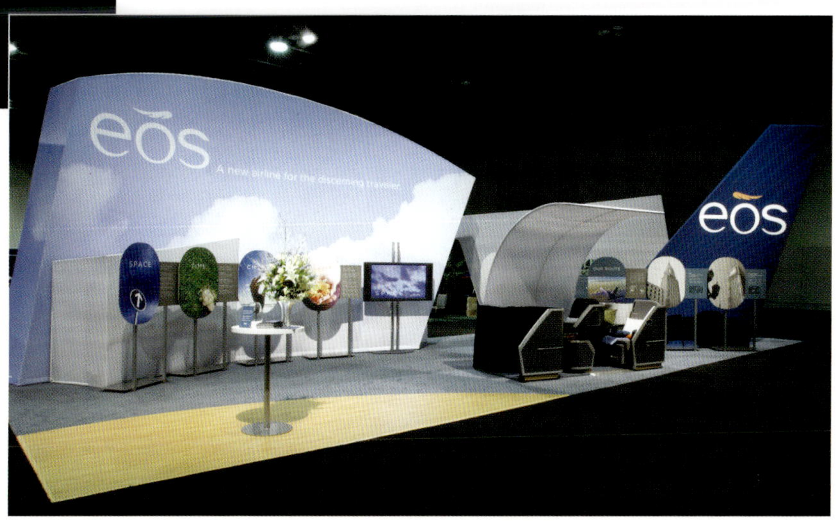

client
Eos Airlines
design firm
Hornall Anderson Design Works
designers
Jack Anderson, Mark Popich,
David Bates, Andrew Wicklund,
Jacob Carter, Leo Raymundo,
Hans Krebs, Yuri Shvets,
Jamie Monberg, Michele Godfrey,
Joe King, Nathan Young, Don Kenoyer

Brand Engine

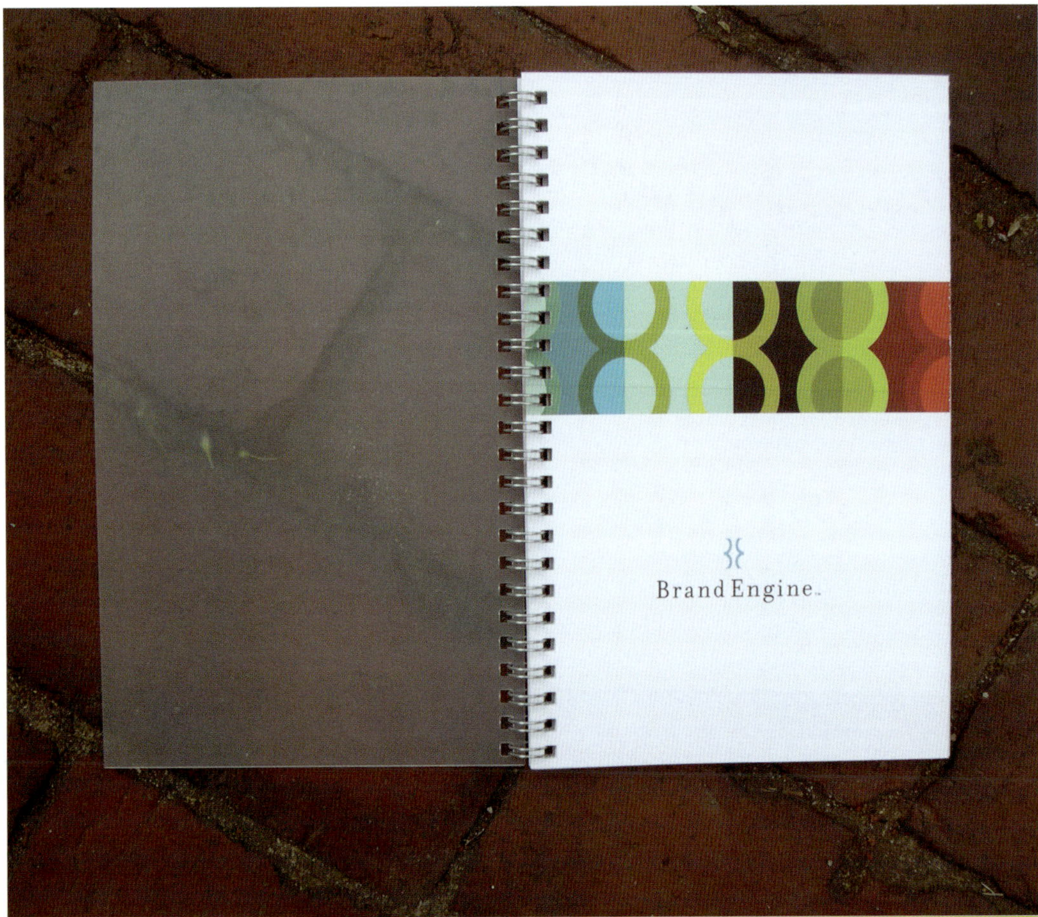

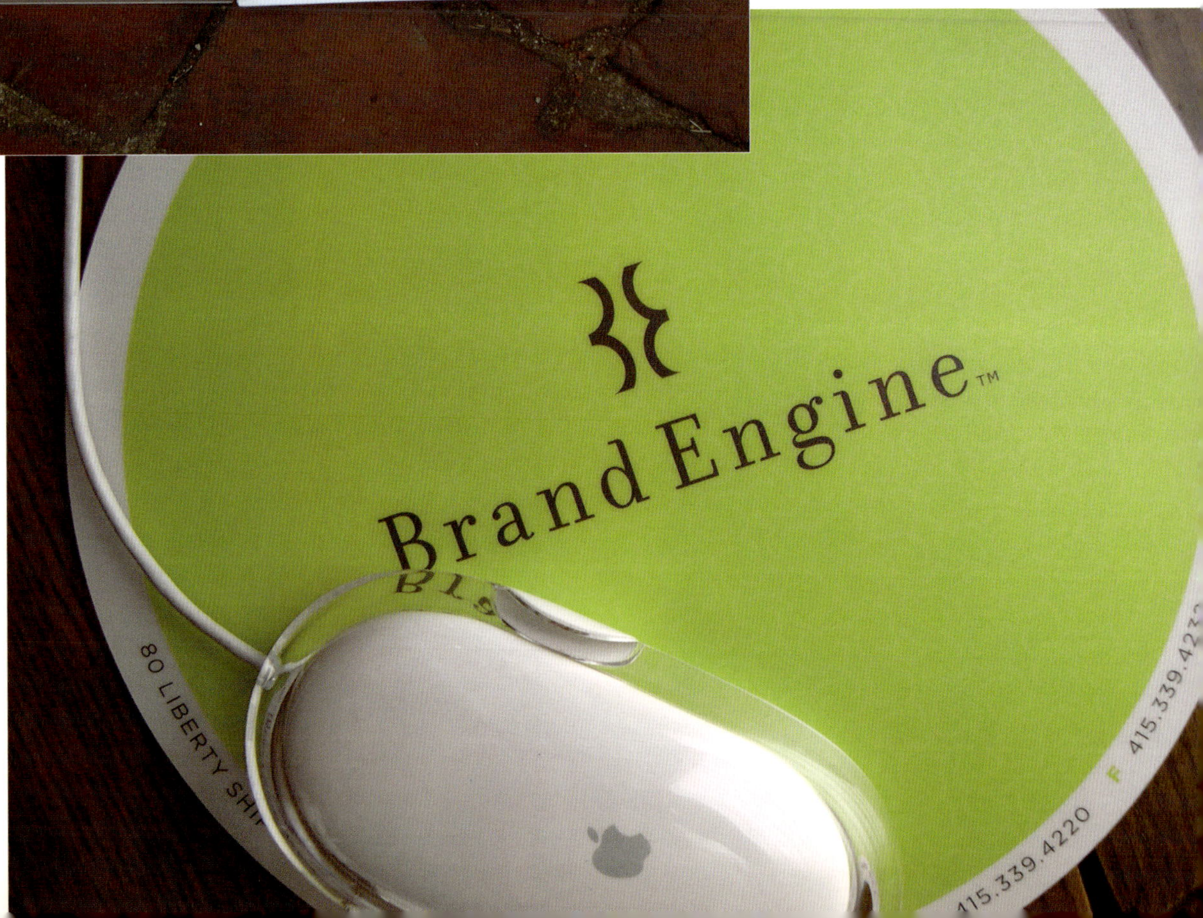

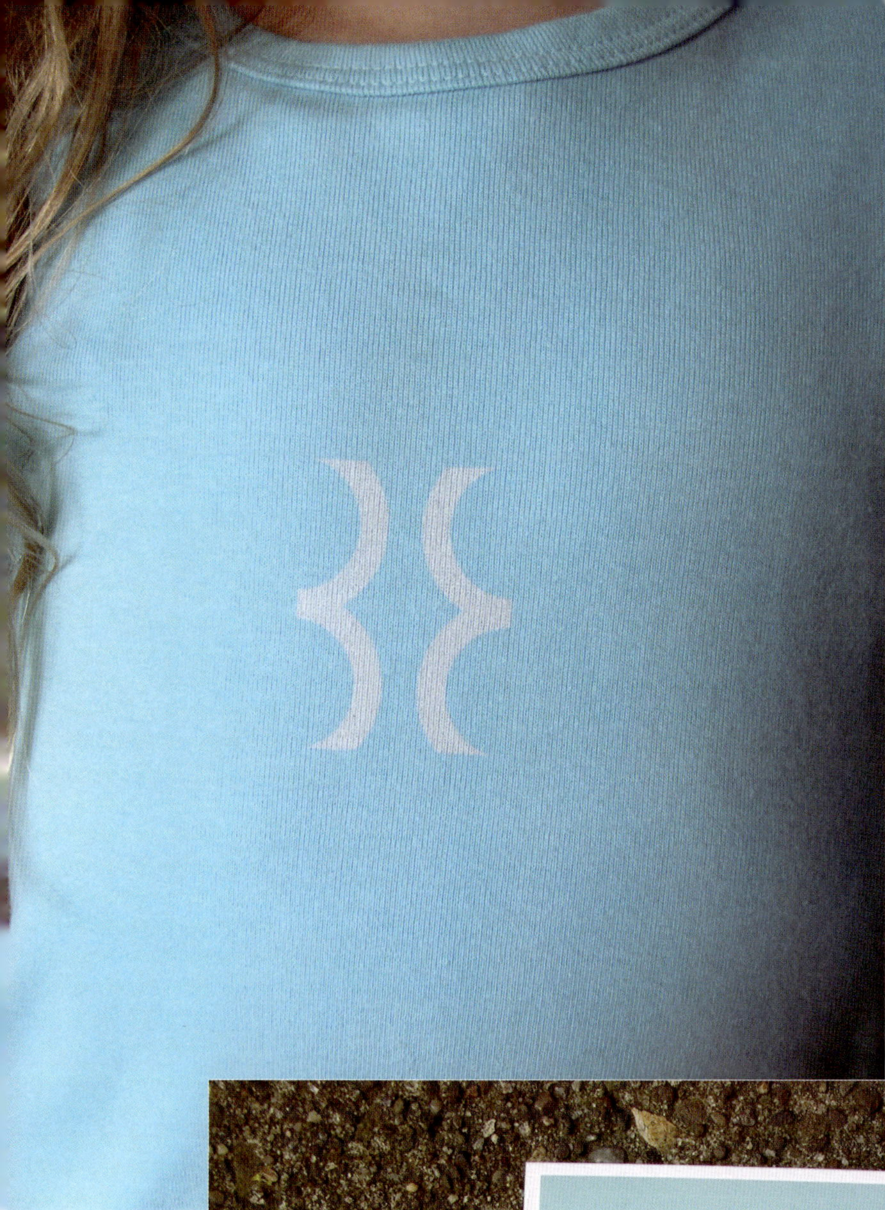

client
Brand Engine
design firm
Brand Engine
art director
Will Burke
designers
Eric Read, Robert Burns, Yusuke Asaka

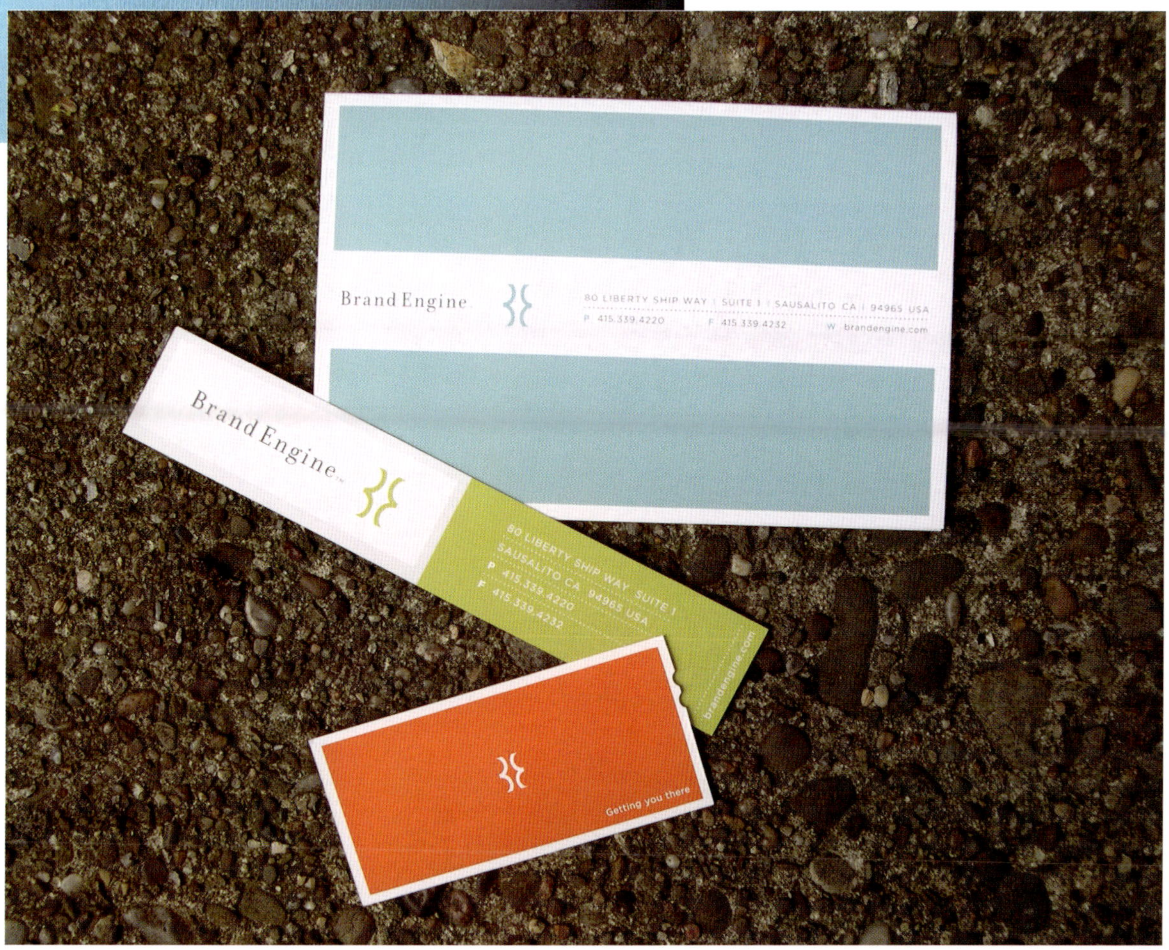

Free
LIBRARY OF PHILADELPHIA

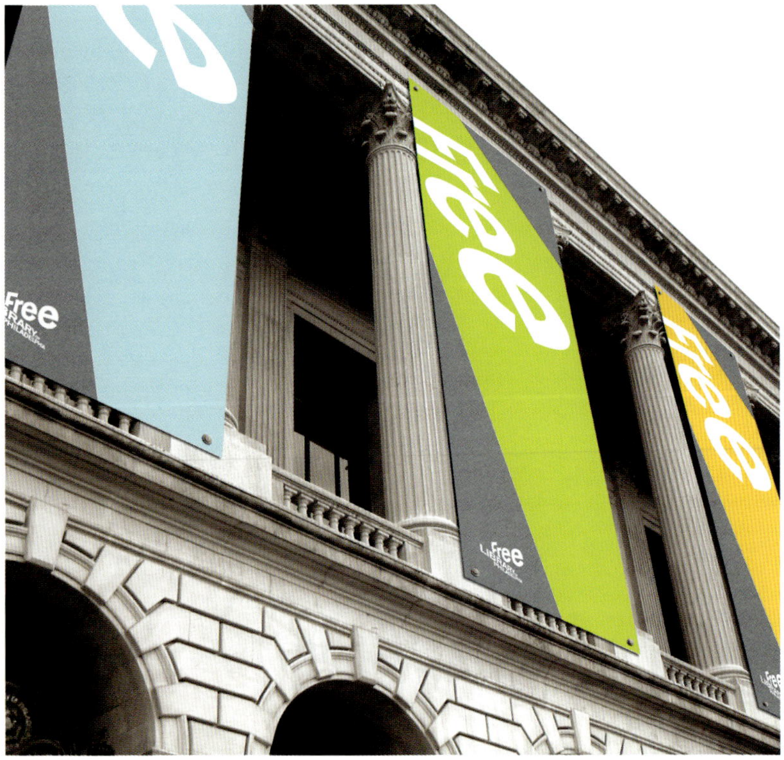

client
Free Library of Philadelphia
design firm
Siegel & Gale
creative director
Steve Rank
designer
Daniel Johnston
illustrator
Joe Finocchiaro

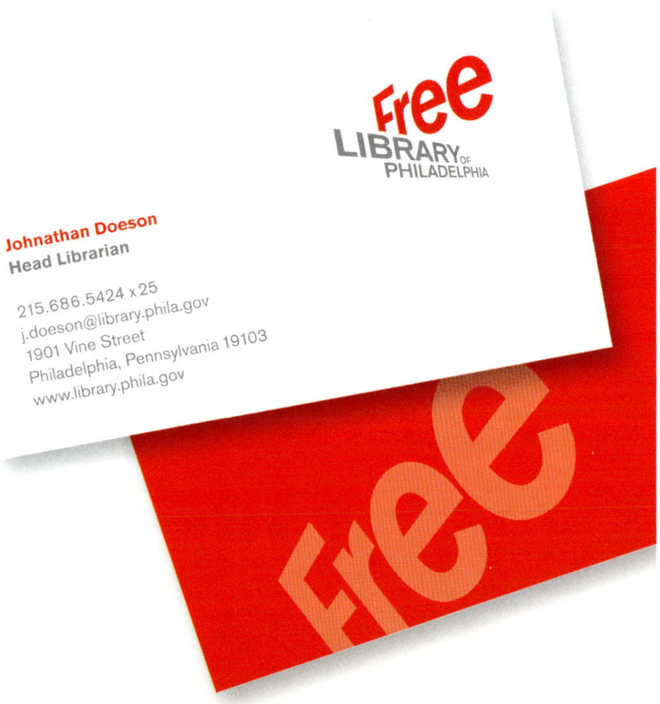

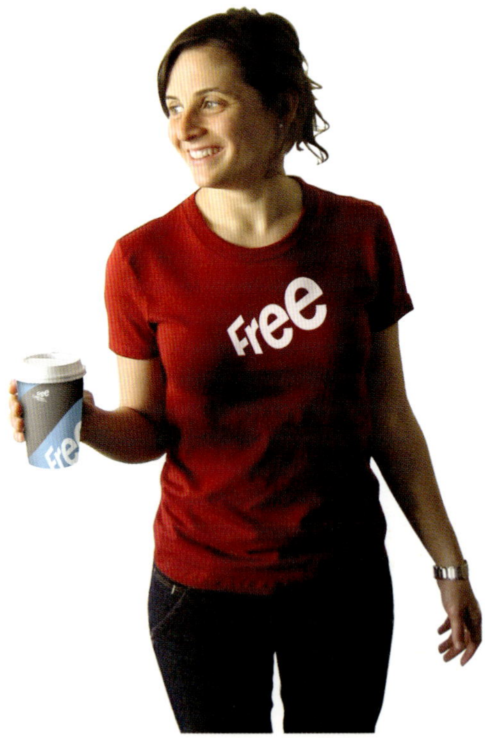

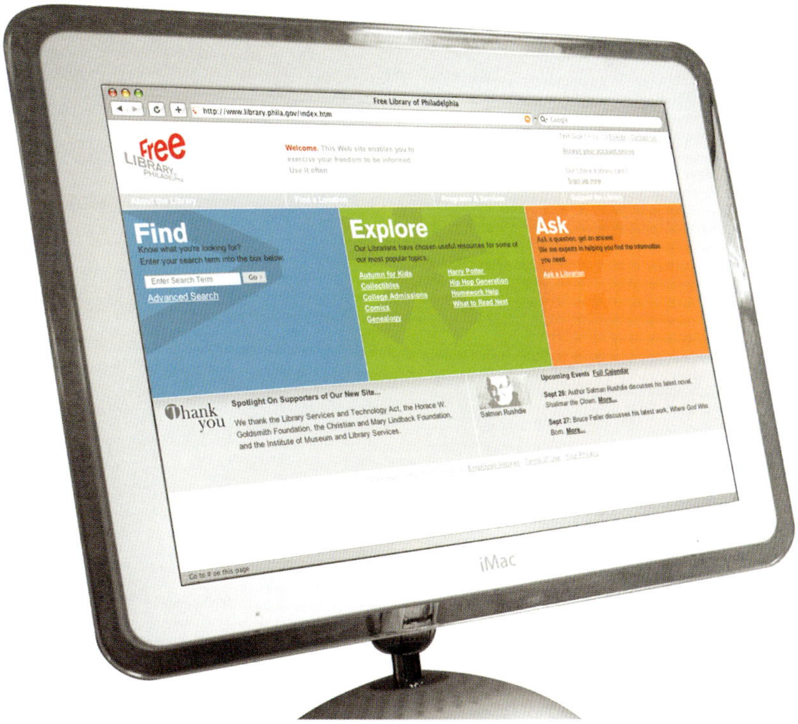
Free Library of Philadelphia
http://www.library.phila.gov/index.htm
Free
LIBRARY
Find
Know what you're looking for?
Enter your search term into the box below.
Advanced Search
Explore
Ask
Thank you
Spotlight On Supporters of Our New Site...
Upcoming Events
iMac

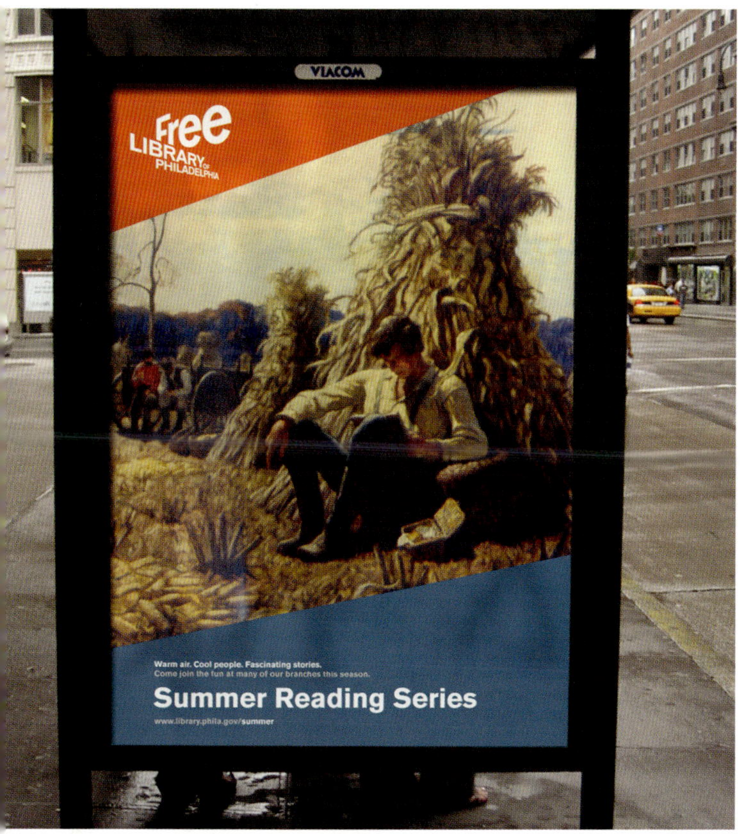
VIACOM
Free
LIBRARY OF PHILADELPHIA
Warm air. Cool people. Fascinating stories.
Come join the fun at many of our branches this season.
Summer Reading Series
www.library.phila.gov/summer

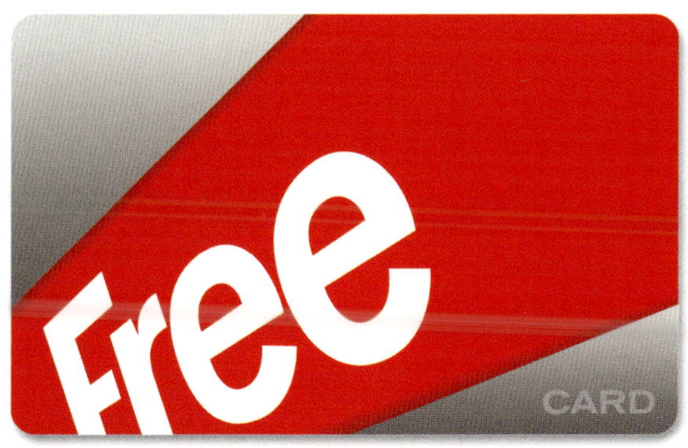
Free
CARD

Free
LIBRARY OF PHILADELPHIA
This card enables you to exercise your freedom to be informed. Use it often.
X
I am free.
www.library.phila.gov
ACCESS PENNSYLVANIA

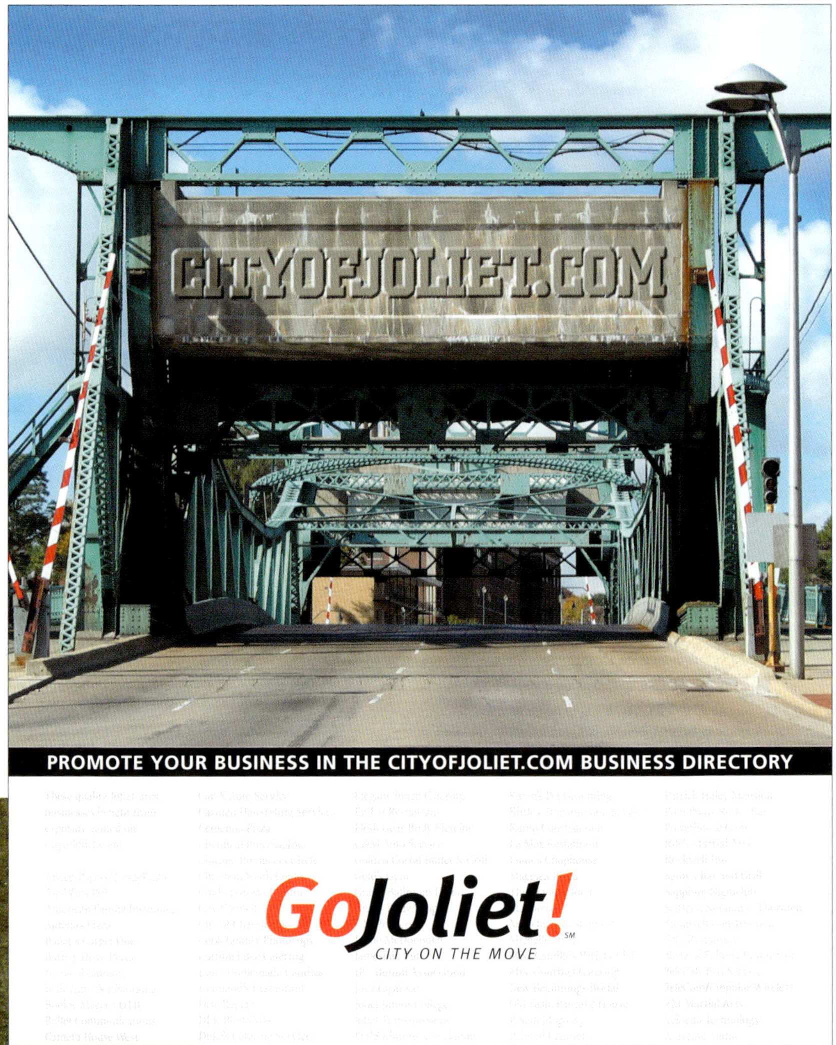

client
CITYOFJOLIET.COM
design firm
Bullet Communications, Inc.
designer
Tim Scott Kump

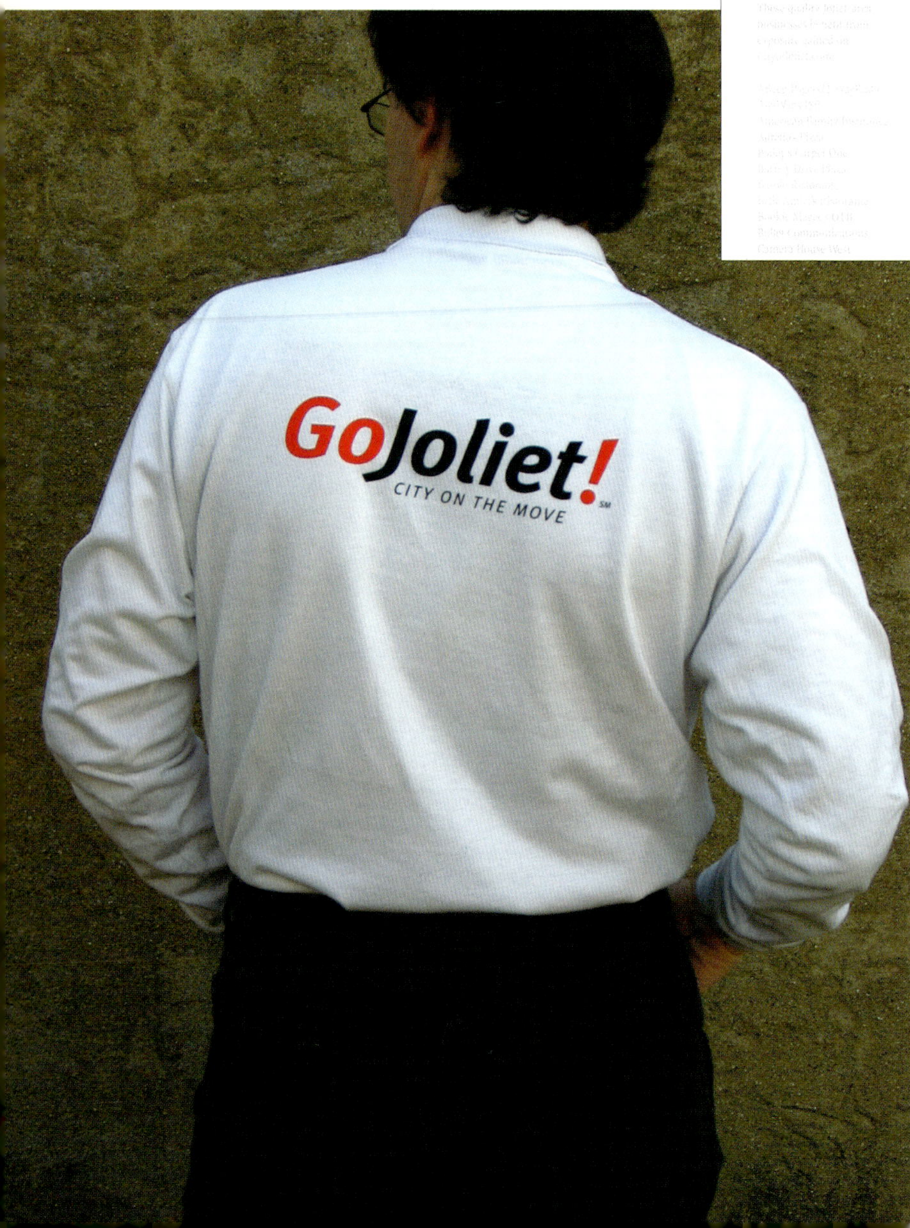

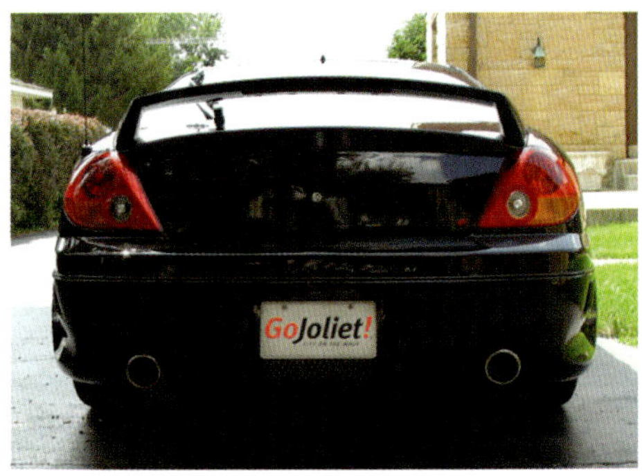

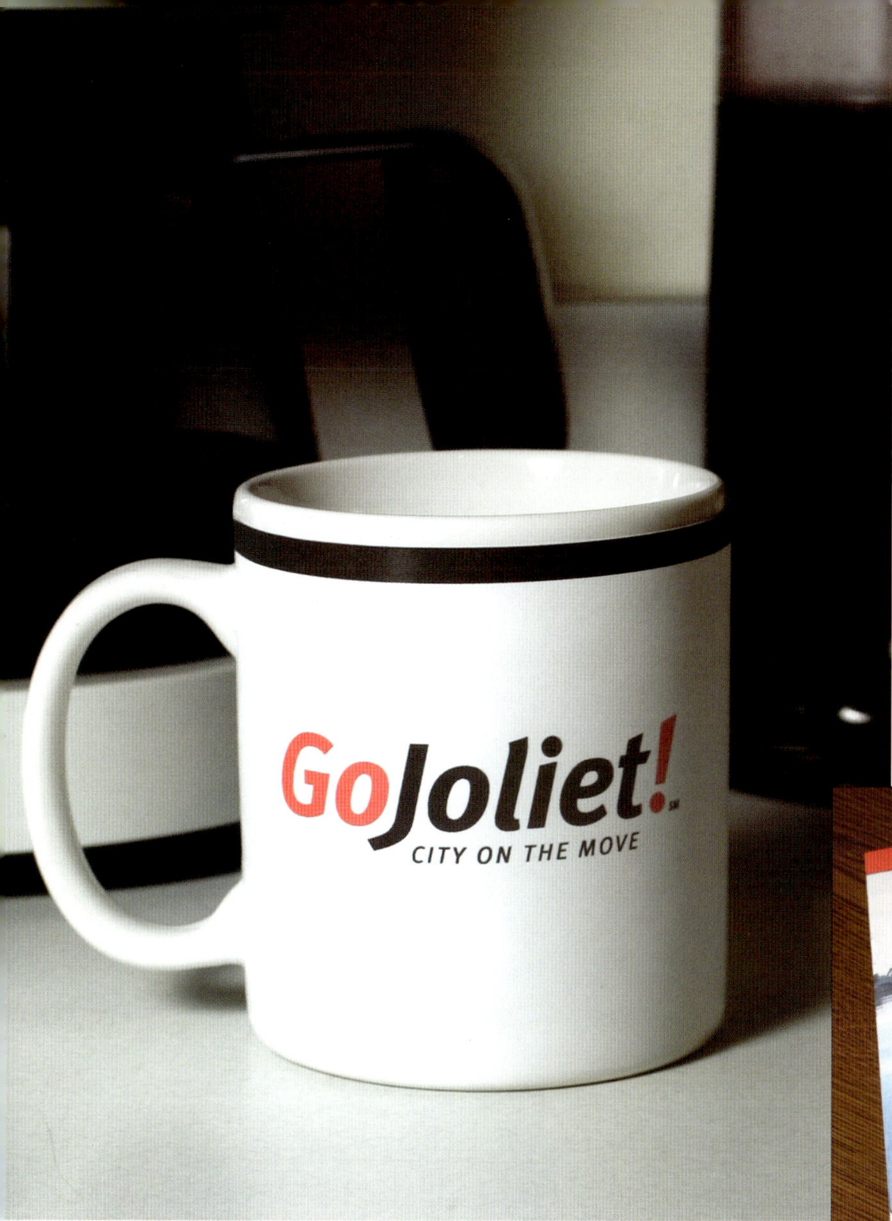

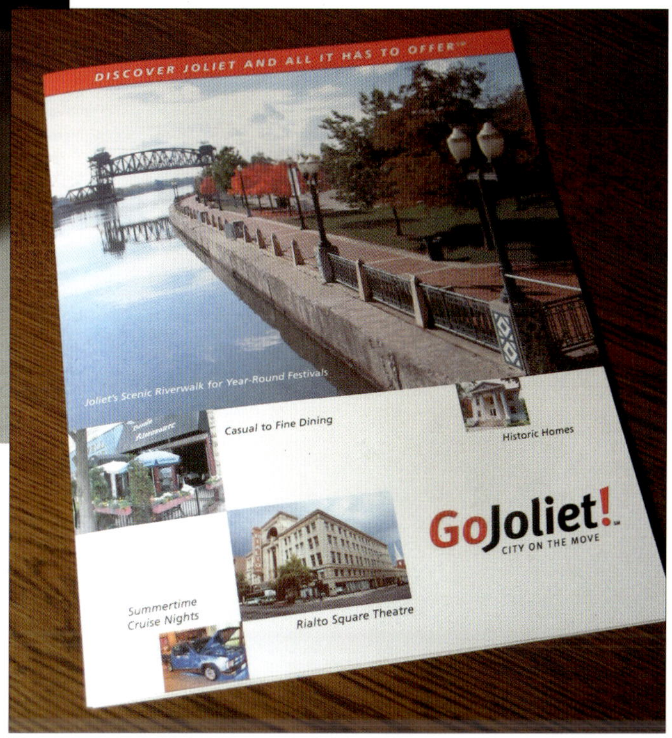

GoJoliet!
SM
CITY ON THE MOVE

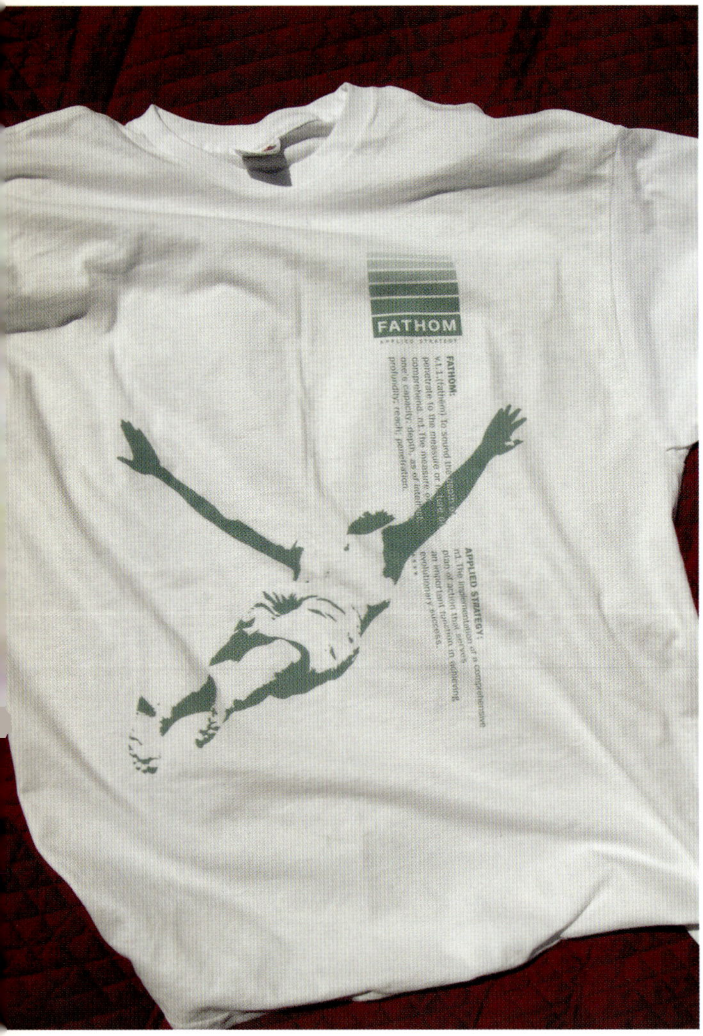

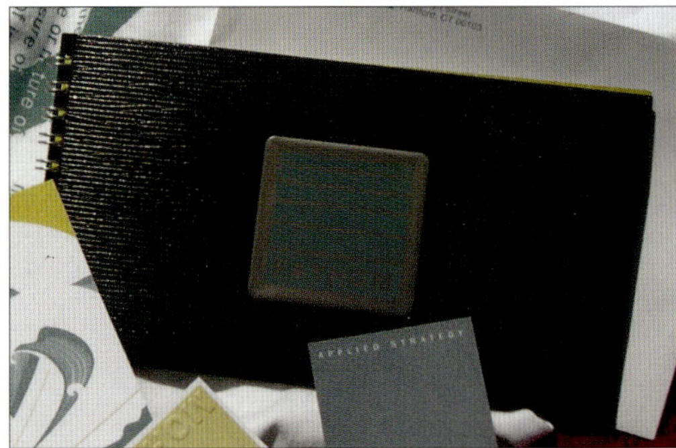

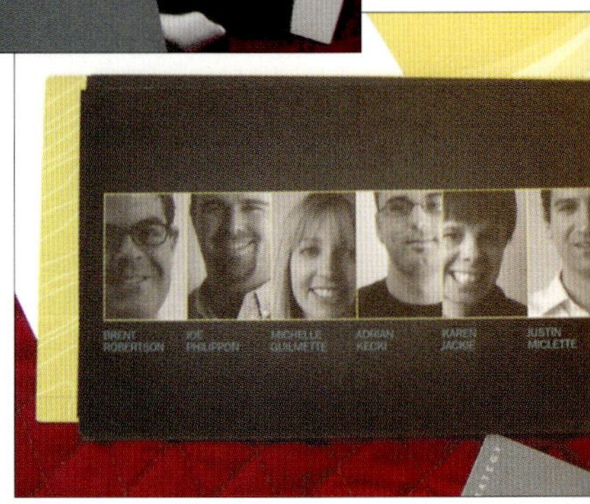

client
Fathom
design firm
Fathom
designers
Brent Robertson,
Bil Jenak, Vaughn Fender

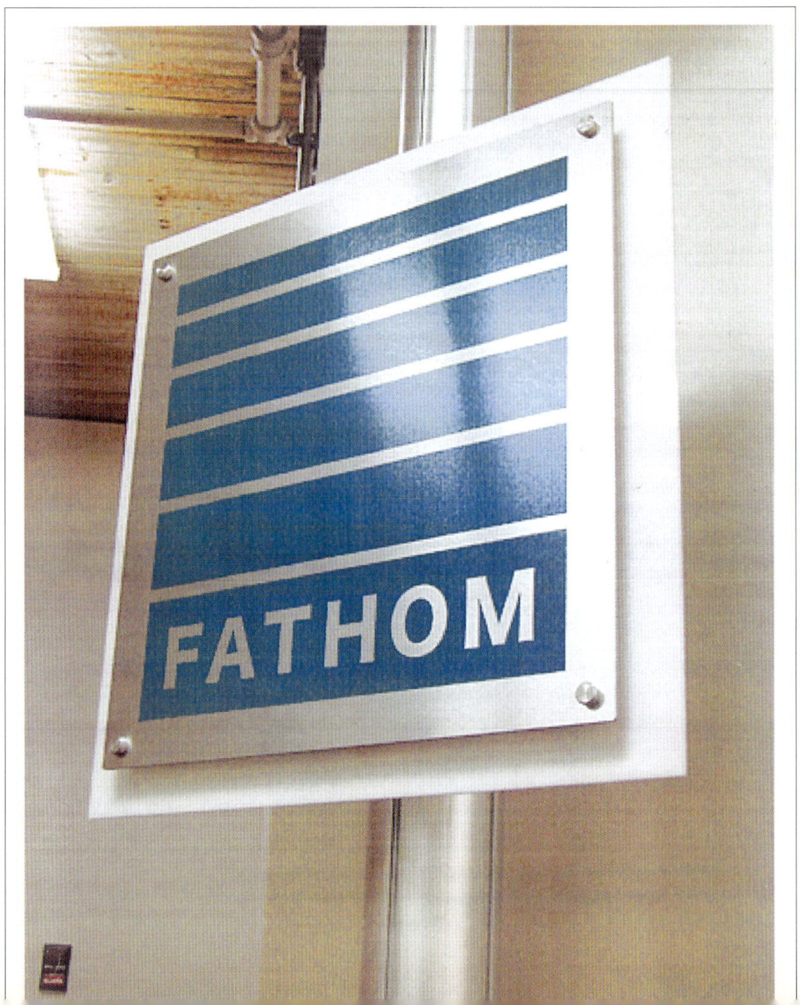

FATHOM

APPLIED STRATEGY

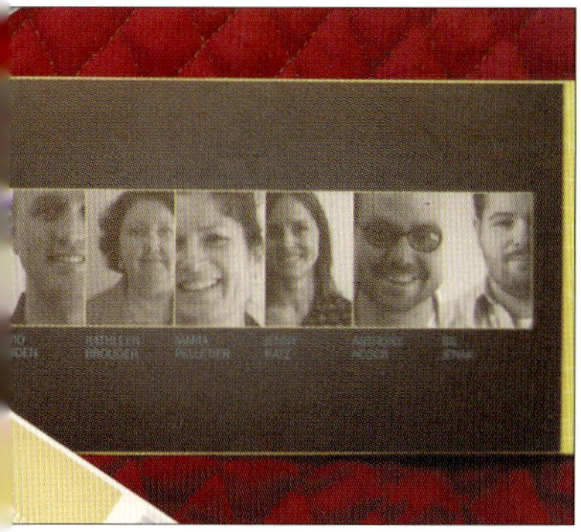

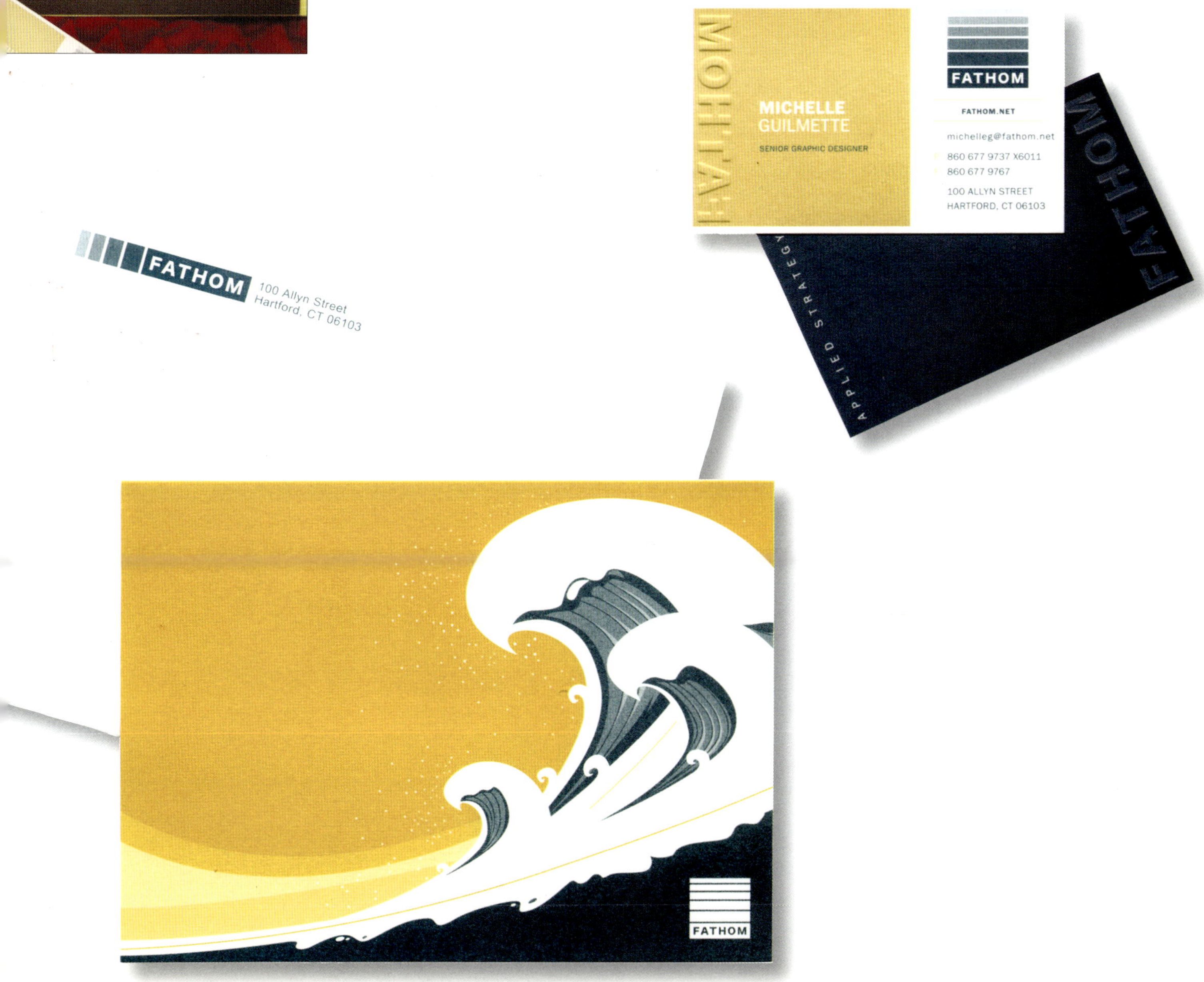

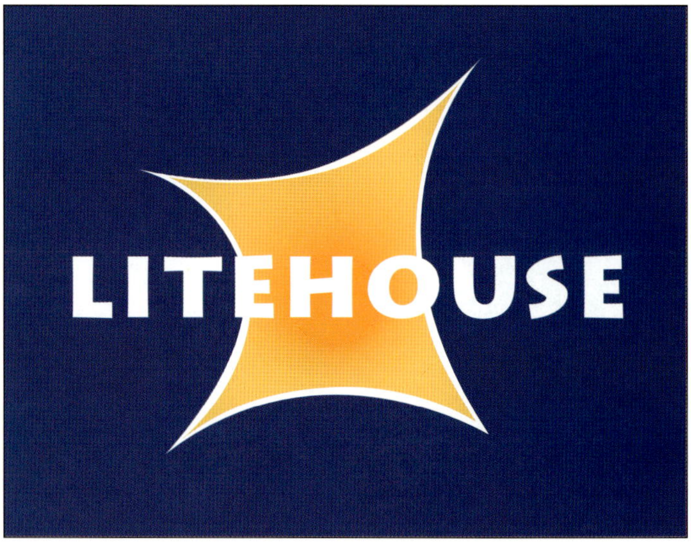

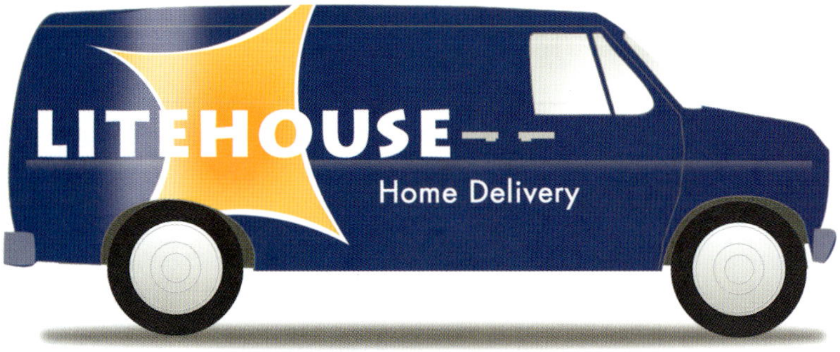

client
Litehouse
design firm
King-Casey
designers
John Chrzanowski, Carolina Guimarey, Jeff Redston, Art Crisci

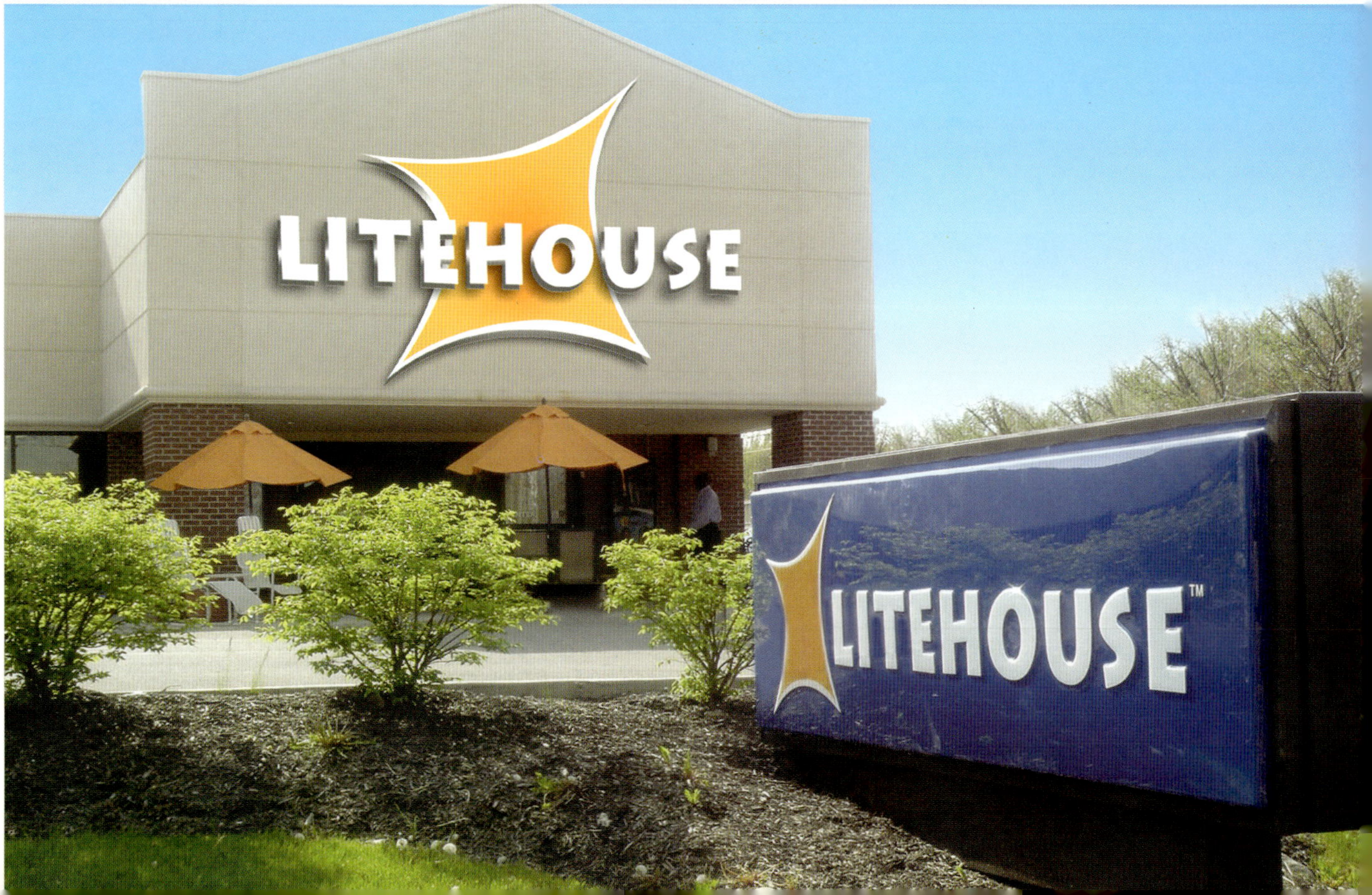

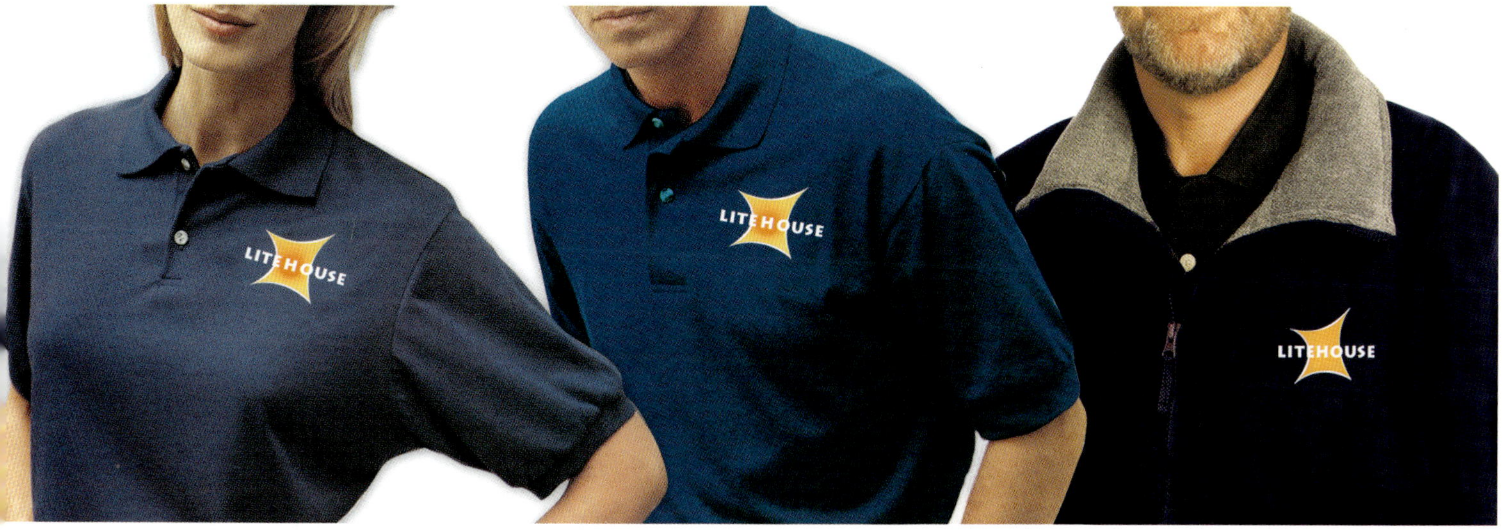
LITEHOUSE
LITEHOUSE
LITEHOUSE

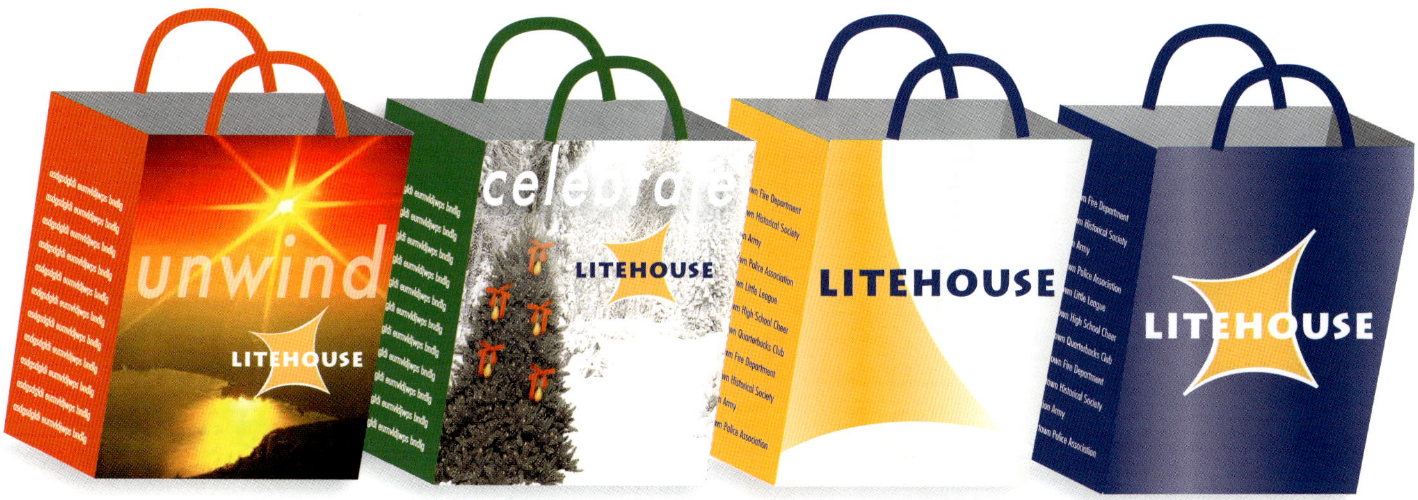
unwind
LITEHOUSE
celebrate
LITEHOUSE
LITEHOUSE
LITEHOUSE

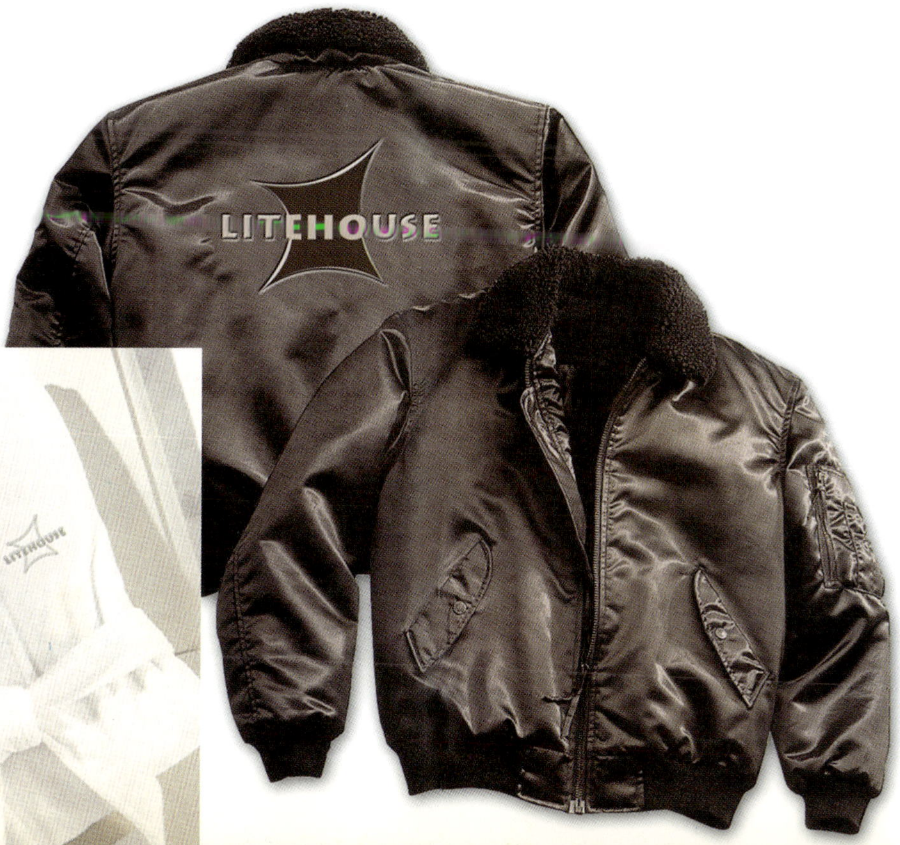
LITEHOUSE

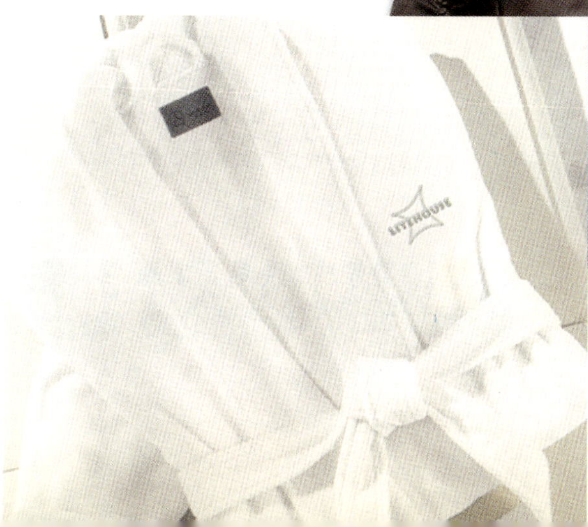

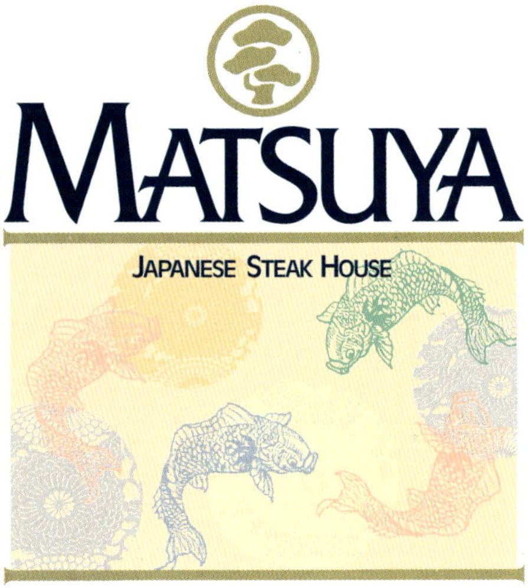
MATSUYA
JAPANESE STEAK HOUSE

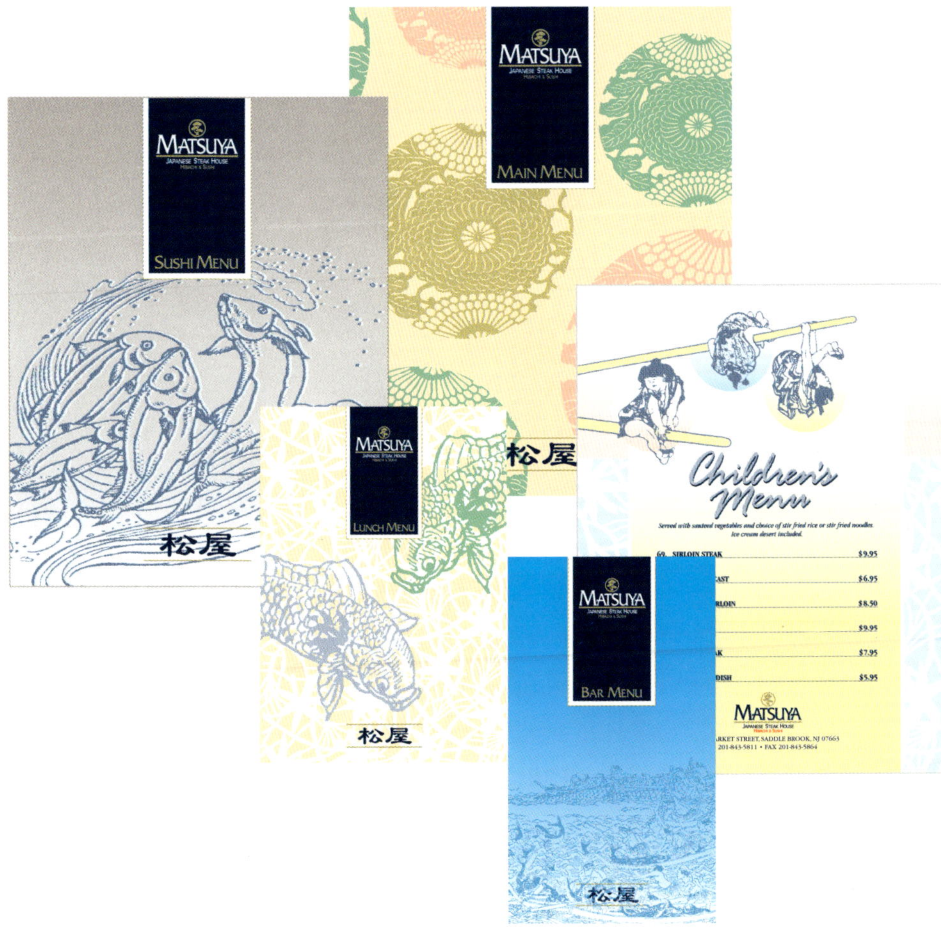
MATSUYA
SUSHI MENU
松屋
MATSUYA
MAIN MENU
松屋
MATSUYA
LUNCH MENU
松屋
Children's Menu
MATSUYA
MATSUYA
BAR MENU
松屋

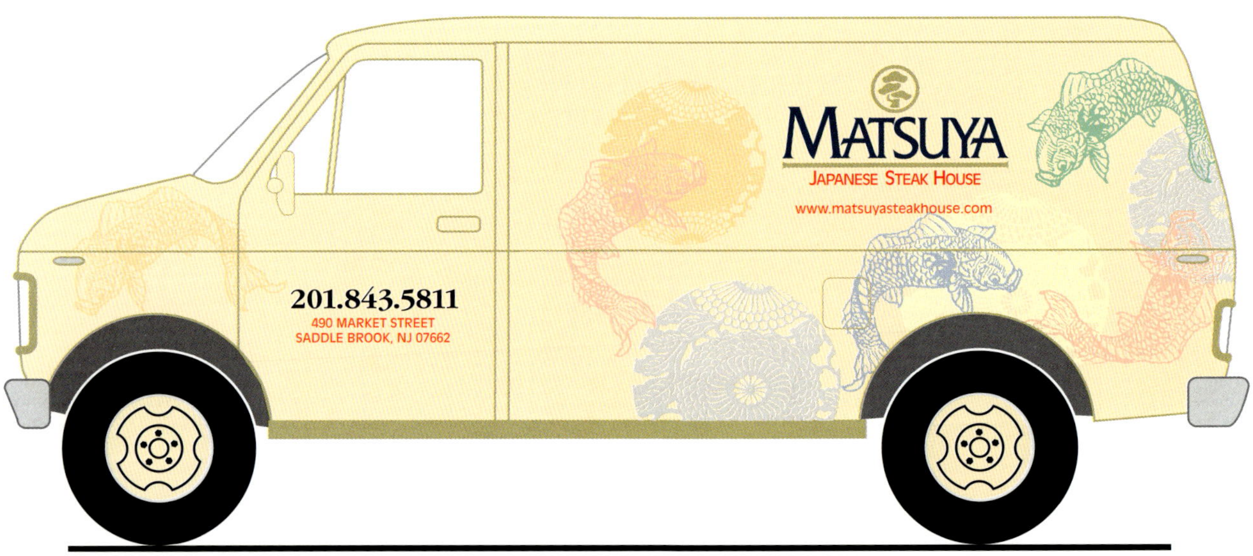
MATSUYA
JAPANESE STEAK HOUSE
www.matsuyasteakhouse.com
201.843.5811
490 MARKET STREET
SADDLE BROOK, NJ 07662

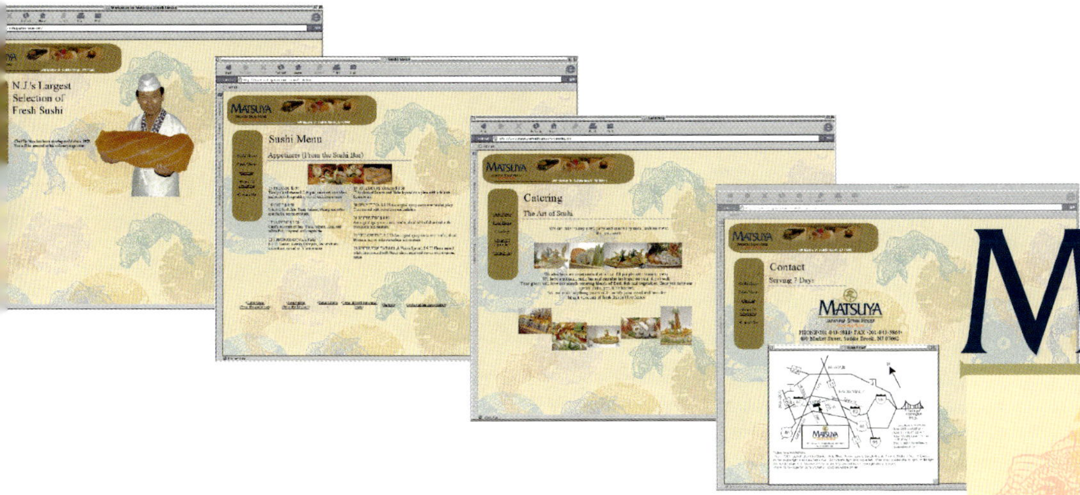

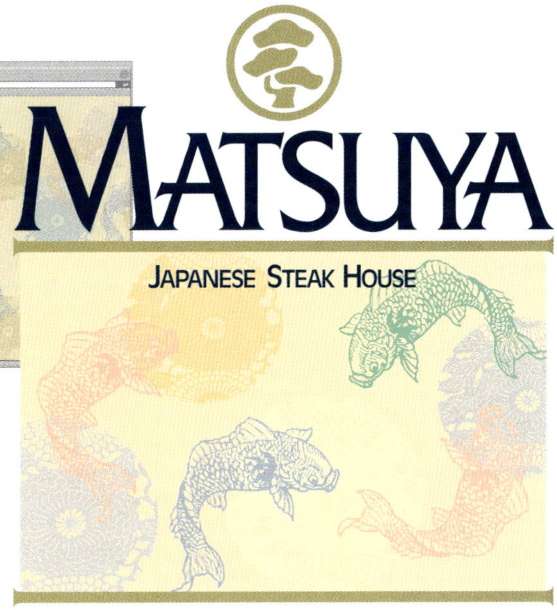

client
Matsuya Japanese Steakhouse
design firm
Stephen Longo Design Assoc.
designer
Stephen Longo

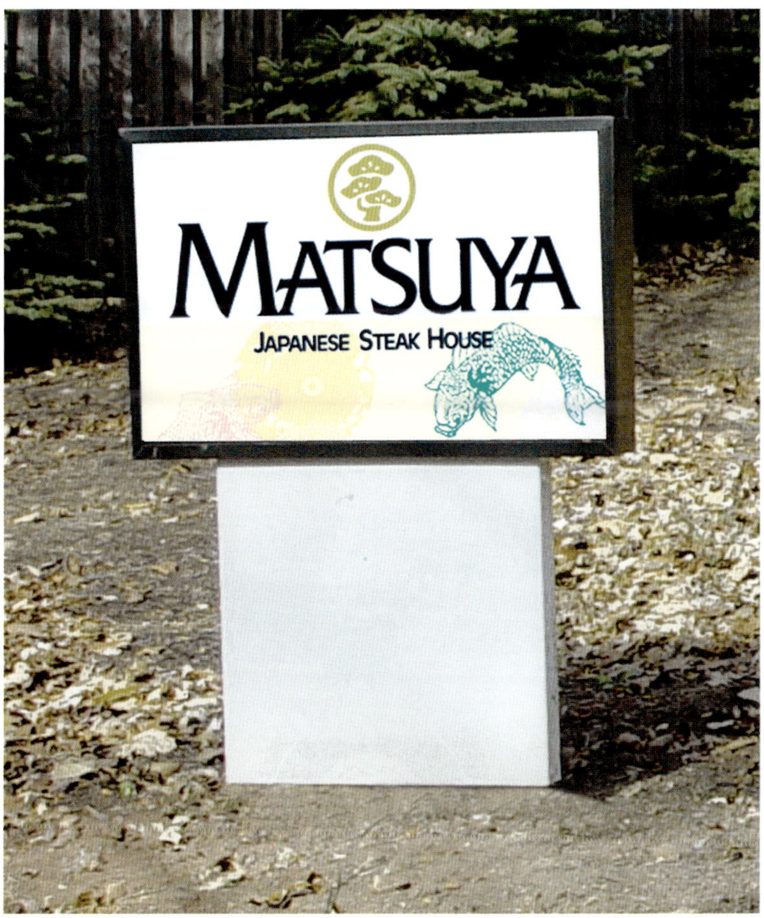

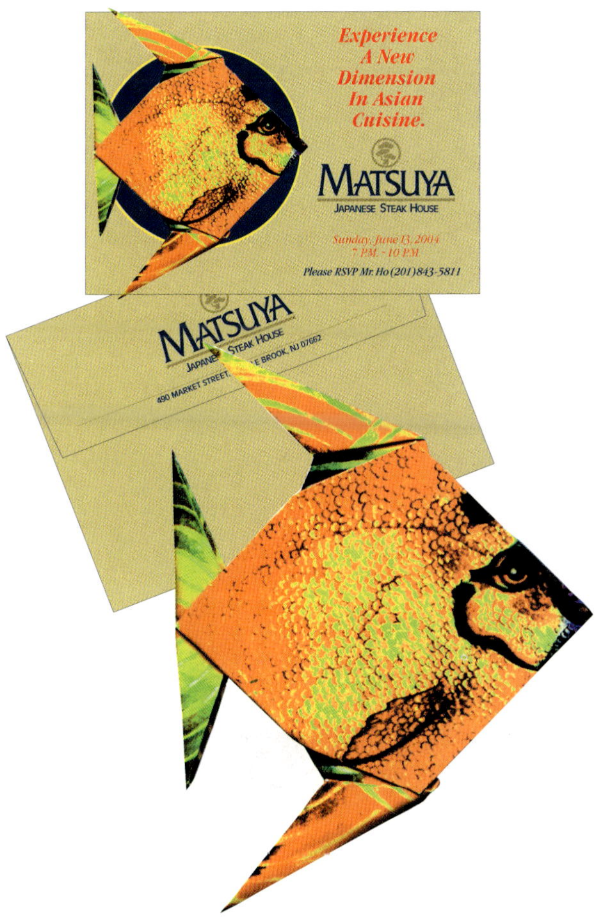

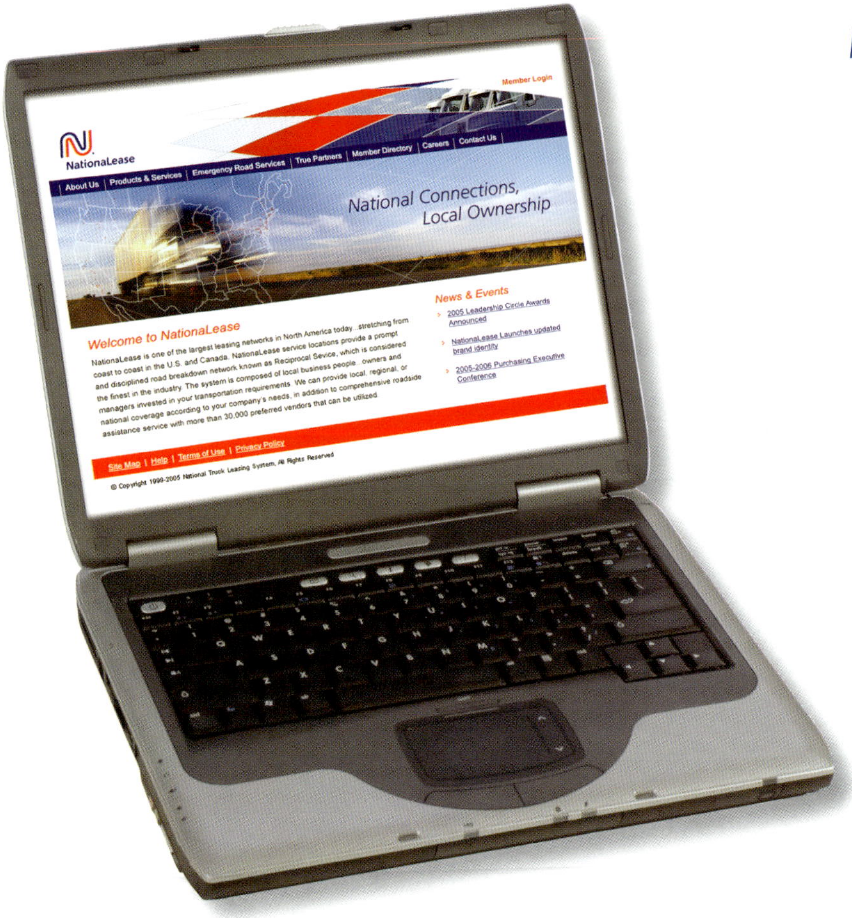

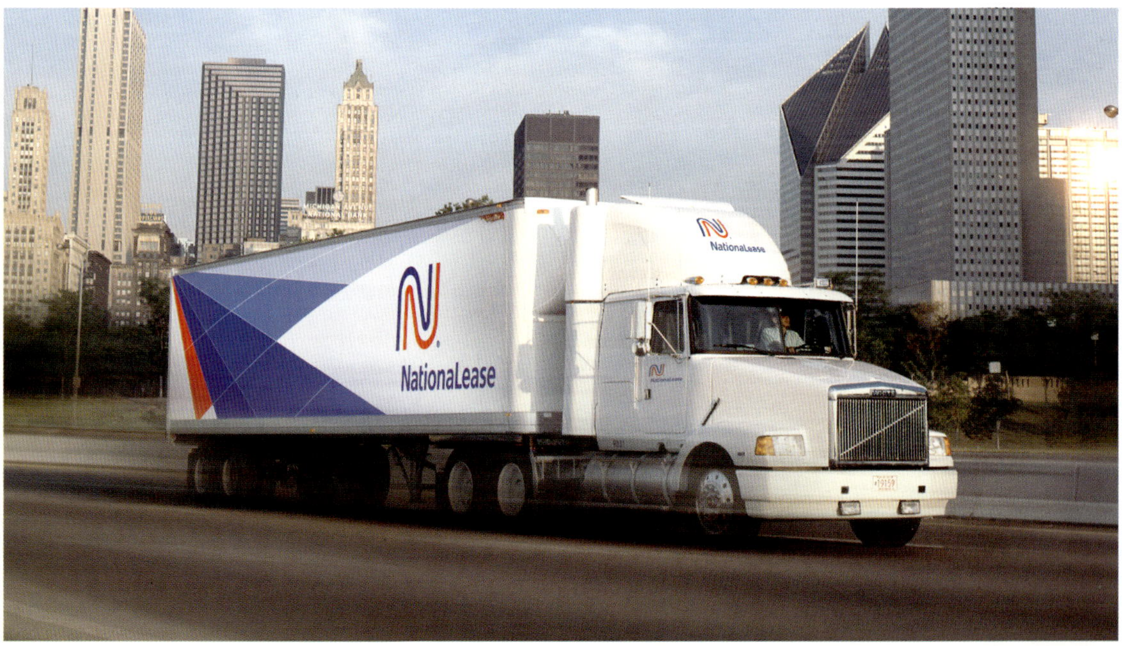

client
NationaLease
design firm
BrandSavvy Inc.
designer
Karl Peters

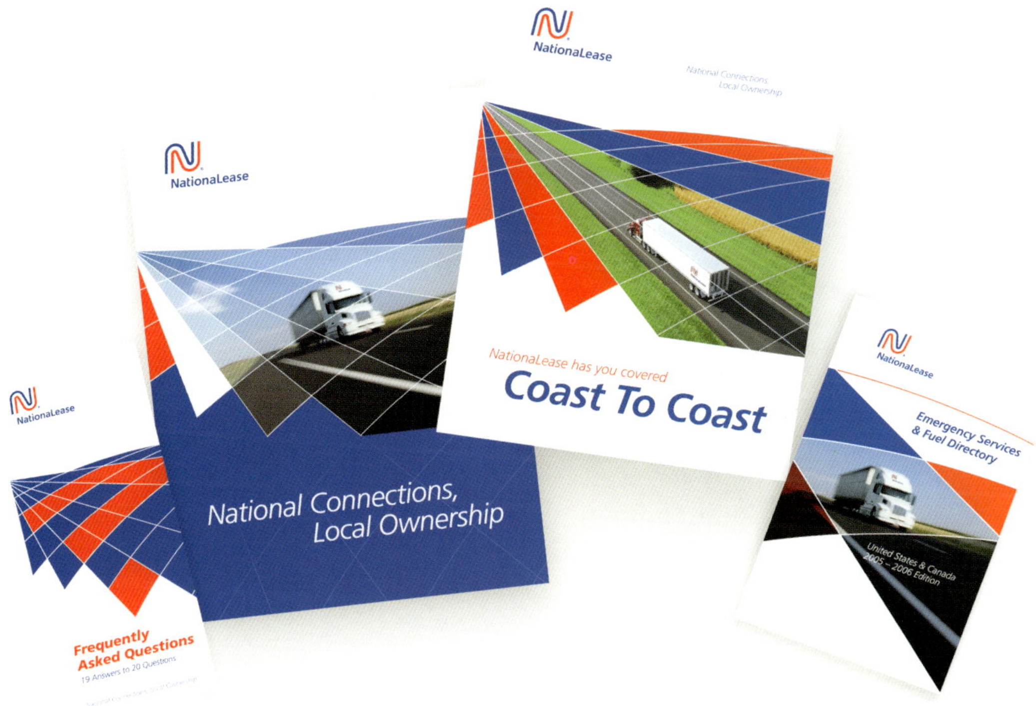
NationaLease
National Connections, Local Ownership
NationaLease has you covered
Coast To Coast
Frequently Asked Questions
19 Answers to 20 Questions
Emergency Services & Fuel Directory
United States & Canada
2005 – 2006 Edition

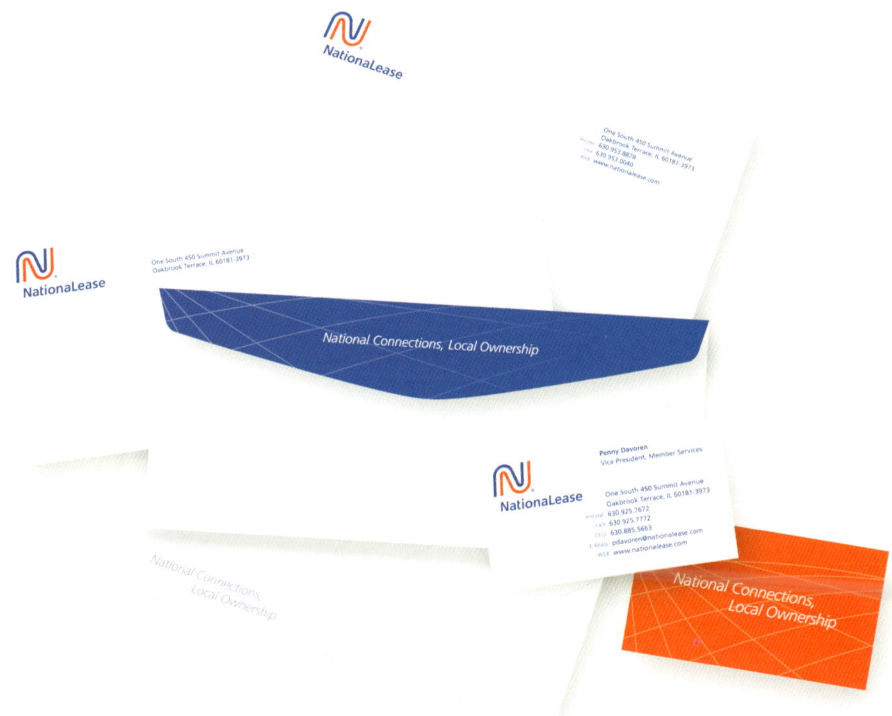
NationaLease
National Connections, Local Ownership
Penny Davoren
Vice President, Member Services
National Connections, Local Ownership

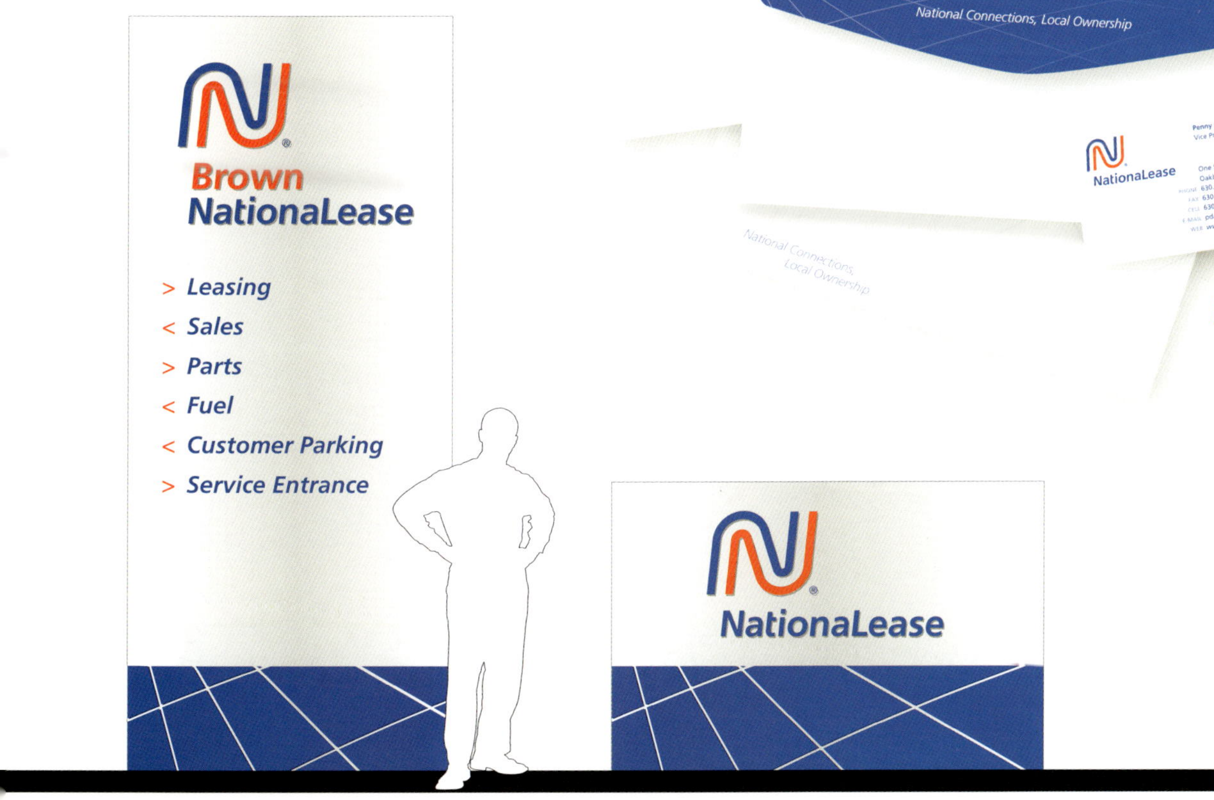
Brown
NationaLease
Leasing
Sales
Parts
Fuel
Customer Parking
Service Entrance
NationaLease

THE NEW SCHOOL
A UNIVERSITY

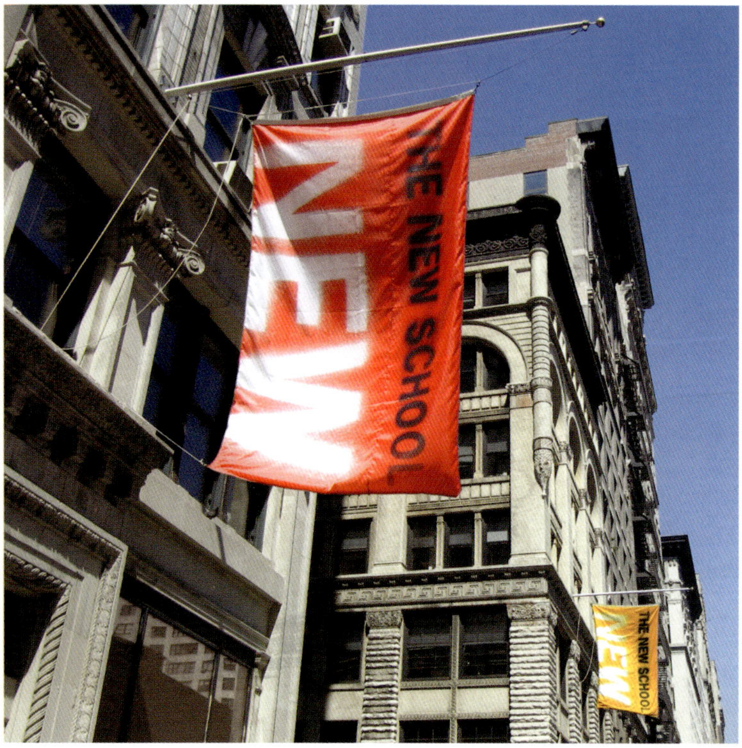

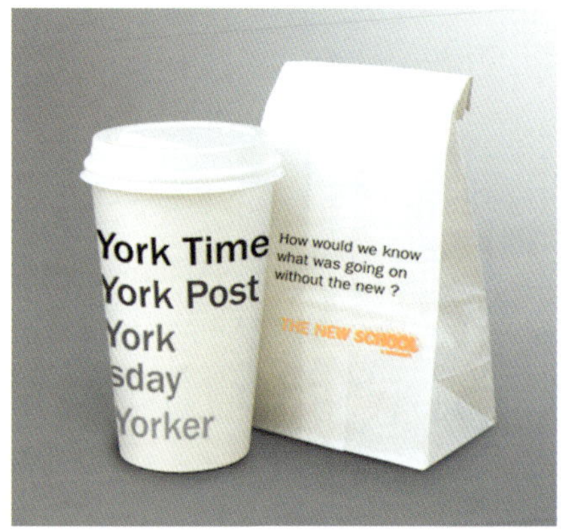

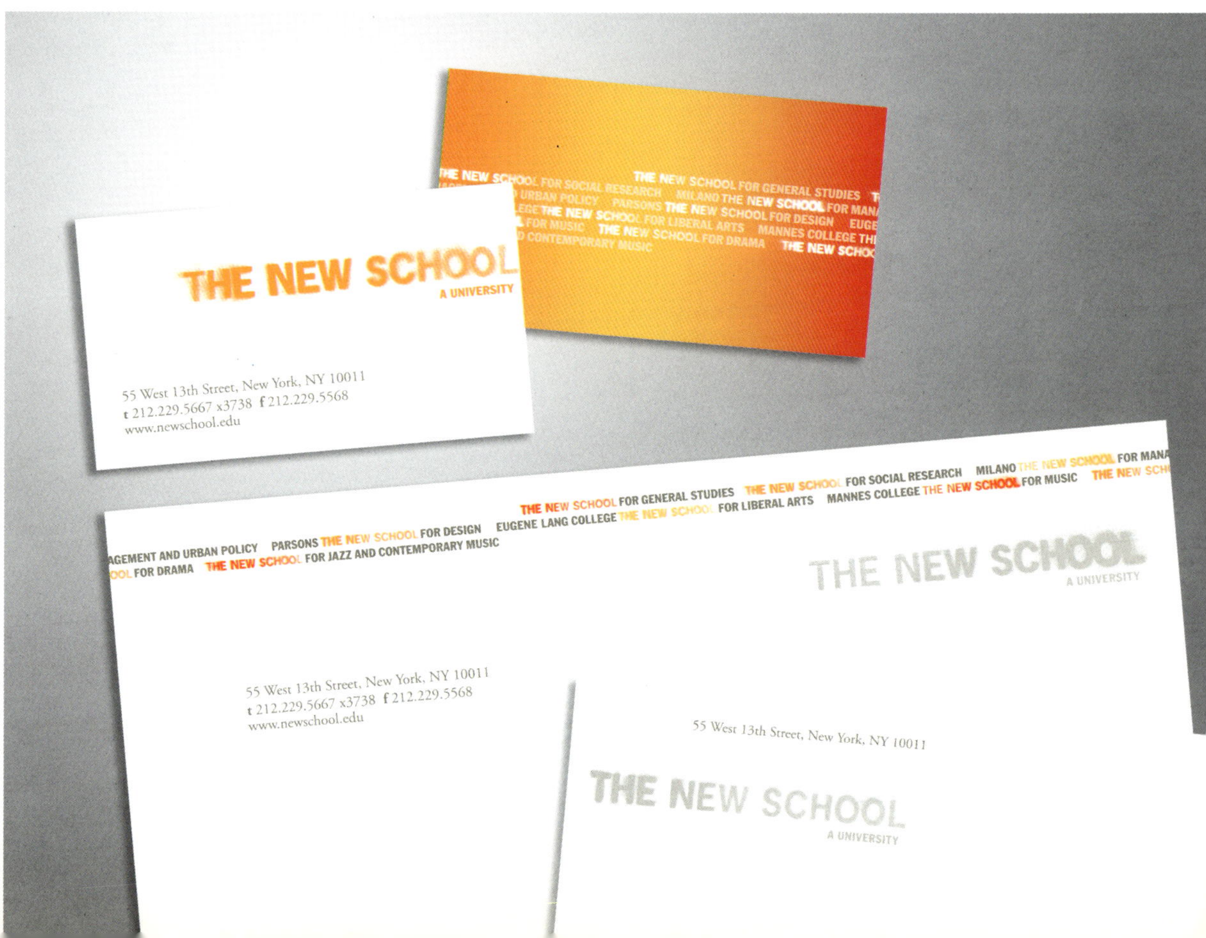

client
The New School
design firm
Siegel & Gale
creative director
Howard Belk
design directors
Young Kim, Anne Swan
designer
Lloyd Blander
copywriter
Peter Swerdloff
project manager
Jim Justice

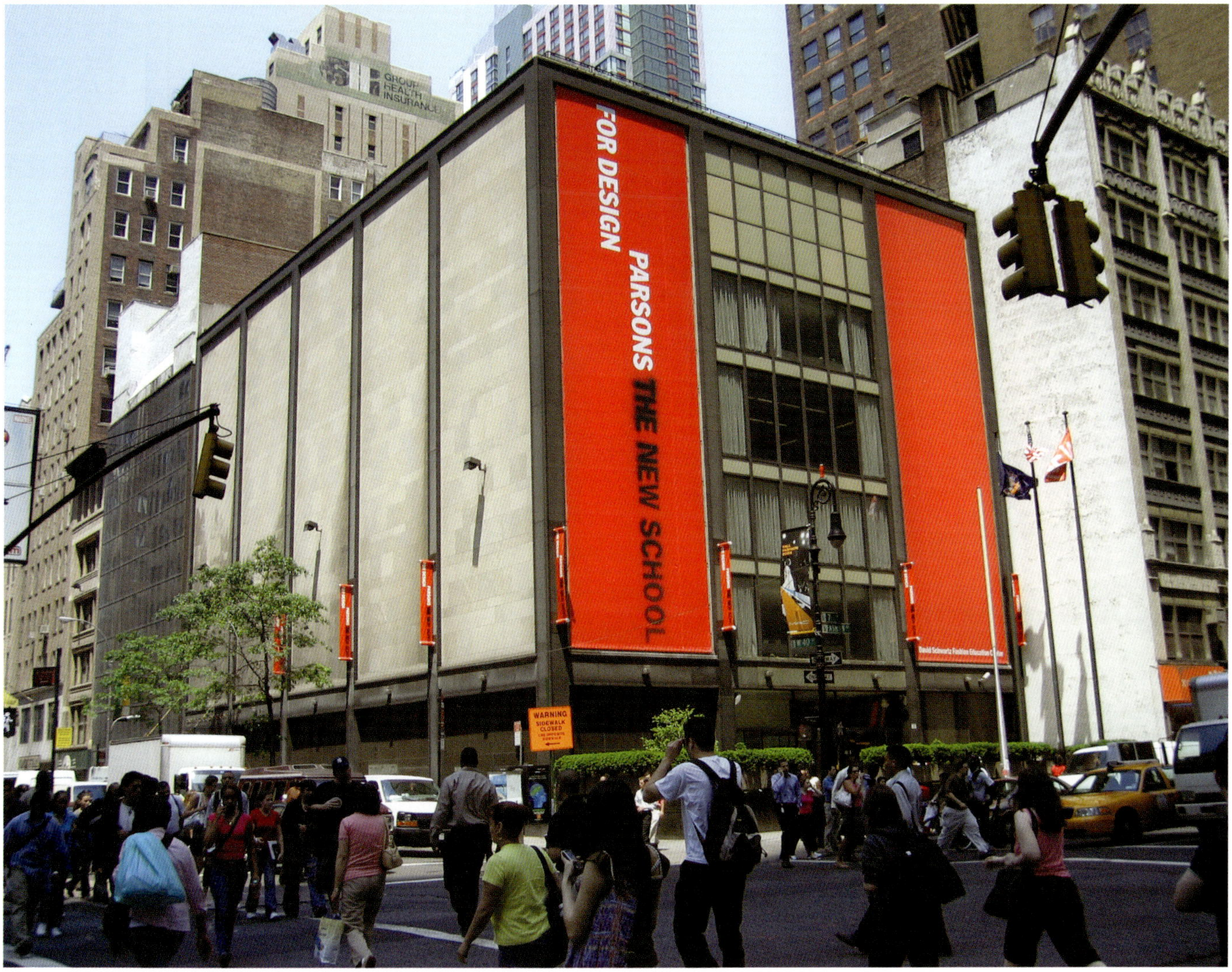

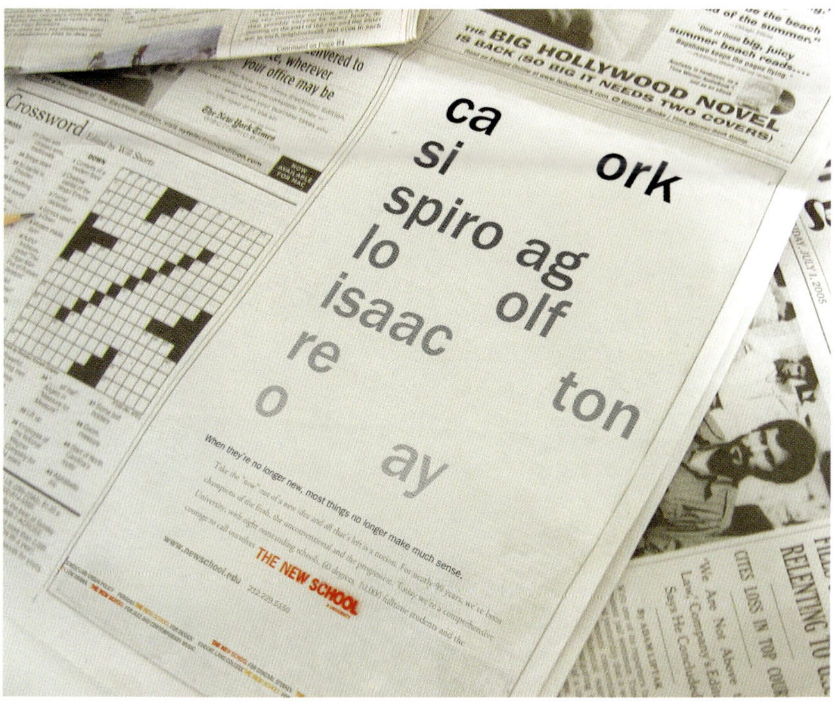

THE NEW SCHOOL FOR GENERAL STUDIES

THE NEW SCHOOL FOR SOCIAL RESEARCH

MILANO THE NEW SCHOOL FOR MANAGEMENT AND URBAN POLICY

PARSONS THE NEW SCHOOL FOR DESIGN

EUGENE LANG COLLEGE THE NEW SCHOOL FOR LIBERAL ARTS

MANNES COLLEGE THE NEW SCHOOL FOR MUSIC

THE NEW SCHOOL FOR DRAMA

THE NEW SCHOOL FOR JAZZ AND CONTEMPORARY MUSIC

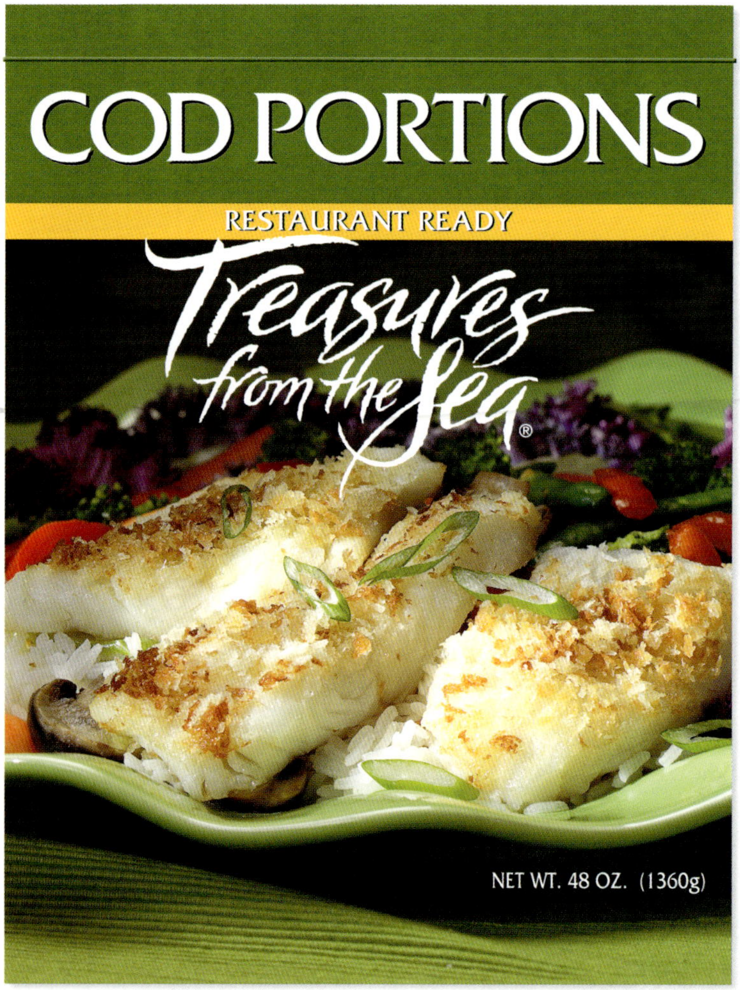

client
Odyssey Enterprises
design firm
Walsh Design
designer
Miriam Lisco

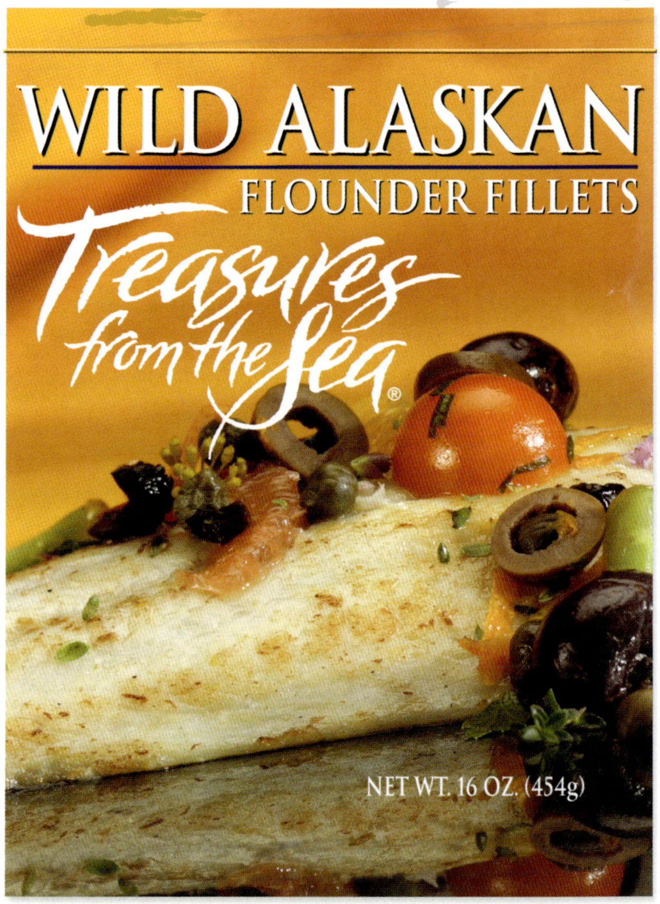

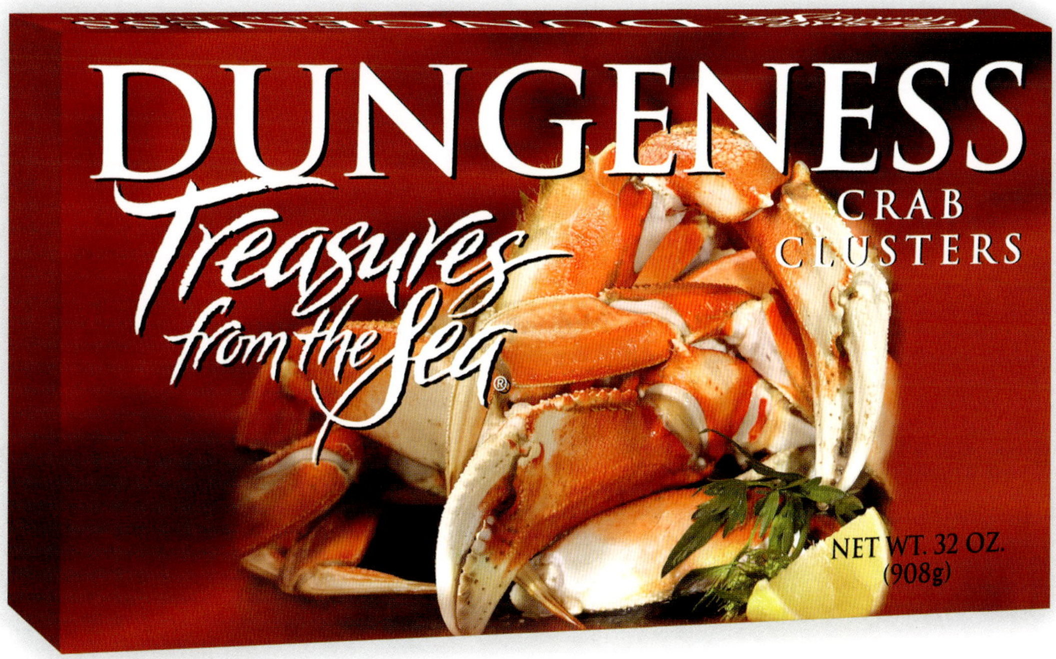
DUNGENESS
Treasures from the Sea®
CRAB CLUSTERS
NET WT. 32 OZ. (908g)

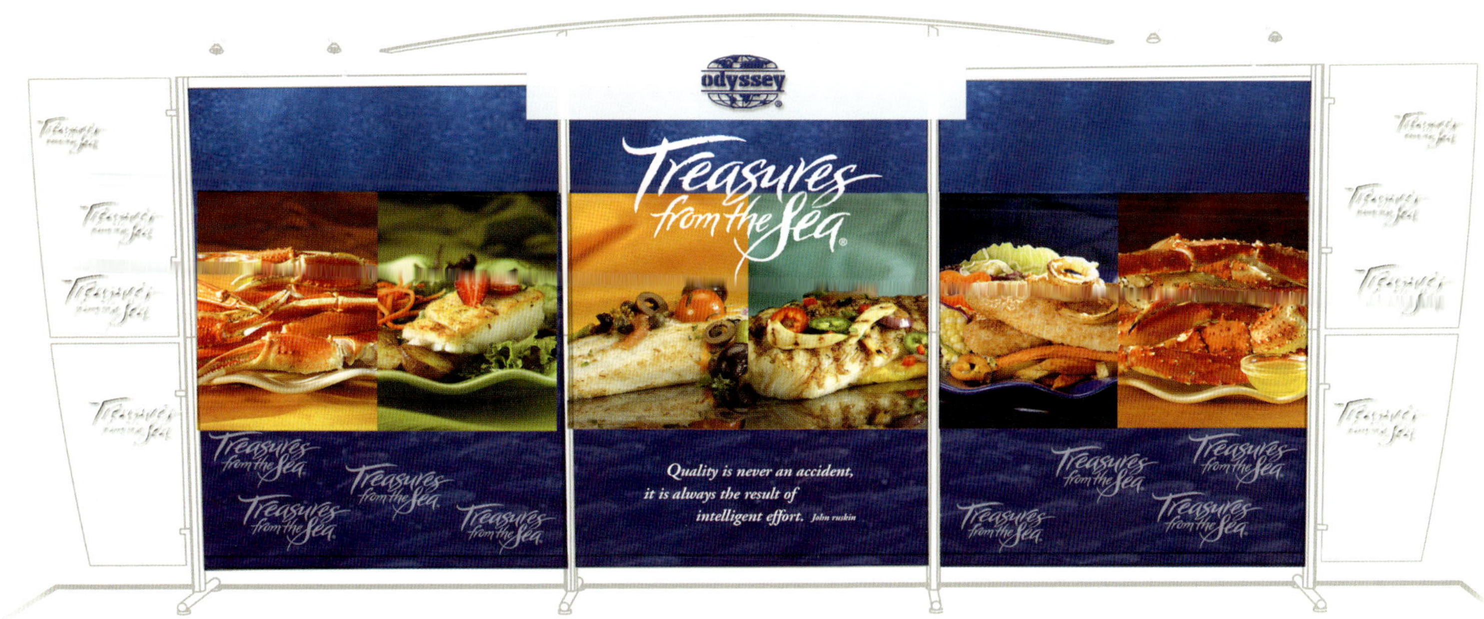
odyssey
Treasures from the Sea®
Quality is never an accident,
it is always the result of
intelligent effort. John ruskin

TEXAS
MANOR®
Bakery

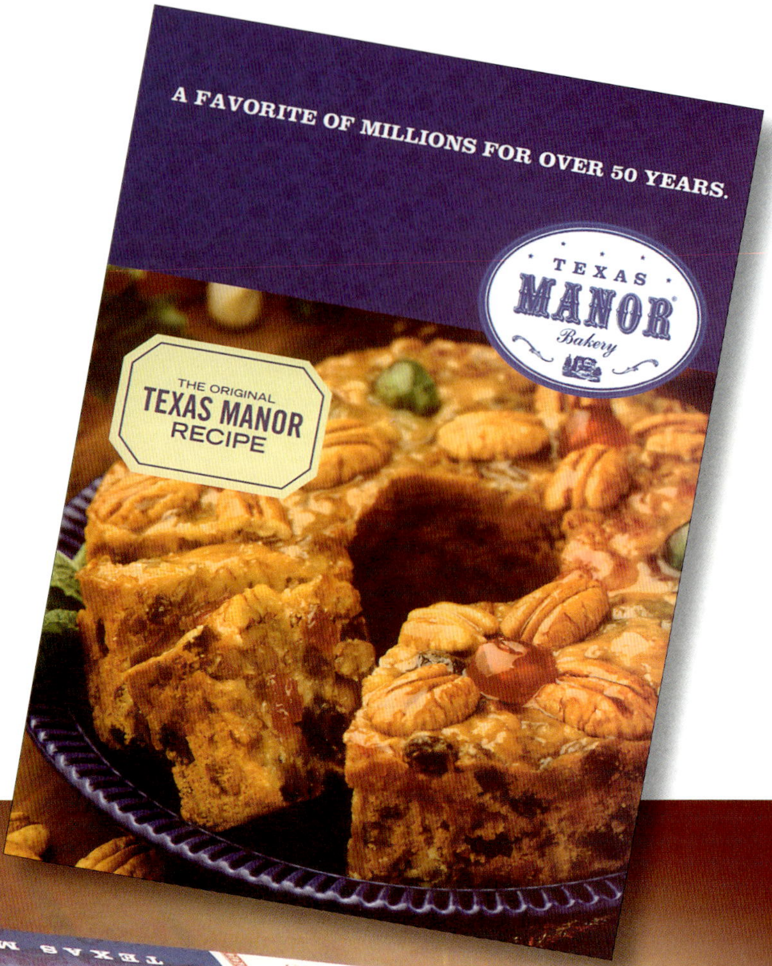

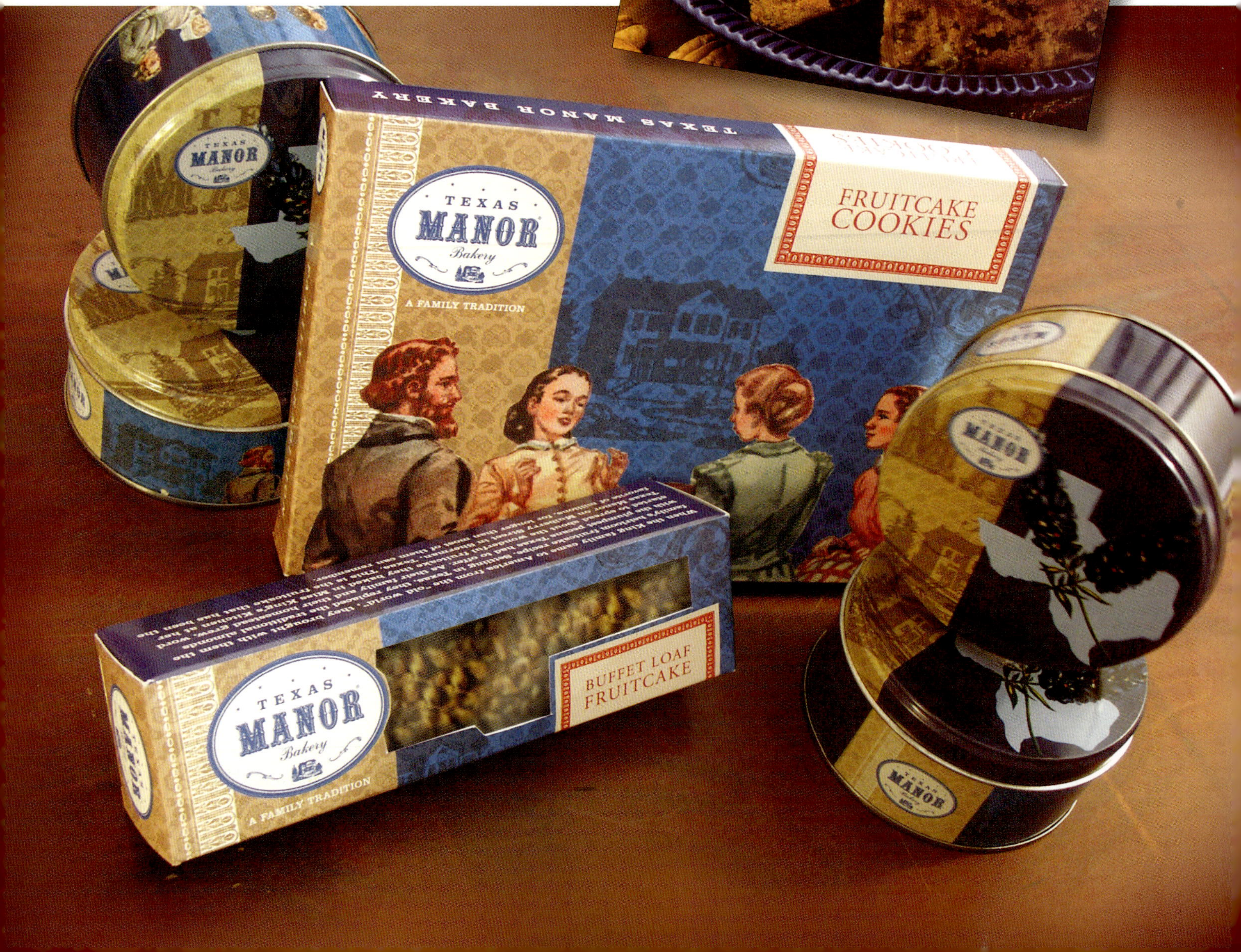

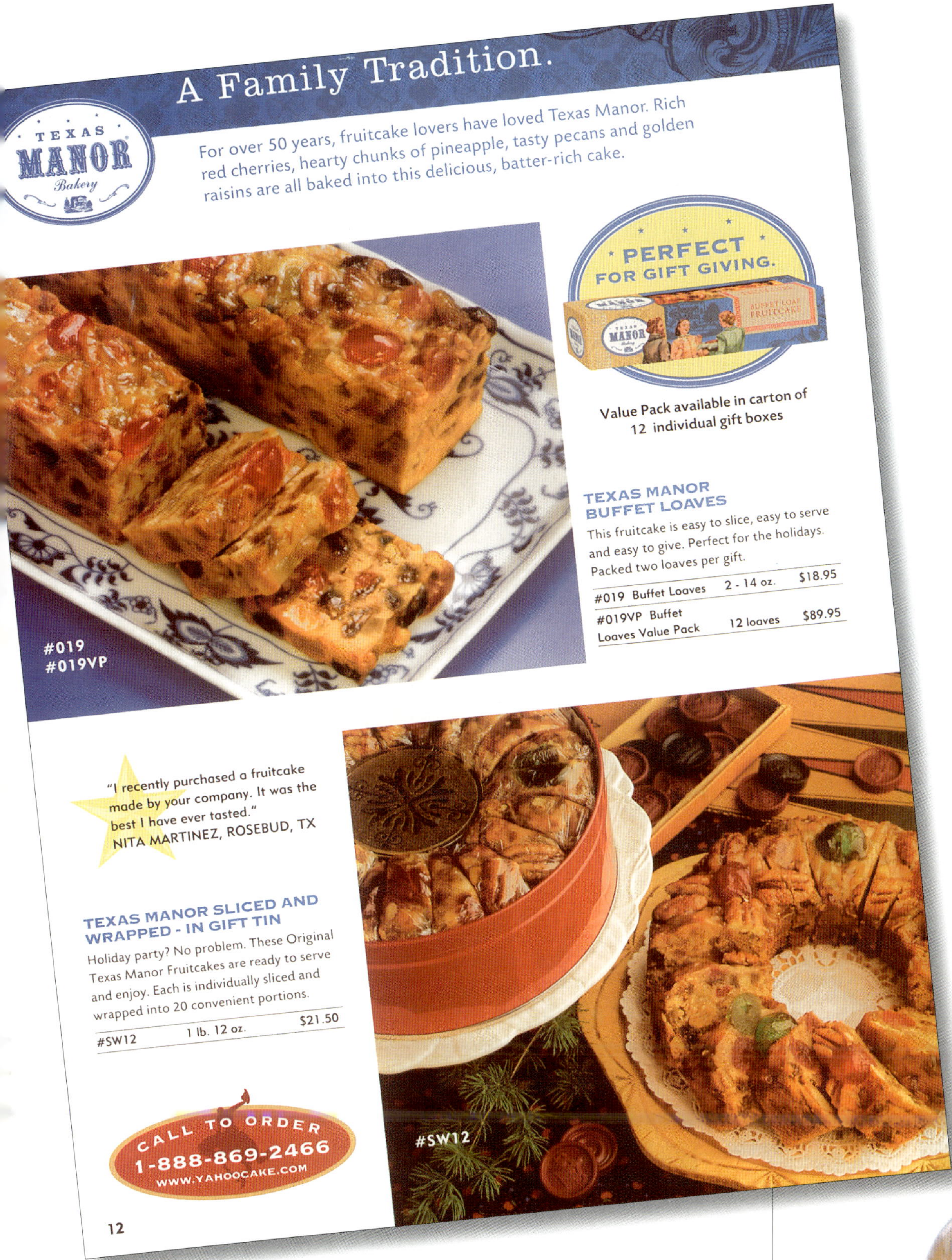

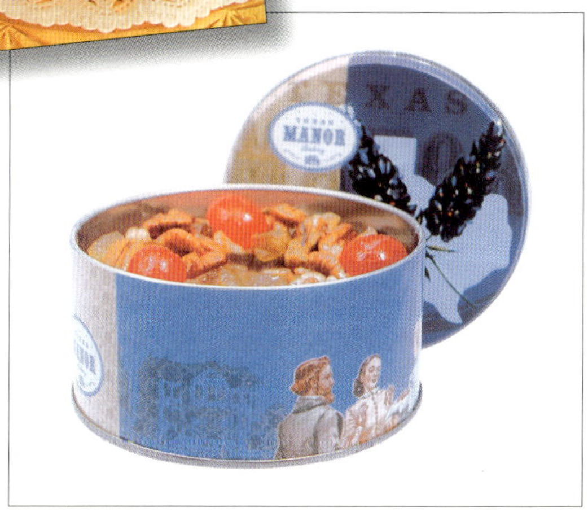

client
The Original Ya-Hoo! Baking Co.
design firm
Marcantel LeBlanc Brand Partnership
designers
Richard LeBlanc, Tom Marcantel

pathways

client
Pathways Church
design firm
Marcantel LeBlanc Brand Partnership
designers
Richard LeBlanc, Tom Marcantel

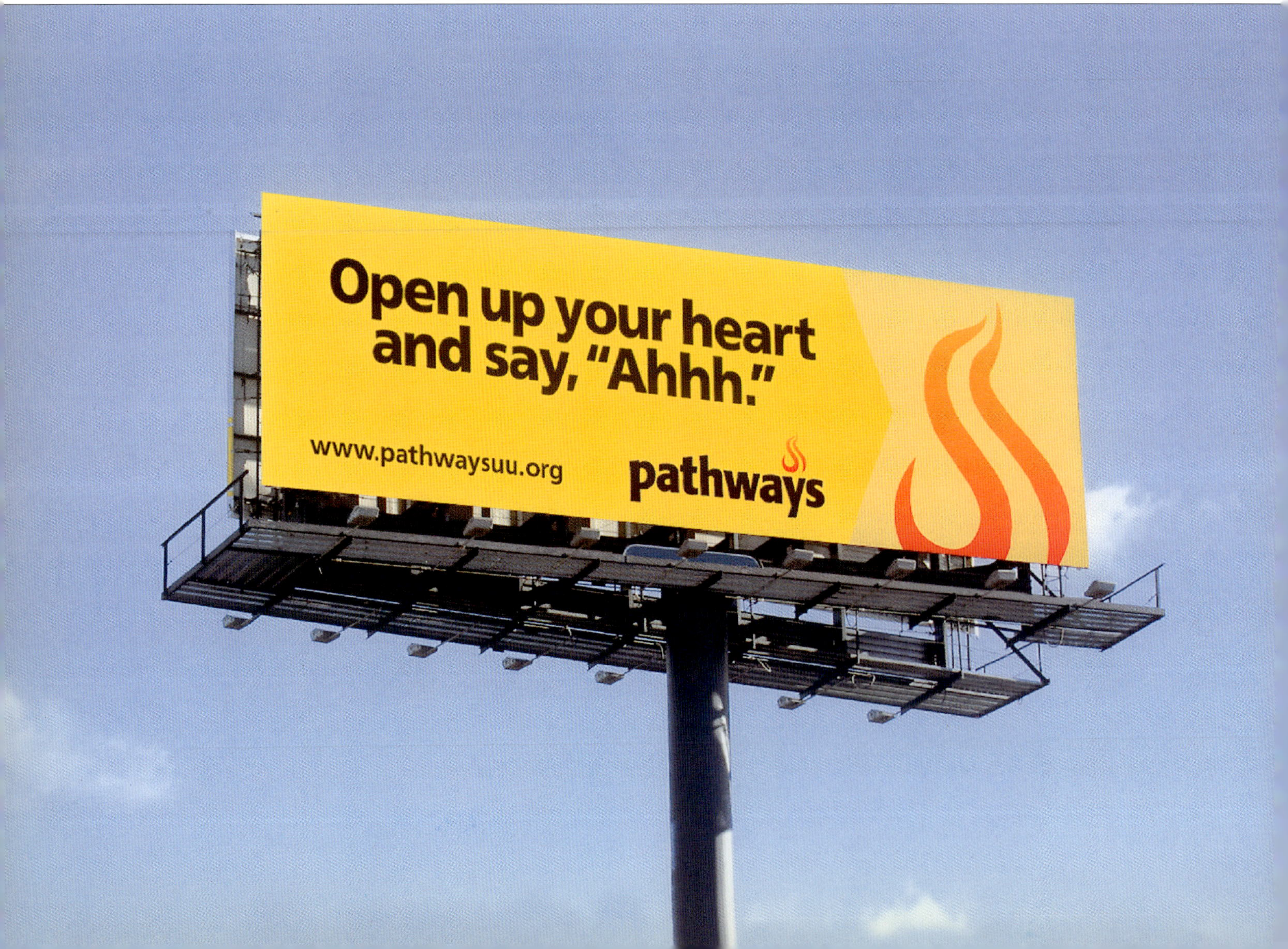

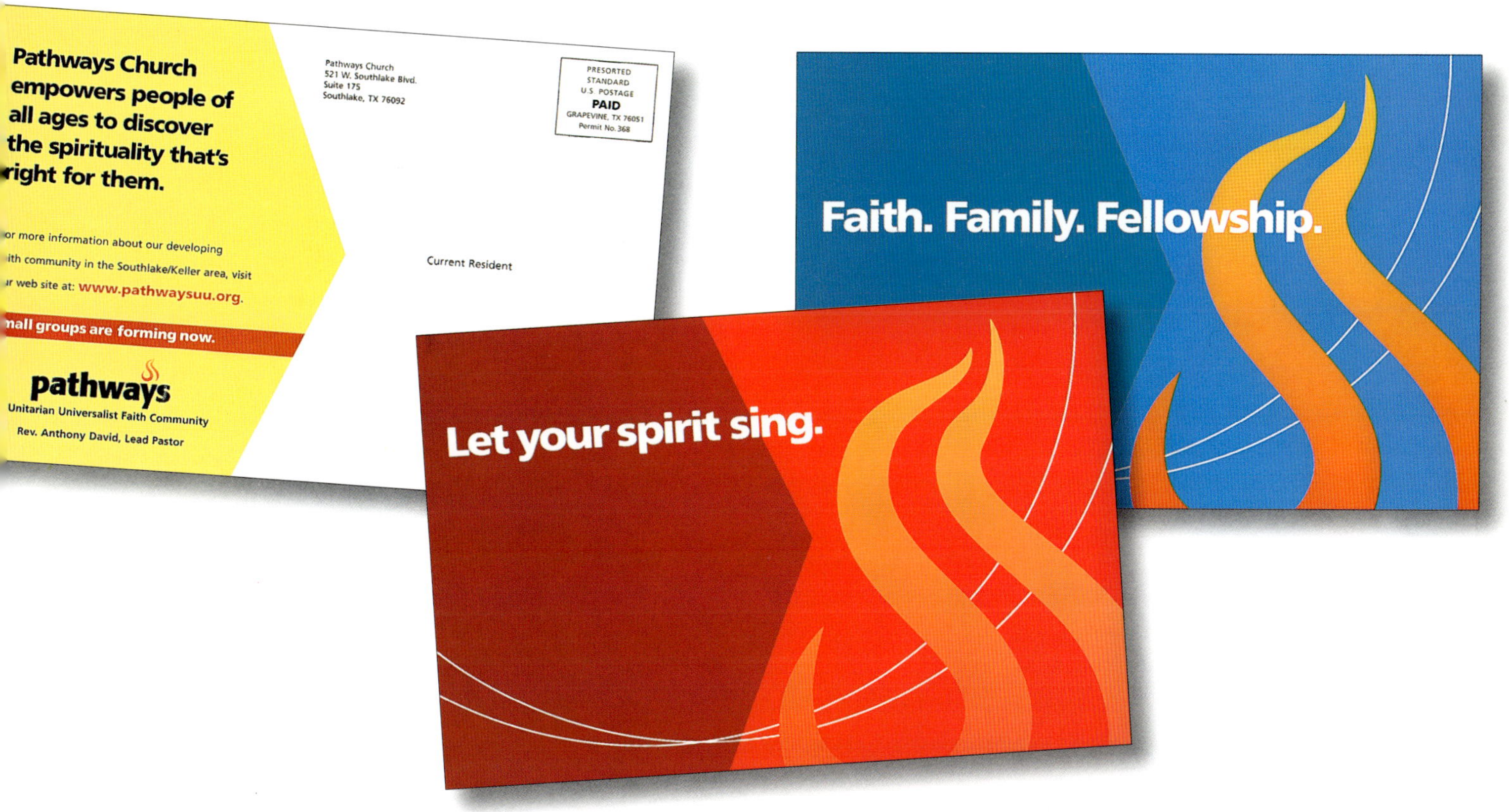
Pathways Church empowers people of all ages to discover the spirituality that's right for them.
or more information about our developing ith community in the Southlake/Keller area, visit r web site at: www.pathwaysuu.org.
mall groups are forming now.
pathways
Unitarian Universalist Faith Community
Rev. Anthony David, Lead Pastor
Pathways Church
521 W. Southlake Blvd.
Suite 175
Southlake, TX 76092
PRESORTED
STANDARD
U.S. POSTAGE
PAID
GRAPEVINE, TX 76051
Permit No. 368
Current Resident
Faith. Family. Fellowship.
Let your spirit sing.

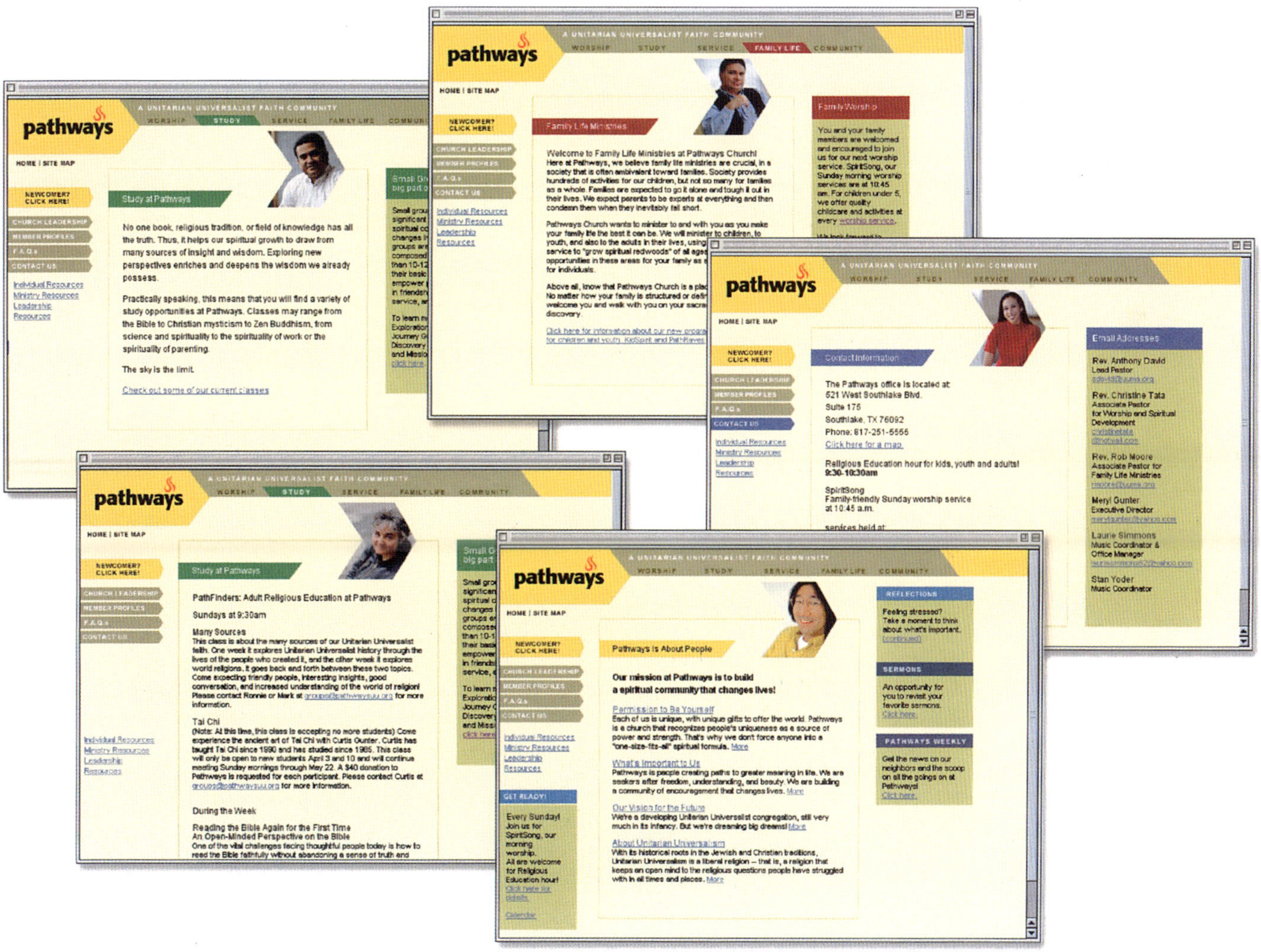
pathways
A UNITARIAN UNIVERSALIST FAITH COMMUNITY
WORSHIP
STUDY
SERVICE
FAMILY LIFE
COMMUNITY
HOME | SITE MAP
NEWCOMER? CLICK HERE!
Study at Pathways
Family Life Ministries
Contact Information
Pathways Is About People

Real Legacy Assurance

client
Real Legacy Assurance Co.
design firm
IDGroup
designers
Abner Gutiérrez,
Jorge Colón,
Mayra Maldonado

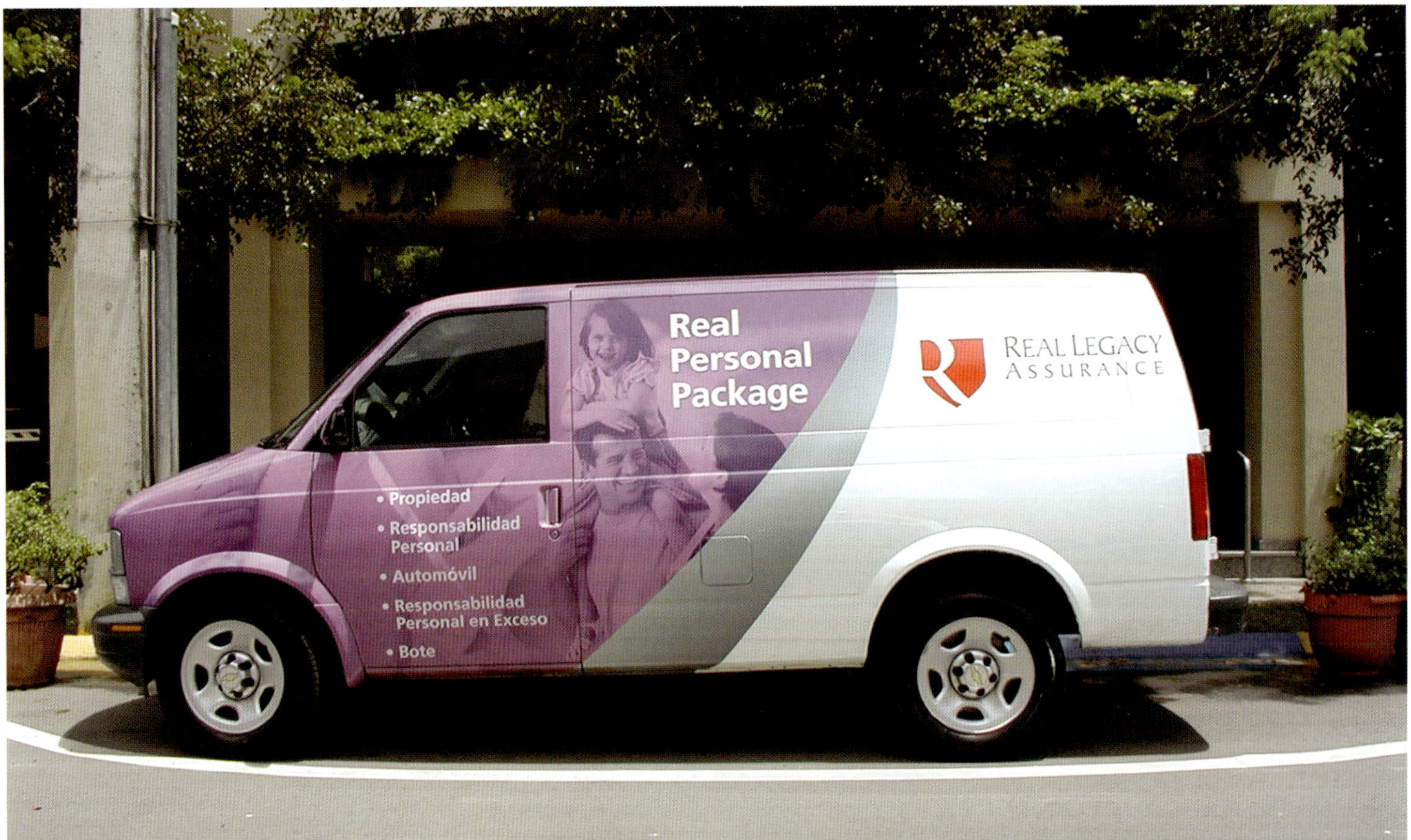

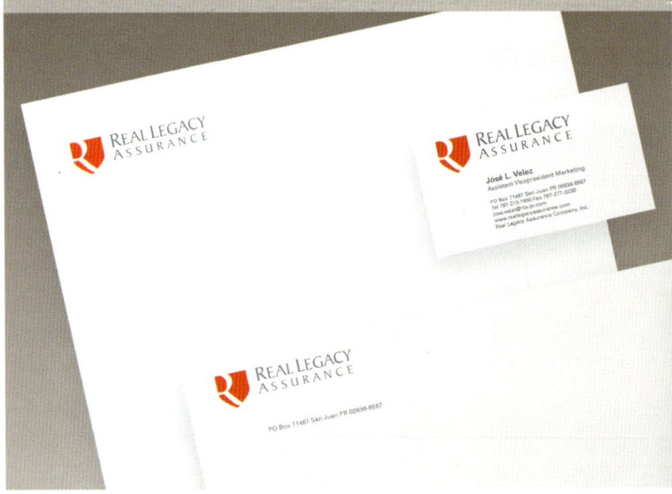

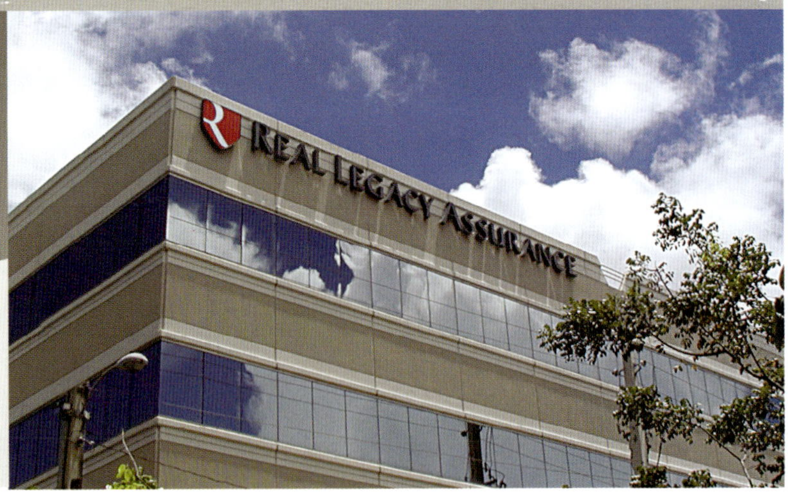

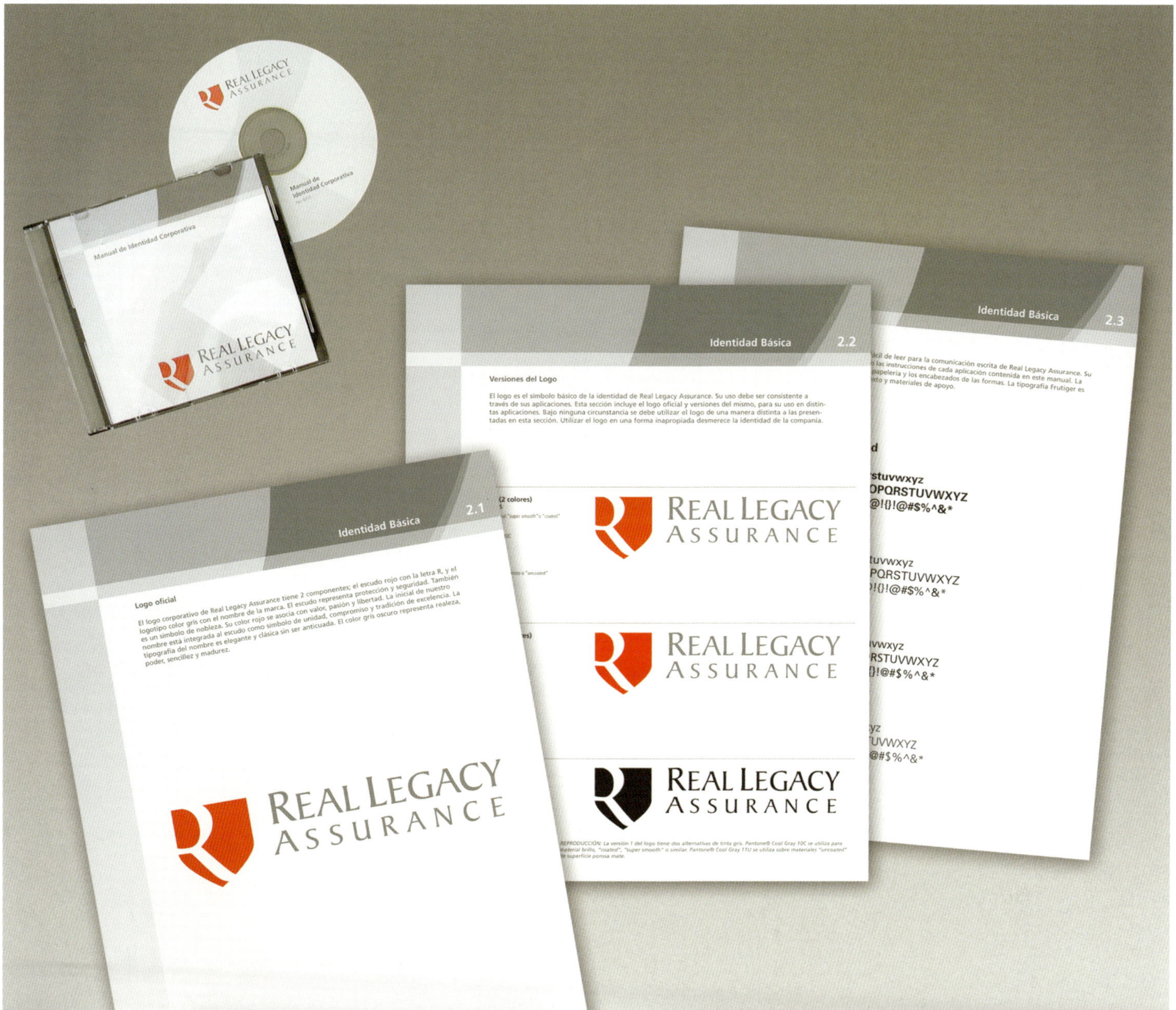
Real Legacy Assurance
Manual de Identidad Corporativa
Real Legacy Assurance
Identidad Básica 2.3
Identidad Básica 2.2
Versiones del Logo
Real Legacy Assurance
Real Legacy Assurance
Real Legacy Assurance
Identidad Básica 2.1
Logo oficial
Real Legacy Assurance

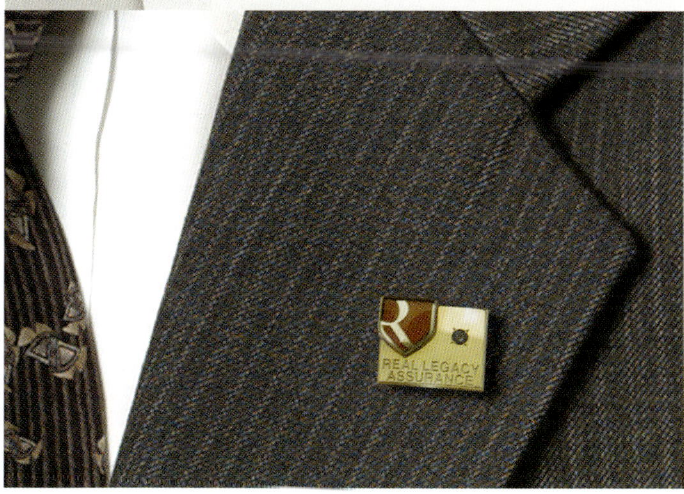
Real Legacy Assurance

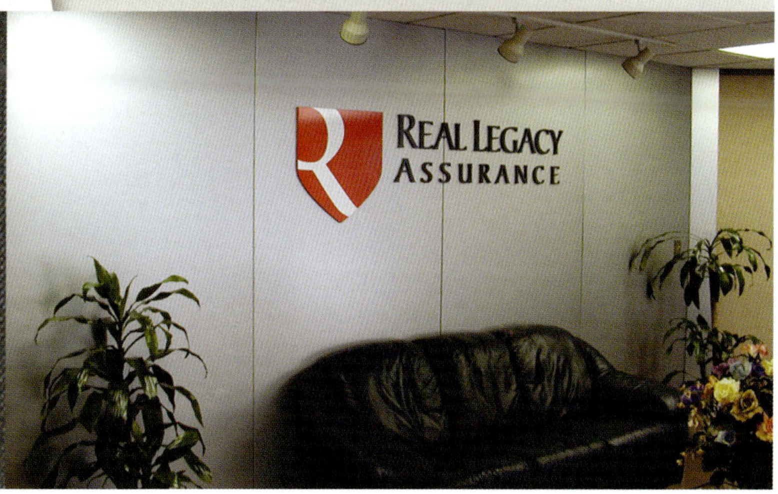
Real Legacy Assurance

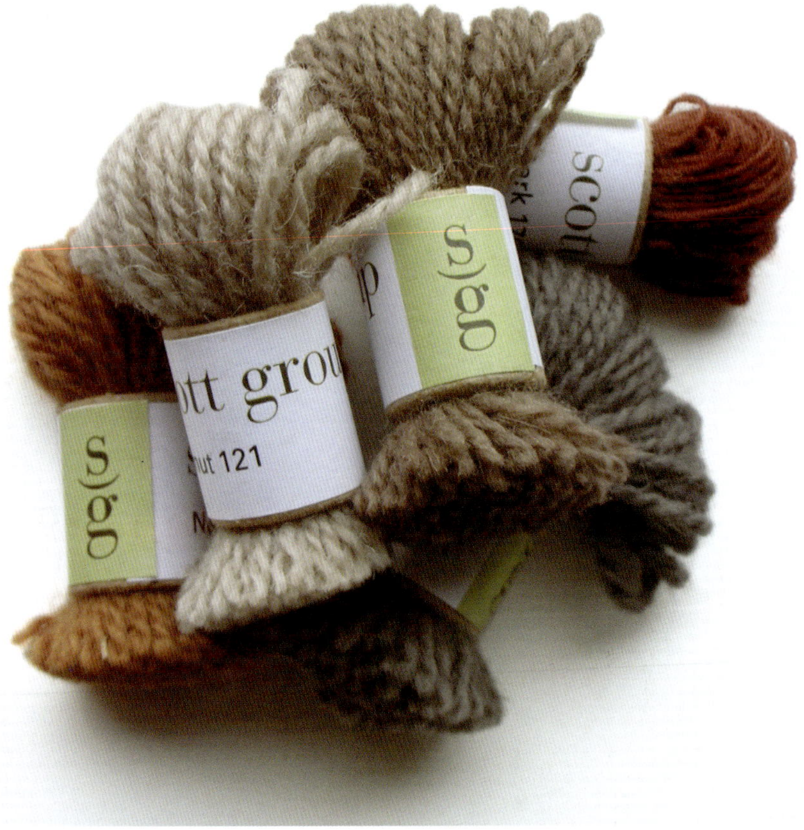

client
Scott Group
design firm
Square One Design
designers
Lin Ver Meulen,
Anna Huddleston

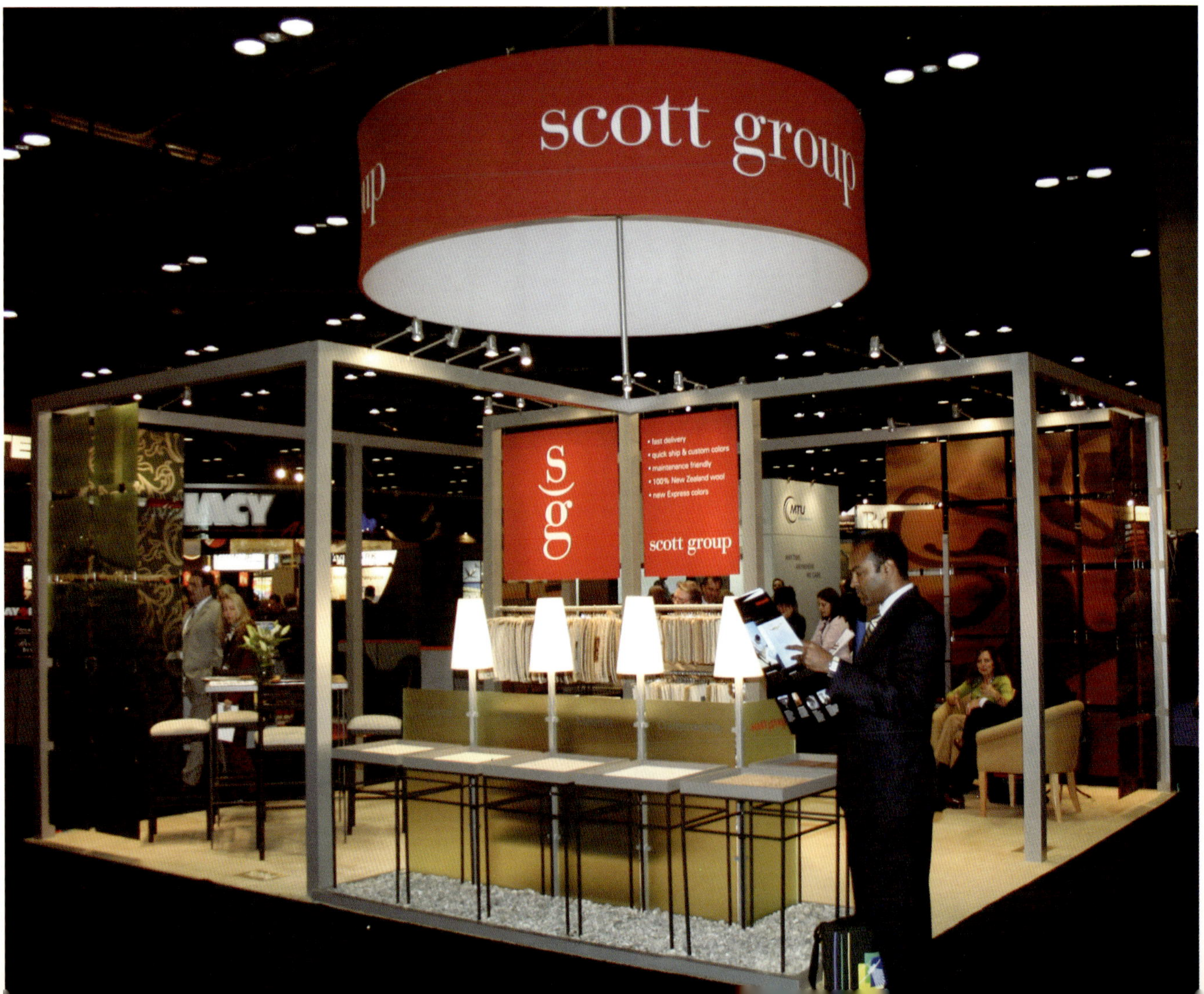

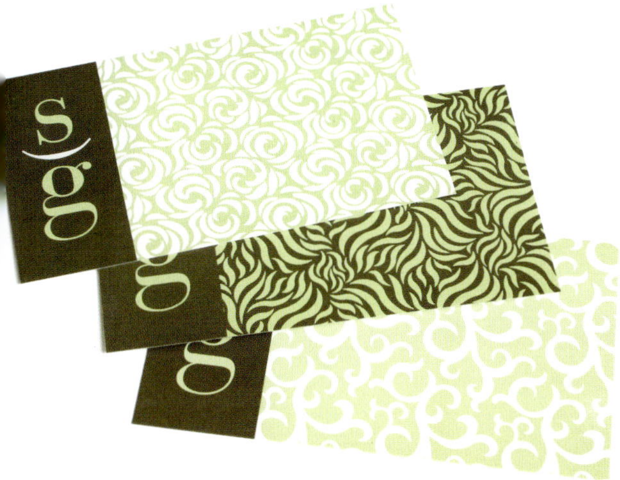

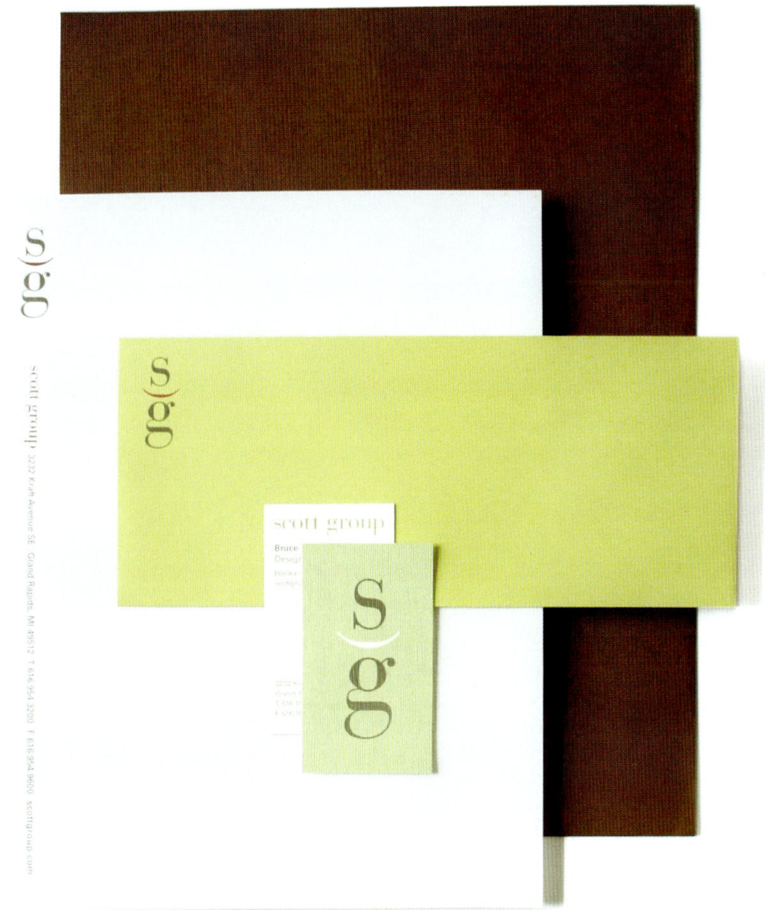
scott group

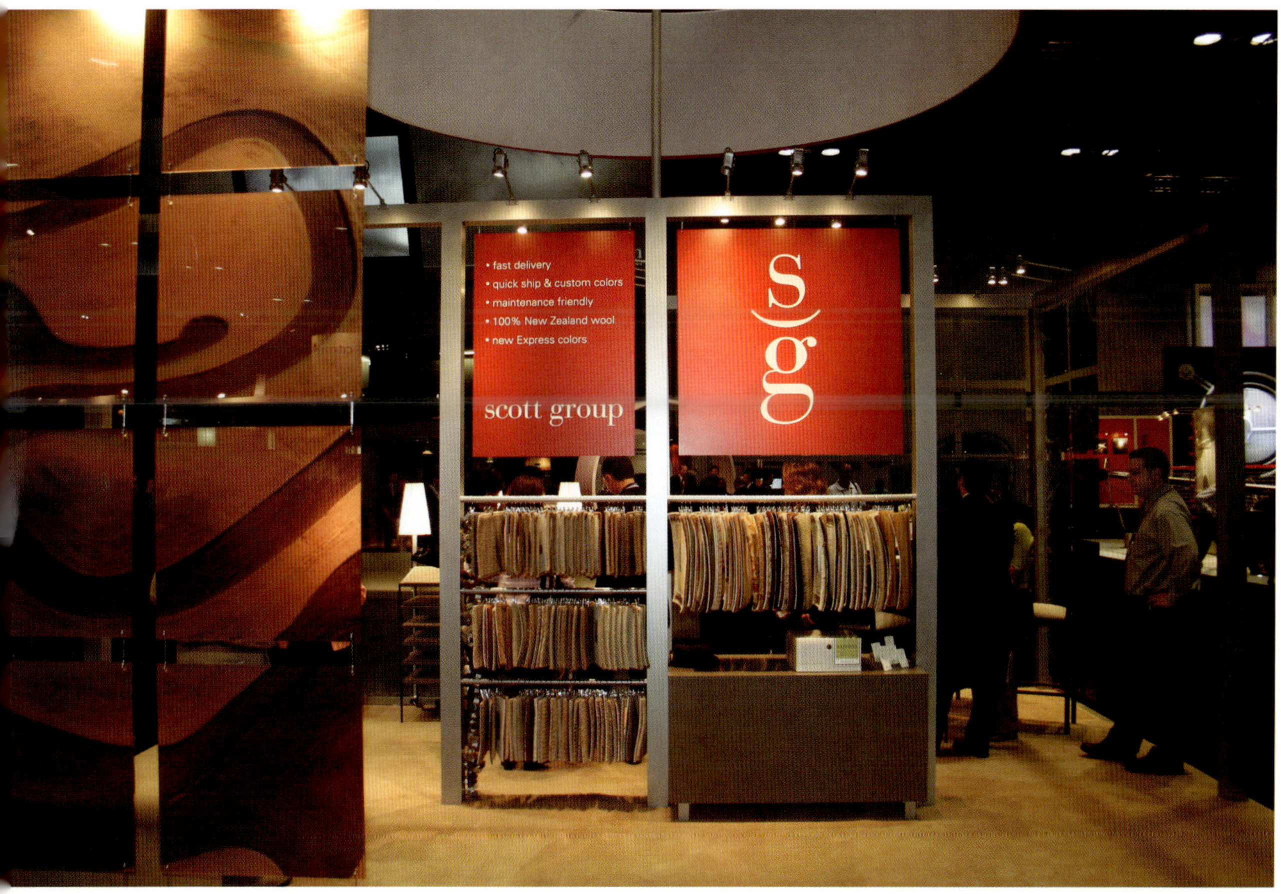
• fast delivery
• quick ship & custom colors
• maintenance friendly
• 100% New Zealand wool
• new Express colors
scott group

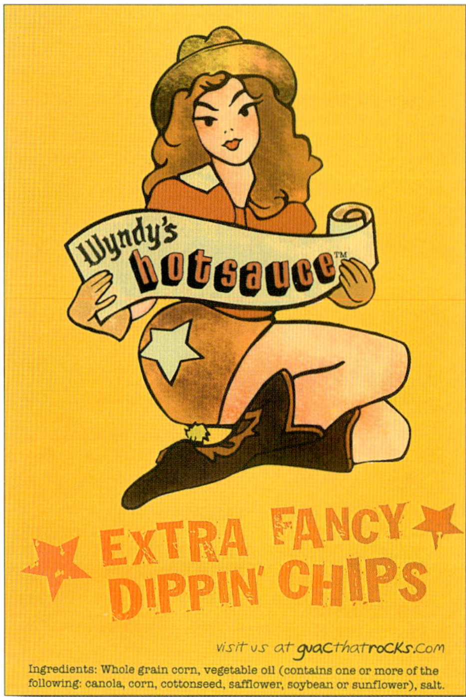

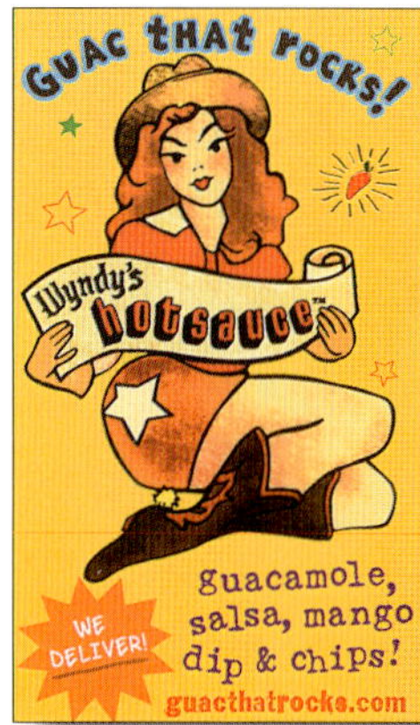

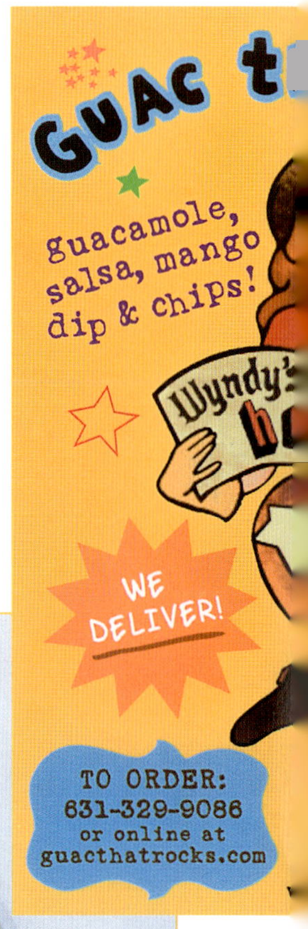

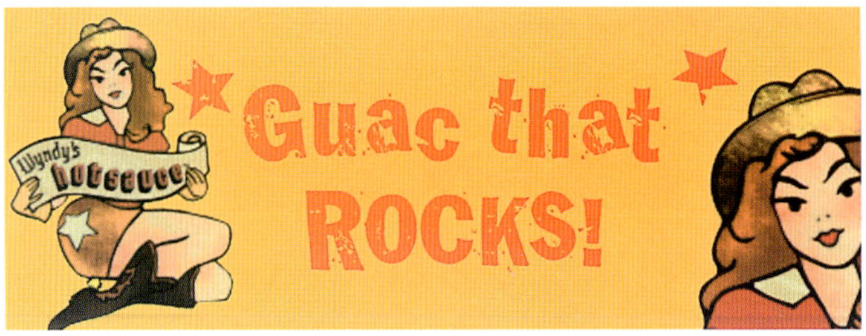

Banner

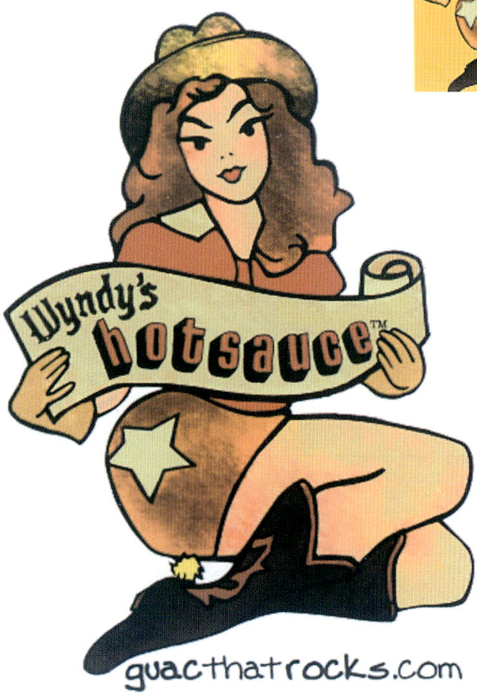

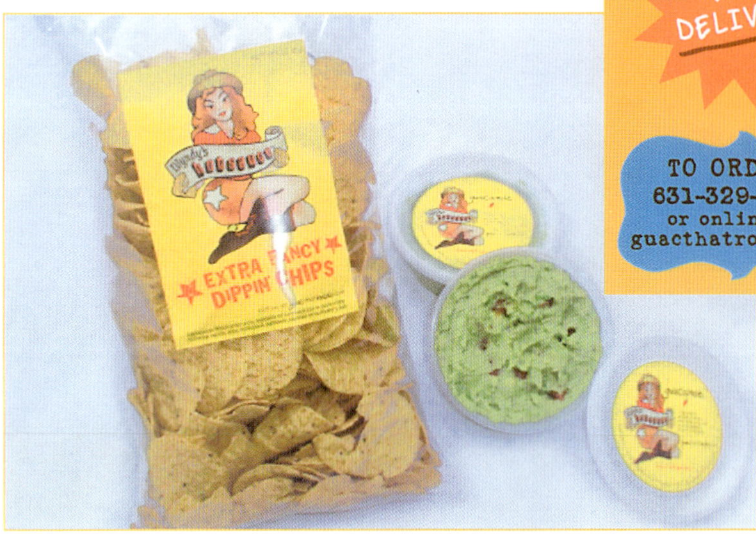

Packaging

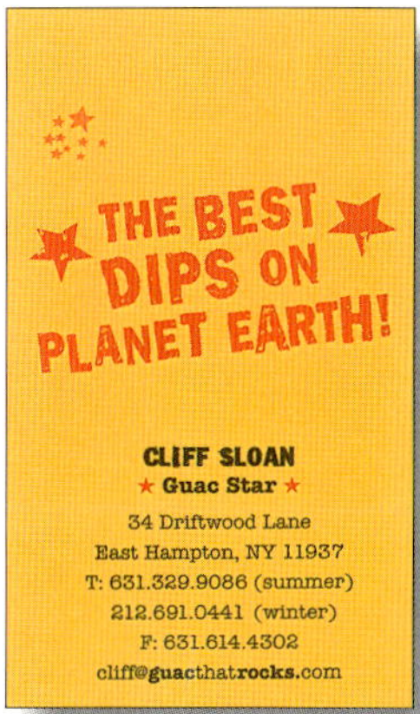

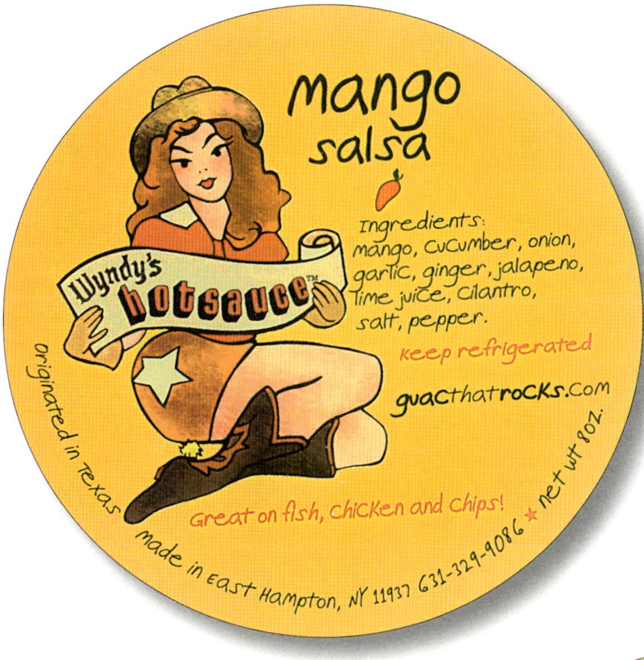

client
Wyndy's Hotsauce
design firm
Hotsauce
designer
Wyndy Wilder Sloan

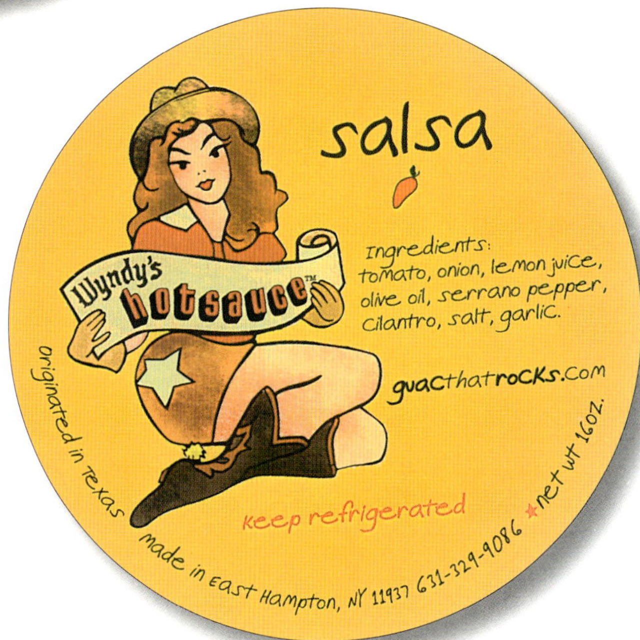

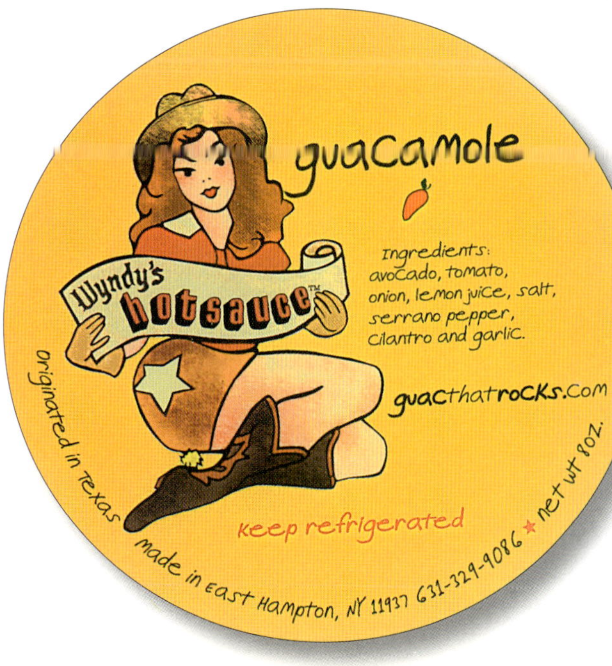

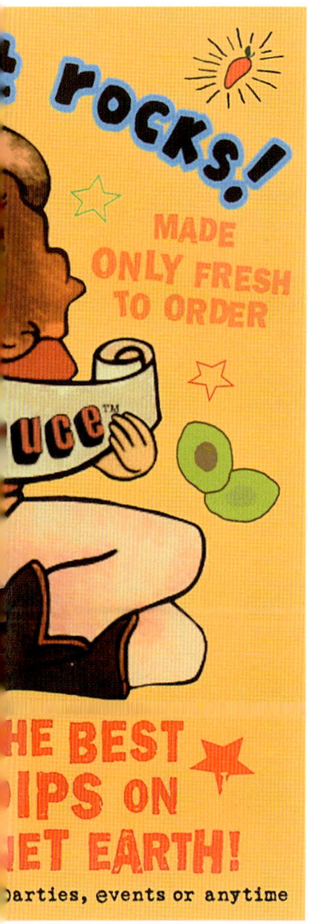

Promotional

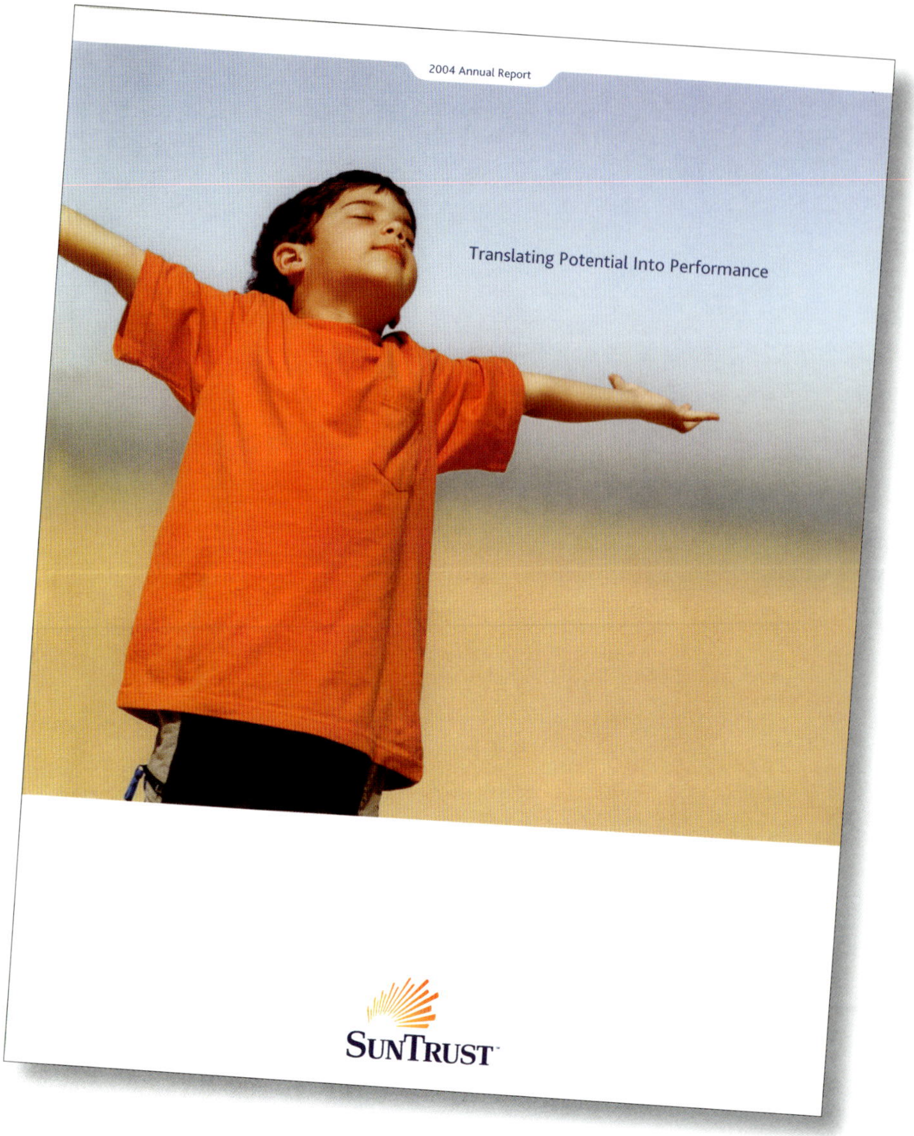
2004 Annual Report
Translating Potential Into Performance
SunTrust

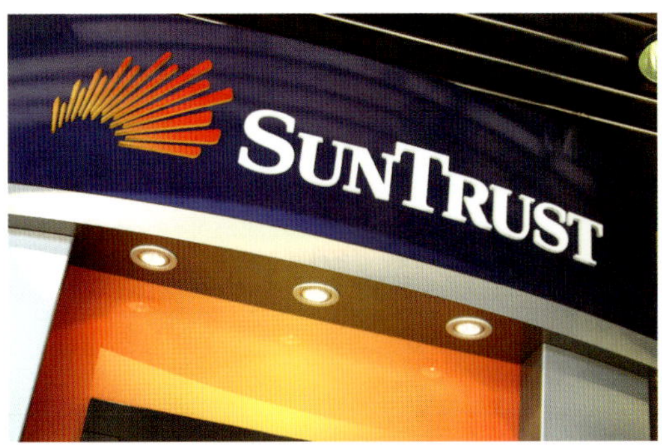
SunTrust

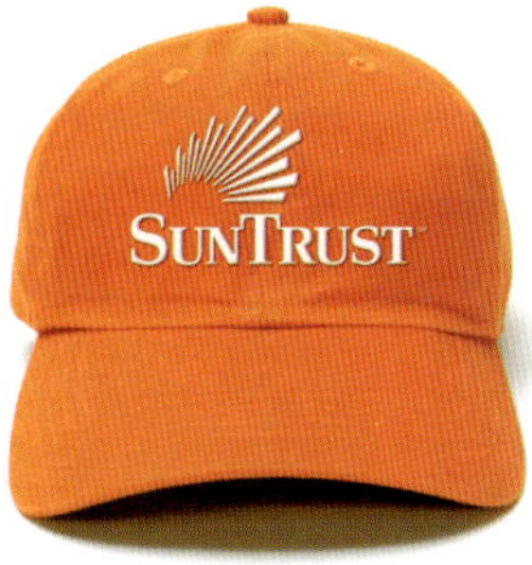

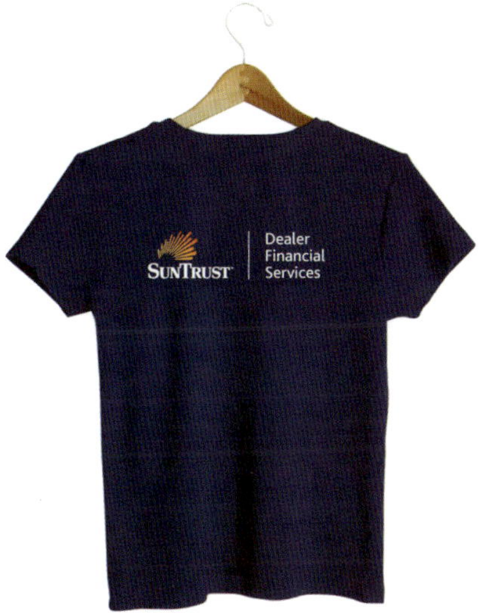

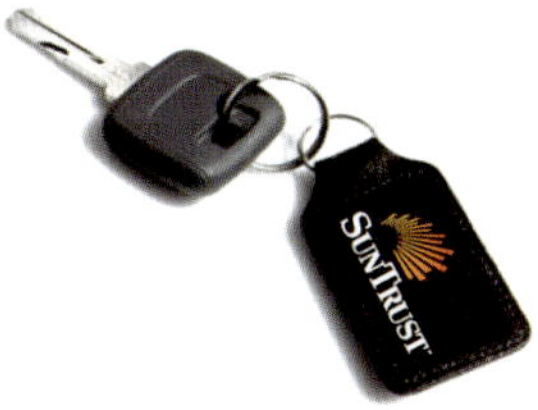

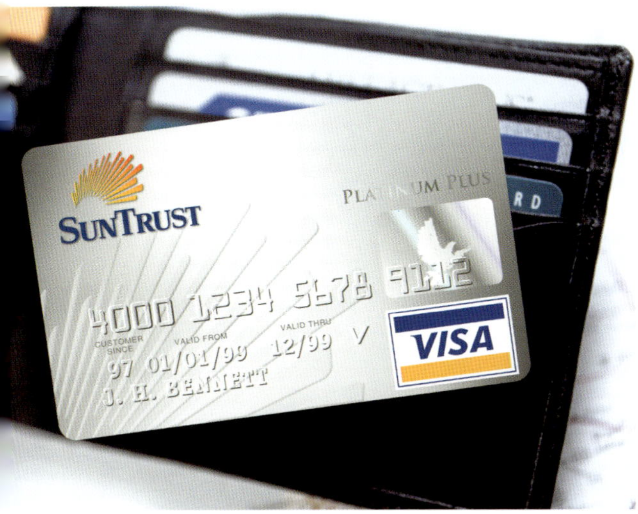

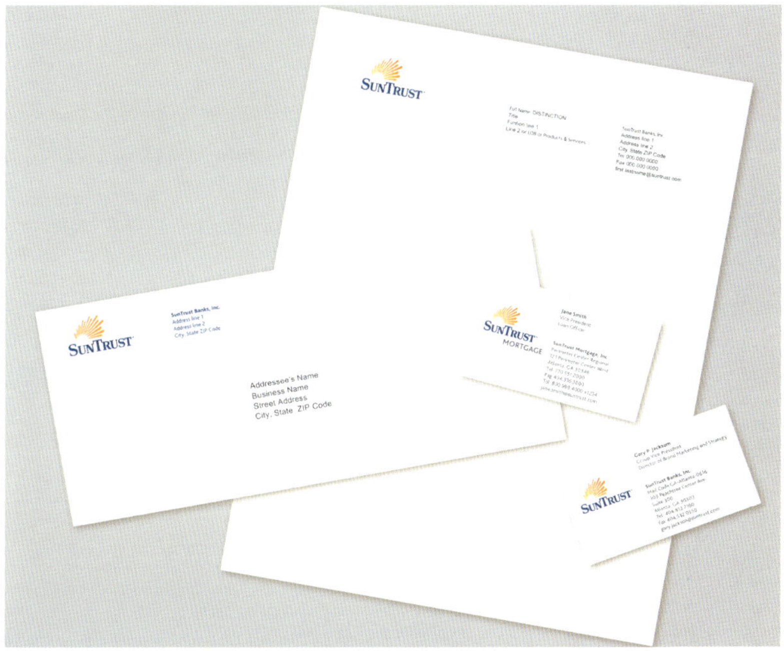

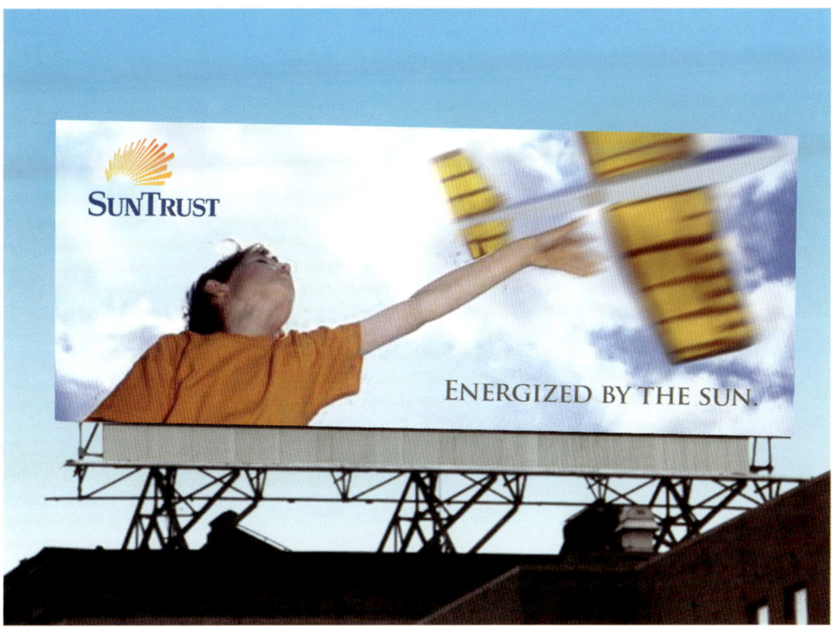

client
SunTrust Bank
design firm
Siegel & Gale
creative director
Howard Belk
design directors
Marie Schabenbeck,
Justin Peters
designer
Glen Barry

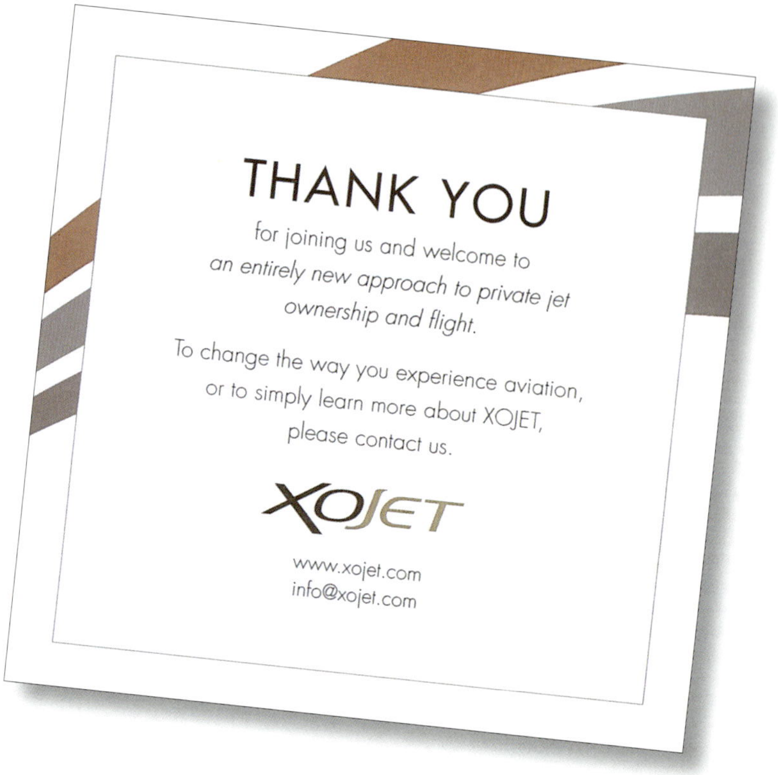

client
XOJET
design firm
brandadvisors
designers
Lindon Leader,
Julia Hencz,
Charles Rashall

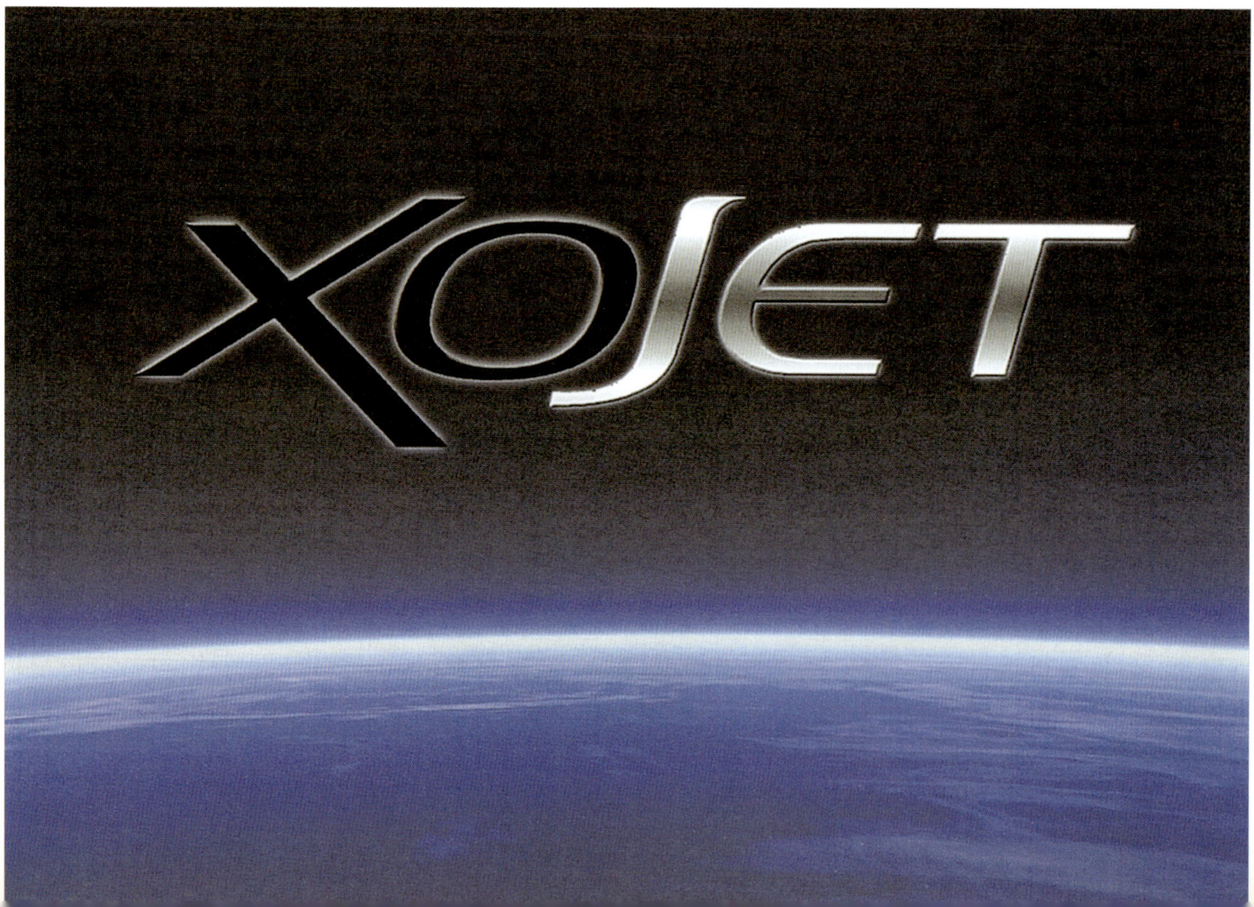

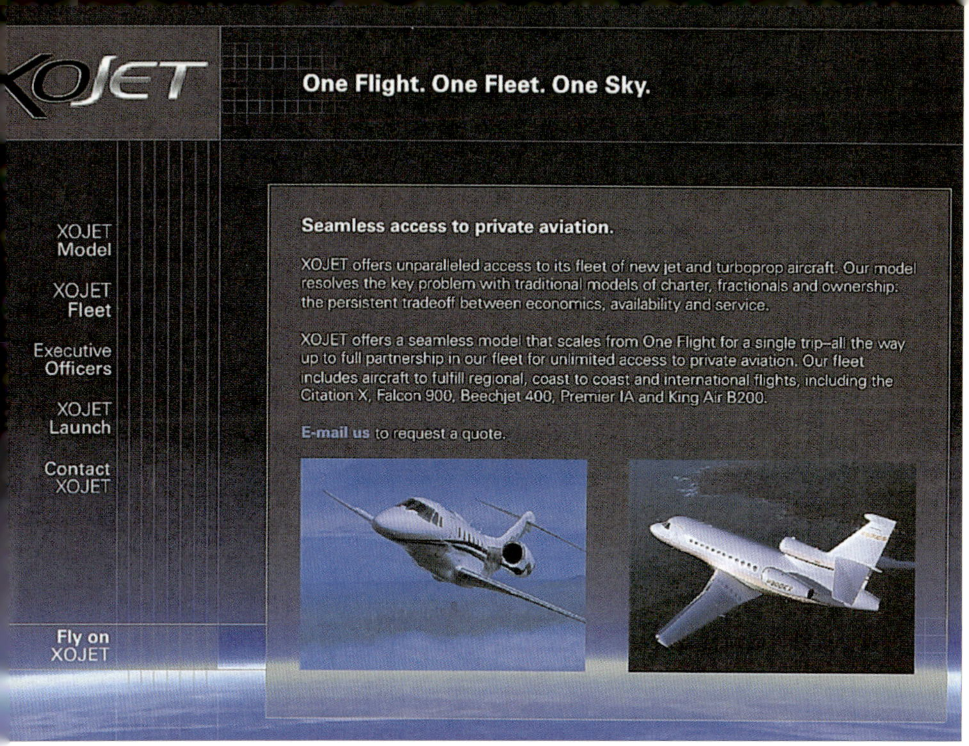
XOJET
One Flight. One Fleet. One Sky.
XOJET Model
XOJET Fleet
Executive Officers
XOJET Launch
Contact XOJET
Fly on XOJET
Seamless access to private aviation.
XOJET offers unparalleled access to its fleet of new jet and turboprop aircraft. Our model resolves the key problem with traditional models of charter, fractionals and ownership: the persistent tradeoff between economics, availability and service.
XOJET offers a seamless model that scales from One Flight for a single trip–all the way up to full partnership in our fleet for unlimited access to private aviation. Our fleet includes aircraft to fulfill regional, coast to coast and international flights, including the Citation X, Falcon 900, Beechjet 400, Premier IA and King Air B200.
E-mail us to request a quote.

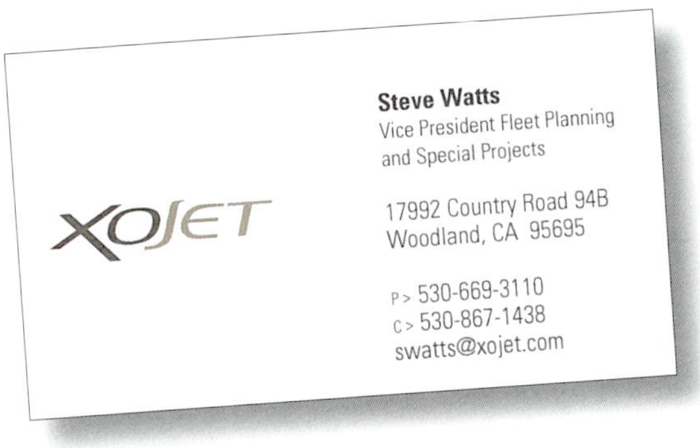
XOJET
Steve Watts
Vice President Fleet Planning and Special Projects
17992 Country Road 94B
Woodland, CA 95695
P> 530-669-3110
C> 530-867-1438
swatts@xojet.com

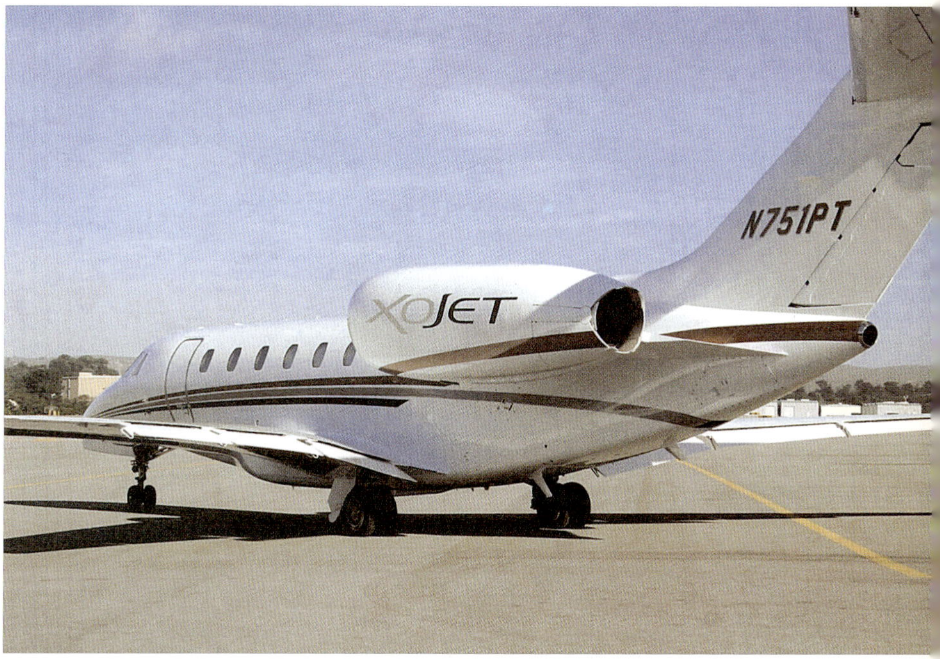
N751PT
XOJET

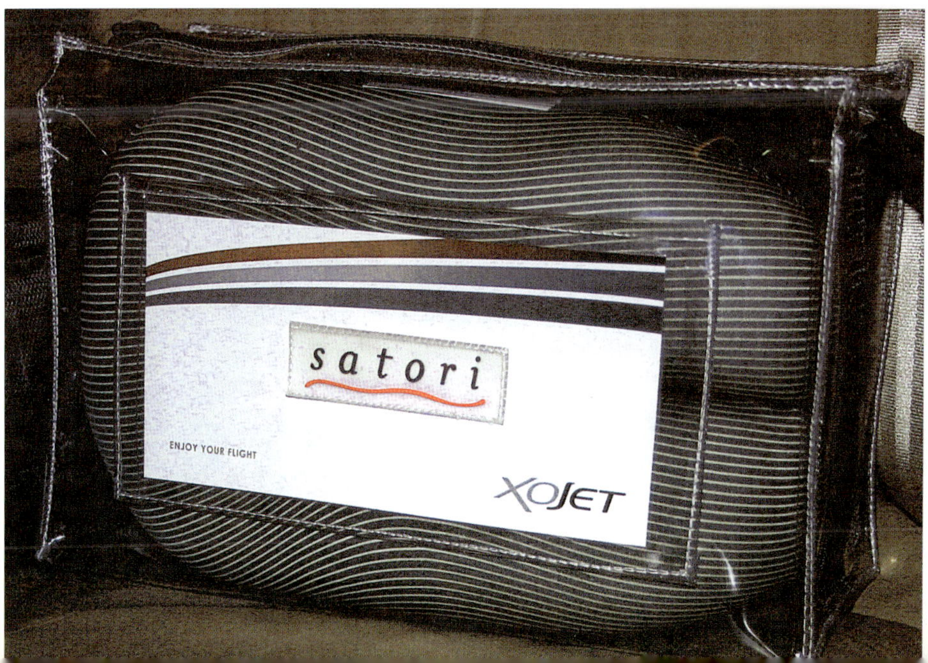
satori
ENJOY YOUR FLIGHT
XOJET

starlight starbright
children's foundation

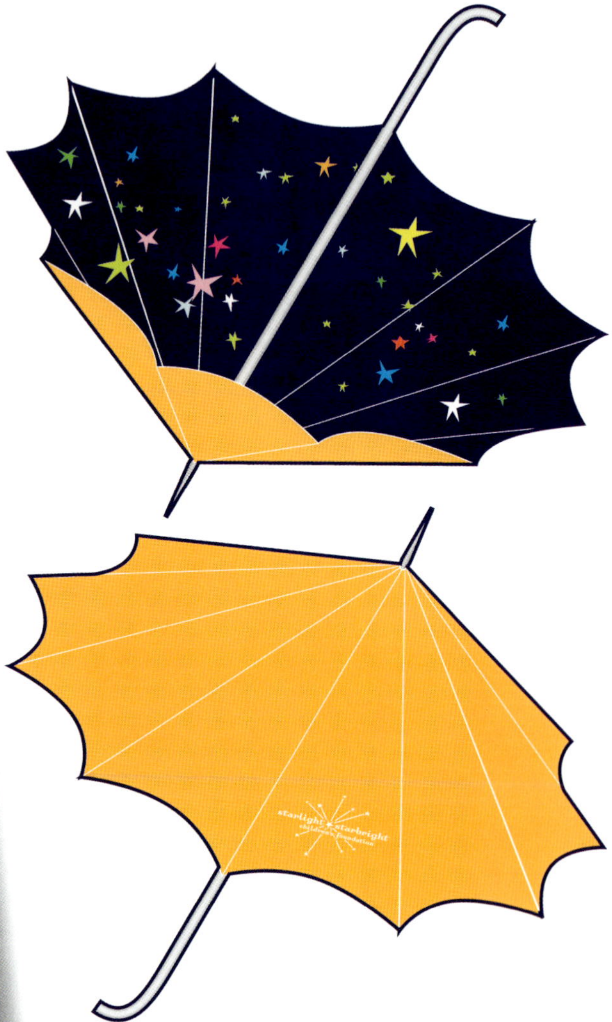

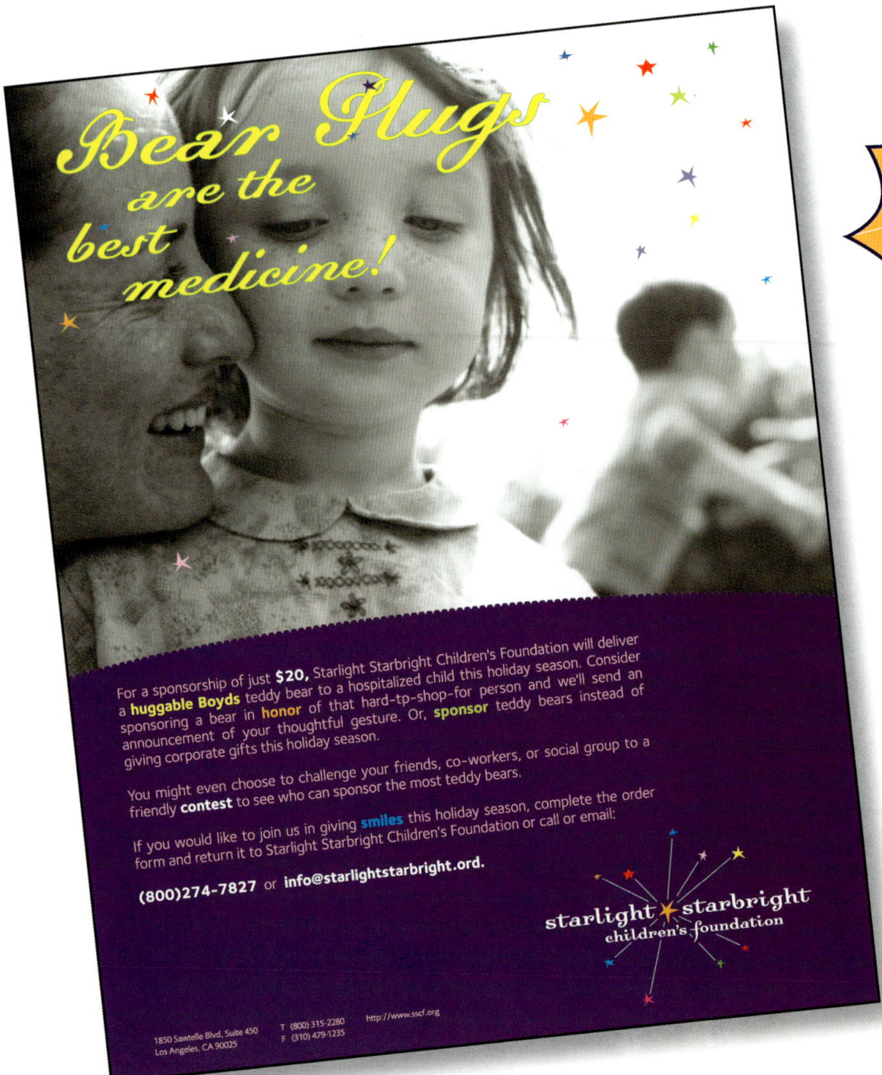

client
Starlight Starbright Children's Foundation
designers
Christina Antonopoulos,
Miho Nishimaniwa

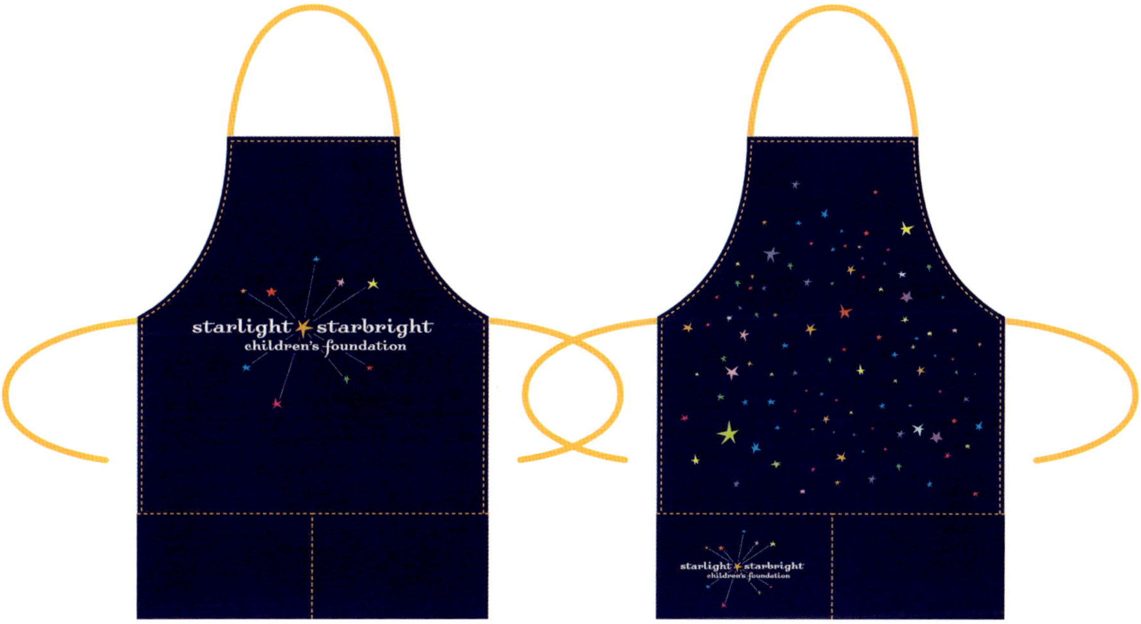
starlight starbright
children's foundation
starlight starbright
children's foundation

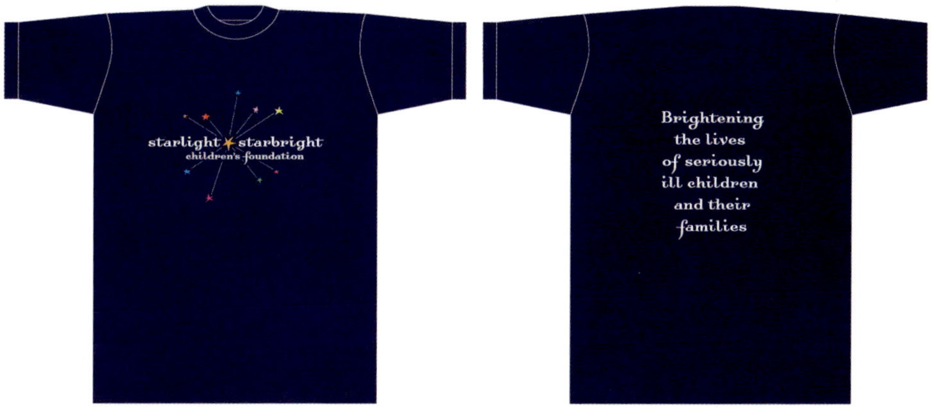
starlight starbright
children's foundation
Brightening
the lives
of seriously
ill children
and their
families

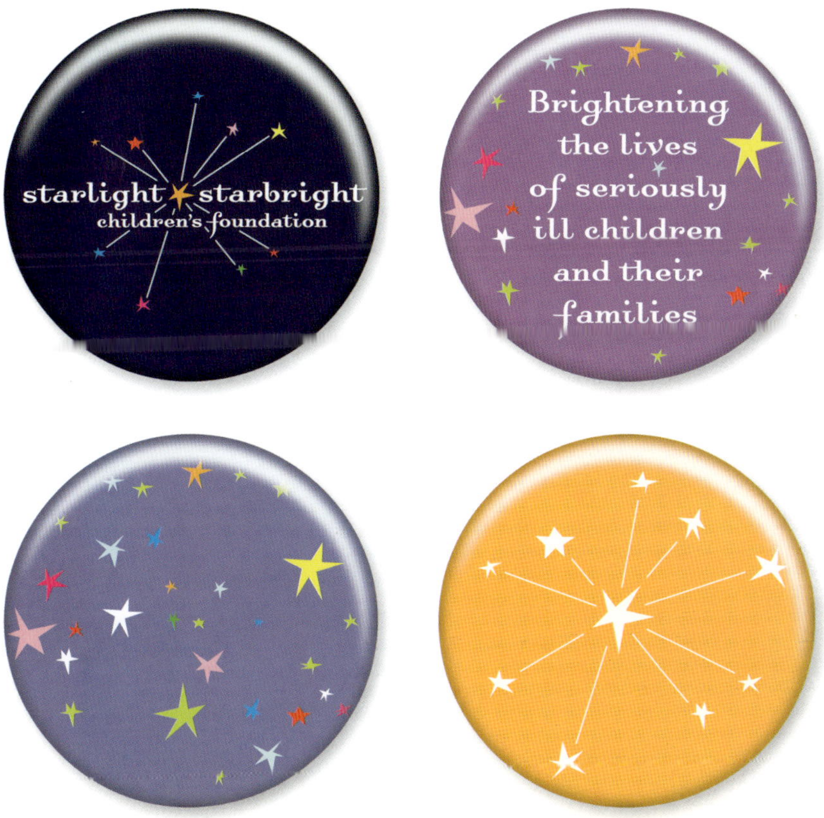
starlight starbright
children's foundation
Brightening
the lives
of seriously
ill children
and their
families

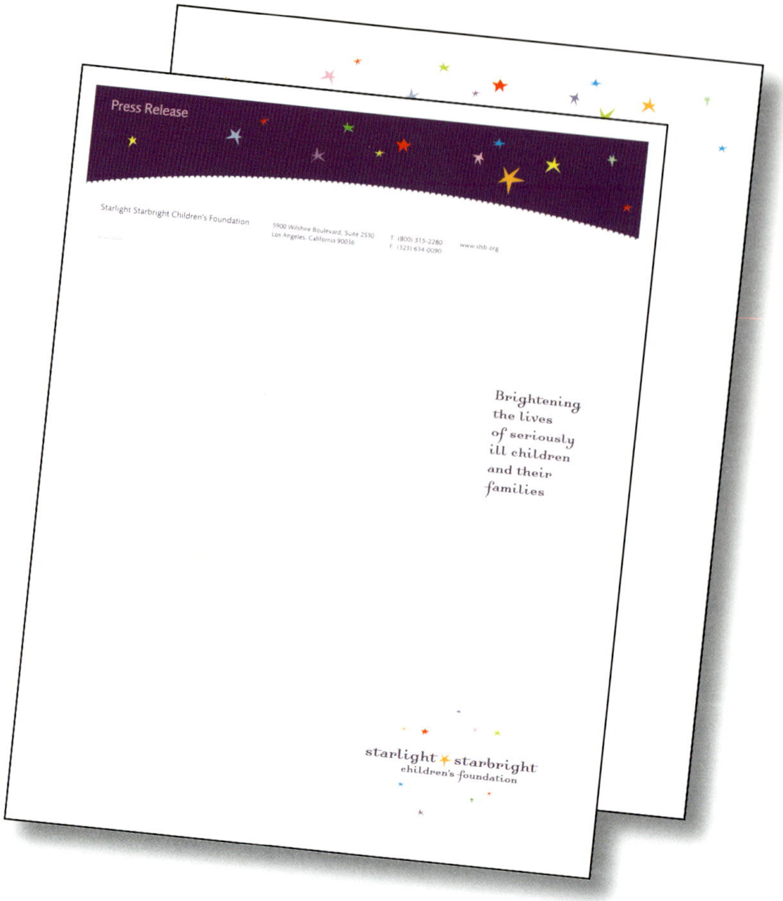

(continued)
client
Starlight Starbright Children's Foundation

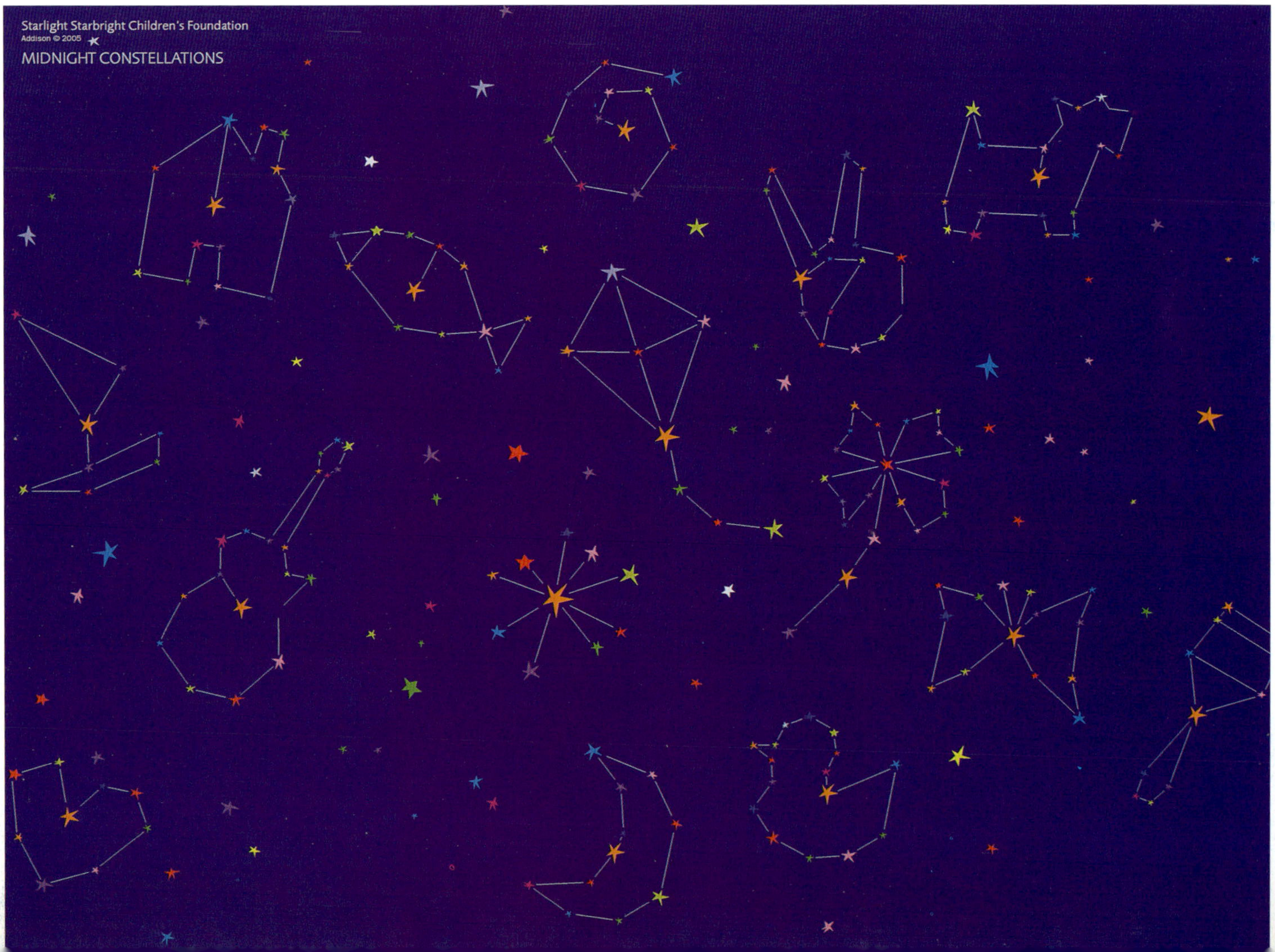

Package Design

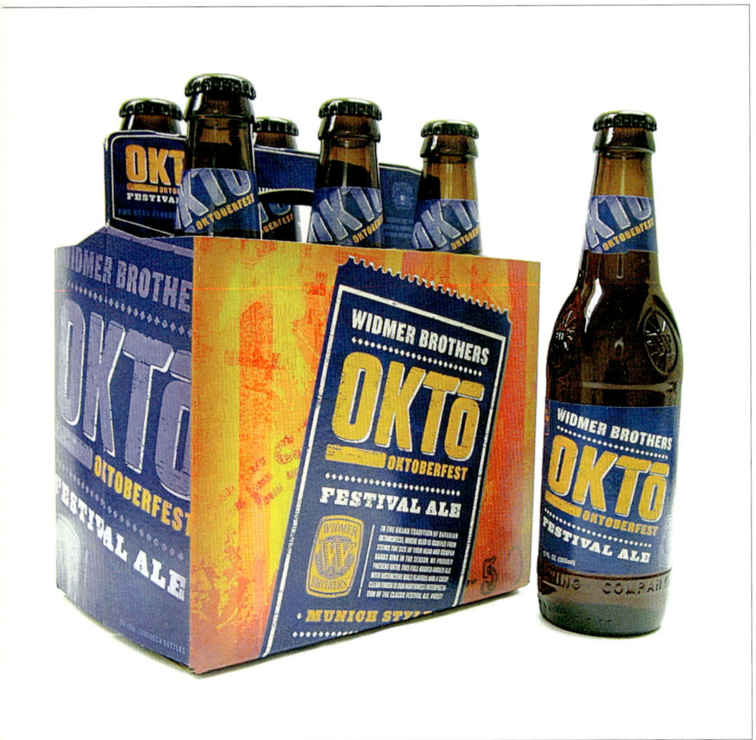

client
Widmer Brothers Brewery
design firm
Hornall Anderson Design Works
designers
Larry Anderson, Jack Anderson,
Jay Hilburn, Bruce Stigler, Henry Yiu,
Elmer dela Cruz, Bruce Branson-Meyer

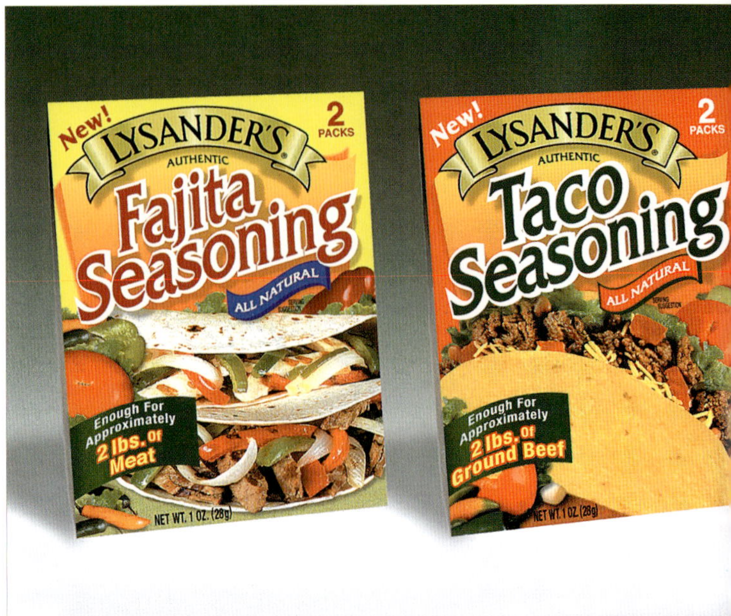

client
Geneva Foods, LLC (Sanford, FL)
design firm
J. Roy Parcels Associates
designers
J. Roy Parcels Associates

client
Jennie-O Turkey Store
design firm
Semmer Group
designers
Emily Oberg, Roger Remaley

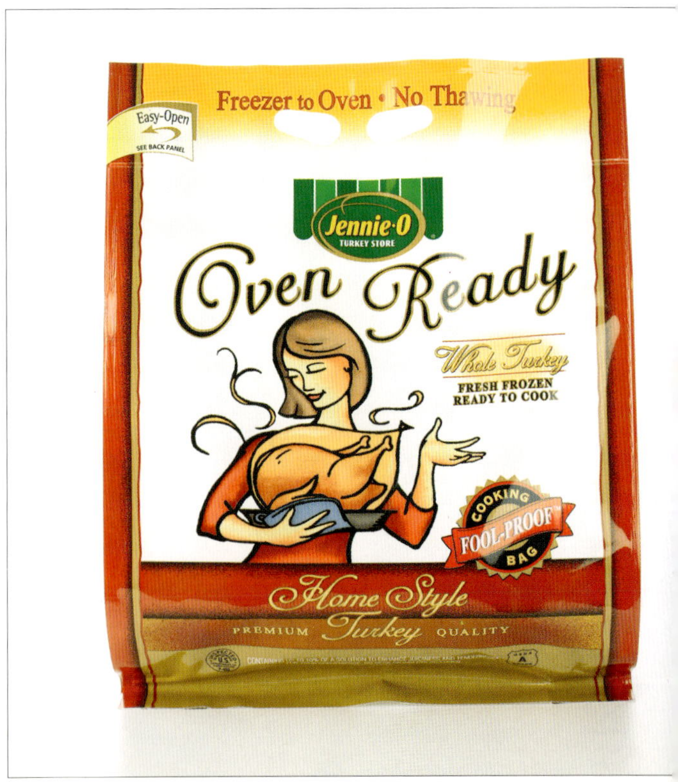

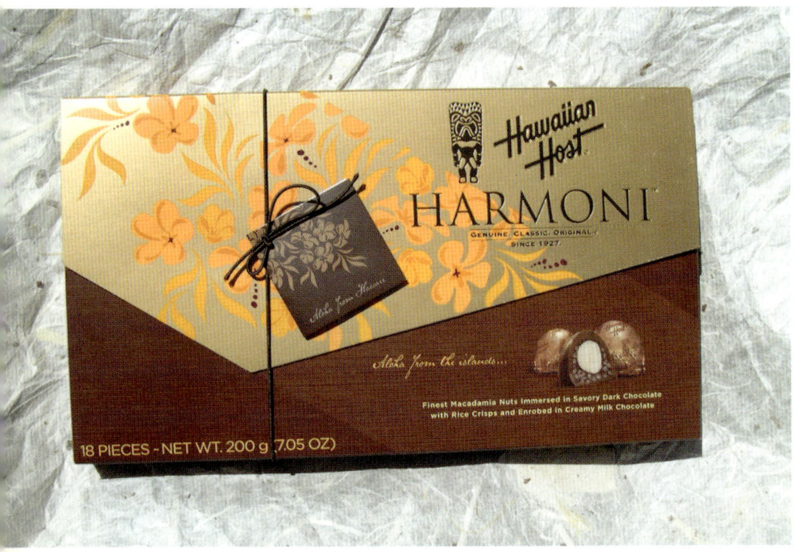

client
Hawaiian Host
design firm
Hornall Anderson Design Works
designers
Larry Anderson, Jay Hilburn,
Holly Craven, Jacob Carter,
Beth Grimm, Bruce Stigler,
Chris Freed, Yuri Shvets

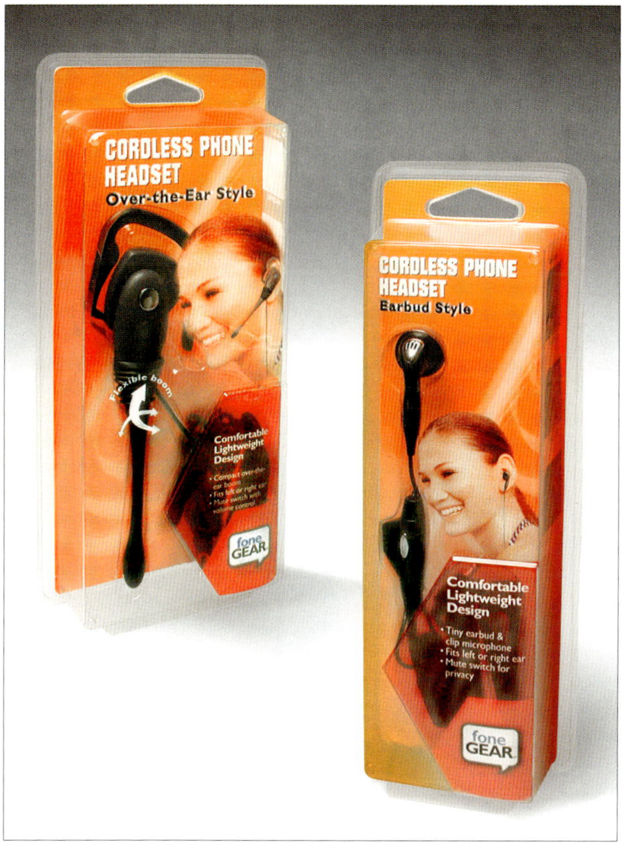

client
foneGEAR
design firm
Zen Design Group
designers
Kok Hwa Chung,
David Perrin,
Matt Chapman

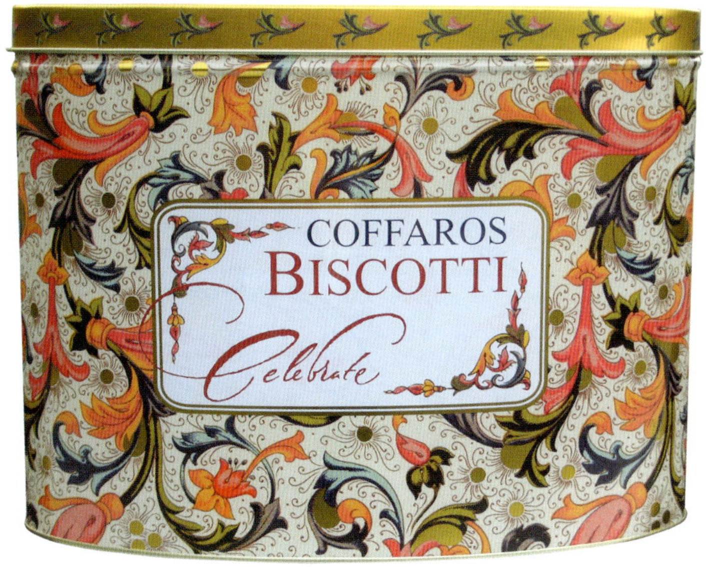

client
Coffaros Baking Company
design firm
Walsh Design
designer
Miriam Lisco

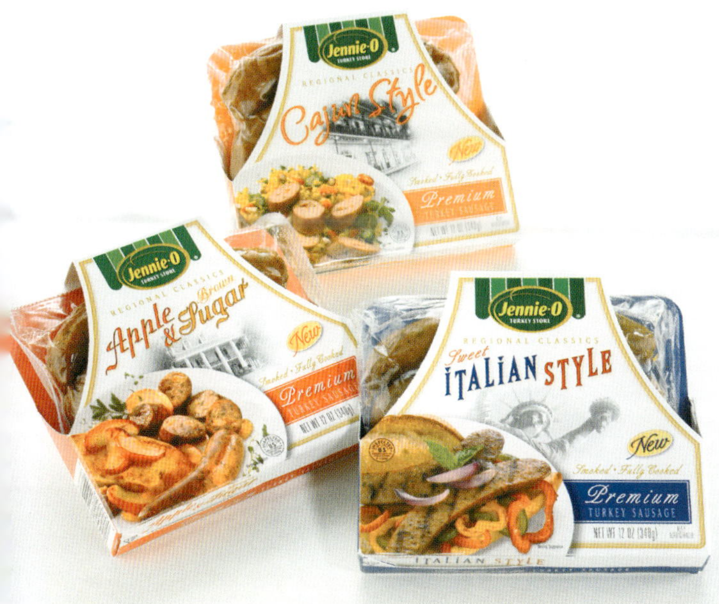

client
Jennie-O Turkey Store
design firm
Semmer Group
designers
Emily Oberg, Matt McKee

client
Nancy's Specialty Foods
design firm
Brand Engine
art director
Eric Read
designer
Coralie Russo

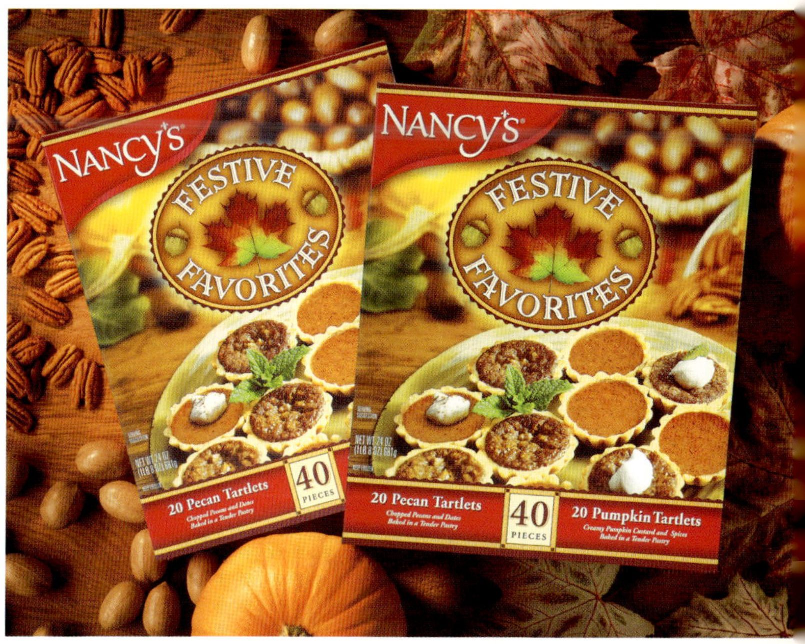

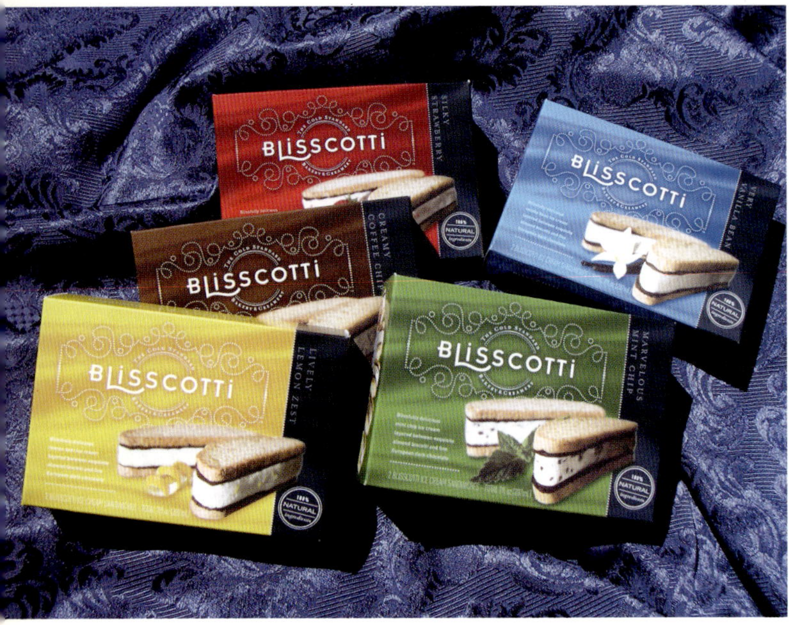

client
Bliscotti
design firm
Hornall Anderson Design Works
designers
Larry Anderson, Jack Anderson,
Holly Craven, Jay Hilburn, Chris Freed

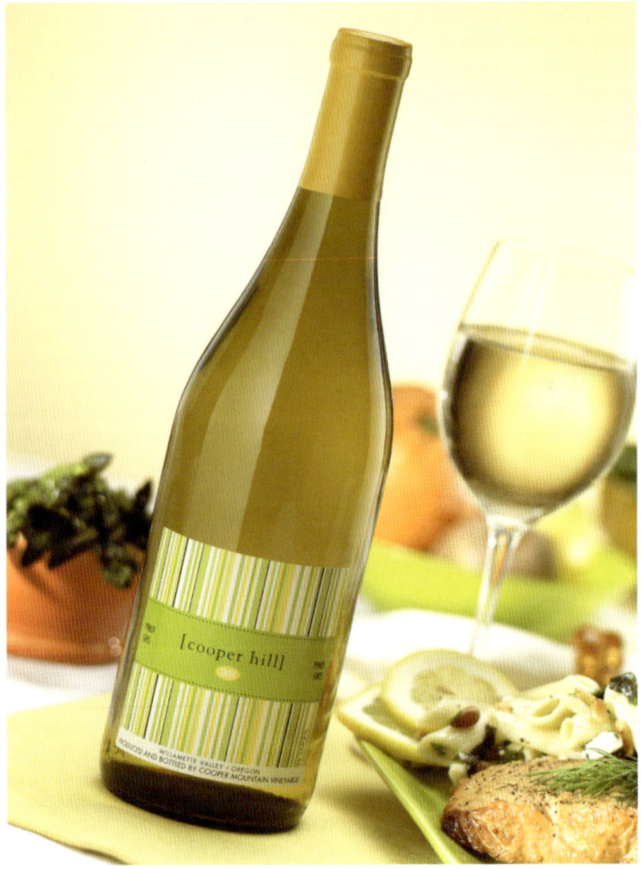

client
Cooper Mountain Vineyards
design firm
Defteling Design
designer
Alex Wijnen

client
Nordstrom
design firm
Hornall Anderson Design Works
designers
Jack Anderson, David Bates,
Sonja Max, Holly Craven

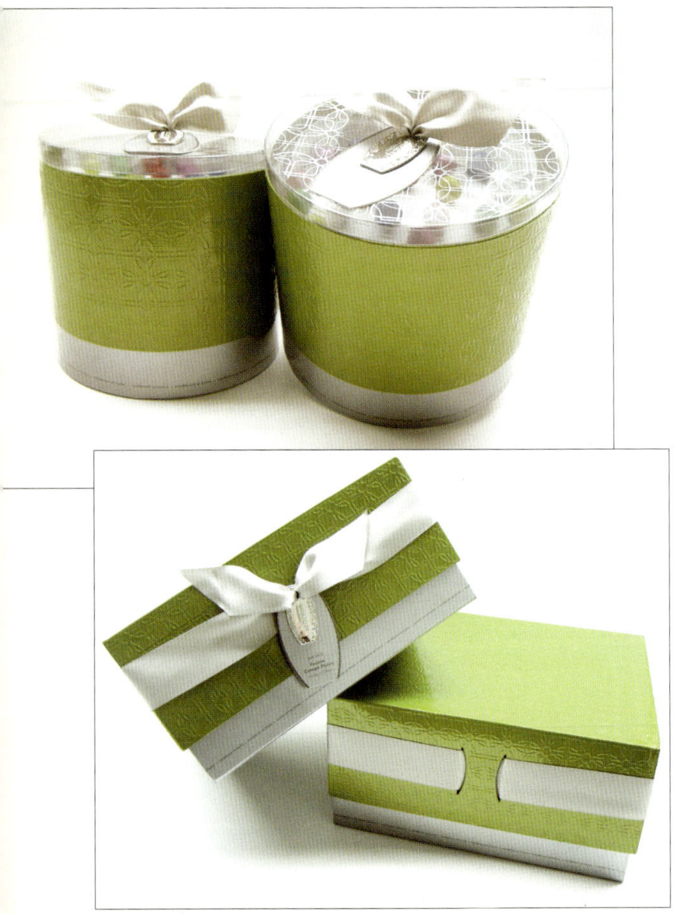

client
Wegmans
design firm
McElveney & Palozzi Design Group
designers
Lisa Gates, Mike Johnson

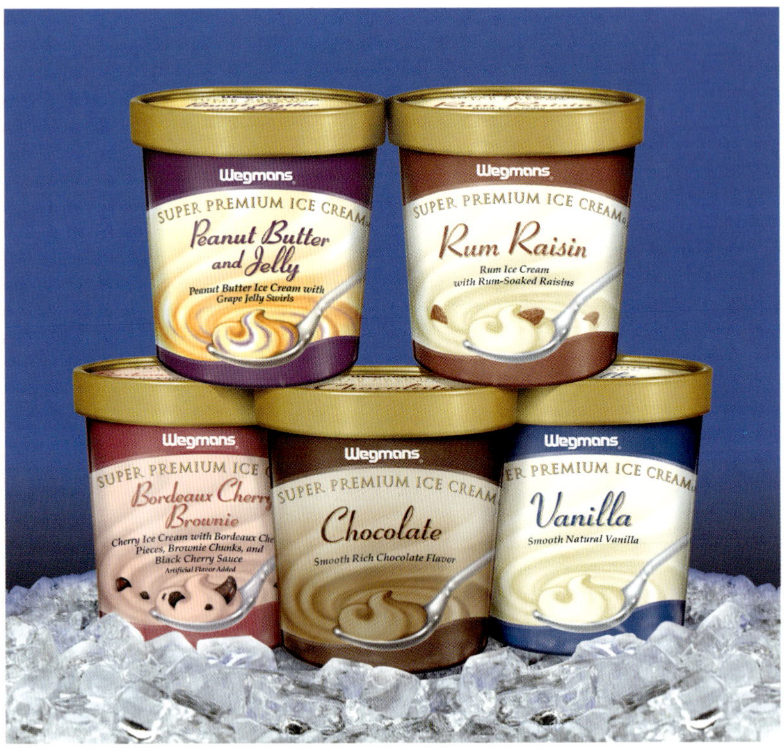

client
Nikon
design firm
Chevalier Packaging
designer
Robin Kizzar

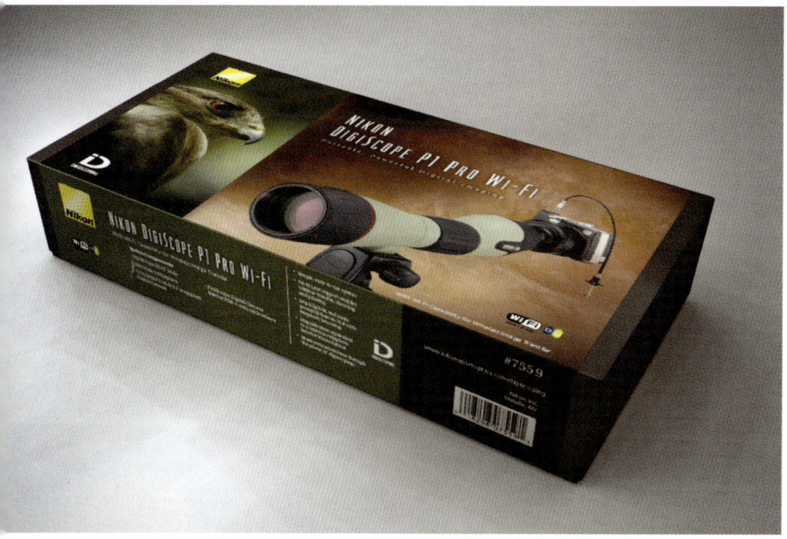

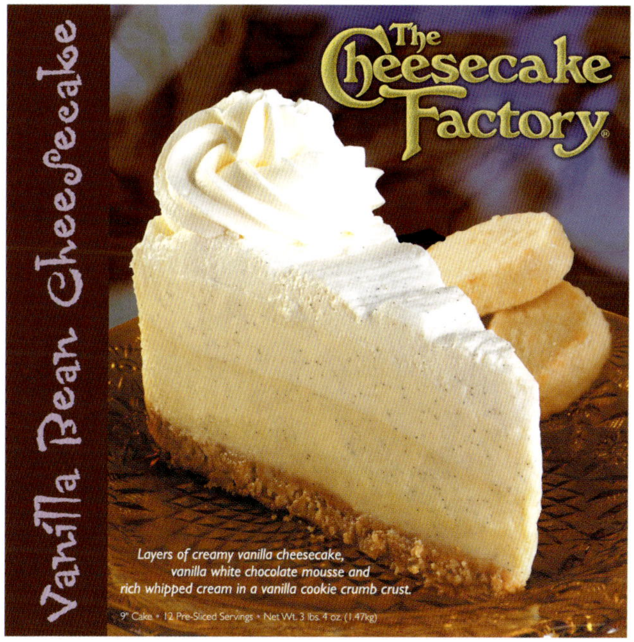

client
The Cheesecake Factory
design firm
Olson Communication
designer
Holly Stein

client
Mighty Leaf Tea Company
design firm
Brand Engine
art directors
Will Burke, Eric Read
designers
Eric Read, Lisa Brussel, Yusuke Asaka

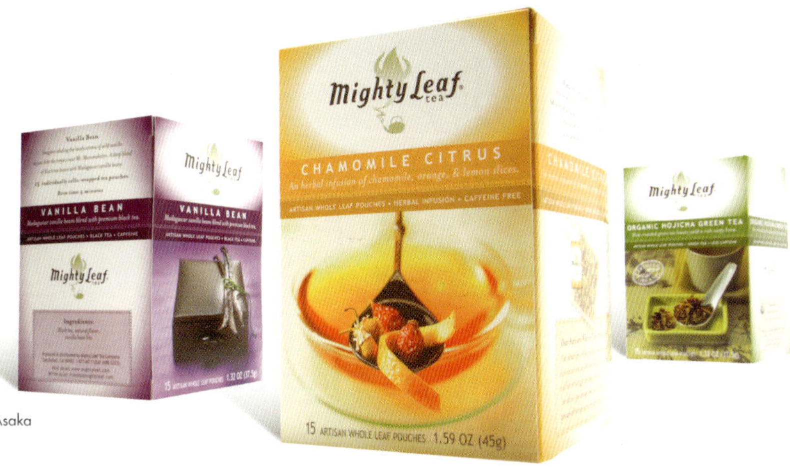

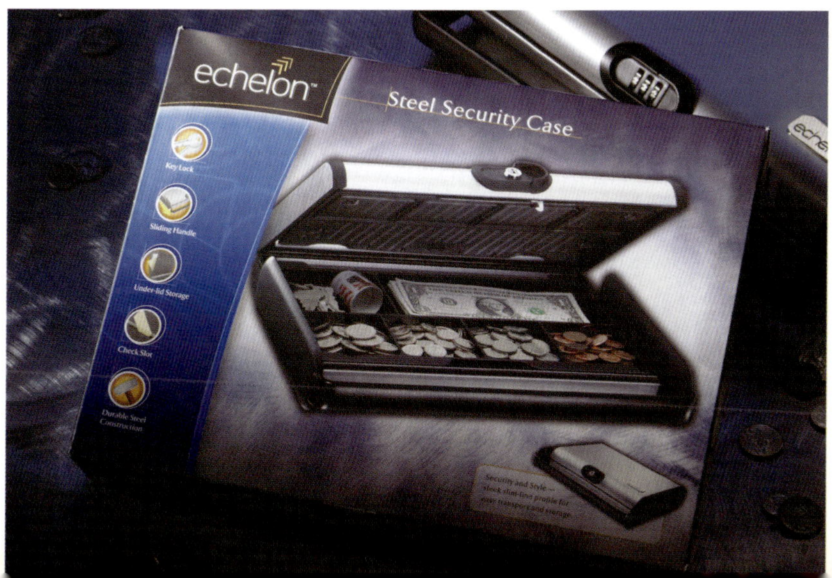

client
MMF Industries
design firm
Design North
designer
Jane Marcussen

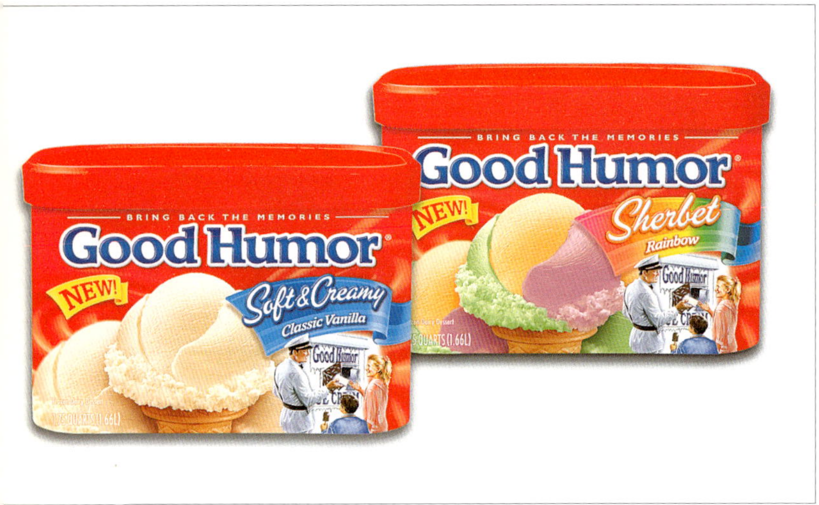

client
Good Humor-Breyers
design firm
Smith Design
designer
Laura Markley

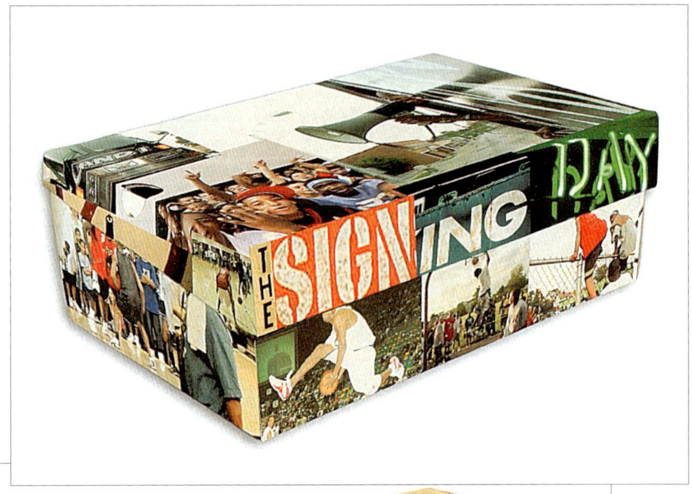

client
And 1
design firm
160over90
designers
Darryl Cilli, Dan Shepelavy,
Steve Penning, Jerrod Modica

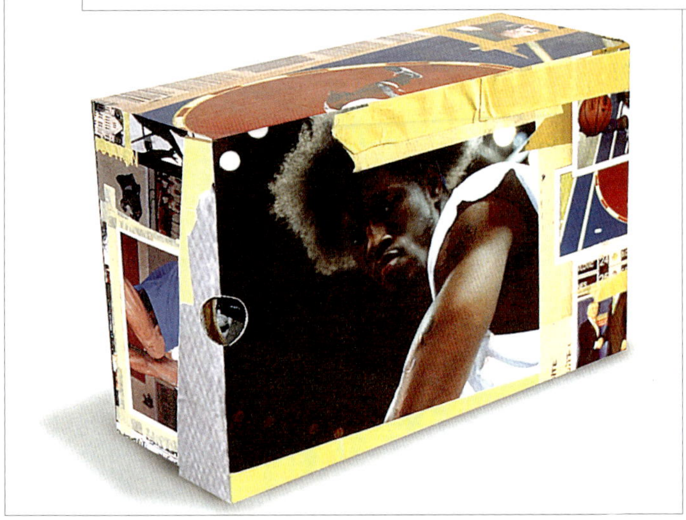

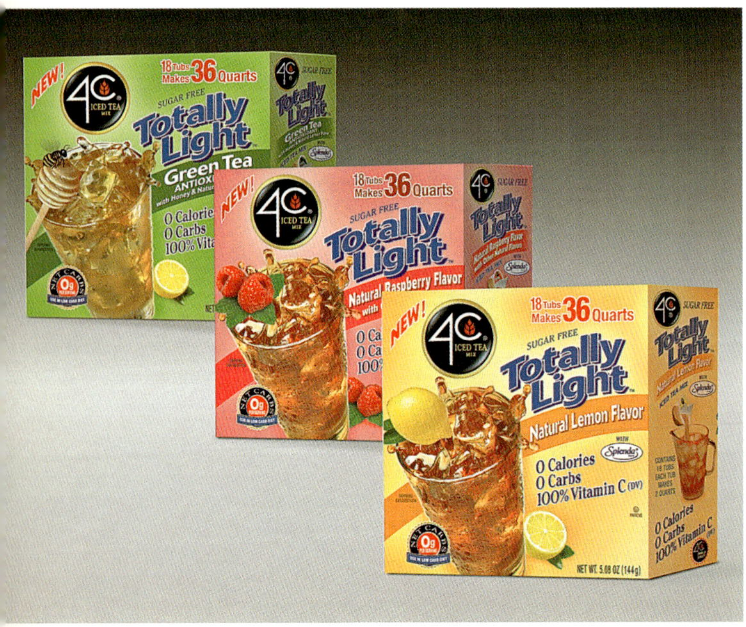

client
4C Foods Corp. (Brooklyn, NY)
design firm
J. Roy Parcels Associates
designers
J. Roy Parcels Associates

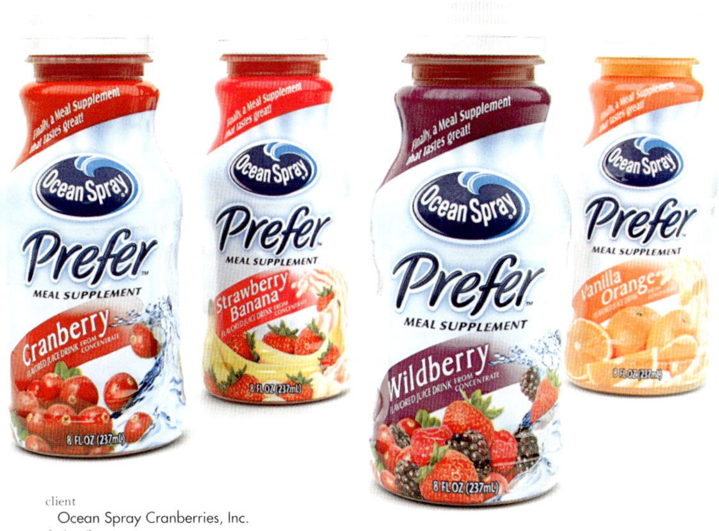

client
Ocean Spray Cranberries, Inc.
design firm
The Bailey Group
designers
Dave Fiedler, Steve Perry,
Jerry Corcoran, Wendy Slavish

client
PowerBar Inc.
design firm
The Thompson Design Group
designers
The Thompson Design Group

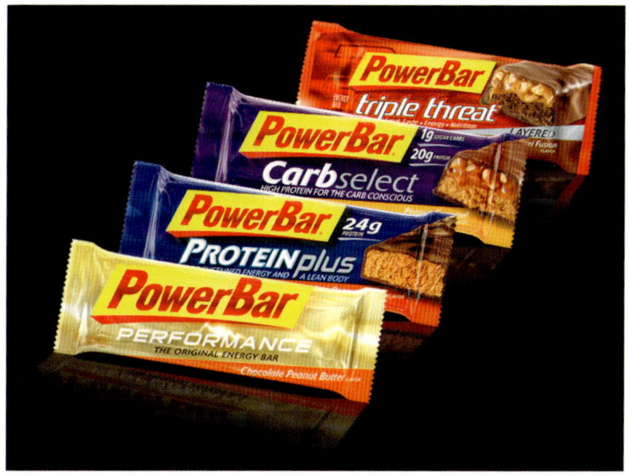

client
SkylarHaley
design firm
Brand Engine
art director
Eric Read
designers
Eric Read, Josh Levine, Yusuke Asaka

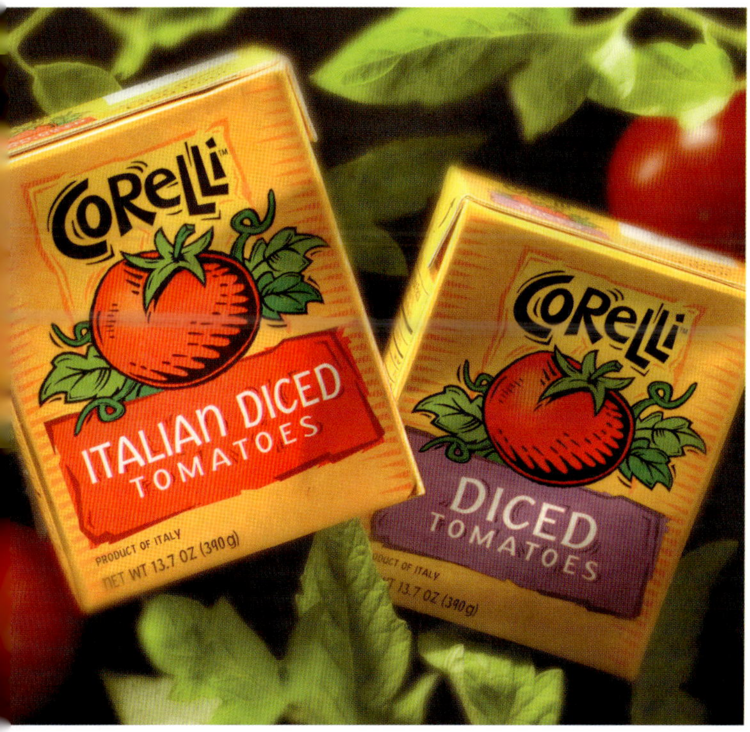

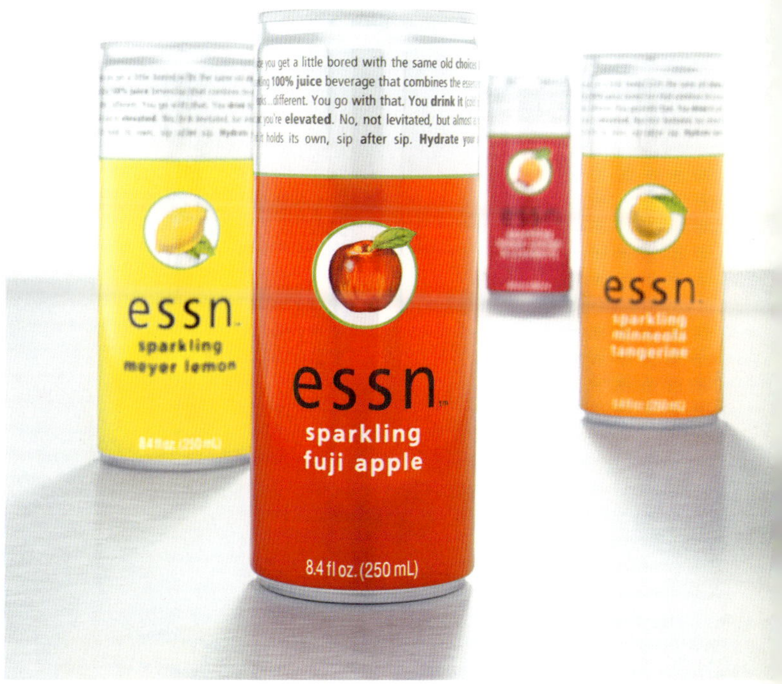

client
Tetra Pak
design firm
Design North
designers
Gwen Granzow

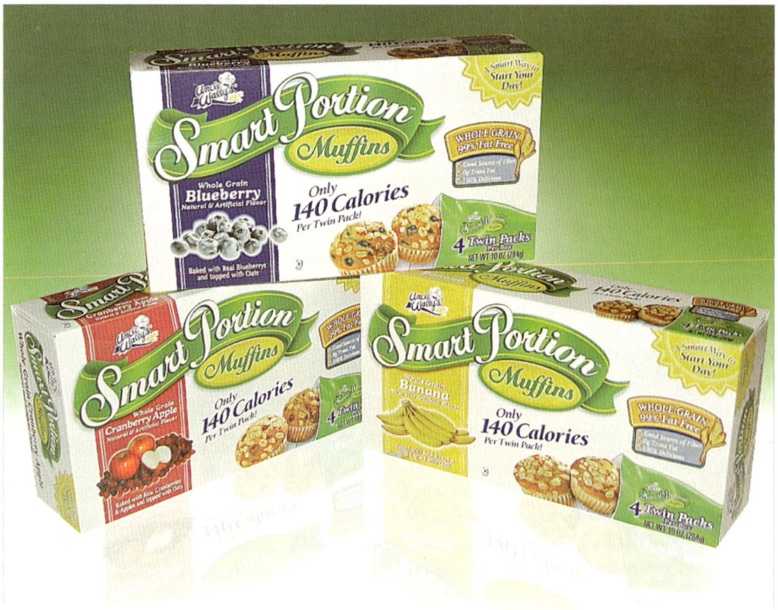

client
Uncle Wally's
design firm
McElveney & Palozzi Design Group
designers
Lisa Gates, Mike Johnson

client
Dreyer's Grand Ice Cream Company
design firm
The Thompson Design Group
designers
The Thompson Design Group

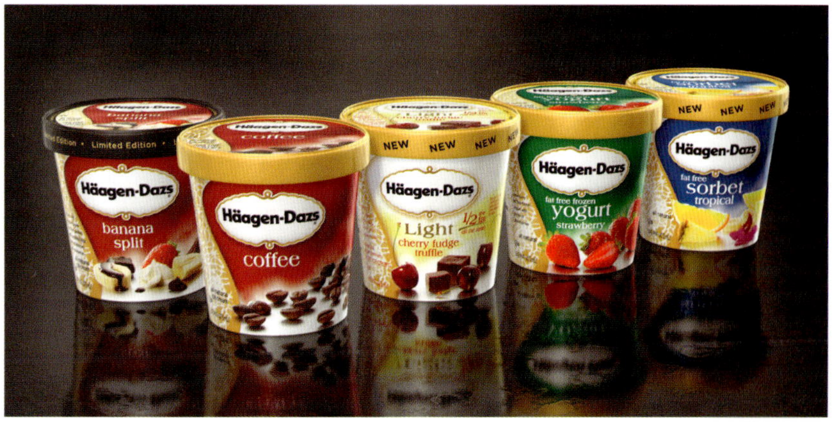

client
Kehe Food Distributors, Inc.
design firm
Design Resource Center
designers
John Norman,
Melanie Gibb,
Marc Rumaner

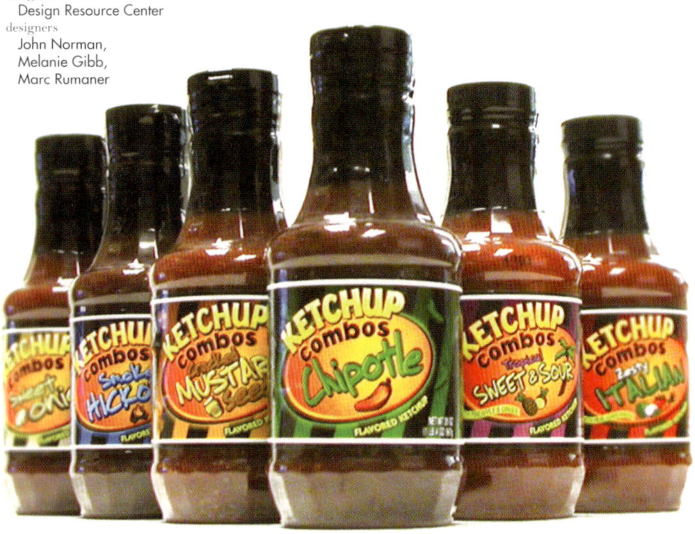

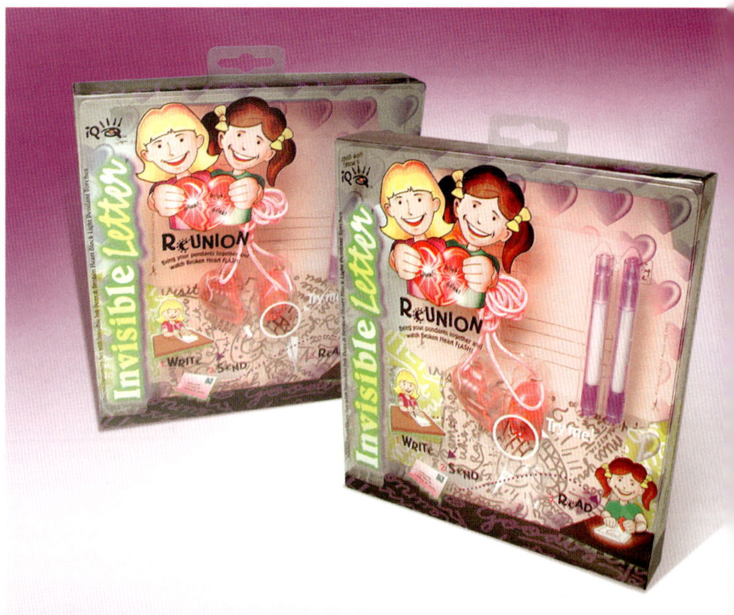

client
IQ Hong Kong
design firm
Zen Design Group
designers
David Perrin,
Kok Hwa Chung

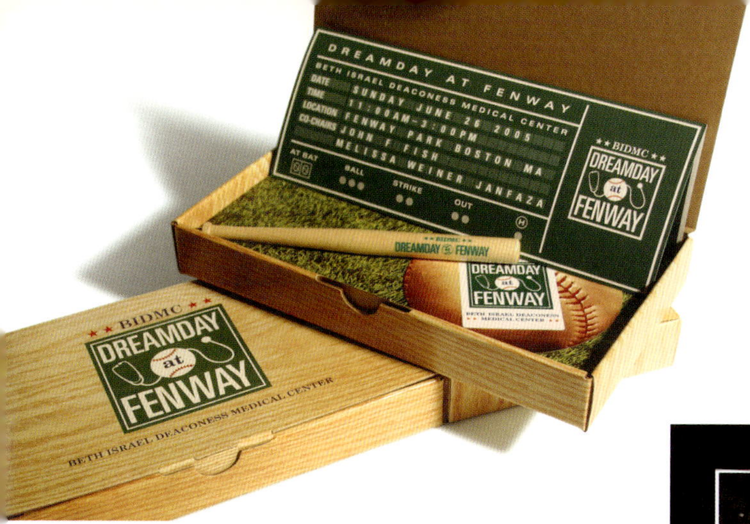

client
Beth Israel Deaconess Medical Center
design firm
kor group
designers
Kjerstin Oh, James Grady

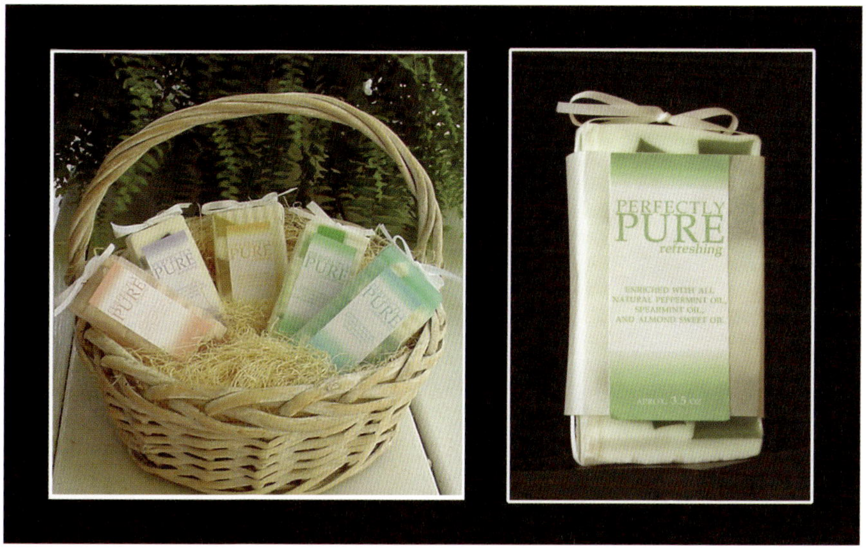

client
Perfectly Pure
design firm
ArrDesign
designers
Angela Ryczkowski

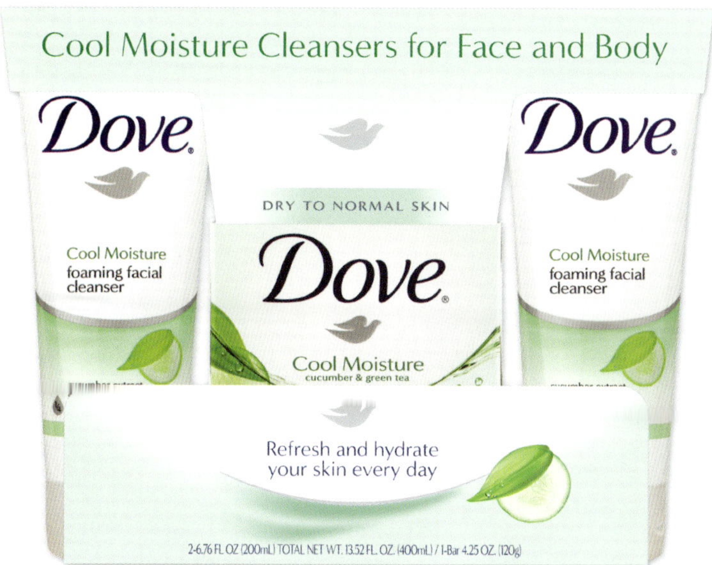

client
Unilever Home & Personal Care NA
design firm
Tom Fowler, Inc.
art director
Elizabeth P. Ball
designers
Chris Plaisted, Elizabeth P. Ball

client
The Hain Celestial Group
design firm
Smith Design
designer
Carol Konkowski

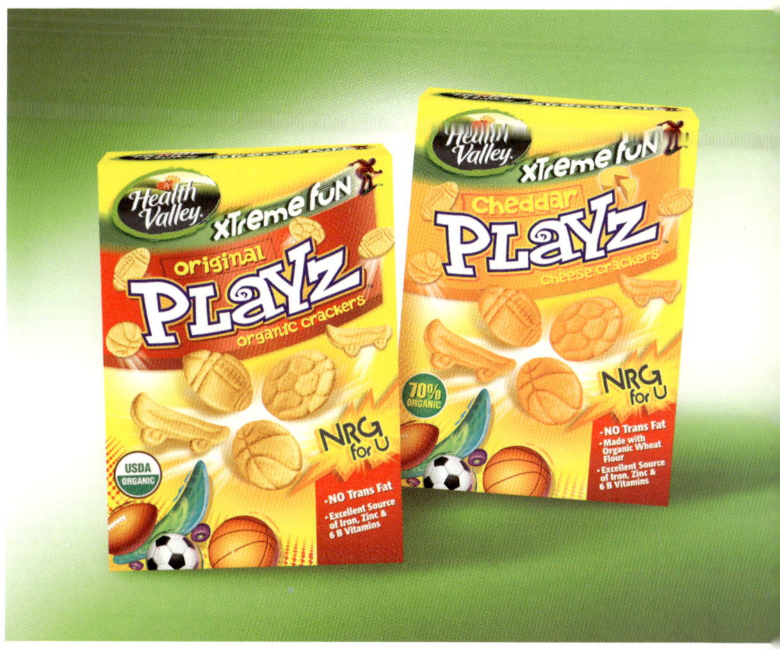

client
Horizon Group USA
design firm
Design Trends
designers
Tree Trapanese, David Un

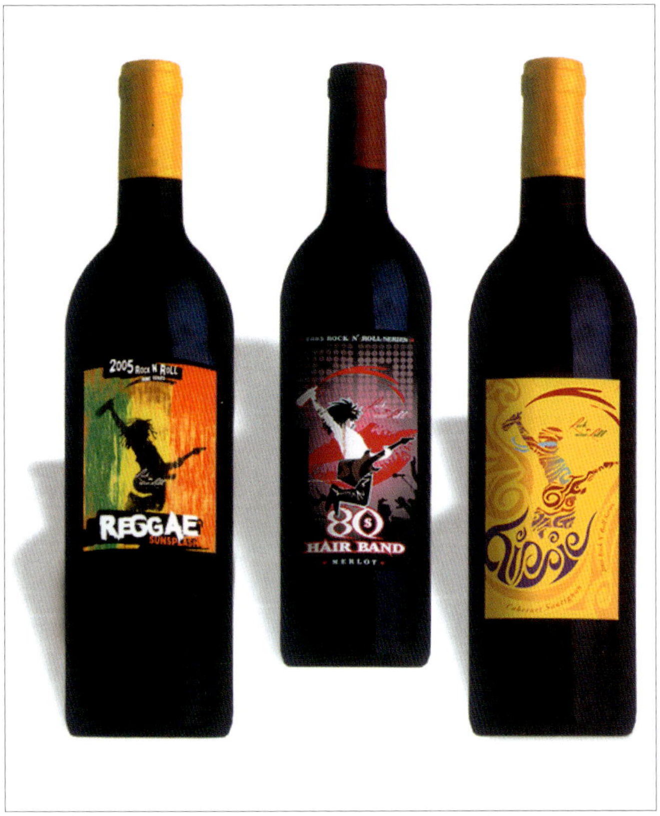

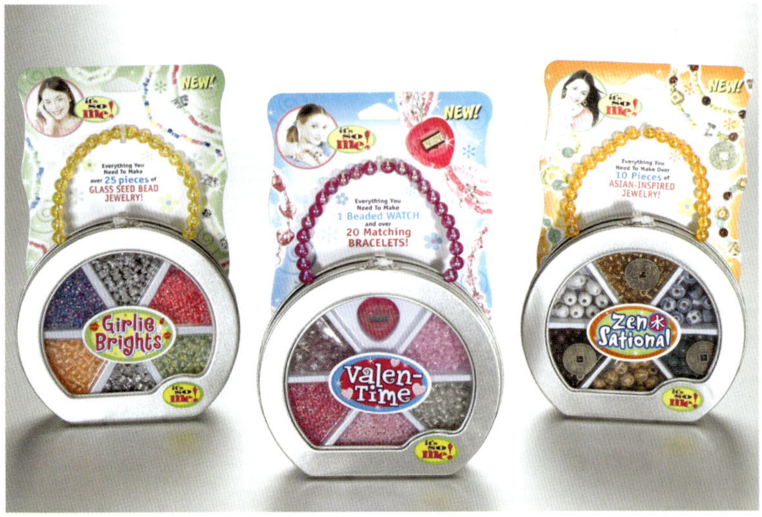

client
Chris Hammond/www.rocknrollwine.com
design firm
CDI Studios
designer
Dan McElhattan III
illustrator
David Araujo

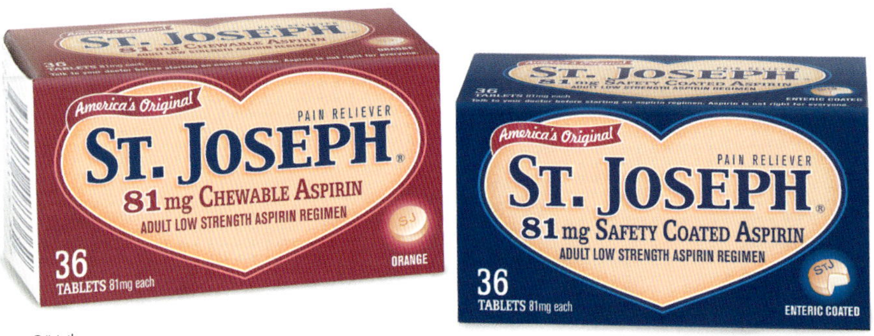

client
McNeil Pharmaceutical
design firm
The Bailey Group
designers
Dave Fiedler, Ken Cahill, Janet O'Neil

client
The Four Twenty Company
design firm
Gold Forest
designers
Pat Cowan, Bibiana Pulido,
Ana Teresa Mellet Suarez

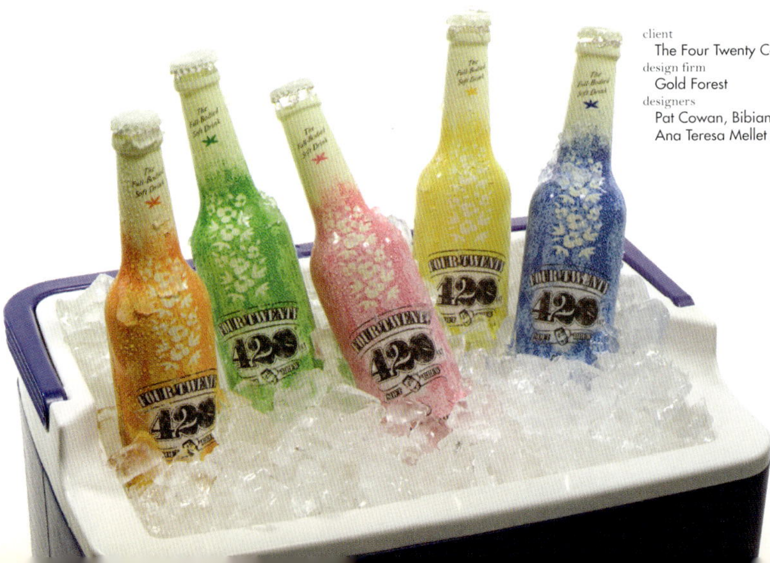

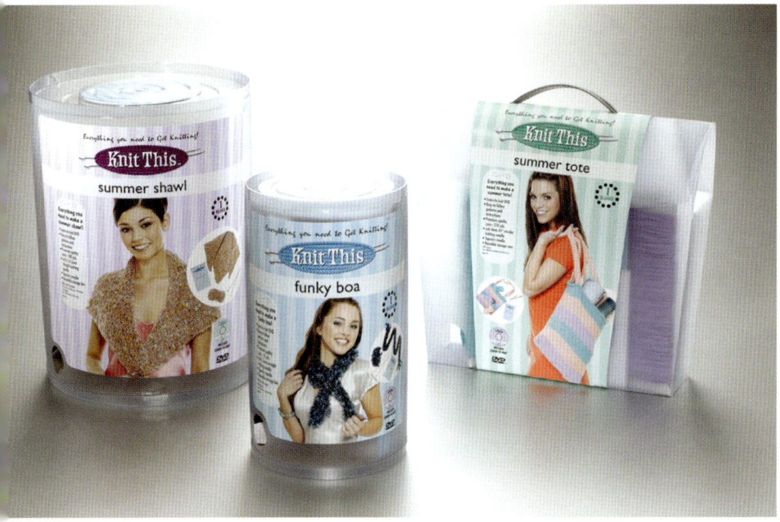

client
Horizon Group USA
design firm
Design Trends
designers
Tree Trapanese, David Un

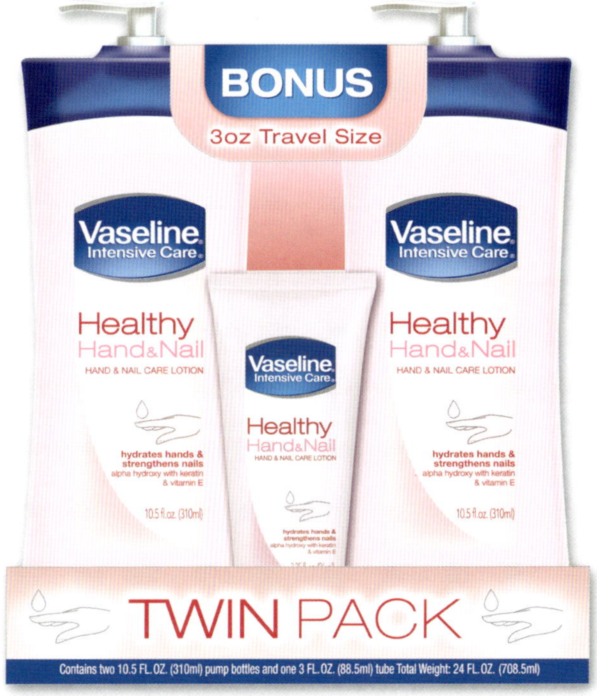

client
Unilever Home & Personal Care NA
design firm
Tom Fowler, Inc.
art director
Elizabeth P. Ball
designers
Mary Ellen Butkus, Vicki Naftali

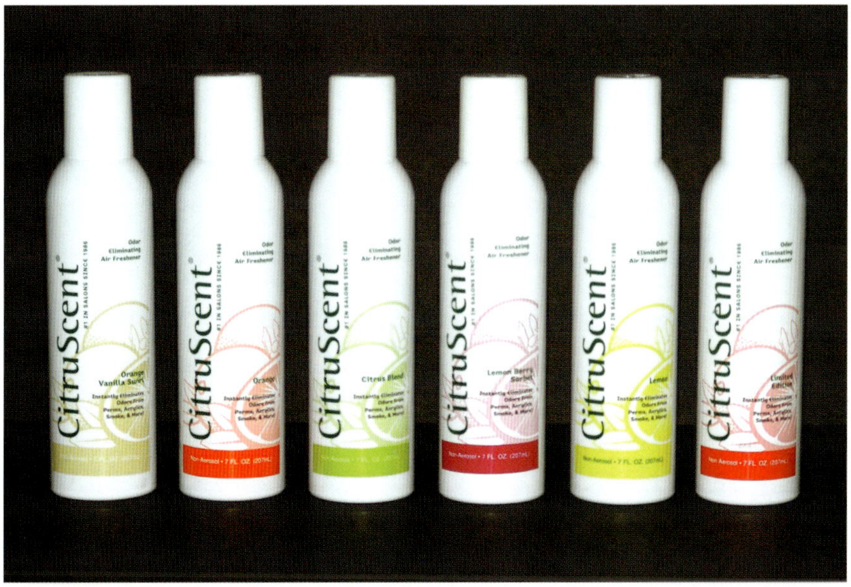

client
Beaumont Products
design firm
Octavo Designs
designer
Sue Hough

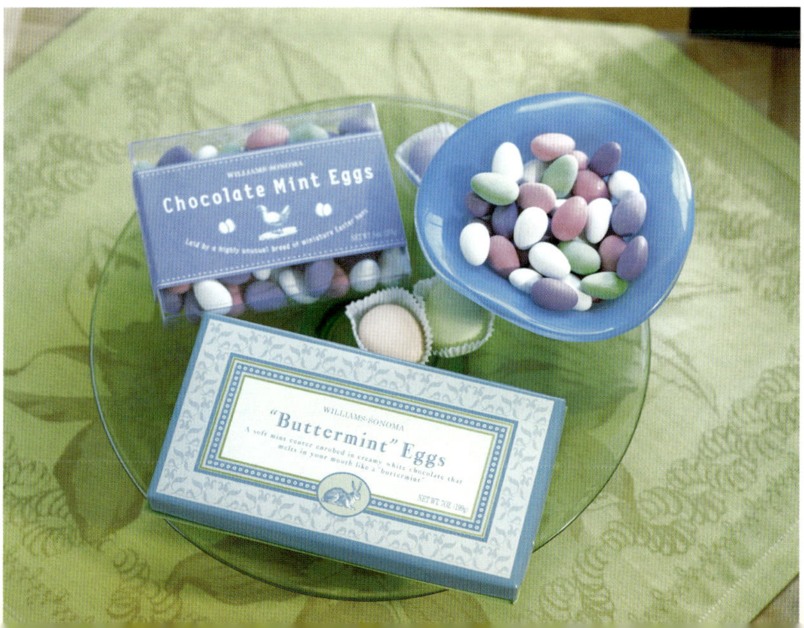

client
Williams-Sonoma
design firm
Brand Engine
art director
Eric Read
designers
Eric Read, Coralie Russo, Yusuke Asaka

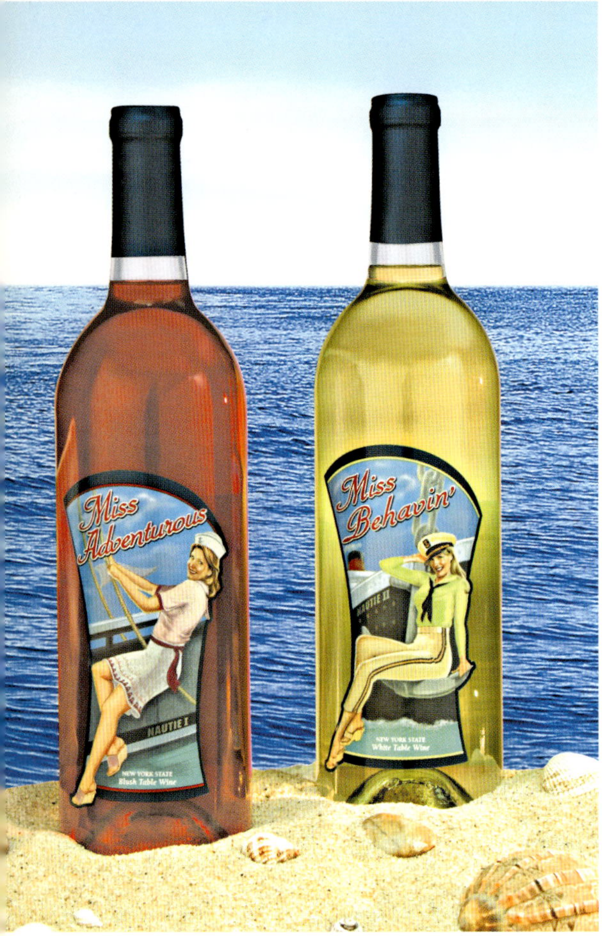

client
Lucas Vineyards
design firm
McElveney & Palozzi Design Group
designers
Lisa Gates, Mike Johnson

client
Tahitian Noni
design firm
Hornall Anderson Design Works
designers
Lisa Cerveny, James Tee,
Tiffany Place, Mark Popich,
Jana Nishi, Leo Raymundo,
Yuri Shvets, Belinda Bowling

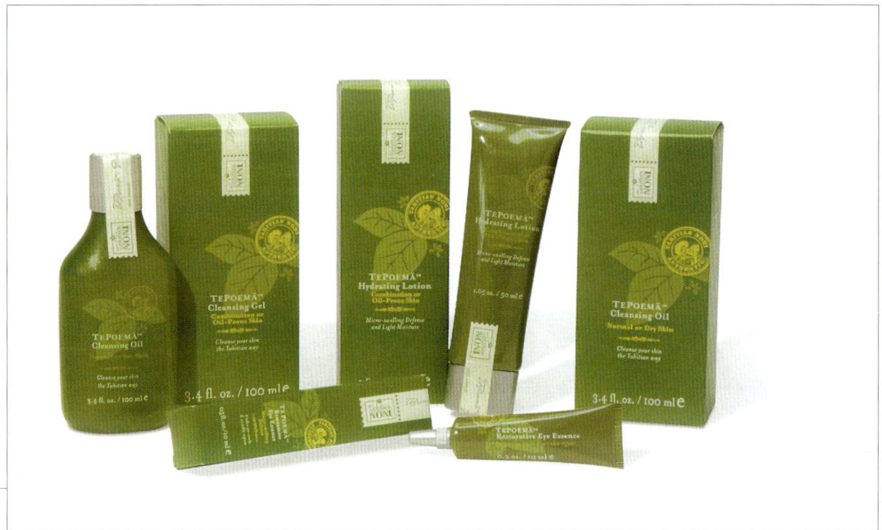

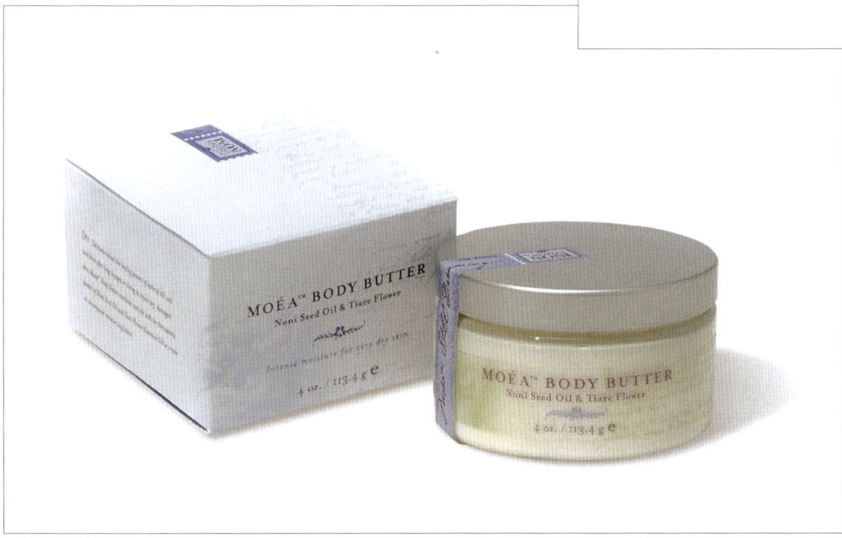

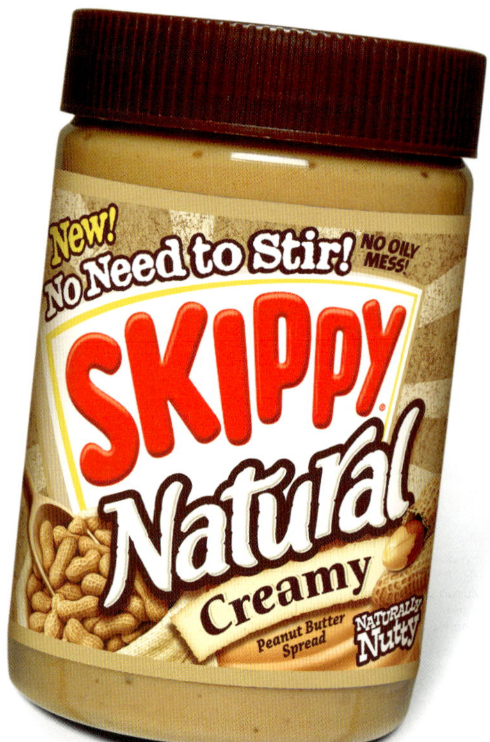

client
Unilever
design firm
Smith Design
designer
Laura Markley

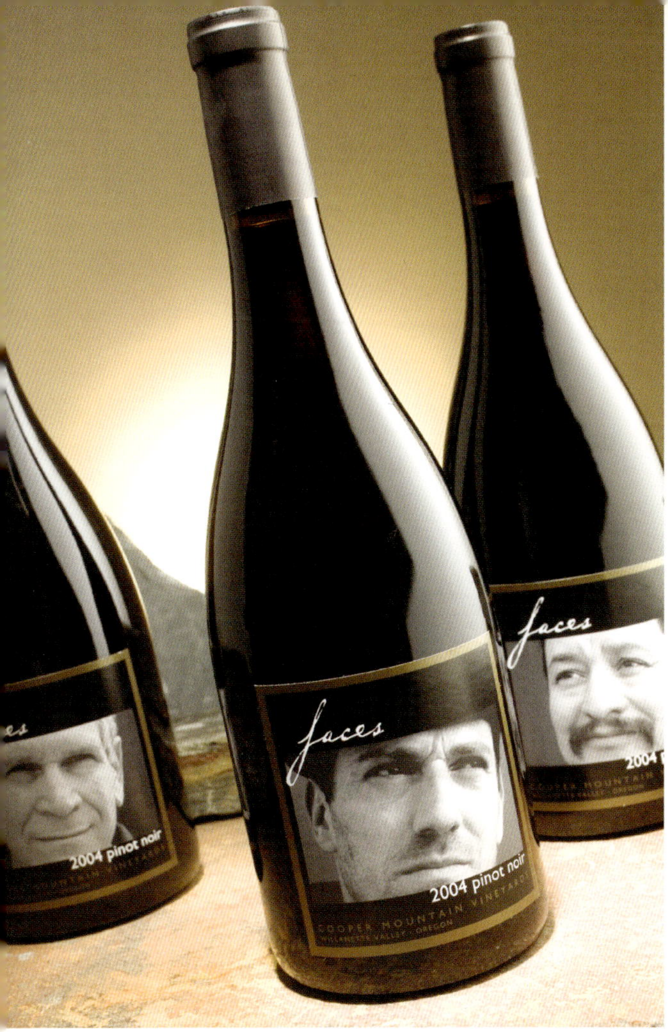

client
Cooper Mountain Vineyards
design firm
Defteling Design
designer
Alex Wijnen

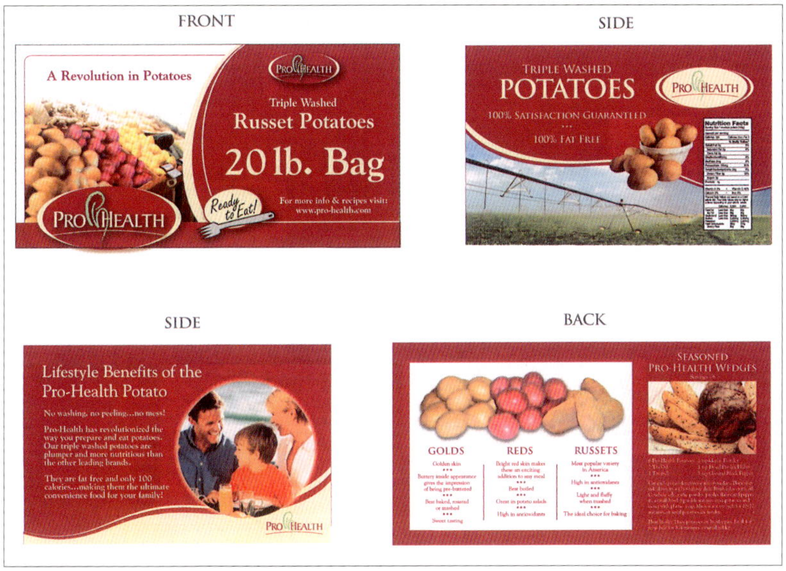

client
Pro-Health
design firm
Duncan/Day Advertising
designer
Leigh Finney

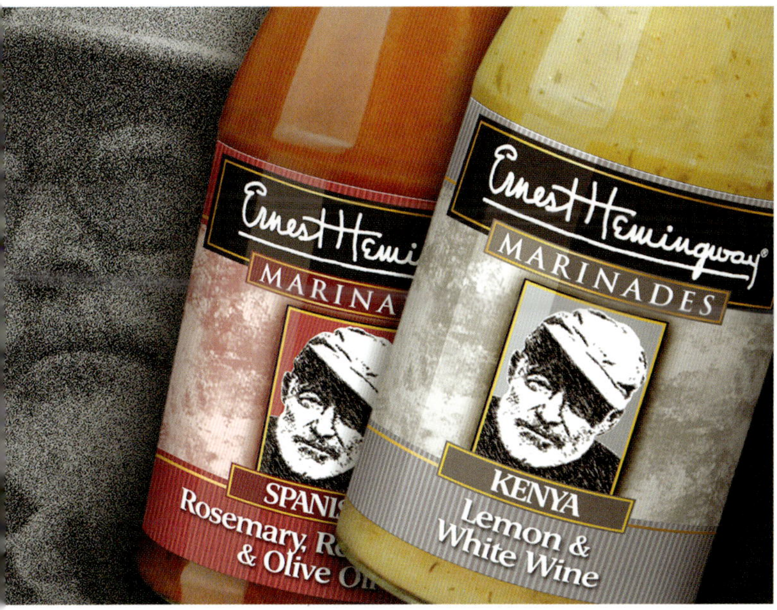

client
World Finer Foods, Inc.
design firm
Zunda Design Group
designers
Charles Zunda, Lauren Millar

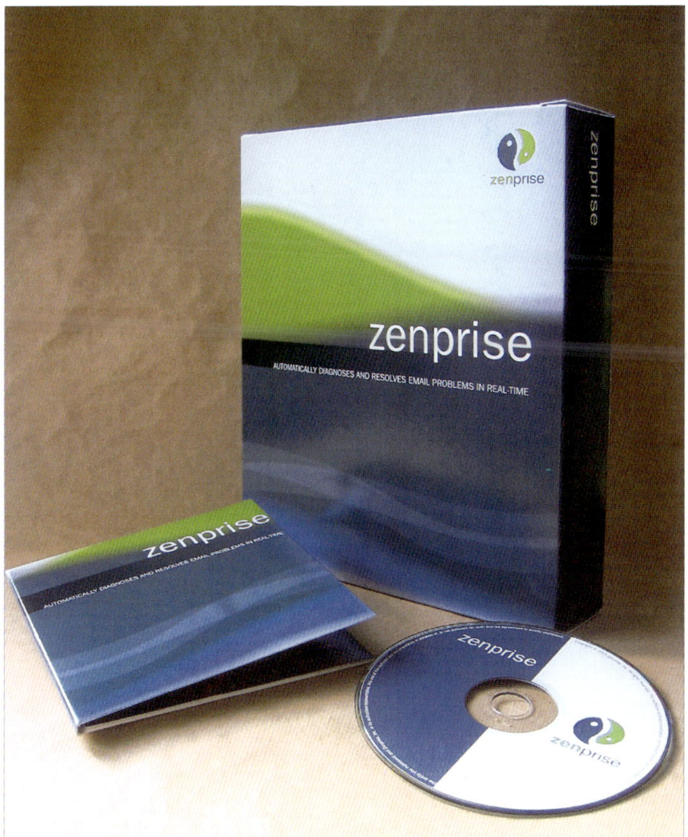

client
Zenprise, Inc.
design firm
Connie Hwang Design
designer
Connie Hwang

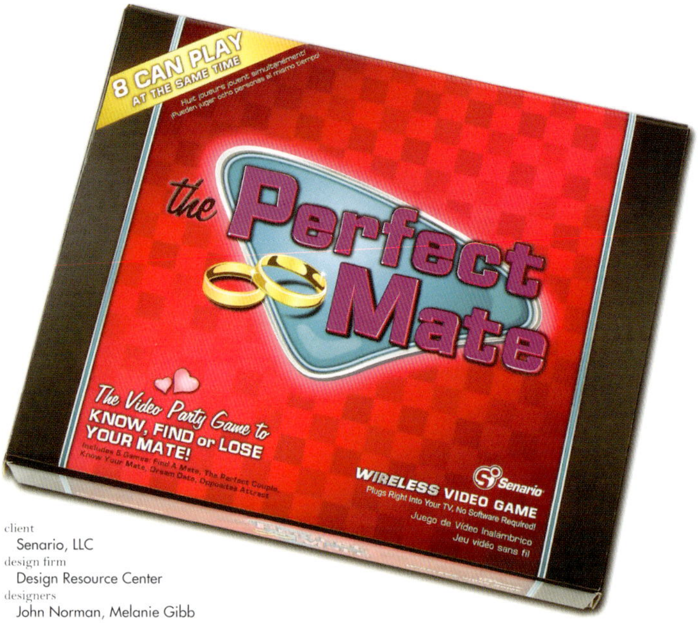

client
Senario, LLC
design firm
Design Resource Center
designers
John Norman, Melanie Gibb

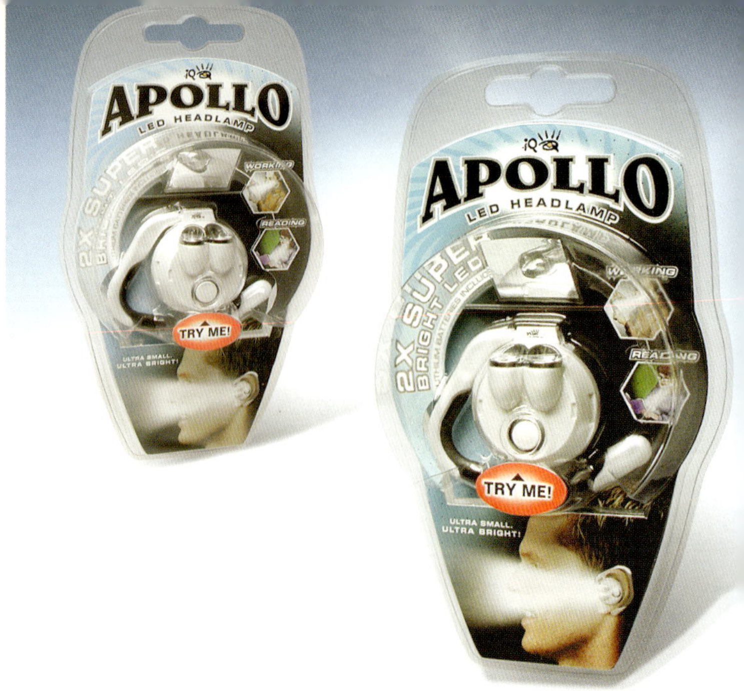

client
IQ Hong Kong
design firm
Zen Design Group
designers
David Perrin, Matt Chapman

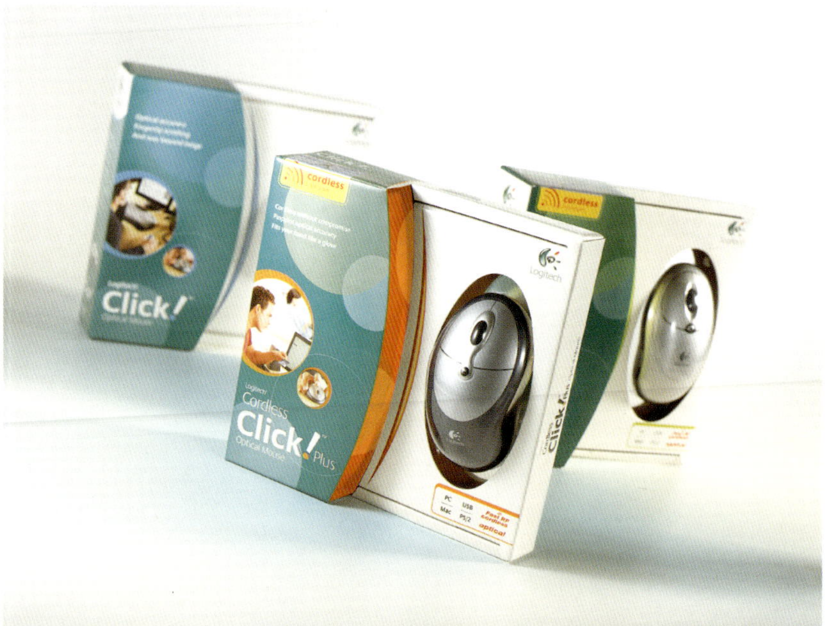

client
Logitech
design firm
Brand Engine
art director
Will Burke
designers
Monica Schlaug,
Shinichi Eguchi,
Yusuke Asaka

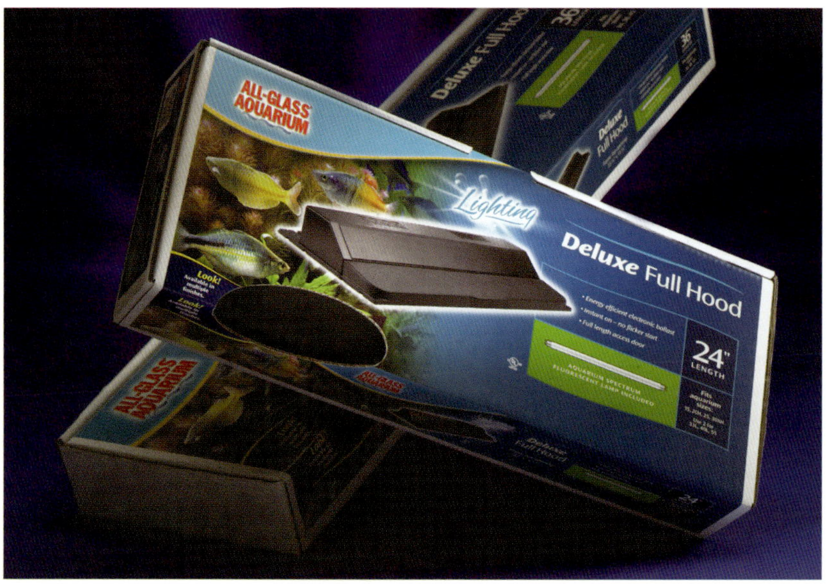

client
All-Glass Aquarium
design firm
Design North
designer
Kaytee Mosher

client
Garrity
design firm
Zen Design Group
designers
Matt Chapman,
David Perrin

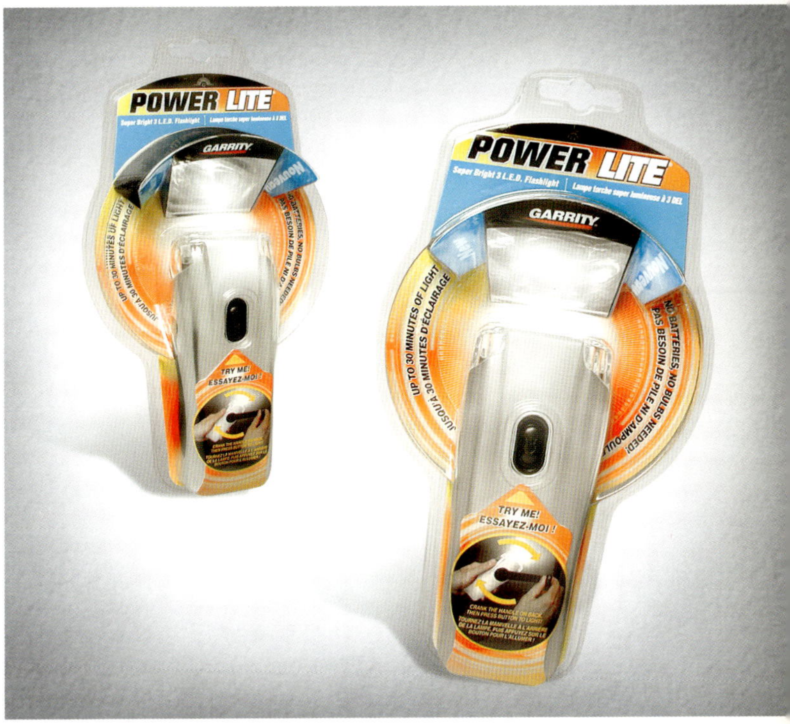

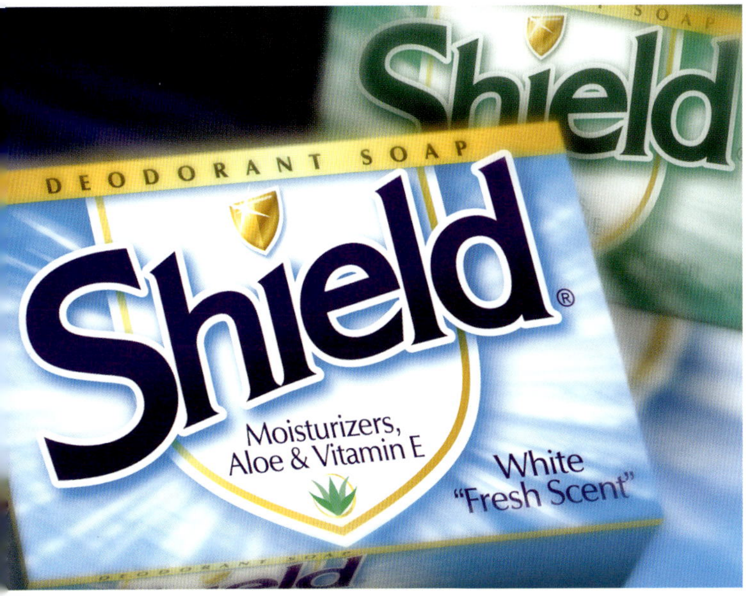

client
Supreme Brands, Inc.
design firm
Zunda Design Group
designer
Charles Zunda

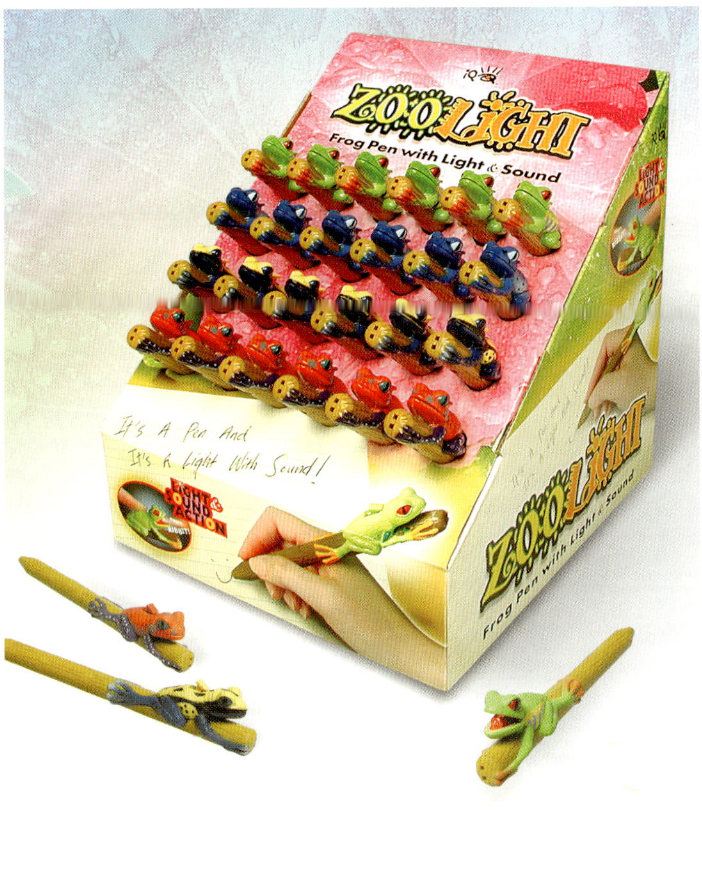

client
IQ Hong Kong
design firm
Zen Design Group
designers
Kok Hwa Chung,
Joe Braschayko,
David Perrin

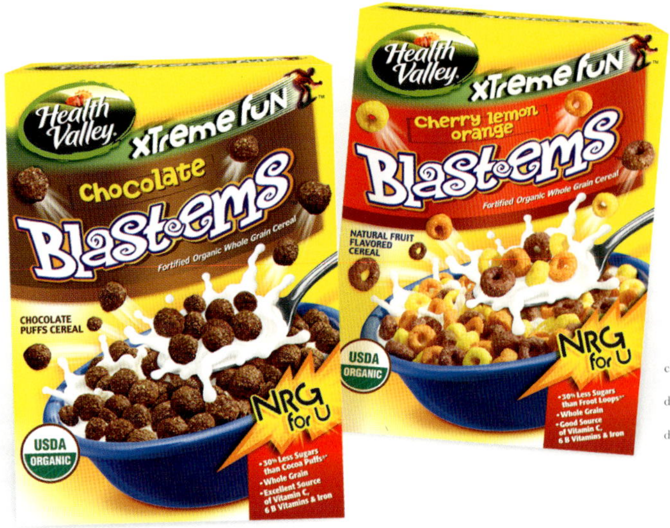

client
The Hain Celestial Group
design firm
Smith Design
designer
Carol Konkowski

client
Unilever Home & Personal Care NA
design firm
Tom Fowler, Inc.
designer
Elizabeth P. Ball

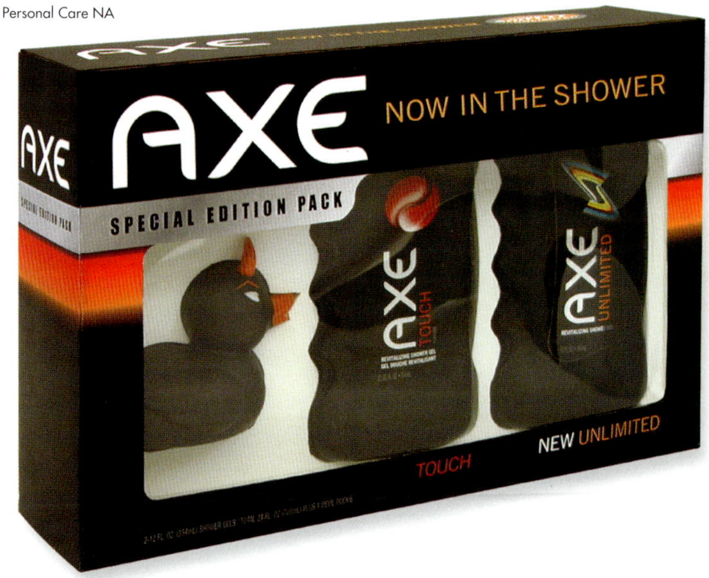

client
Widmer Brothers Brewery
design firm
Hornall Anderson Design Works
designers
Jack Anderson, Bruce Stigler,
Larry Anderson, Jay Hilburn,
Elmer dela Cruz

client
Heinz
design firm
DuPuis
creative director
Steven DuPuis
designers
Lindsay Evans, Jack Halpern,
Al Nanakonpanom

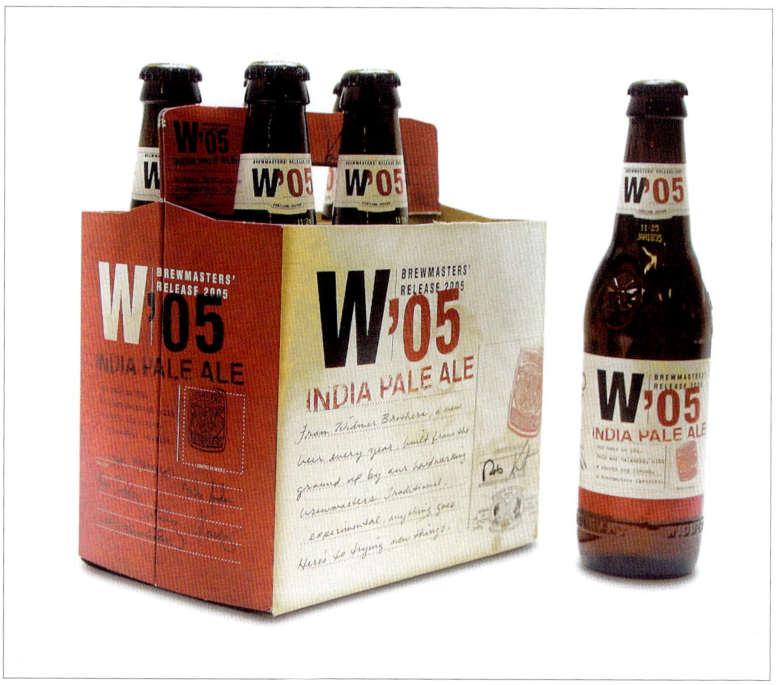

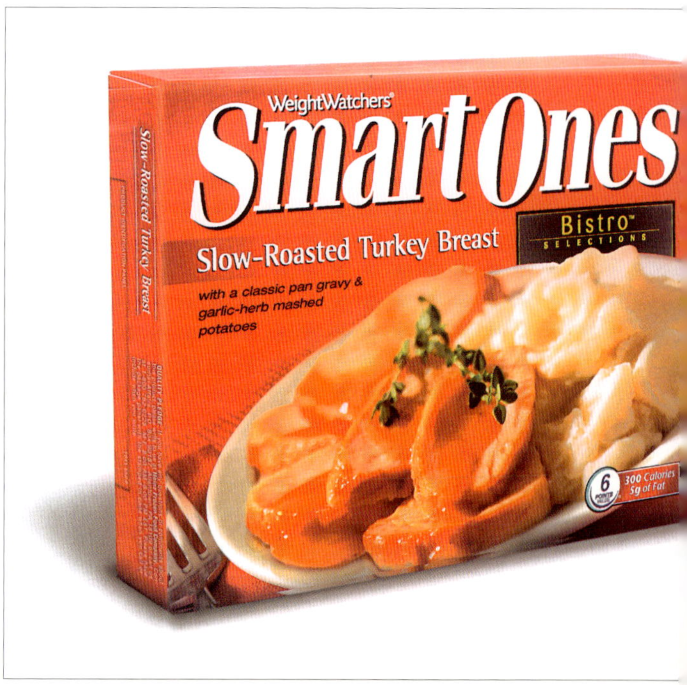

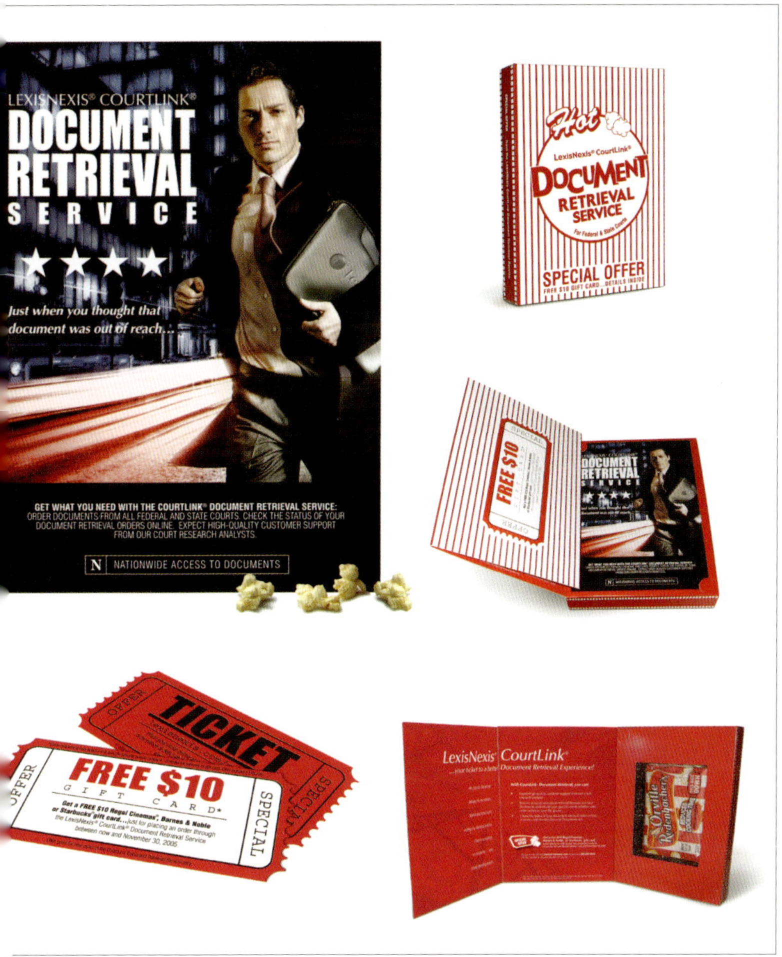

client
LN Document Retrieval
design firm
Marcomm Kop
designers
Jonathan Georgopulos,
Craig Brewster,
Travis Hanmer, Dawn Nye

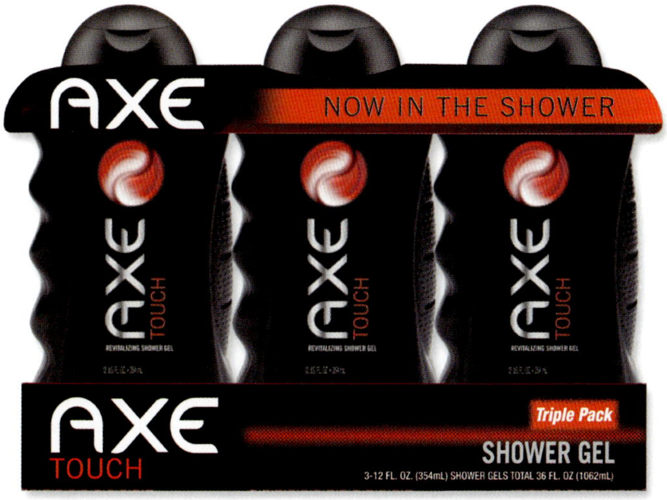

client
Unilever Home & Personal Care NA
design firm
Tom Fowler, Inc.
art directors
Elizabeth P. Ball, Mary Ellen Butkus
designers
Mary Ellen Butkus, Vicki Naftali

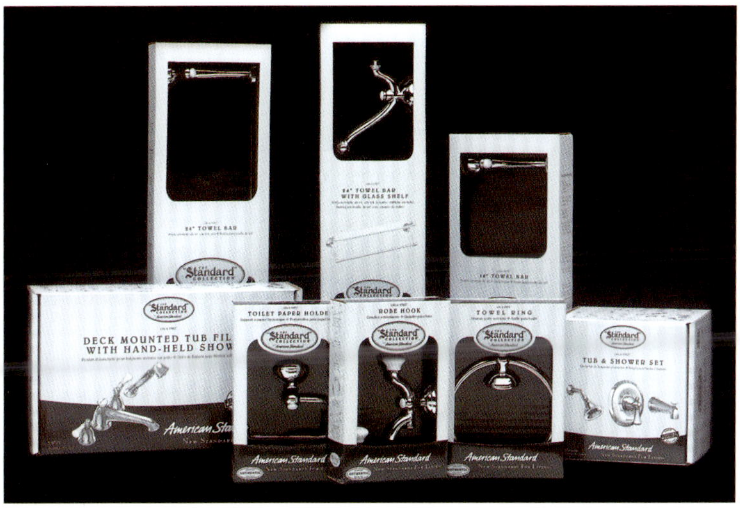

client
American Standard
design firm
Options By Design
creative director
Jeff Wright
designer
Kathy Smyth

client
Senario, LLC
design firm
Design Resource Center
designers
John Norman, Melanie Gibb

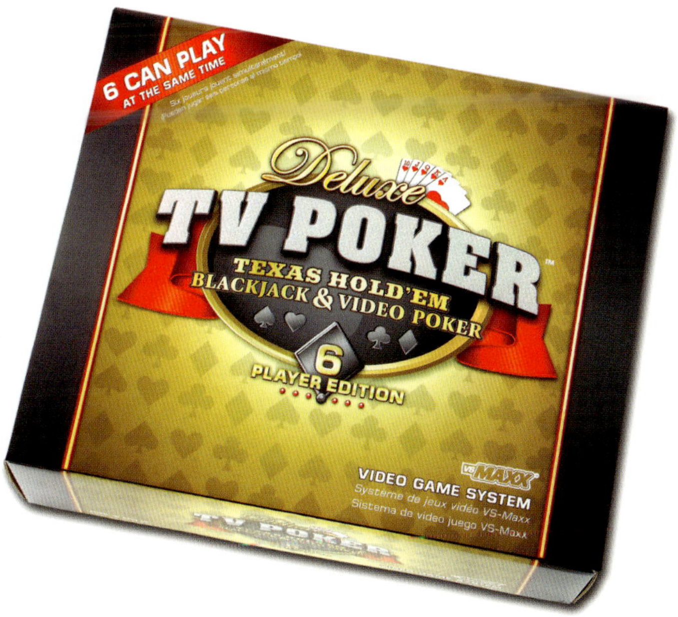

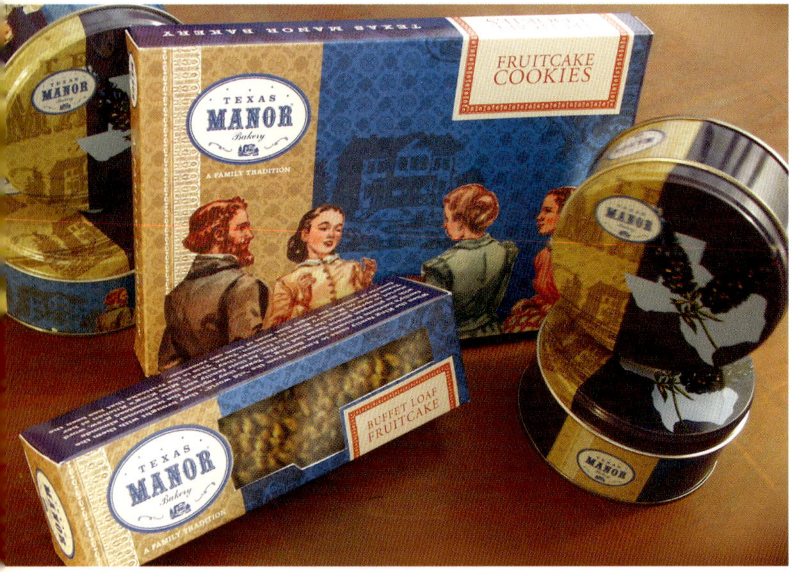

client
The Original Ya-Hoo! Baking Co.
design firm
Marcantel LeBlanc Brand Partnership
designers
Richard LeBlanc, Tom Marcantel

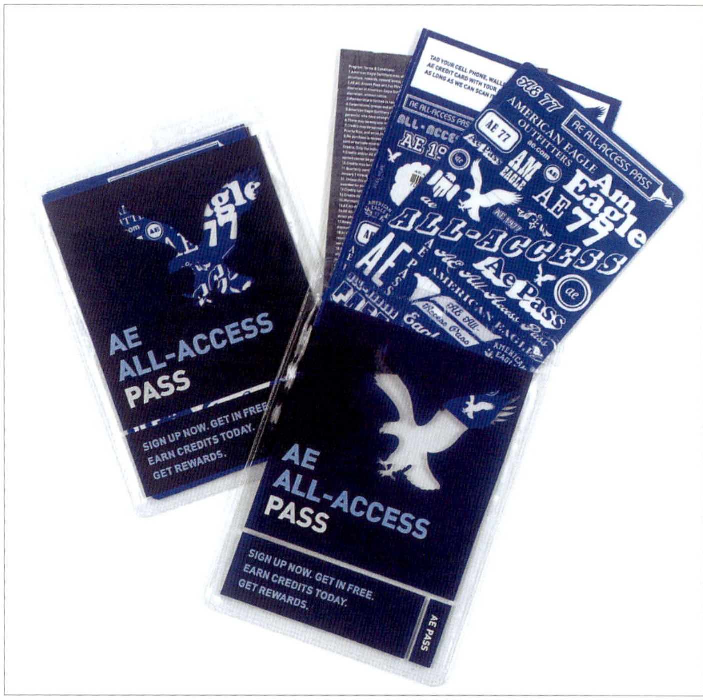

client
American Eagle
design firm
160over90
designers
Darryl Cilli, Dan Shepelavy,
Steve Penning, Brendan Quinn

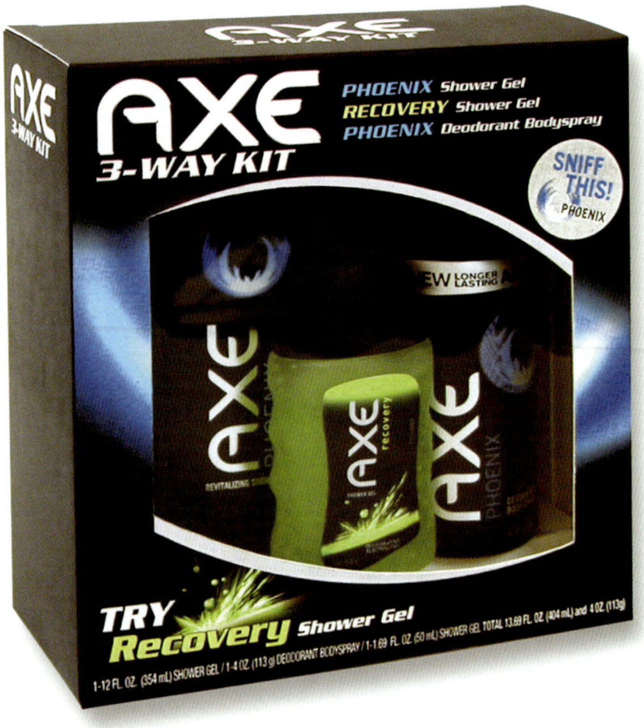

client
Unilever Home & Personal Care NA
design firm
Tom Fowler, Inc.
art director
Elizabeth P. Ball
designer
Vicki Naftali

client
Blue Diamond Growers
design firm
The Thompson Design Group
designers
The Thompson Design Group

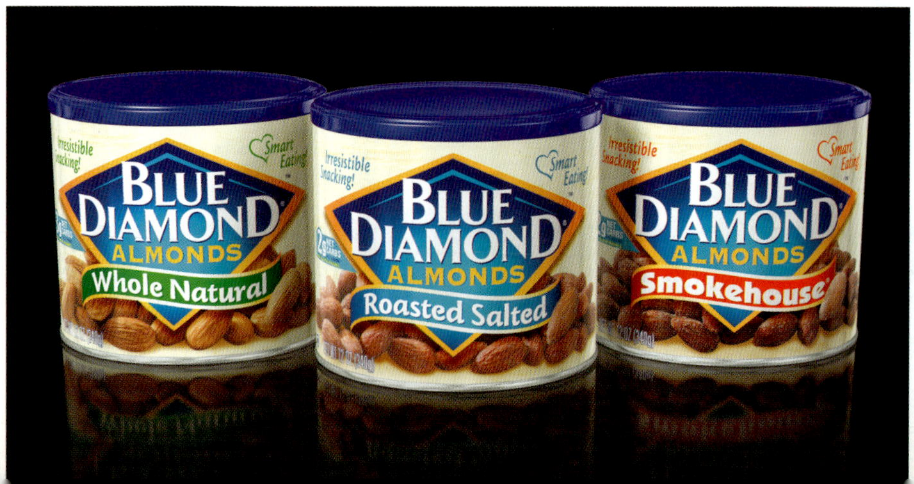

Stationery

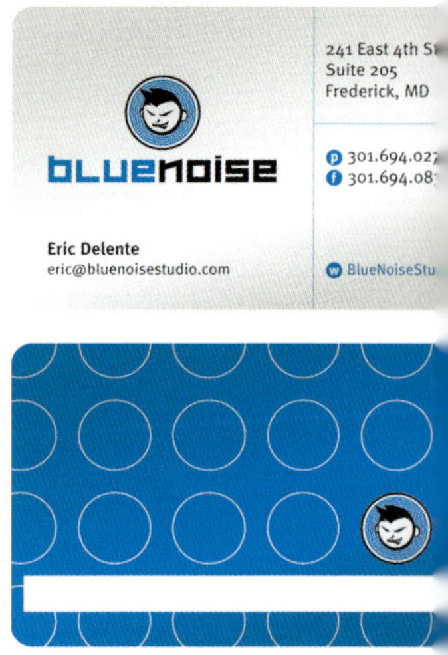

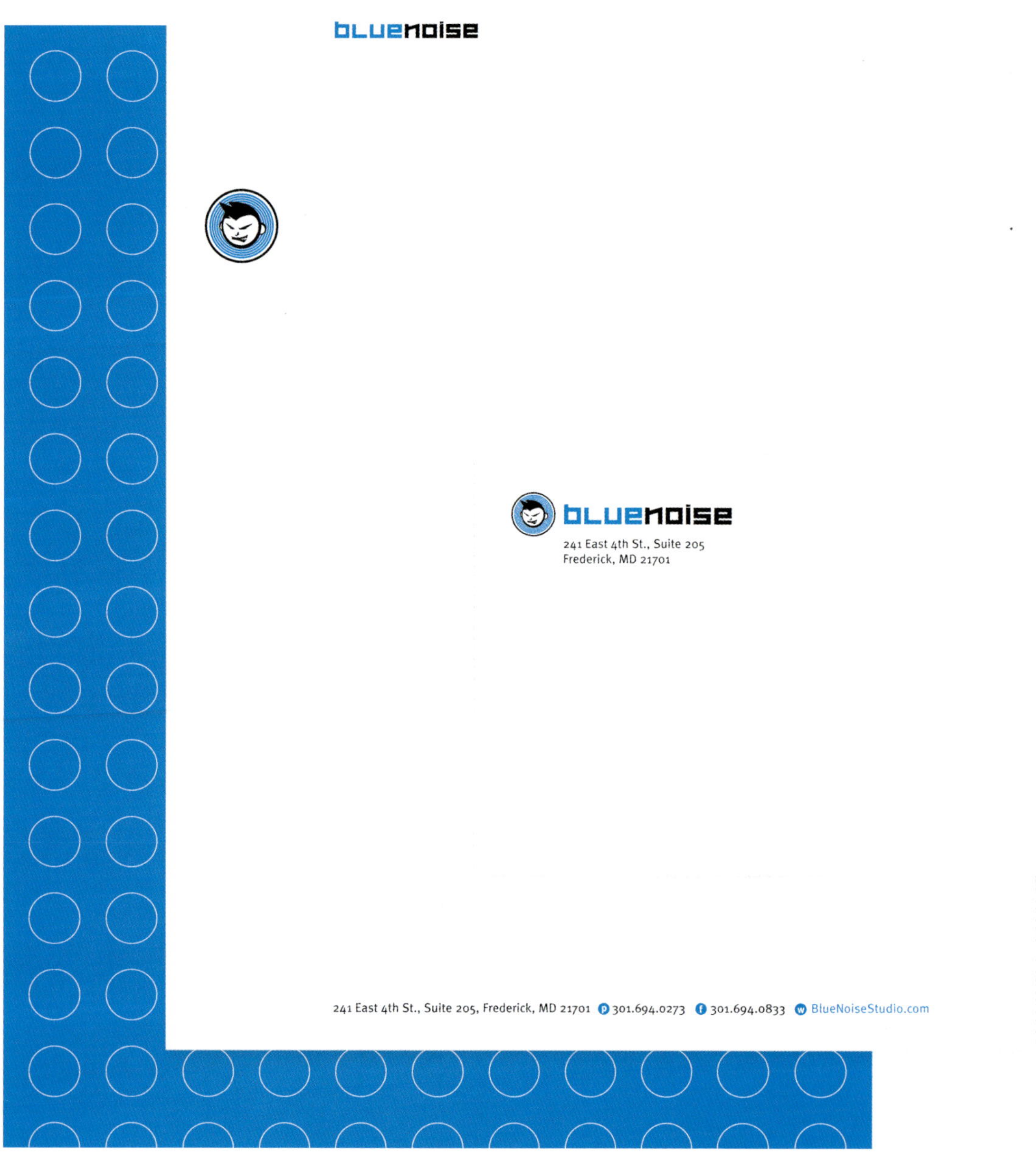

client
Blue Noise
design firm
Octavo Designs
designers
Sue Hough, Mark Burrier

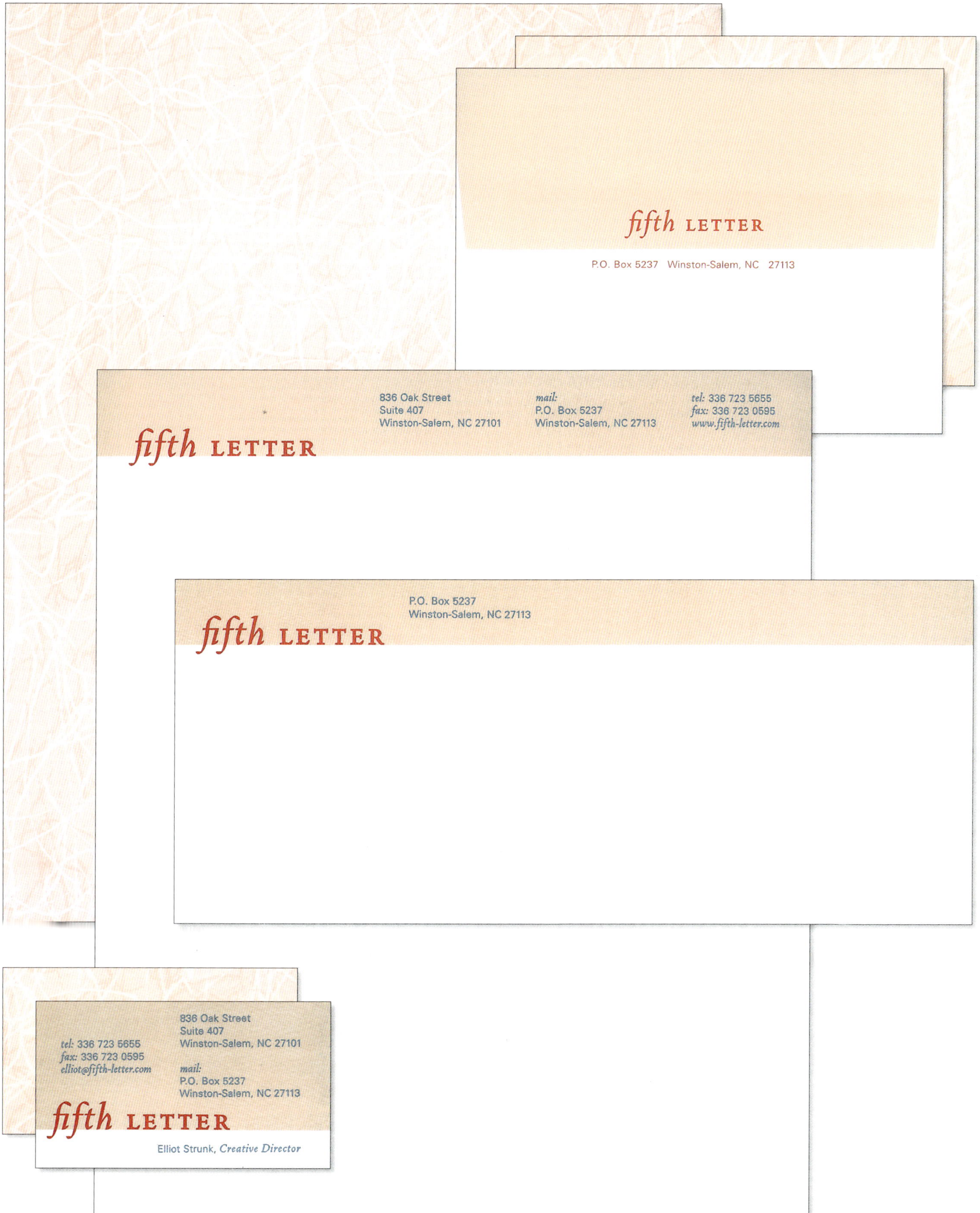

client
Fifth Letter
design firm
Fifth Letter
designer
Elliot Strunk

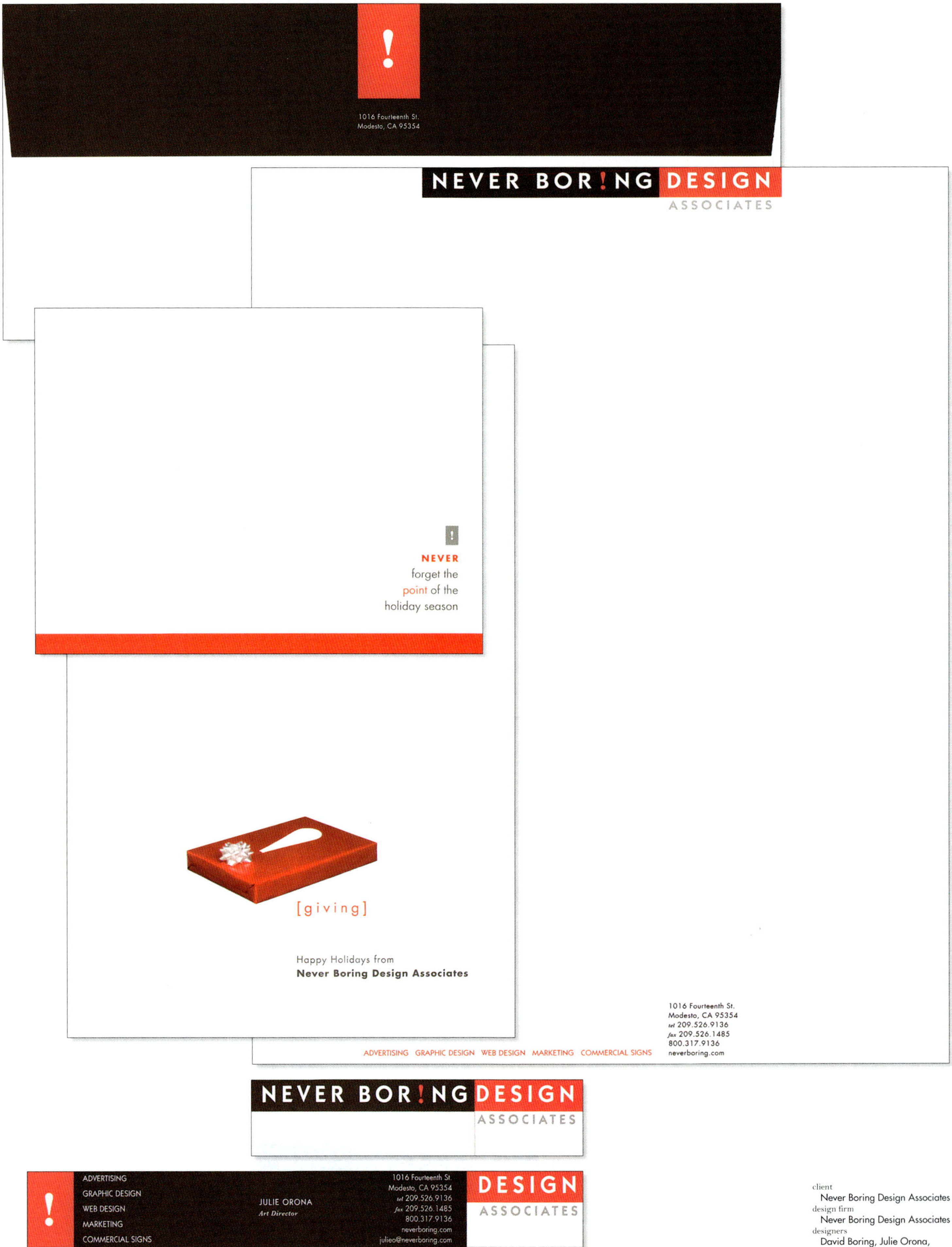

client
Never Boring Design Associates
design firm
Never Boring Design Associates
designers
David Boring, Julie Orona, Katrina Furton, Shawna Bayers

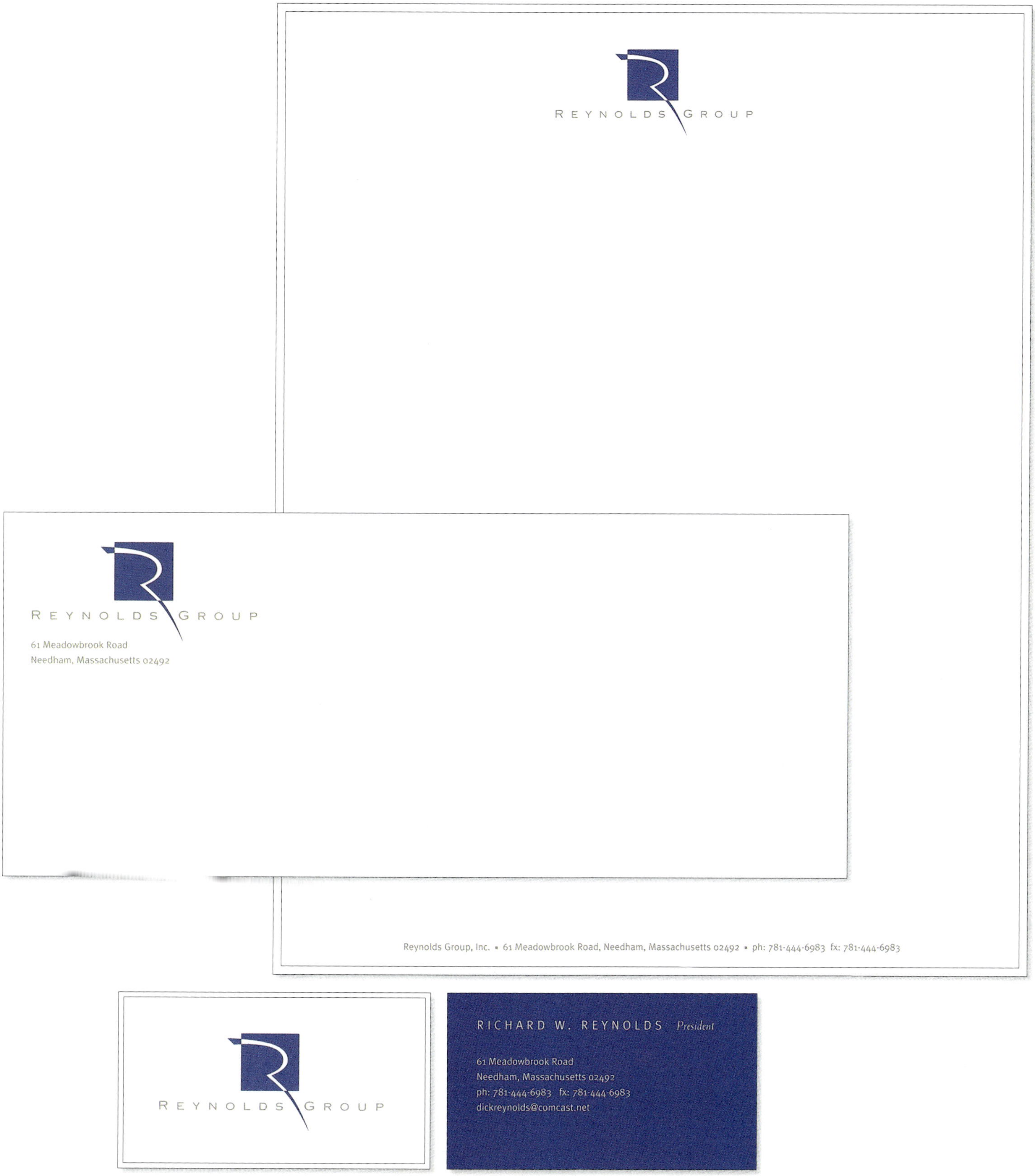

client
Reynolds Group
design firm
Doerr Associates
designer
Linda Blacksmith

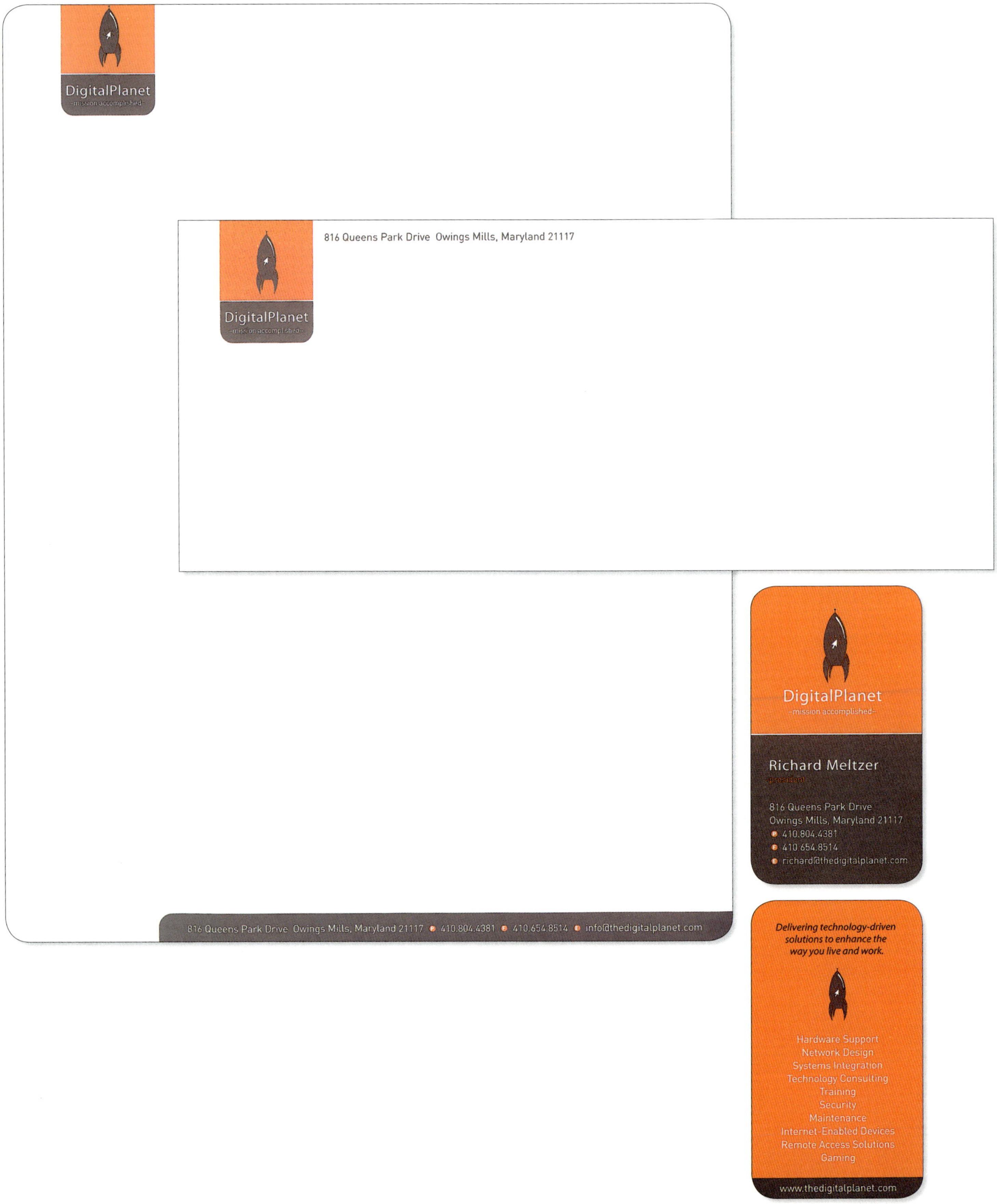

client
Digital Planet
design firm
Round 2 Communications
designer
Christopher Ciesielski

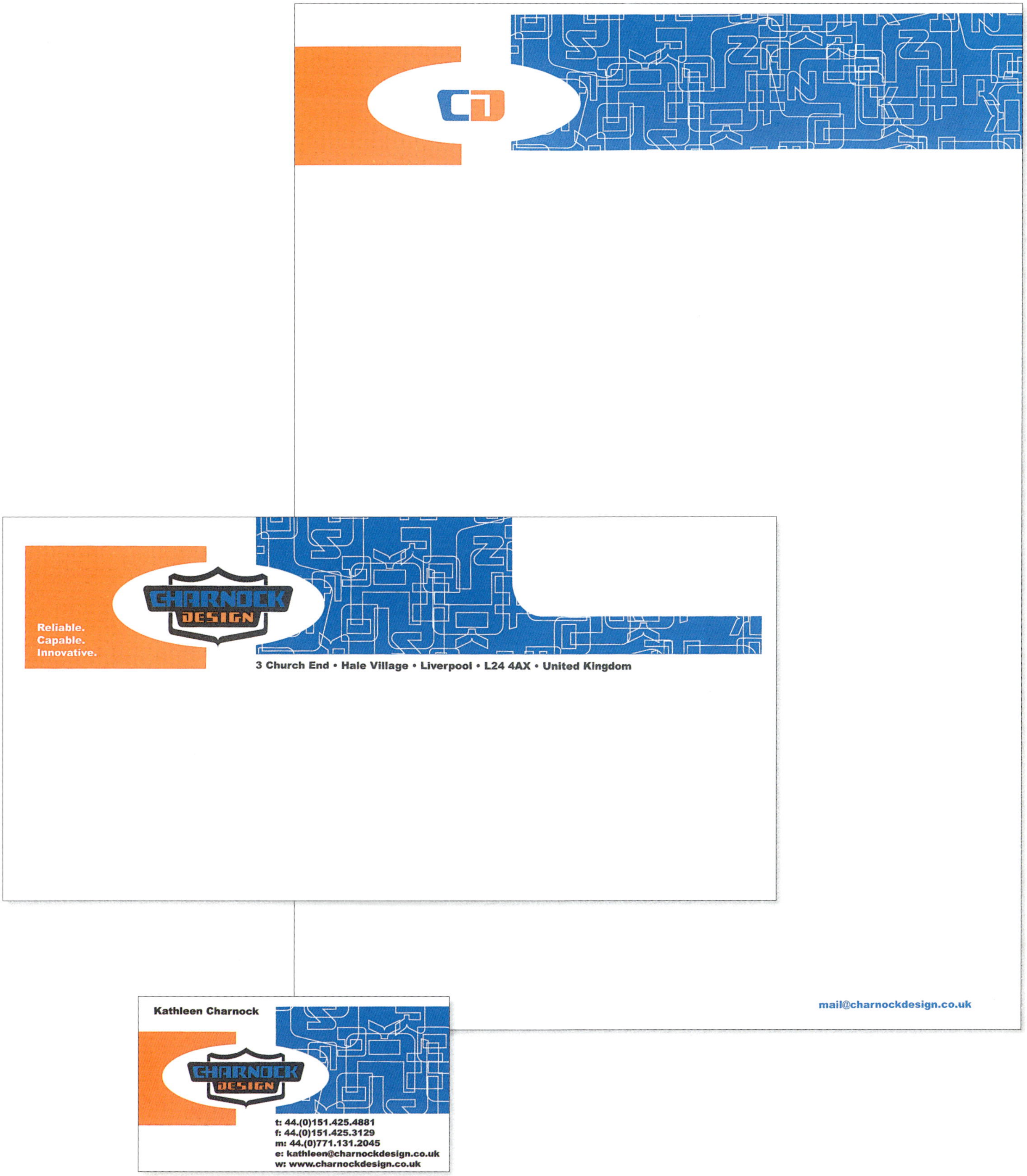

client
Charnock Design
design firm
Sayles Graphic Design
designers
John Sayles, Kelly Bittner

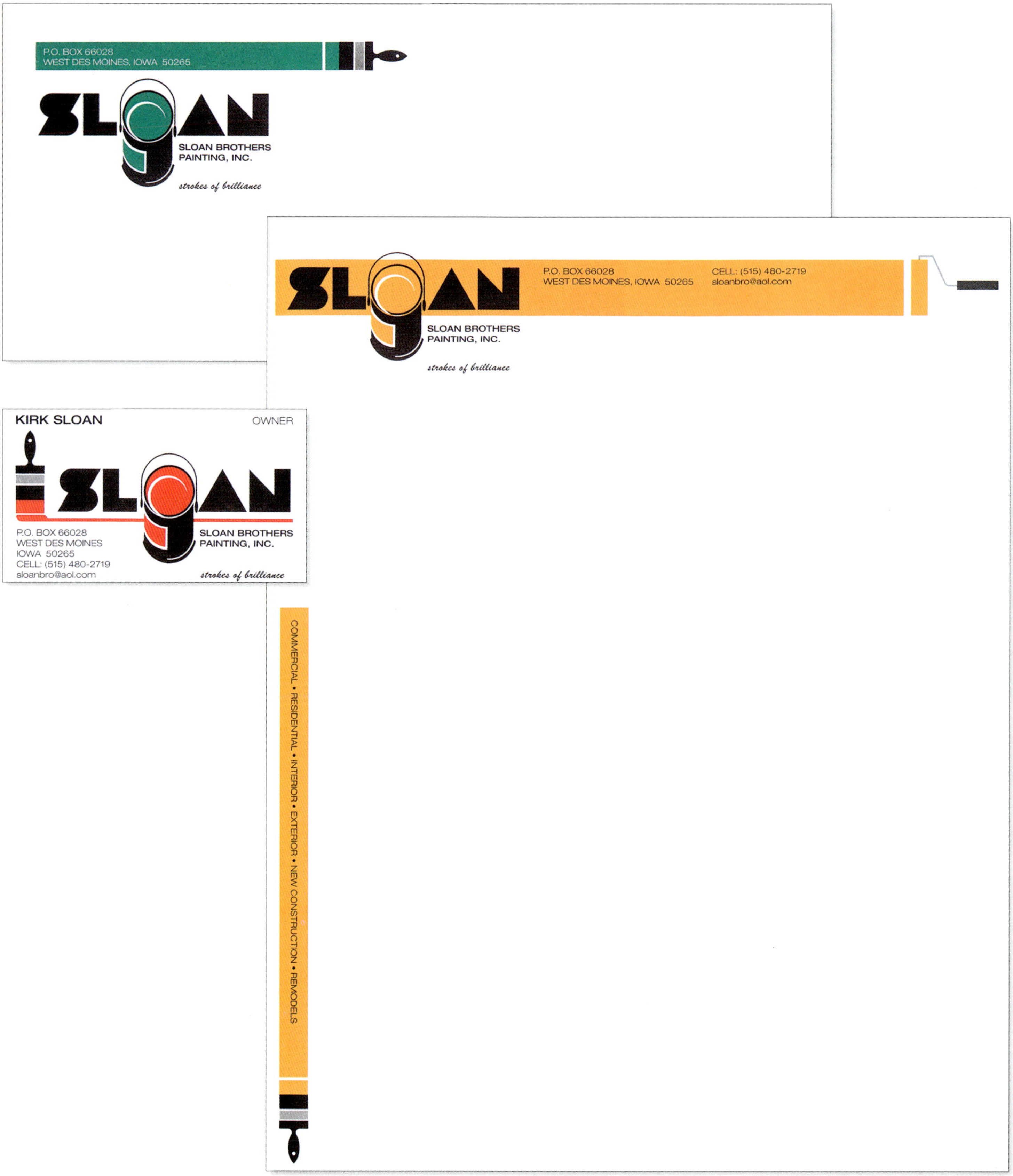

client
Sloan Brothers Painting, Inc.
design firm
Sayles Graphic Design
designers
John Sayles, Kelly Bittner

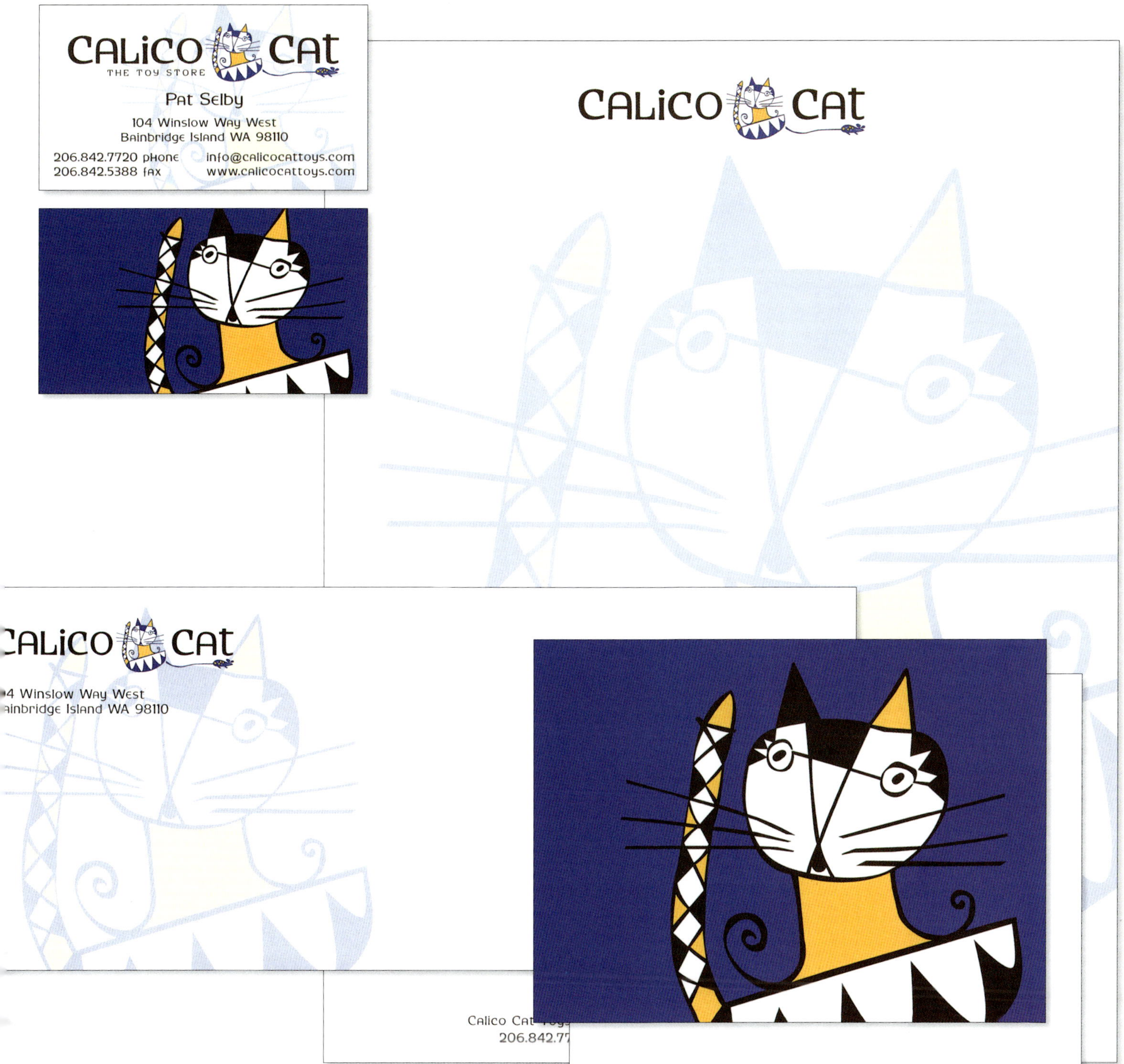

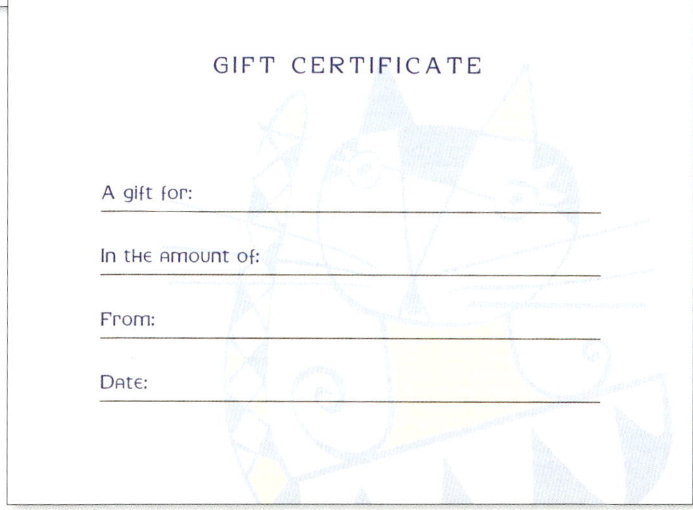

client
Calico Cat
design firm
Daigle Design
art director
Candace Daigle
designers
Paul Dunning, Jessi Carpenter
illustrator
Callie Butler Goodrich

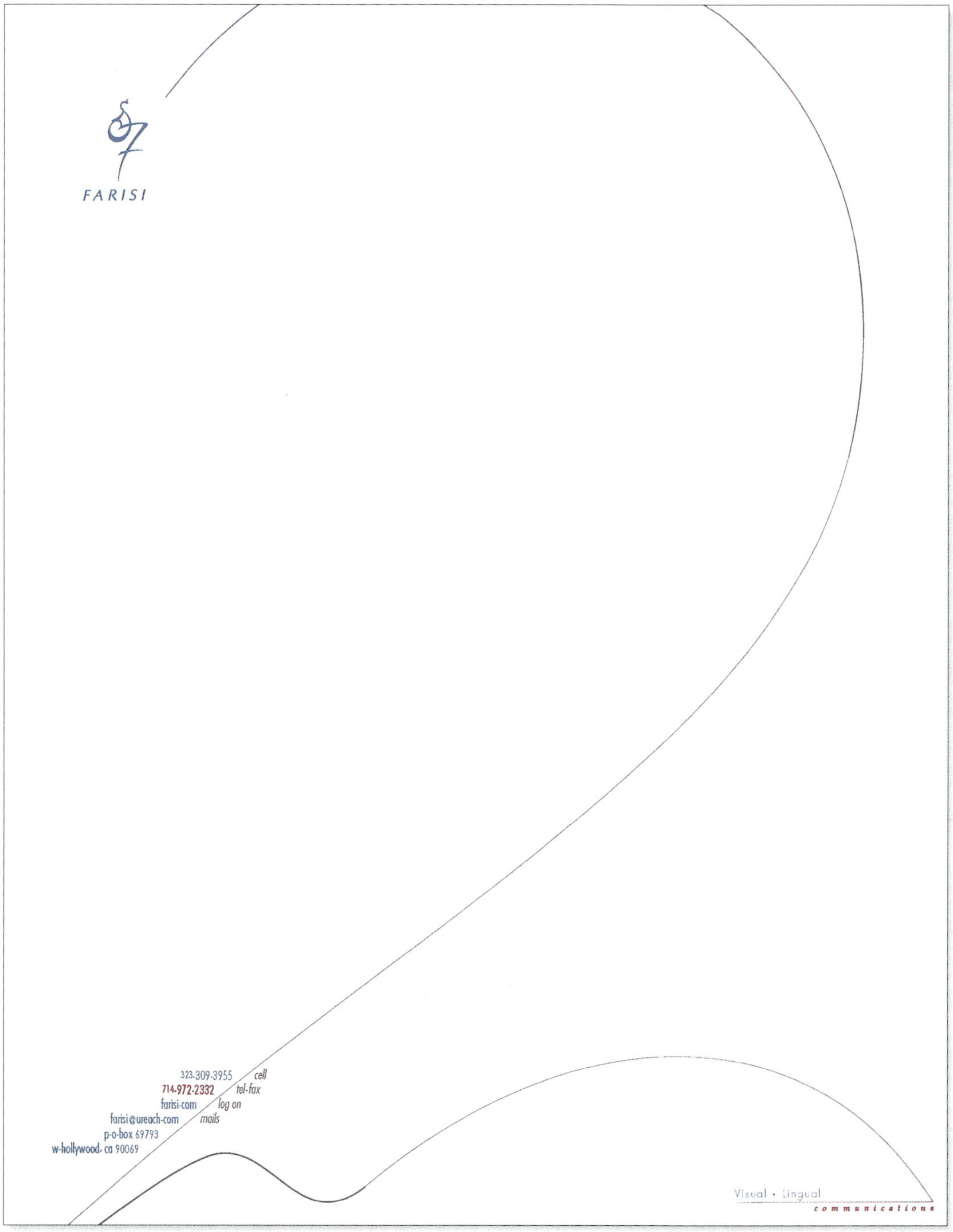

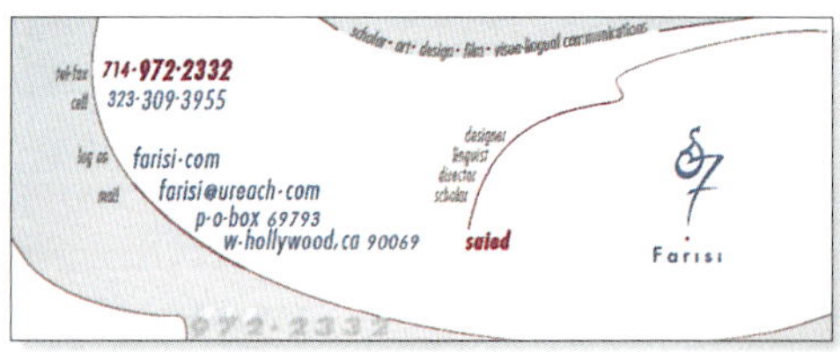

client
Farisi
design firm
Farisi
designer
Saied Farisi

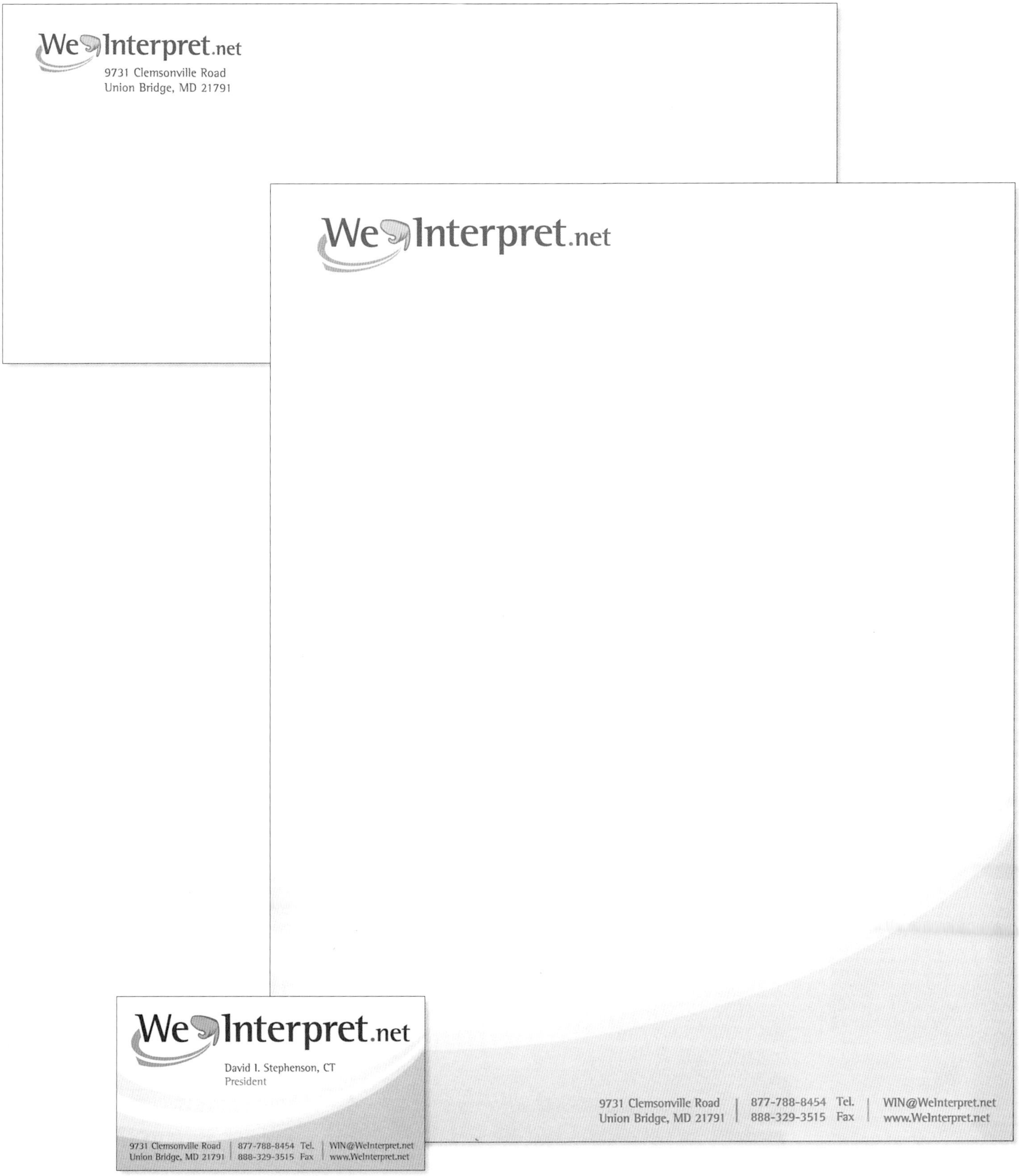

client
WeInterpret.net
design firm
Octavo Designs
designer
Sue Hough

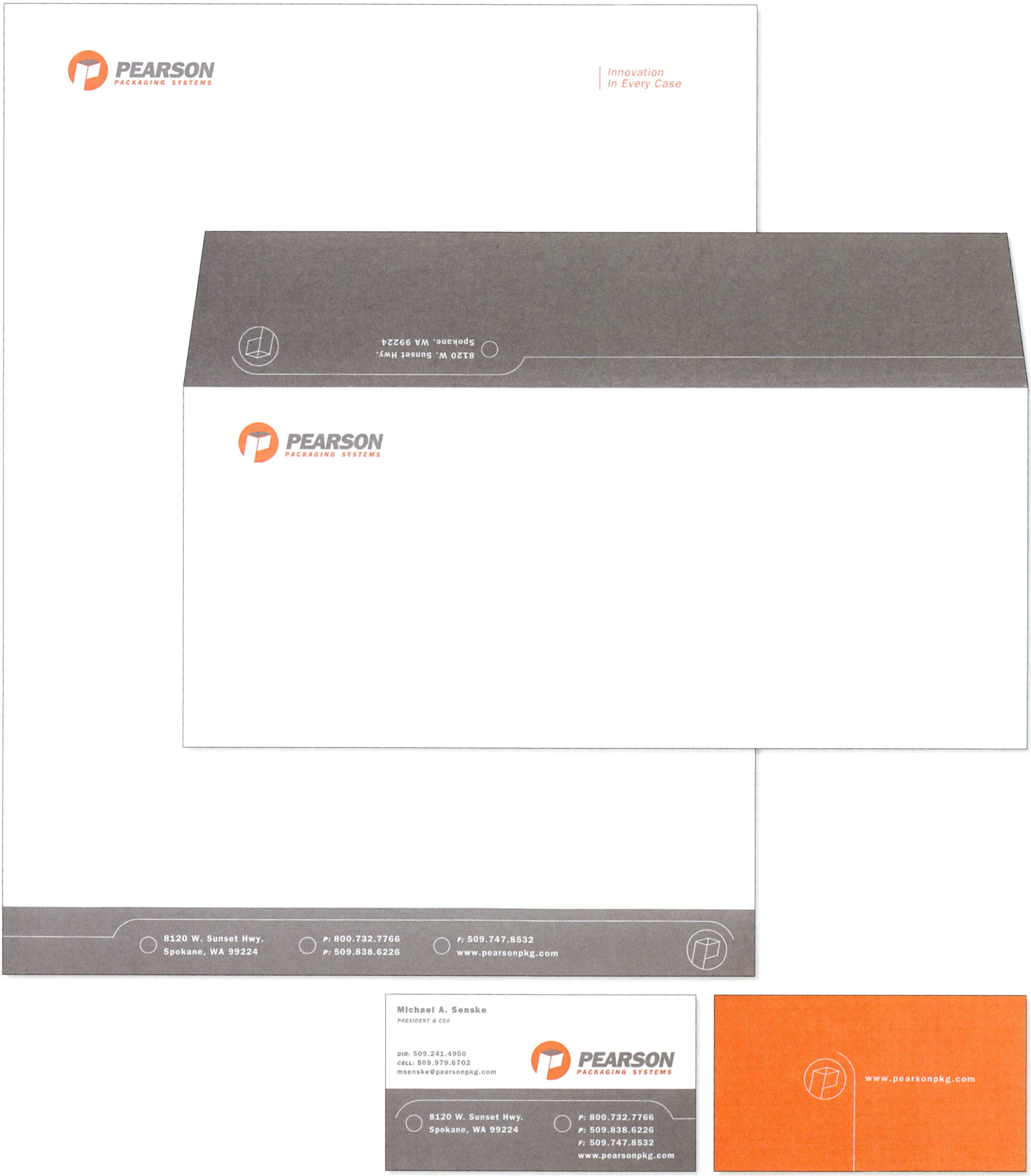

client
Pearson Packaging Systems
design firm
Klündt Hosmer
designers
Judy Heggem-Davis,
Darin Klündt

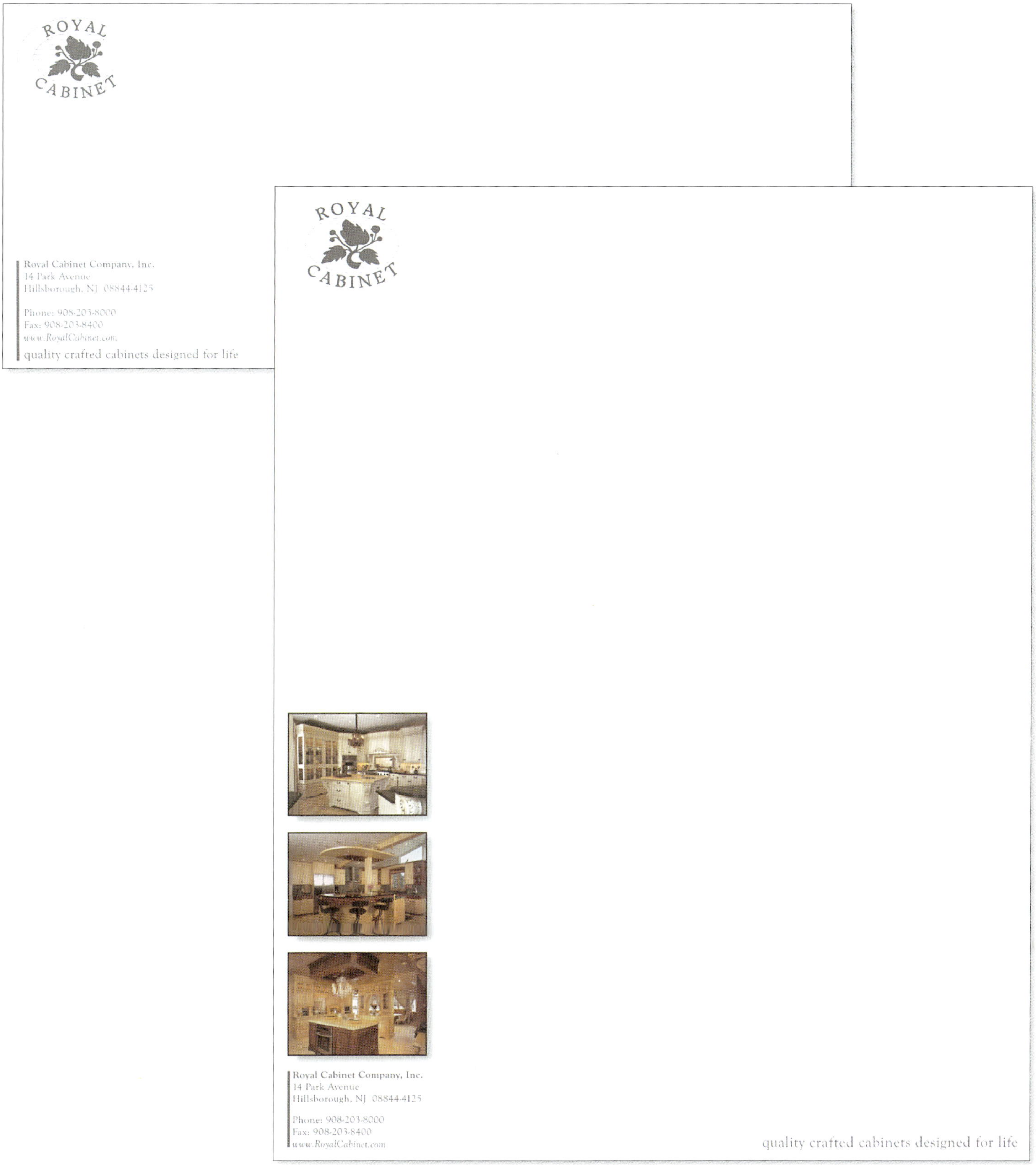

client
Royal Cabinet Company
design firm
Z promotion & design
designer
Philip D. Zaleon

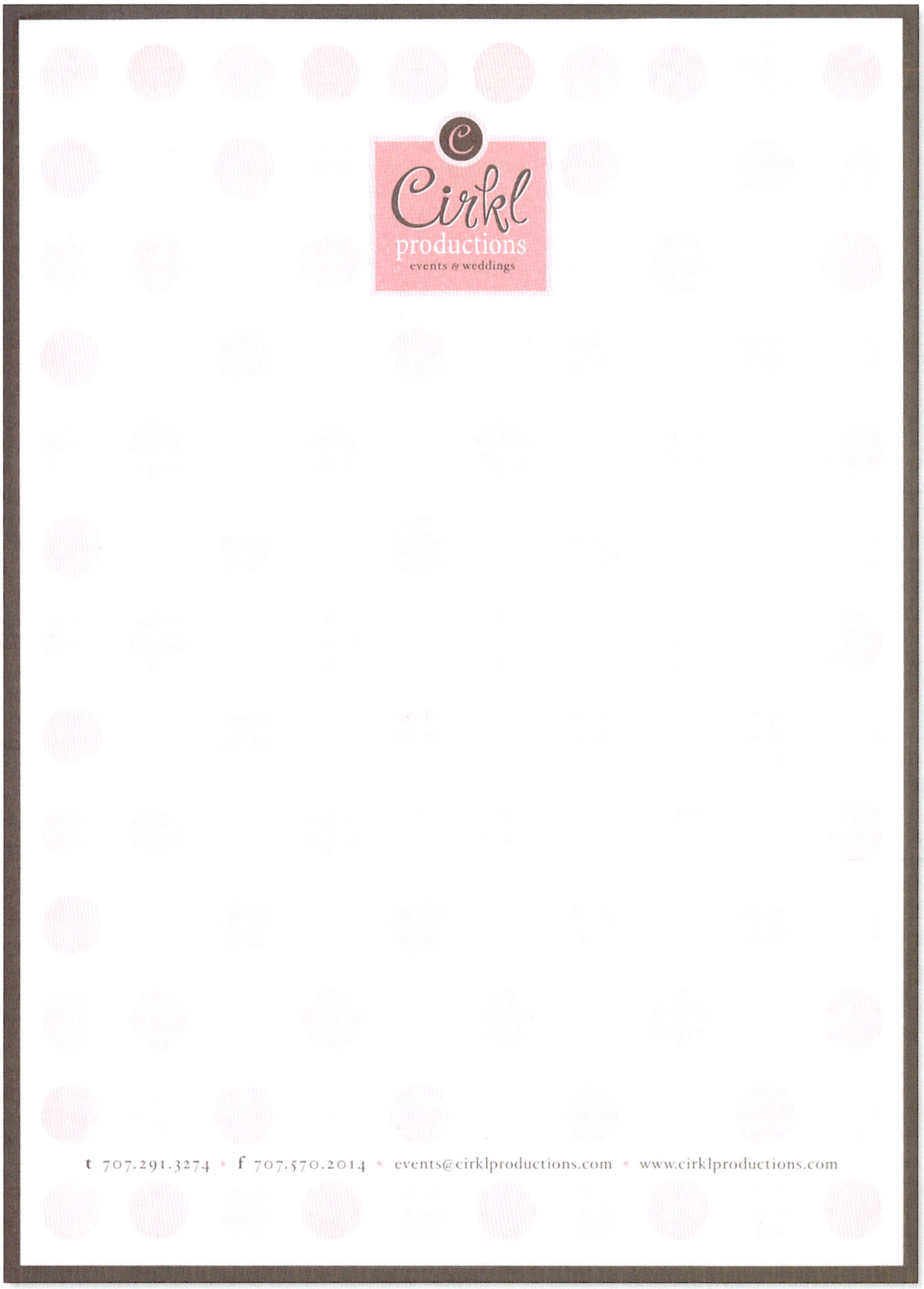

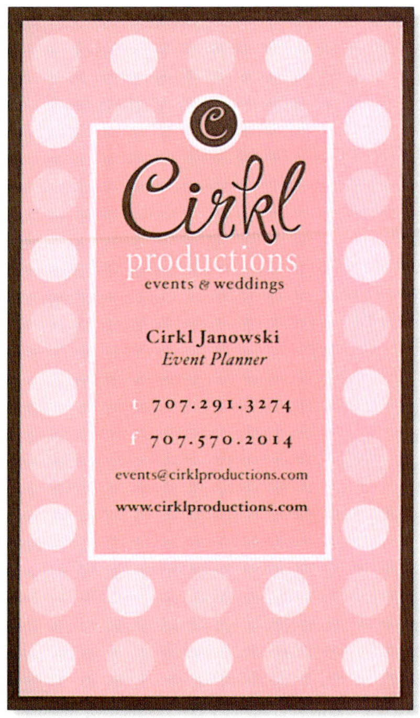

client
Cirkl Productions—Events & Weddings
design firm
Tristano Design
designer
Sara Tristano

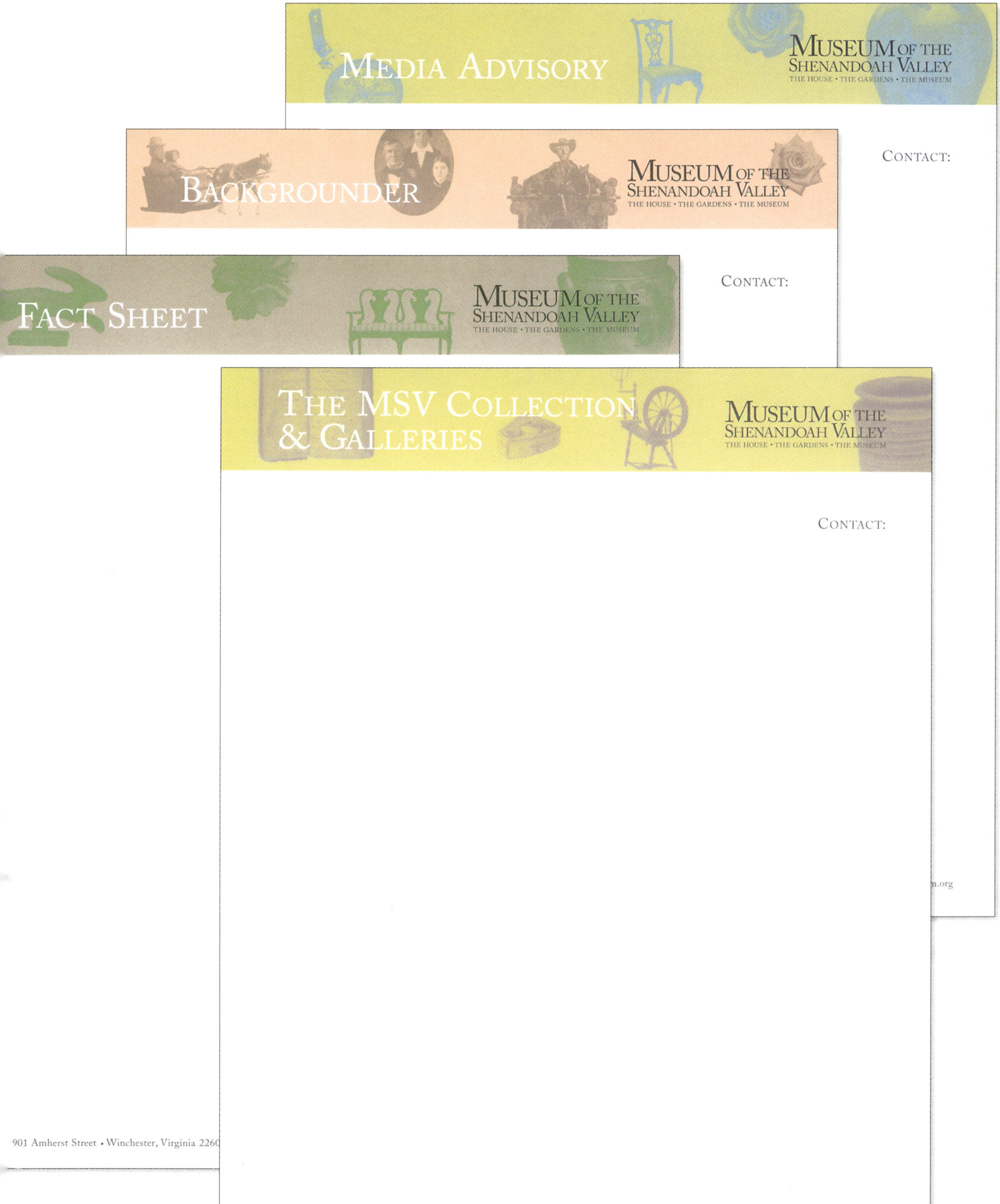

client
Museum of the Shenandoah Valley
design firm
Beth Singer Design, LLC
designer
Sucha Snidvongs

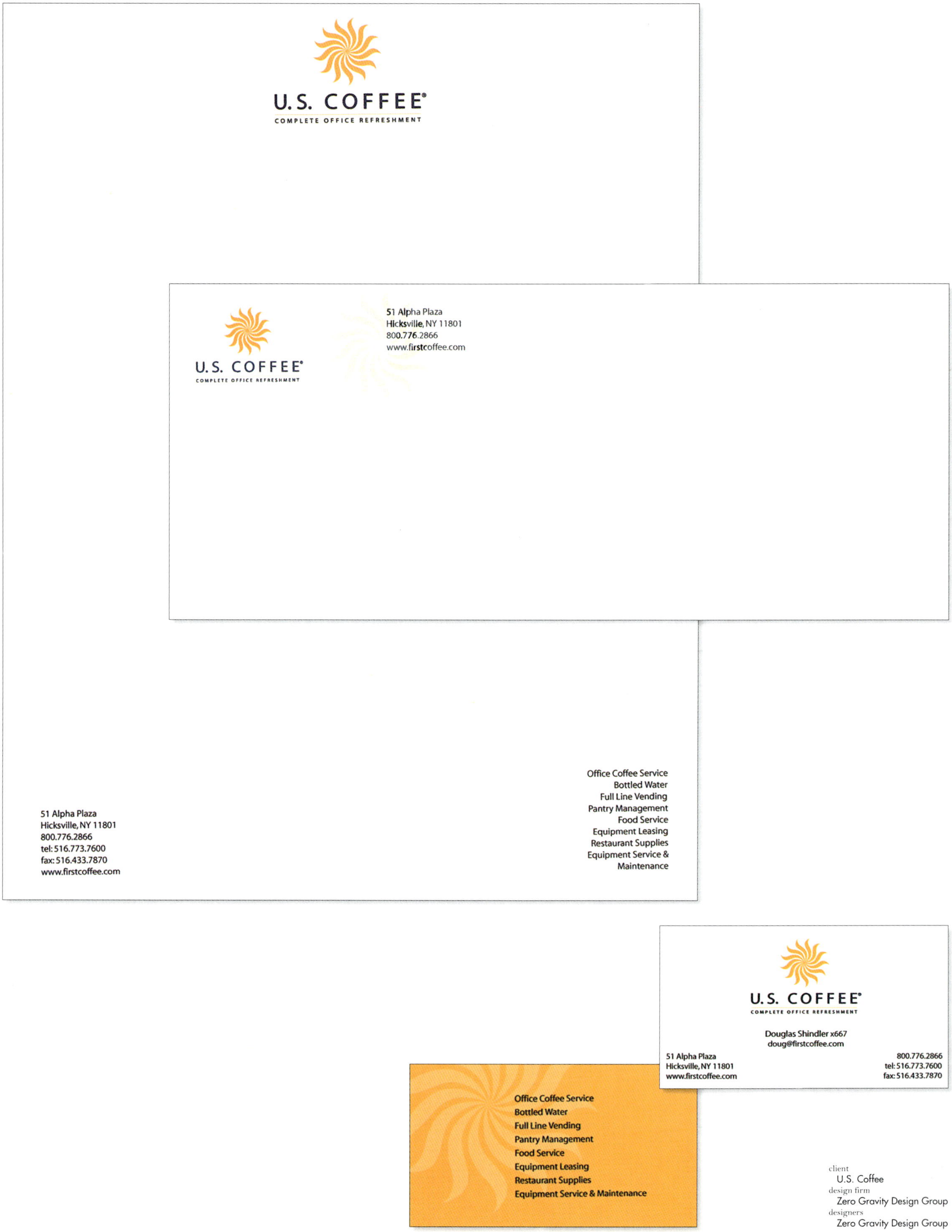

client
U.S. Coffee
design firm
Zero Gravity Design Group
designers
Zero Gravity Design Group

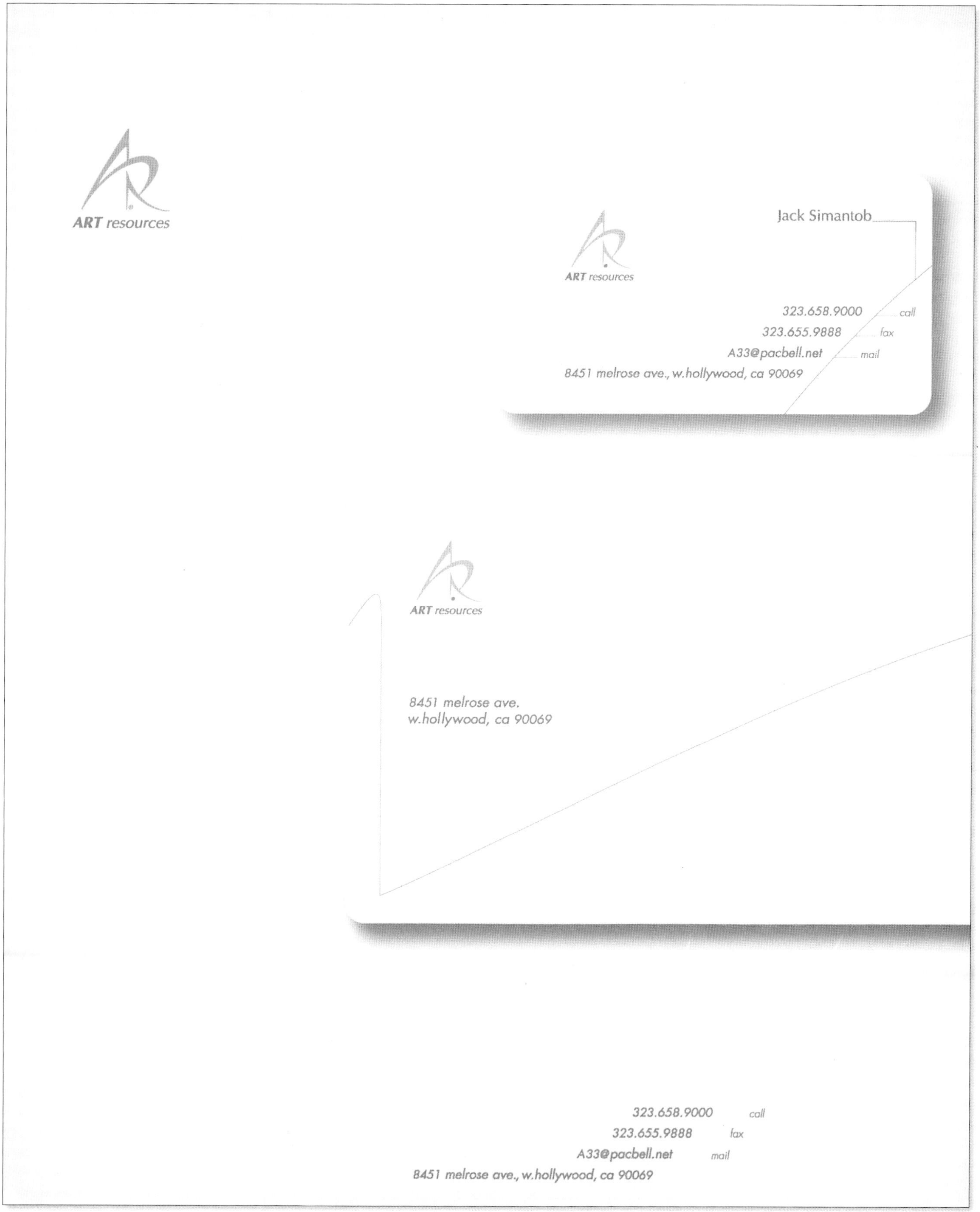

client
Art Resources
design firm
Farisi Design
designer
Saied Farisi

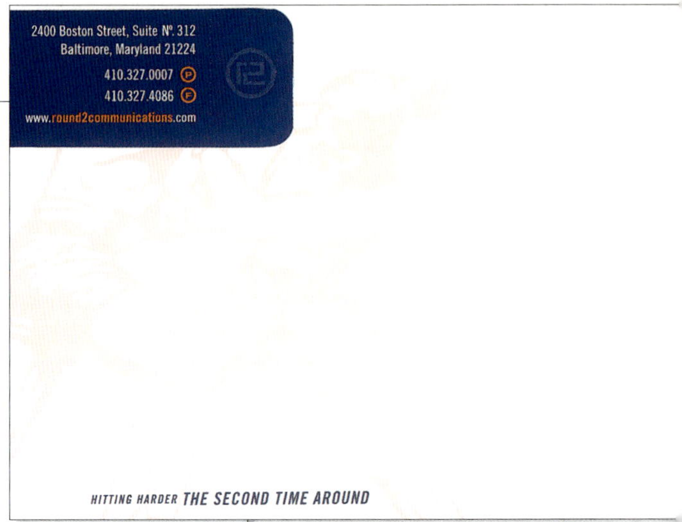

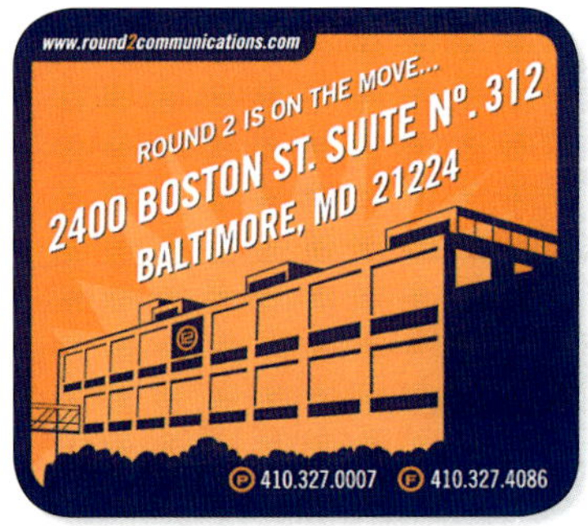

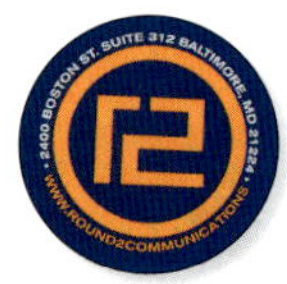

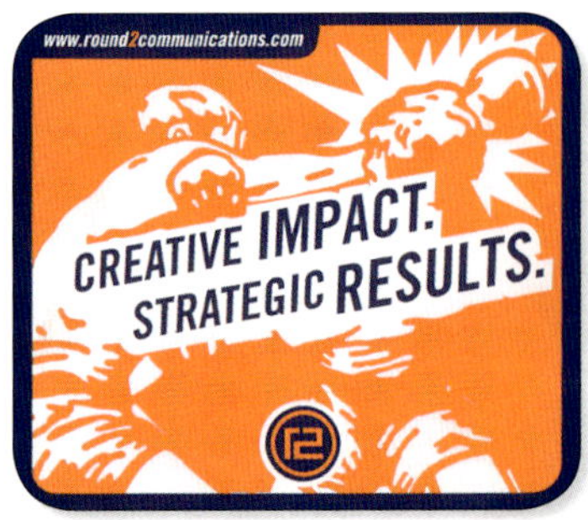

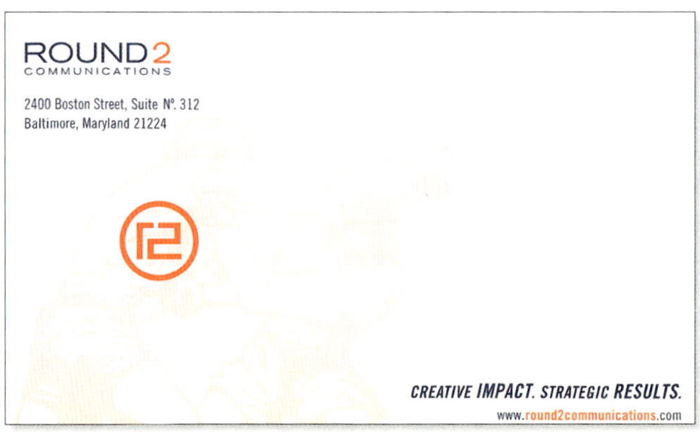

client
Round 2 Communications
design firm
Round 2 Communications
designer
John Welker

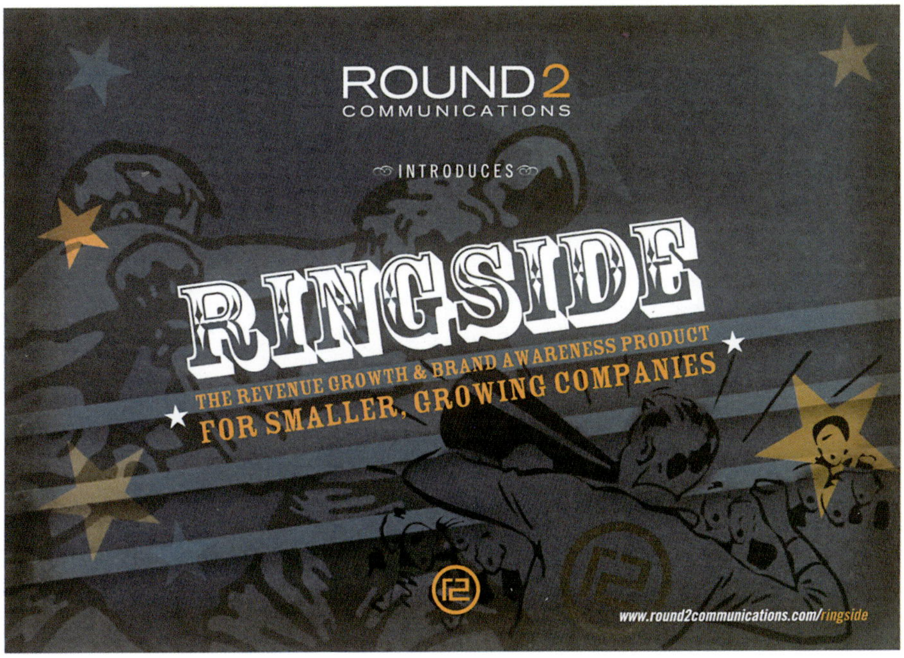

THE BEST SEATS IN THE HOUSE ARE ALWAYS RINGSIDE—CLOSE TO THE ACTION WITH A GREAT POTENTIAL TO BE SEEN!

Smaller growing companies are often overlooked because traditional public relations plans are costly and not always the best fit.
At **Round 2**, we have spent the last 8 years solving this problem.
Our success has led to the development of ***Ringside***, a manageable strategic communication system that will raise your awareness level and at a cost you can afford.

There are a lot of businesses out there—why should the large ones get all the attention?

ROUND 2
2737 Dillon Street
Baltimore, Maryland 21224
P 410.327.0007
F 410.327.8330

ROUND 2

ROUND 2
COMMUNICATIONS

Julie Novak
Assistant Marketing Coordinator
julie@round2communications.com

STRATEGY
MARKETING
CREATIVE

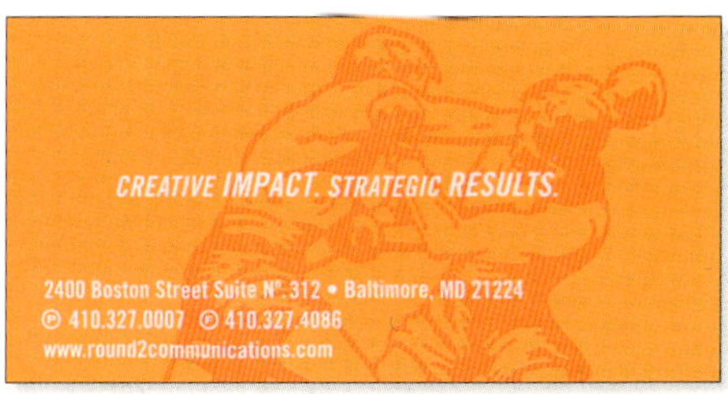

2737 Dillon Street
Baltimore, Maryland 21224
P 410.327.0007
F 410.327.8330
www.round2communications.com

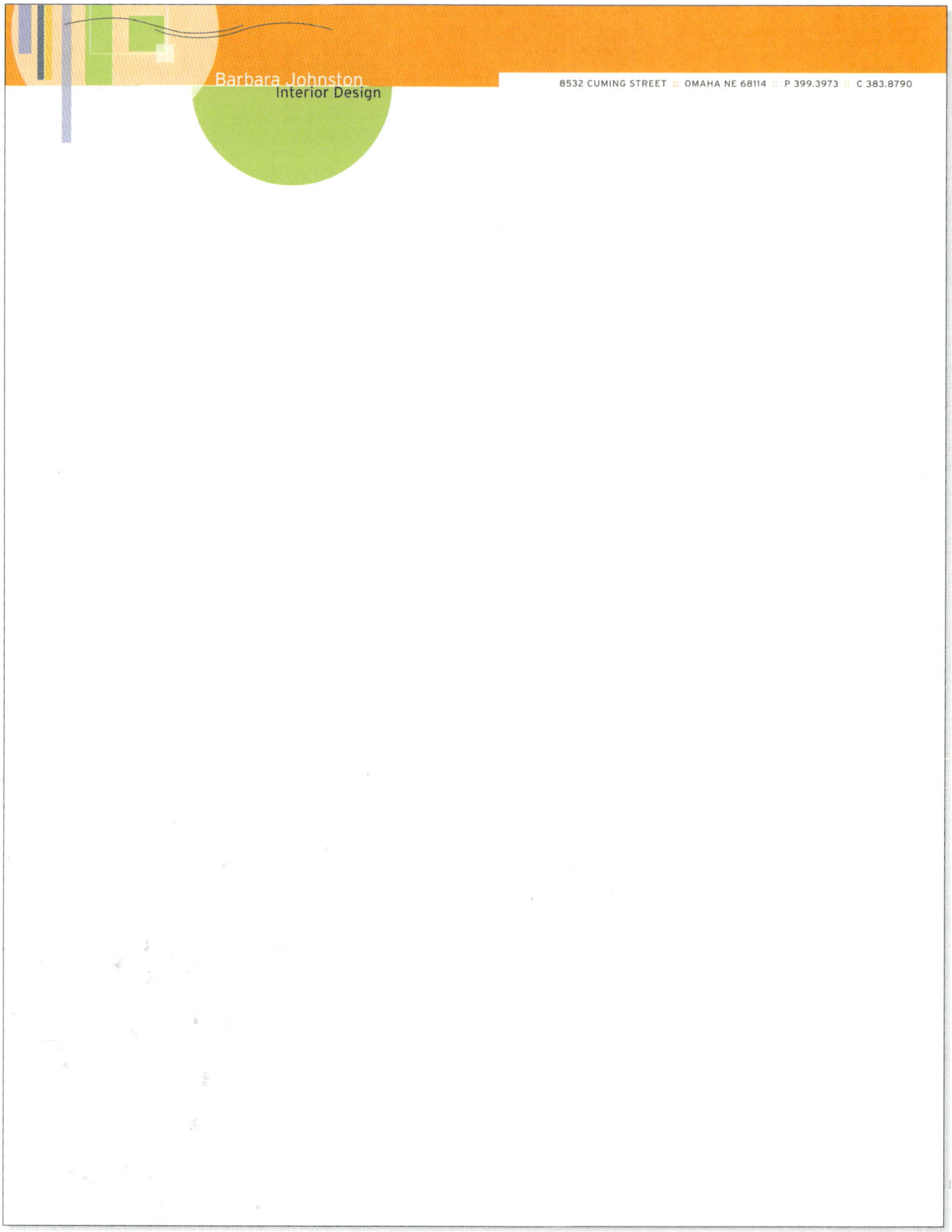

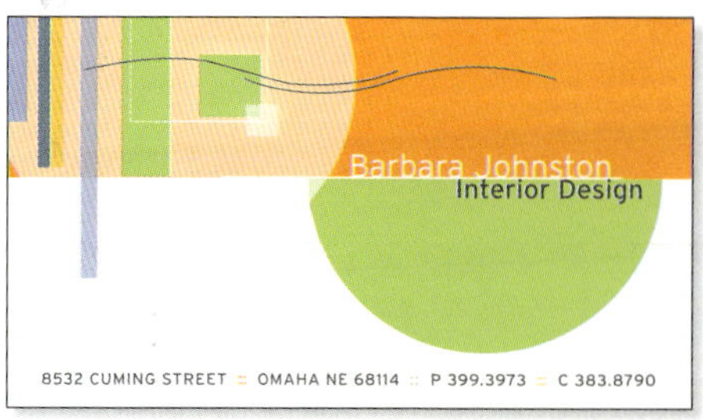

client
Barbara Johnston Interior Design
design firm
HrupekDesign
designer
Michael Hrupek

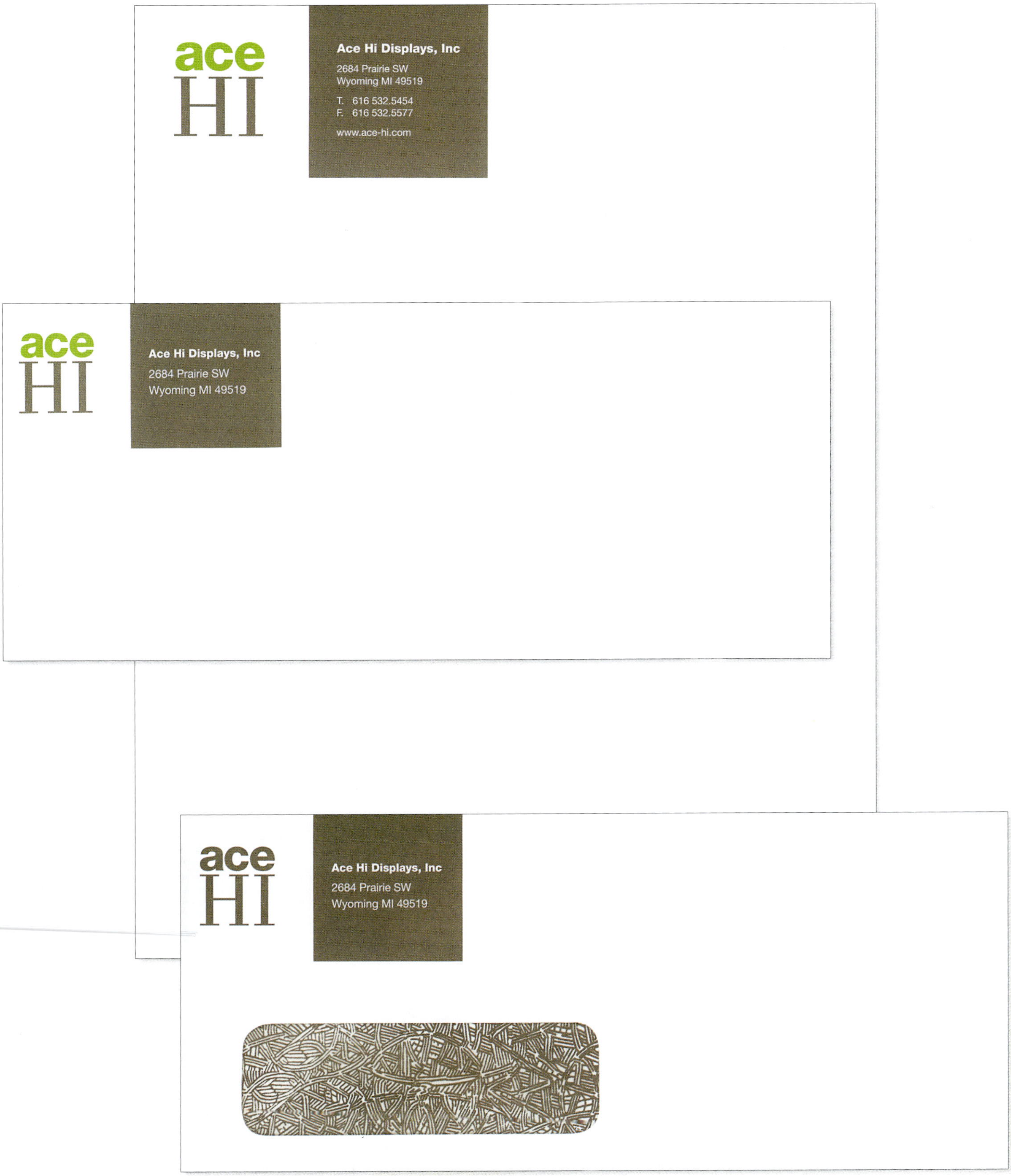

client
AceHi
design firm
Square One Design
designers
Lin Ver Meulen, Martin Schoenborn

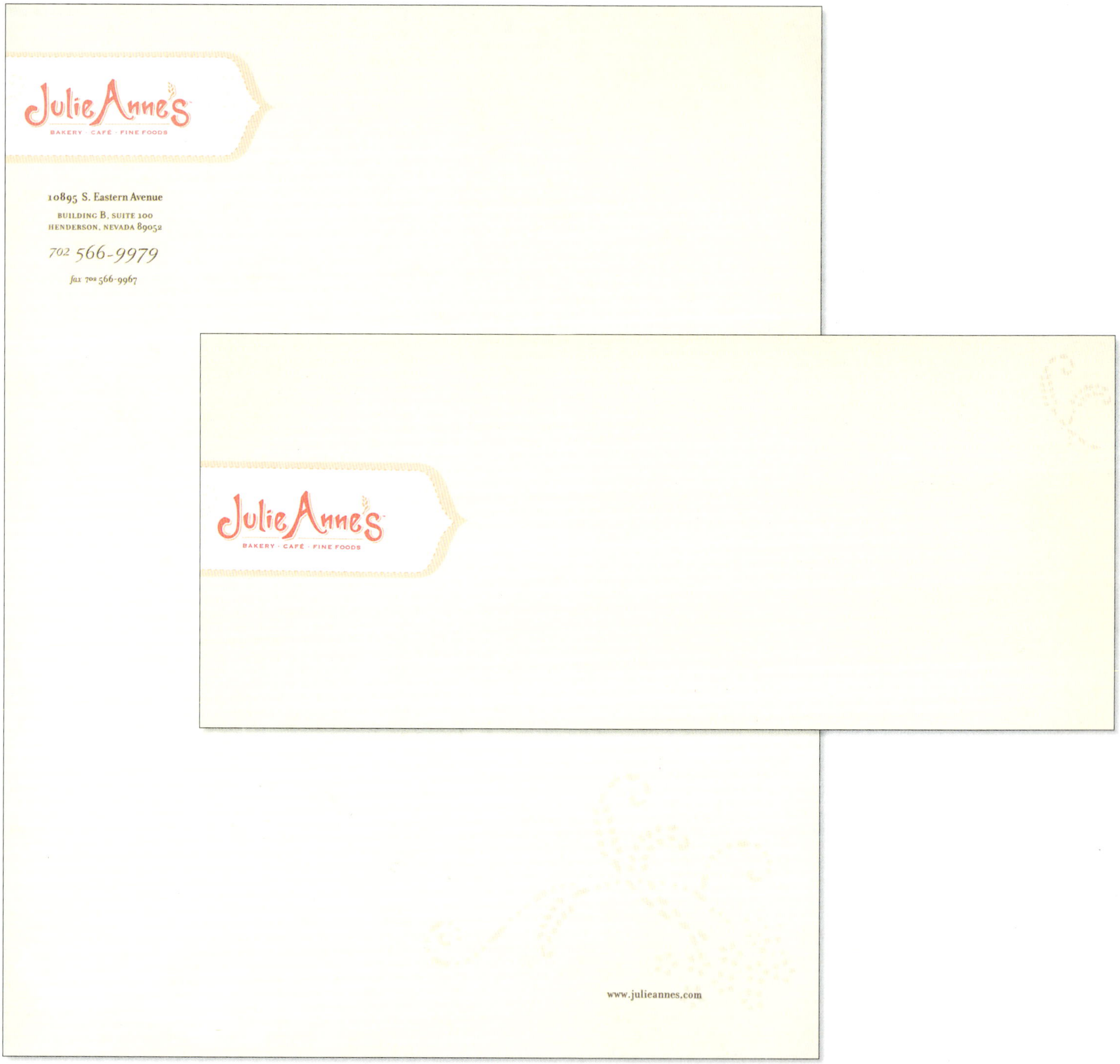

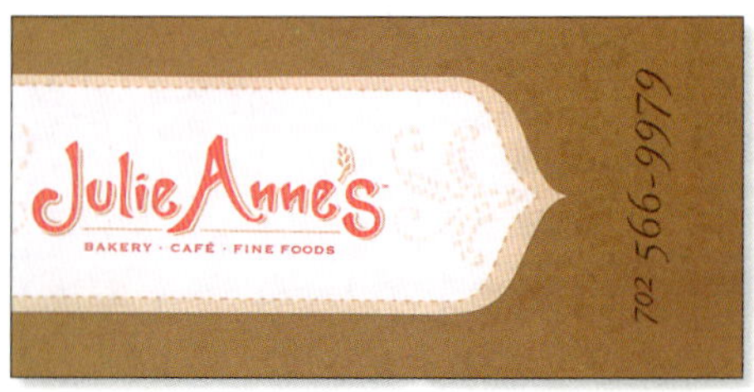

client
Julie Anne's
design firm
CDI Studios
creative director
Victoria Hart
designer
Brian Felgar

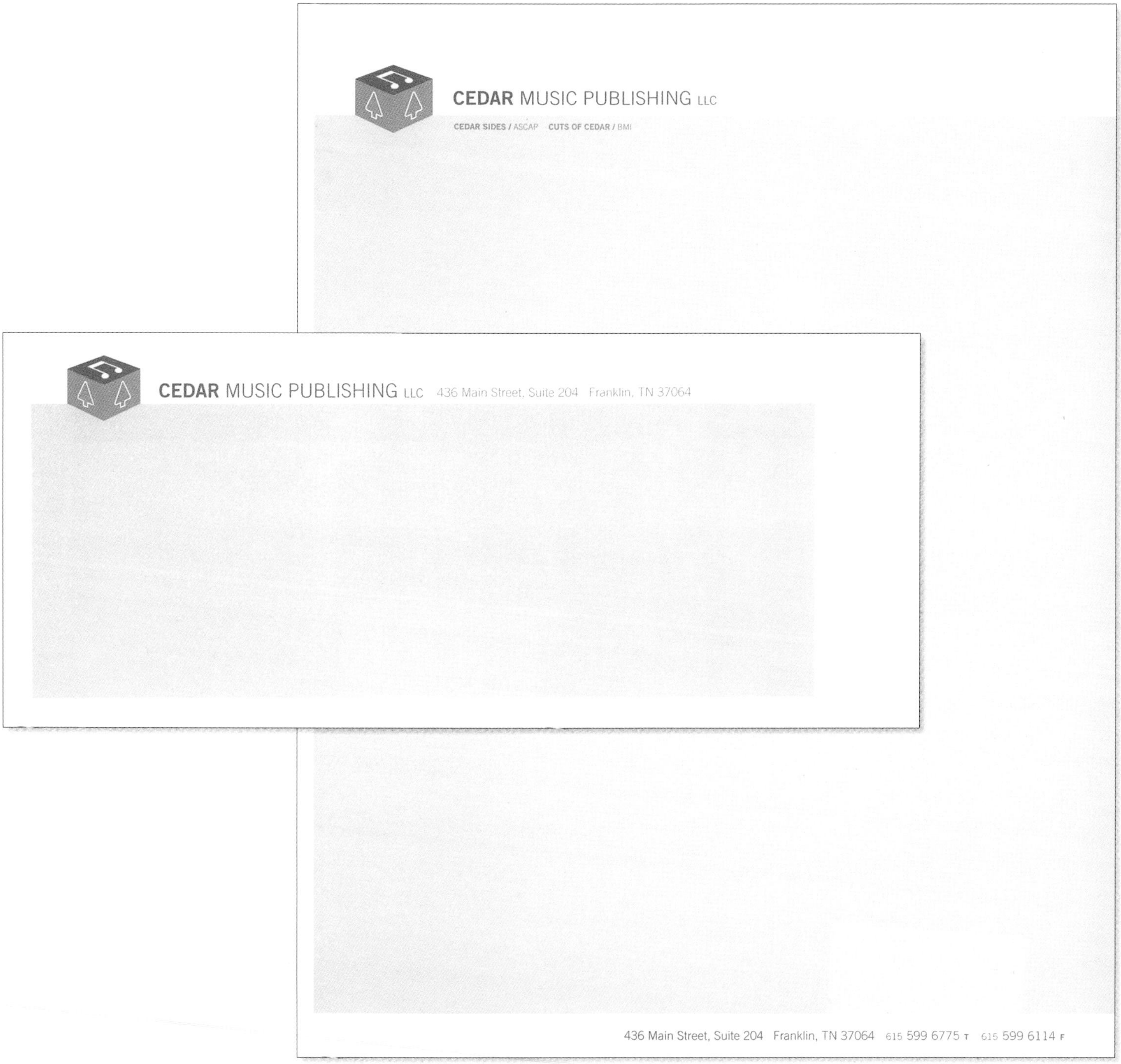

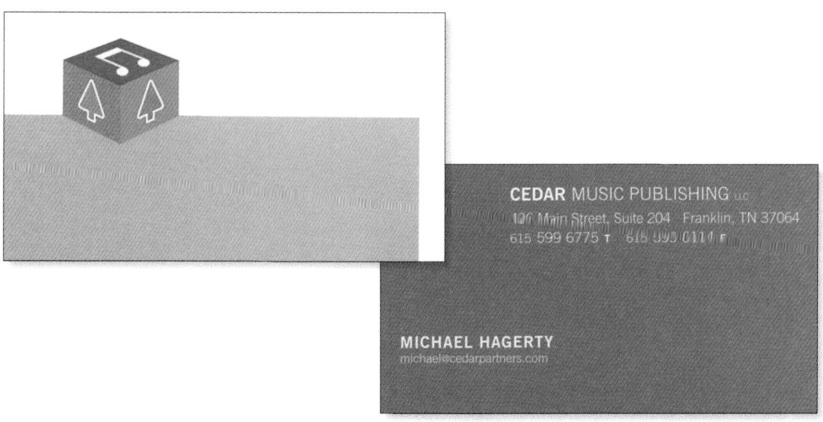

client
Cedar Partners
design firm
Lewis—Nashville
designer
Clark Hook

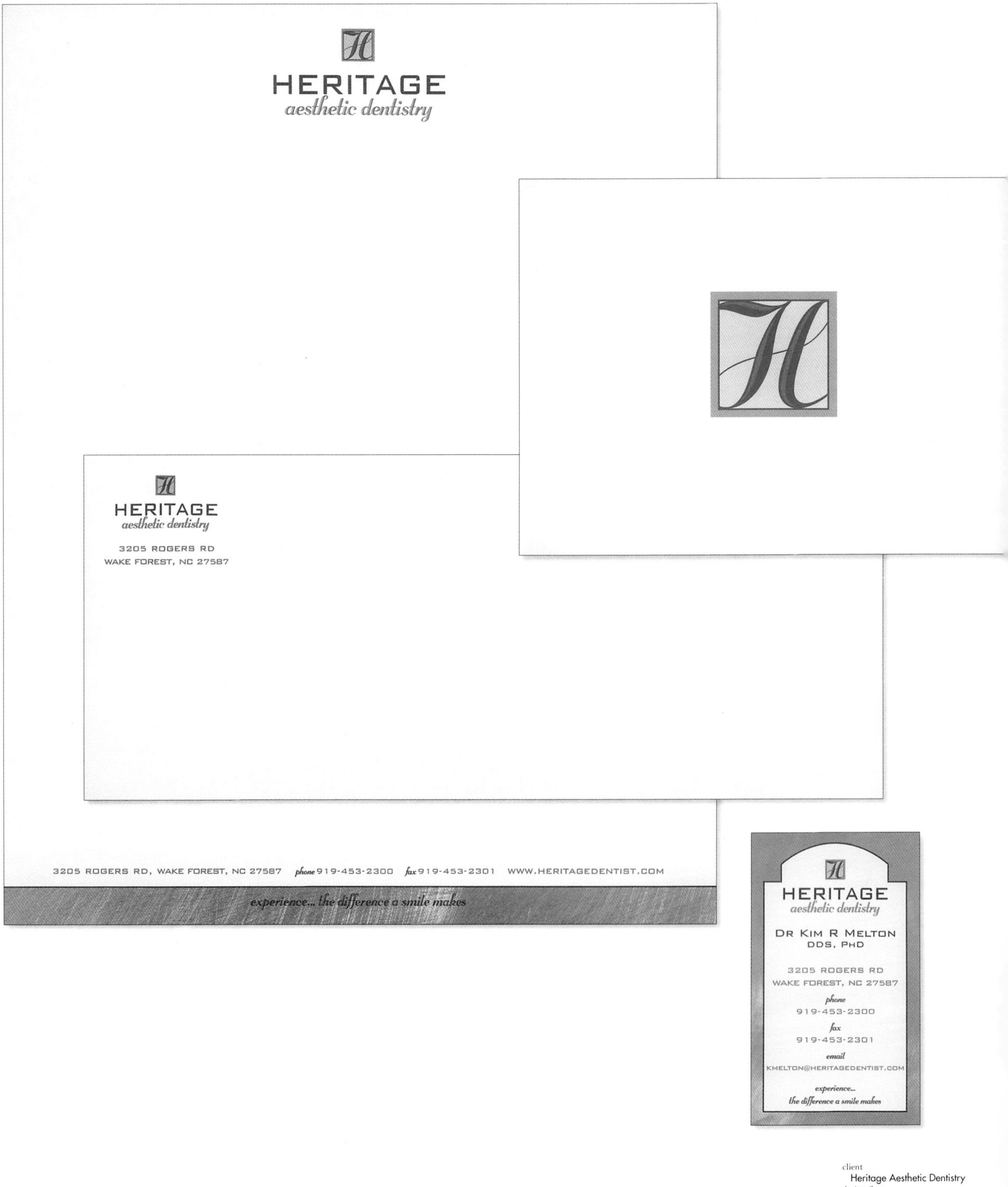

client
Heritage Aesthetic Dentistry
design firm
Hummingbird Creative Group
designers
Sabrina Frasier, Lorana Price

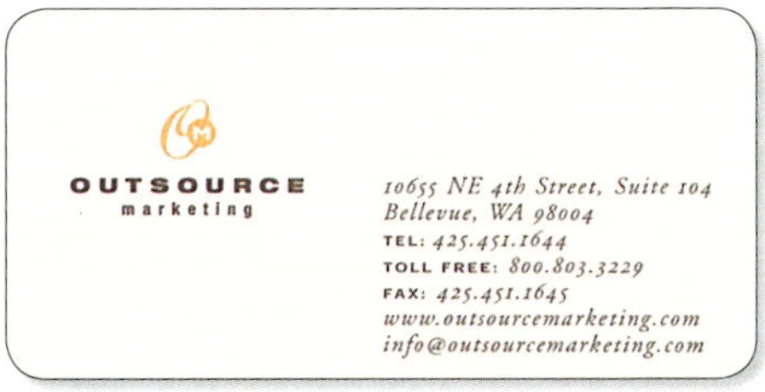

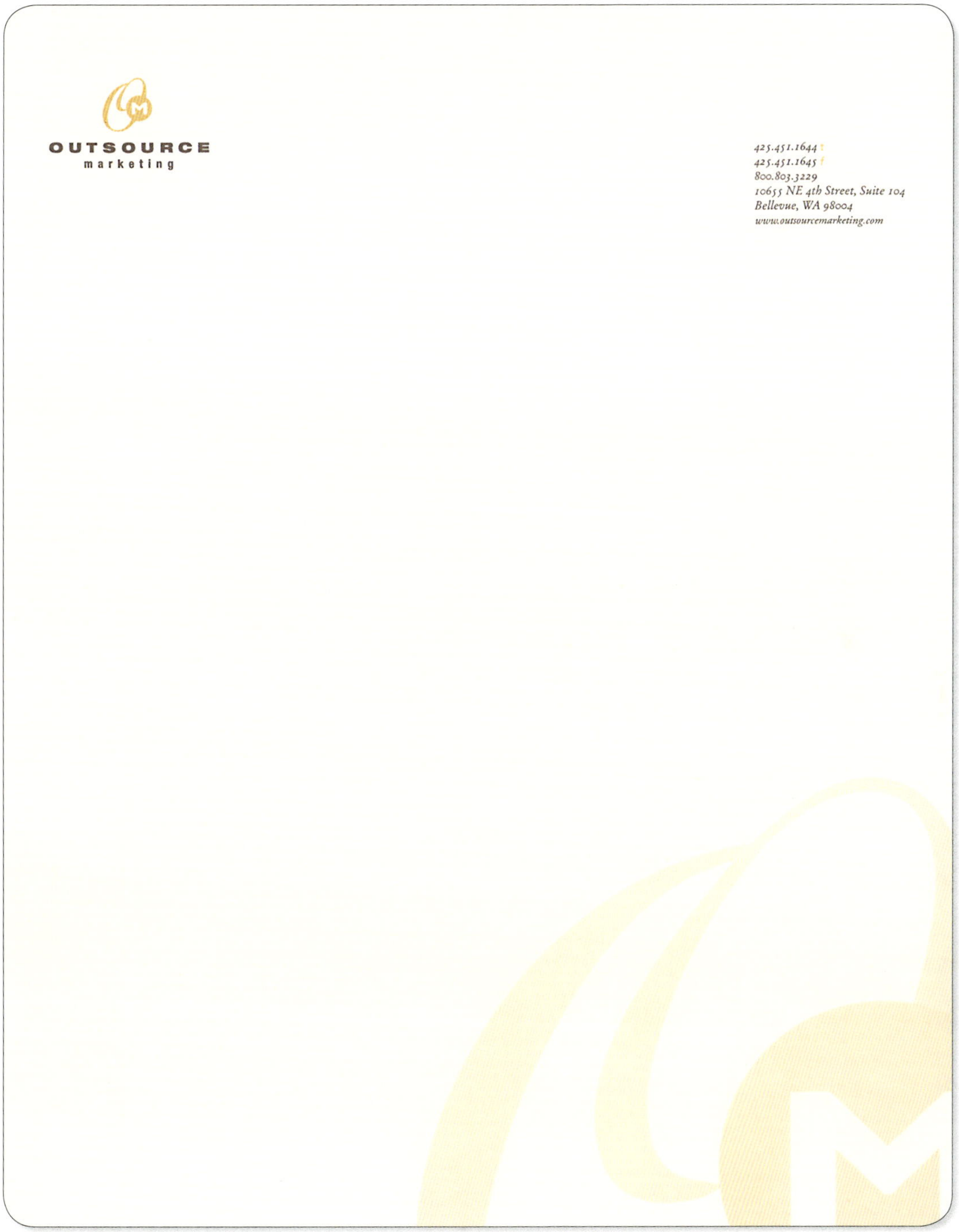

client
Outsource Marketing
design firm
Eben Design
designer
Dan Meehan

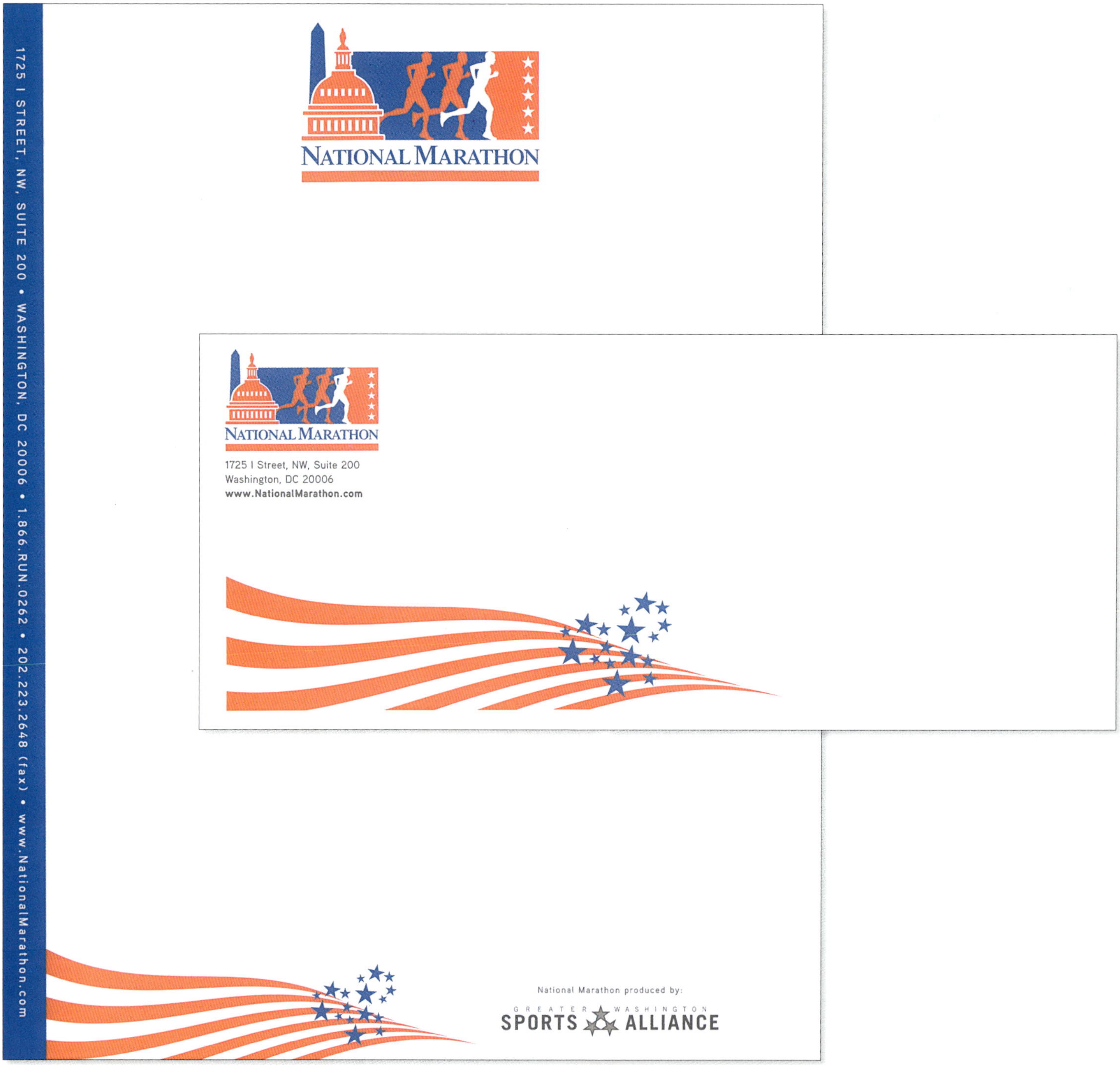

client
Greater Washington Sports Alliance
design firm
Fixation Marketing
designers
John Frantz, Bruce E. Morgan

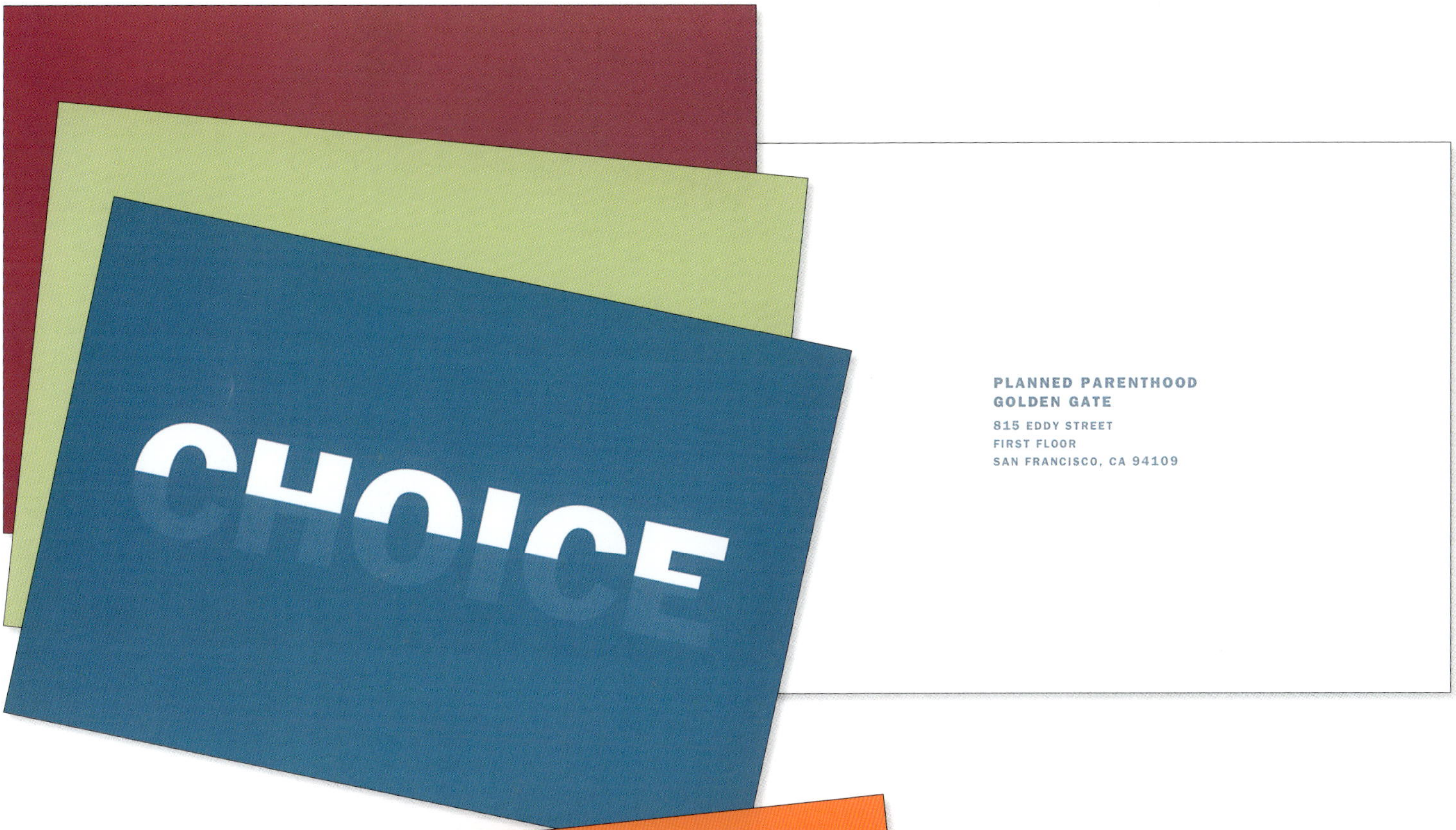

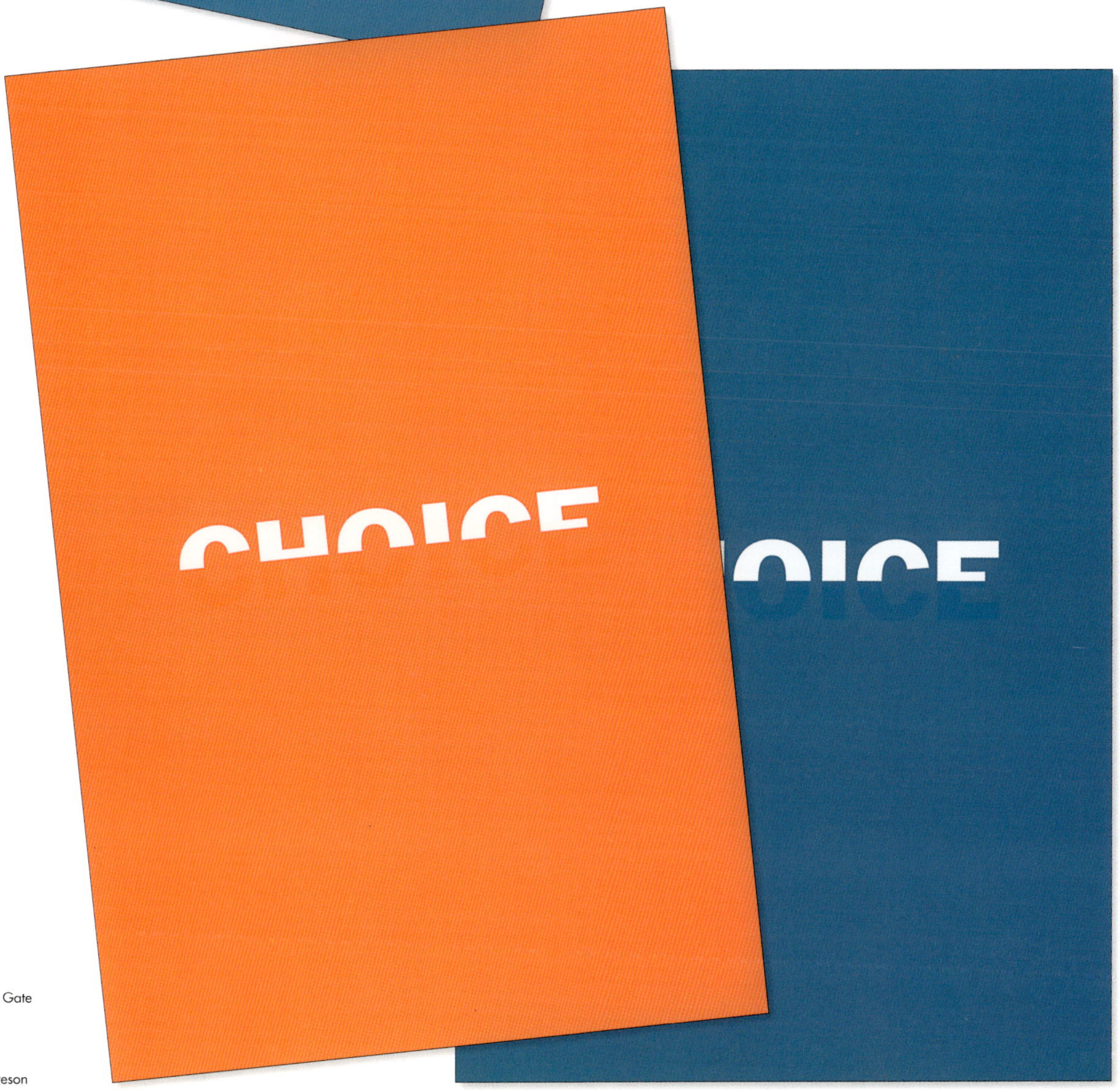

client
Planned Parenthood Golden Gate
design firm
Addis Group
designers
Fabian Falconett,
Magdalena Hladka, John Creson

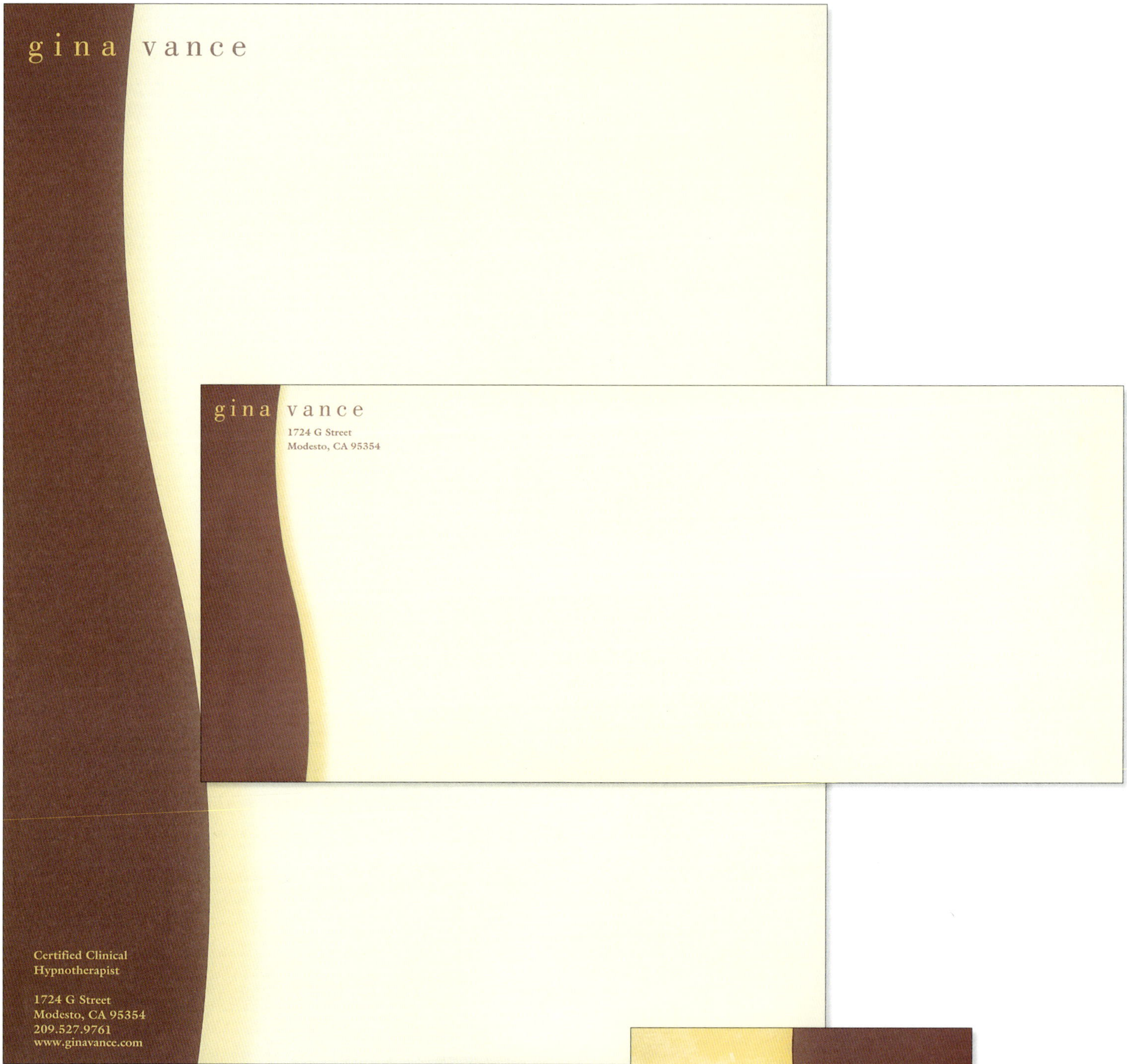

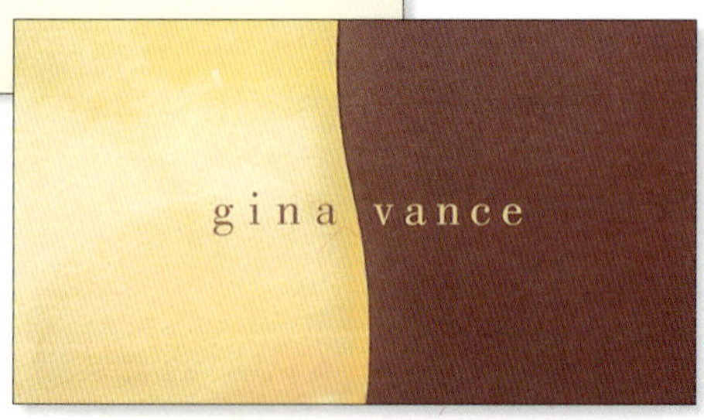

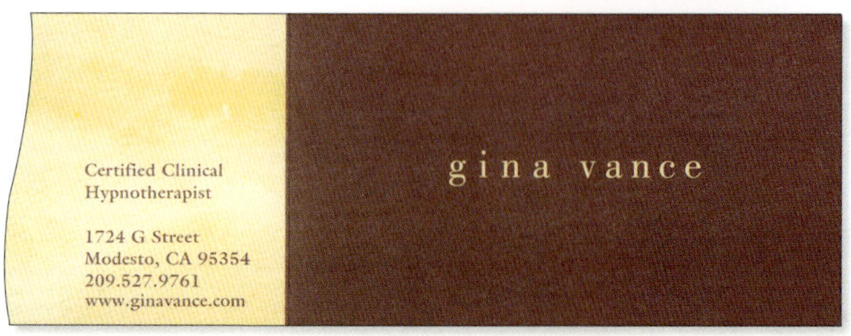

client
Gina Vance
design firm
Never Boring Design Associates
designer
Julie Orona

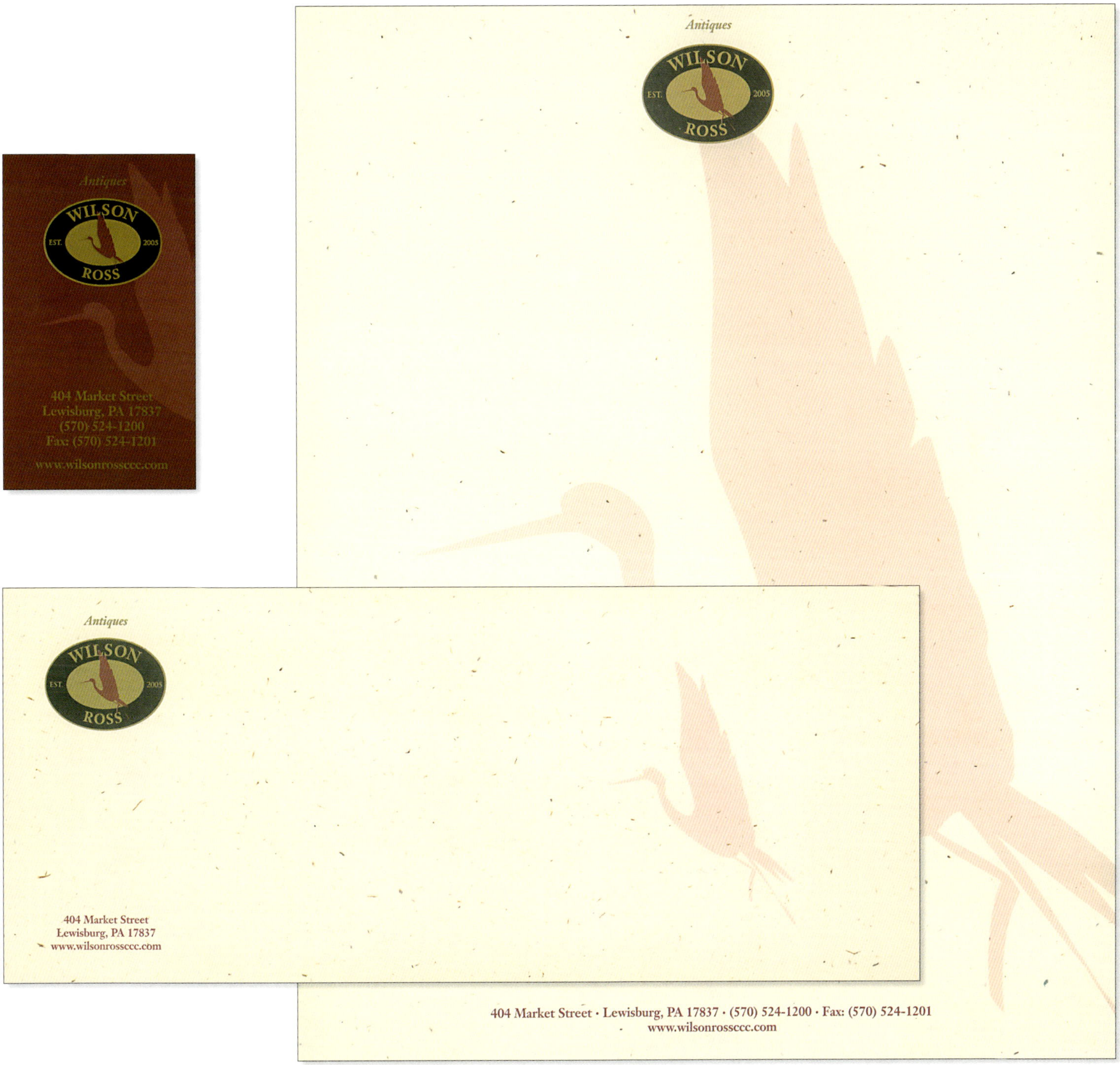

client
Wilson Ross
design firm
Sire Advertising
designer
Shawn Felty

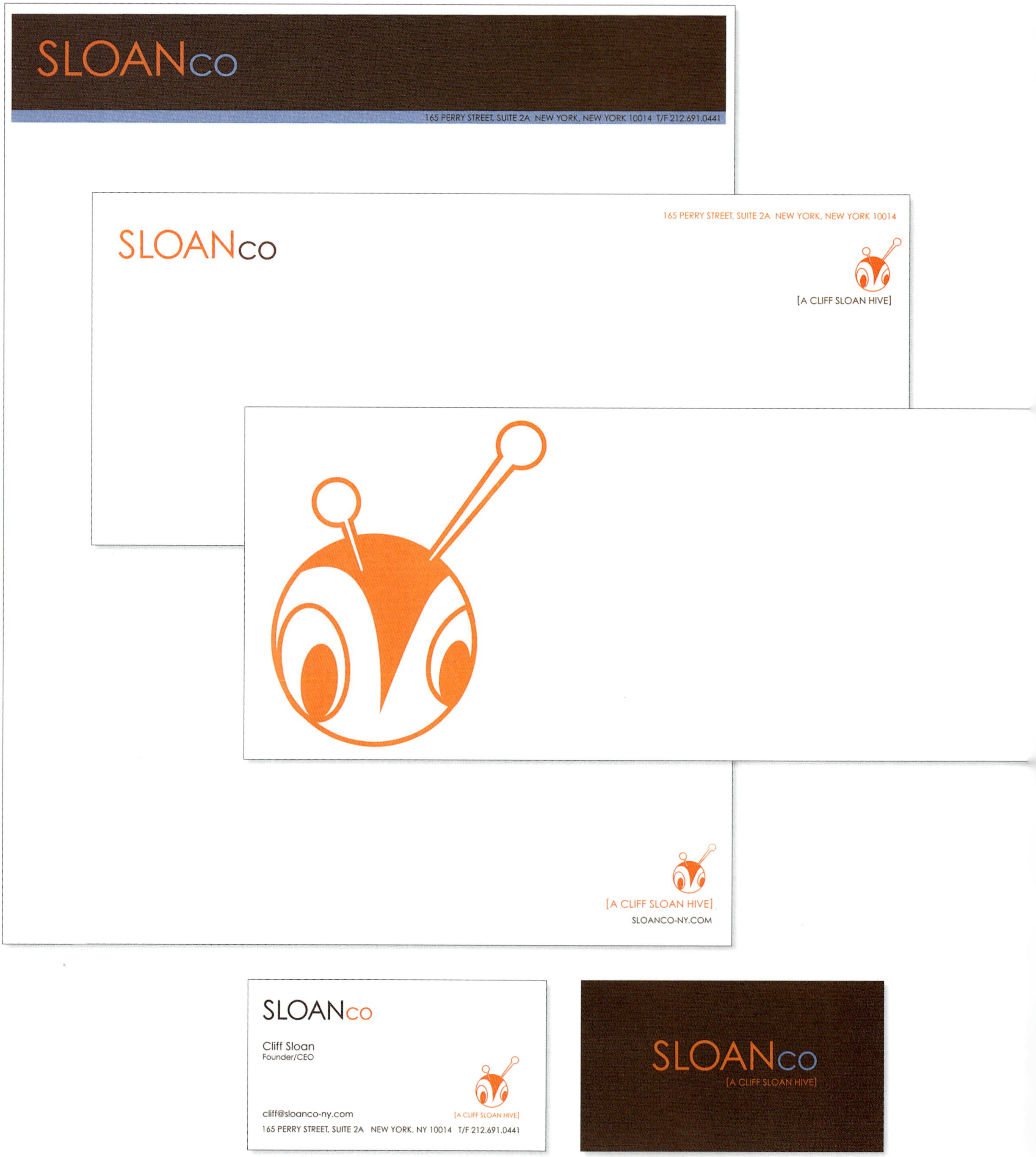

client
SloanCo
design firm
Hotsauce
designer
Wyndy Wilder Sloan

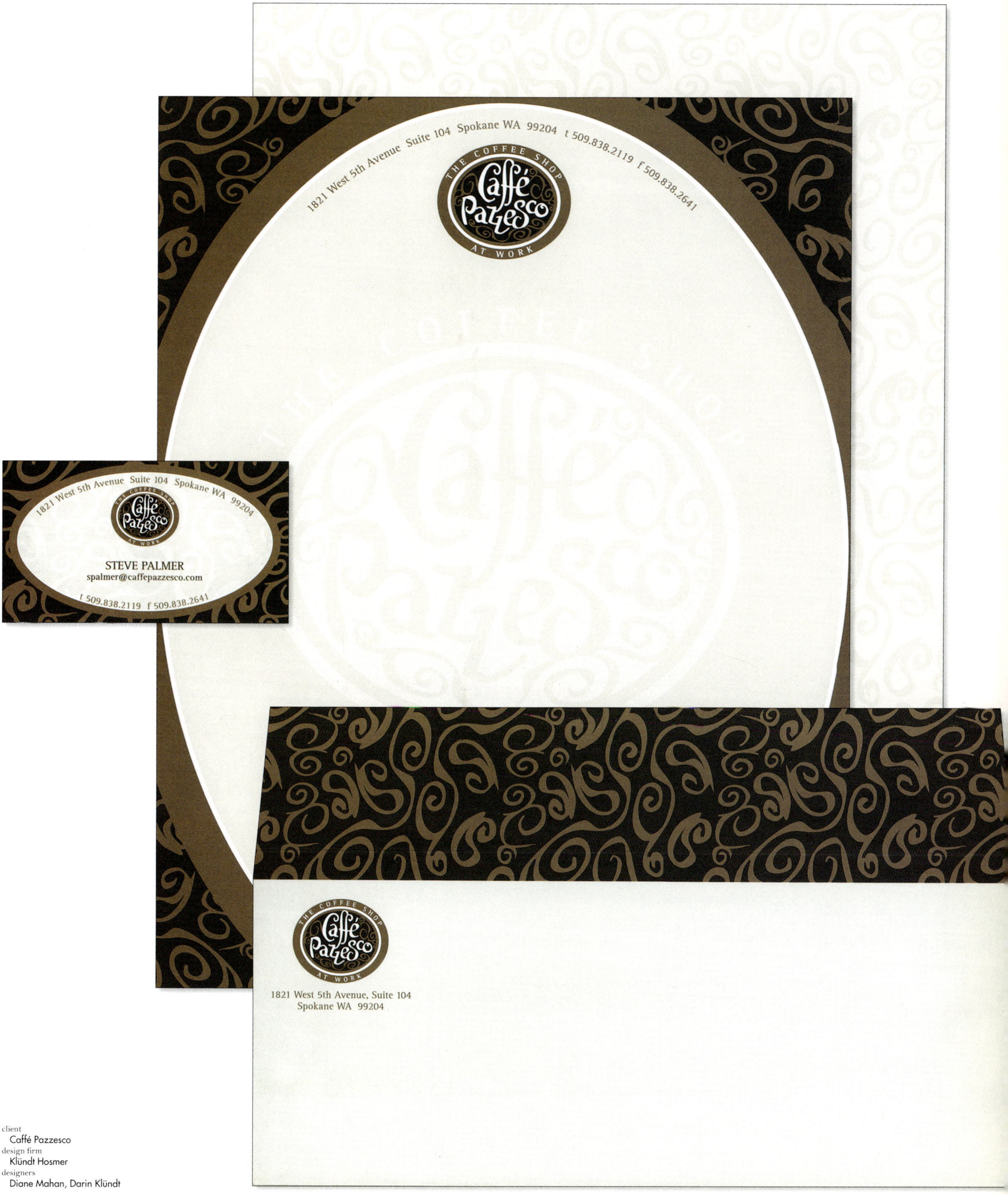

client
Caffé Pazzesco
design firm
Klündt Hosmer
designers
Diane Mahan, Darin Klündt

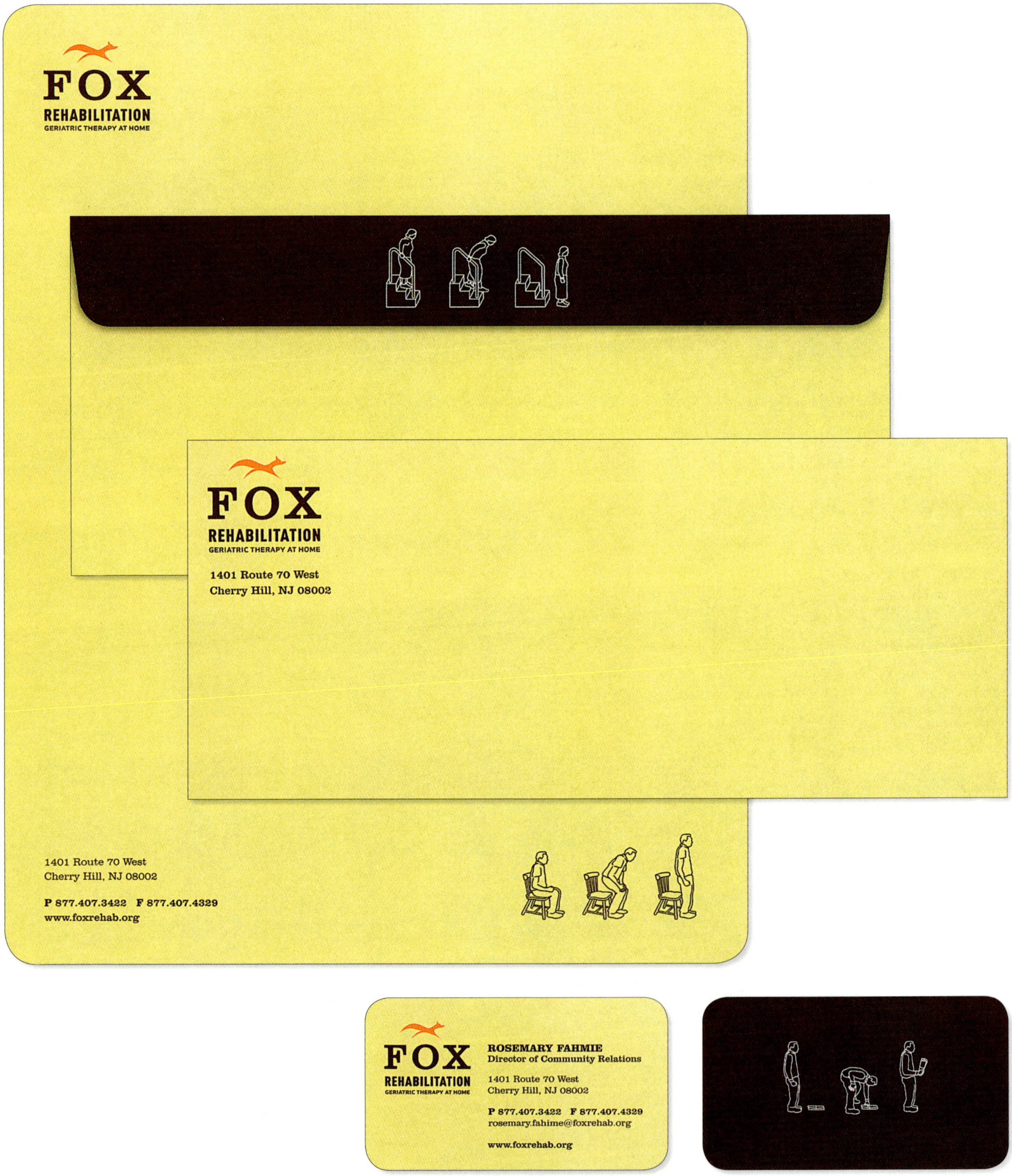

client
Fox Rehabilitation
design firm
160over90
designers
Darryl Cilli, Jim Walls, Stephen Penning

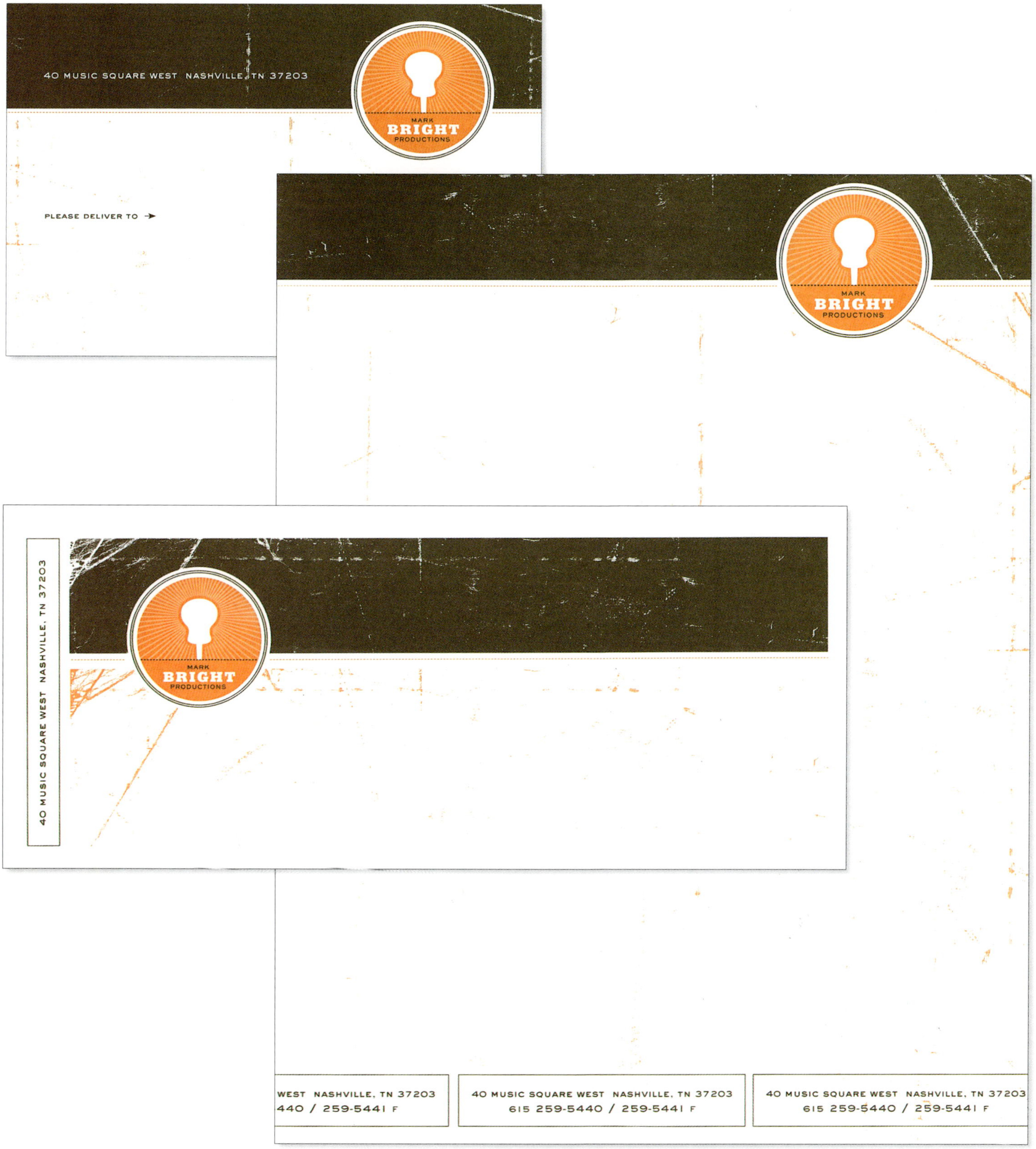

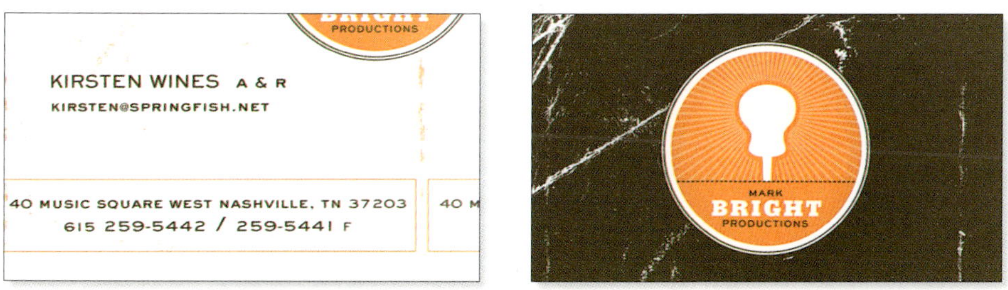

client
Mark Bright
design firm
Lewis—Nashville
designer
Clark Hook

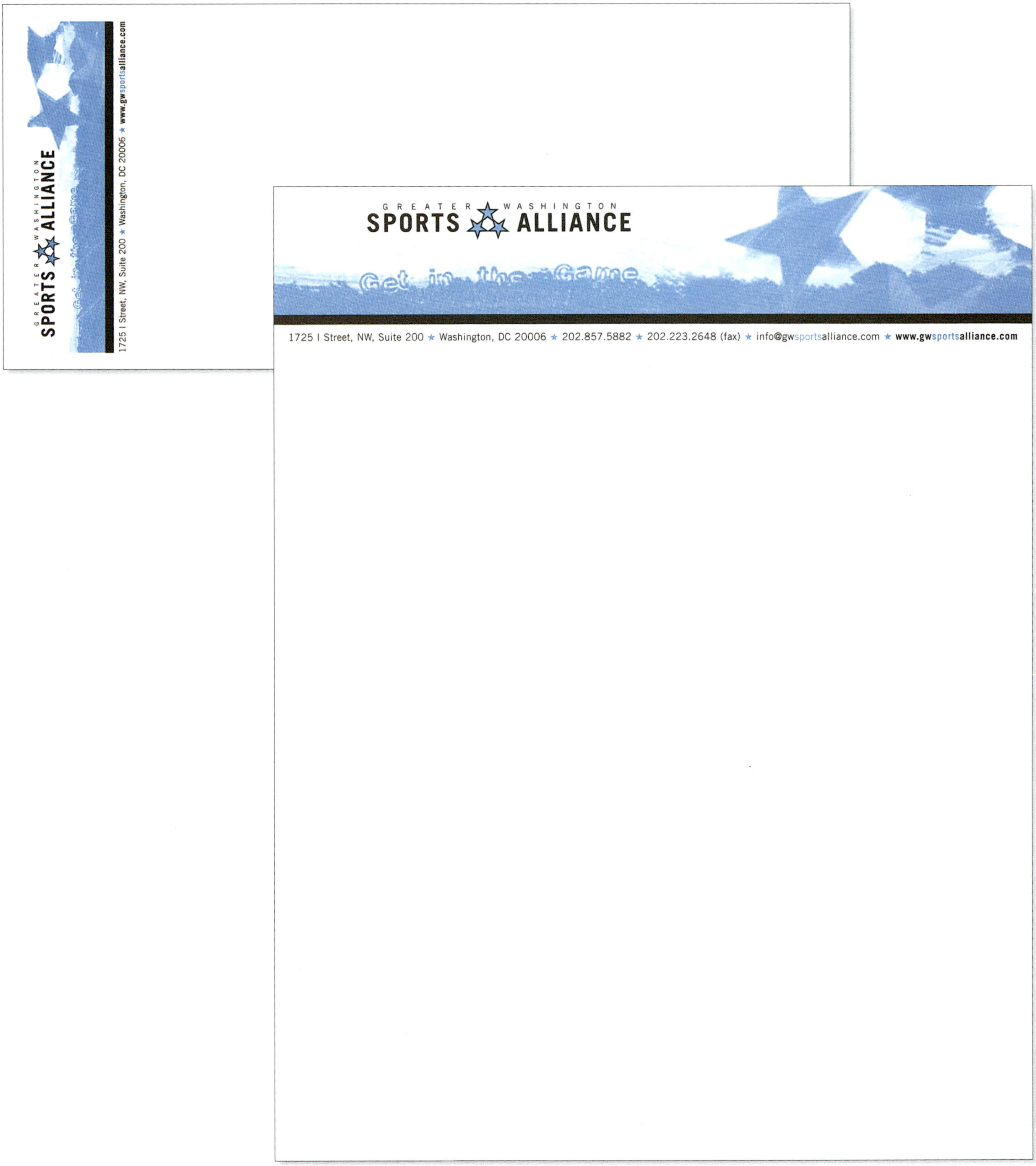

client
Greater Washington Sports Alliance
design firm
Fixation Marketing
designer
Bruce E. Morgan

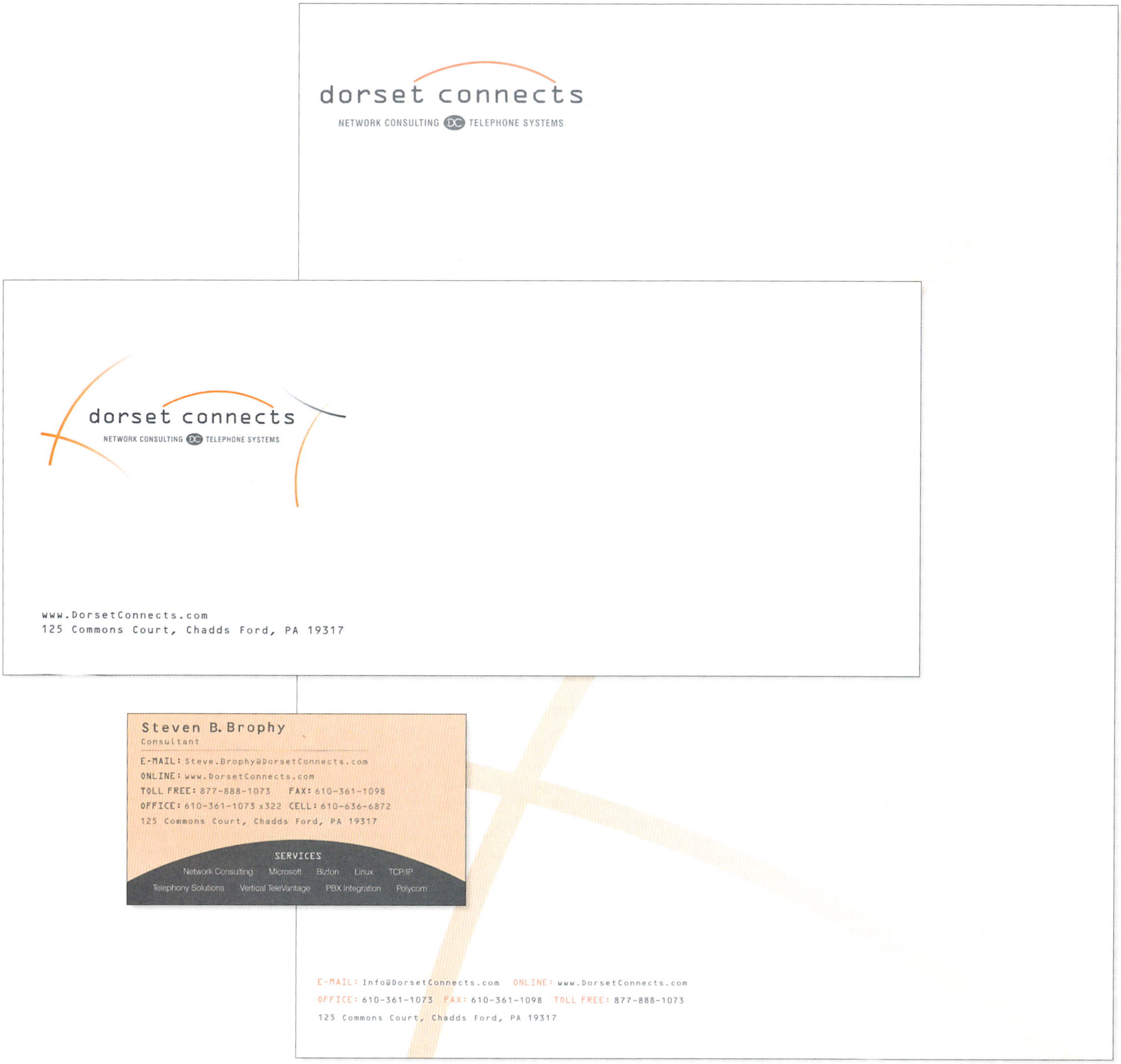

client
Dorset Connects
design firm
Verve Marketing and Design
principal, creative director
Diane Lemonides
art director
Nancy Nguyen
designer
David Eberly

PAGE 2
CEDAR PARTNERS
SHOW BUSINESS | GROW BUSINESS
SHOW BUSINESS
GROW BUSINESS
108 4th Avenue South Suite 207 Franklin, TN 37064 615 599-6775 T 615 599-6114 F

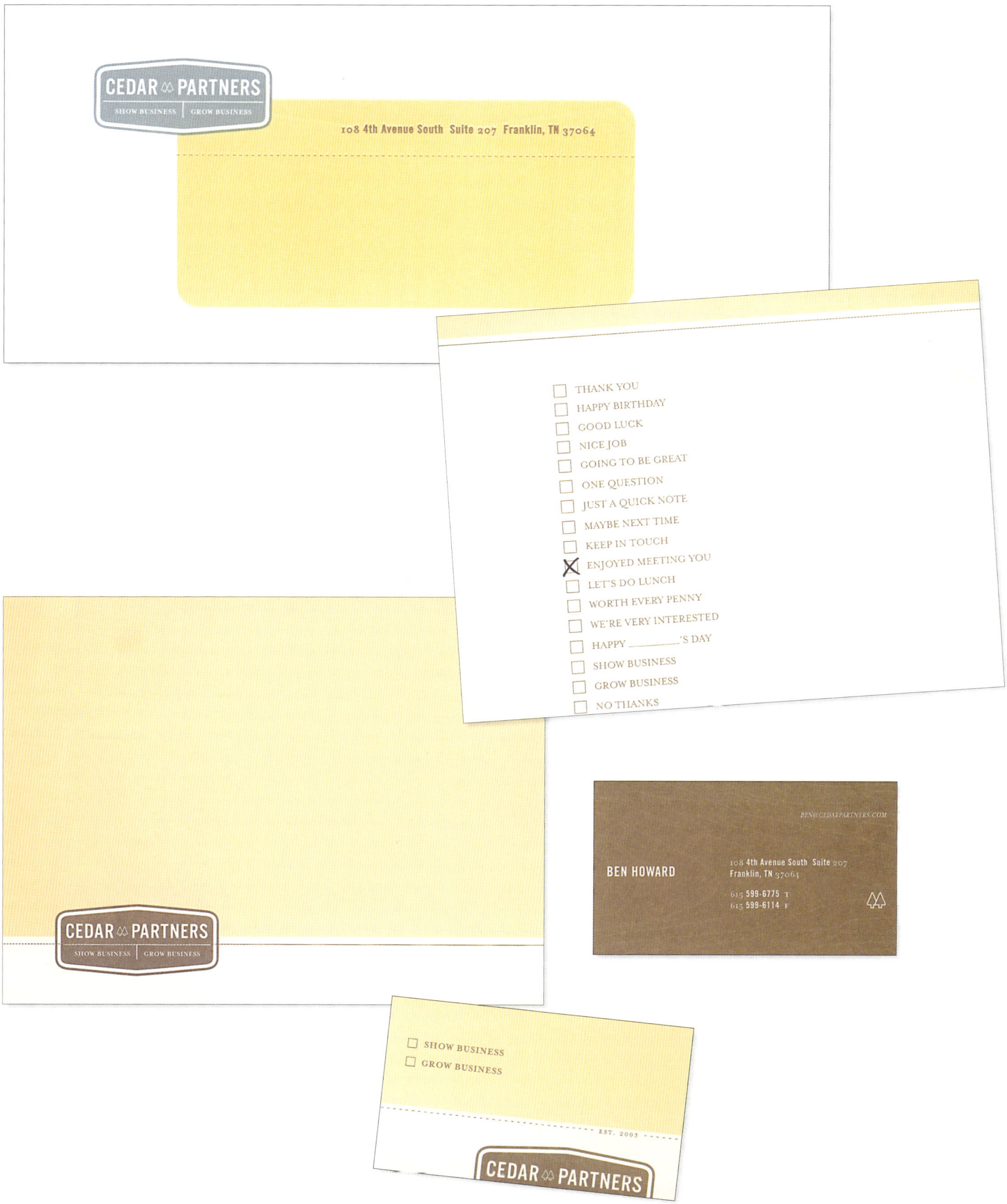

client
Cedar Partners
design firm
Lewis—Nashville
designer
Clark Hook

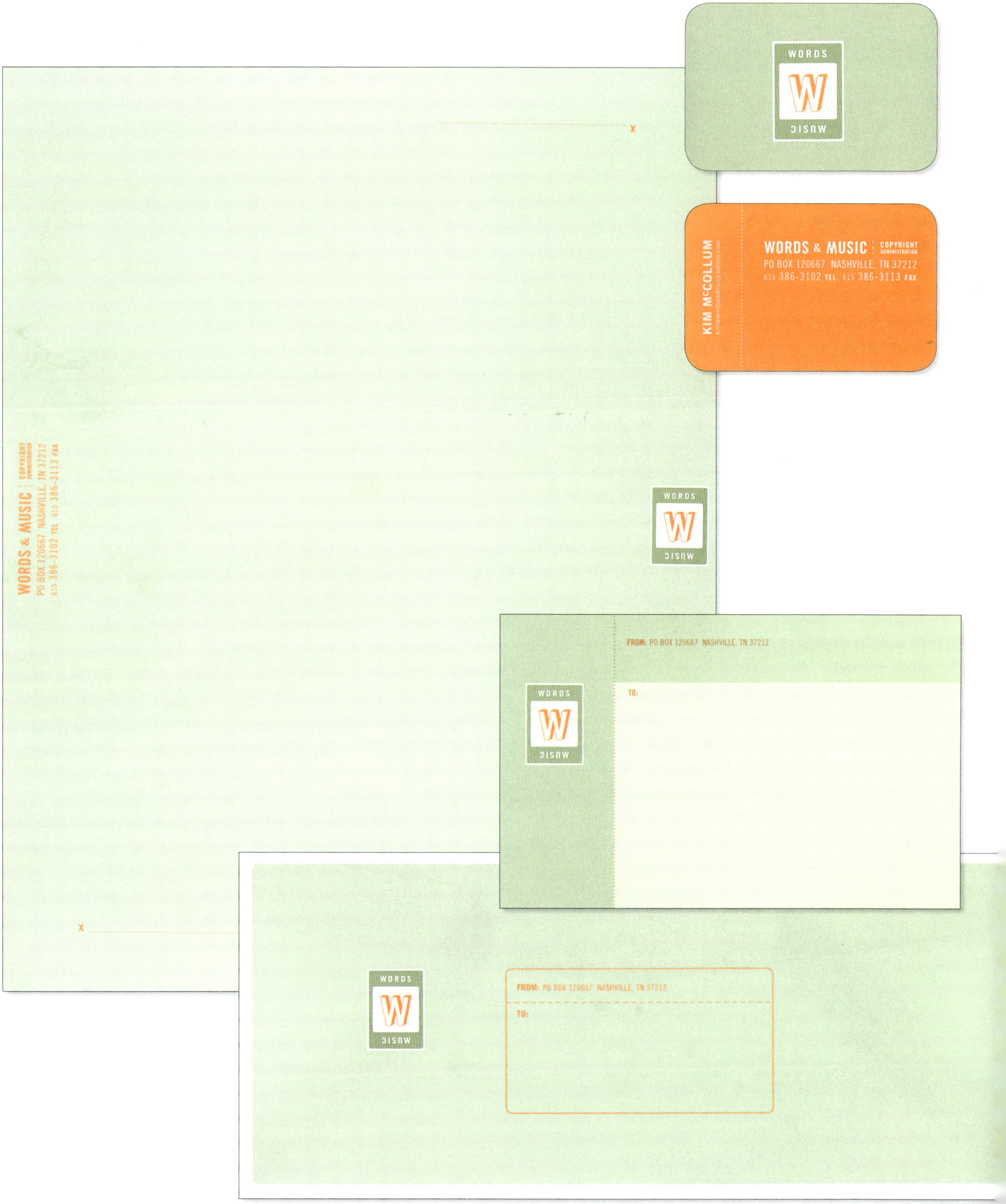

client
Kim McCollum
design firm
Lewis—Nashville
designer
Clark Hook

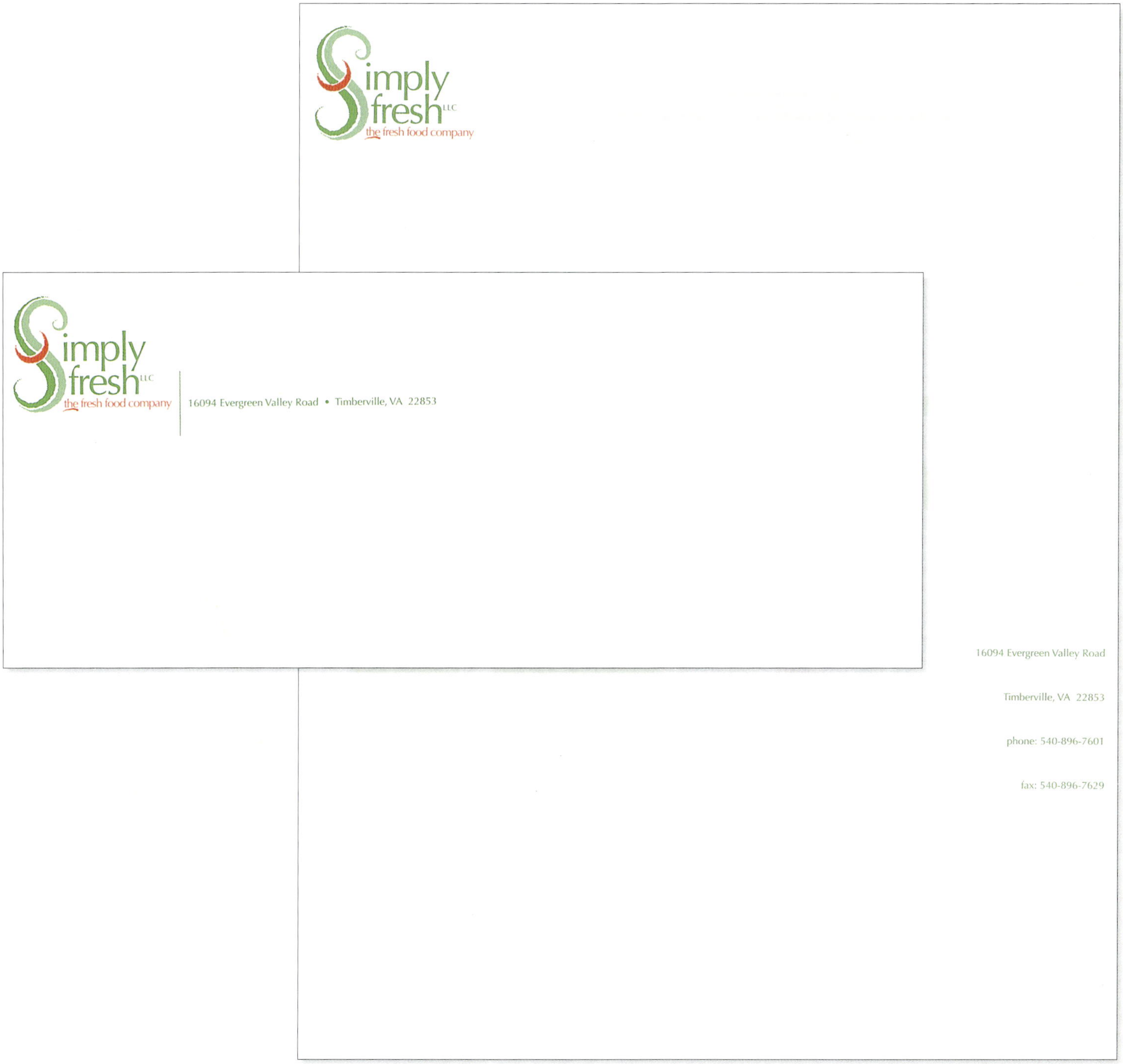

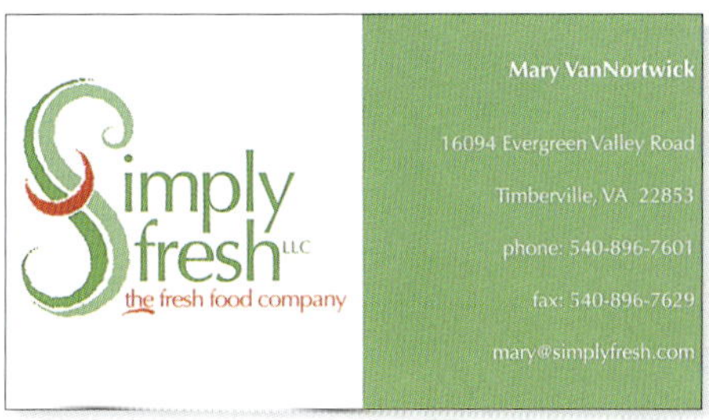

client
Simply Fresh
design firm
Mind's Eye Creative
designer
Stephen Brown

client
Boettcher Media Group
design firm
McDill Design
designer
Joel Harmeling

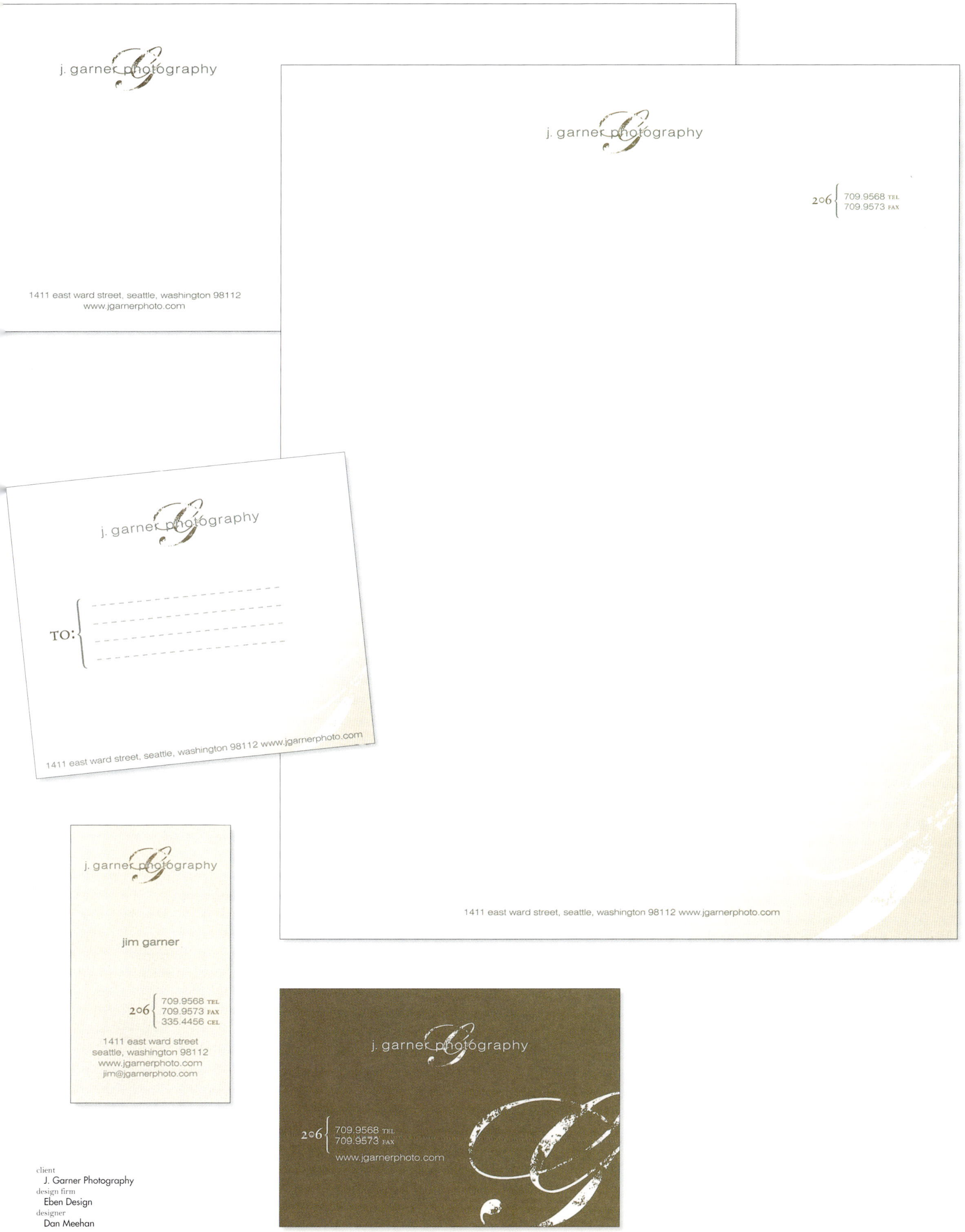

client
J. Garner Photography
design firm
Eben Design
designer
Dan Meehan

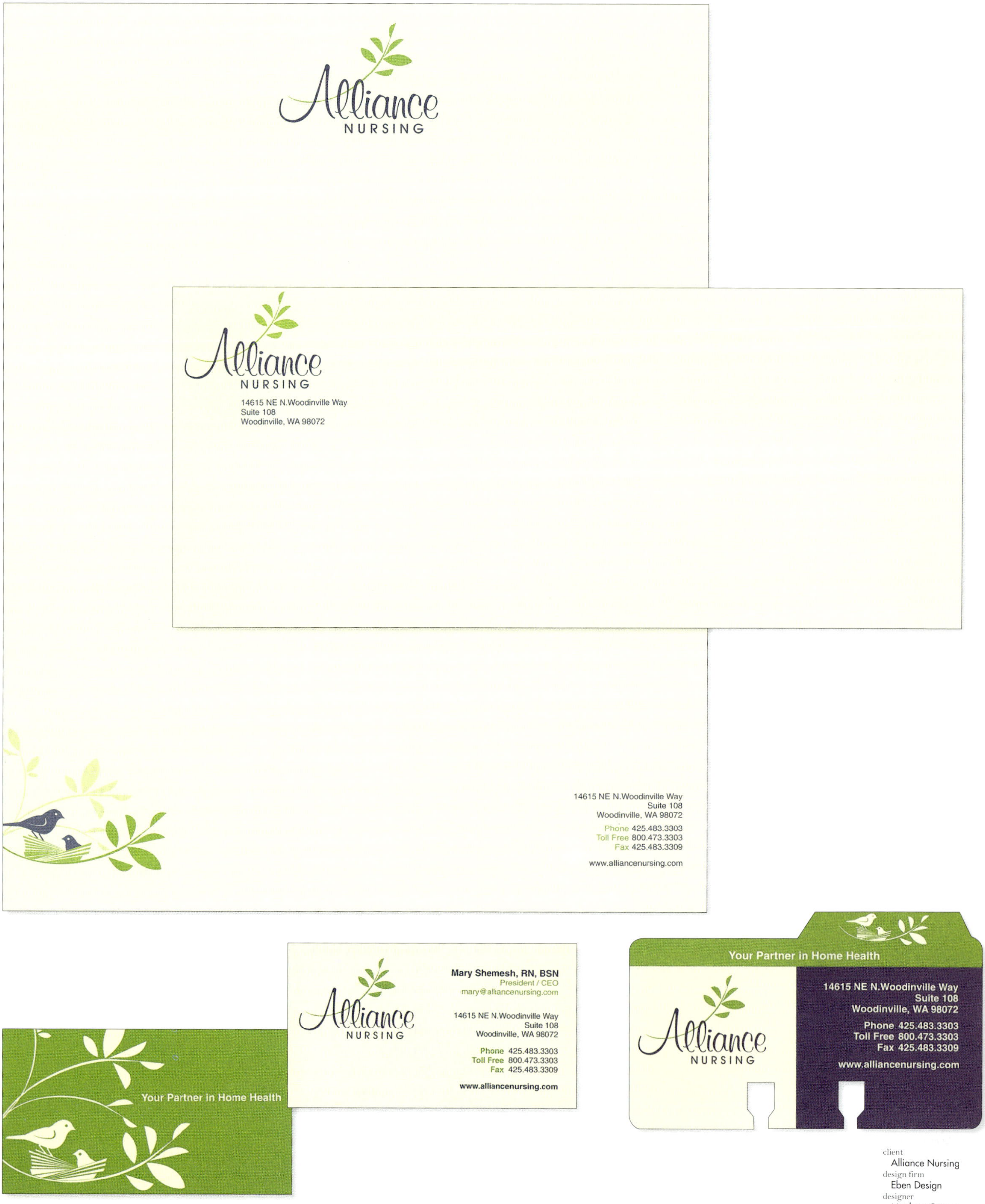

client
Alliance Nursing
design firm
Eben Design
designer
Matthew Grimes

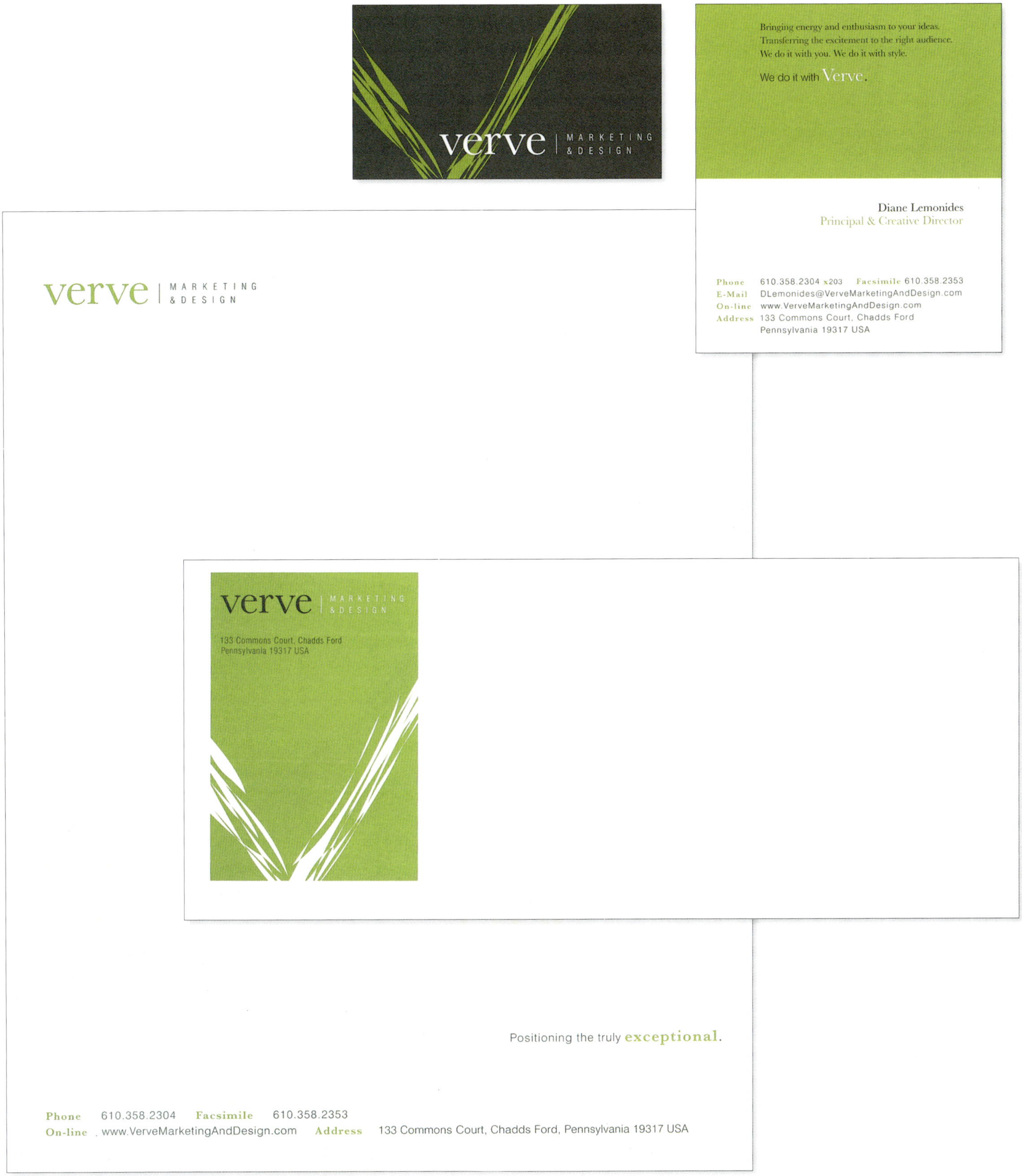

client
Verve Marketing and Design
design firm
Verve Marketing and Design
principal, creative director
Diane Lemonides
art director, designer
Nancy Nguyen

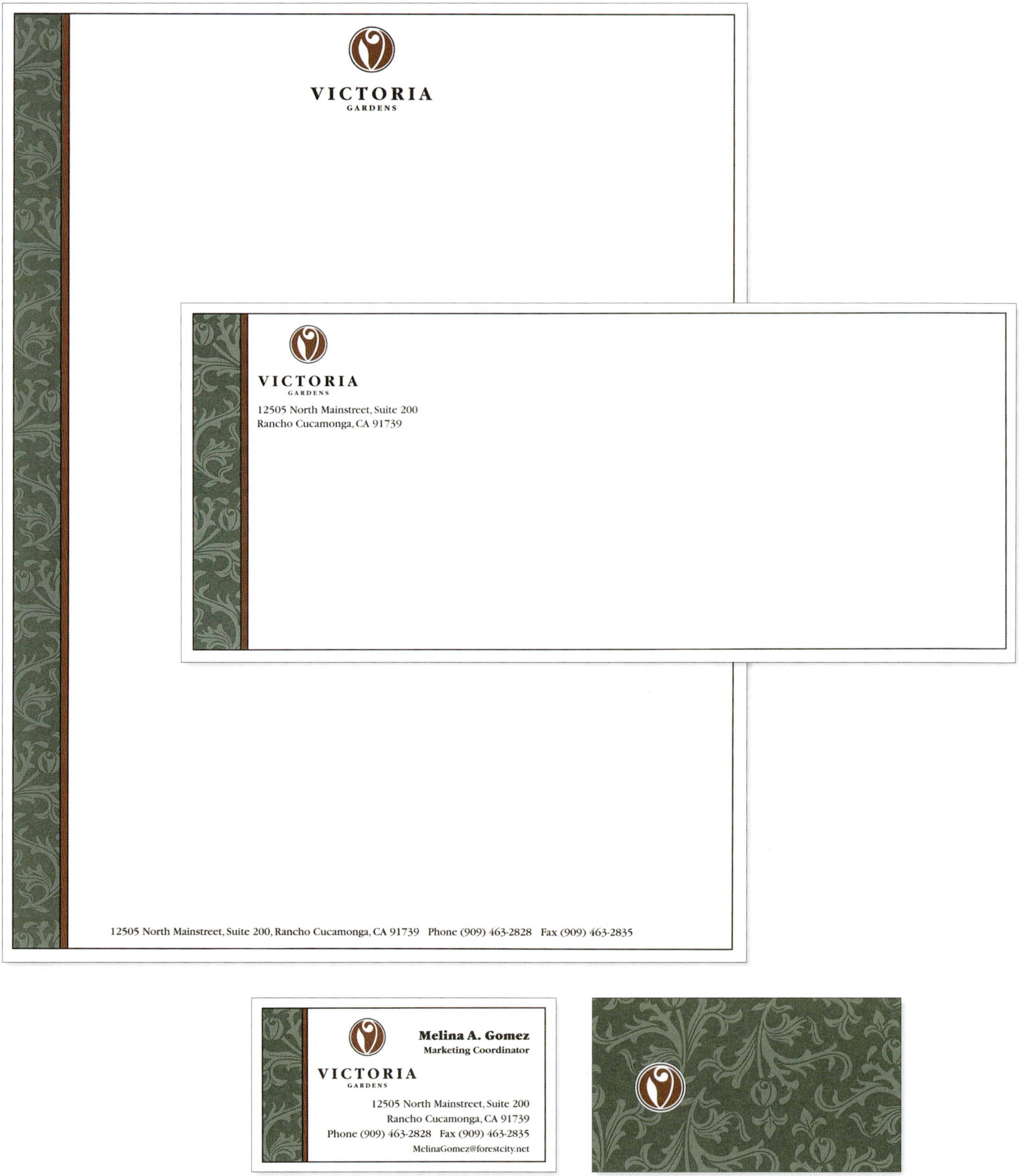

client
Victoria Gardens
design firm
Think Tank Designs
designers
Heath C. Meyette,
Robin Lindblom

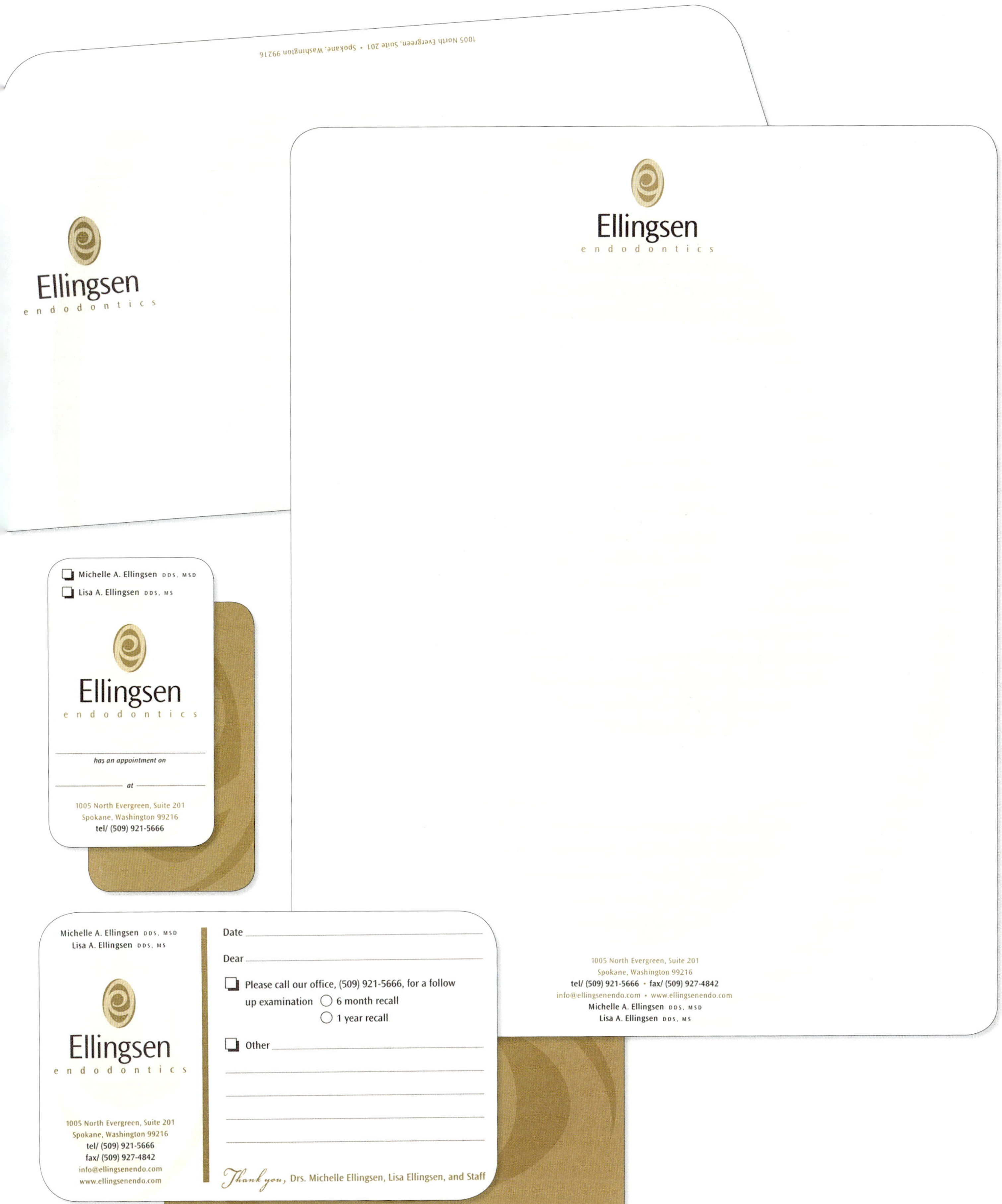

client
Ellingsen Endodontics
design firm
Klündt Hosmer
designers
Lorri Johnston, Darin Klündt

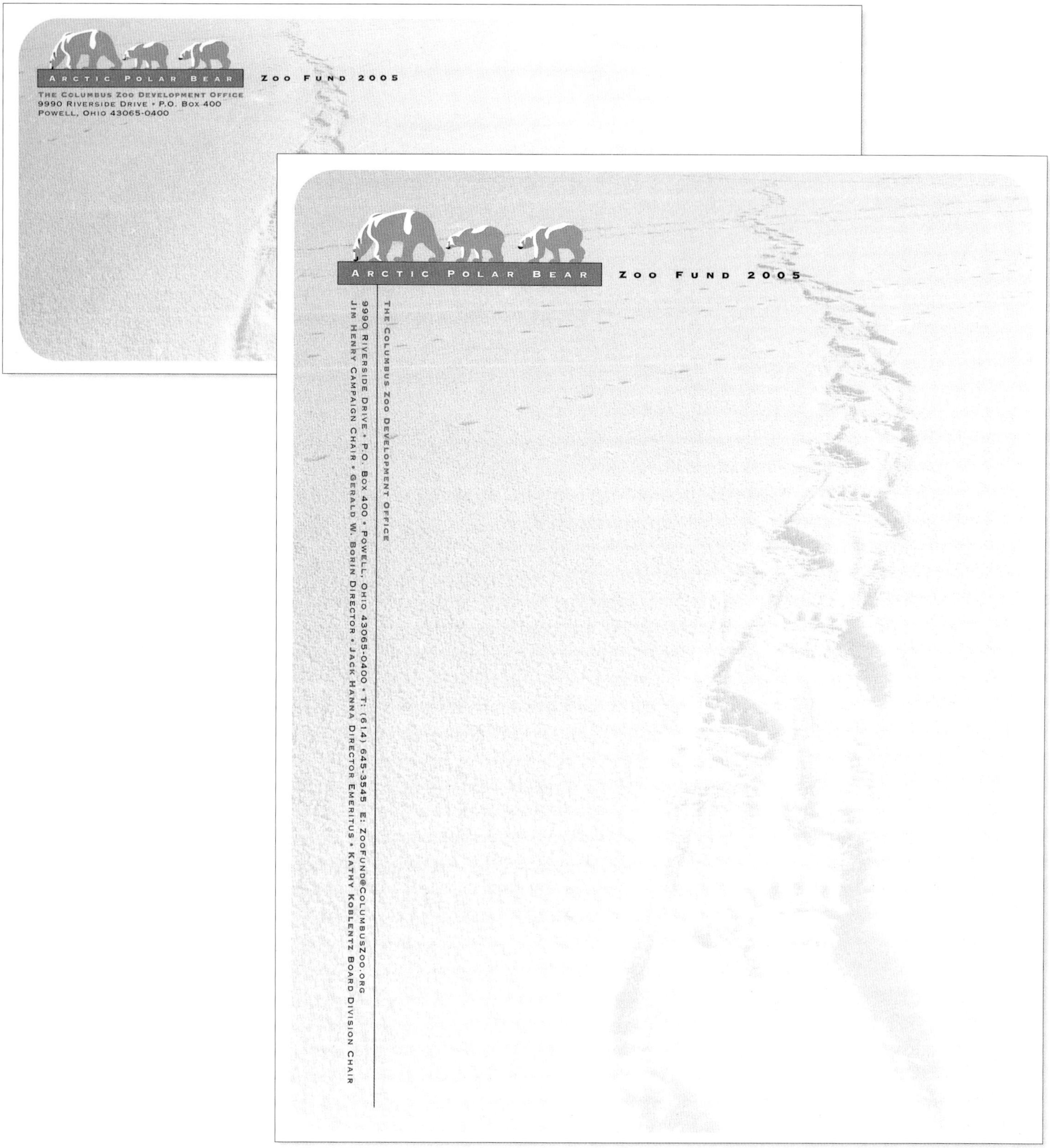

client
Columbus Zoo & Aquarium
design firm
VMA, Inc.
creative director
Doug Knopp
account manager
Kenneth Botts
production designer
Patrick Londergan
graphic designer
Tim Frank/WDD

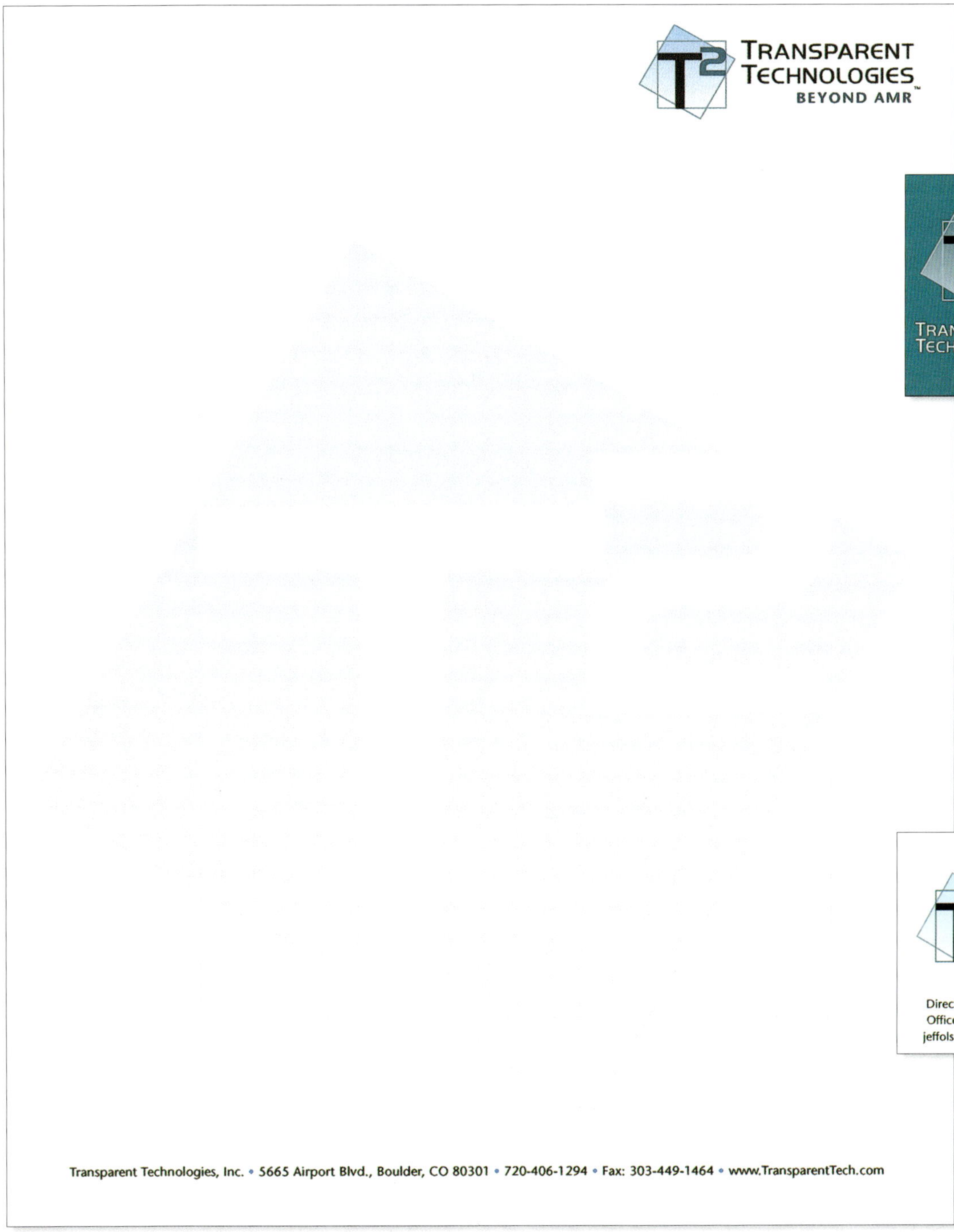

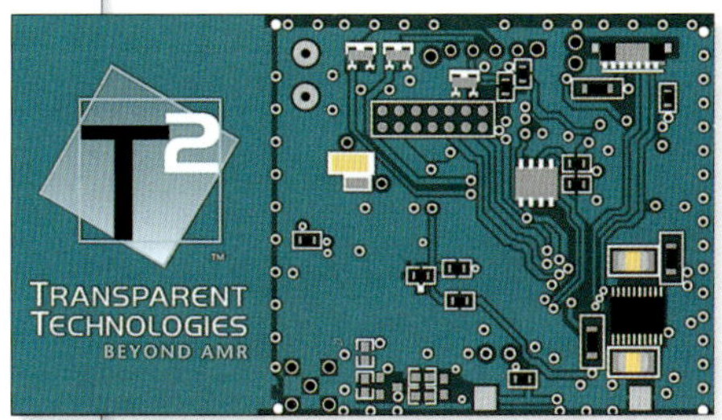

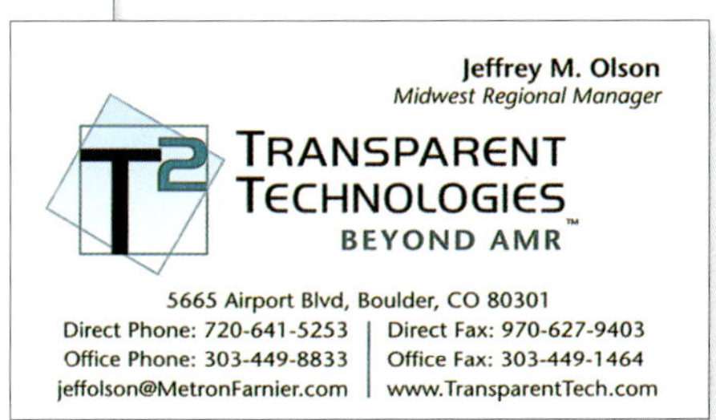

client
Metron-Farnier
design firm
Lightspeed Commercial Arts
designer
Michael J. Hamers

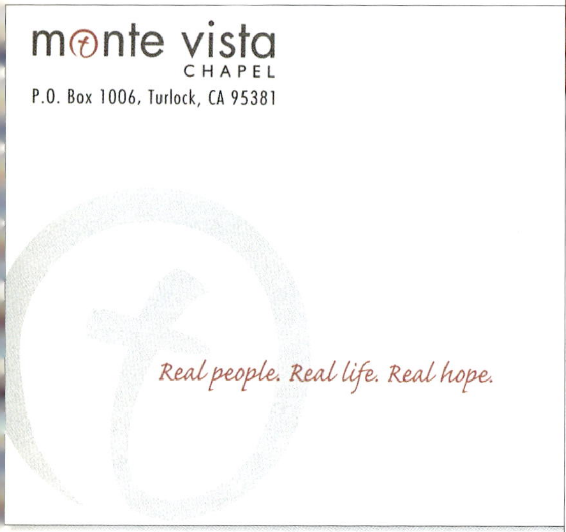

client
Monte Vista Chapel
design firm
Never Boring Design Associates
designer
Shawna Bayers

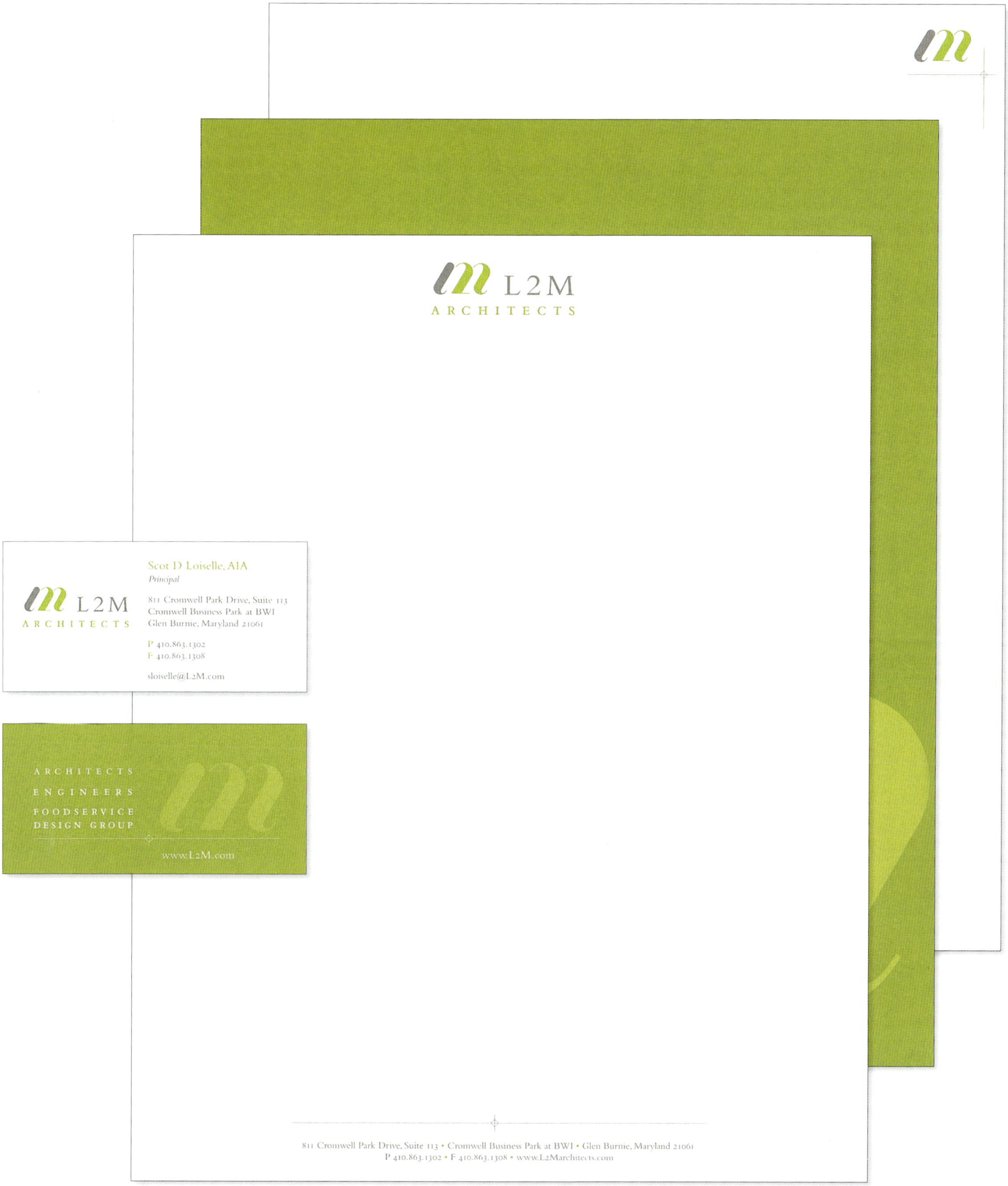

client
L2M Architects
design firm
Round 2 Communications
designer
Glen Villegas

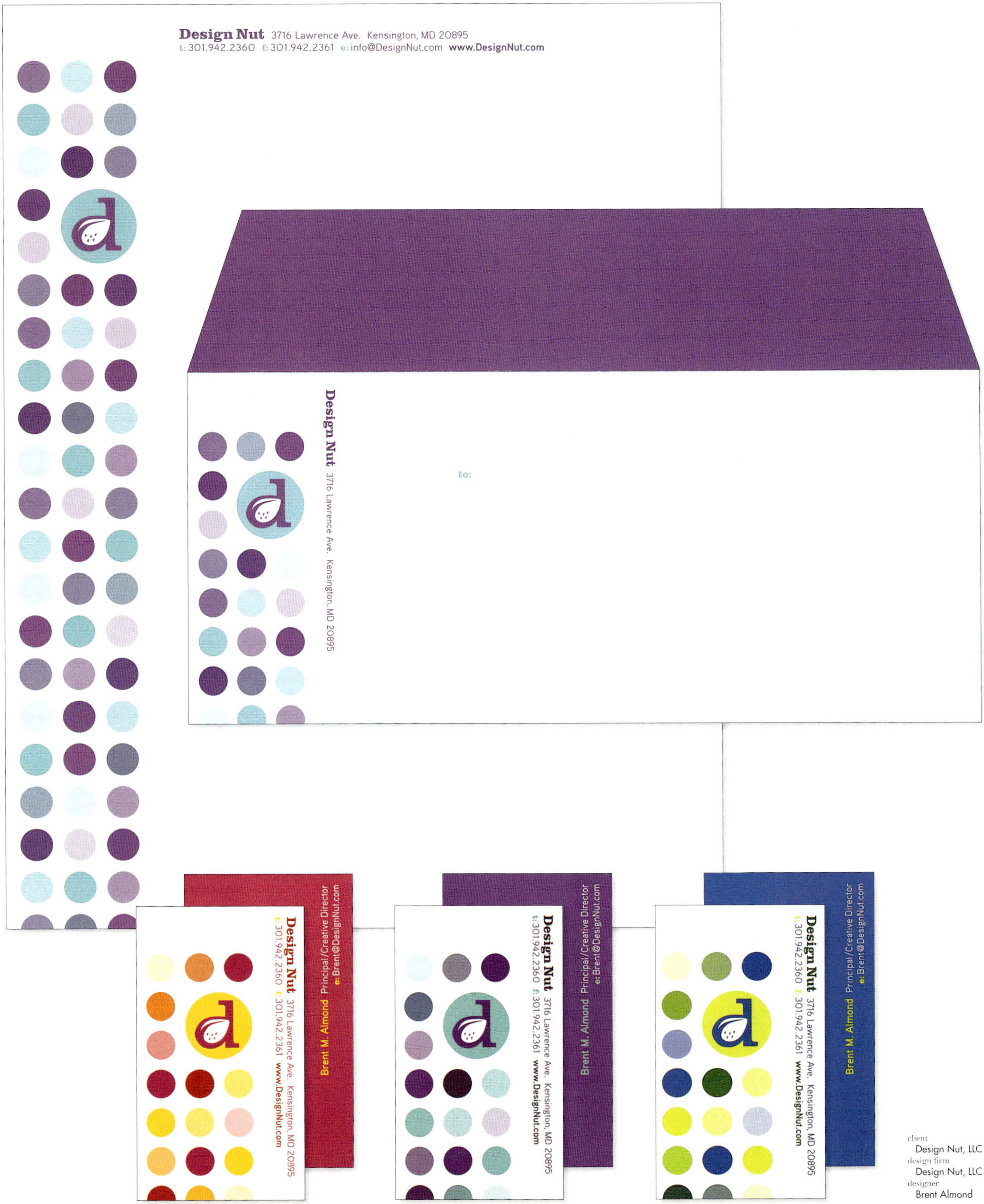

client
Design Nut, LLC
design firm
Design Nut, LLC
designer
Brent Almond

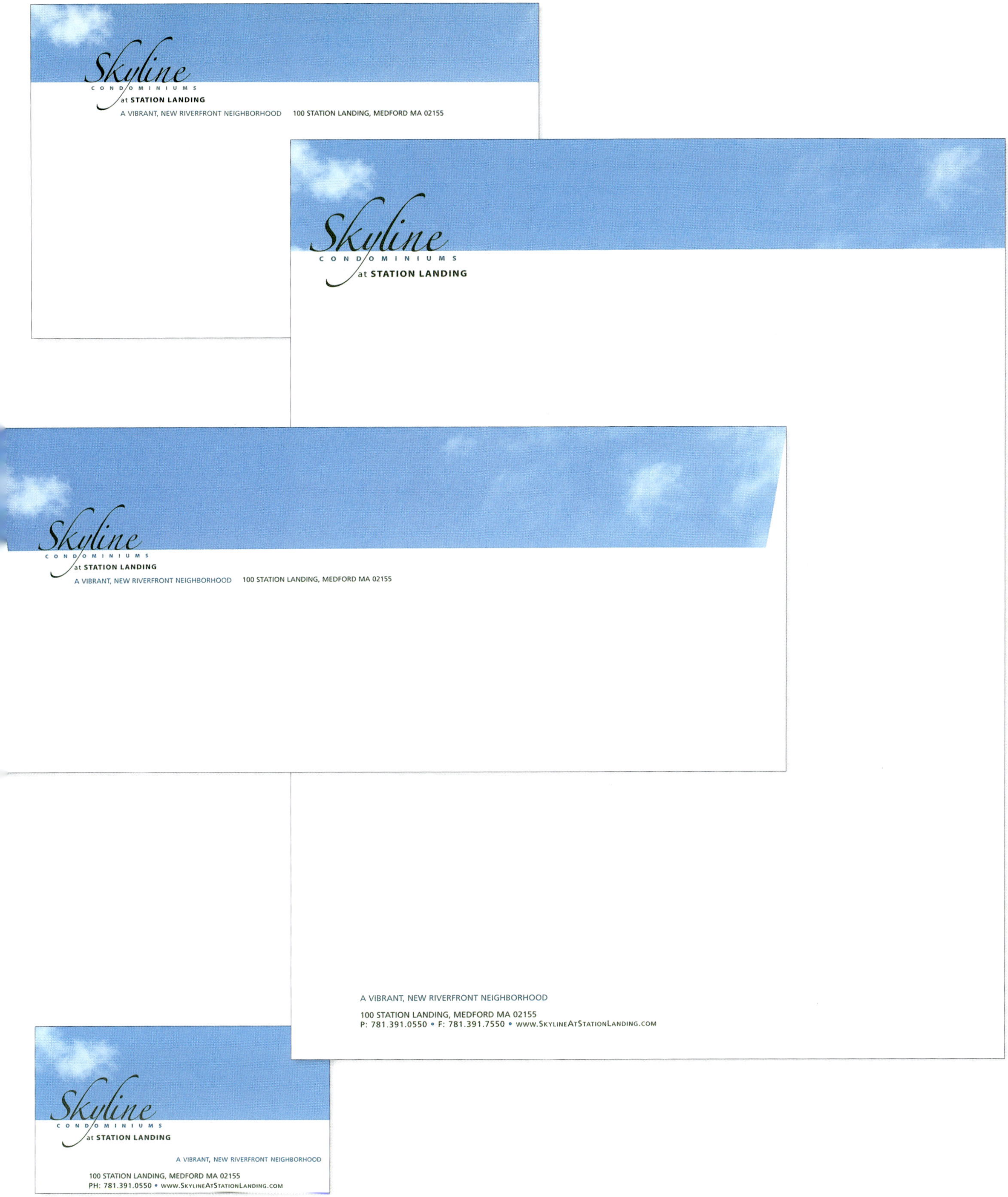

client
National Development
design firm
Doerr Associates, Inc.
designer
Joan Wilking

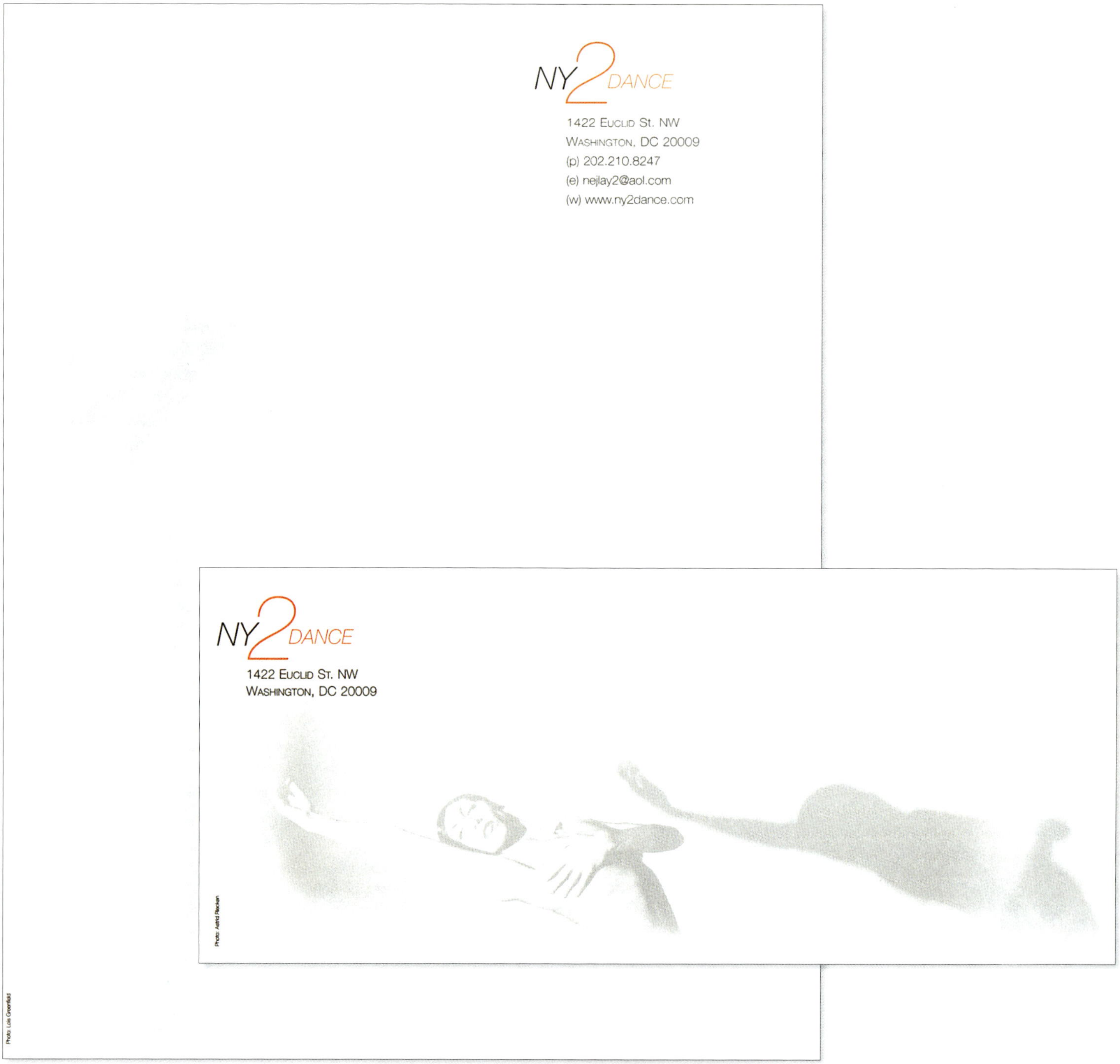

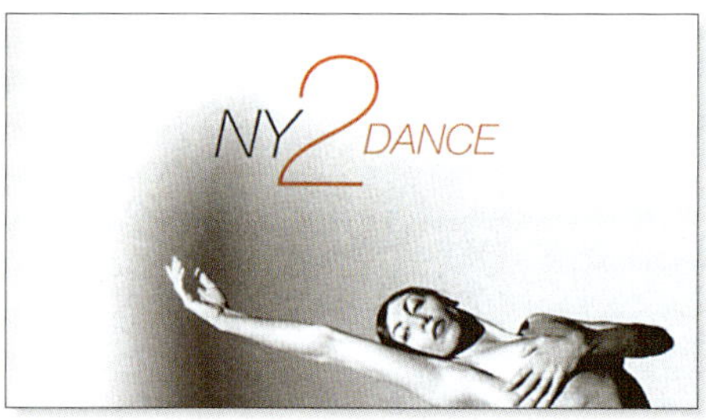

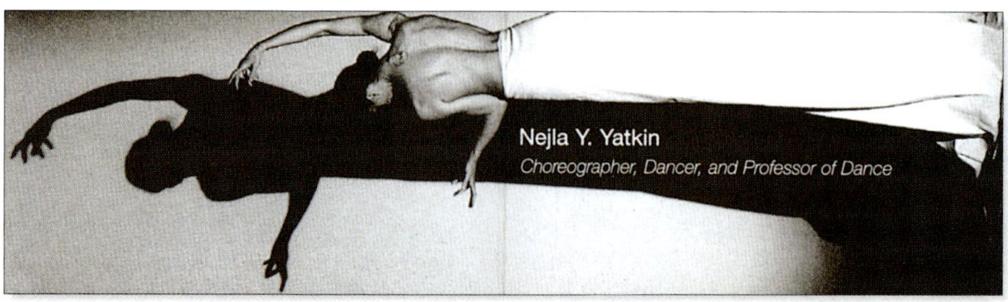

client
NY2 Dance
design firm
RCW Communication Design INC
designers
Richard McDade, Rodney Williams

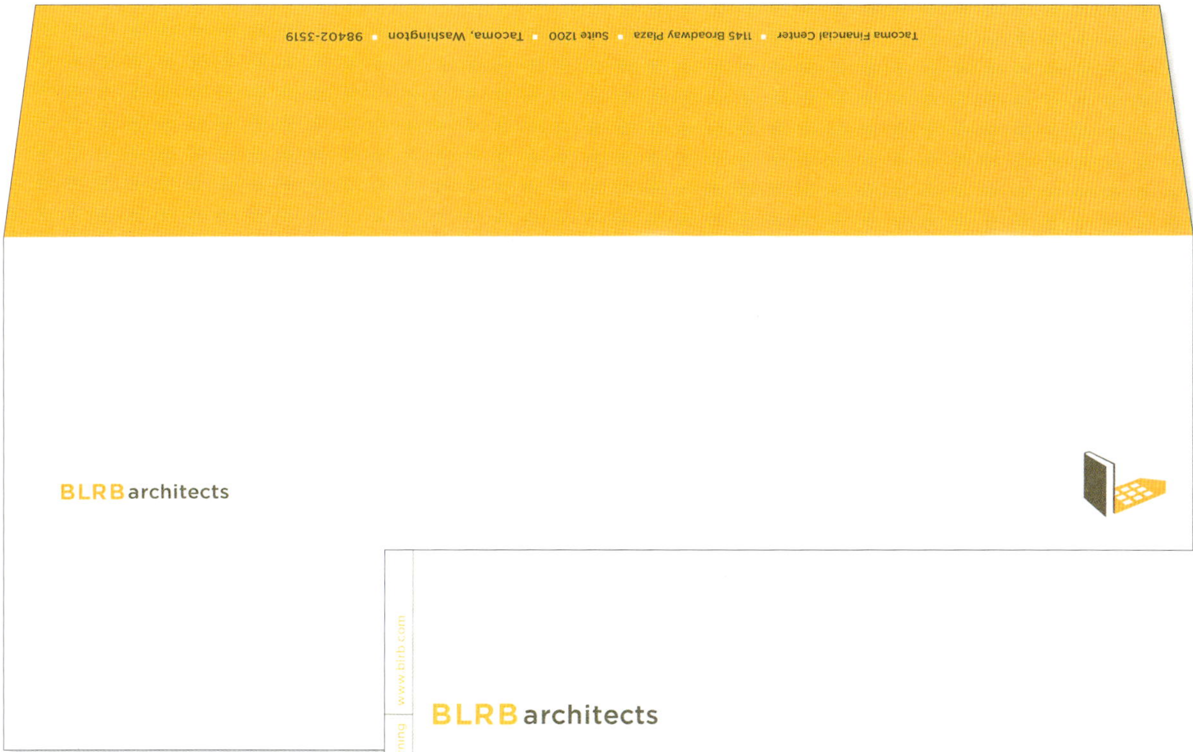

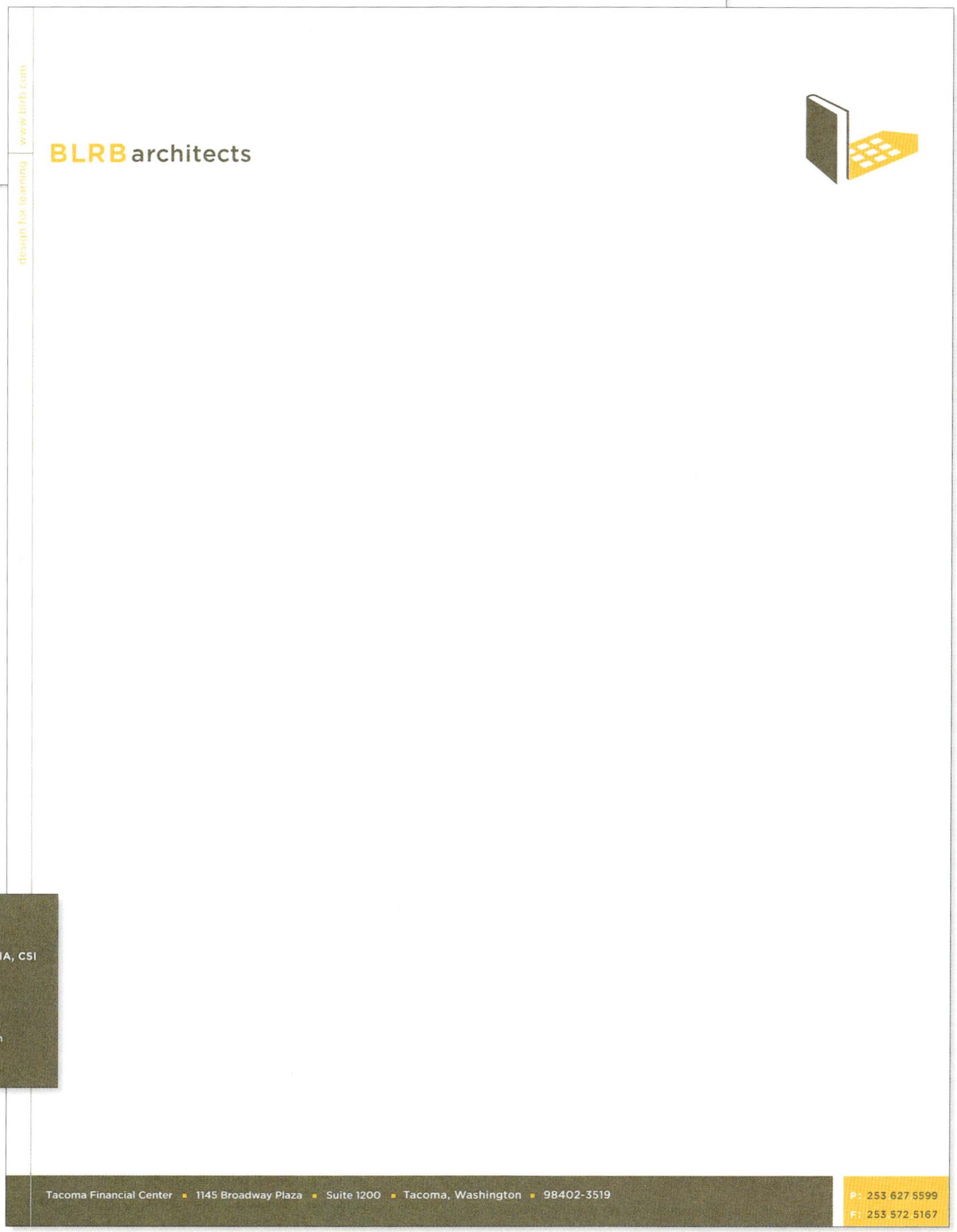

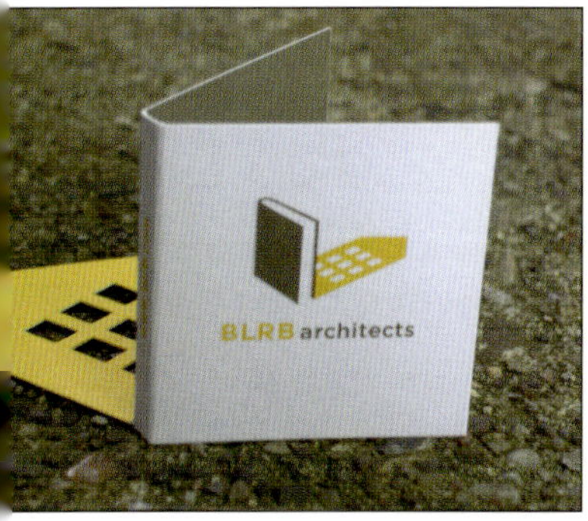

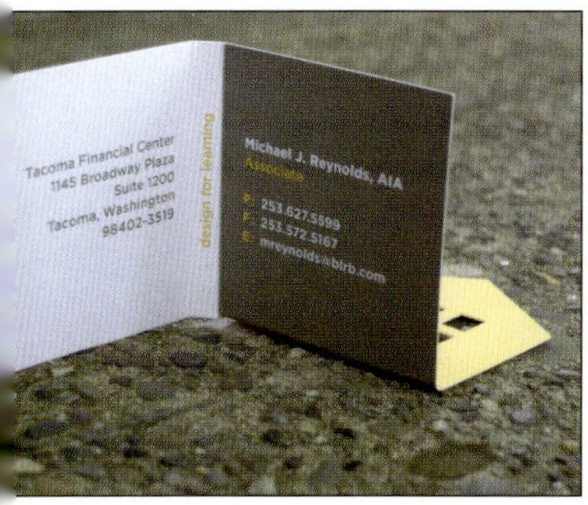

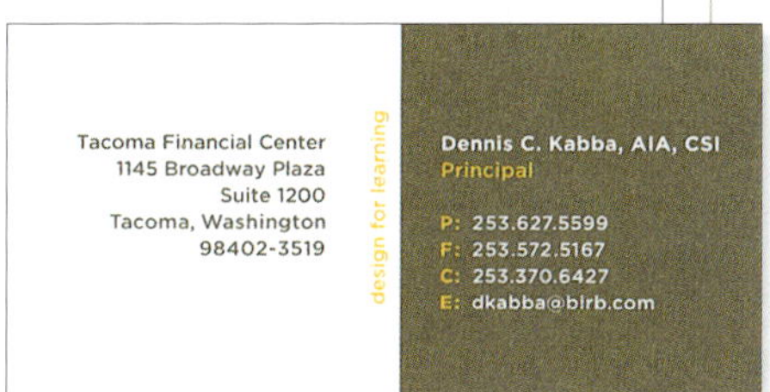

client
BLRB Architects
design firm
Hornall Anderson Design Works
designers
Daymon Bruck,
Yuri Shvets, Hillary Radbill

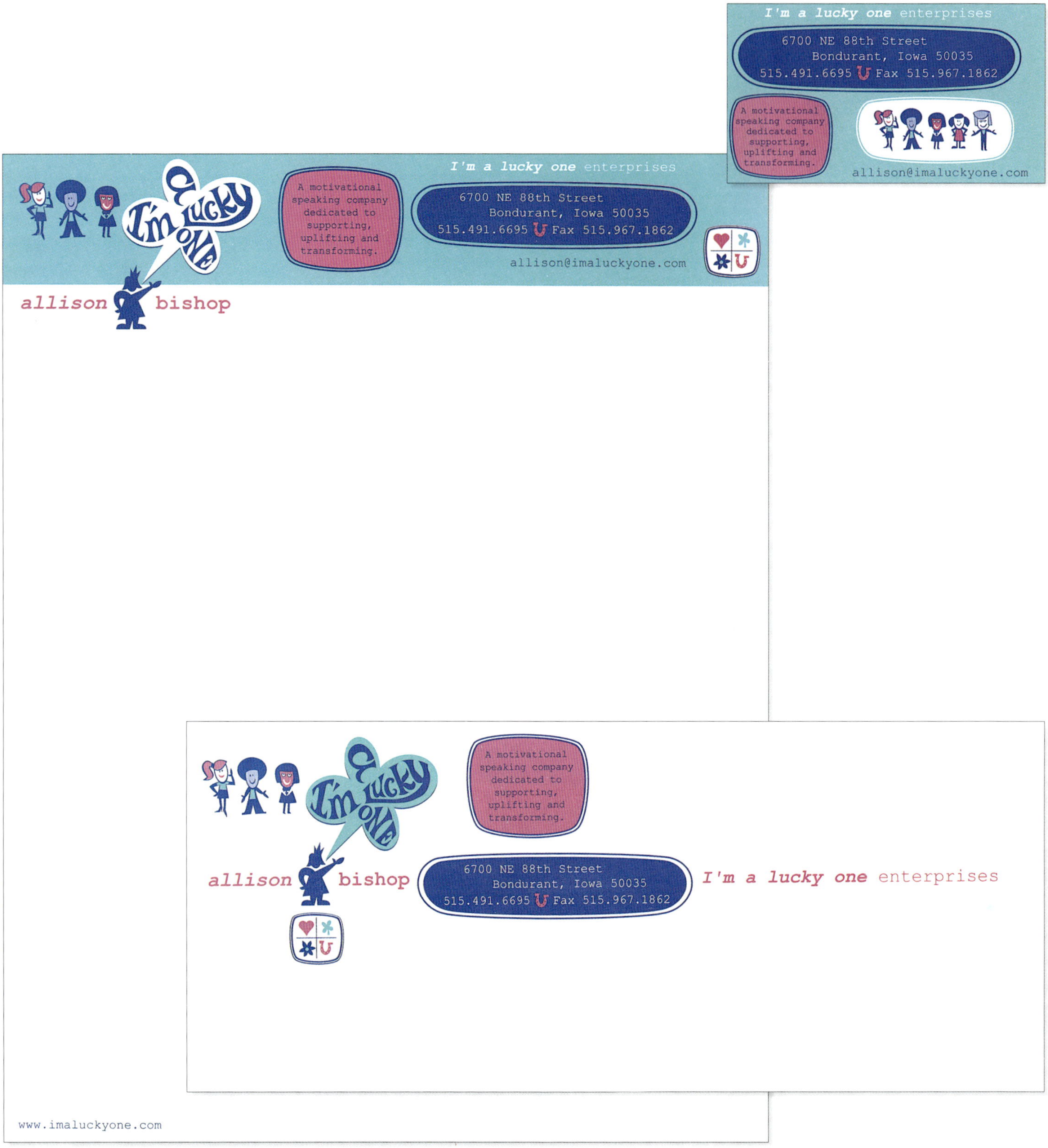

client
I'm A Lucky One
design firm
Sayles Graphic Design
designers
John Sayles, Kelly Bittner

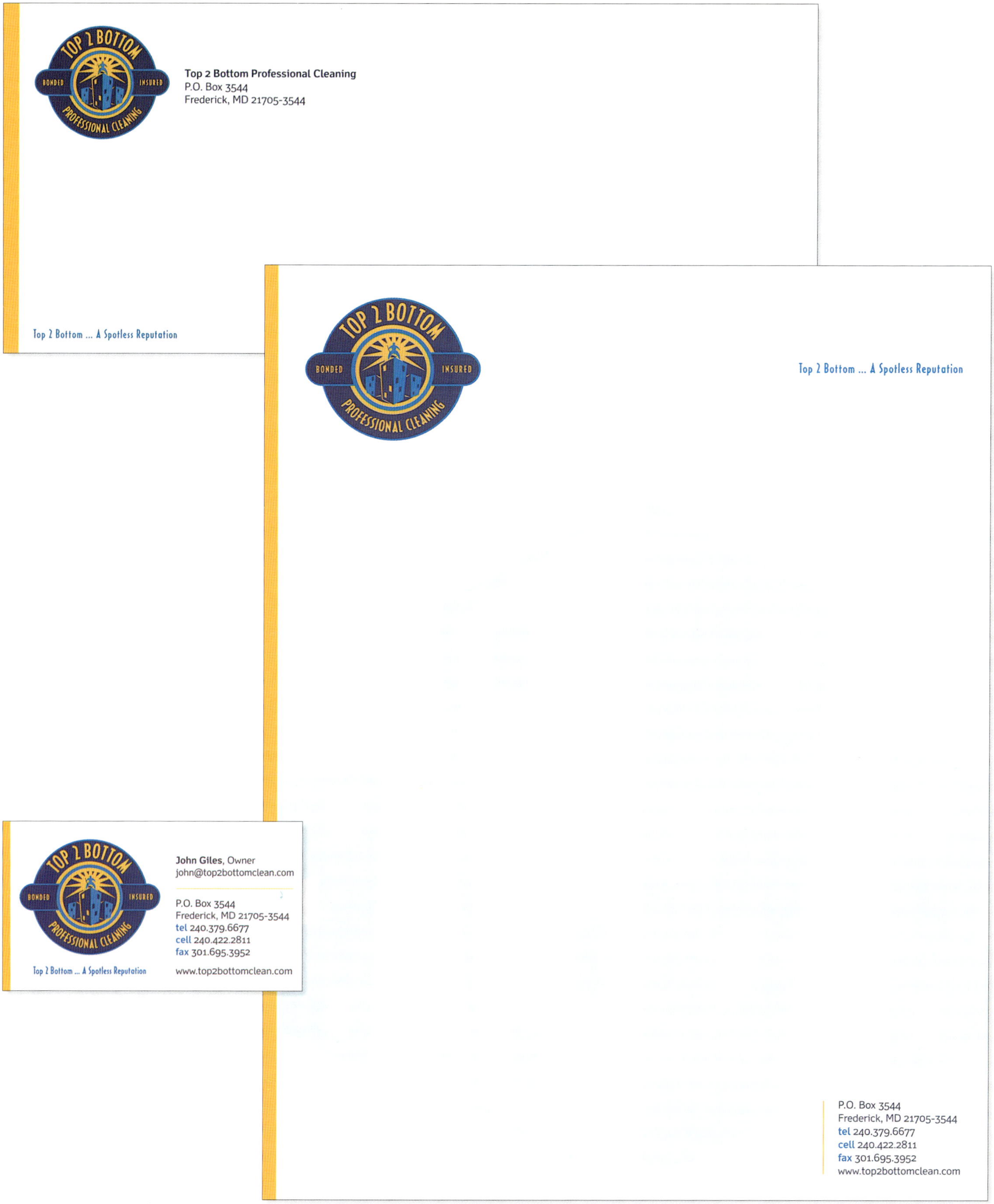

client
Top 2 Bottom Professional Cleaning
design firm
Octavo Designs
designer
Sue Hough

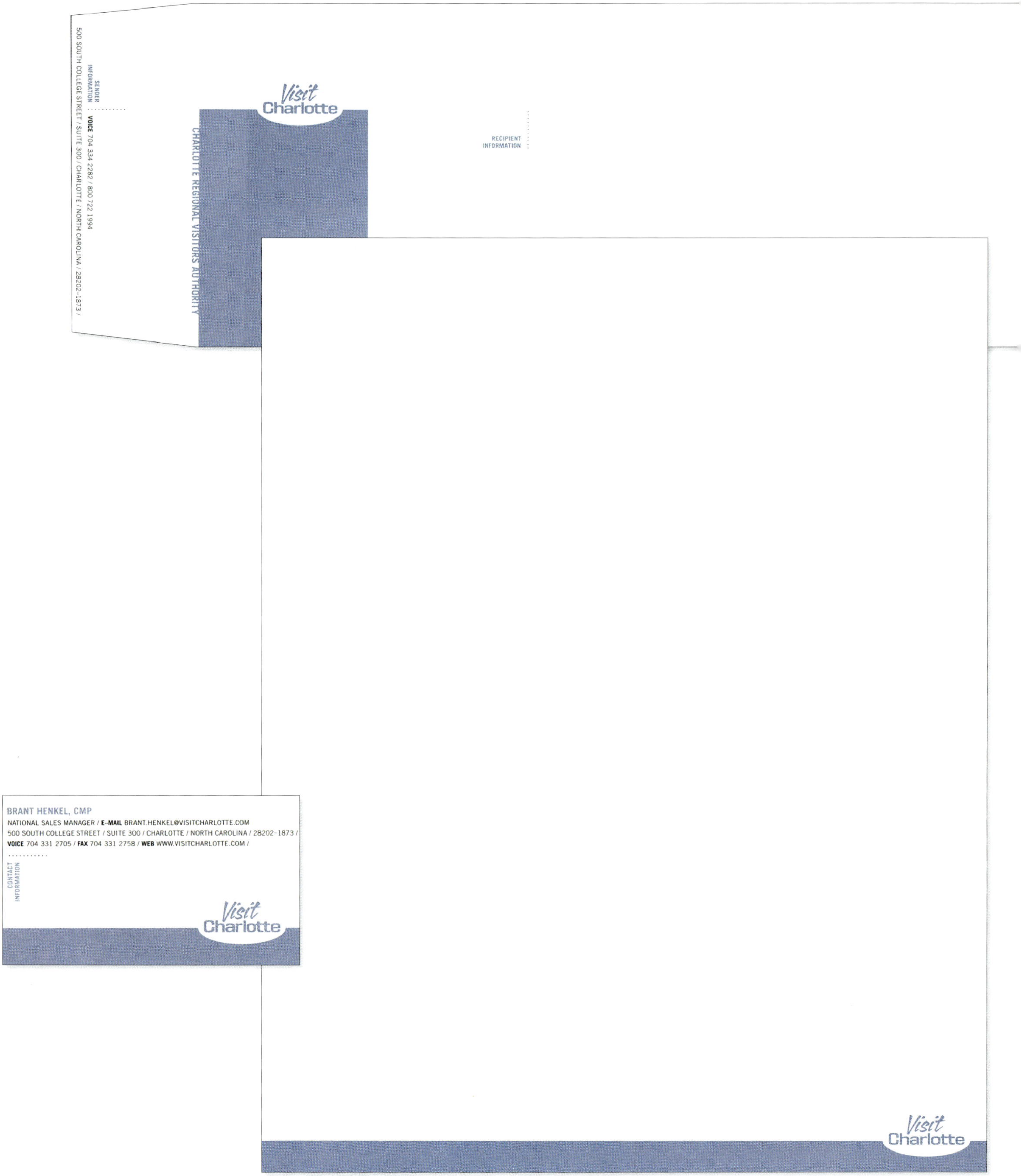

client
Visit Charlotte
design firm
A3 Design
designers
Alan Altman,
Amanda Altman

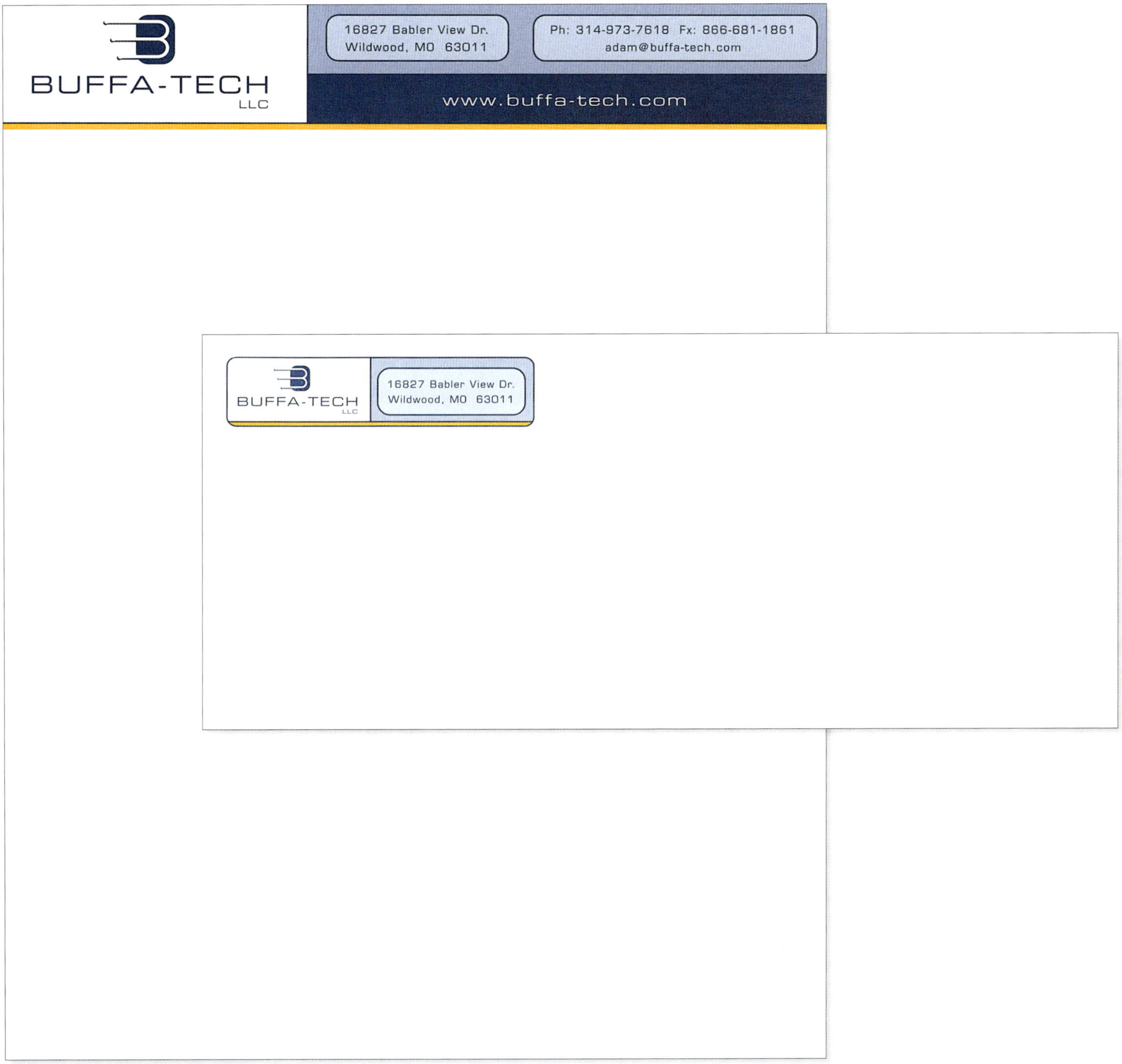

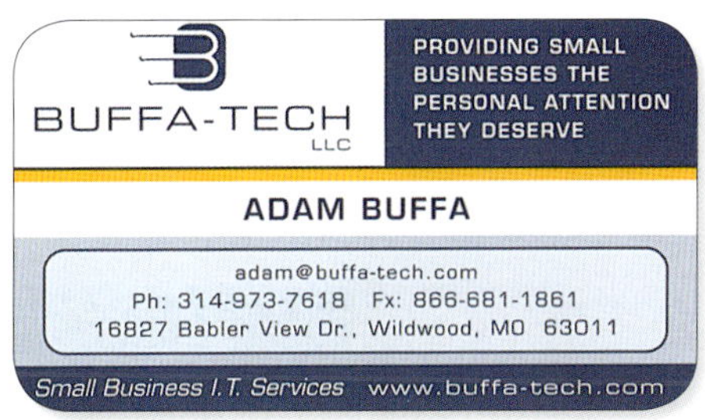

client
Buffa-Tech, LLC
design firm
Bright Rain Creative
designer
Matt Marino

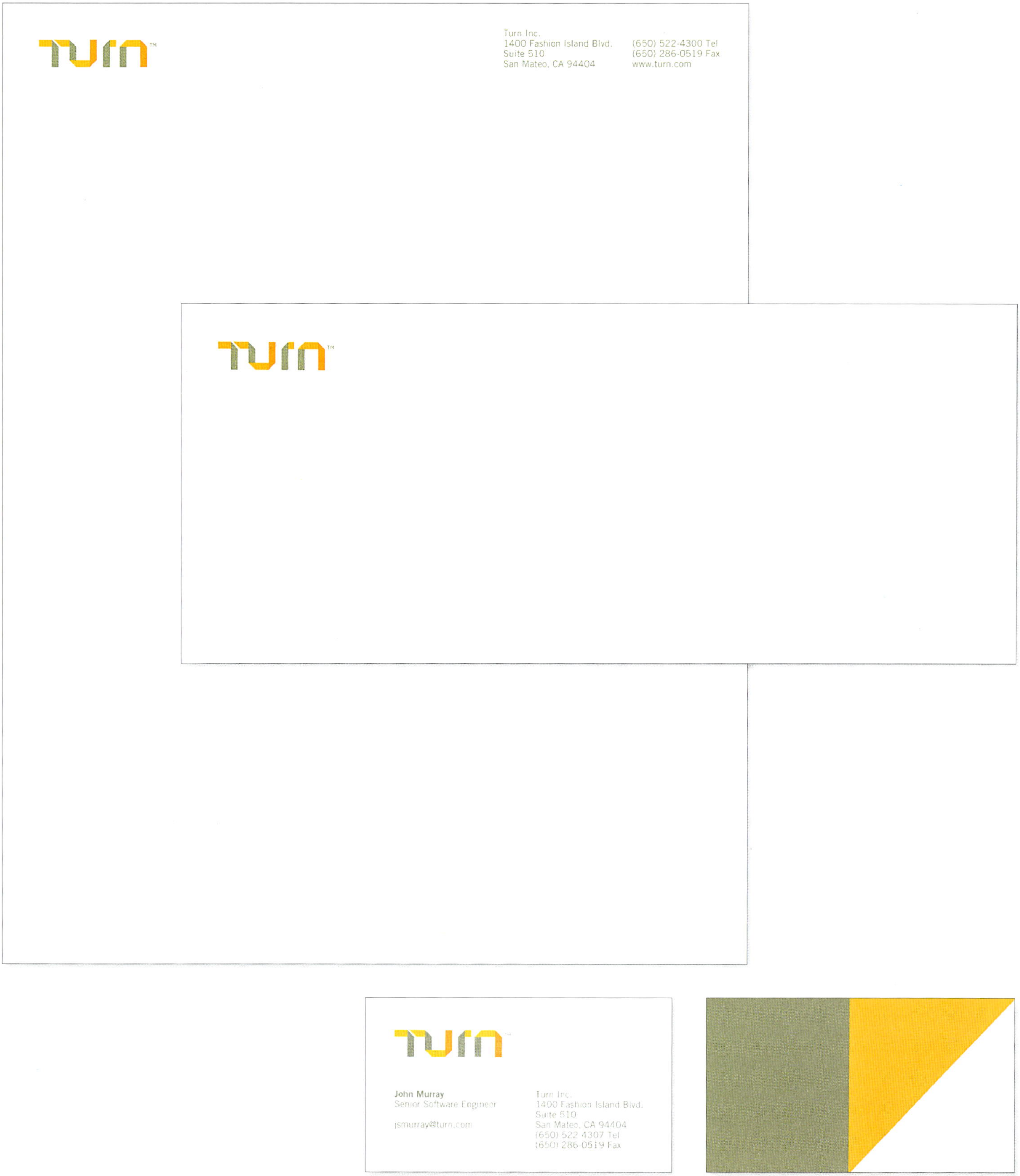

client
Turn
design firm
Addis Group
designer
John Creson

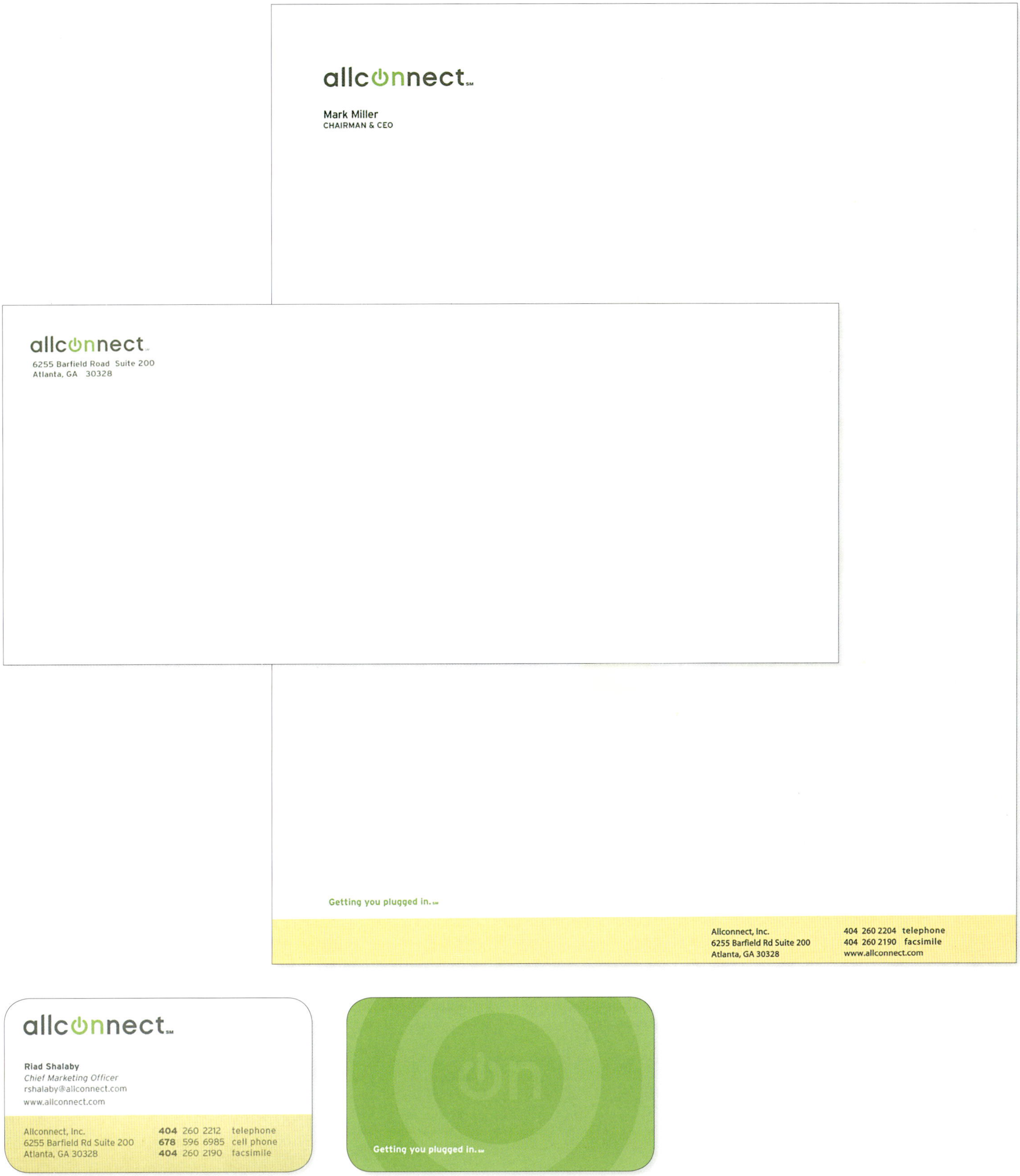

client
Allconnect
design firm
Hornall Anderson Design Works
designers
Jack Anderson, James Tee,
Tiffany Place, Yuri Shvets, Sonja Max,
Belinda Bowling, Stephanie Cooper

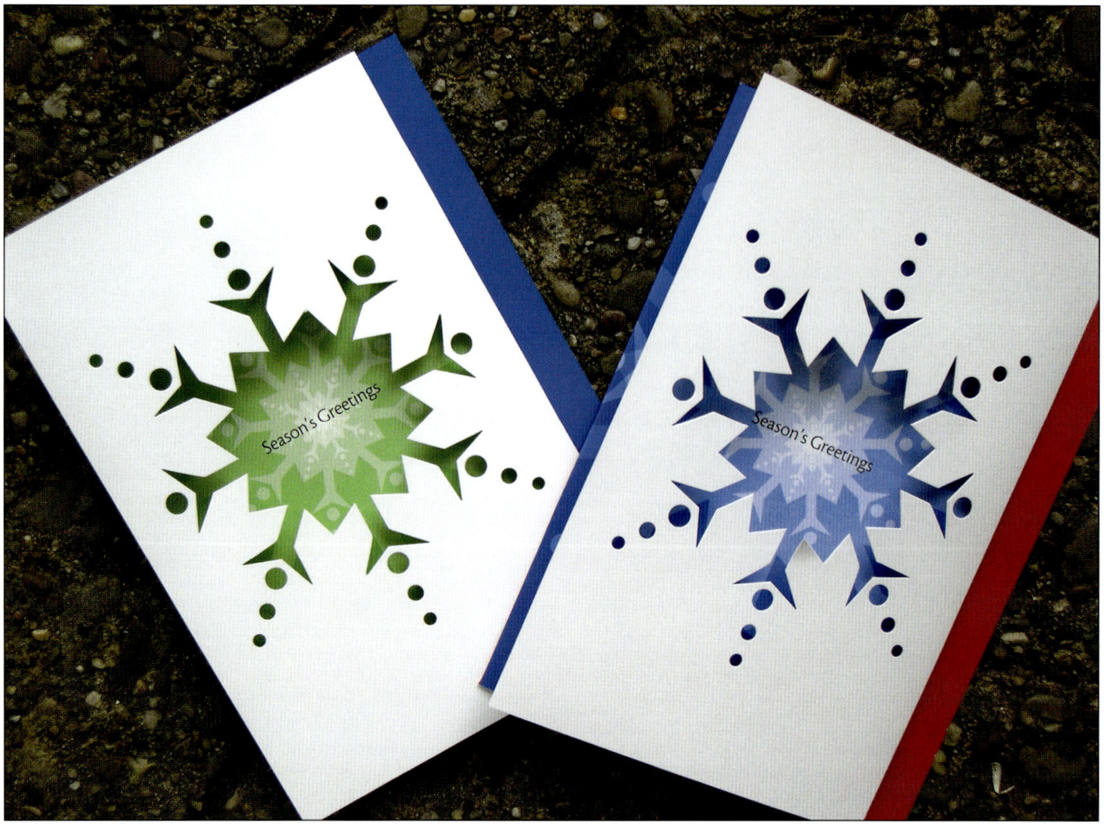

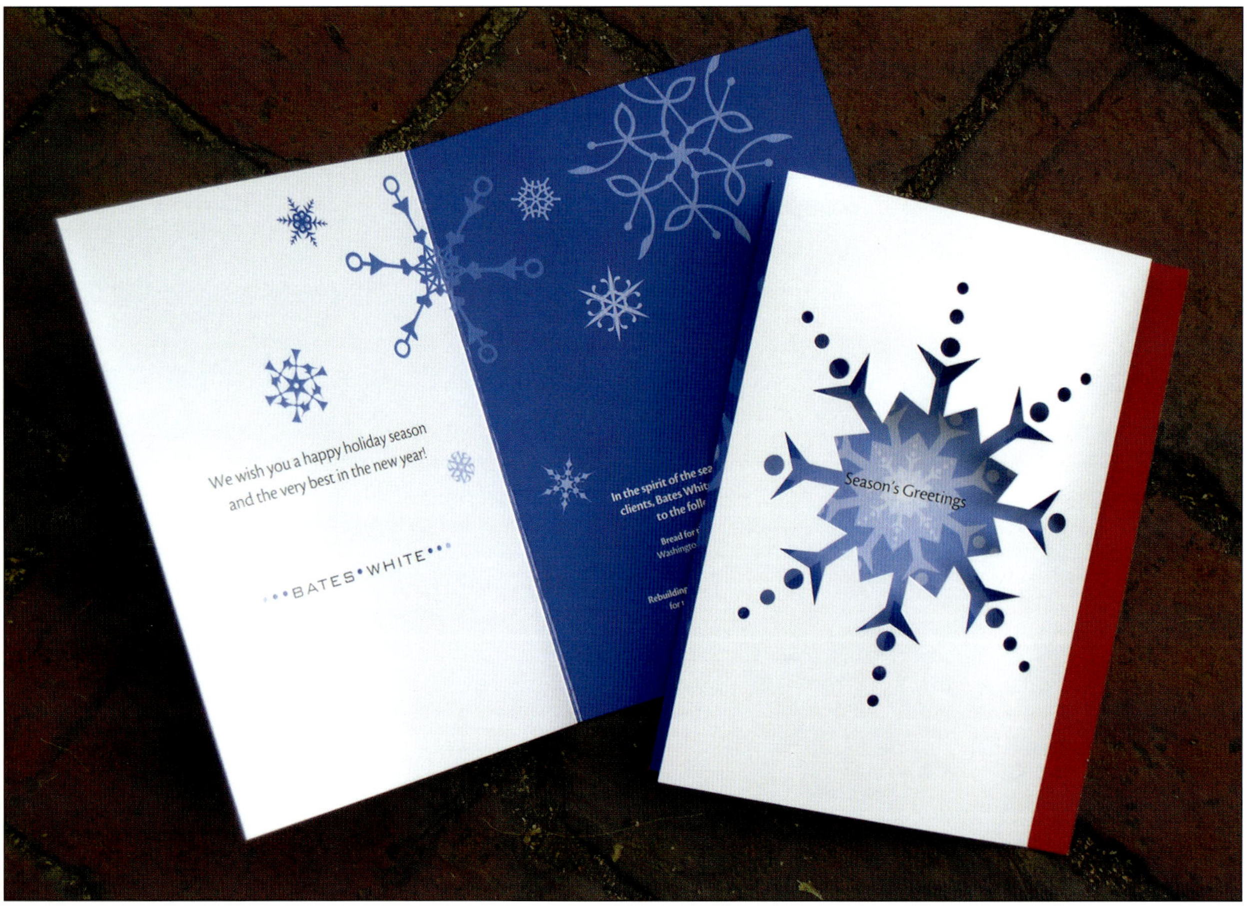

client
Bates White
design firm
Phoenix Creative Group
designer
Sean Mullins

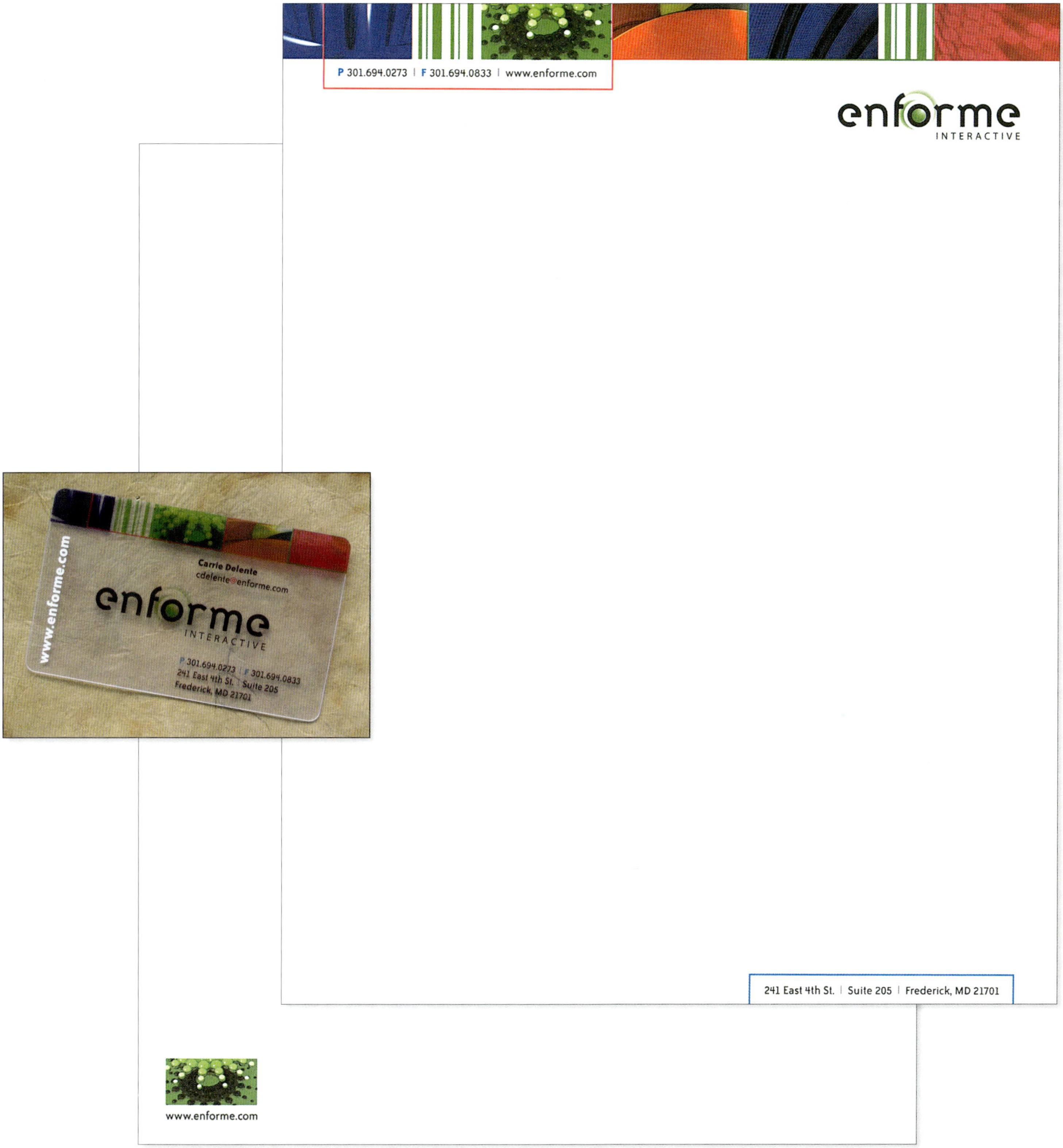

client
Enforme Interactive
design firm
Octavo Designs
designer
Sue Hough

client
Chris Gorney Design
design firm
Chris Gorney Design
designer
Chris Gorney

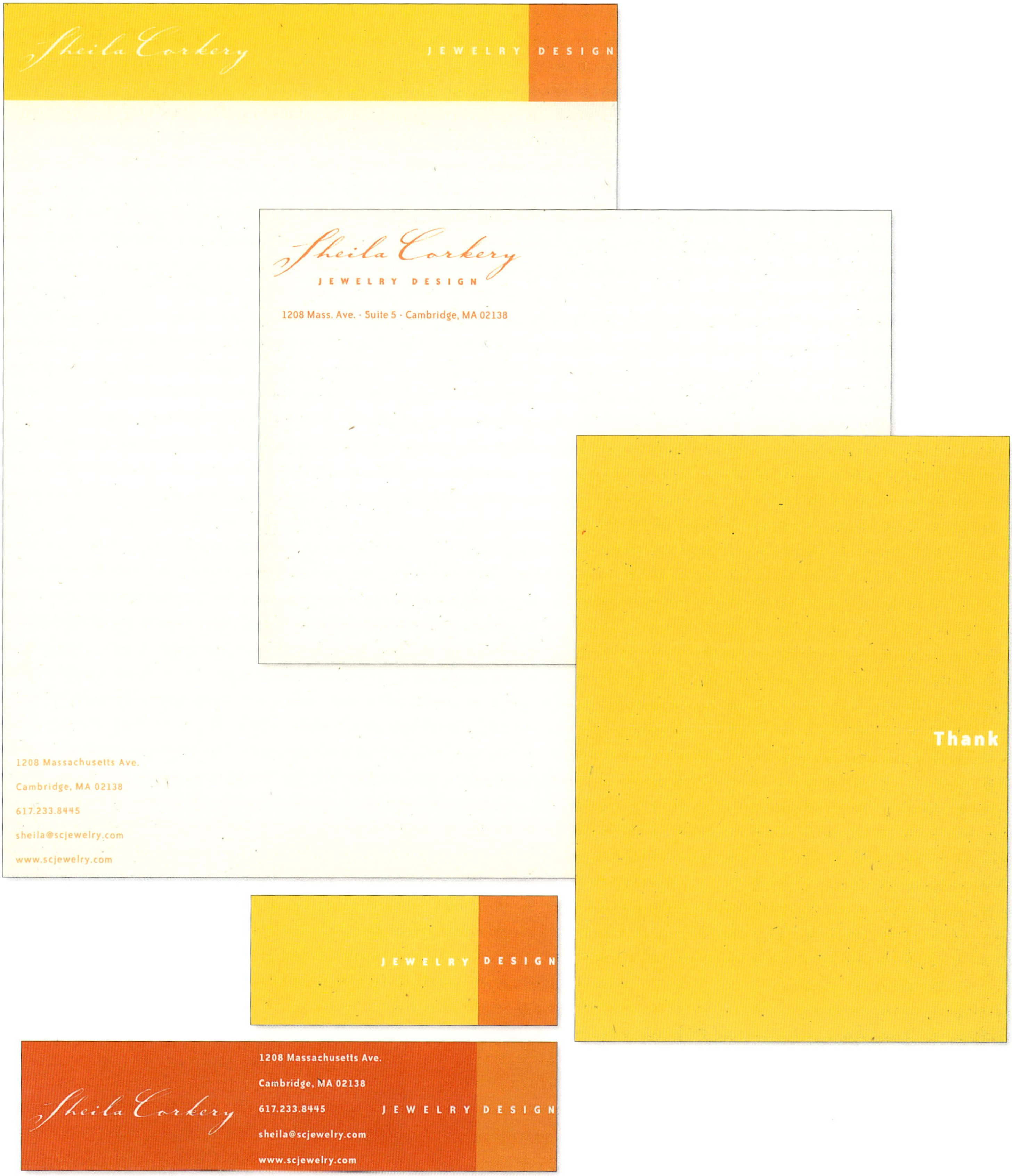

client
Sheila Corkery Jewelry Design
design firm
Martin Randal Communications
designers
Eric Rotramel

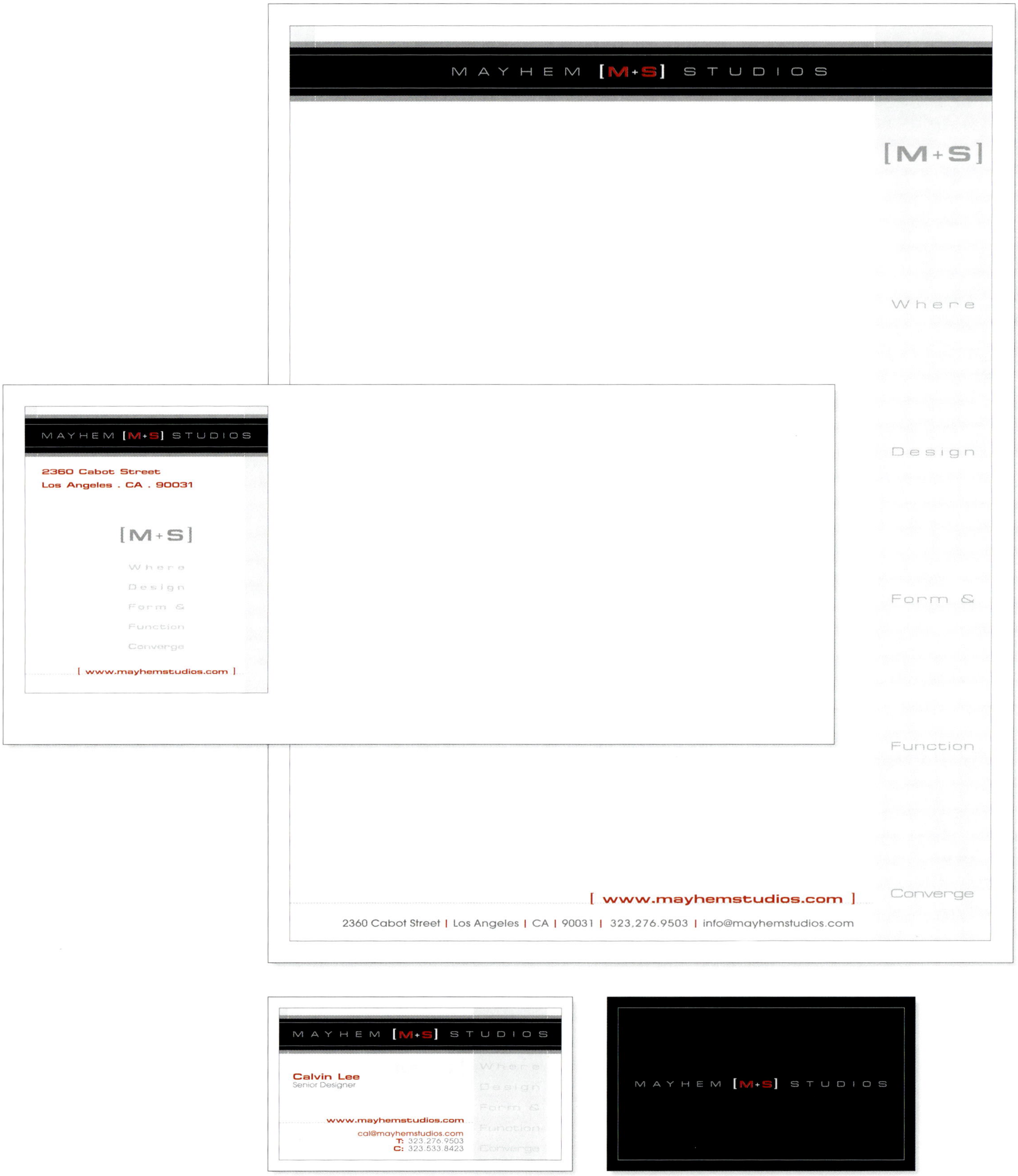

client
Mayhem Studios
design firm
Mayhem Studios
designer
Calvin Lee

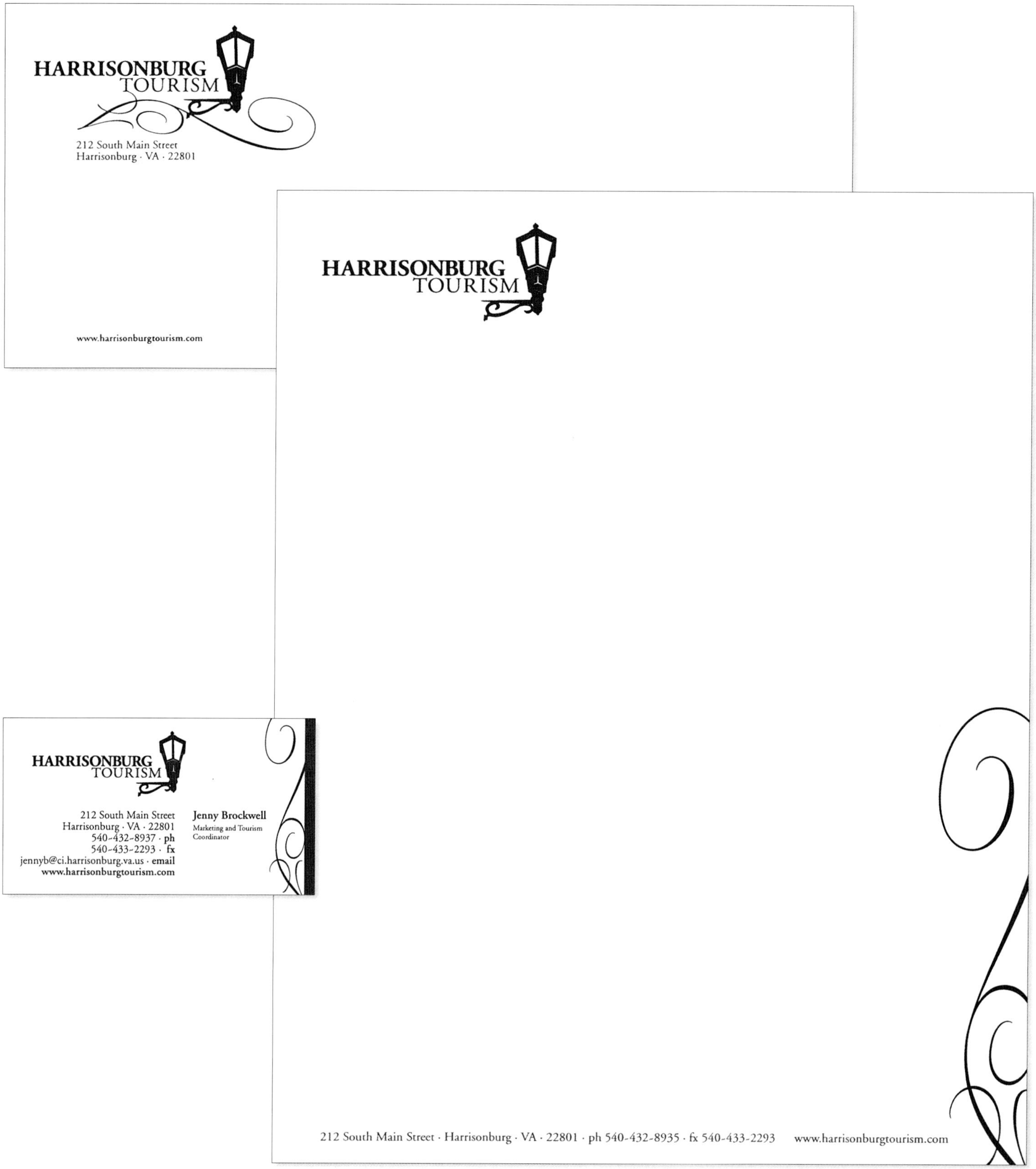

client
Harrisonburg Tourism
design firm
Grafix Dezine
designer
Oleg Yagolnikov

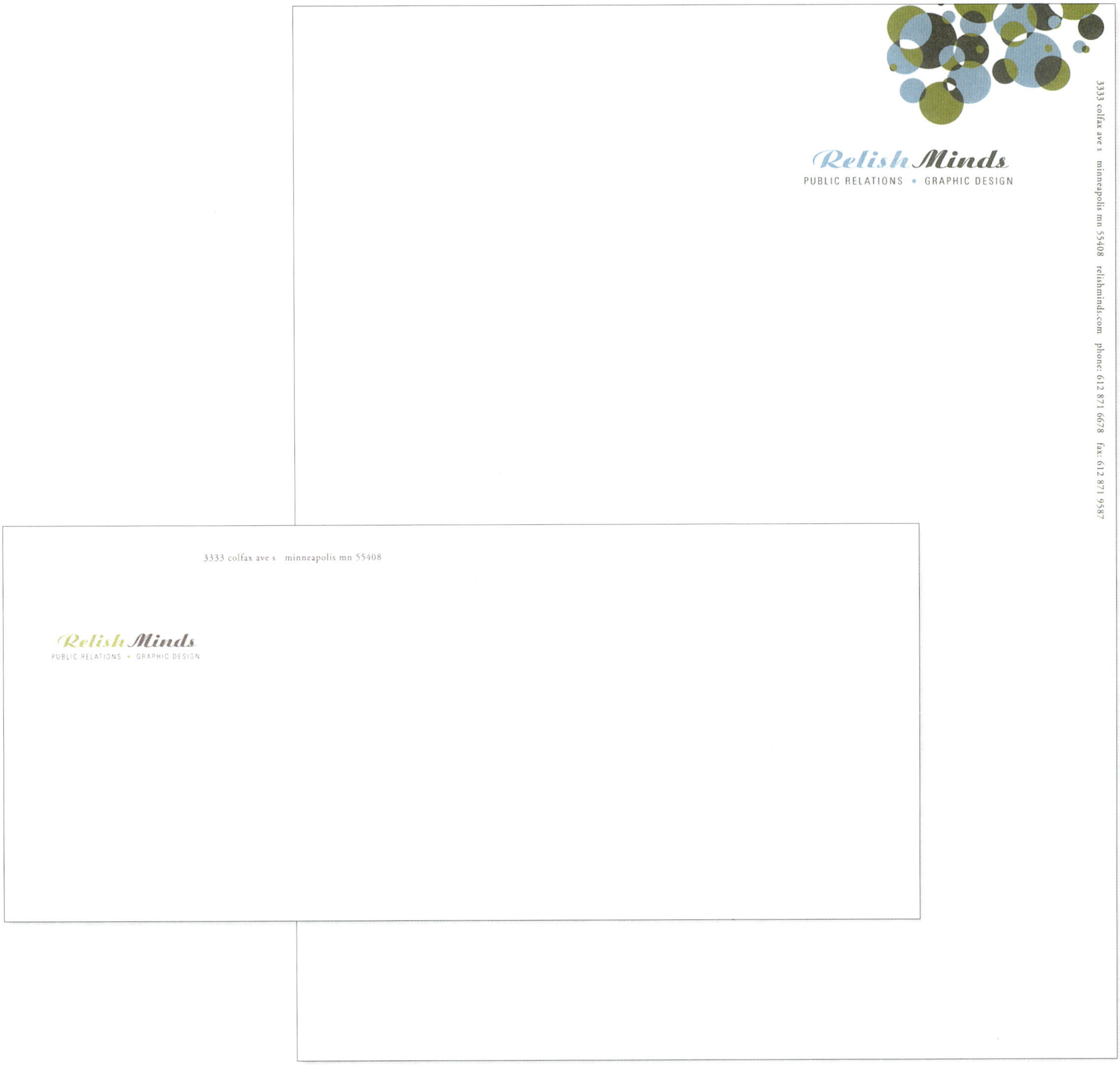

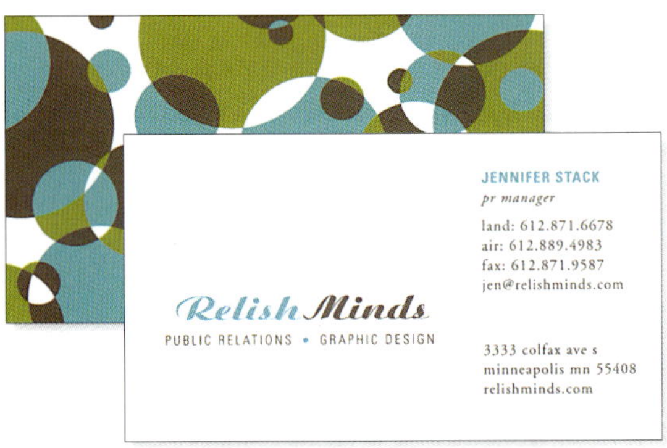

client
Relish Minds, Inc.
design firm
Chris Gorney Design
designer
Chris Gorney

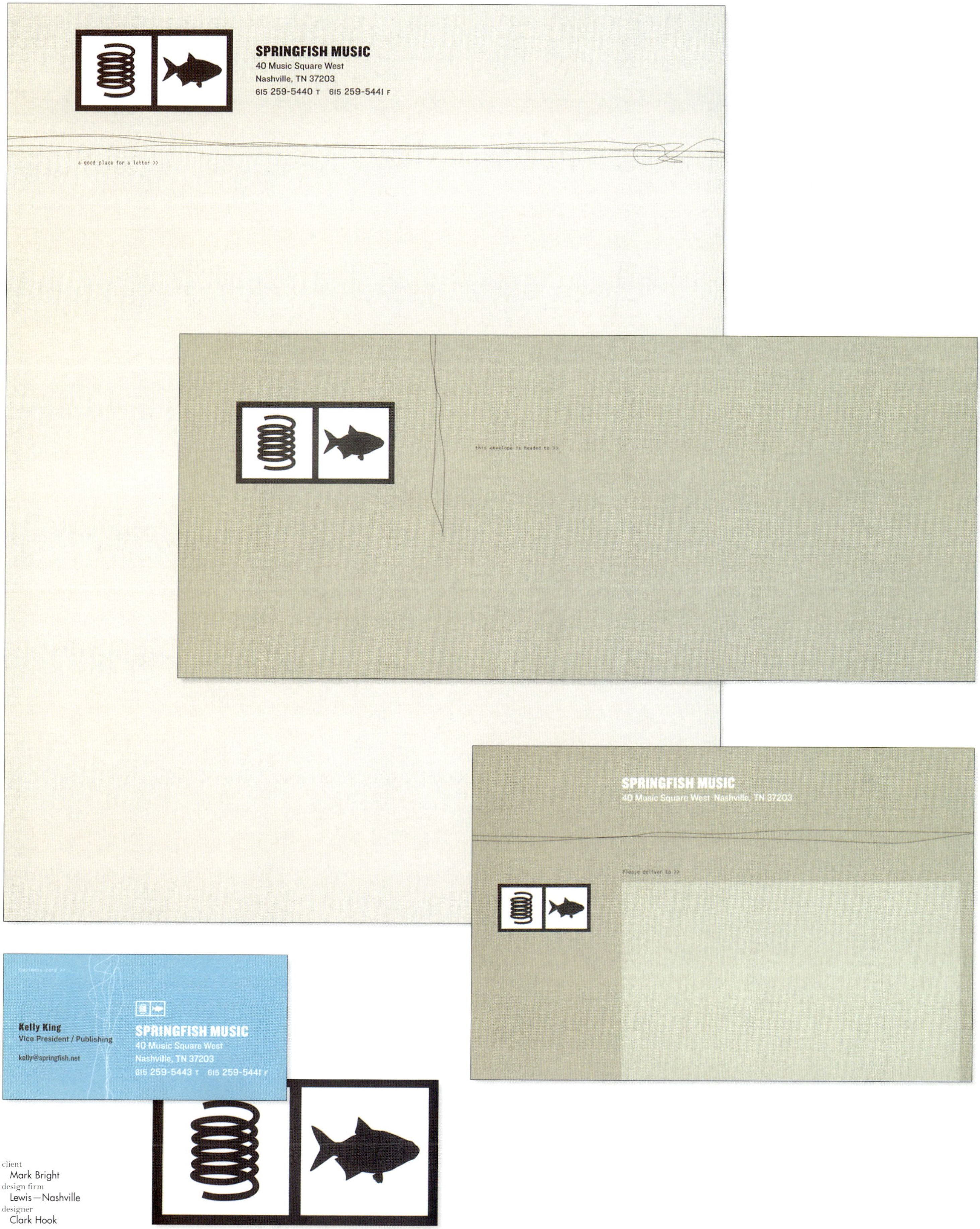

client
Mark Bright
design firm
Lewis—Nashville
designer
Clark Hook

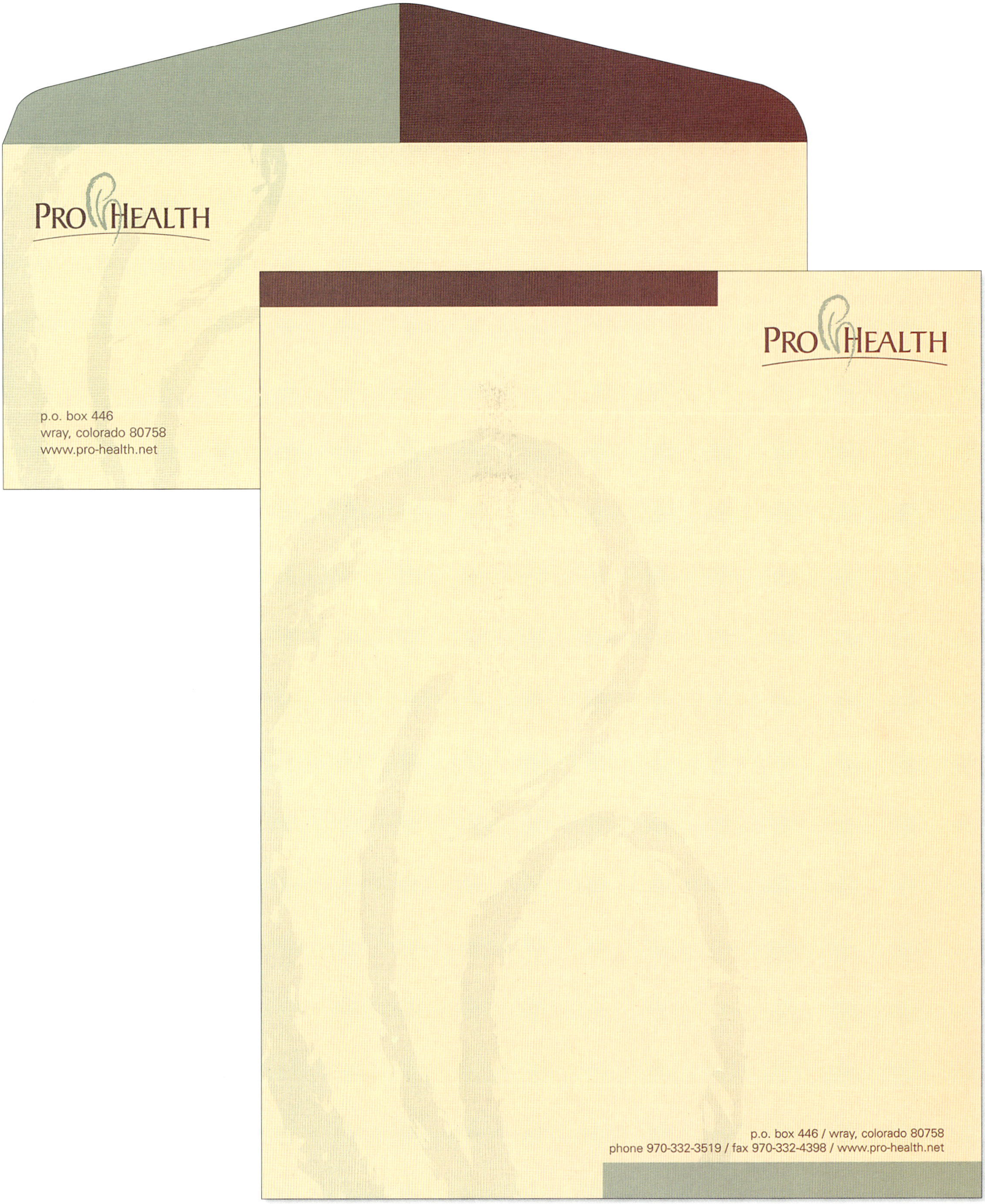

client
Pro-Health
design firm
Duncan/Day Advertising
designer
Leigh Finney

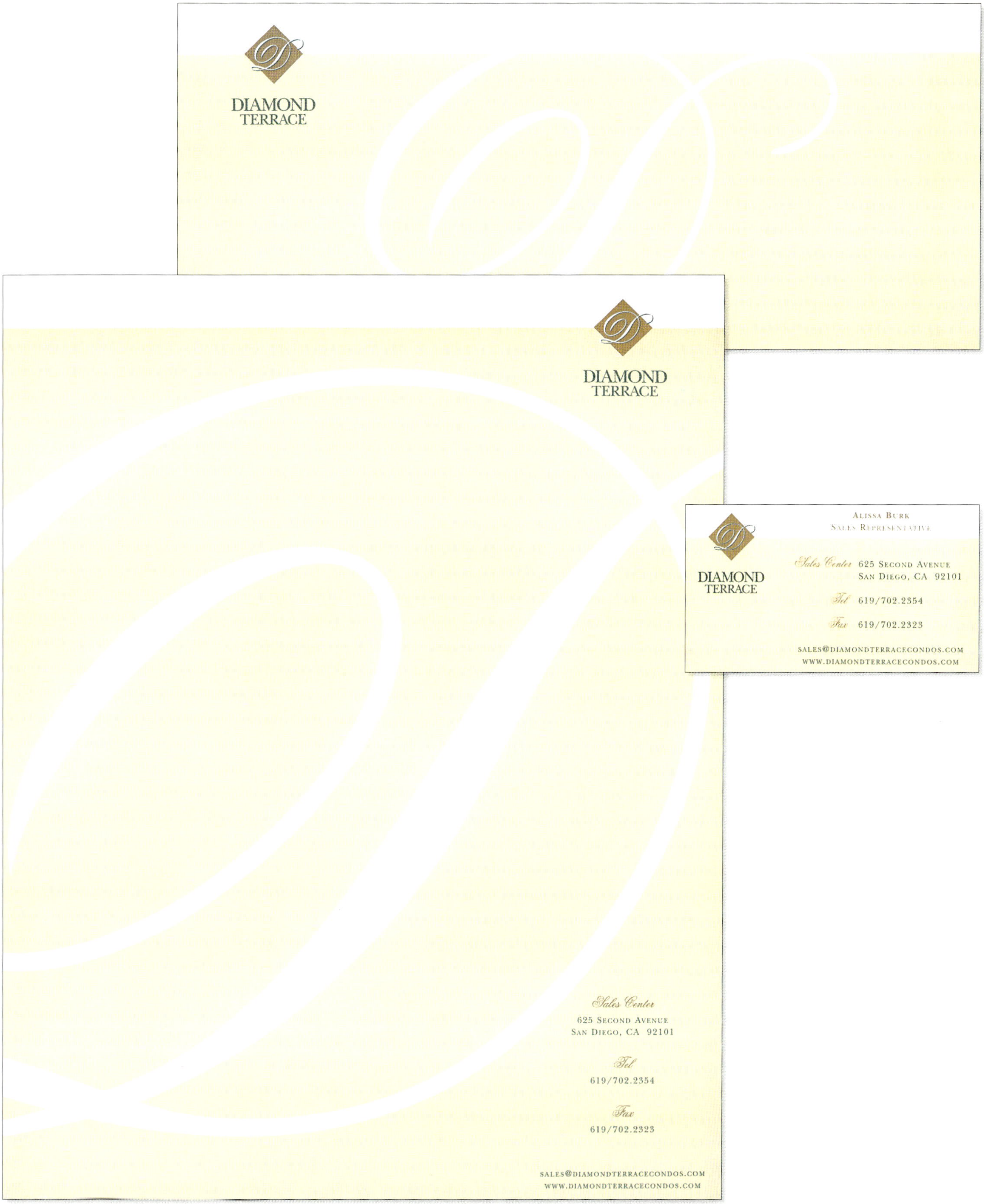

client
Intracorp
design firm
Lorenz Advertising
designer
Arne Ratermanis

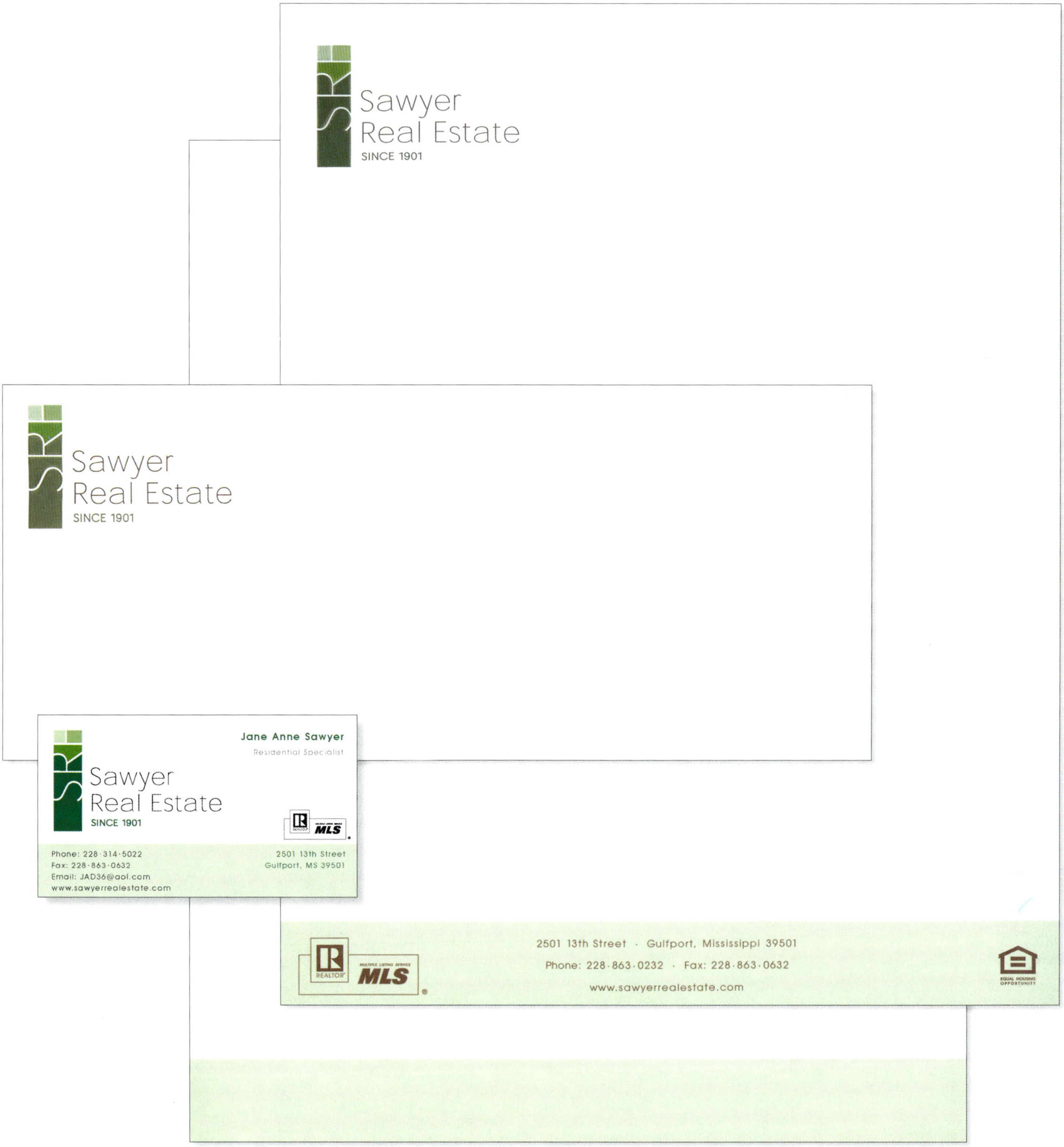

client
Sawyer Real Estate
design firm
The Prime Time Agency, LLC
designers
John Seymour

Corporate Identity Manuals

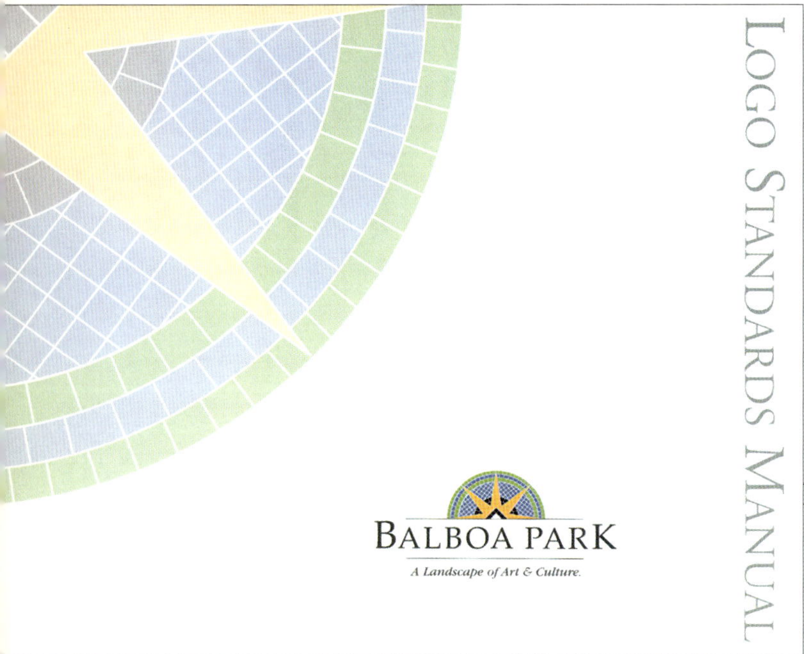

client
Balboa Park
design firm
Design Group West
designer
Jim Naegeli

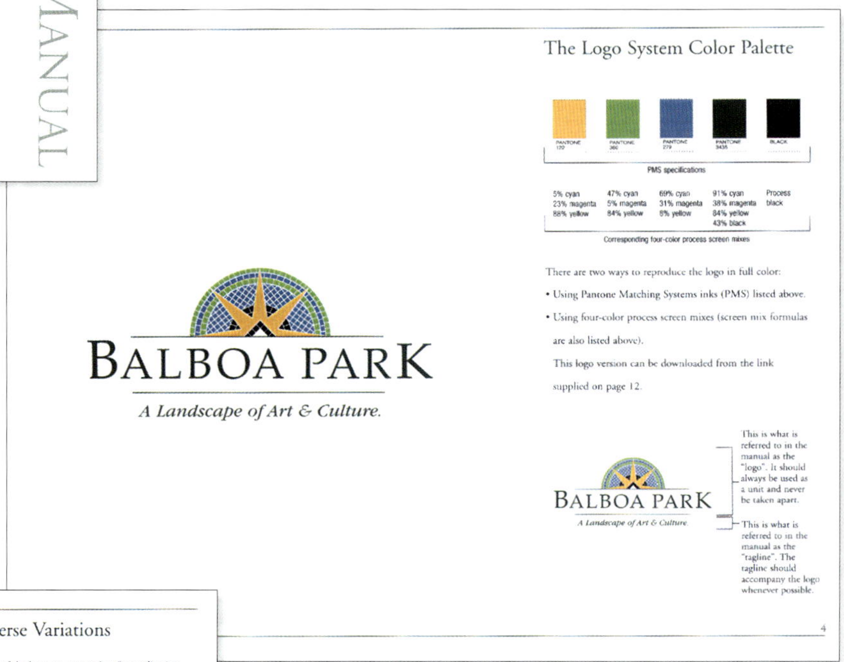

Balboa Park
A Landscape of Art & Culture.

The Logo System Color Palette

Pantone 122	Pantone 360	Pantone 279	Pantone 3435	Black
5% cyan 23% magenta 88% yellow	47% cyan 5% magenta 84% yellow	69% cyan 31% magenta 8% yellow	91% cyan 38% magenta 84% yellow 43% black	Process black

PMS specifications

Corresponding four-color process screen mixes

There are two ways to reproduce the logo in full color:

- Using Pantone Matching Systems inks (PMS) listed above.
- Using four-color process screen mixes (screen mix formulas are also listed above).

This logo version can be downloaded from the link supplied on page 12.

This is what is referred to in the manual as the "logo". It should always be used as a unit and never be taken apart.

This is what is referred to in the manual as the "tagline". The tagline should accompany the logo whenever possible.

4

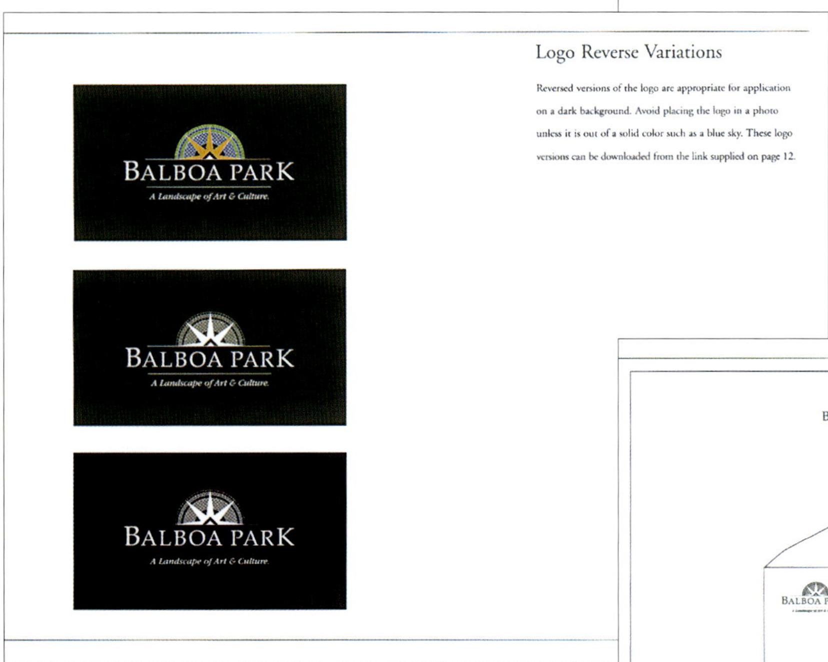

Logo Reverse Variations

Reversed versions of the logo are appropriate for application on a dark background. Avoid placing the logo in a photo unless it is out of a solid color such as a blue sky. These logo versions can be downloaded from the link supplied on page 12.

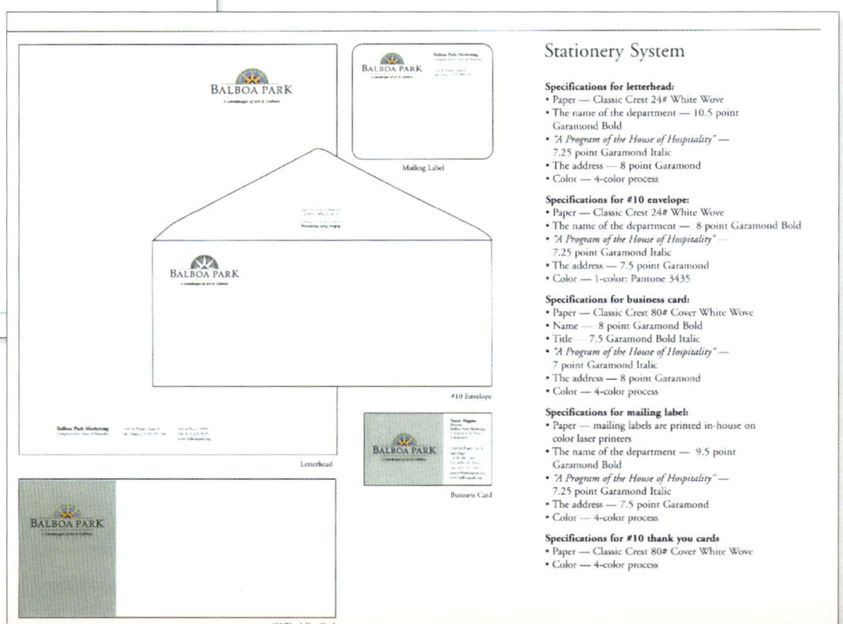

Stationery System

Specifications for letterhead:
- Paper — Classic Crest 24# White Wove
- The name of the department — 10.5 point Garamond Bold
- *"A Program of the House of Hospitality"* — 7.25 point Garamond Italic
- The address — 8 point Garamond
- Color — 4-color process

Specifications for #10 envelope:
- Paper — Classic Crest 24# White Wove
- The name of the department — 8 point Garamond Bold
- *"A Program of the House of Hospitality"* — 7.25 point Garamond Italic
- The address — 7.5 point Garamond
- Color — 1-color: Pantone 3435

Specifications for business card:
- Paper — Classic Crest 80# Cover White Wove
- Name — 8 point Garamond Bold
- Title — 7.5 Garamond Bold Italic
- *"A Program of the House of Hospitality"* — 7 point Garamond Italic
- The address — 8 point Garamond
- Color — 4-color process

Specifications for mailing label:
- Paper — mailing labels are printed in-house on color laser printers
- The name of the department — 9.5 point Garamond Bold
- *"A Program of the House of Hospitality"* — 7.25 point Garamond Italic
- The address — 7.5 point Garamond
- Color — 4-color process

Specifications for #10 thank you cards
- Paper — Classic Crest 80# Cover White Wove
- Color — 4-color process

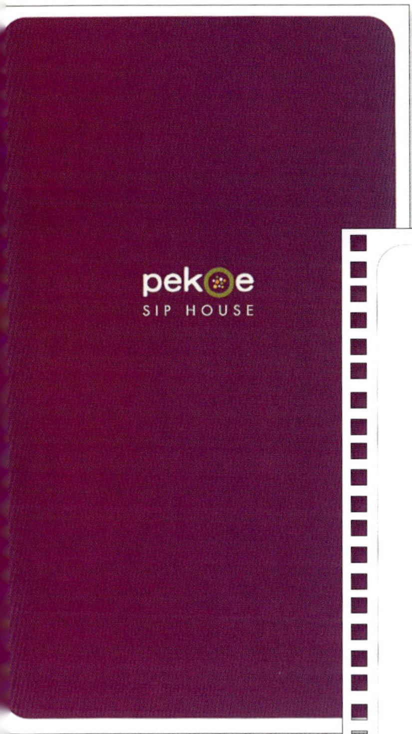

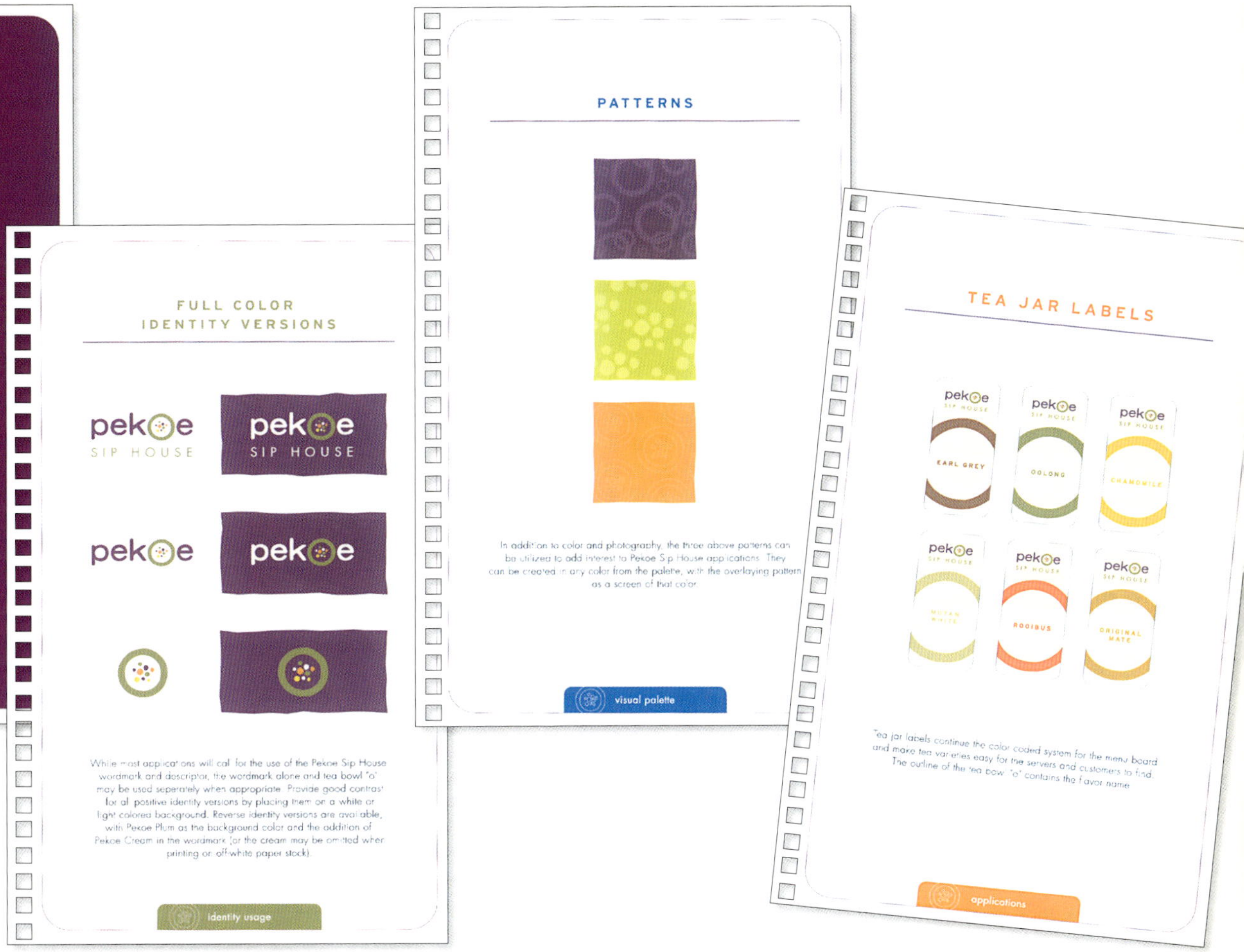

client
Pekoe Siphouse
design firm
Brand Engine
art director
Will Burke
designers
Yusuke Asaka, Monica Schlaug
copywriter
Monica Schlaug

client
Pixie Maté
design firm
Brand Engine
art director
Will Burke
designers
Yusuke Asaka, Casey Coyle, Kinkel Rowan
copywriter
David Eichhorn

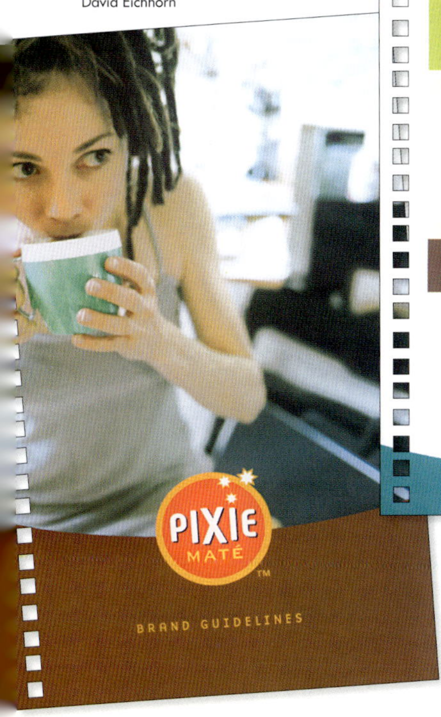

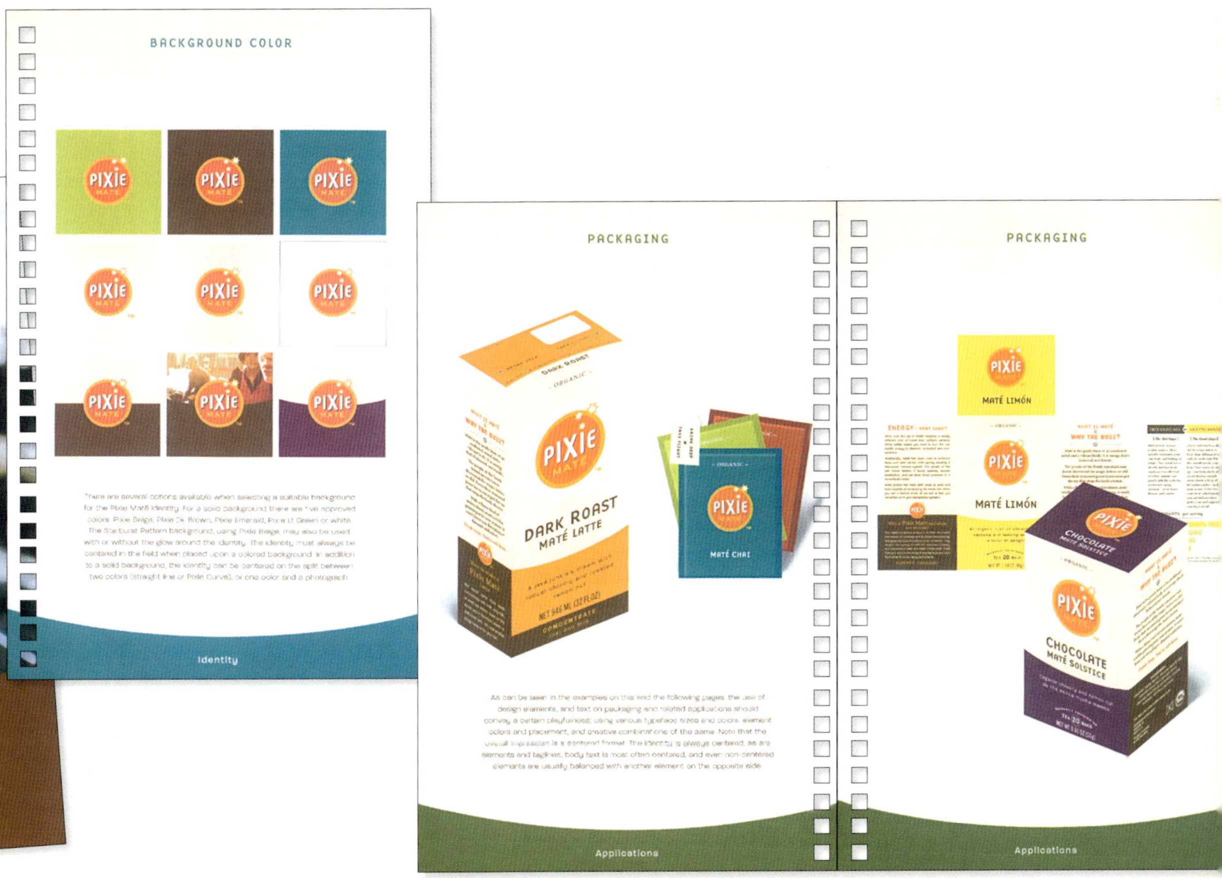

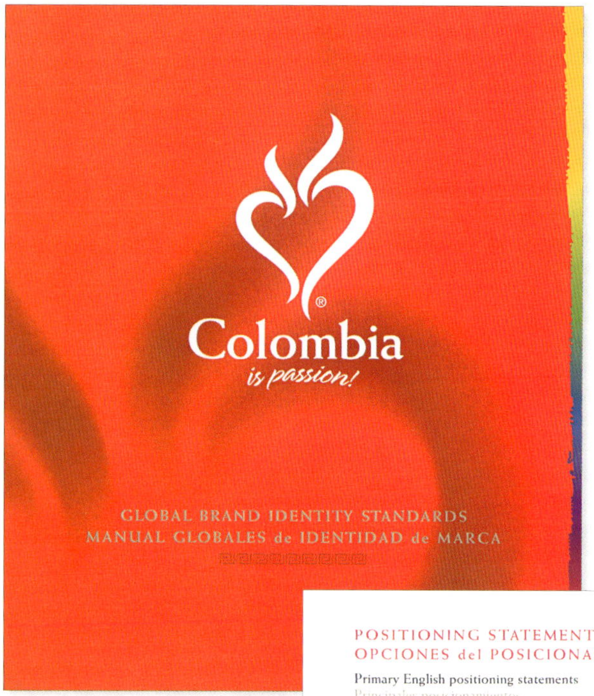

client
Fiducoldex-Proexport
design firm
VMA, Inc.
creative director
Doug Knopp
account manager
Steve Goubeaux
project manager
Kenneth Botts
production designer
Patrick Londergan

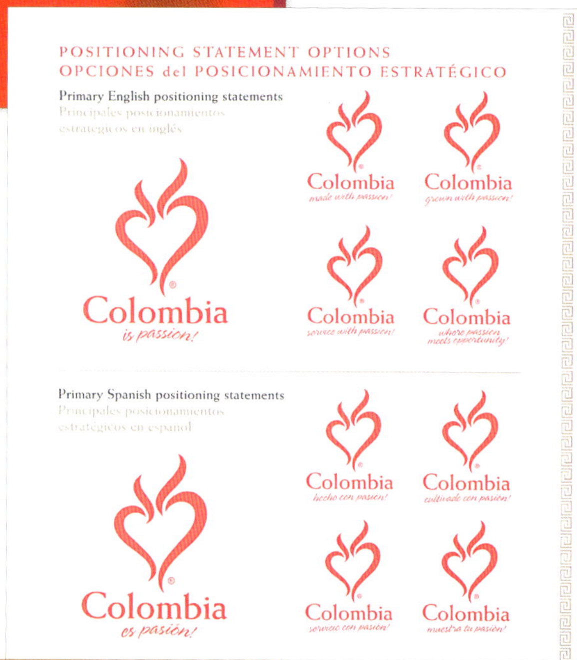

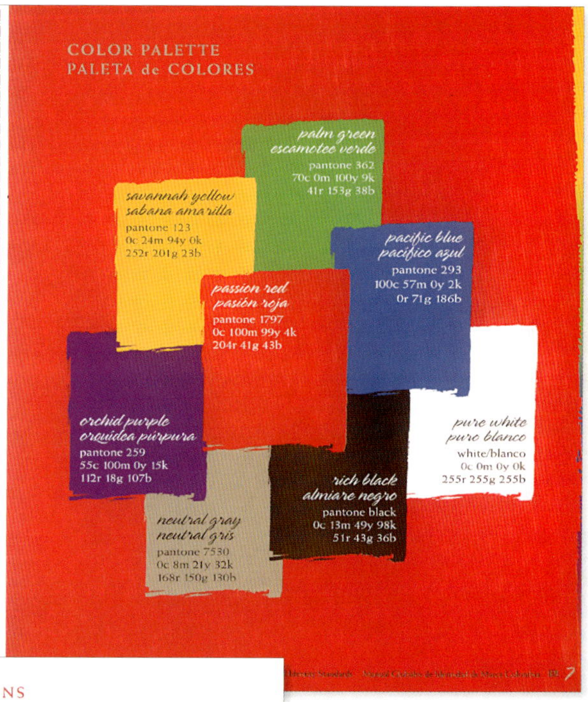

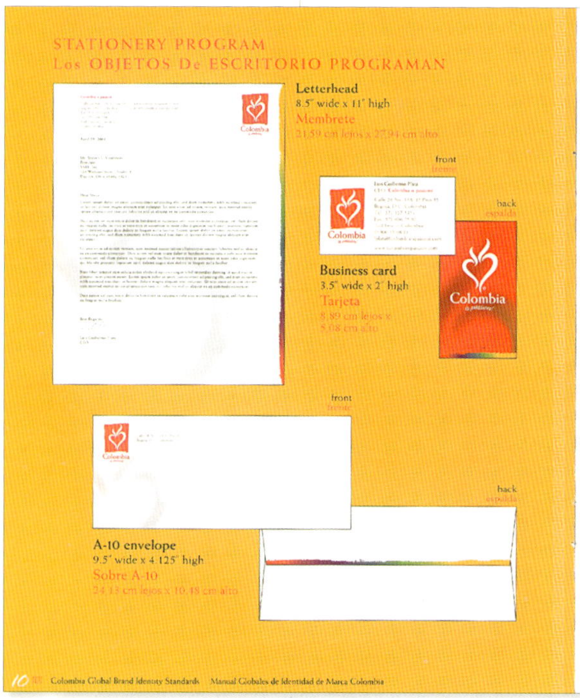

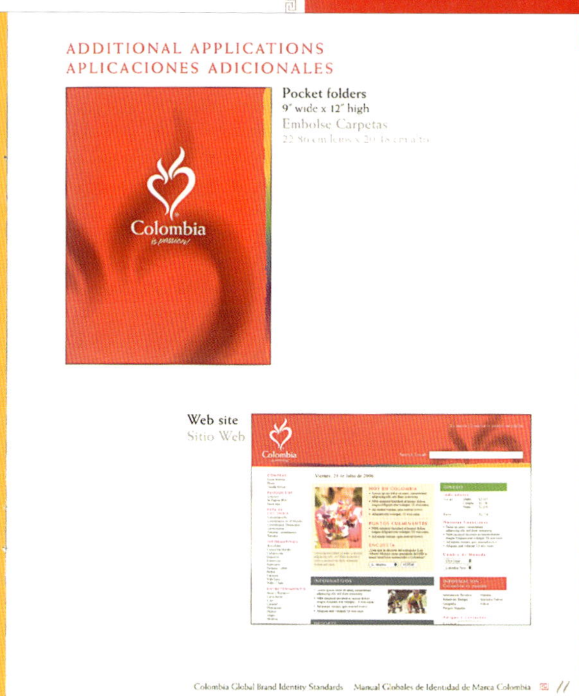

Signage & Environmental Graphics

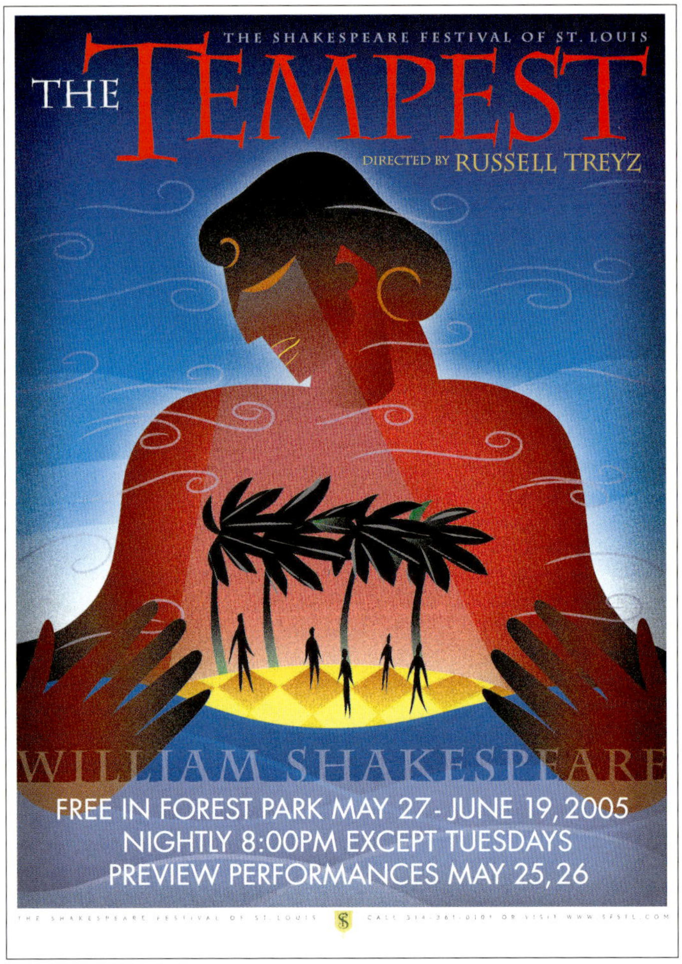

client
Shakespeare Festival of St. Louis
design firm
Kiku Obata + Company
designer
Rich Nelson

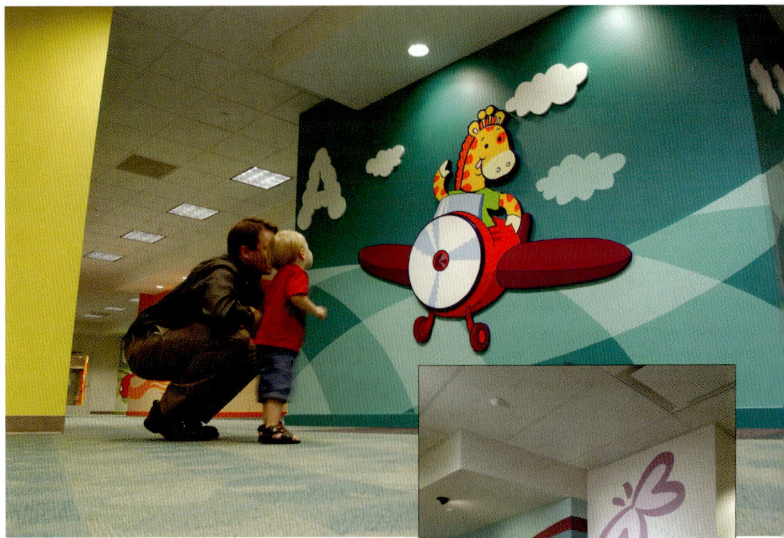

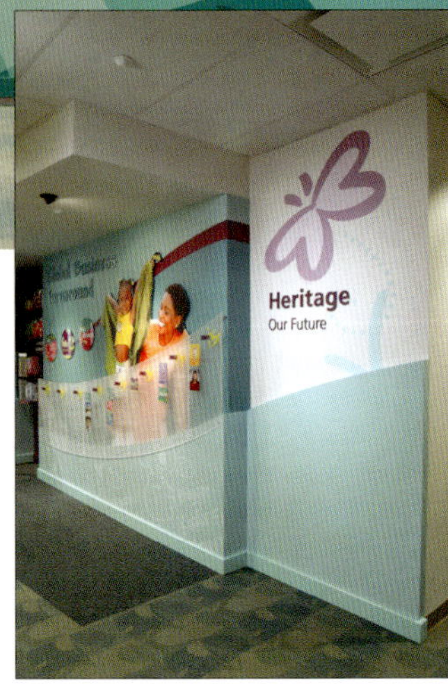

client
Procter & Gamble
design firm
Kolar Design, Inc.
project team
Brent Beck, Donald Carson, Matt Corbin, Mary Dietrich, David Eyman, Leisa Graham, Kelly Kolar, Matt Oscar, Janice Radlove, Nicole Roberts, Amy Scheid, TJ Schmidlin, Stacy Sims, Ric Snodgrass, Annelle Suszkiw, Aggie Toppins
collaborative partners
CUH2A Architecture, BHDP Architecture

client
Loop Island Wetlands
design firm
Mind's Eye Creative
designer
Stephen Brown

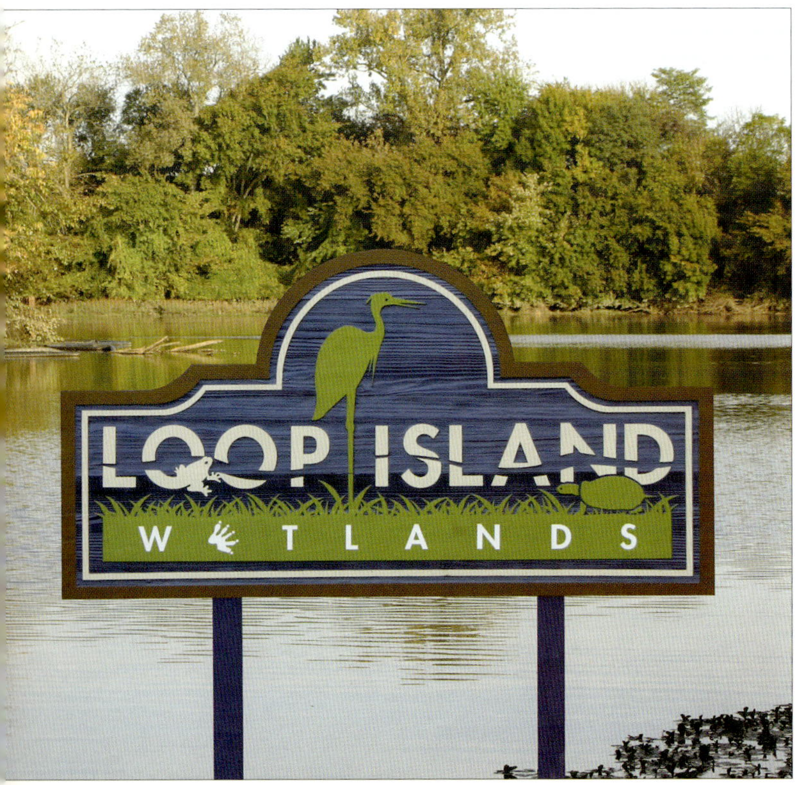

client
Earthplace Nature Center
design firm
Acme Communications, Inc.
designers
Kiki Boucher, Andrea Ross Boyle

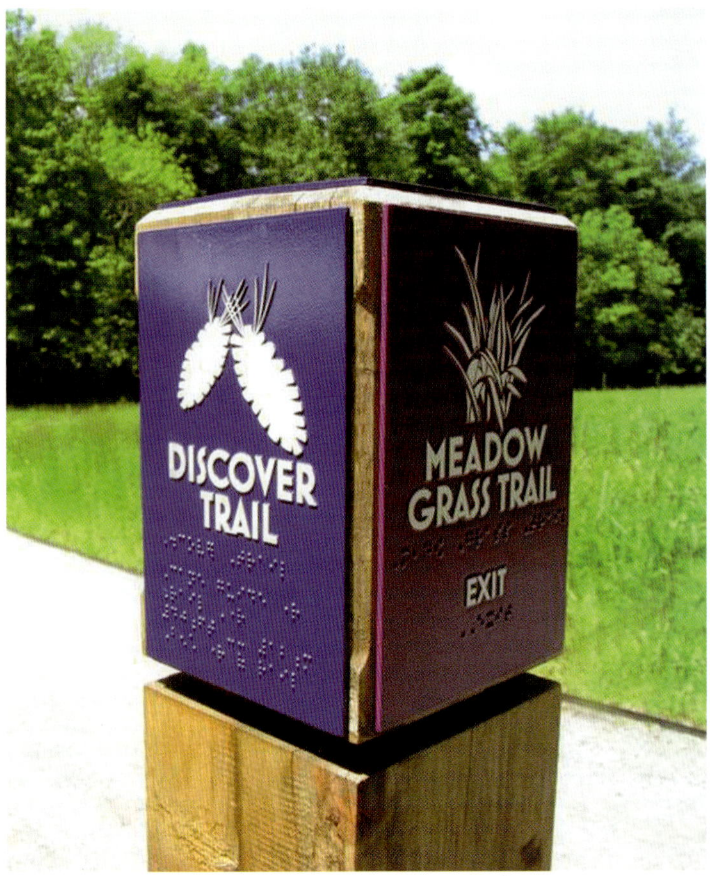

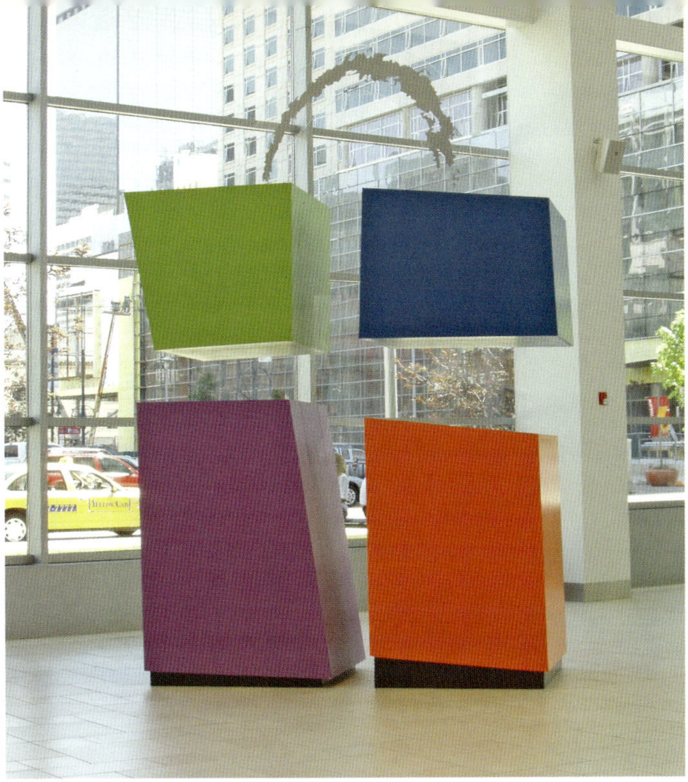

client
Christian Booksellers Association
design firm
Fixation Marketing, Freeman
designers
Bruce E. Morgan, Jim Moore

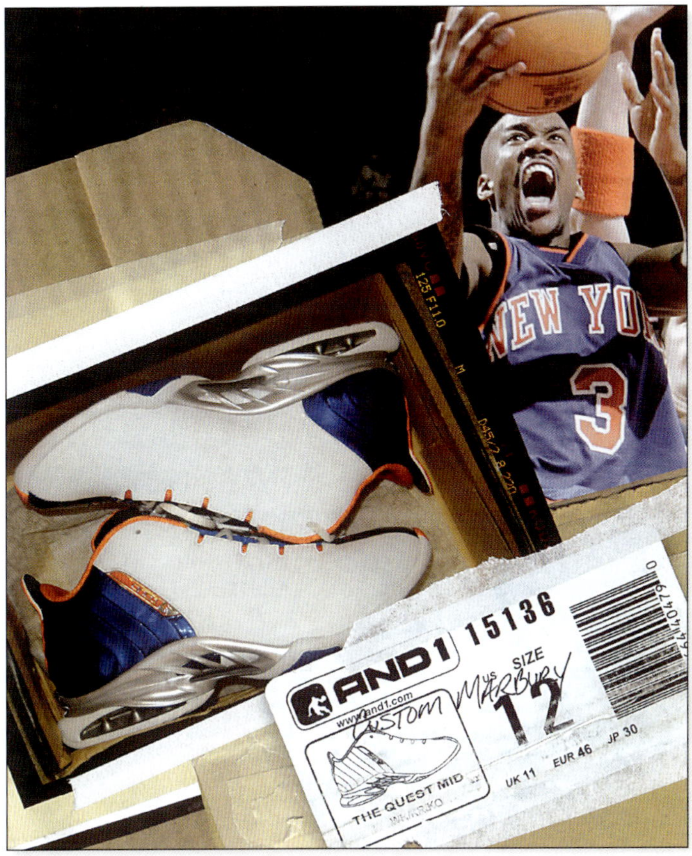

client
And 1
design firm
160over90
designers
Darryl Cilli, Dan Shepelavy, Jim Walls, Adam Flanagan, Giacomo Ciminello, Steve Penning, Jerrod Modica, Brendan Quinn

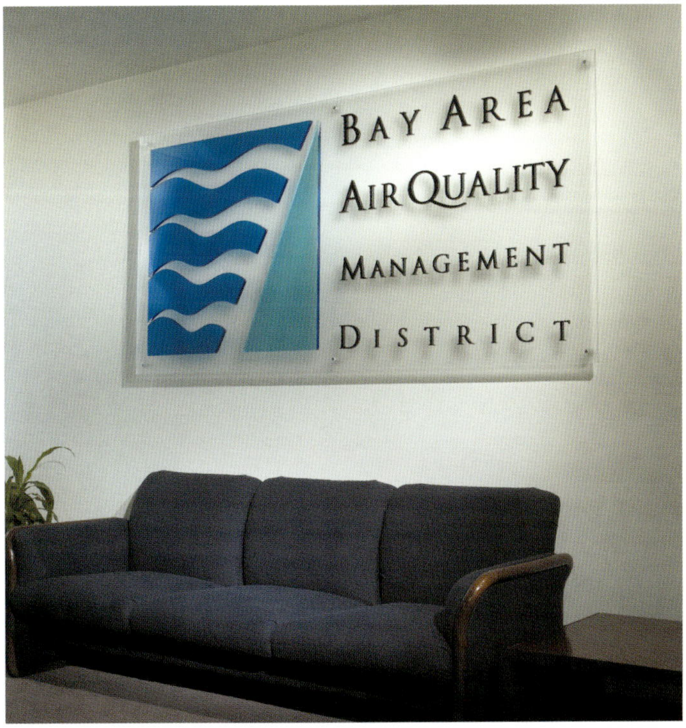

client
Bay Area Air Quality Management District
design firm
Gee + Chung Design
designer
Earl Gee

client
Las Vegas Odyssey
design firm
Brand, ltd.
designers
Virginia Martino, Mark V. Martino, Annie Manning, Jack Johnson, Pam Cirulli, Ginger Tatoya

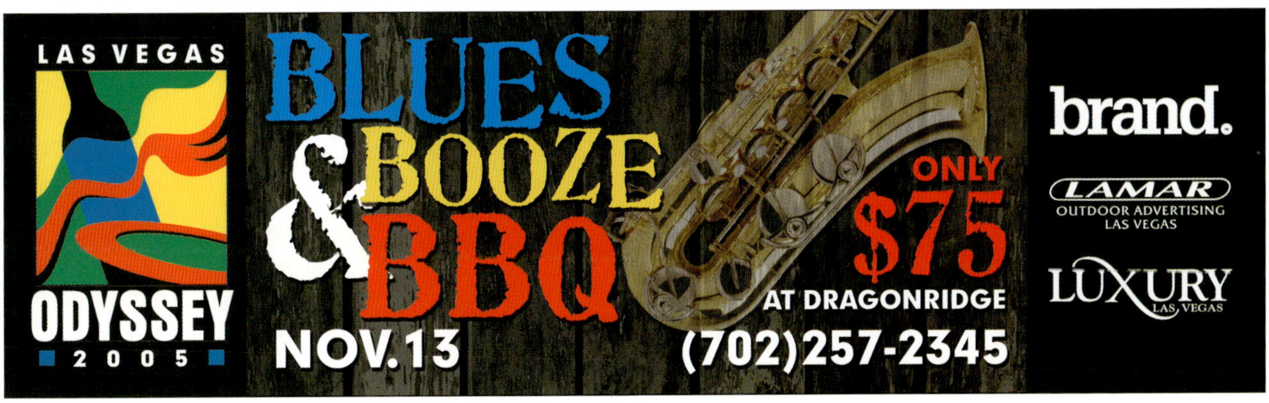

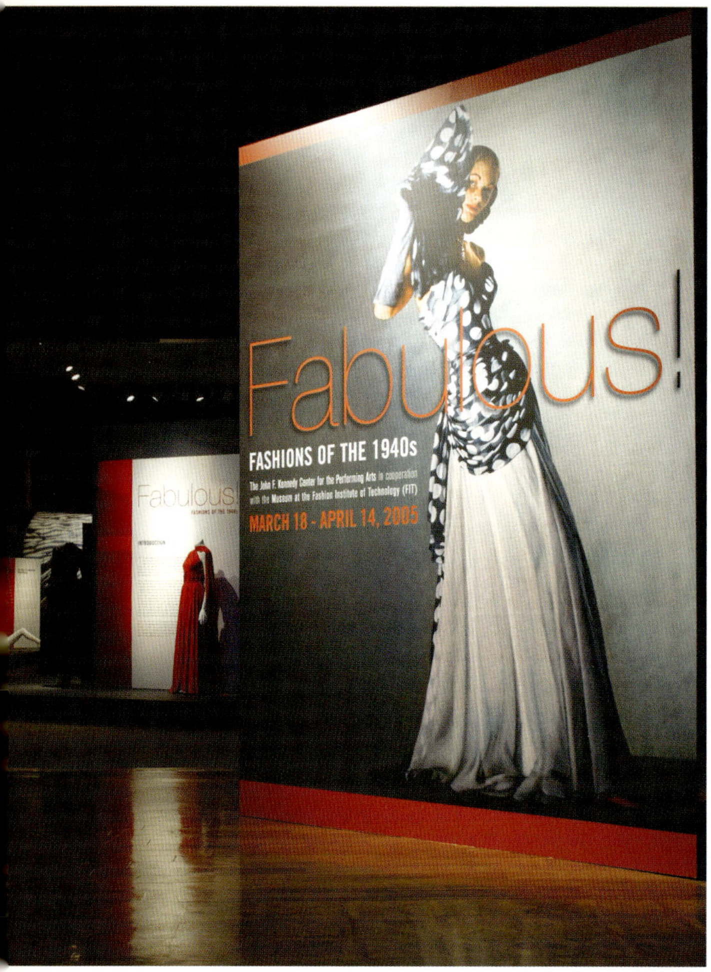

client
The John F. Kennedy Center for the Performing Arts
design firm
Design Nut, LLC
designer
Brent Almond
illustrator
Eileen Ritter

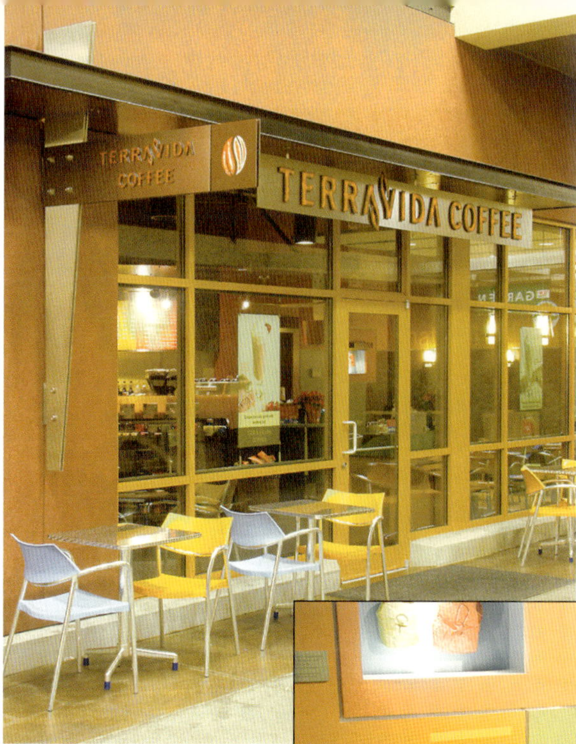

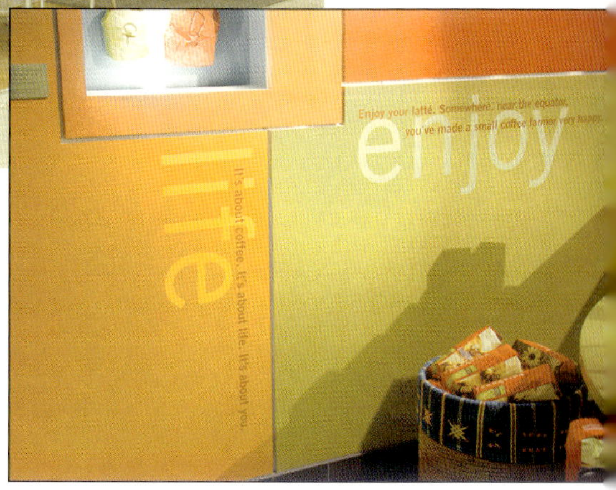

client
TerraVida Coffee
design firm
Hornall Anderson Design Works
designers
Jack Anderson, James Tee, Sonja Max

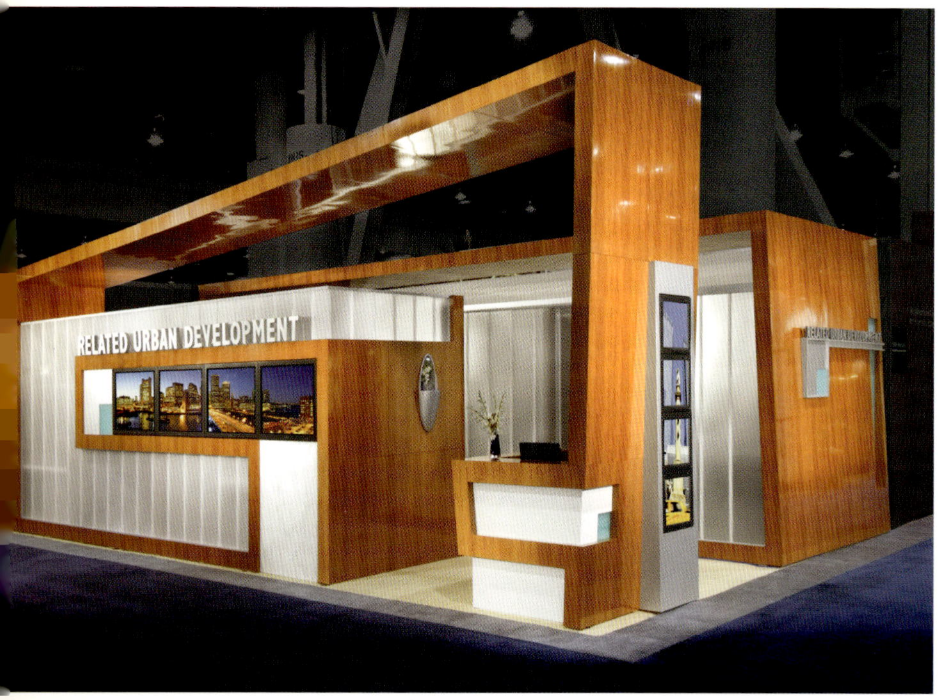

client
The Related Companies
design firm
Lorenc + Yoo Design/
Journey Communications
designers
Jan Lorenc, Steve McCall, Ken Boyd

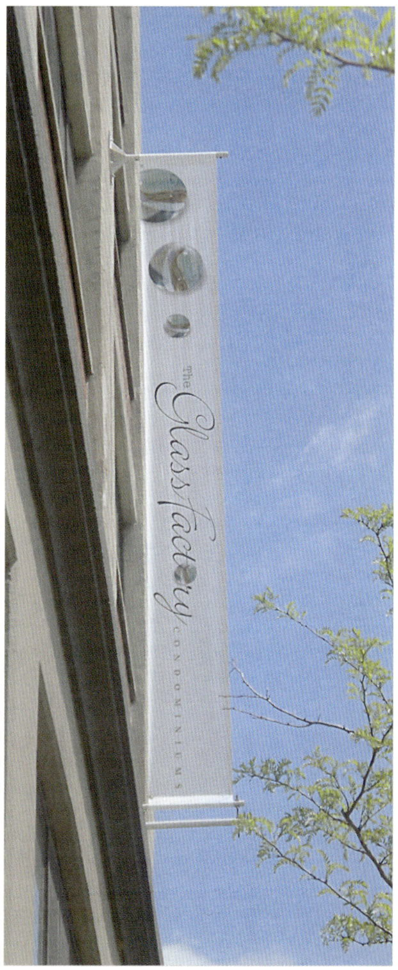

client
Crescent Heights
design firm
Doerr Associates
designer
Joan Wilking

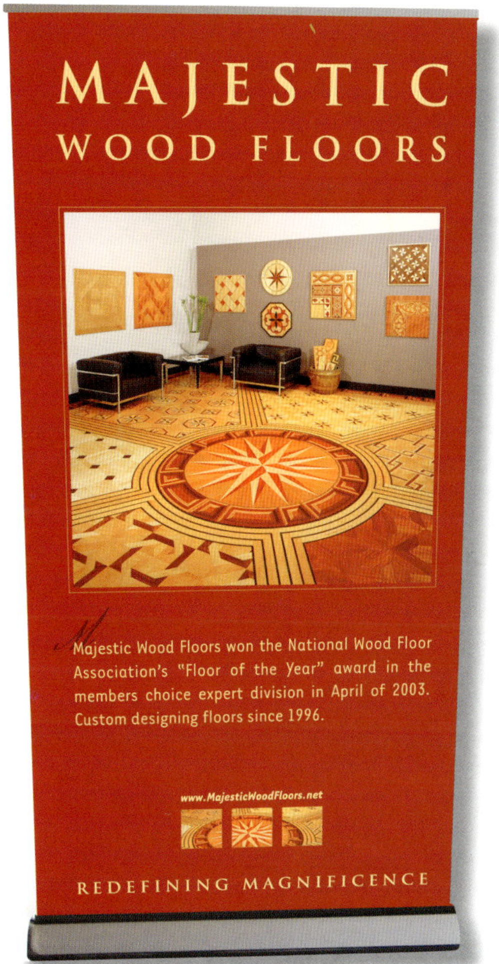

client
Majestic Wood Floors
design firm
Octavo Designs
designer
Sue Hough

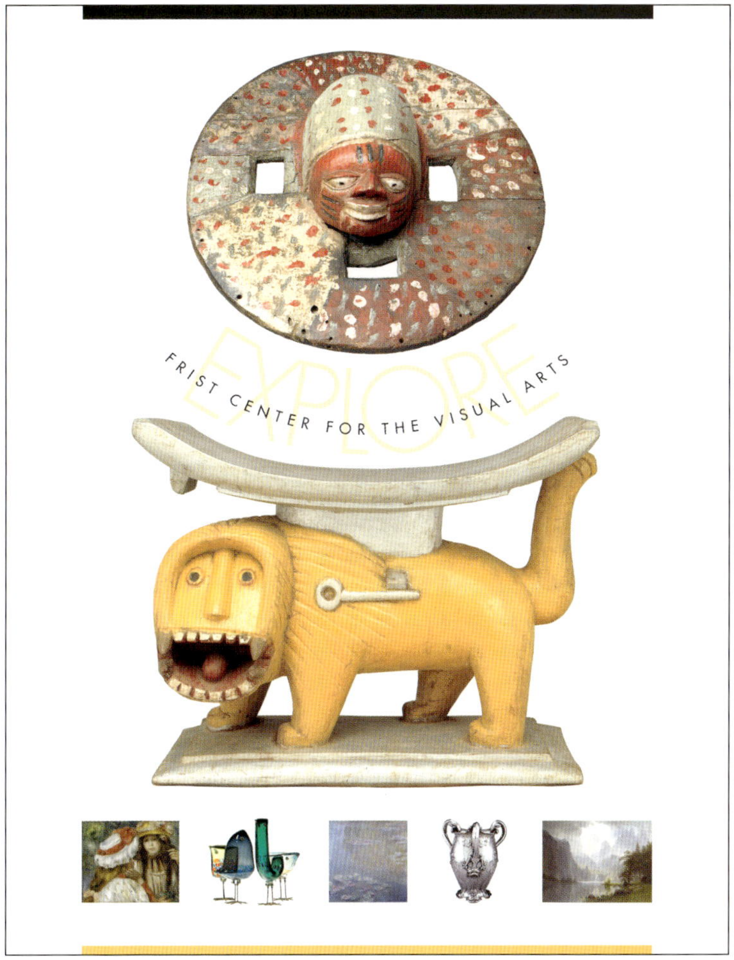

client
Frist Center for the Arts
design firm
Ventress Design Group
designers
Tom Ventress,
Eric Ventress

client
Phillips Edison & Company
design firm
Lorenc + Yoo Design/
Journey Communications
designers
Jan Lorenc, Steve McCall, David Park

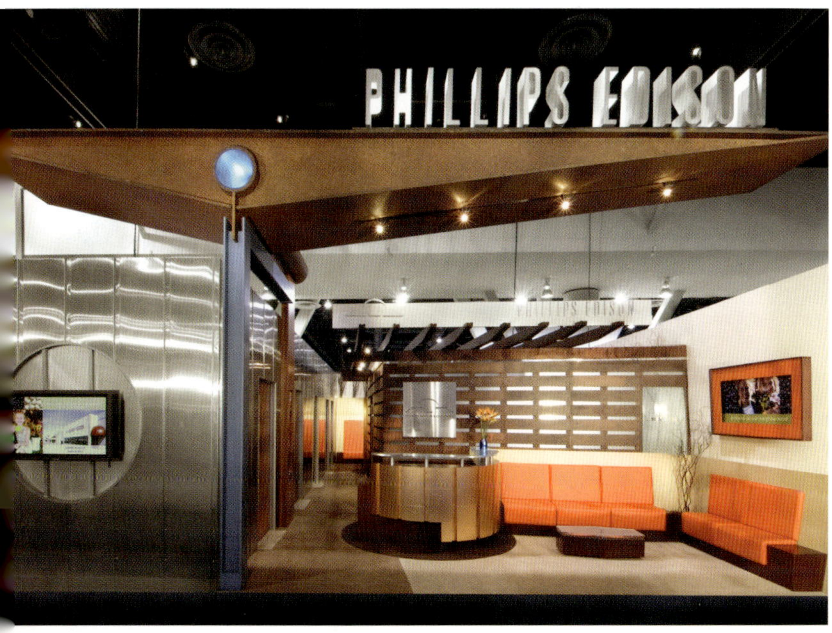

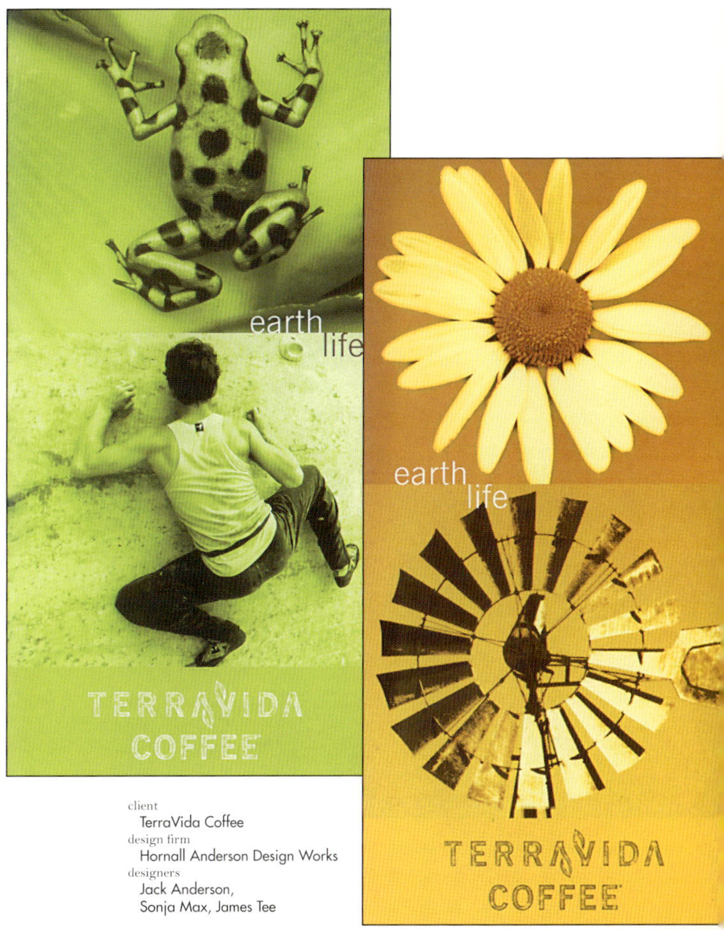

client
TerraVida Coffee
design firm
Hornall Anderson Design Works
designers
Jack Anderson,
Sonja Max, James Tee

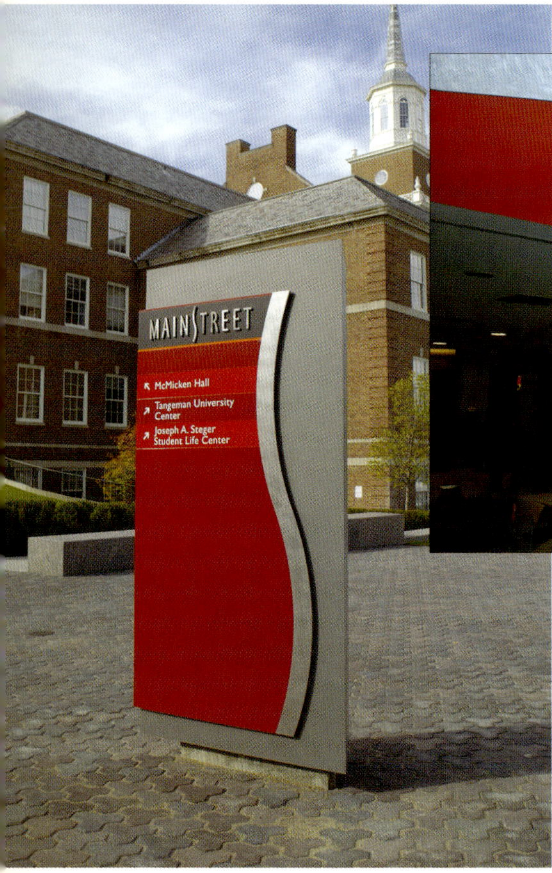

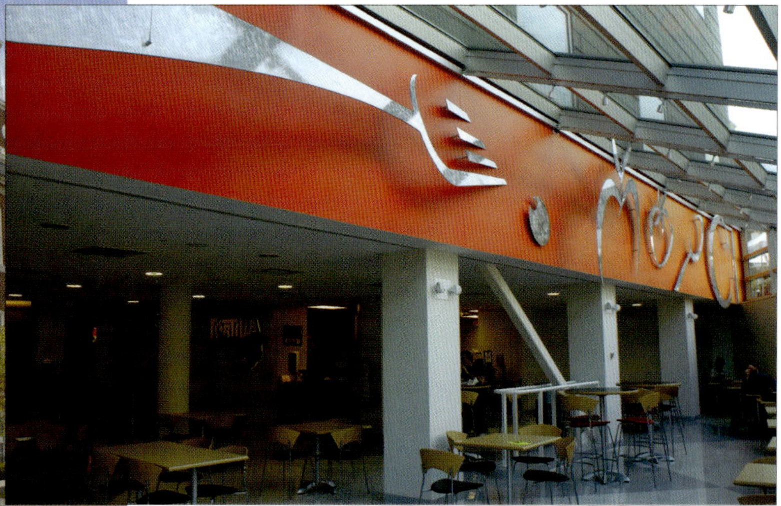

client
University of Cincinnati
design firm
Kolar Design, Inc./Shortt Design
project team
Kelly Kolar, Marcia Shortt, Brent Beck, Maren Carpenter, Donald Carson, Mary Dietrich, Jeff Dudero, David Eyman, Charlie Hartman, Laura Martin, Katy McCormick, Nicole Roberts, Becky Ruehl, Kelly Salchow, TJ Schmidlin, Lori Seibert, Paul Shortt, Ric Snodgrass
consultants
Hargreaves Associates, Moore Ruble Yudel, Morphosis Architects, Glaserworks, KZF Design, Gwathmey Siegel & Associates, GBBN Architects, Leers Weinzapfel Associates, University of Cincinnati Architect's Office

client
Microsoft Corporation
design firm
Hornall Anderson Design Works
designers
Andrew Wicklund, Jay Hilburn, Lauren DiRusso, Chris Freed, Ed Lee

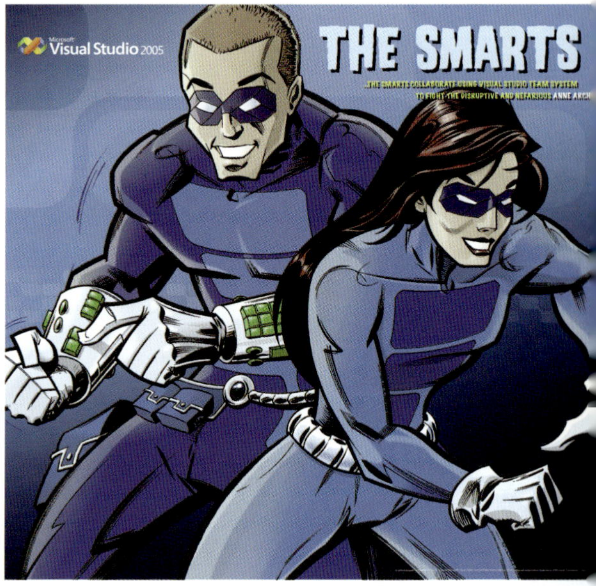

client
National Association of Realtors
design firm
Smith Strategic, Inc./
Beth Singer Design, LLC
designers
Beth Singer, Howard Smith

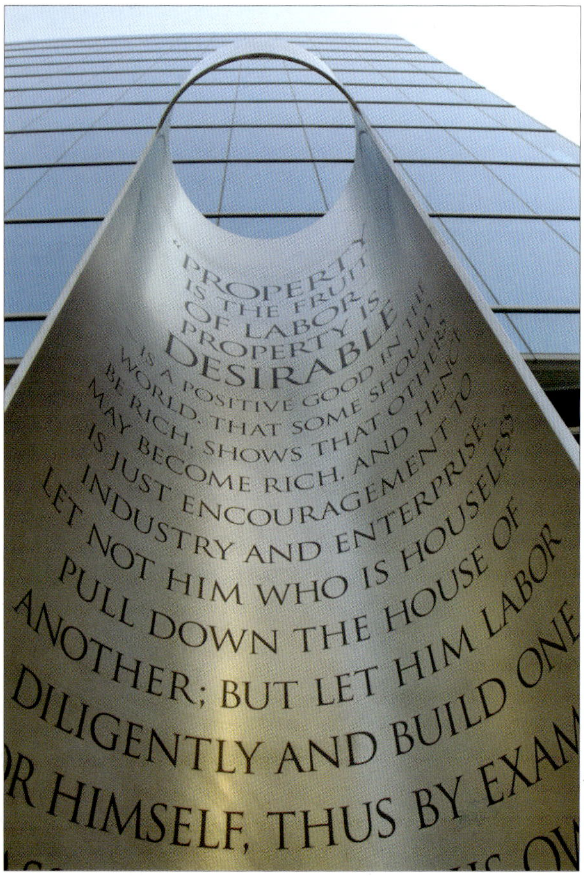

client
Mayo Clinic
design firm
Lorenc + Yoo Design
designers
Jan Lorenc, Chung Youl Yoo, Steve McCall, David Park, Jisun An, Ken Boyd

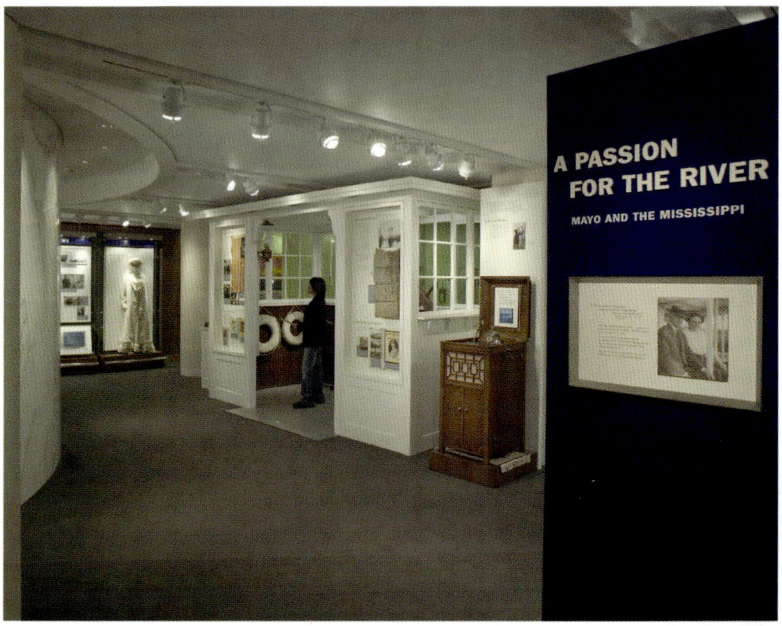

Corporate Image Brochures

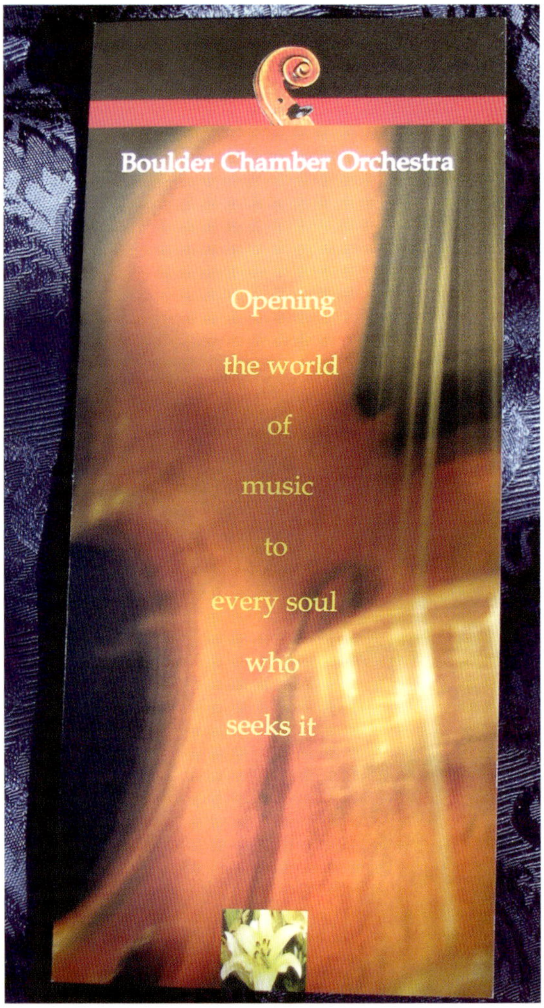

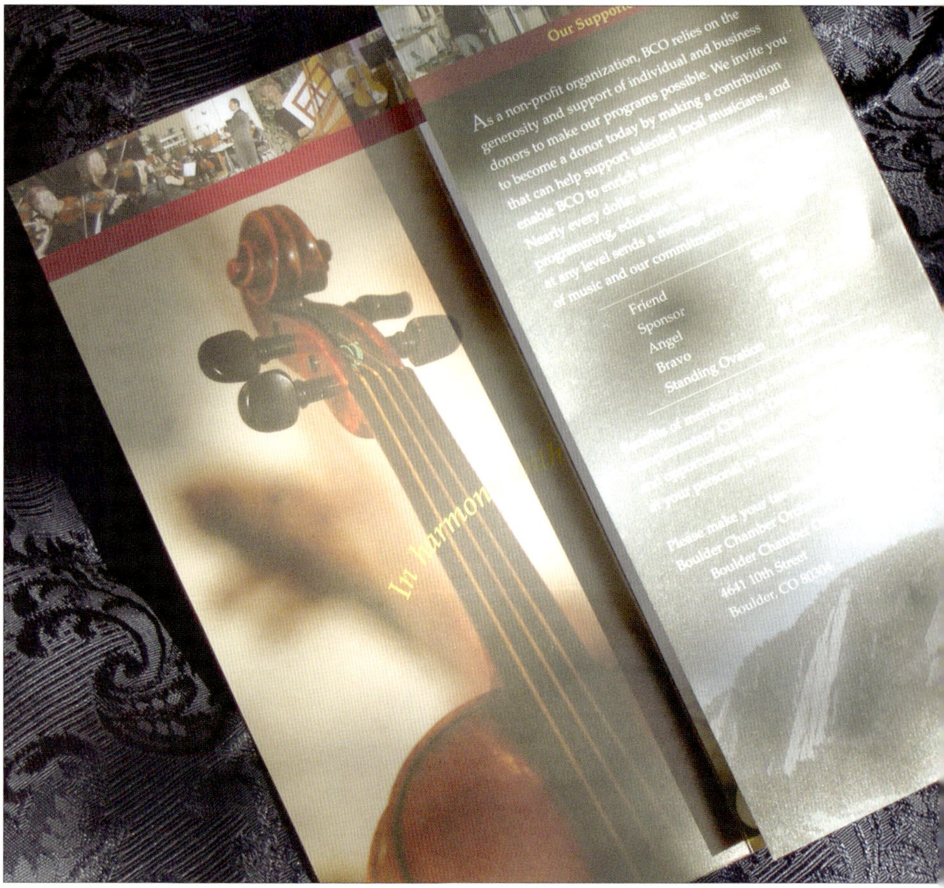

client
Boulder Chamber Orchestra
design firm
Uppercase Design
designer
Justin Deister

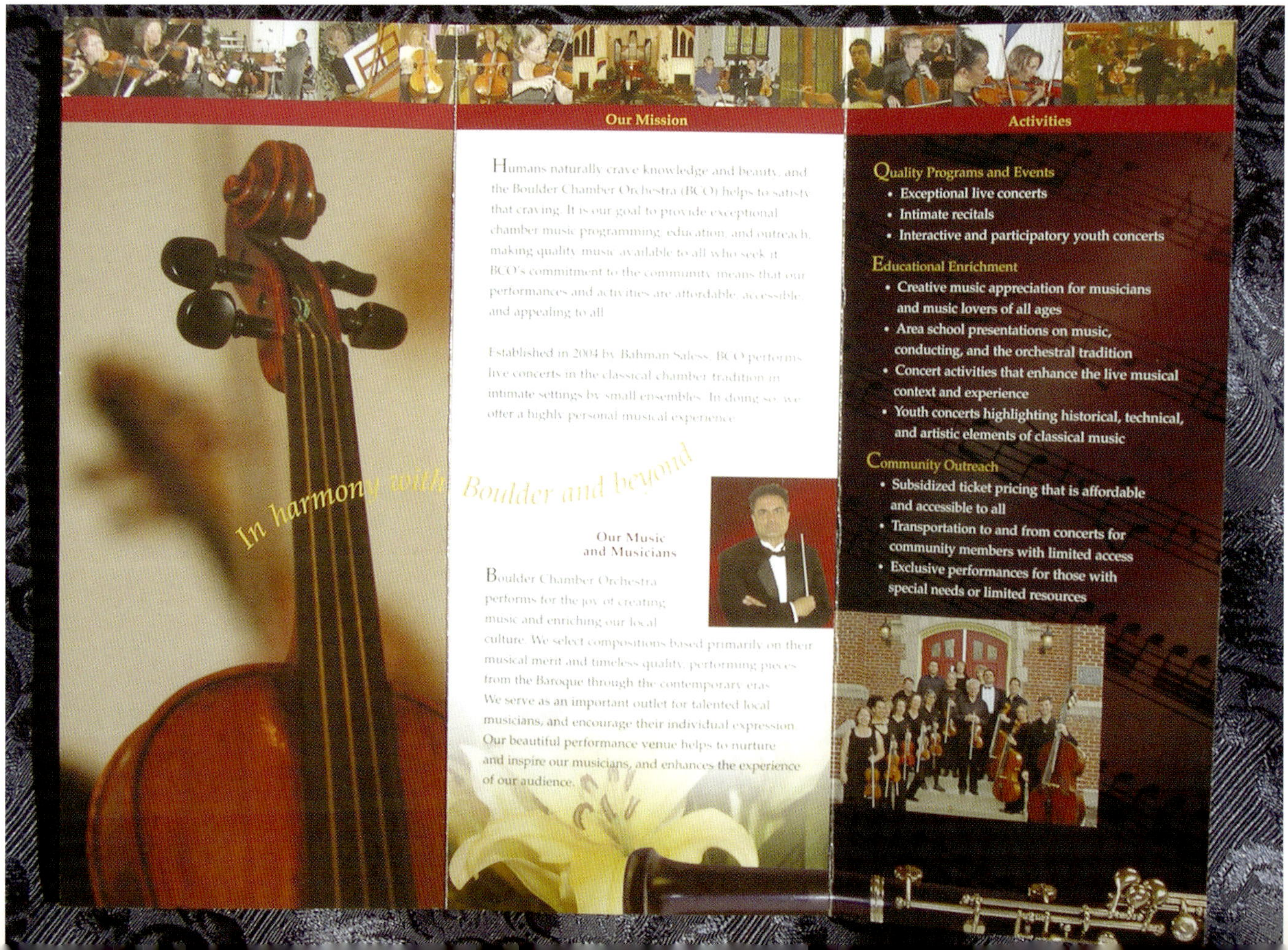

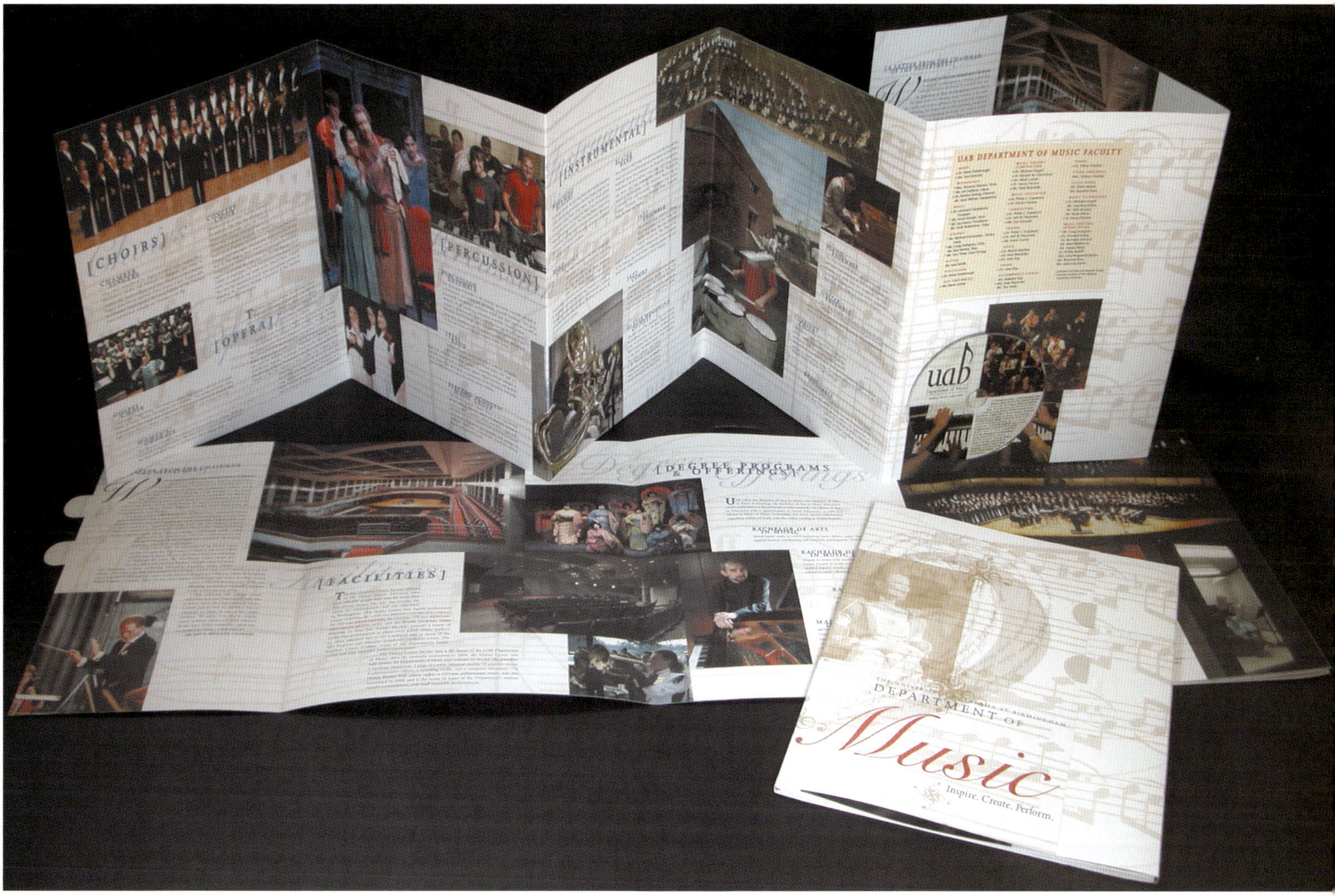

client
University of Alabama at
Birmingham Department of Music
design firm
Audra Buck Design Associates
designer
Audra Buck

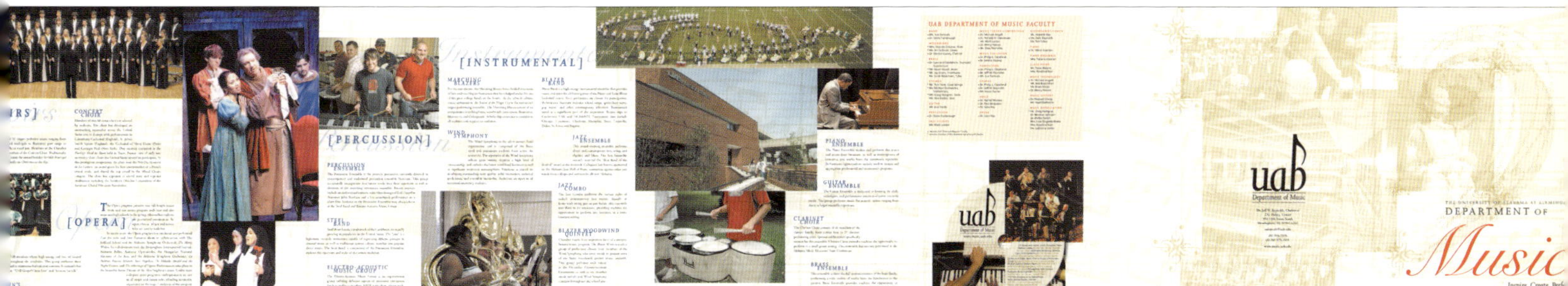

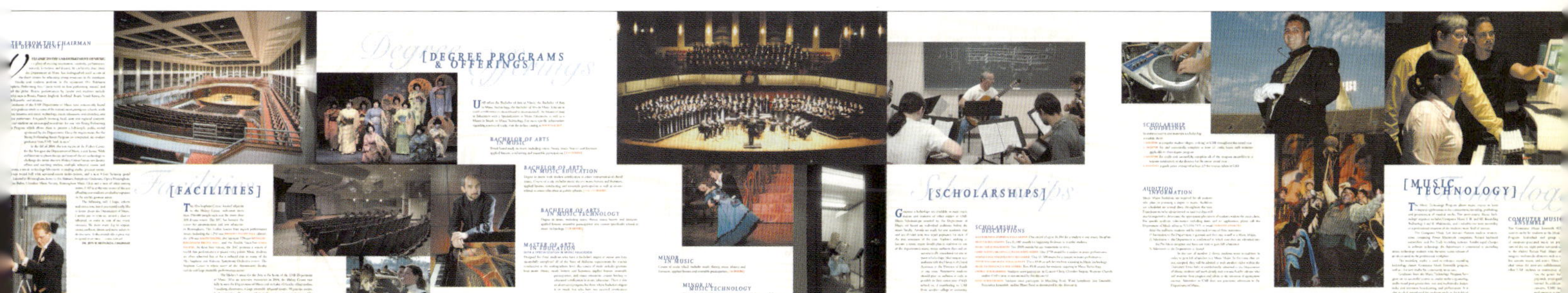

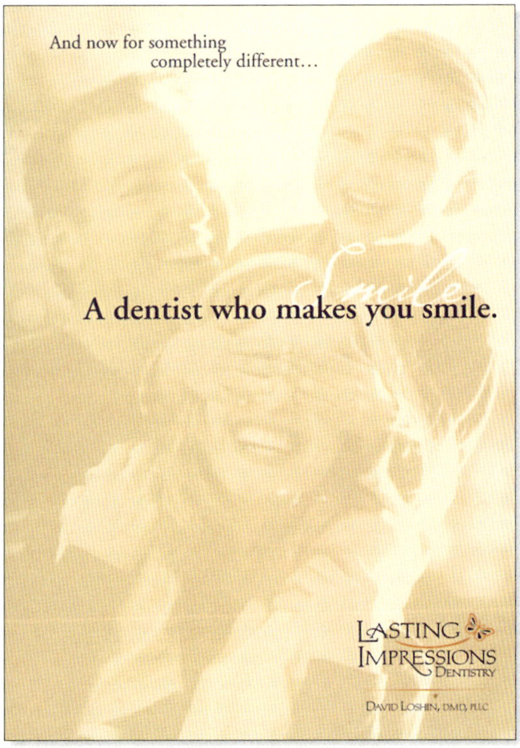

client
Lasting Impressions Dentistry
design firm
Eben Design
designer
Masako Takeda

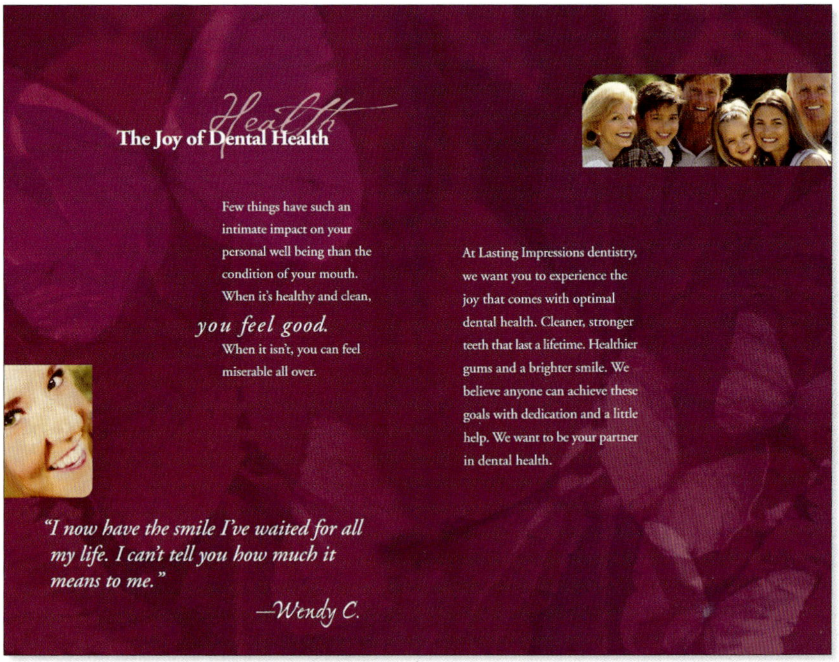

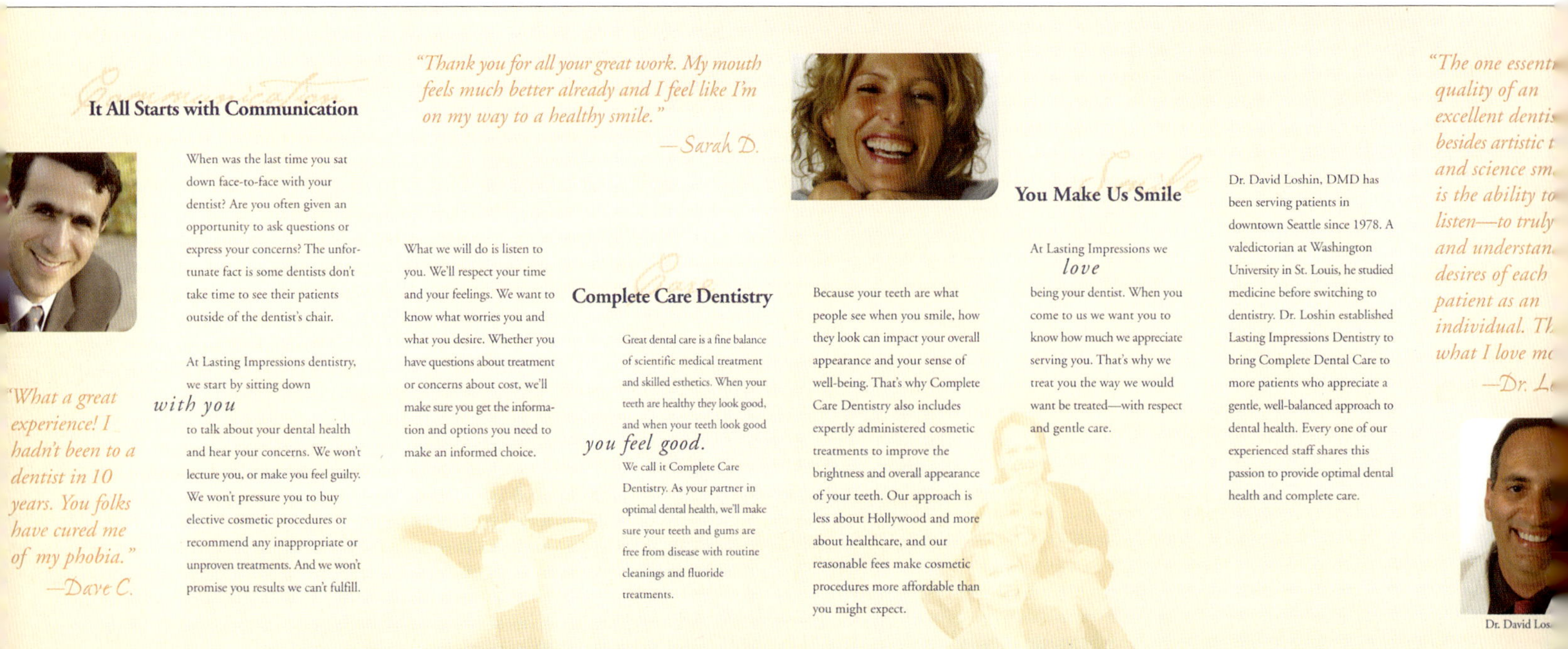

client
Civitas Group
design firm
Kiku Obata + Company
designer
Rich Nelson

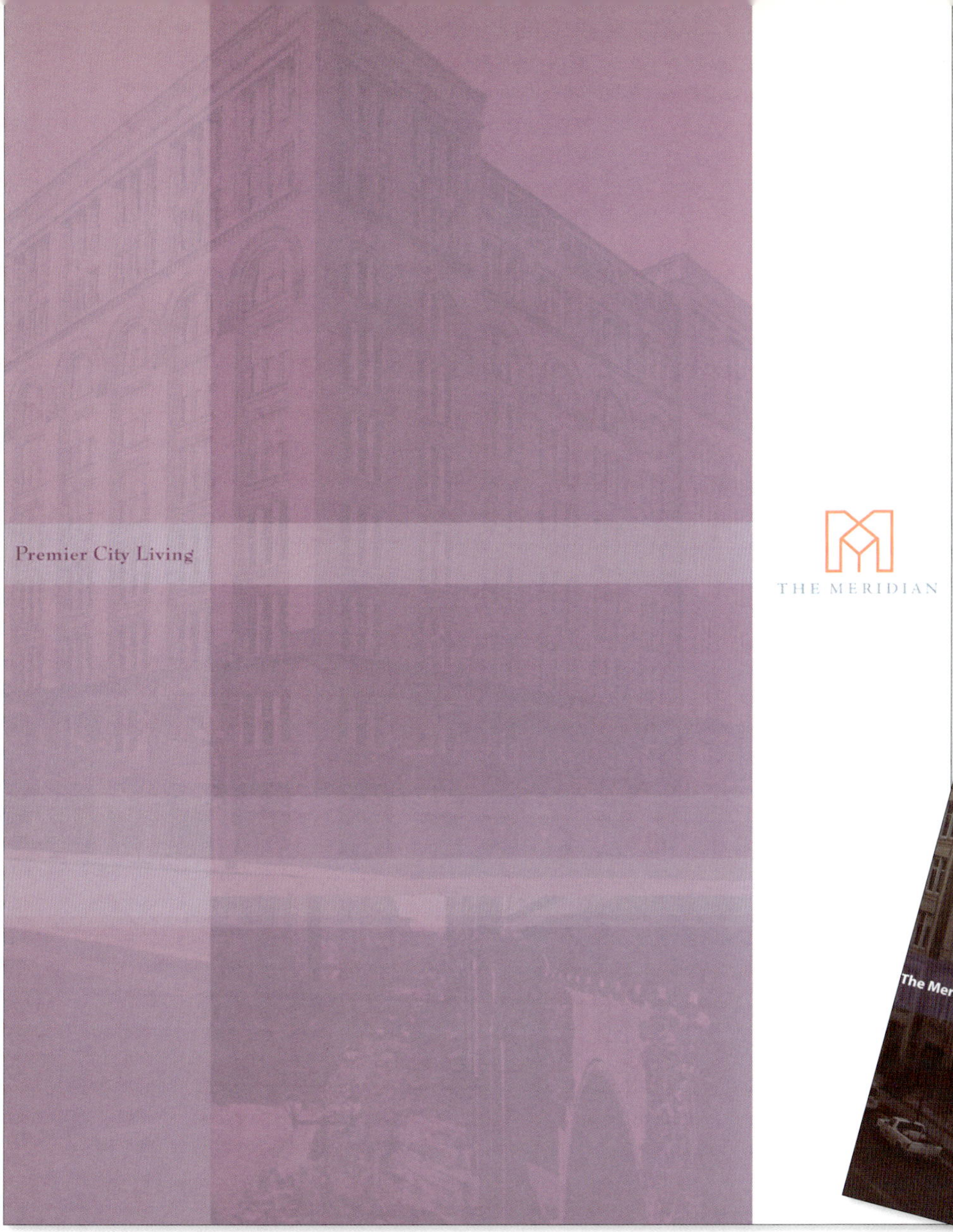

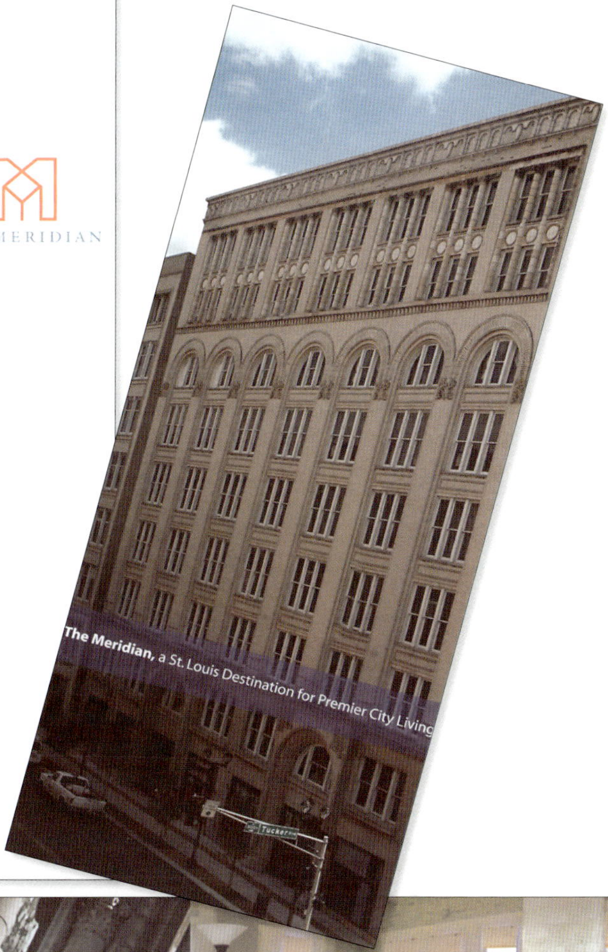

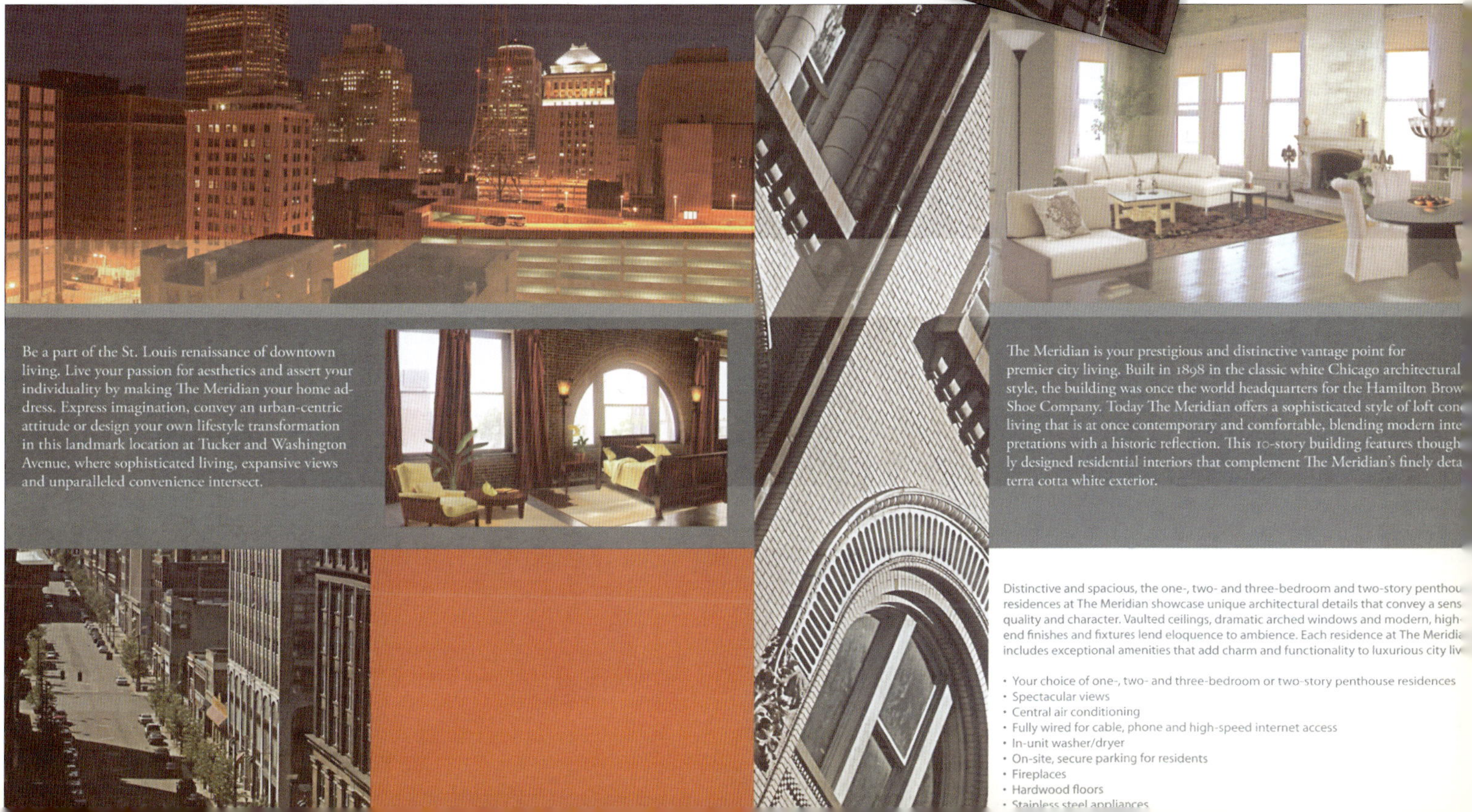

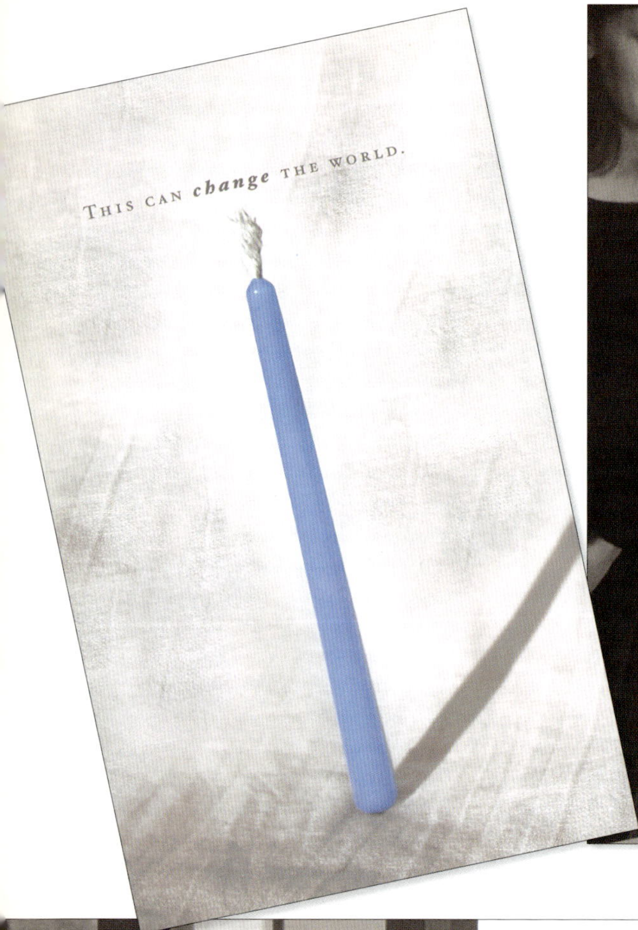

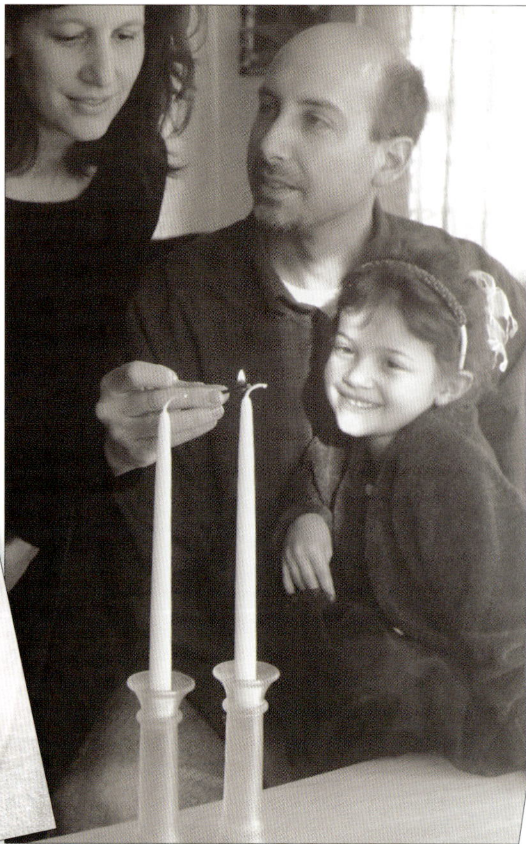

A FLAME *can spread & grow* **POWERFUL.**

Once energized, a flame has the potential to transform what's around it. At the core of aishSeattle is a focus to help Jewish leaders find a sense of community and to see their ability to make a difference within it. Our programs help professionals be a part of an active force in both Seattle and Israel.

-4-

The test of a Jewish leader is not to push away darkness, it is to ... using their light.

KESHER@MICROSOFT

A project of aishSeattle to engage over 2,000 Jewish employees on Microsoft's campus

KESHER@MICROSOFT is committed to strengthening the Jewish community by educating leaders from the pool of exceptionally bright and talented young Jewish employees at Microsoft:

CONNECTING them to Judaism's core values

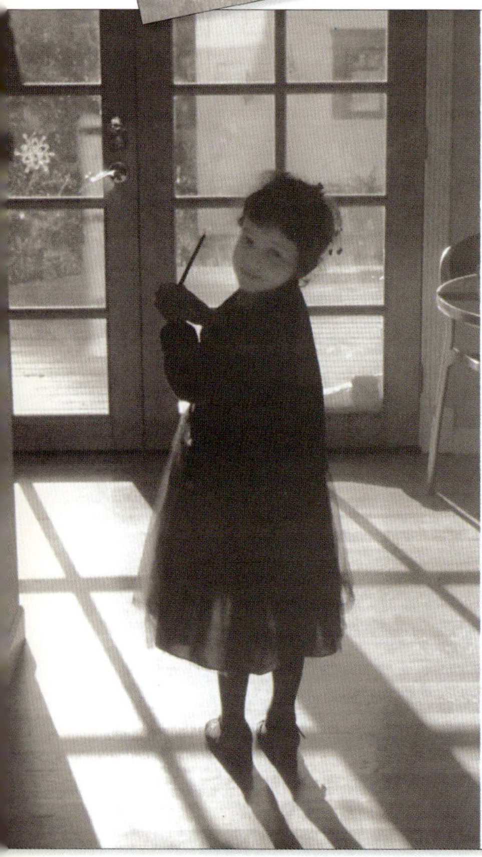

-1-

Ignite the **SPARK**

aishSeattle's Jewish Family Institute is a traditionally observant organization dedicated to connecting individuals to relevant Judaism and the Jewish community in both Seattle and Israel. If you determine the JFI merits your partnership, please help us build a community of young Jewish people who are fanning the spark to change the world.

Learning is recognizing for the first time something you knew to be true your whole life.

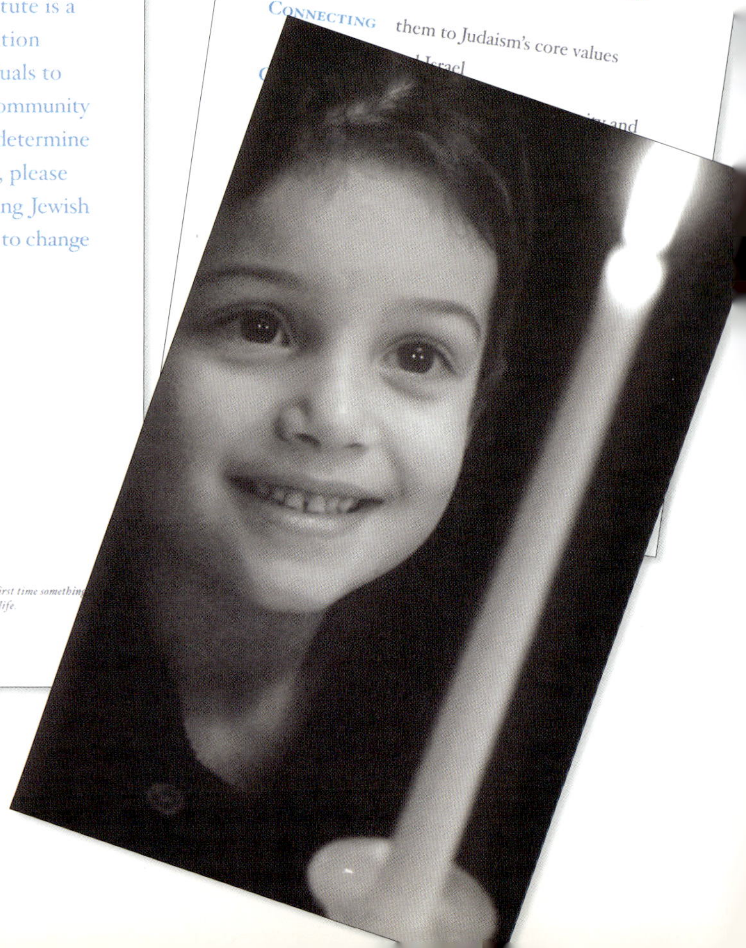

client
aishSeattle
design firm
Hornall Anderson Design Works
designers
Jack Anderson, Yuri Shvets, Katha Dalton

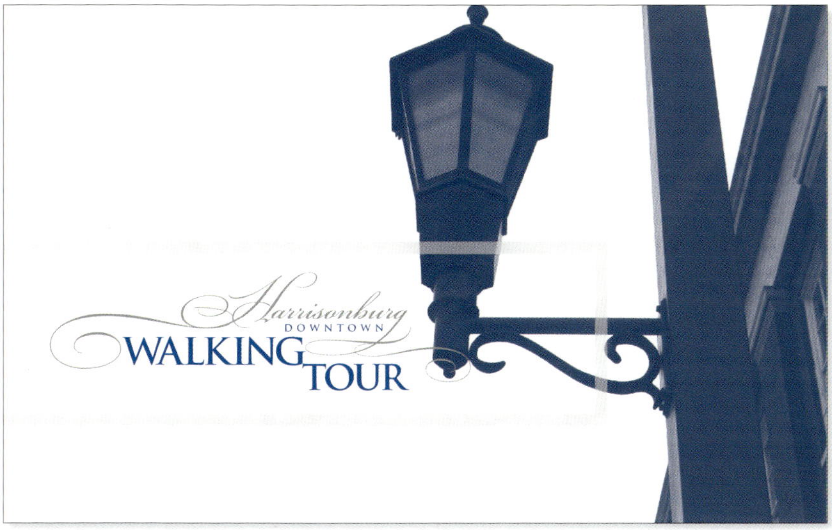

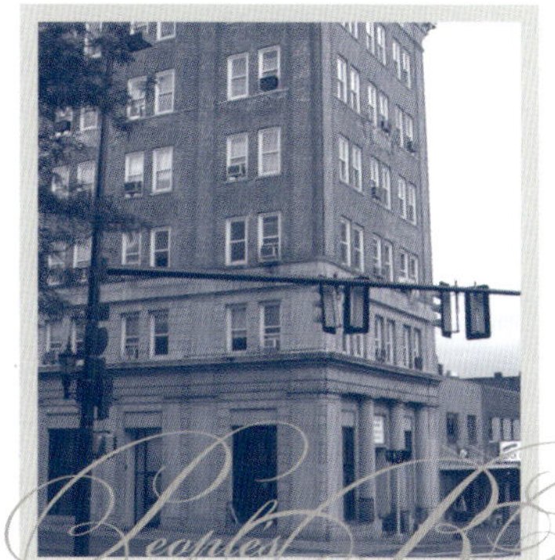

PEOPLE'S BANK BUILDING

2 South Main Street

This six-story corner building opened in 1916 as The People's Bank. Designed by Alfred Charles Bossom of New York, the architect was one of the pioneer skyscraper builders in America. The structure, with an elaborate cornice and floral patterns on the Main Street side, was Valley National Bank's headquarters until the 1960s. The Rockingham County school system had administrative offices in the building for years before selling the structure recently. The current owner may use the building for offices and residences.

People's Bank Building

NEWMAN-RUDDLE BUILDING

2 North Main Street

With its arched windows and first use in Harrisonburg of structured steel, the corner building opened as Rockingham National Bank in 1900. The bank moved down the street in 1943. In 1939 the third floor became the home of WSVA, the first radio station in the area. Don Ruddle of nearby Singers Glen bought the building in 1946 for $75,000. The ground floor has had various uses, including restaurants and a church. A restaurant fills the space now.

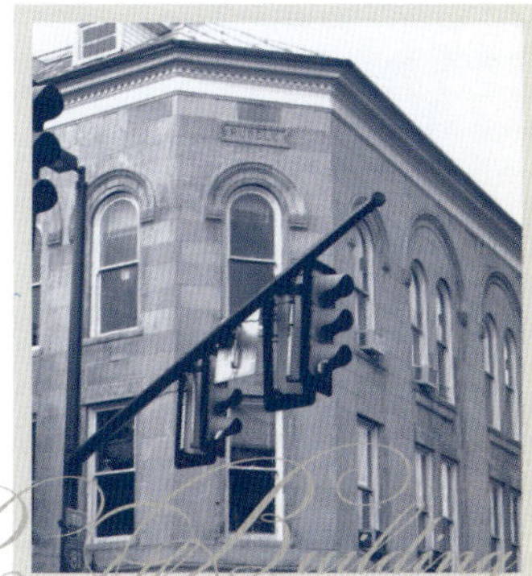

Newman Ruddle Building

HARRISONBURG MUNICIPAL BUILDING

345 South Main Street

This bluestone building designed by Charles M. Robinson of Richmond was constructed in 1908 as Harrisonburg High School and used for that purpose until 1928, when the structure became an elementary school. The brick building attached to the rear dates to 1879 and was also a school. Since about 1960, the building has housed city offices. In the early 1800s, the tract had a barn for stagecoach horses, and shortly before the Civil War, this was the site of a school for girls.

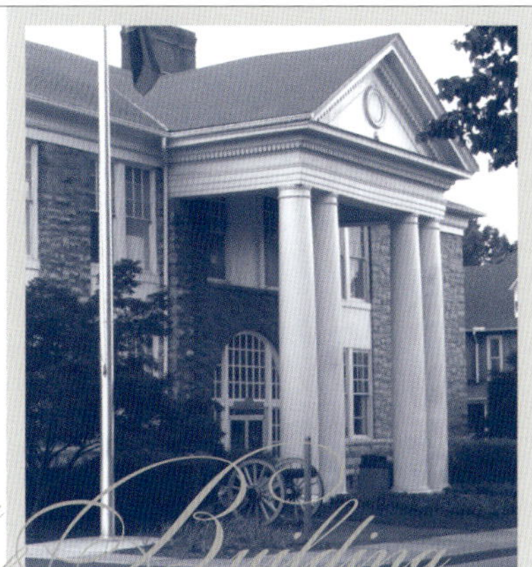

Harrisonburg Municipal Building

client
Harrisonburg City
design firm
Grafix Dezine
designer
Oleg Yagolnikov

least the late 1800s, is the Square. The building was T.J. Collins. Members of the Grattan family in the 1800s and early 1900s including a judge, George G. Grattan, and lawyer George G. Grattan II, occupied the building. A real estate company is in the building now.

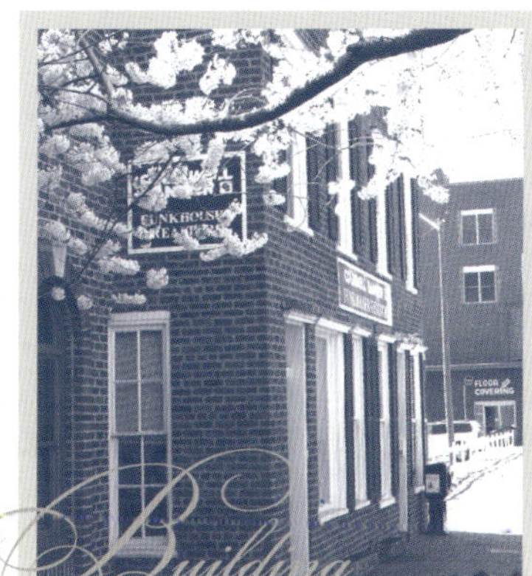

Grattan Building

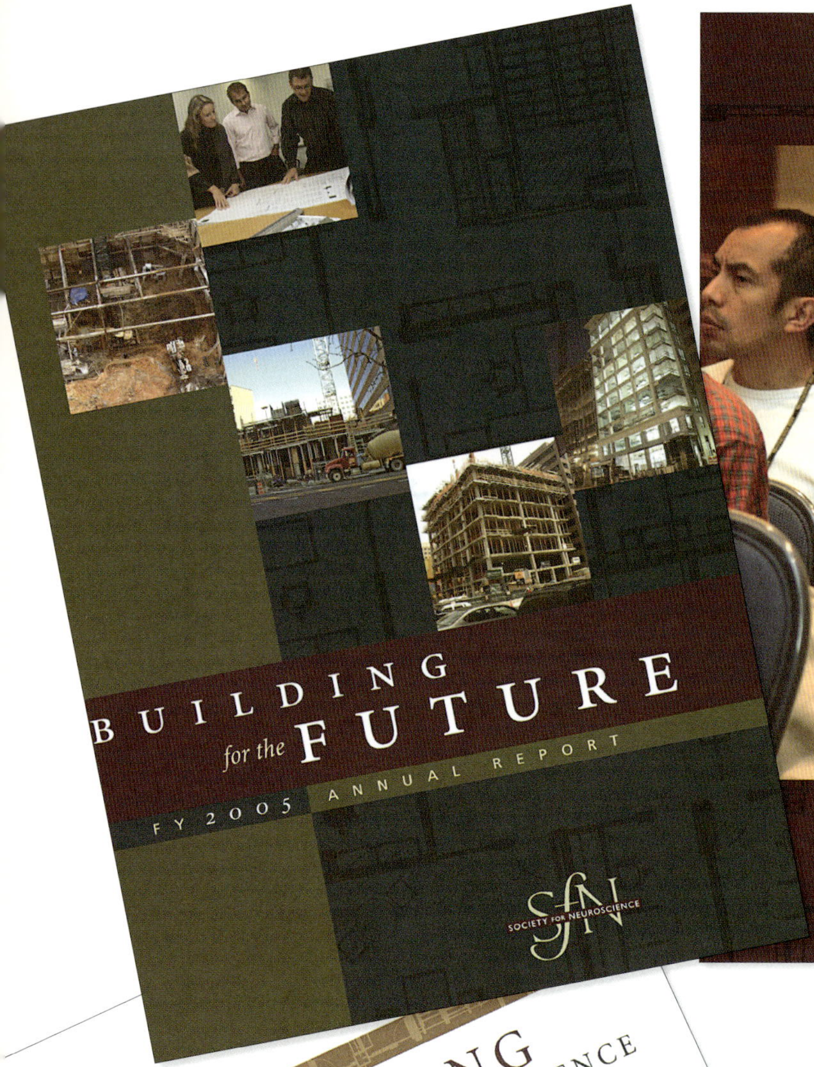

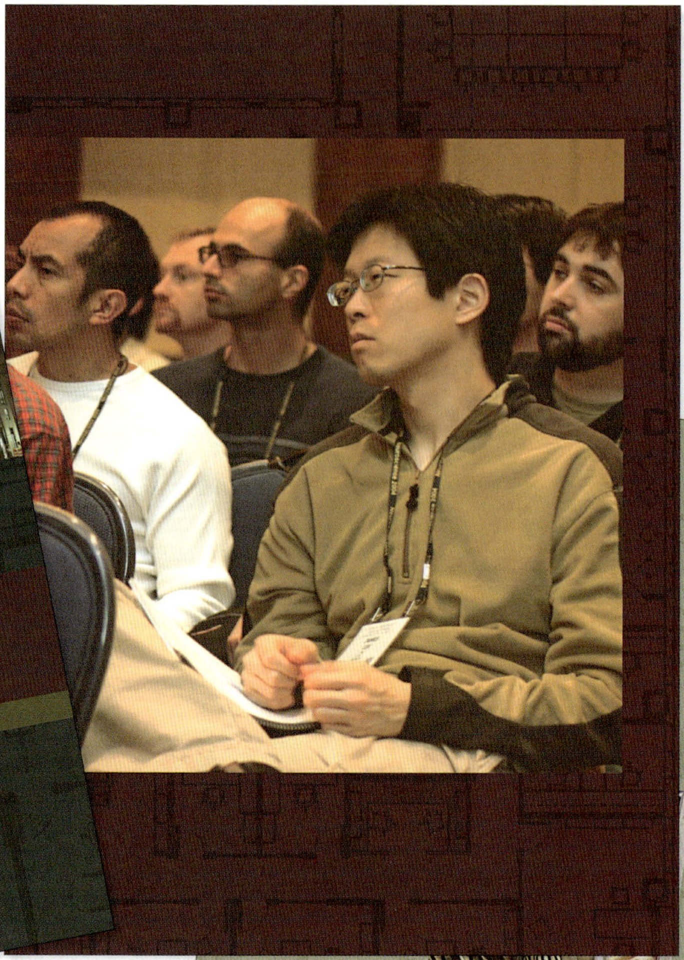

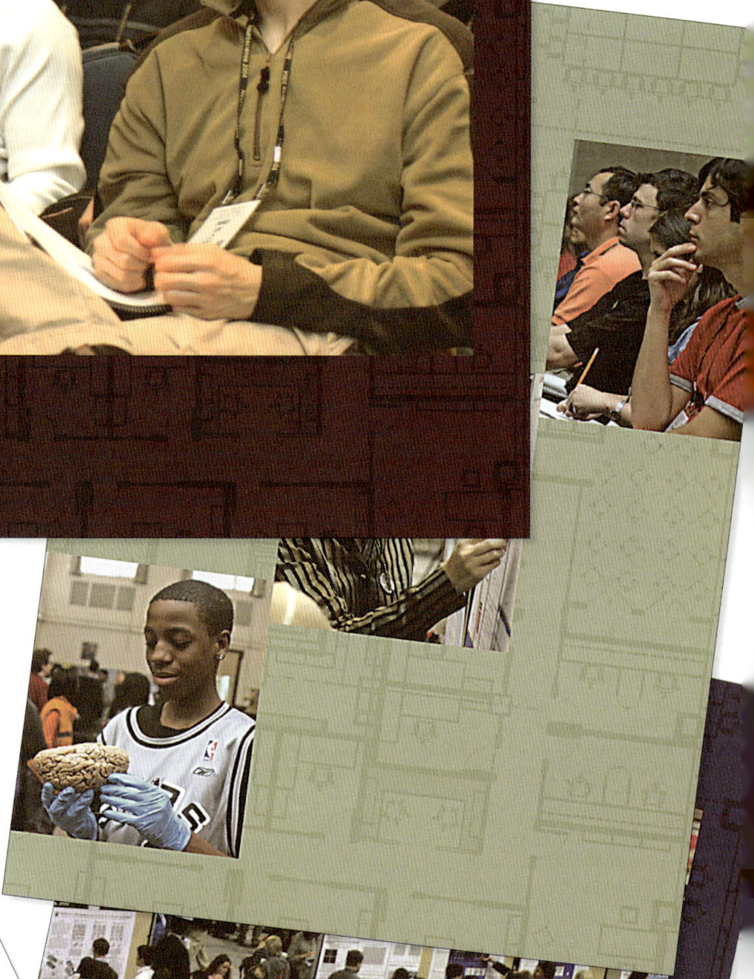

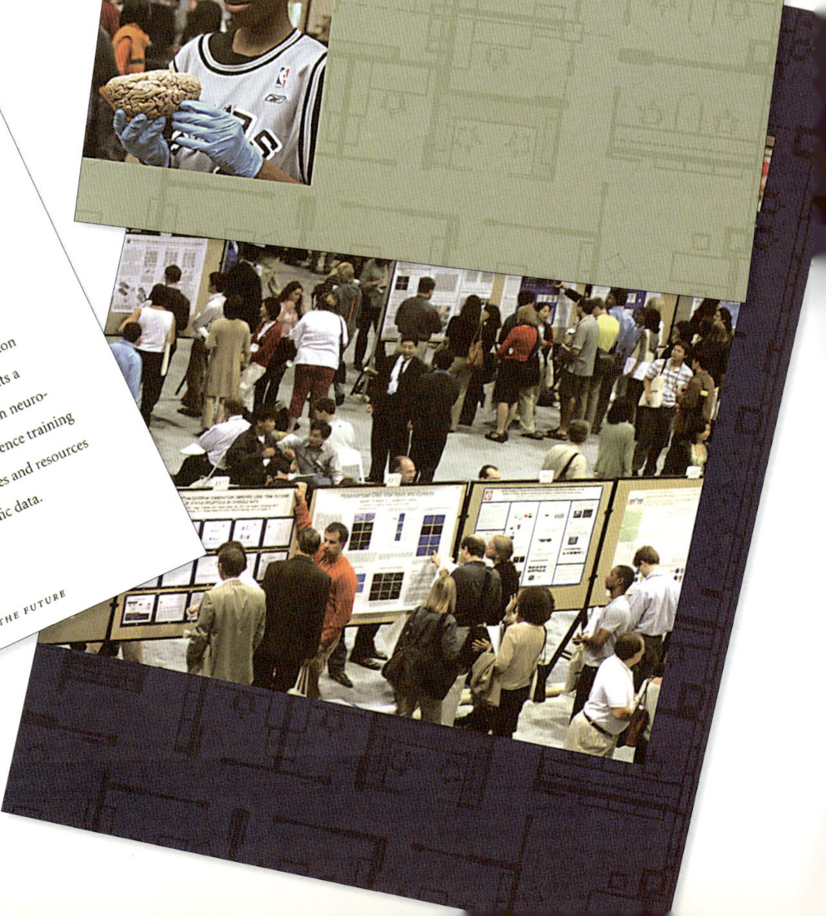

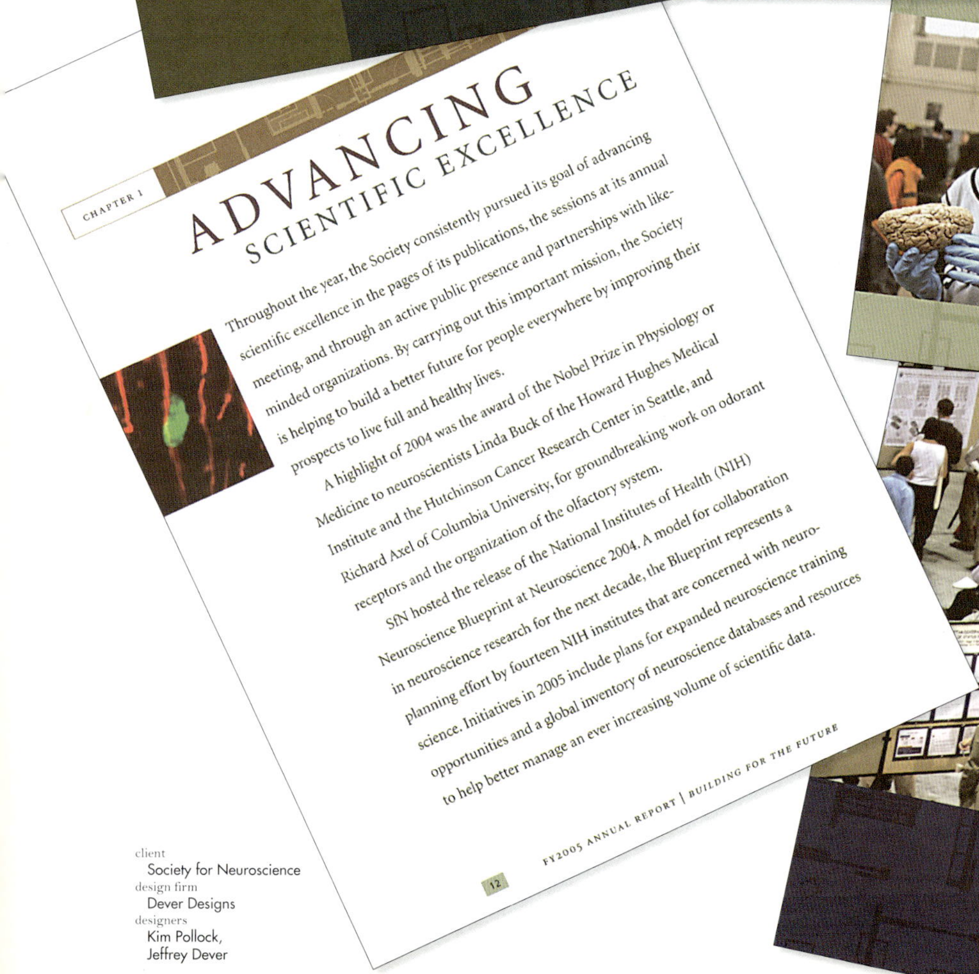

CHAPTER 1

ADVANCING
SCIENTIFIC EXCELLENCE

Throughout the year, the Society consistently pursued its goal of advancing scientific excellence in the pages of its publications, the sessions at its annual meeting, and through an active public presence and partnerships with like-minded organizations. By carrying out this important mission, the Society is helping to build a better future for people everywhere by improving their prospects to live full and healthy lives.

A highlight of 2004 was the award of the Nobel Prize in Physiology or Medicine to neuroscientists Linda Buck of the Howard Hughes Medical Institute and the Hutchinson Cancer Research Center in Seattle, and Richard Axel of Columbia University, for groundbreaking work on odorant receptors and the organization of the olfactory system.

SfN hosted the release of the National Institutes of Health (NIH) Neuroscience Blueprint at Neuroscience 2004. A model for collaboration in neuroscience research for the next decade, the Blueprint represents a planning effort by fourteen NIH institutes that are concerned with neuroscience. Initiatives in 2005 include plans for expanded neuroscience training opportunities and a global inventory of neuroscience databases and resources to help better manage an ever increasing volume of scientific data.

12 FY2005 ANNUAL REPORT | BUILDING FOR THE FUTURE

client
Society for Neuroscience
design firm
Dever Designs
designers
Kim Pollock,
Jeffrey Dever

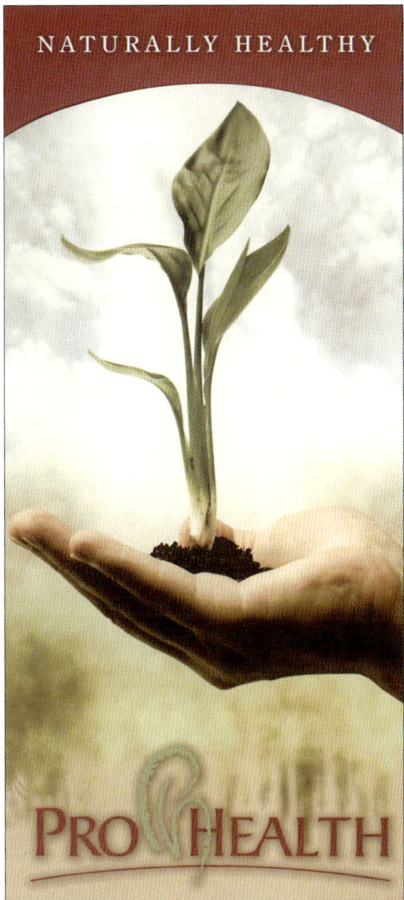

client
Pro-Health
design firm
Duncan/Day Advertising
designer
Leigh Finney

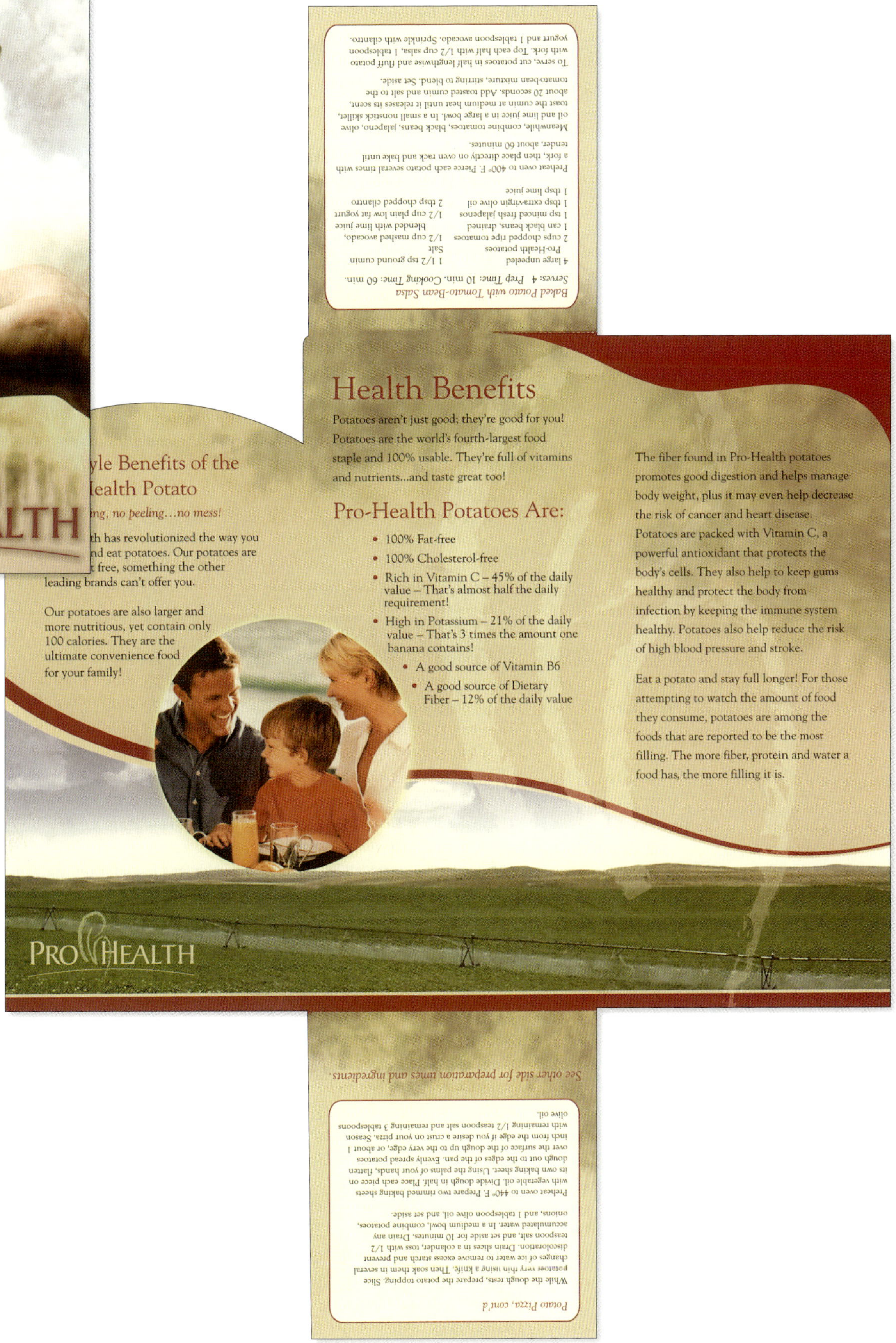

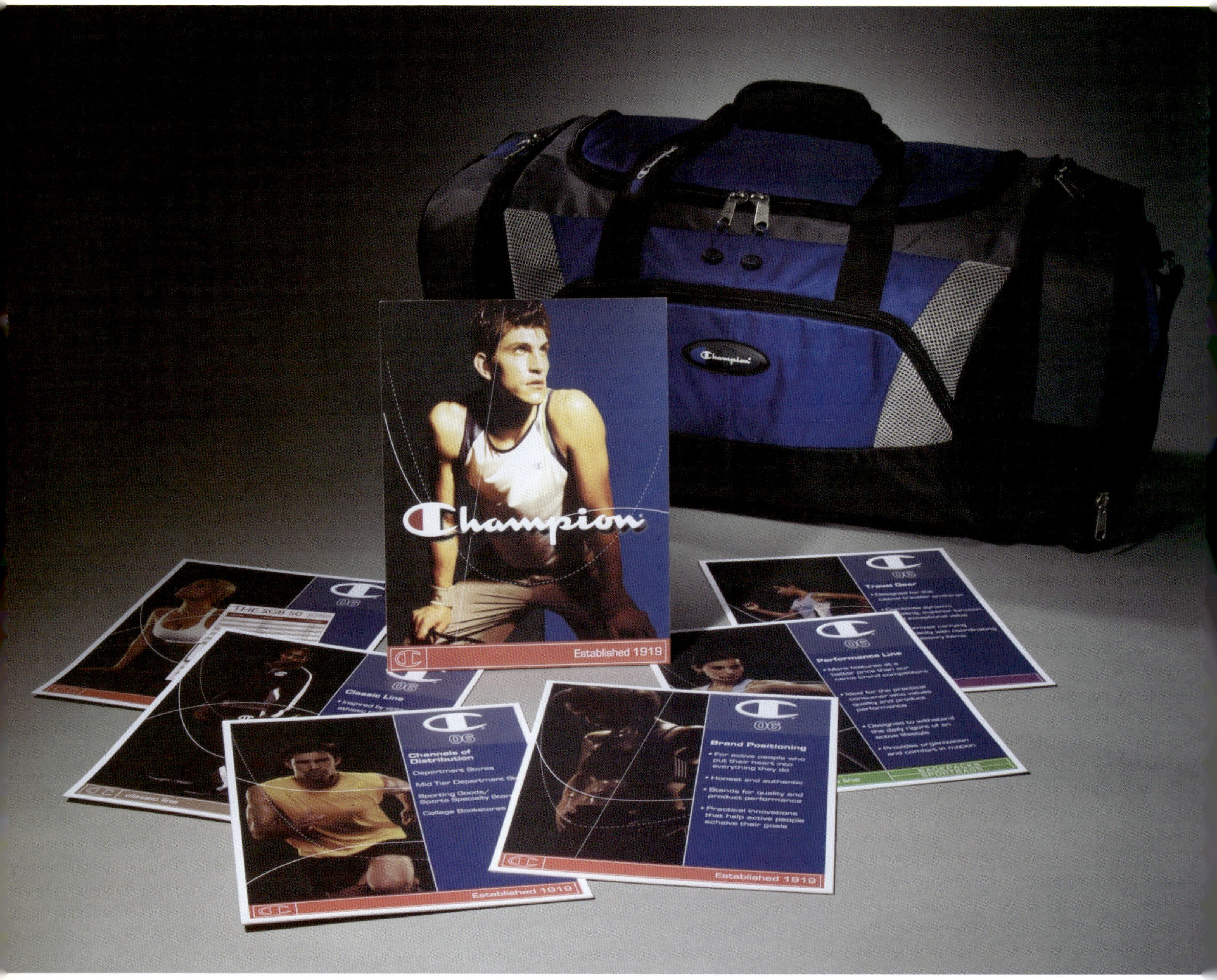

client
Champion®
design firm
InGEAR In-House Design Department
senior designer
Jeremy Swanson
marketing team
Tom Hinkle, Michelle Varland, Sarah Paikai, Julie Garwood, Heather Tvrdik

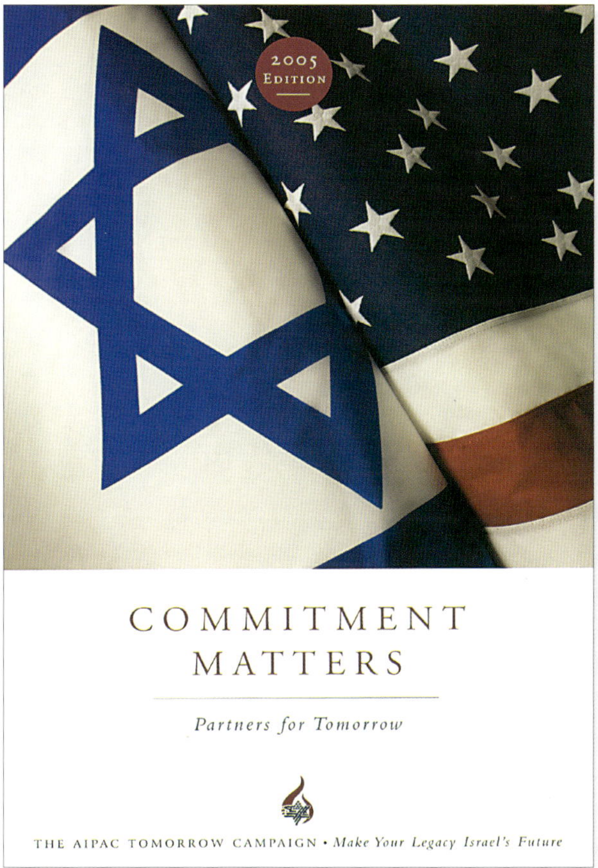

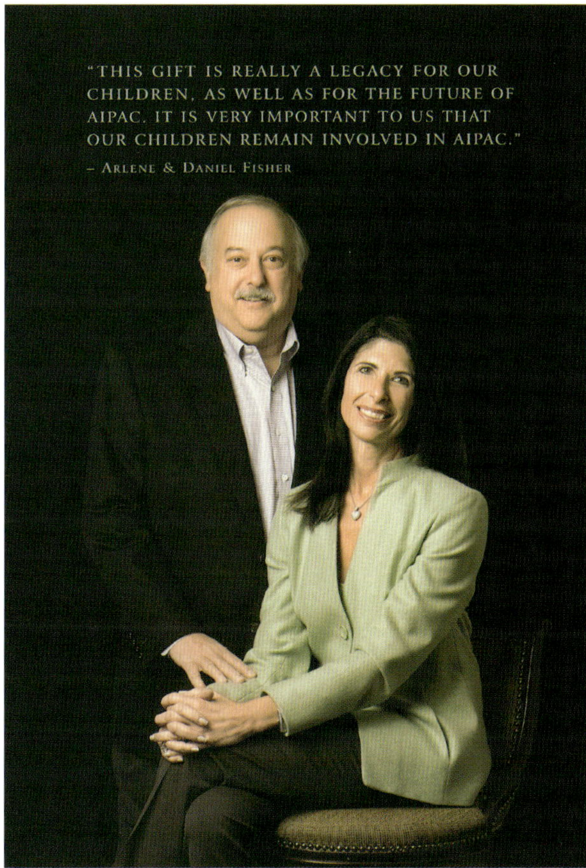

client
American Israel Public Affairs Committee
design firm
Beth Singer Design, LLC
designer
Sucha Snidvongs

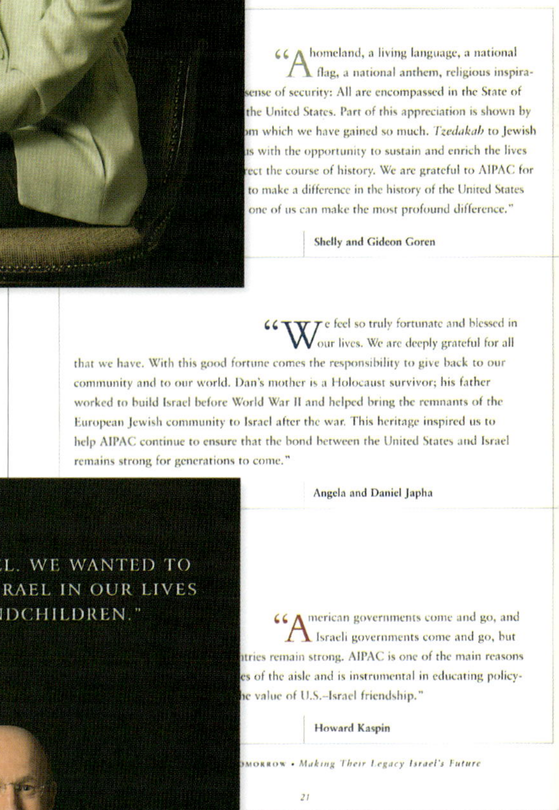

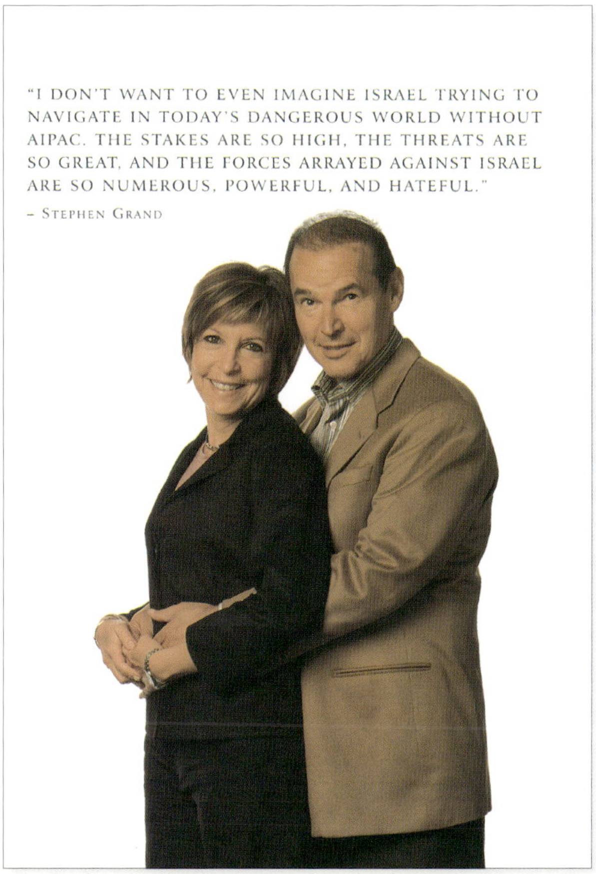

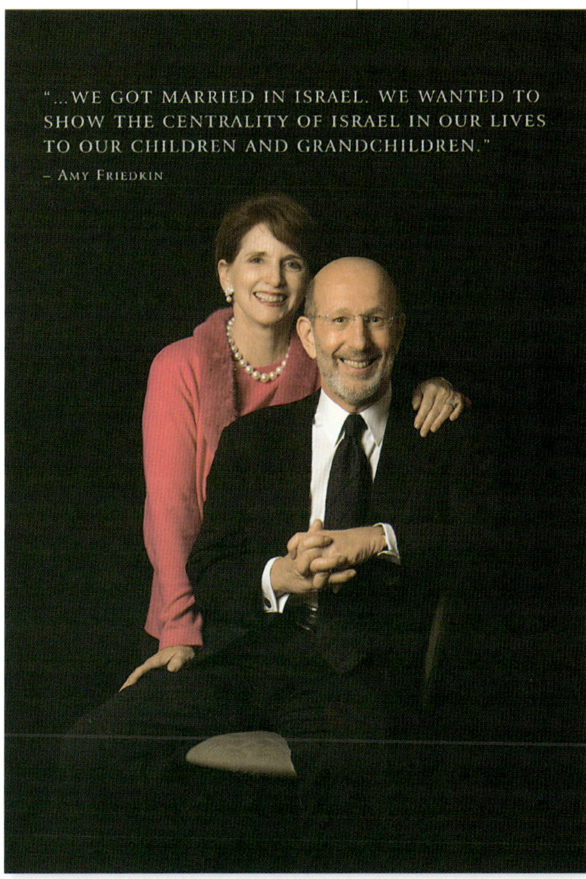

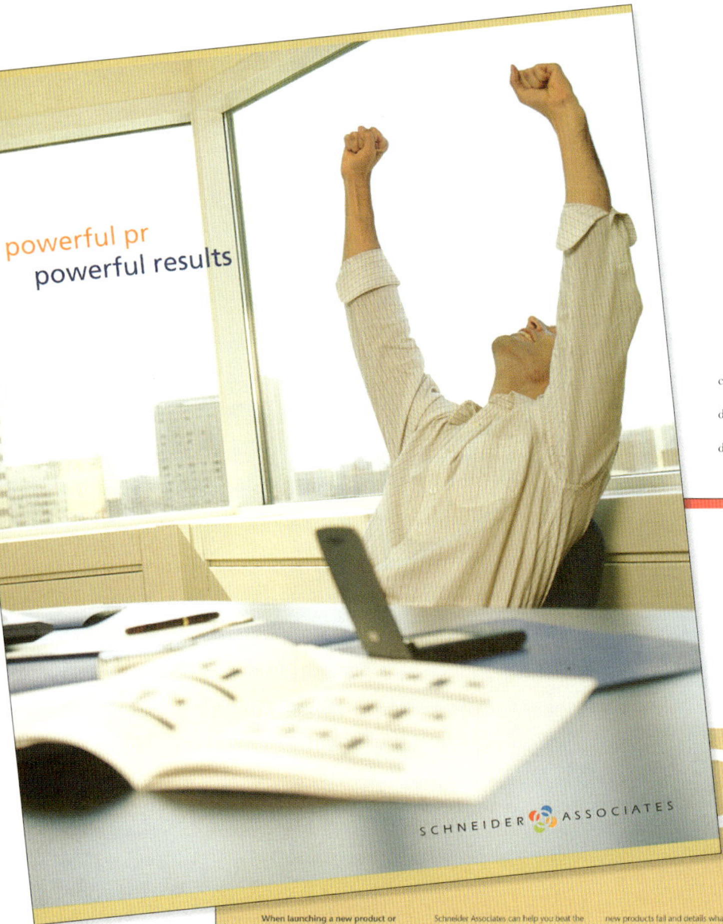

client
Schneider
design firm
Gill Fishman Associates
designer
Alicia Ozyjowski

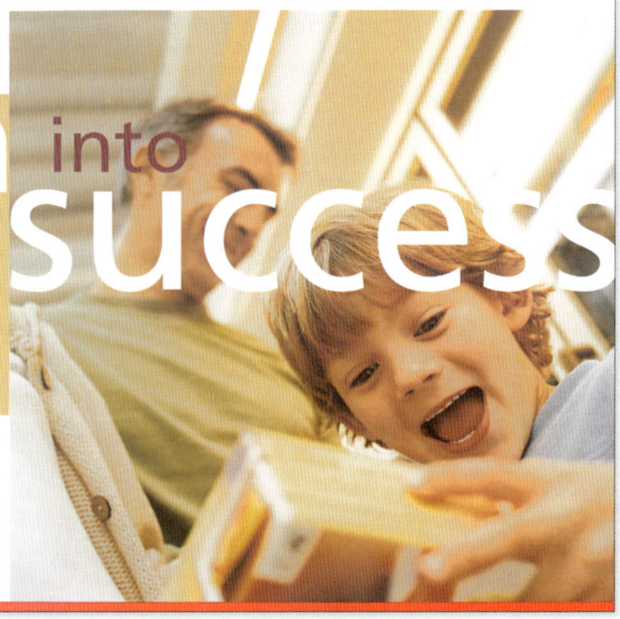

In a burger and fries world, Subway® Restaurants stand out as the healthy alternative to traditional fatty fast foods. Schneider Associates launched the Subway partnership with the American Heart Association's Heart Walks and generated media attention for weight-loss hero, Jared Fogle. We helped craft Subway's childhood obesity prevention program and worked with Jared to create The Jared Foundation, a non-profit organization helping kids live healthy, active lives.

ch into success

When launching a new product or service, it's critical to get it right the first time.

Through proprietary research, a proven track record and authoring a definitive book, Schneider Associates has researched the factors that propel new products to success. In the recent Schneider/Stagnito Most Memorable New Product Launch Survey, 51% of respondents said they are "always looking for new products to try." At the same time, 50% of consumers could not remember a single product launched the previous year.

Schneider Associates can help you beat the high new product failure rate – and create excitement for your product before, during, and after the launch.

Schneider Associates' own Launch Public Relations℠ process propels a product, service or company into the marketplace and sustains it over time, leading to increased market share in today's crowded marketplace.

We wrote the book on launch.

Schneider Associates has unique expertise in launch – we wrote the book on it. *New Product Launch: 10 Proven Strategies* by Joan Schneider addresses why 75% of new products fail and details what factors lead to launch success. Our multi-disciplinary approach is based on groundbreaking research, scores of case histories and revealing interviews with high-level marketing executives.

We practice what we preach.

Our proven Countdown to Launch™ process has propelled scores of new products and services into the marketplace. We apply this methodology to ensure your launch captures the attention of your target customers – and sustains it over time.

TEN

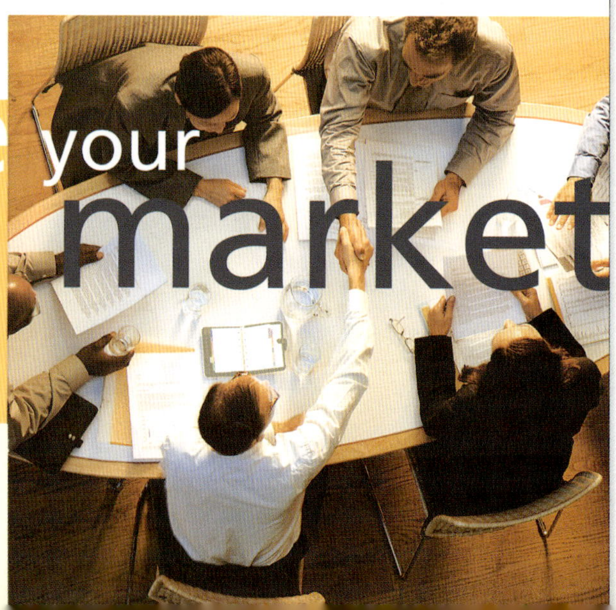

> CORPORATE COMMUNICATIONS SERVICES

When Reebok consolidated its facilities into a 522,000 sq. ft. new world headquarters in Canton, MA, Schneider Associates publicized the merits of unifying Reebok's workforce. As stories appeared in the national and international press, Reebok's stock rose. Media coverage about the new headquarters extolled Reebok's forward thinking, strength and ability to evolve.

capture your market

If you're marketing to other businesses, we know how demanding your customers can be. The competition is fierce and unrelenting.

At Schneider Associates we pride ourselves in quickly understanding business dynamics. We use public relations to craft powerful business solutions to marketing challenges. Schneider Associates helps capture your market by reinforcing credibility and establishing company experts as industry thought leaders.

We've assisted clients in professional services, financial services, biotechnology, technology and manufacturing to stay ahead of the game in an ever-changing competitive landscape.

Turning inquiries into clients.

Our Corporate Communications team has increased awareness to jumpstart business for builders, brokers, mortgage bankers, architects, engineers, entrepreneurs and other professional service visionaries. Our success stems from a deep understanding of business strategy and experience in influencing key stakeholders.

We have strong relationships with the business and trade press, and we understand where the media's needs intersect with client goals.

Our job isn't finished when an article is published or a seminar is well-attended. Our work is complete only when the articles or seminars produce leads and create new clients. Your communications goals are paramount – and our obligation is to continually produce outstanding, measurable results.

SIX

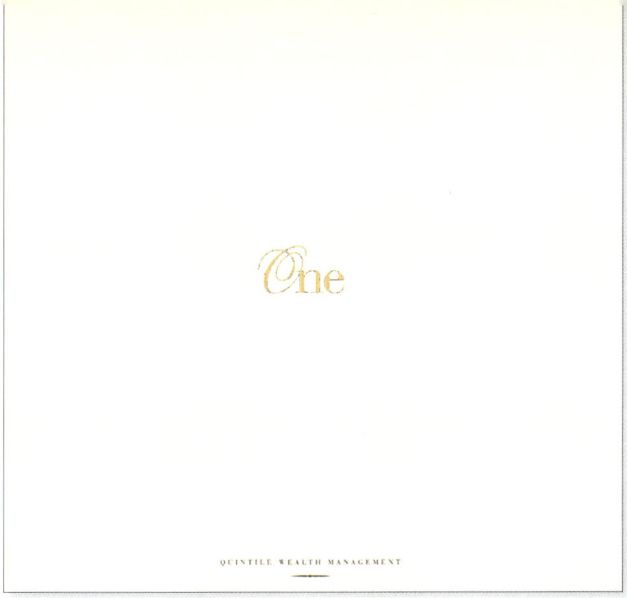

client
Quintile Wealth Management
design firm
IE Design + Communications
designers
Cya Nelson,
Marcie Carson

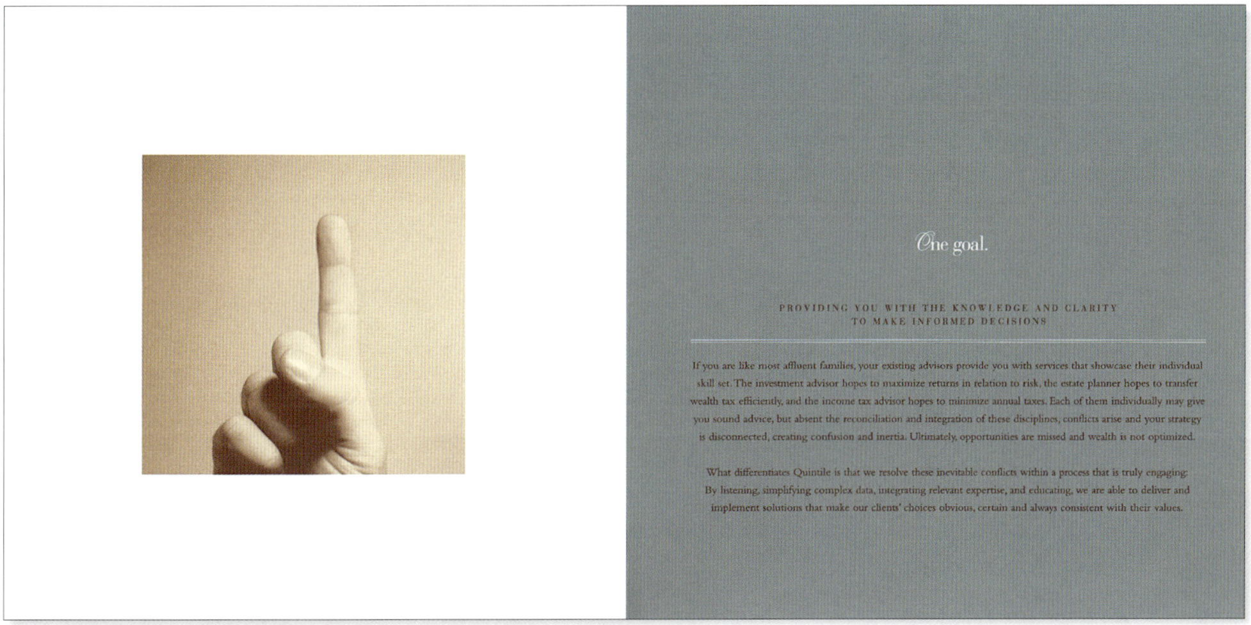

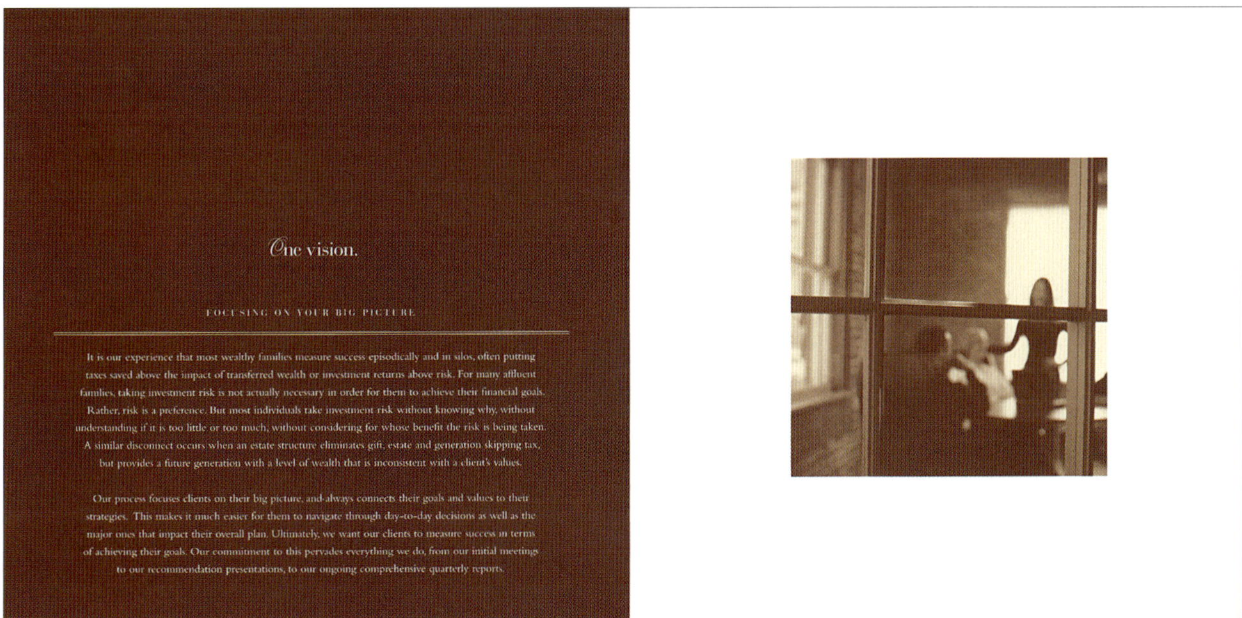

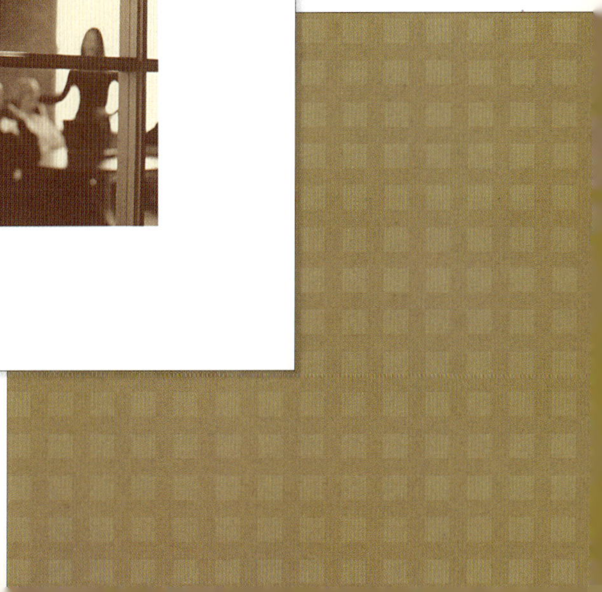

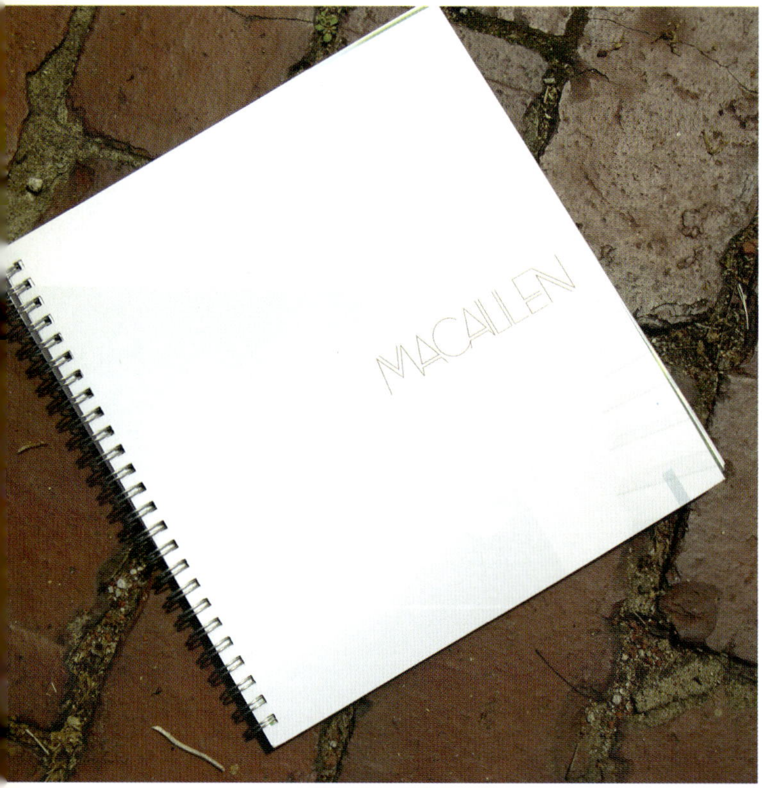

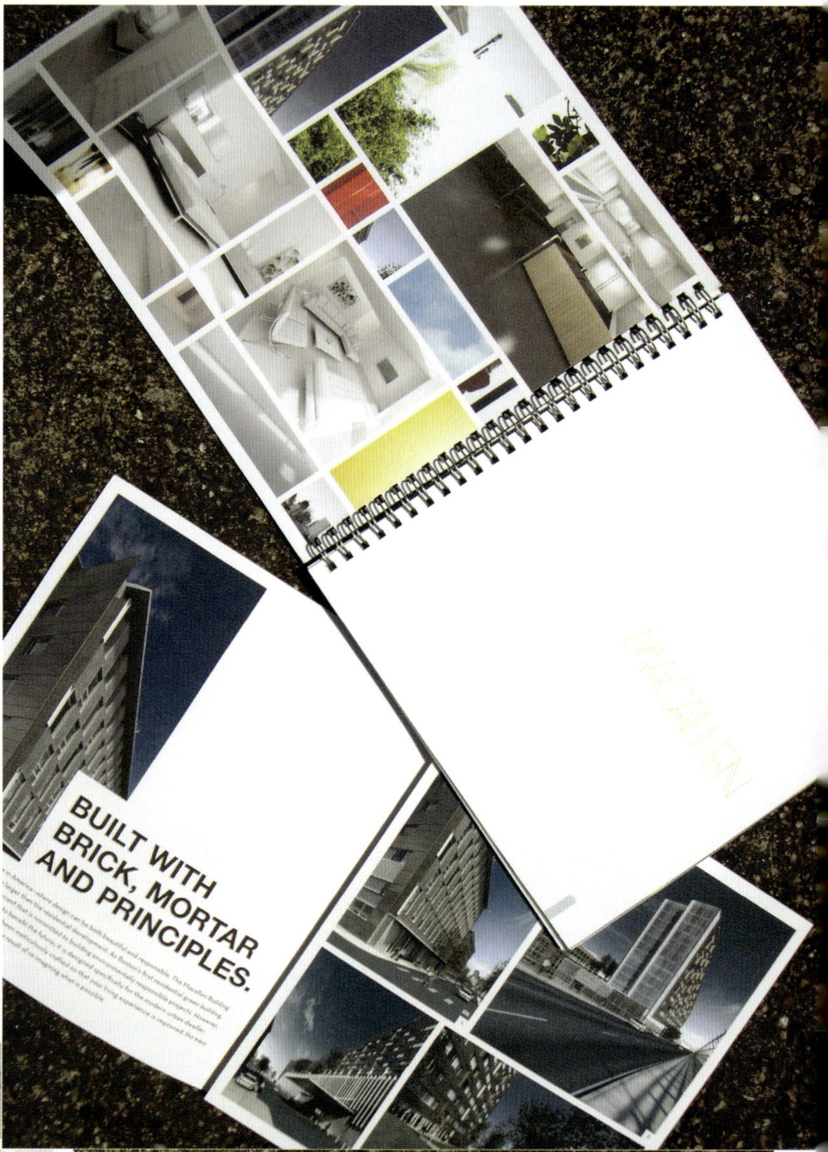

client
Pappas Properties
design firm
160over90
designers
Darryl Cilli, Dan Shepelavy, Steve Penning, Brendan Quinn

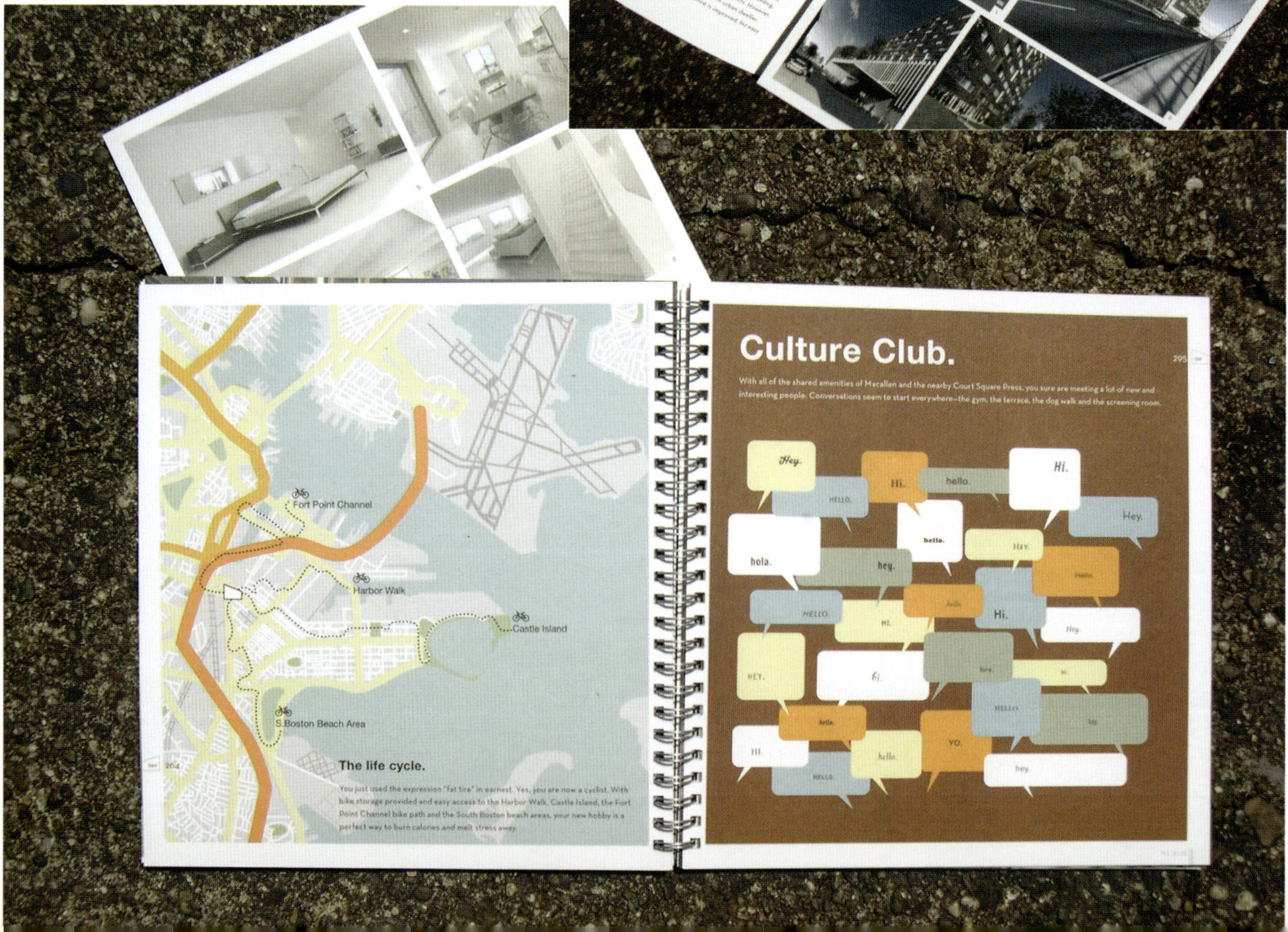

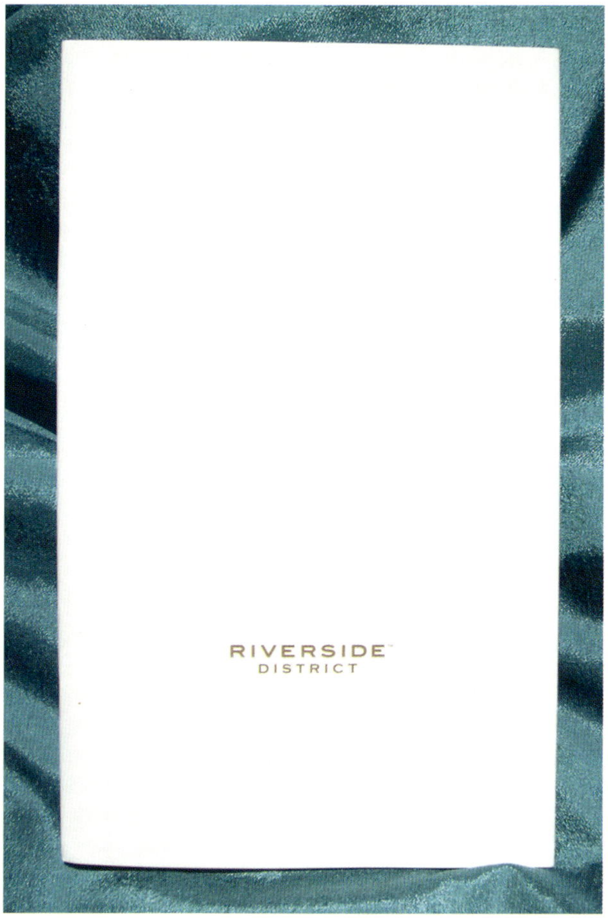

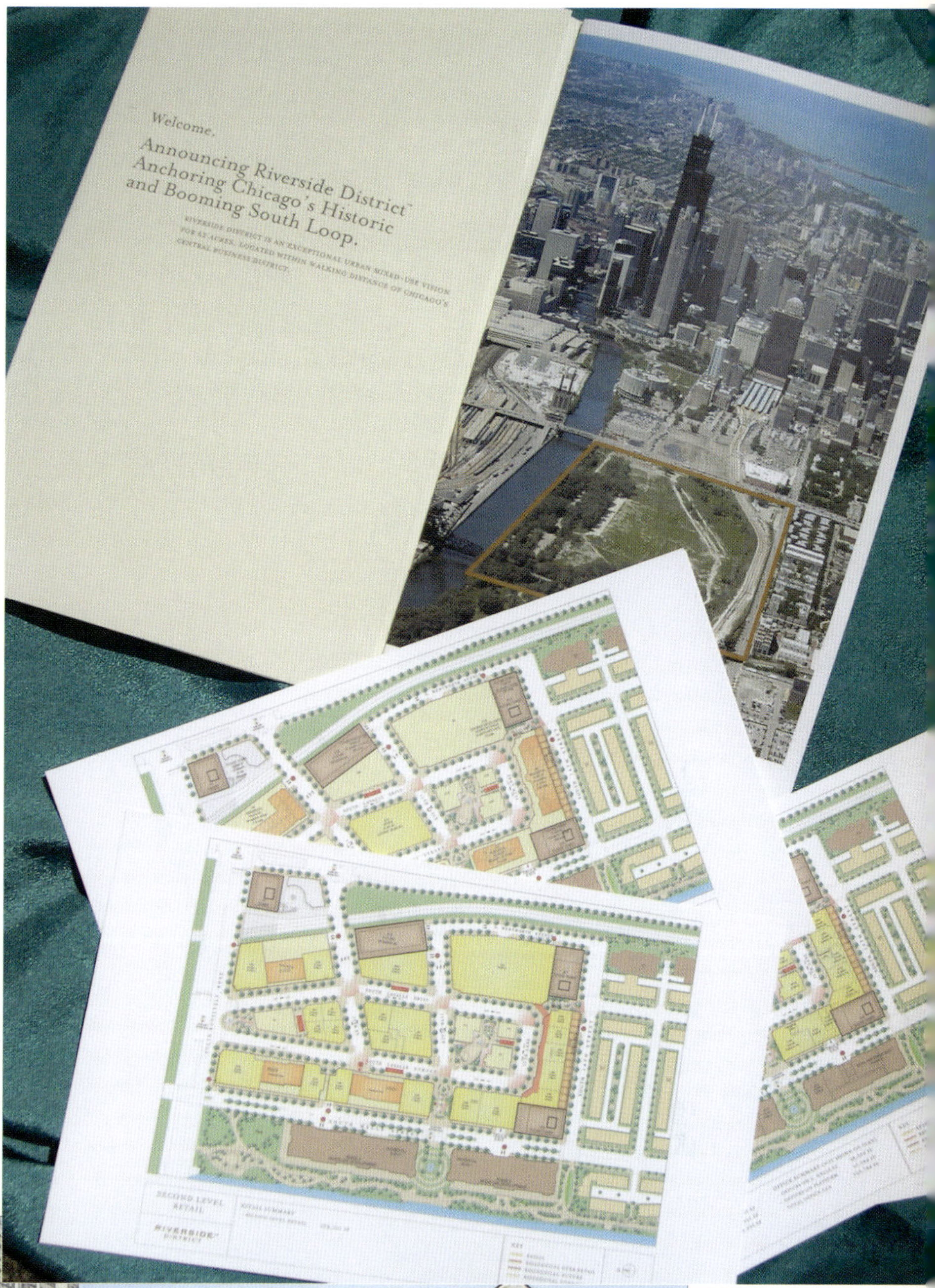

client
Riverside District
design firm
Addis Group
designers
Magdalena Hladka,
John Creson

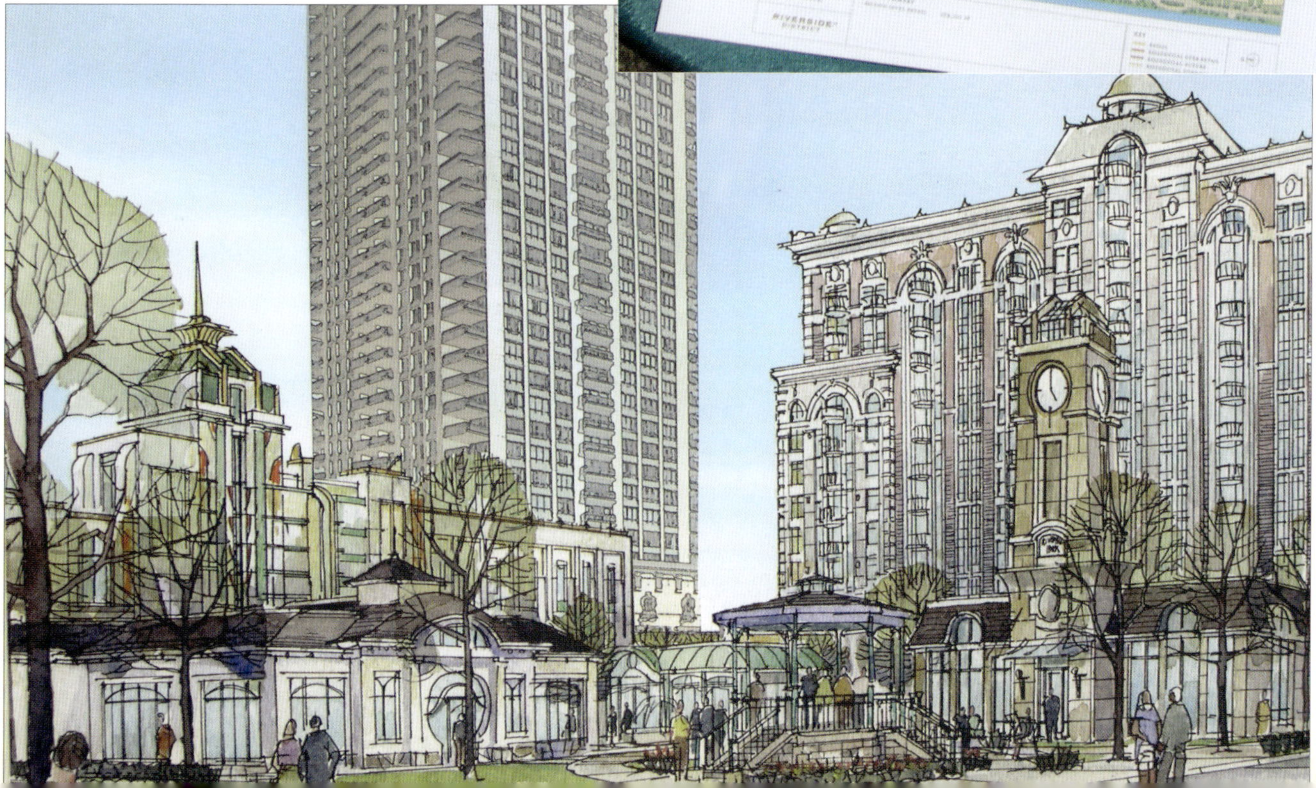

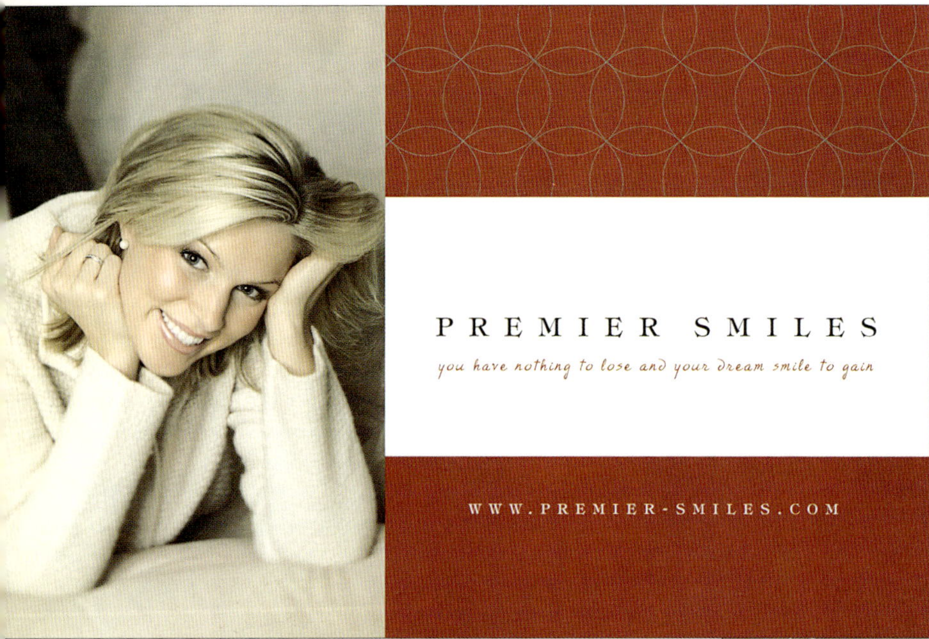

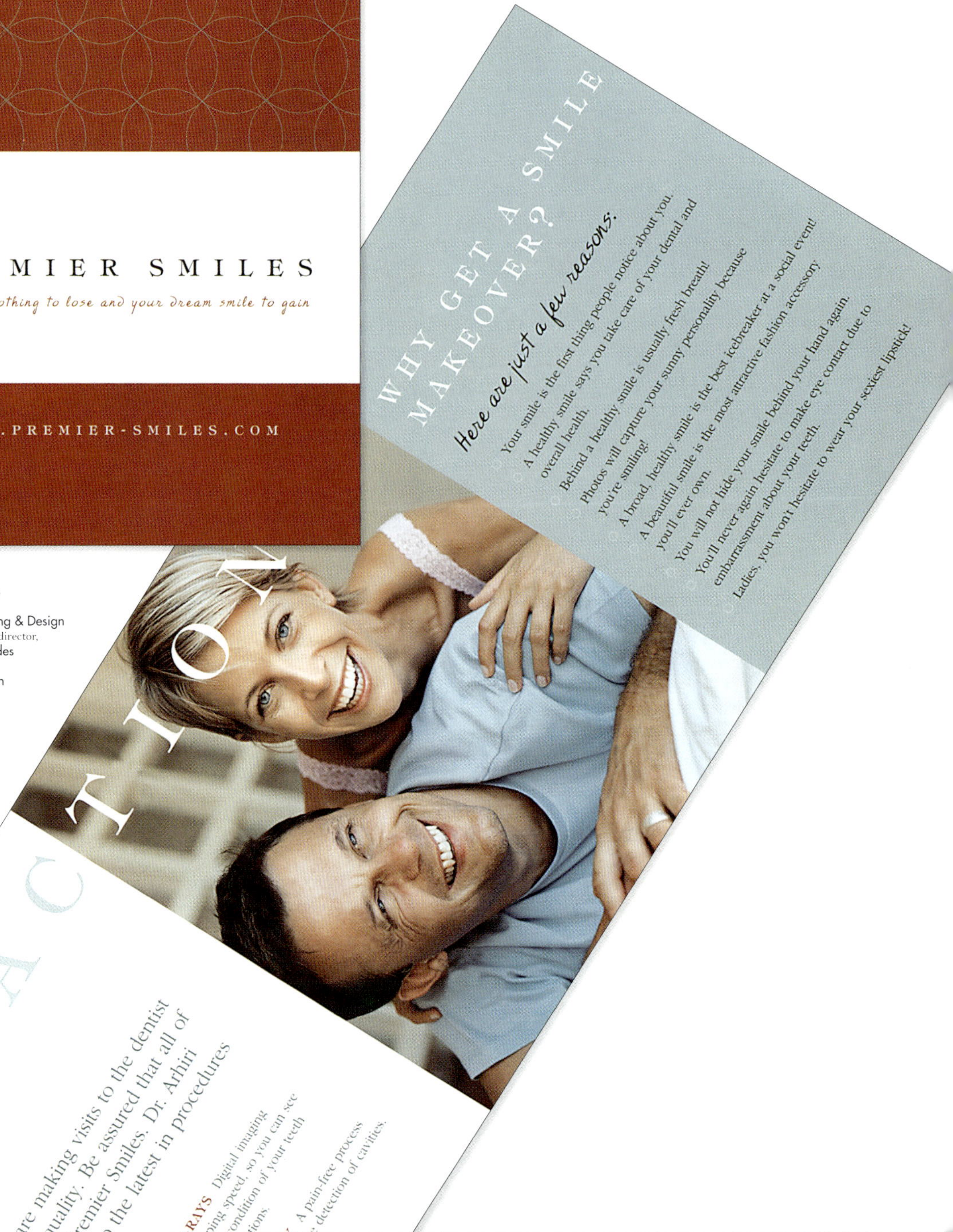

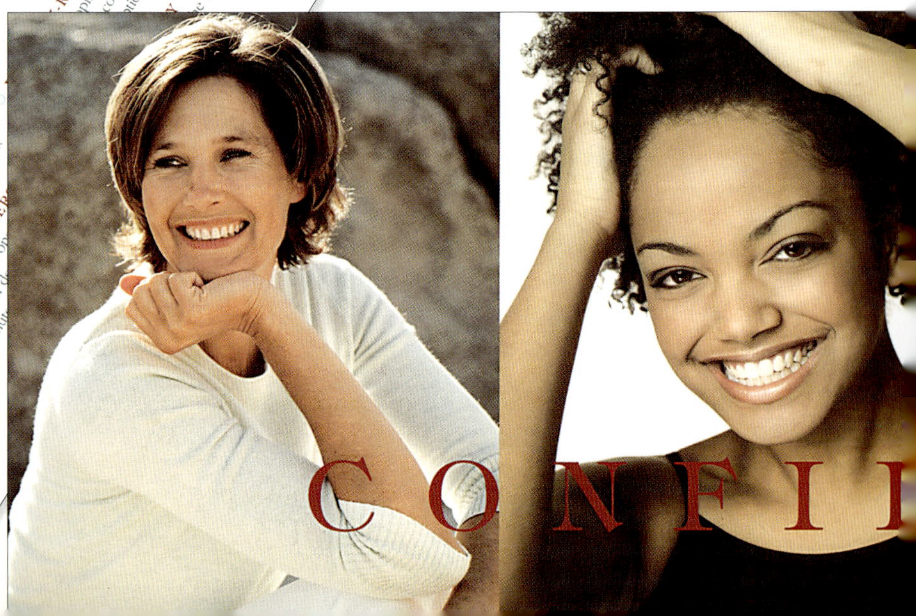

client
Premier Smiles
design firm
Verve Marketing & Design
principle, creative director,
Diane Lemonides
designer
Nancy Nguyen

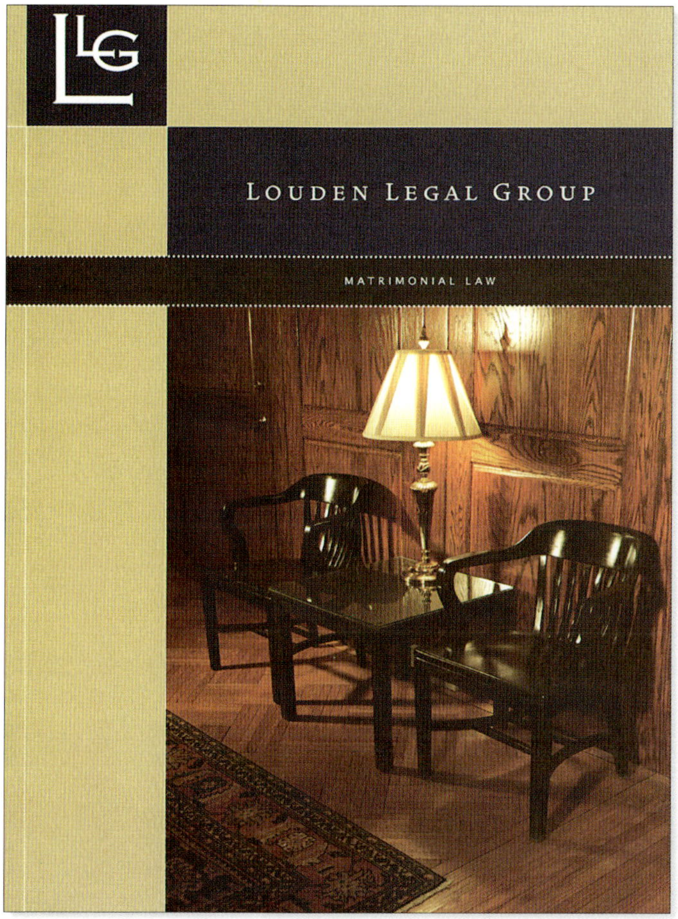

client
Louden Legal Group
design firm
Fathom
designer
Bil Jenak

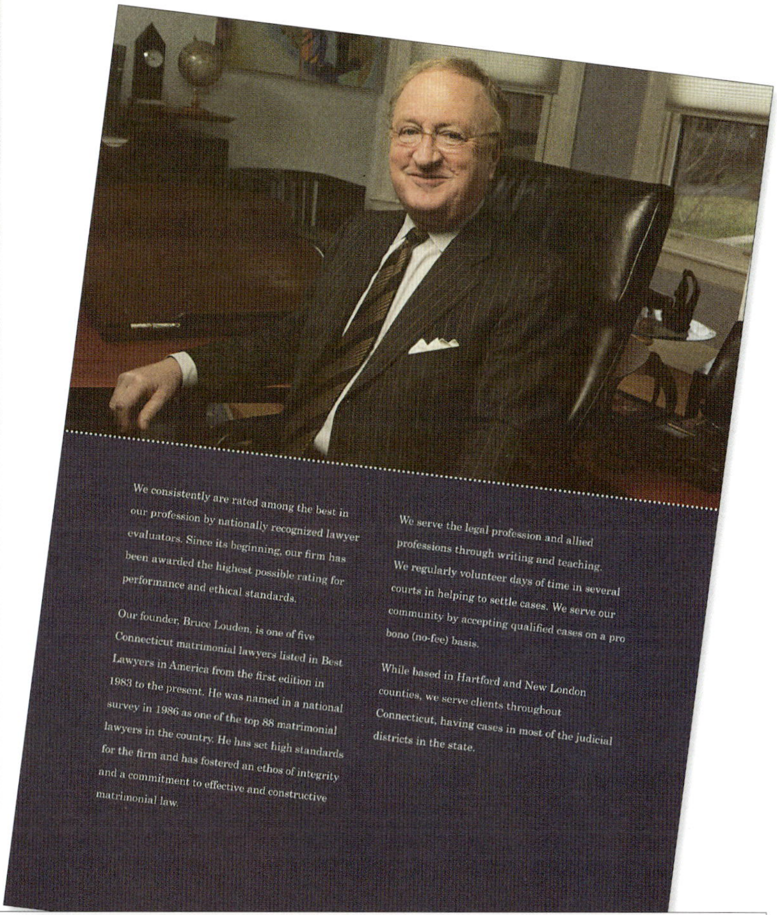

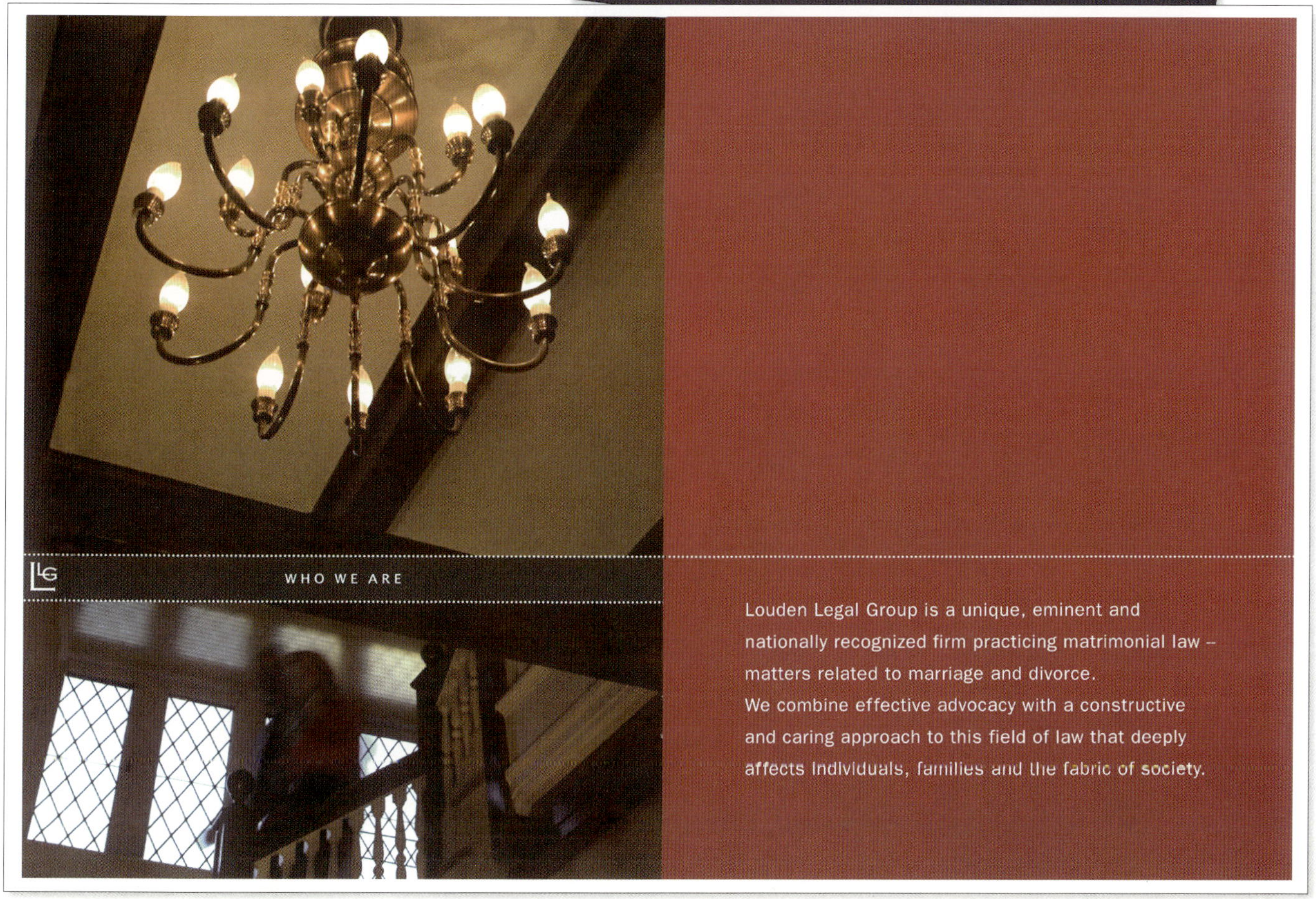

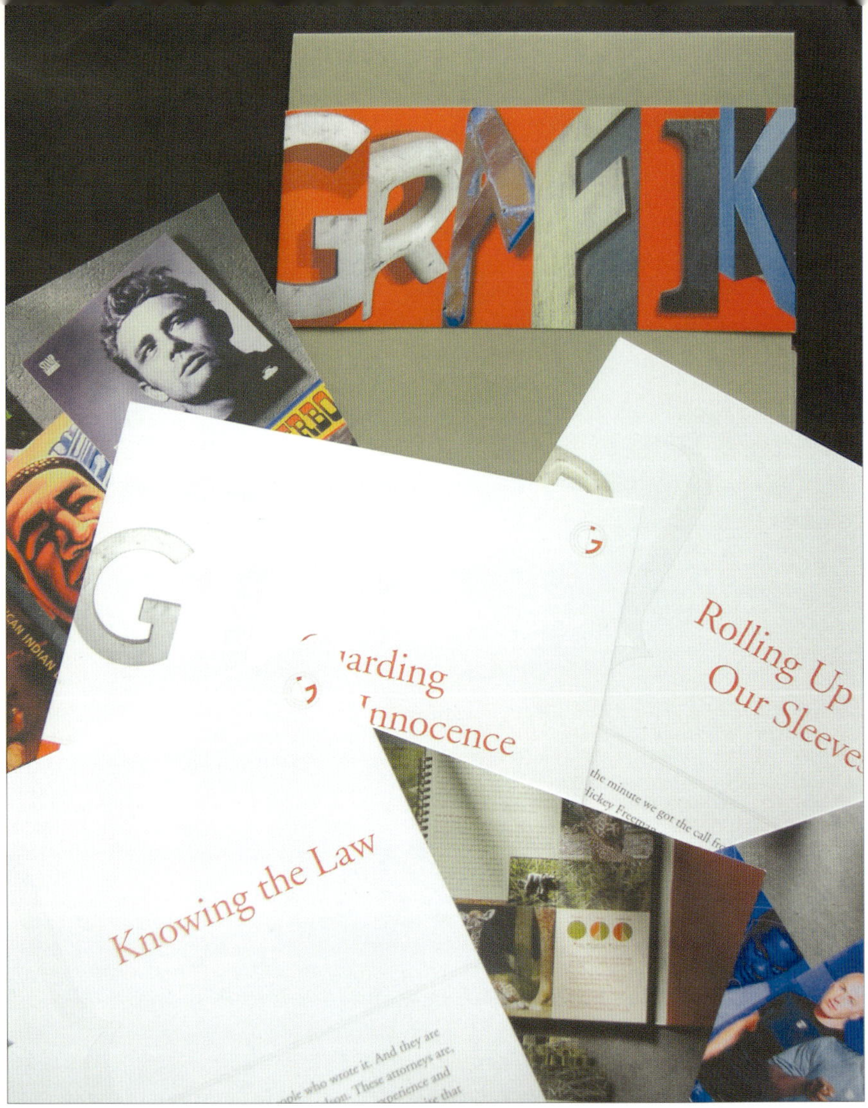

client
Grafik Marketing Communications
design firm
Grafik Marketing Communications
designers
Michael Mateos,
Johnny Vitorovich

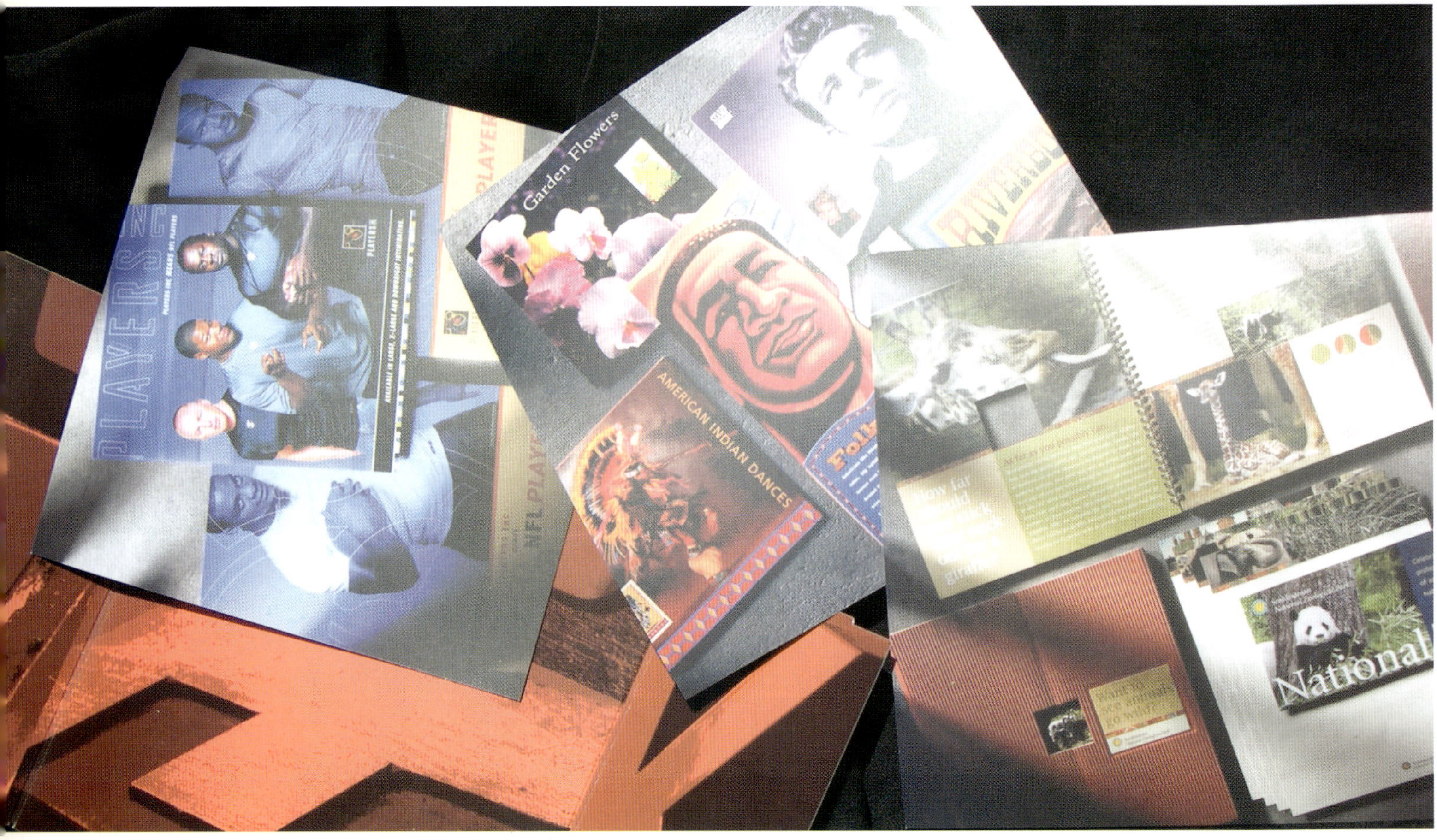

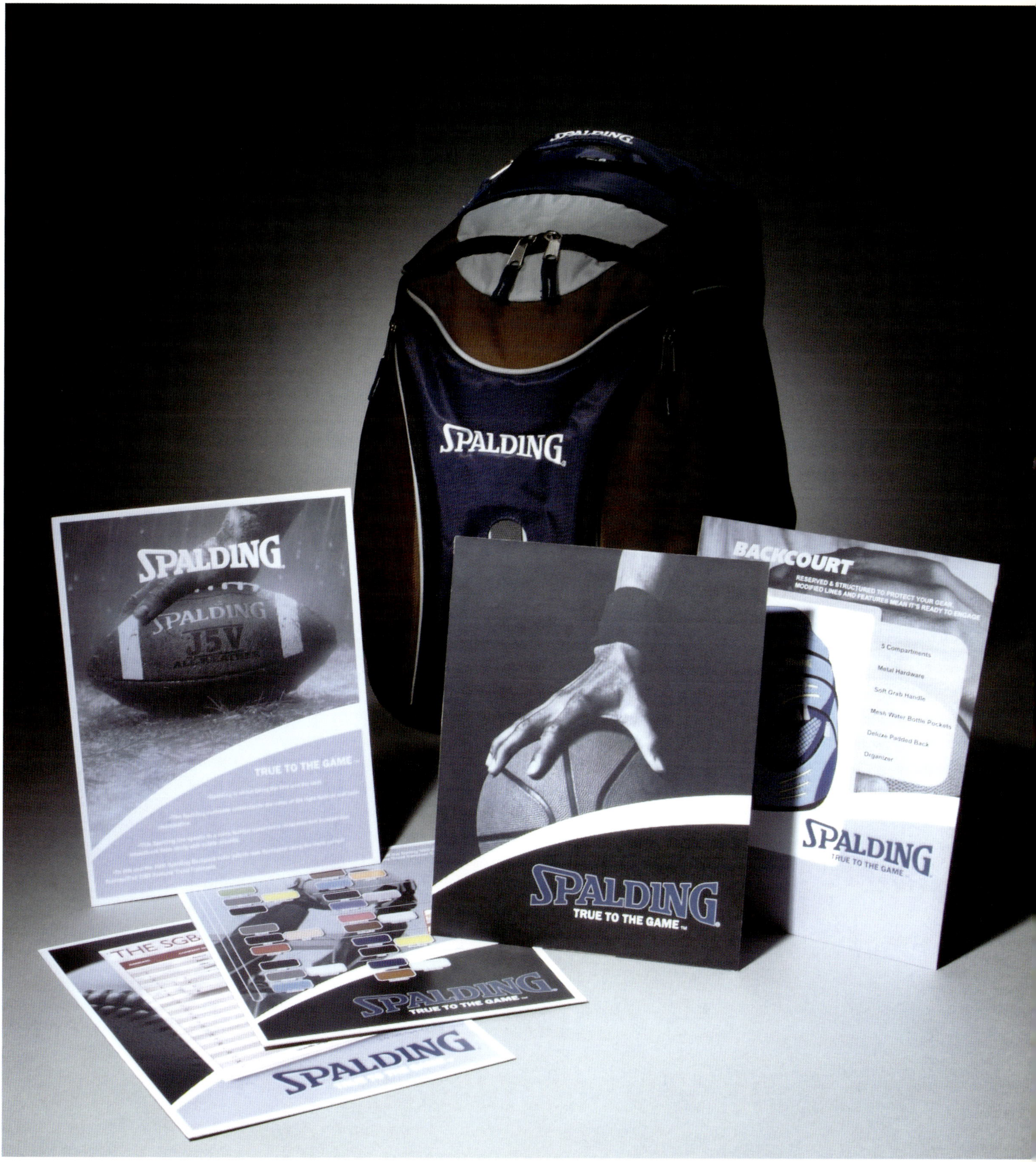

client
Spalding®
design firm
InGEAR In-House Design Department
production design manager, designer
Derek Crenshaw
marketing team
Tom Hinkle, Michelle Varland,
Sarah Paikai, Julie Garwood,
Heather Tvrdik

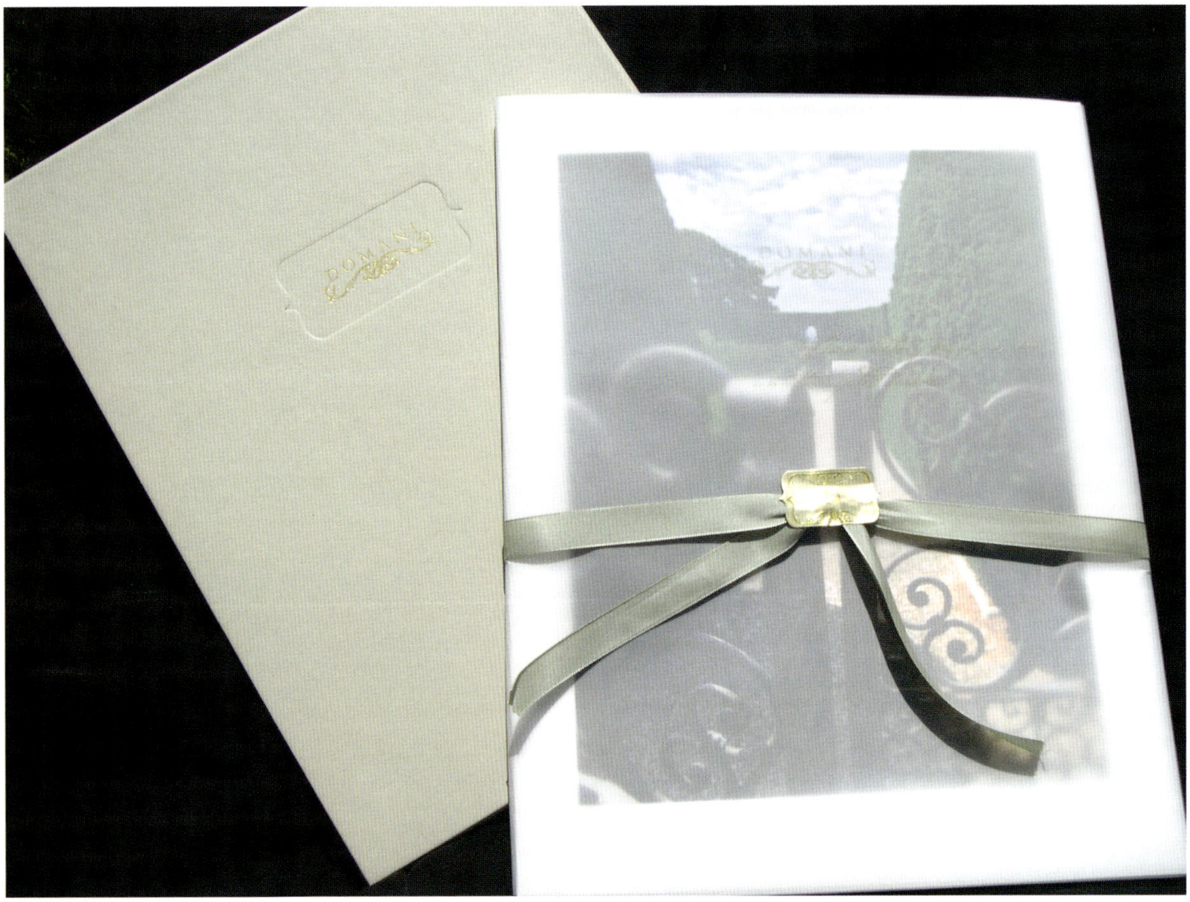

client
Kolter Communities
design firm
Gouthier Design

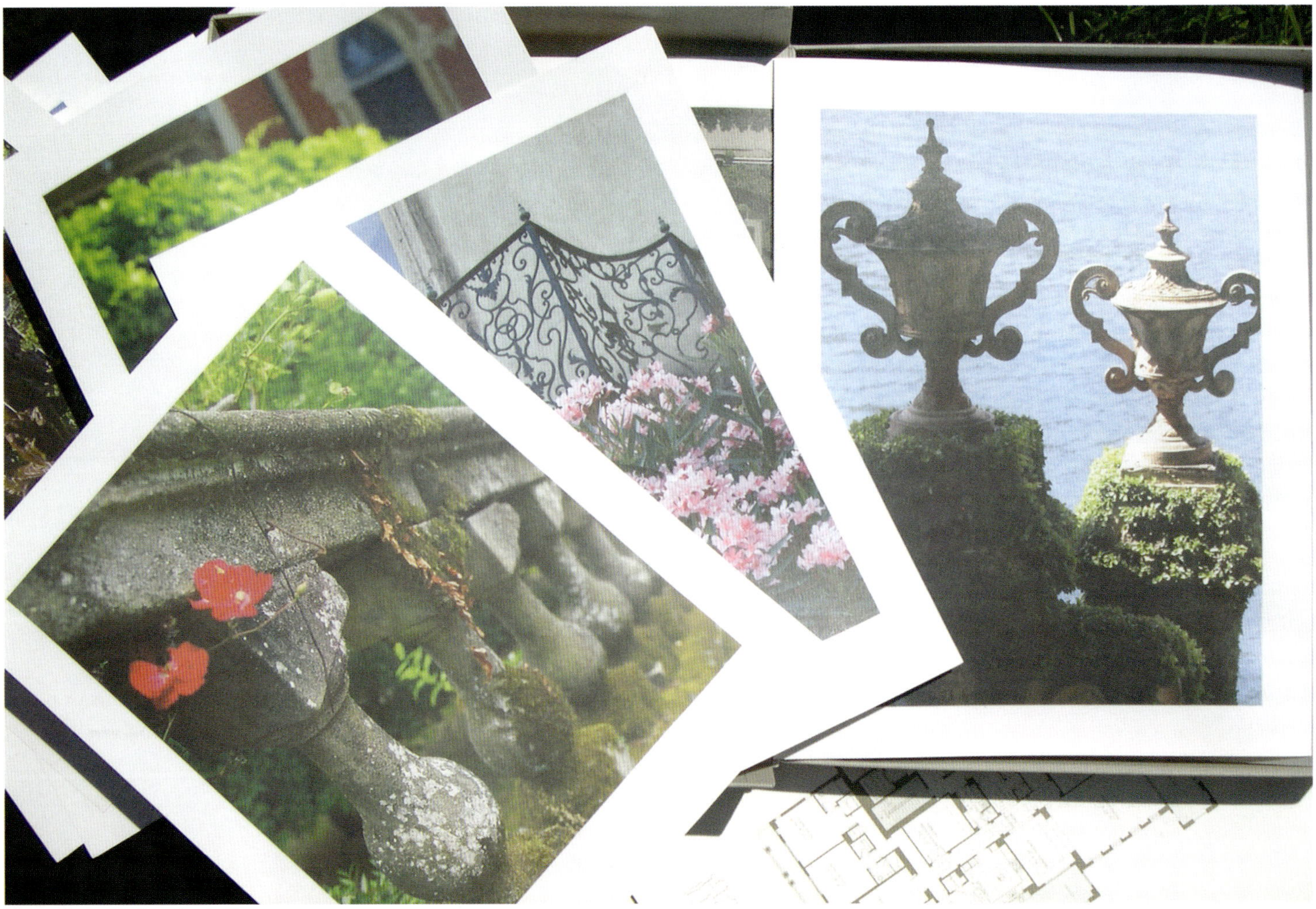

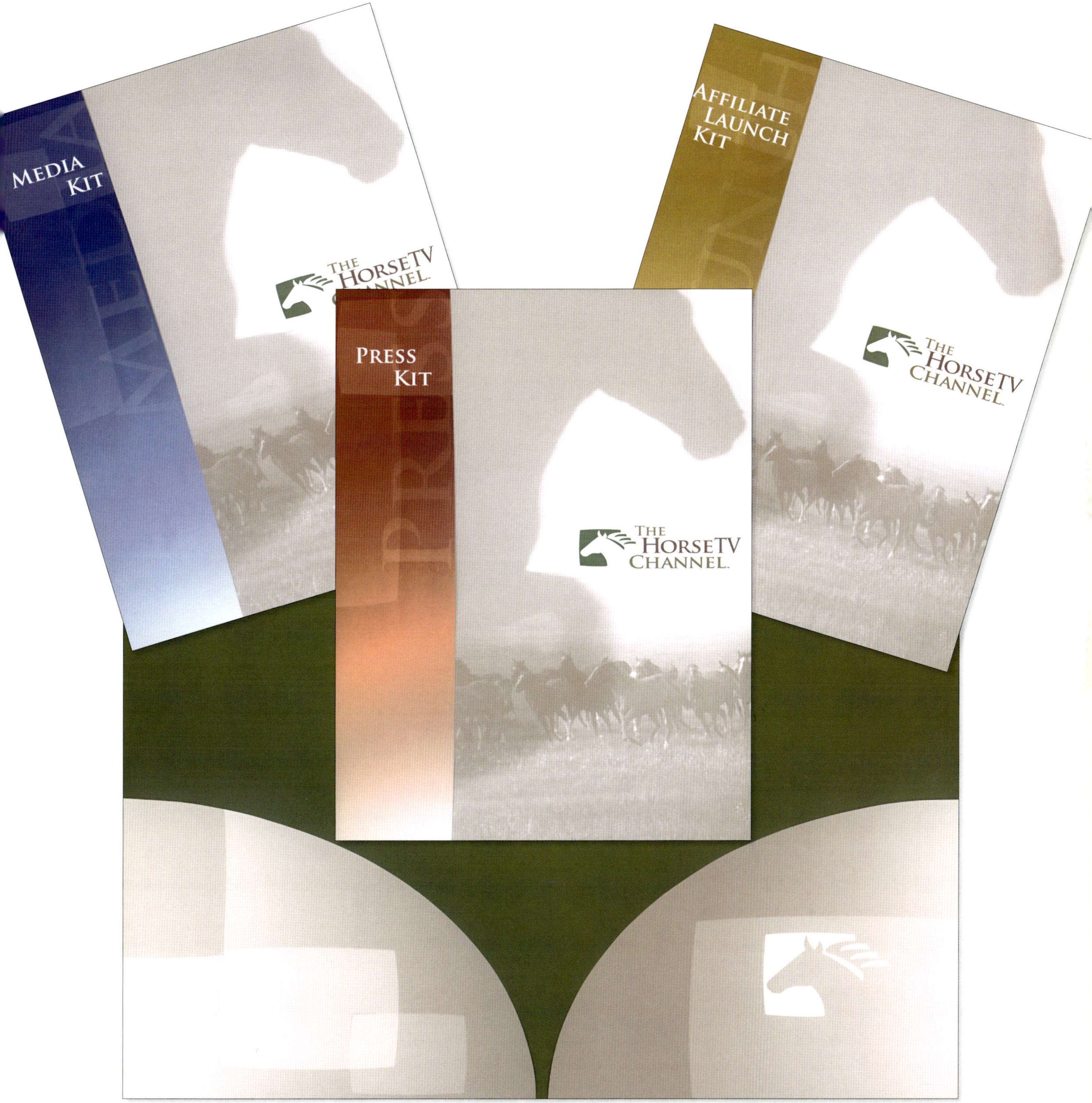

client
The HorseTV Channel
design firm
The HorseTV Channel
designer
Maureen Smullen

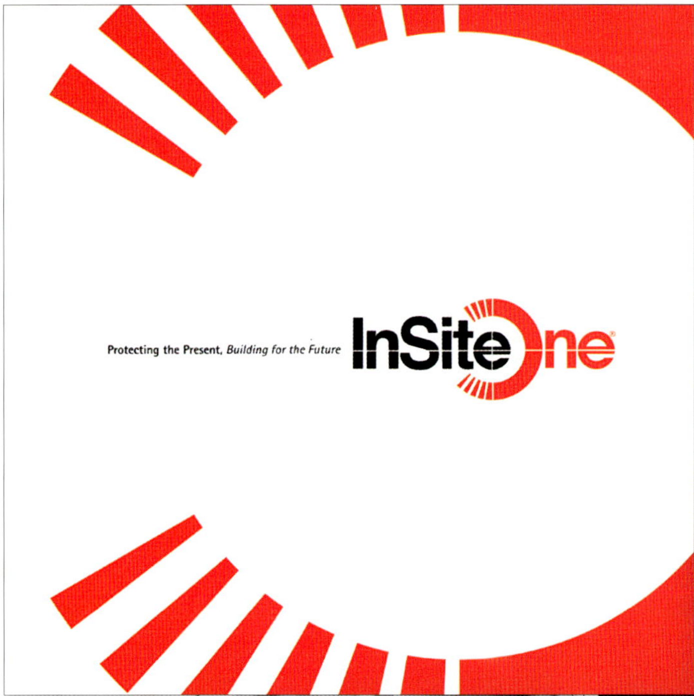

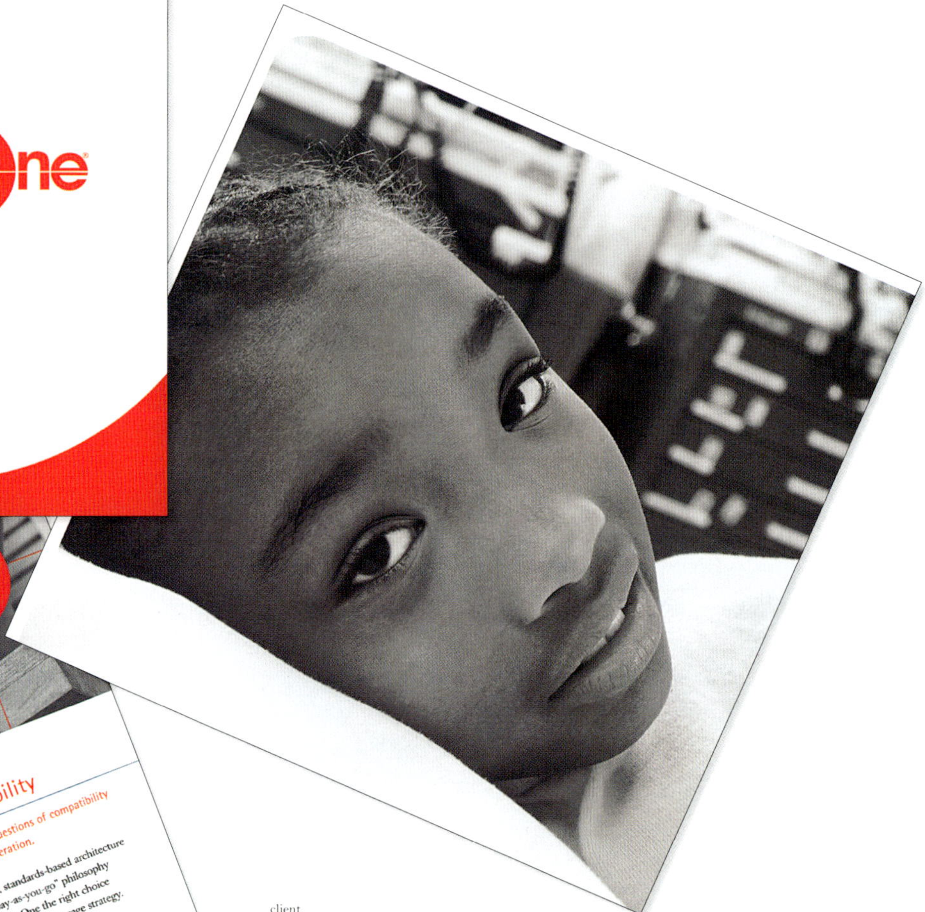

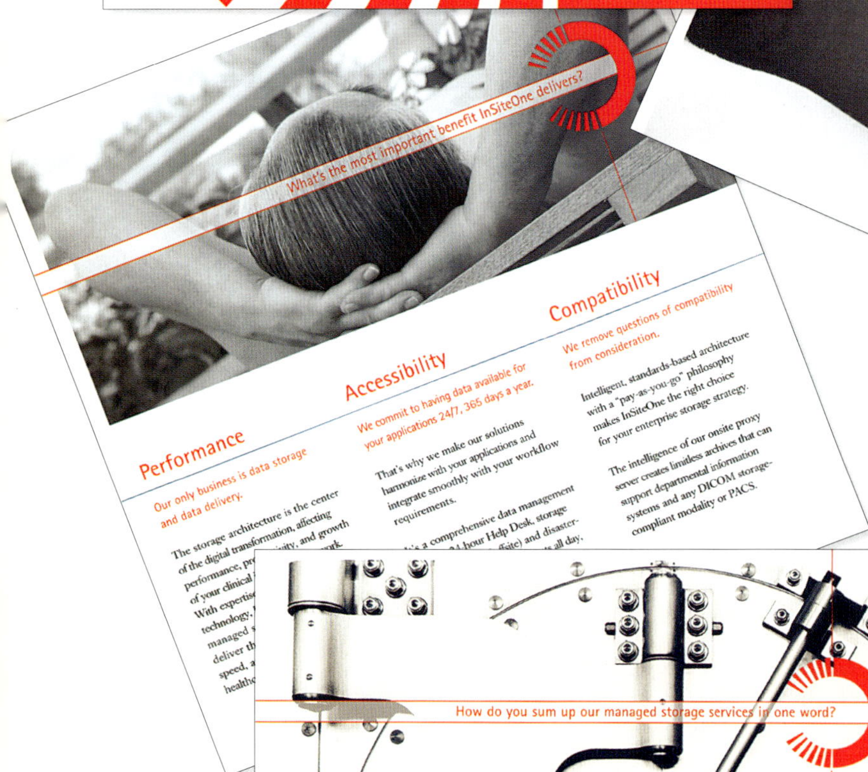

client
InSite One
design firm
Fathom
designers
Brent Robertson,
Anthony Acock,
Bil Jenak

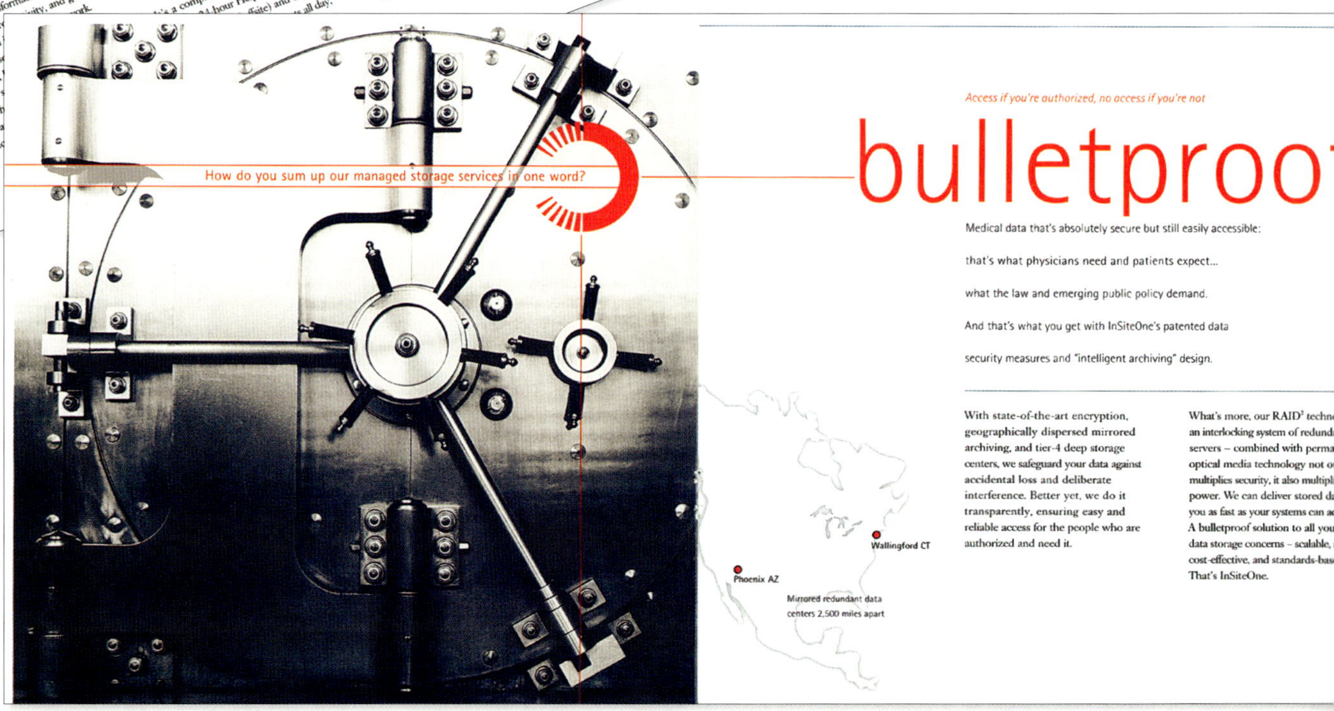

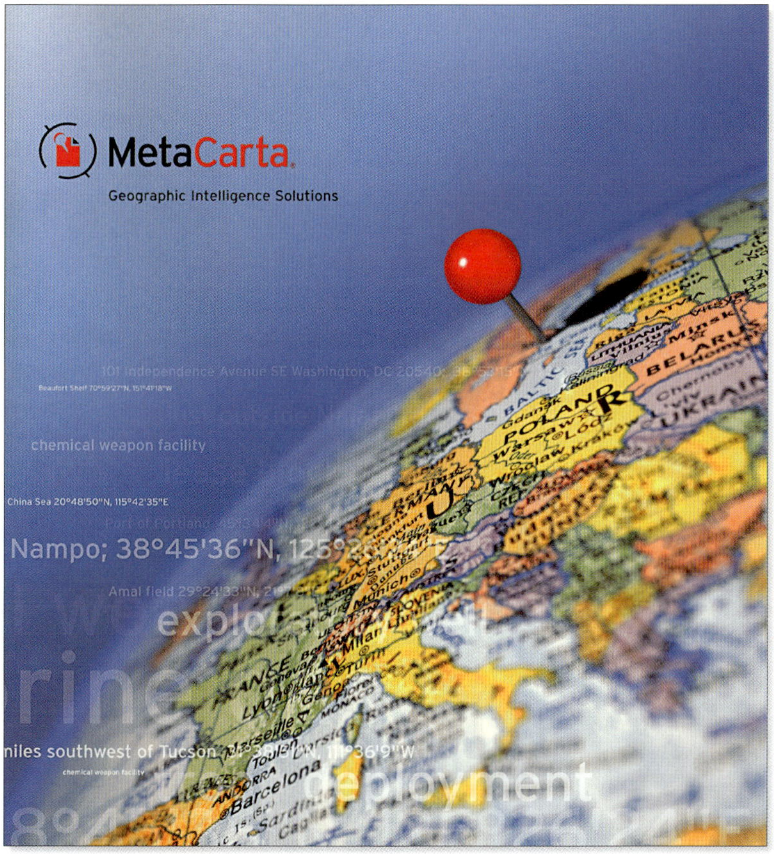

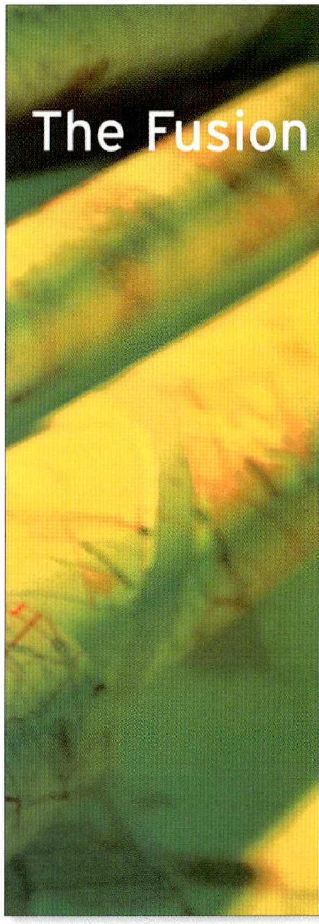

The Fusion of Text, Data and Maps

MetaCarta uses several unique capabilities to allow users to find the information they're looking for:

- **Geographic Text Search** the fastest means of searching text and geography simultaneously to pinpoint the information you're looking for
- **GeoParsing** which makes your documents aware of the locations they reference
- **Geographic Data Module (GDM)** one of the world's largest known digital gazetteers with assigned probabilities by location, and logic and rules that identify places

MetaCarta **Geographic Text Search** allows knowledge workers, analysts, and managers to instantly find documents from massive collections simply by zooming a map into their geographic area of interest. MetaCarta lets users identify a region of interest anywhere on the globe by name or geographic coordinates (latitude/longitude), or by zooming in on the map and entering a search query. In just seconds, GTS presents search results as icons on a map of the selected region.

Users click on the document icons to read the first few lines of text, or click on the embedded link to read the full document. Users can further narrow searches by zooming in to specific geographic locations, modifying the text string, or filtering through time periods.

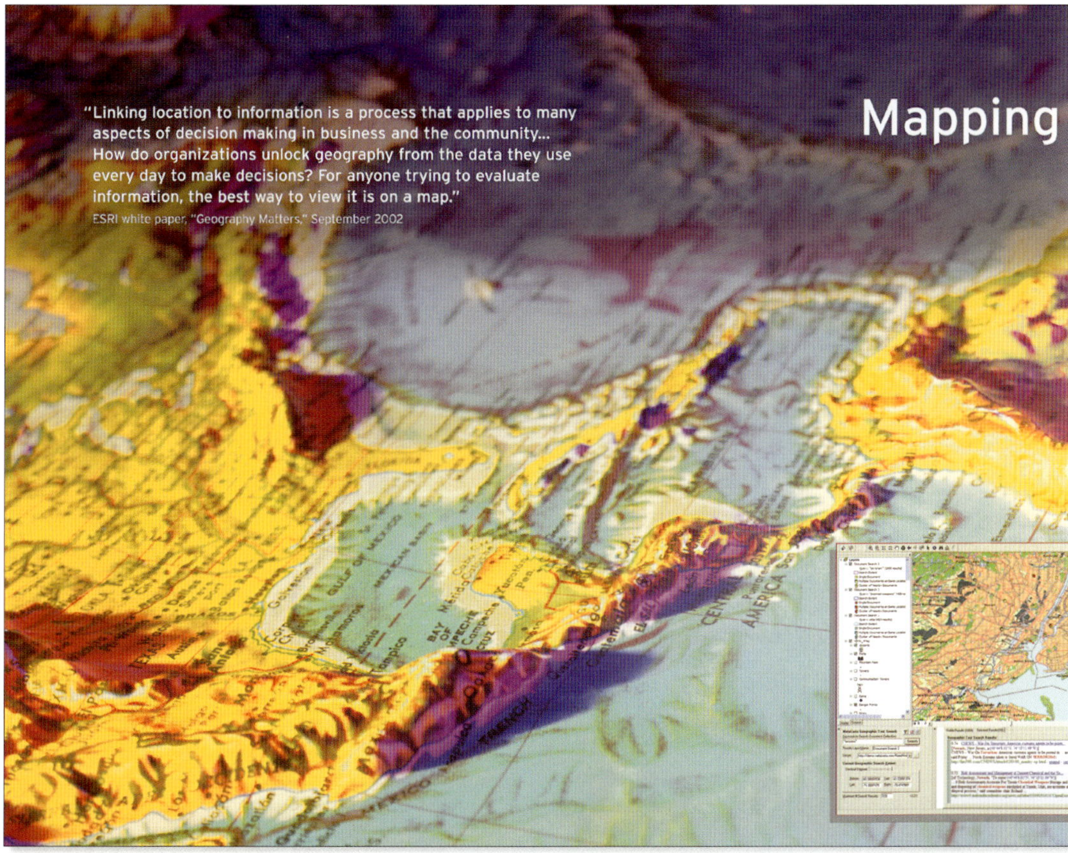

"Linking location to information is a process that applies to many aspects of decision making in business and the community... How do organizations unlock geography from the data they use every day to make decisions? For anyone trying to evaluate information, the best way to view it is on a map."
ESRI white paper, "Geography Matters," September 2002

Mapping Information to Geography

MetaCarta turns digital documents into layers on a map. MetaCarta integrates with document management and GIS systems, such as ESRI ArcMap depicted below.

According to IDC, knowledge workers spend about one third of their time:

- Searching for non-existent information
- Failing to find existing information
- Recreating information that cannot be found

Companies spend hundreds of thousands of dollars or more annually in lost productivity and possibly millions in lost opportunity costs. For some organizations, simply the time to get the information could be too long to impact immediate needs and decisions.

MetaCarta's patent pending technology adds geographic intelligence to information. With its accurate and powerful Geographic Search and Geographic Referencing capabilities, users pinpoint information based on geographic location and view the results on a map. By placing relevant documents on a map, users discover and visualize new geographic relationships and trends, spend less time searching for information, and have more time to make critical decisions.

client
MetaCarta
design firm
kor group
art director
Karen Dendy Smith
designer
James Grady
photographer
Anton Grassl

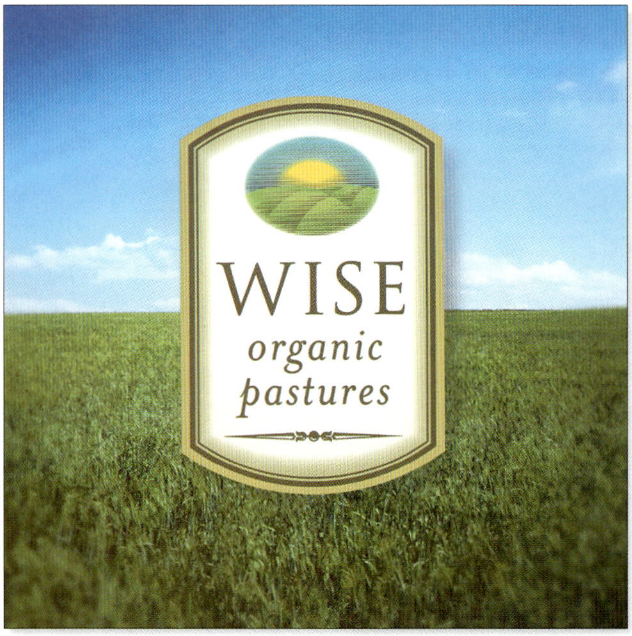

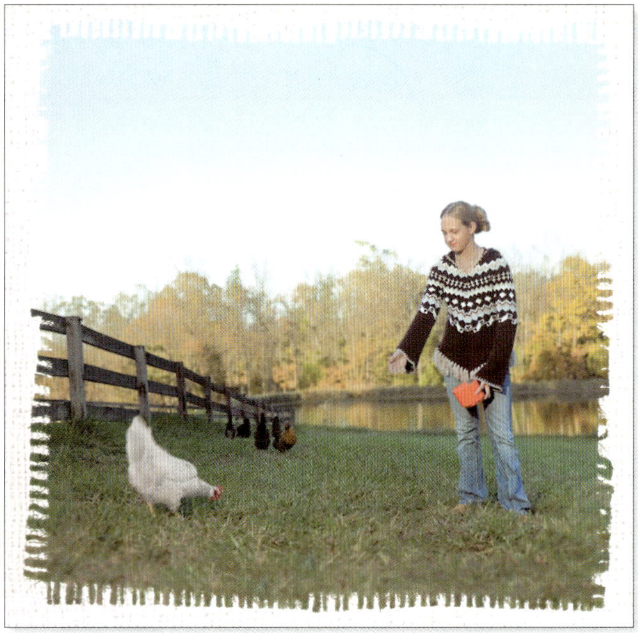

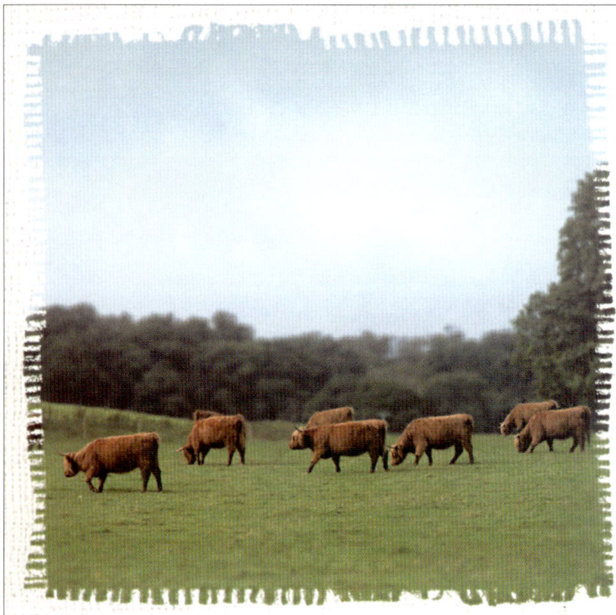

The Organic & Kosher Difference

BESHERT is the Yiddish word for a "match made in heaven" — and that's how we describe Wise Organic Pastures double certification. It's the ideal combination of organic *and* kosher, bringing you a product that is superior in every way.

Certified Organic. Wise Organic Pastures has been certified organic right from the beginning. Our organic meat label was one of the first ever approved by the USDA. Organic certification ensures that animals are given only organic vegetarian feed, free of synthetic pesticides and genetically-modified grains (no animal by-products are allowed, ever), are never given antibiotics or growth hormones, and have access to pasture and fresh air.

Certified Kosher. Kosher processing gives extra attention to purity and wholesomeness in the preparation and handling of food products. Our products are processed under strict supervision of Crown Heights Kosher and the Orthodox Union.

Wise Organic Pastures products are also third-party audited by Steritech for humane handling practices and food safety.

client
Wise Kosher Natural Poultry, Inc.
design firm
Pure Design Co. LLC
designers
Dan Mishkind, Graeme Ritchie

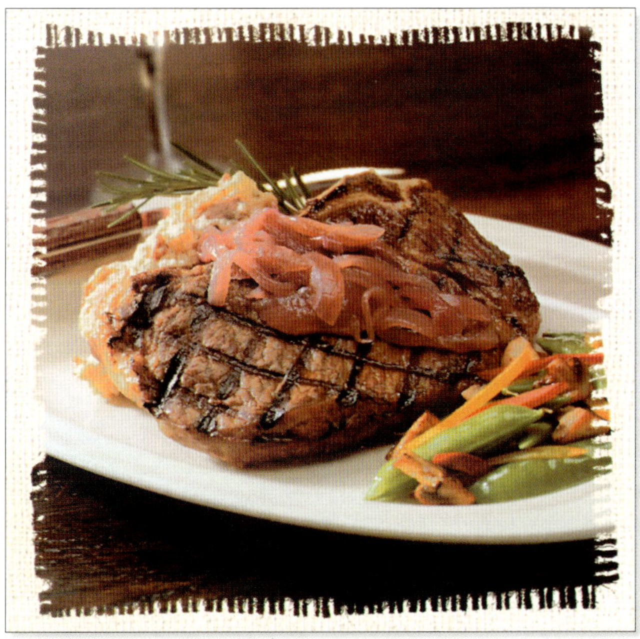

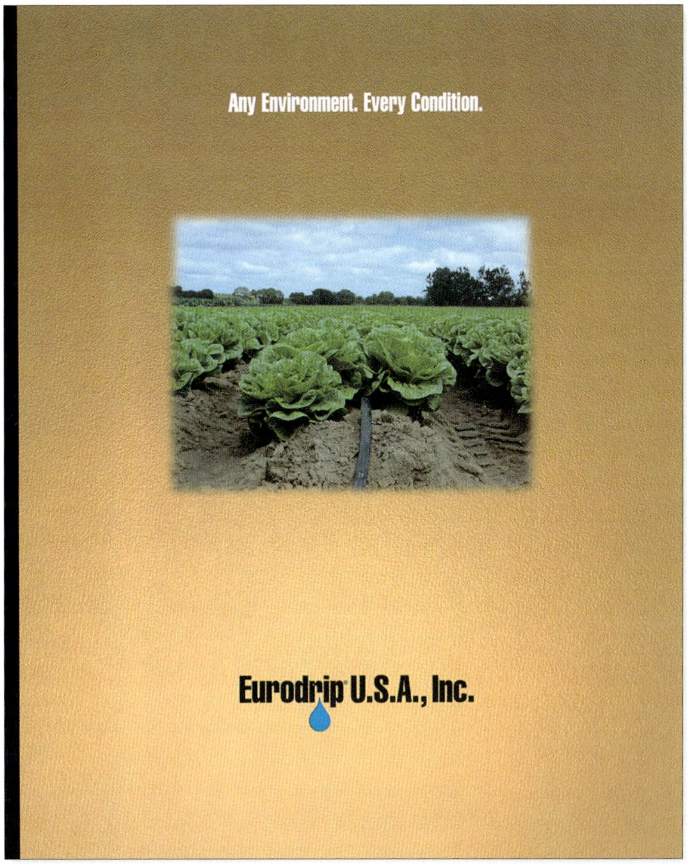

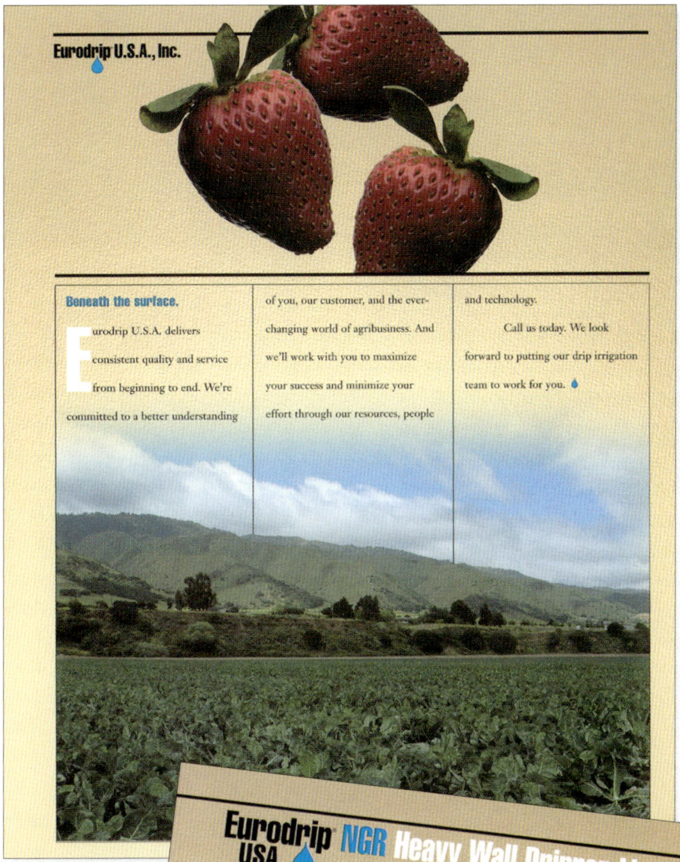

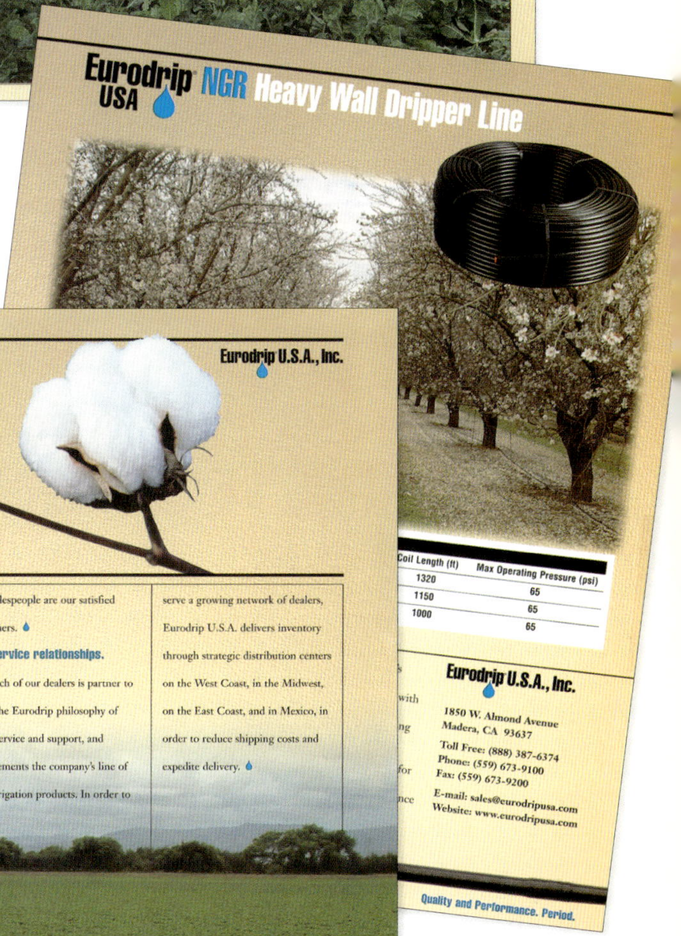

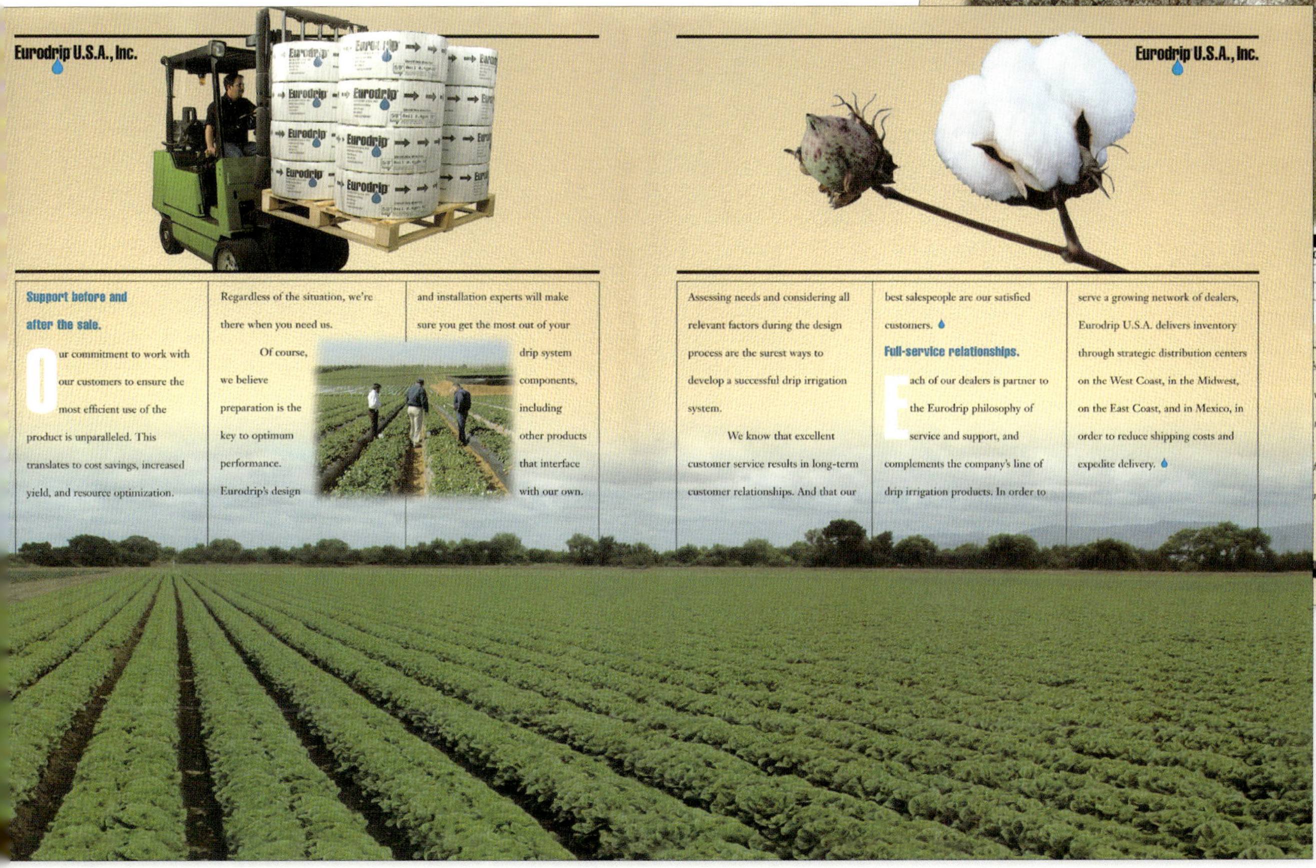

client
Eurodrip USA, Inc.
design firm
Lorenz Advertising
designers
Arne Ratermanis, Brian Lorenz

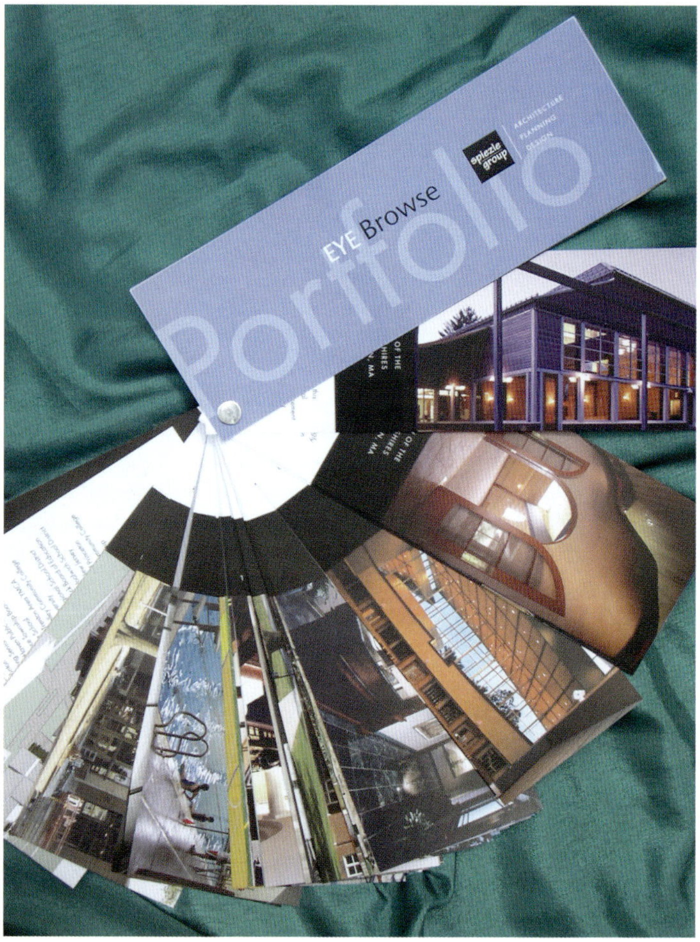

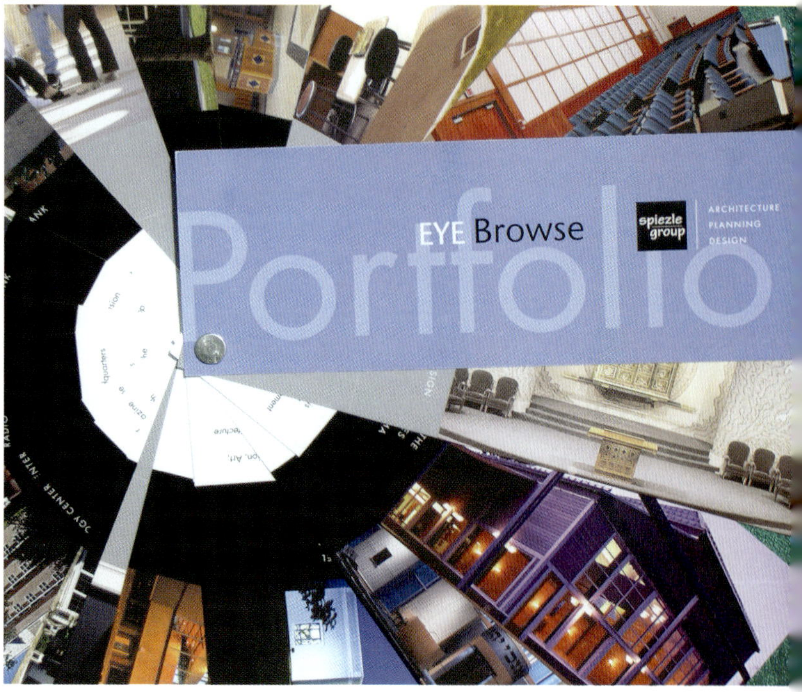

client
spiezle group
design firm
Gill Fishman Associates
designer
Alicia Ozyjowski

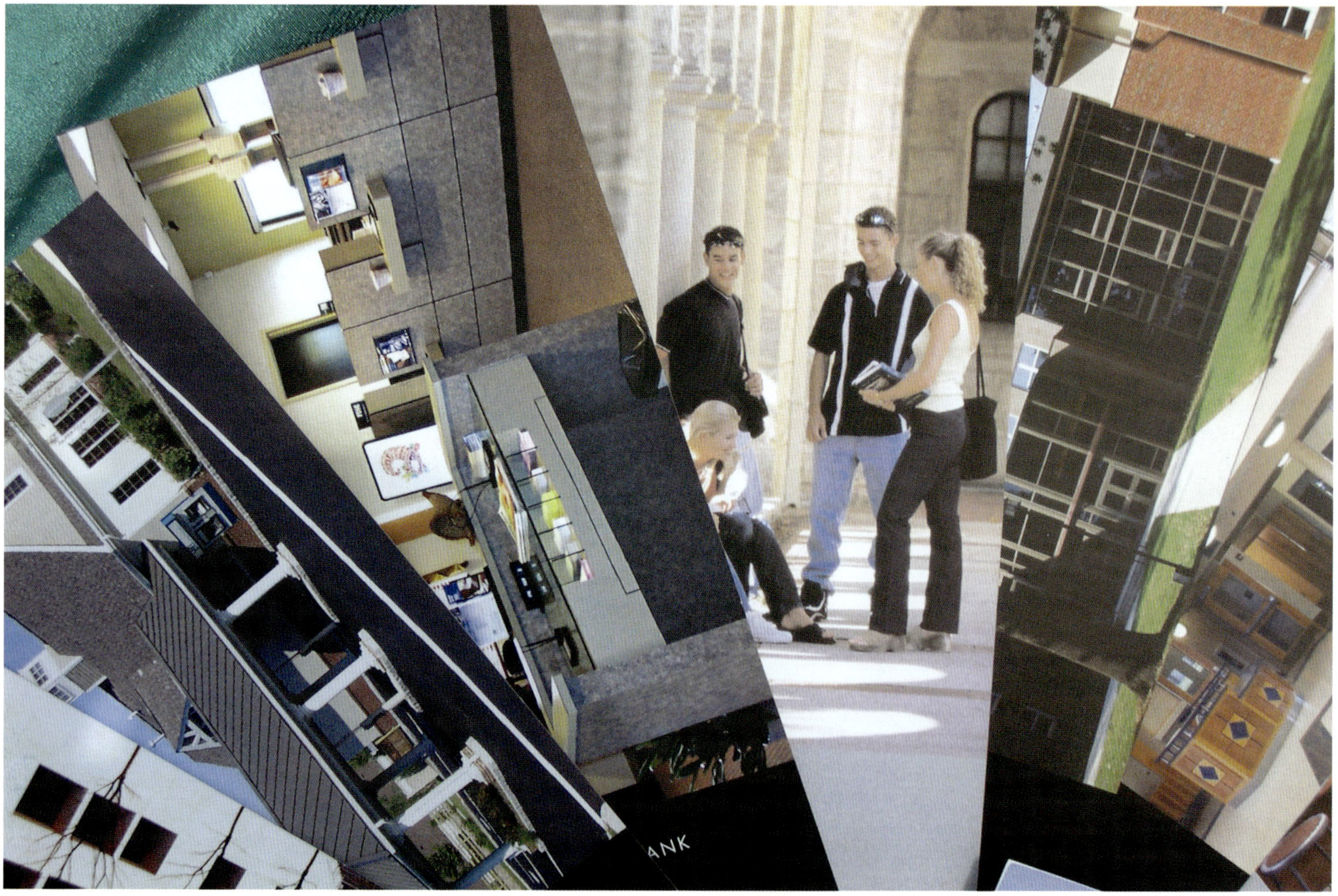

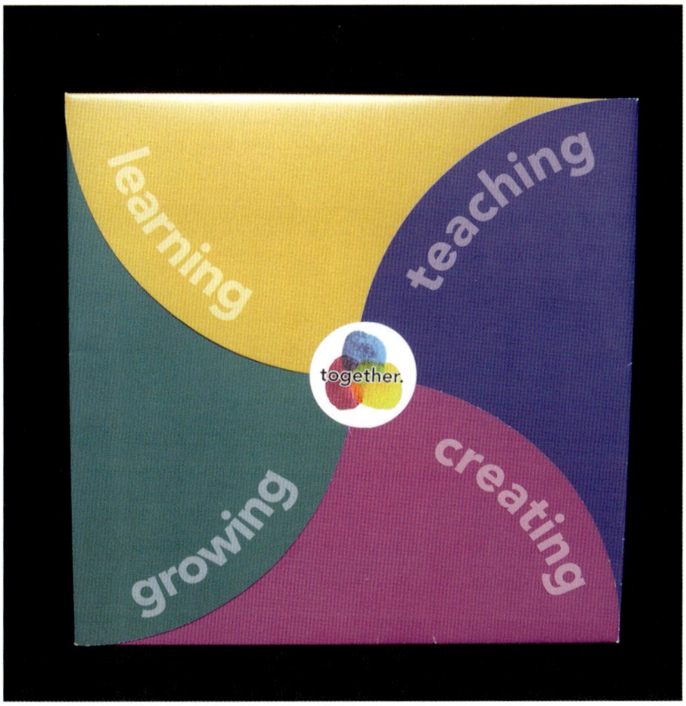

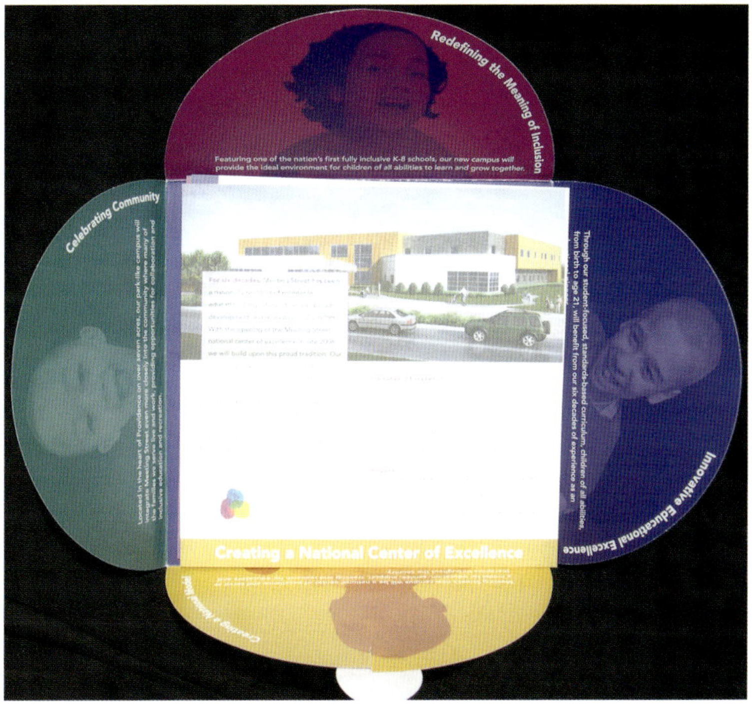

client
Meeting Street
design firm
Im-aj Communications & Design, Inc.
designers
Jami Ouellette,
Leslie Emert

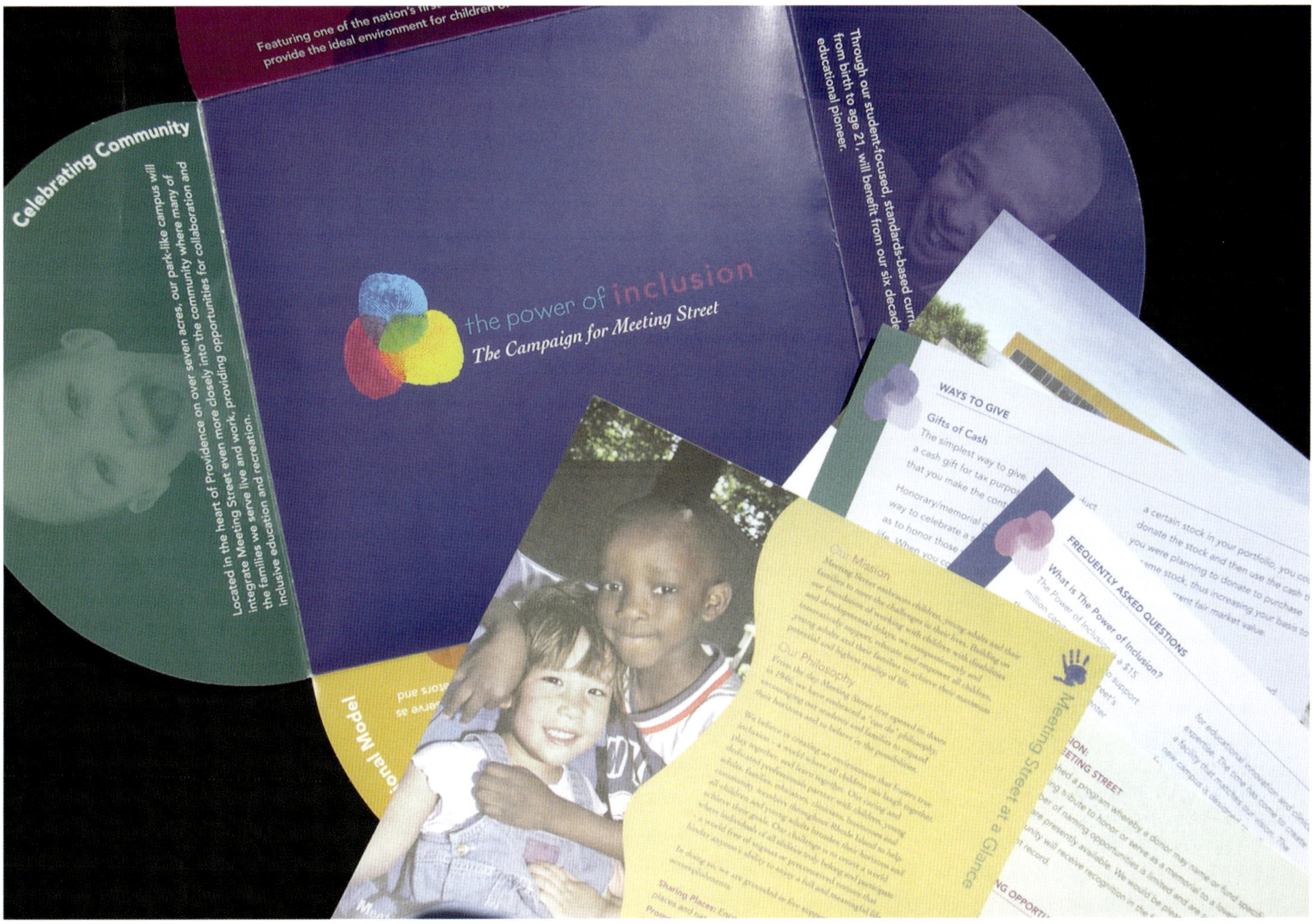

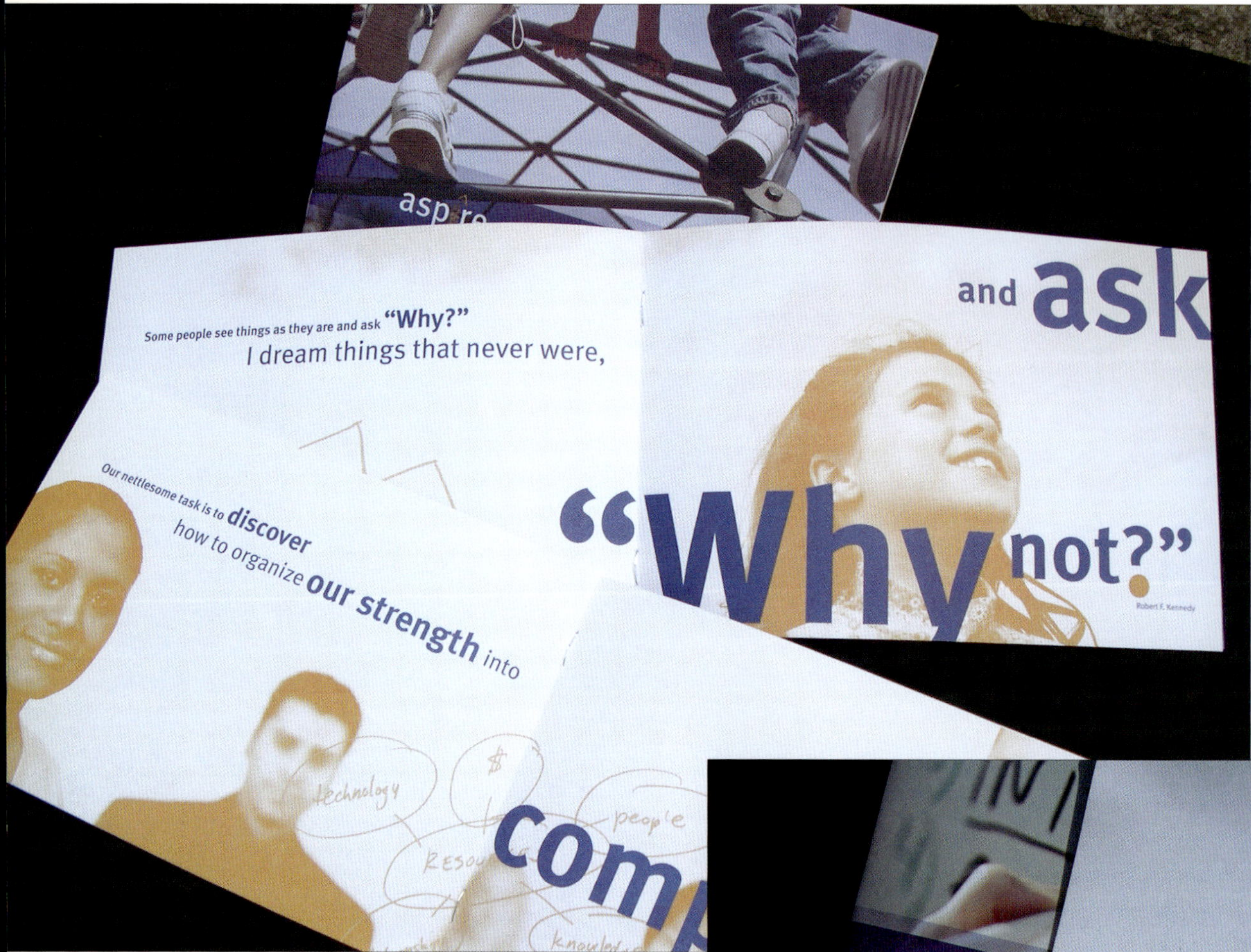

client
United Way
design firm
Grafik Marketing Communications
designers
Gregg Glaviano, Mila Arrisueno, Regina Esposito, Ivan Hooker

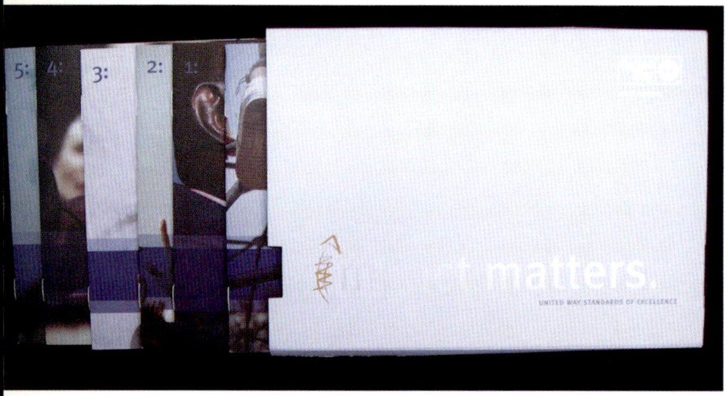

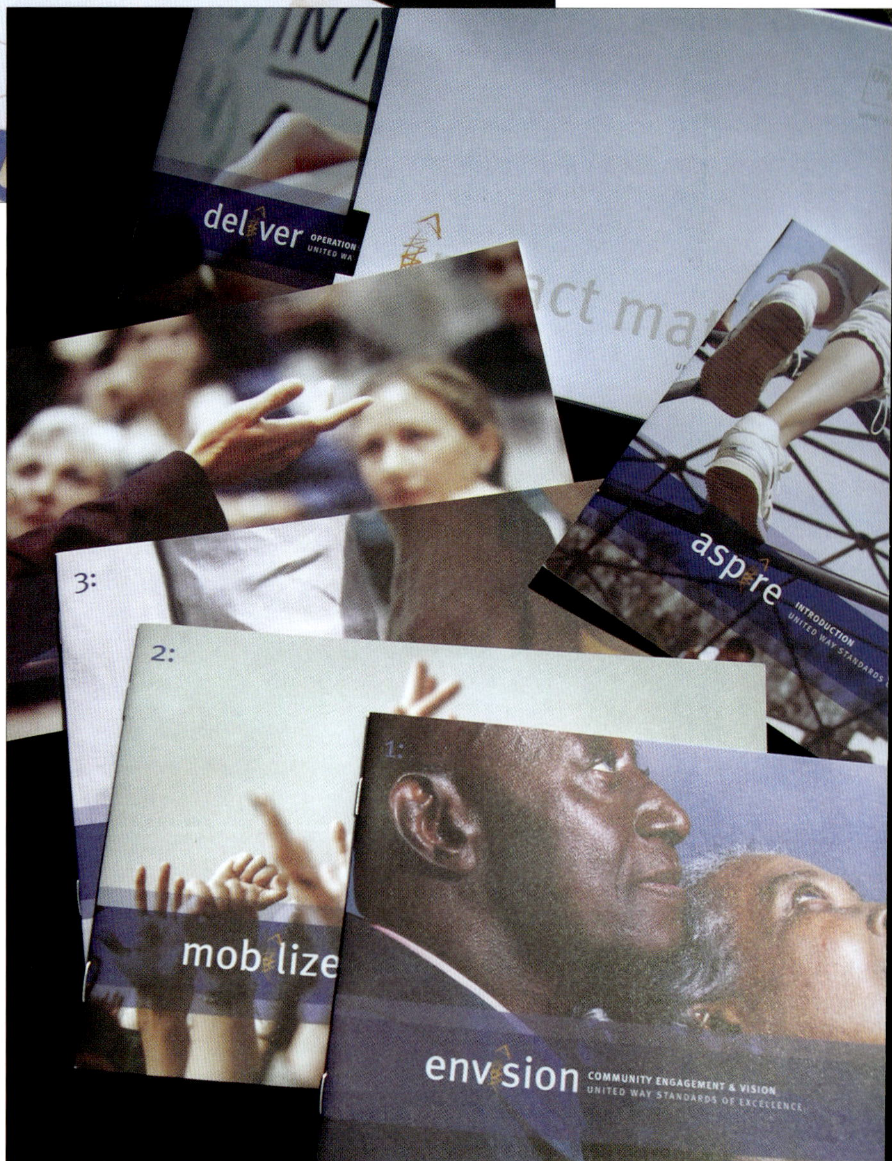

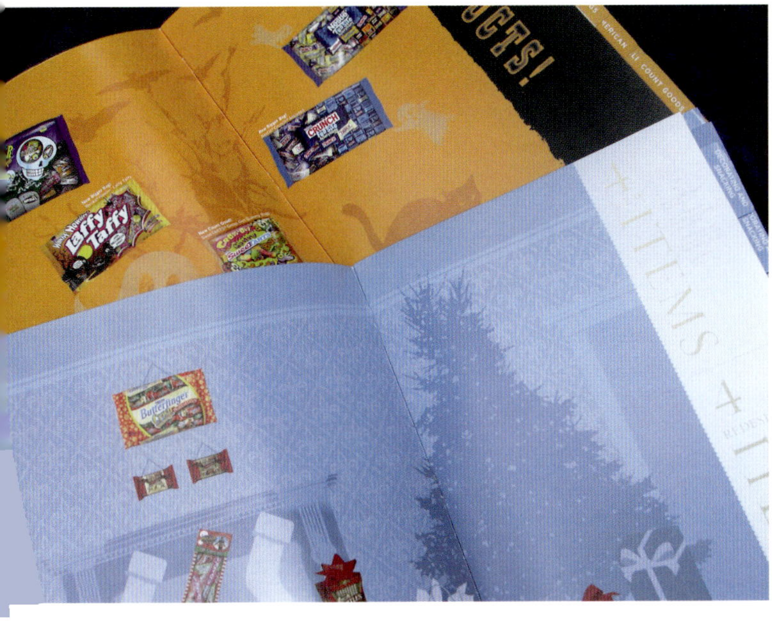

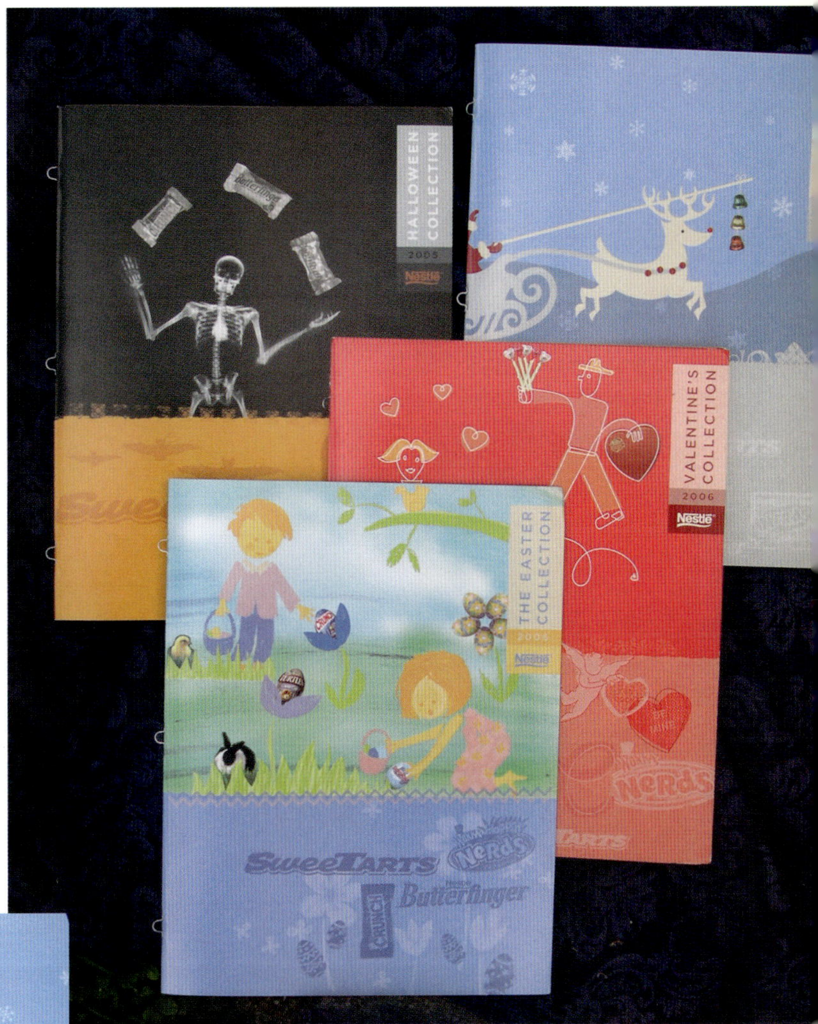

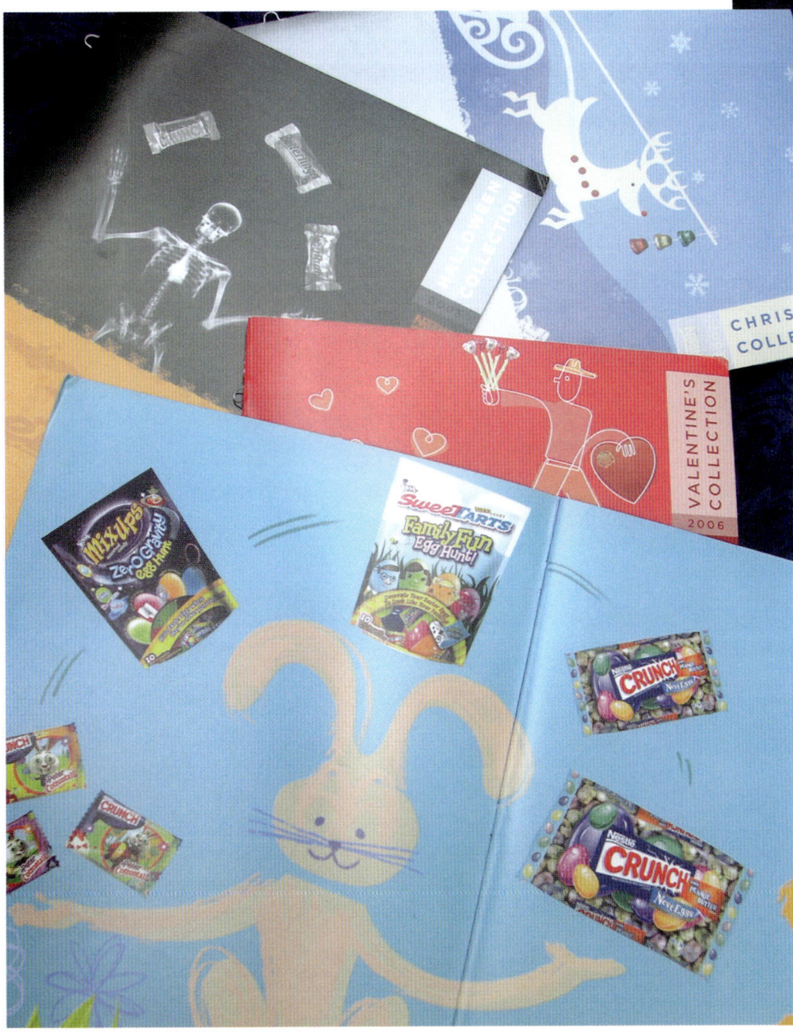

client
Nestle
design firm
Hornall Anderson Design Works
designers
Lisa Cerveny, Sonja Max,
Alan Copeland, Leo Raymundo,
Kris Delaney

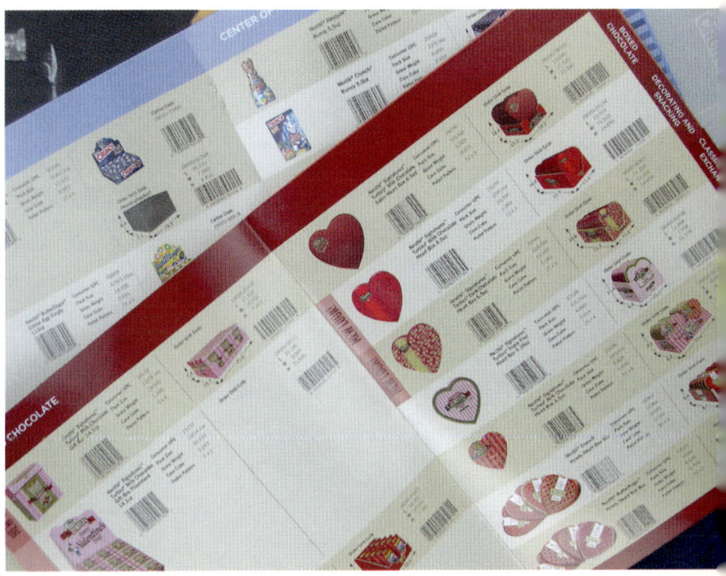

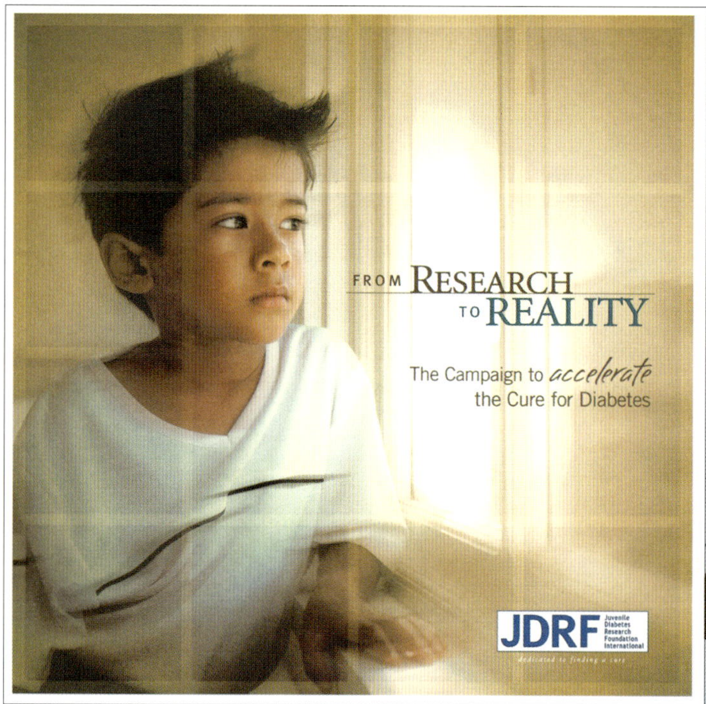

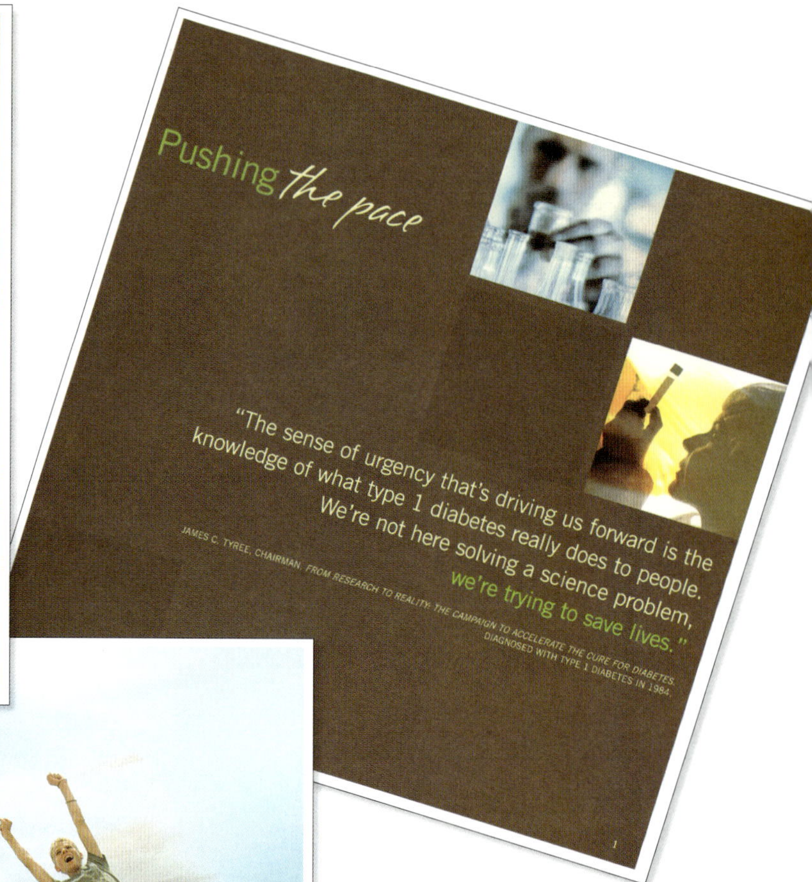

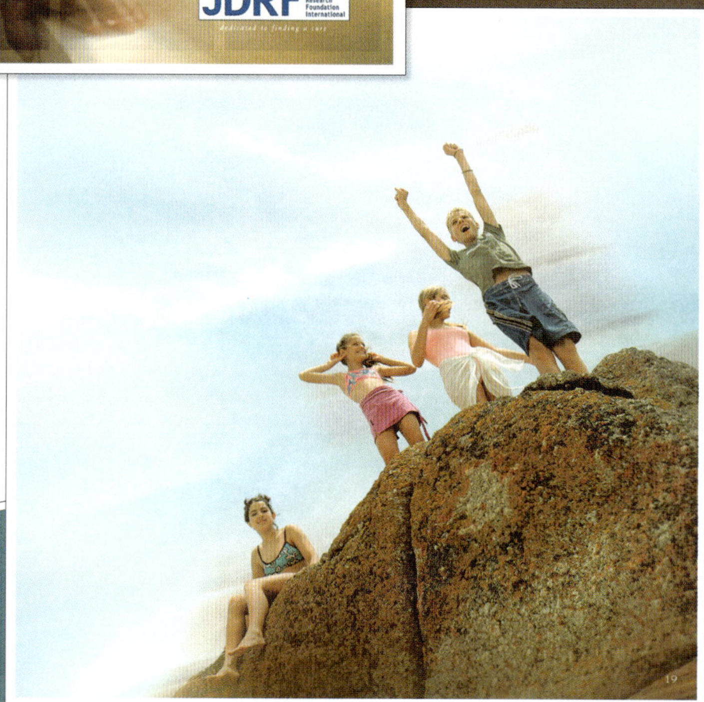

client
Juvenile Diabetes Research Foundation International
design firm
Levine & Associates
designer
Megan Riordan

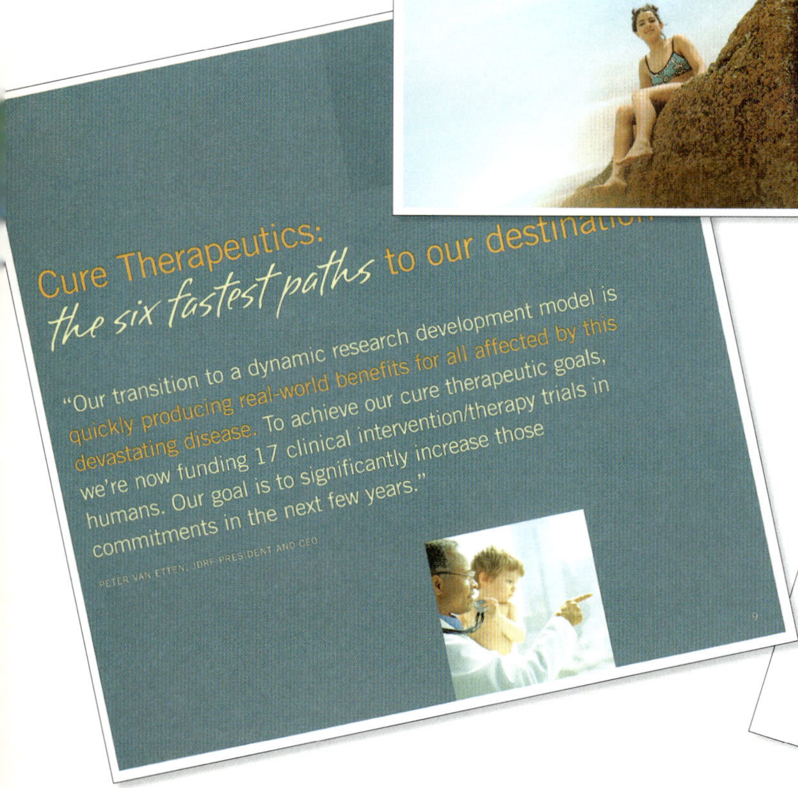

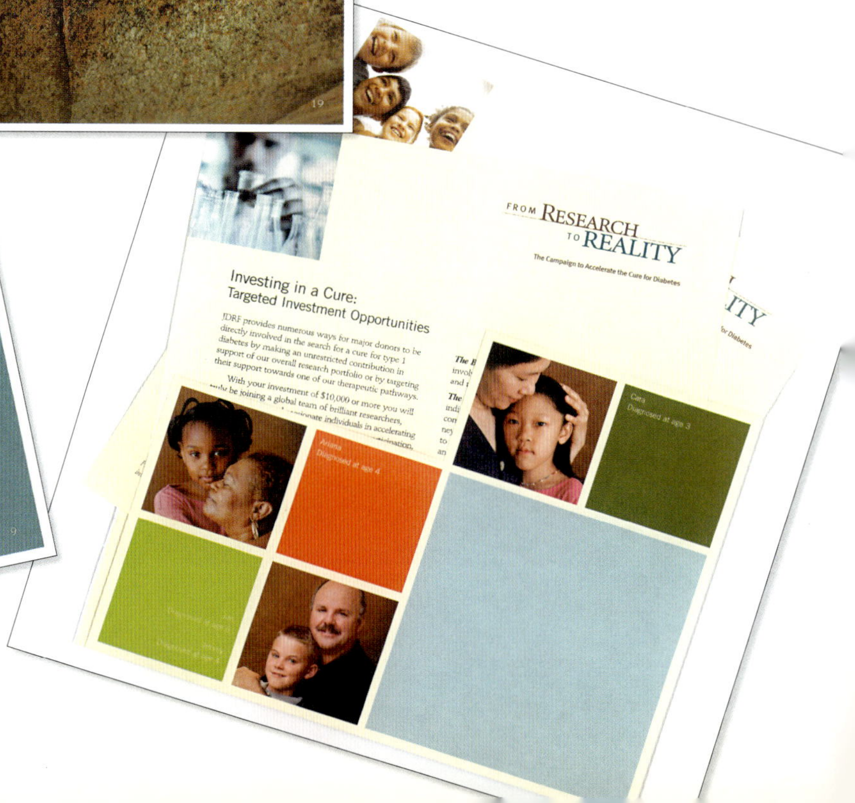

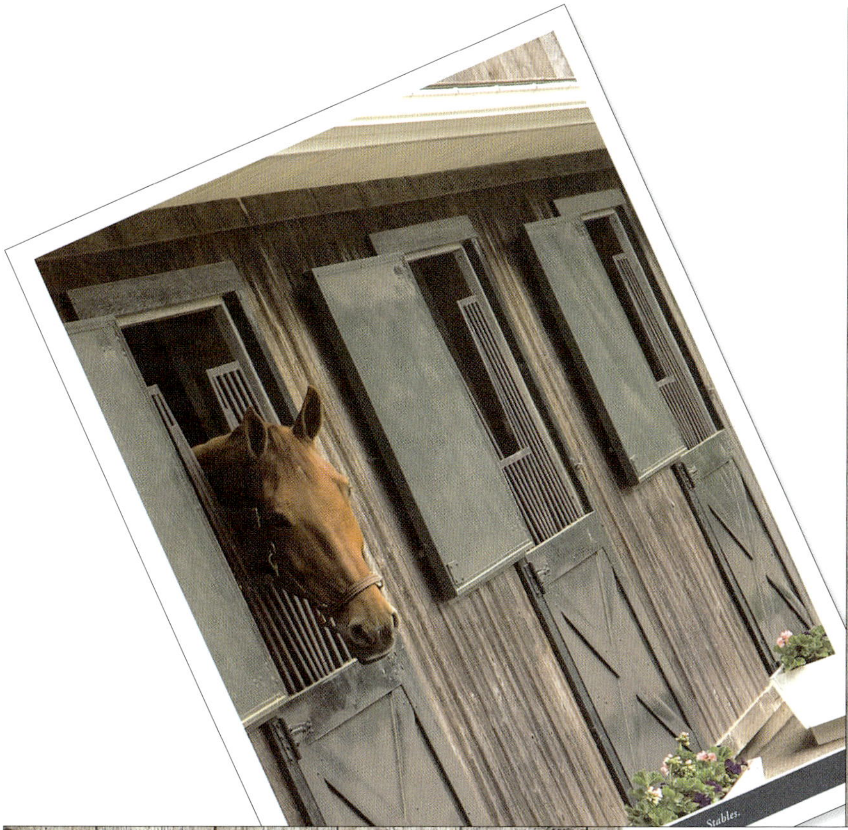

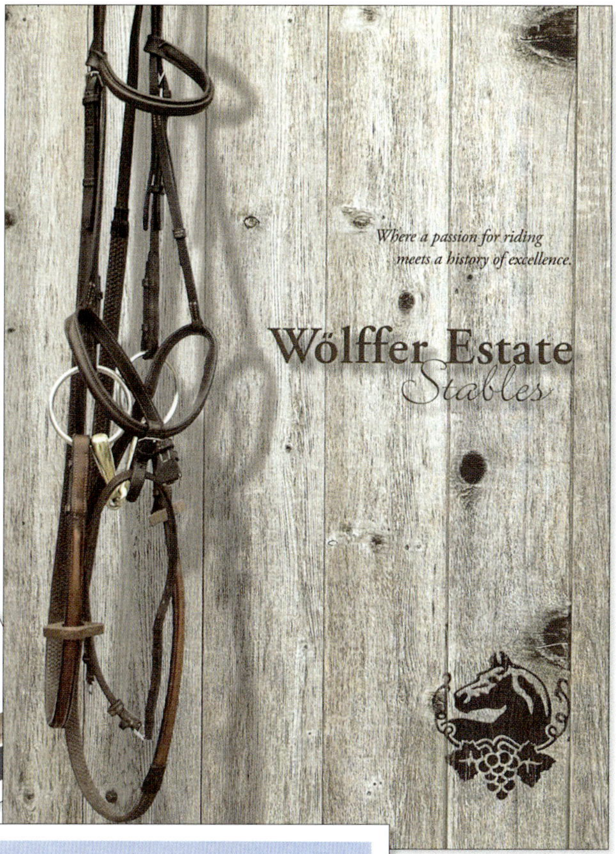

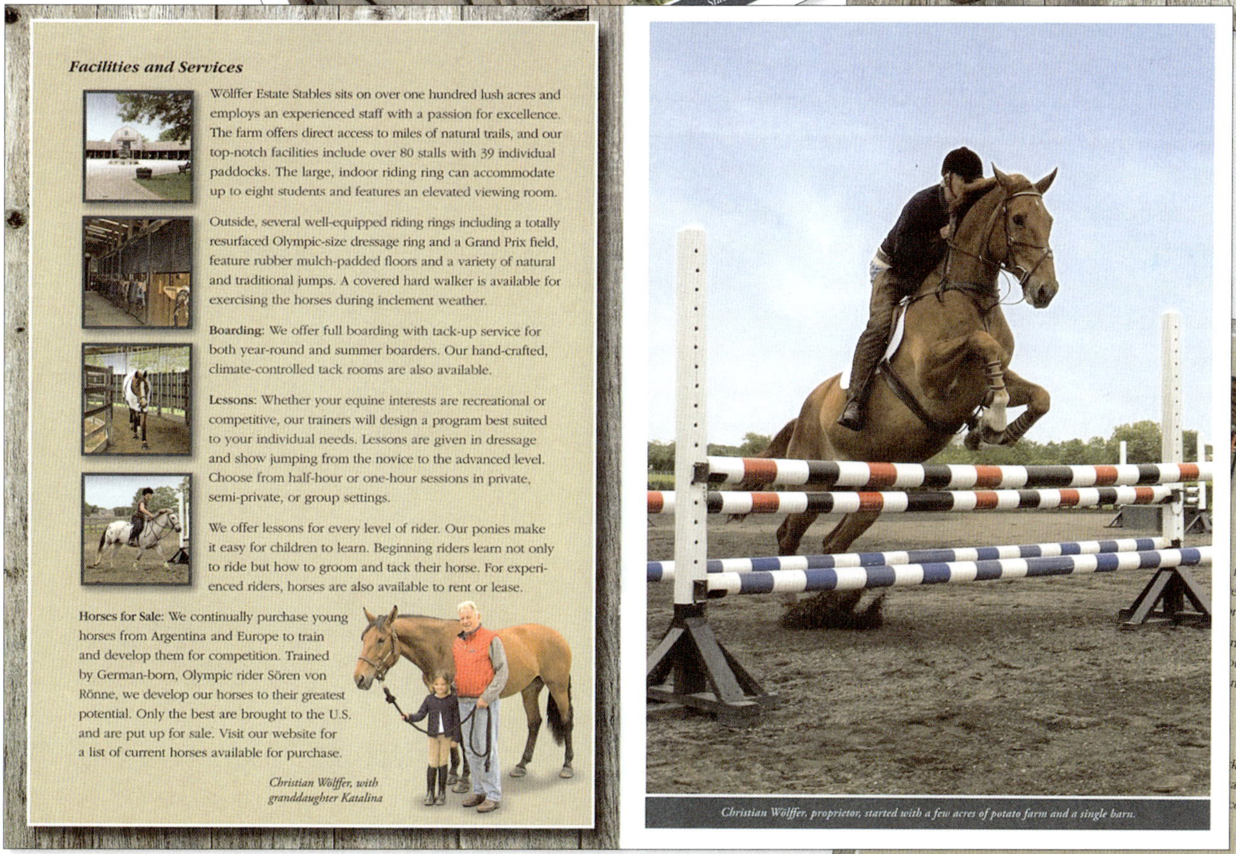

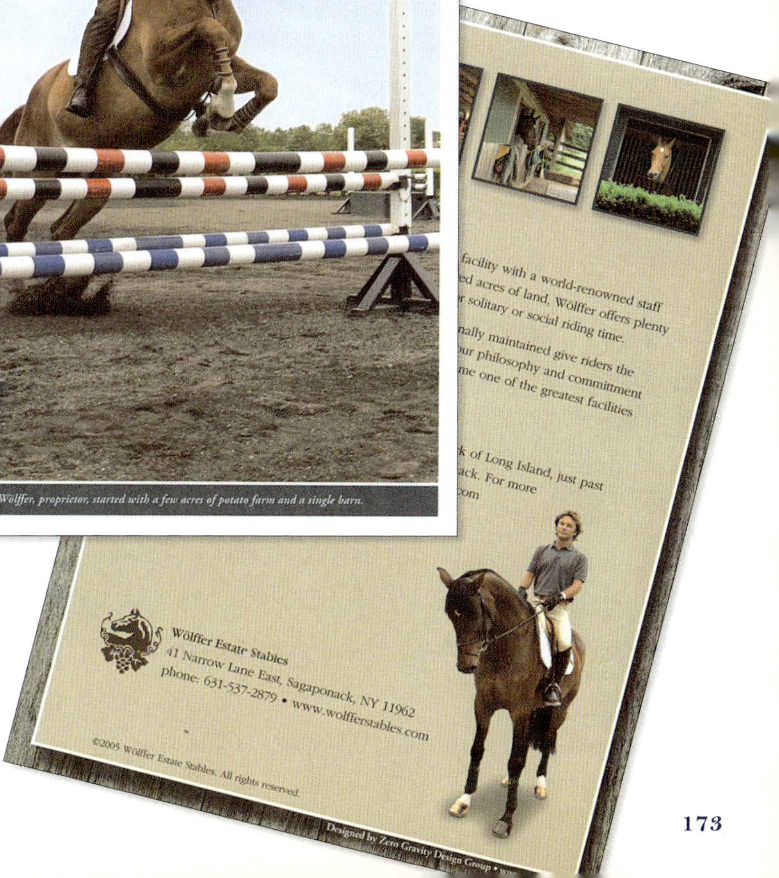

client
Wölffer Estate Stables
design firm
Zero Gravity Design Group
designers
Zero Gravity Design Group

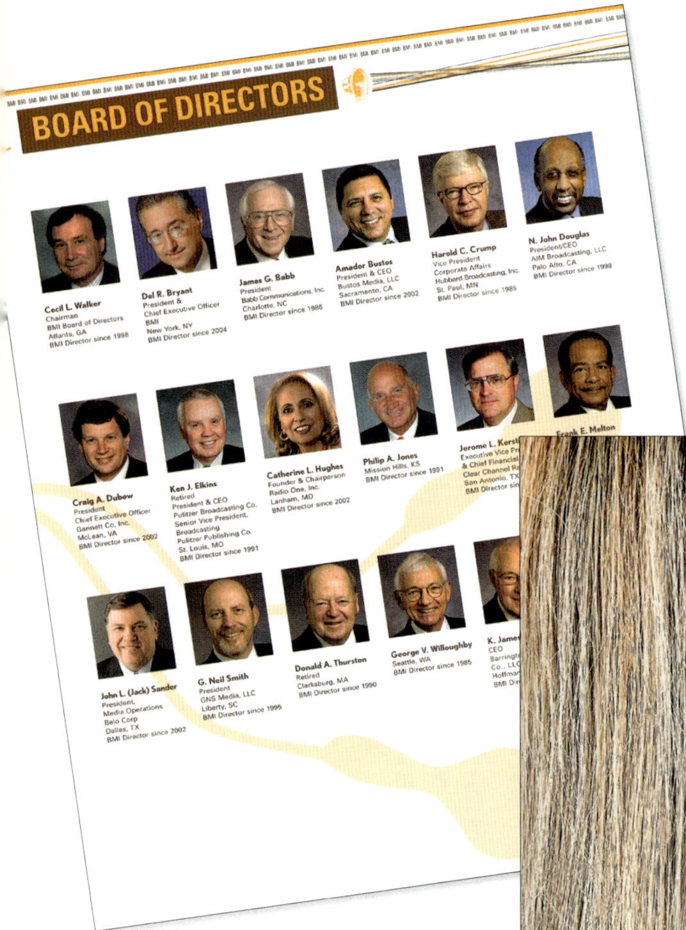

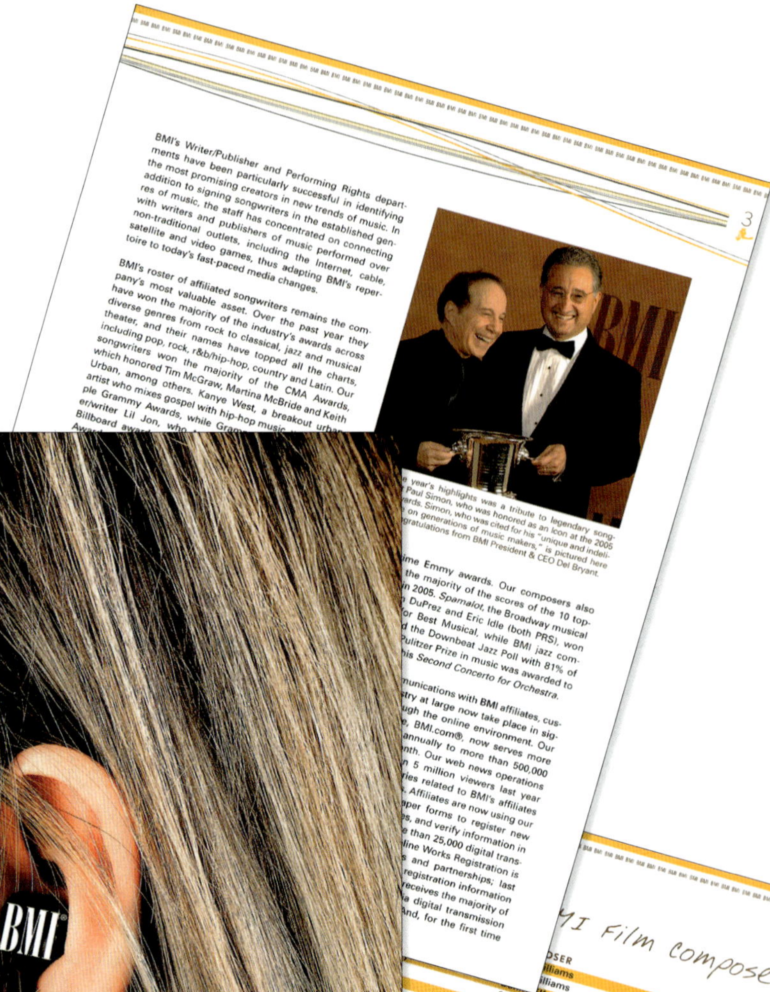

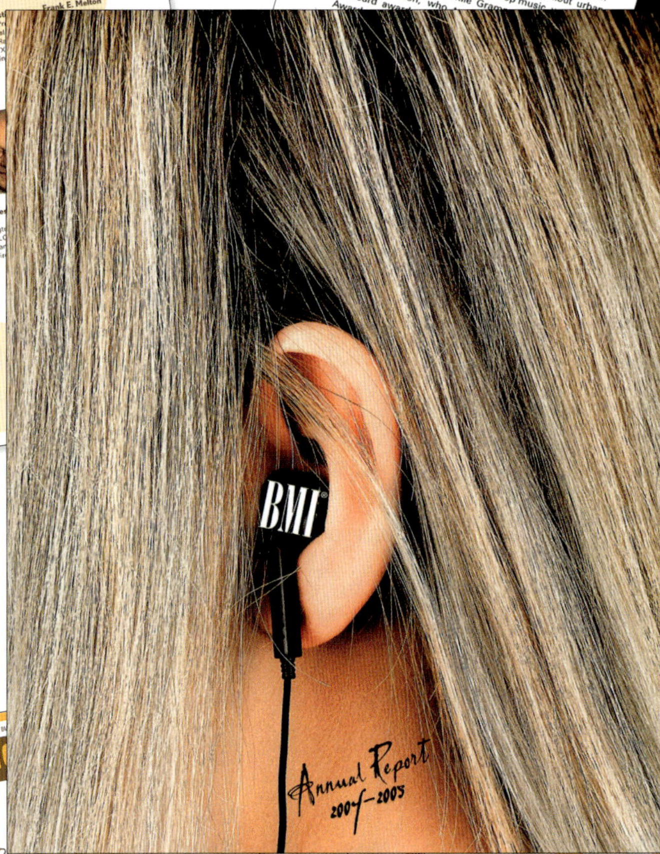

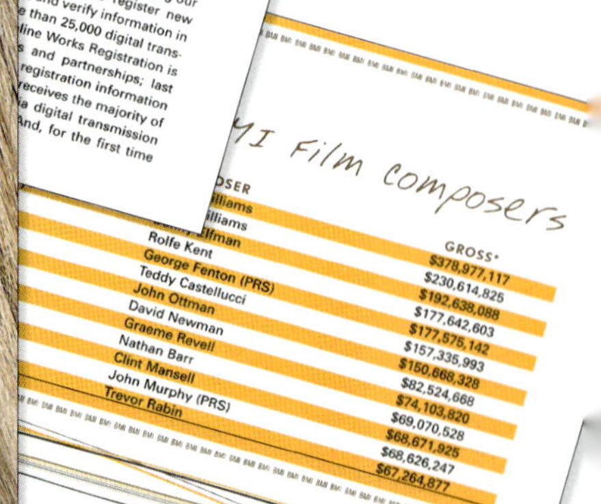

client
BMI
design firm
Hotsauce
designers
Wyndy Wilder Sloan,
Tim Morse

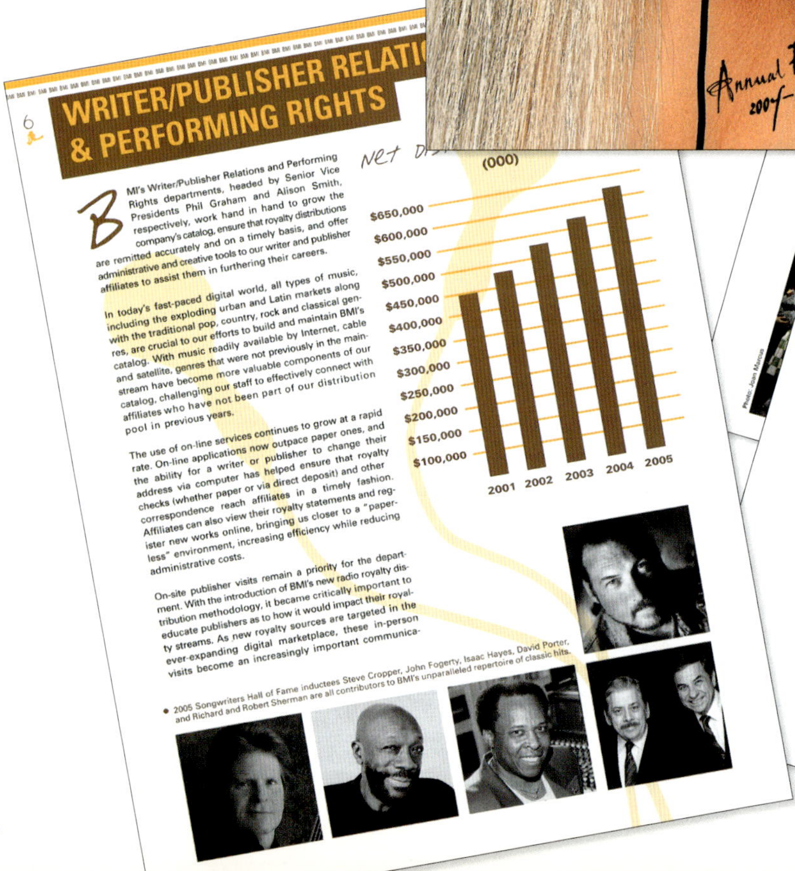

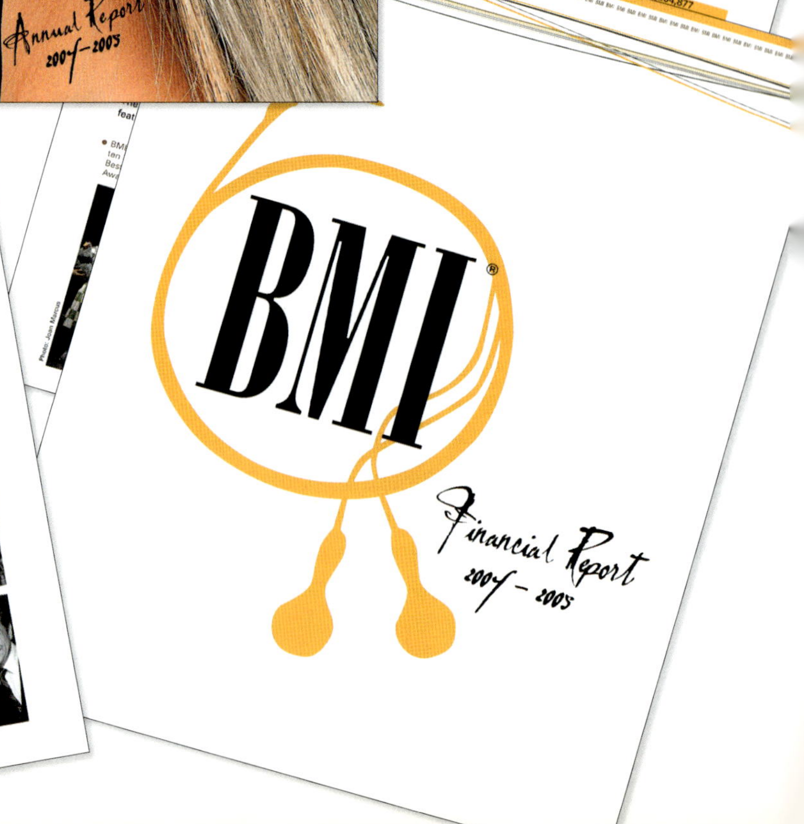

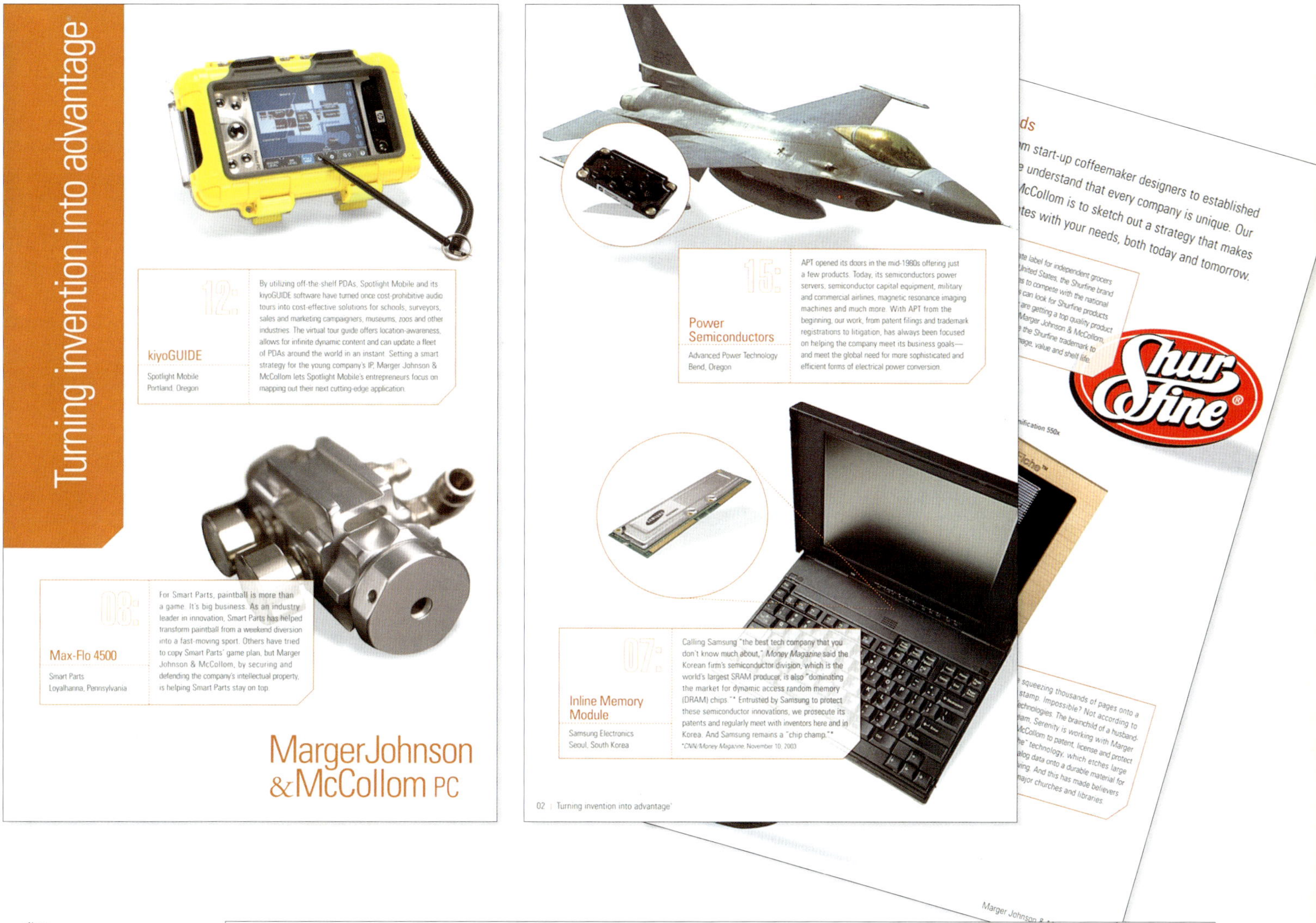

client
Marger Johnson & McCollom PC
design firm
Greenfield/Belser Ltd.
designers
Burkey Belser,
Charlyne Fabi

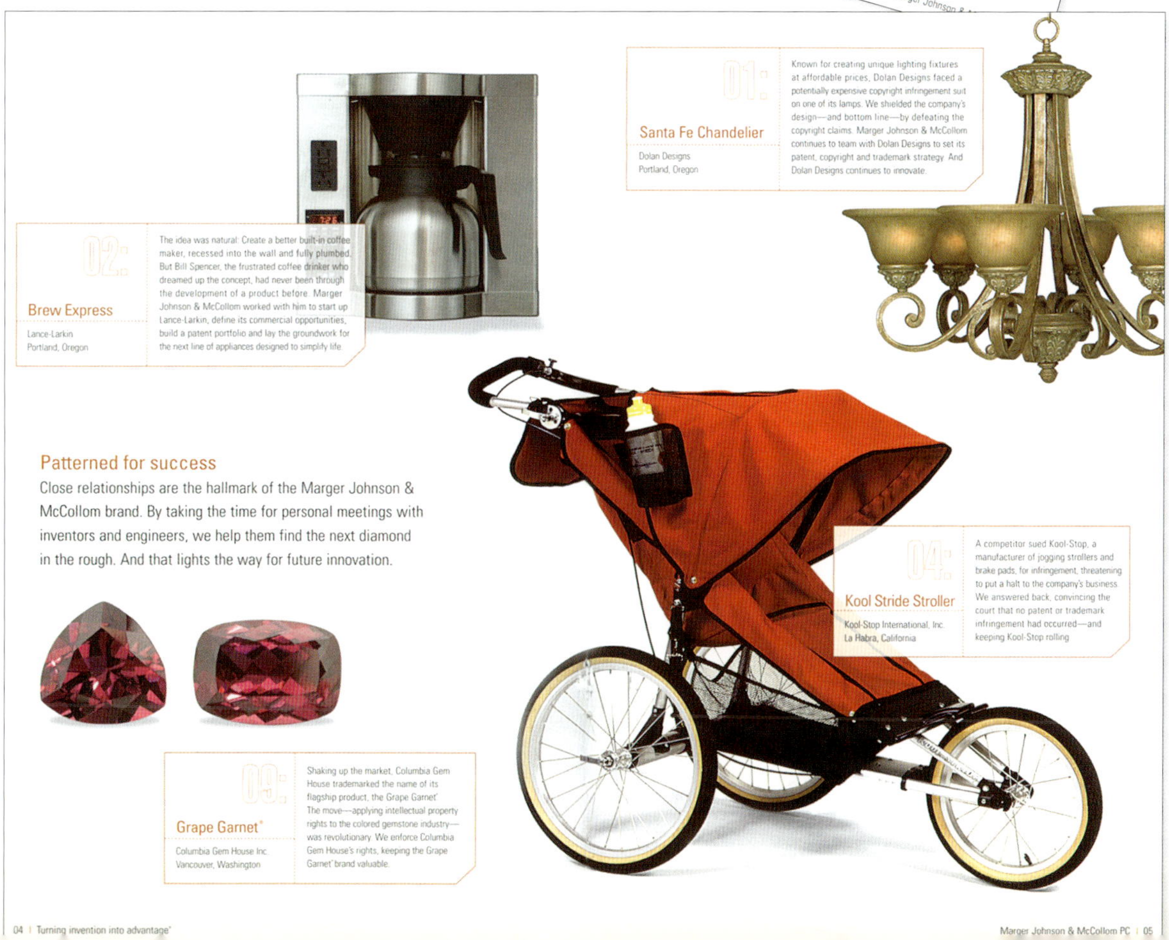

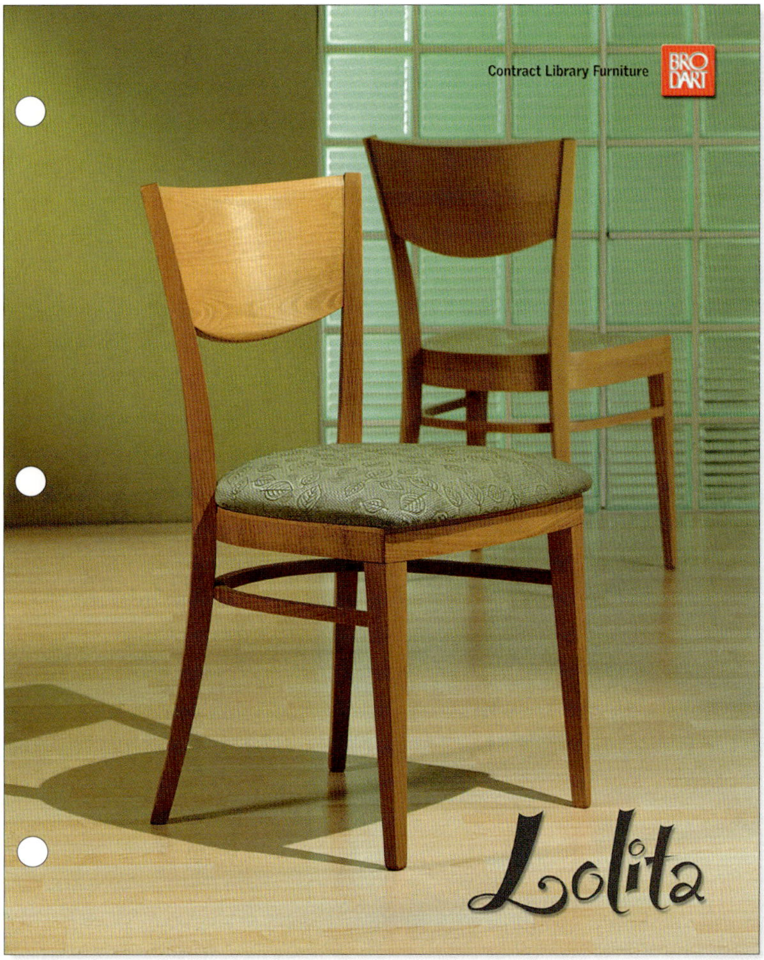

client
Brodart Furniture Company
design firm
Sire Advertising
designers
Shawn Felty,
Jordan Chappell

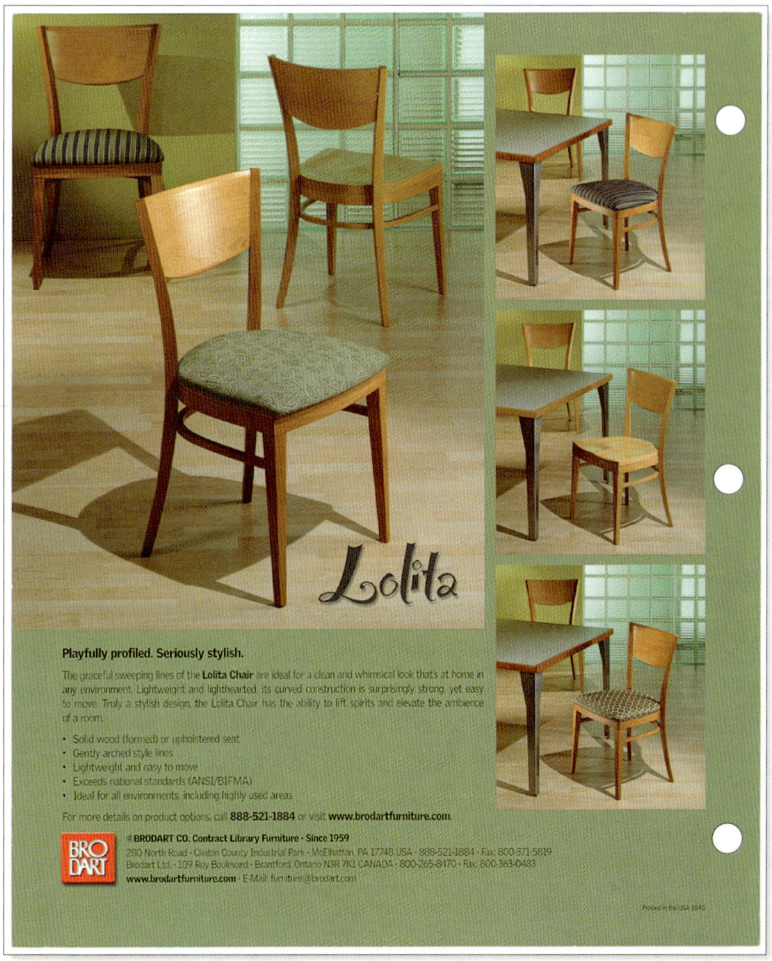

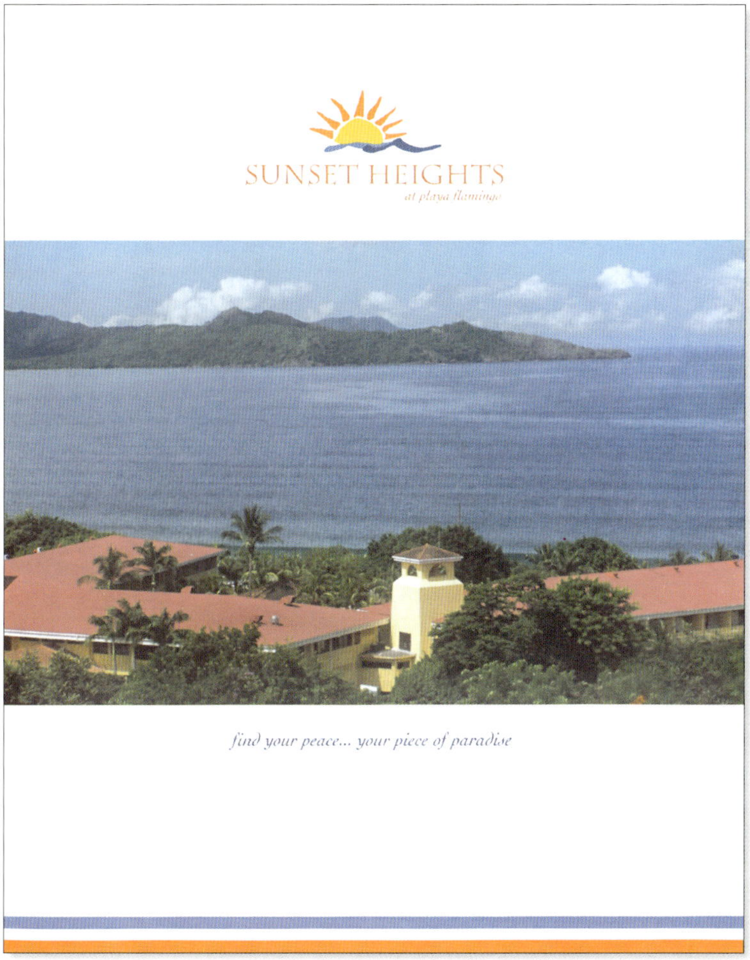

client
Sunset Heights
design firm
Original Impressions
designer
Lisa Cuervo

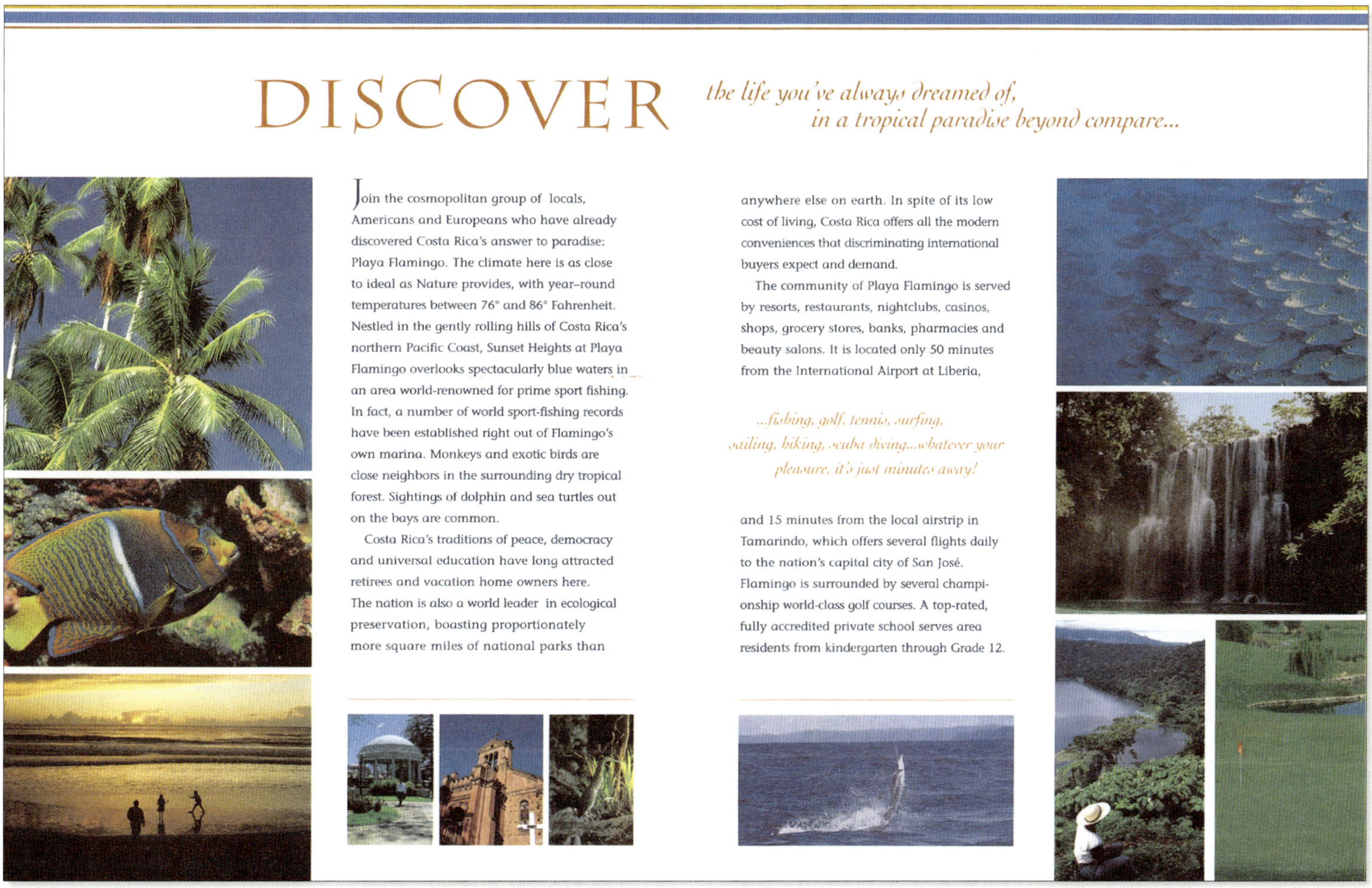

DISCOVER

the life you've always dreamed of, in a tropical paradise beyond compare...

Join the cosmopolitan group of locals, Americans and Europeans who have already discovered Costa Rica's answer to paradise: Playa Flamingo. The climate here is as close to ideal as Nature provides, with year–round temperatures between 76° and 86° Fahrenheit. Nestled in the gently rolling hills of Costa Rica's northern Pacific Coast, Sunset Heights at Playa Flamingo overlooks spectacularly blue waters in an area world-renowned for prime sport fishing. In fact, a number of world sport-fishing records have been established right out of Flamingo's own marina. Monkeys and exotic birds are close neighbors in the surrounding dry tropical forest. Sightings of dolphin and sea turtles out on the bays are common.

Costa Rica's traditions of peace, democracy and universal education have long attracted retirees and vacation home owners here. The nation is also a world leader in ecological preservation, boasting proportionately more square miles of national parks than anywhere else on earth. In spite of its low cost of living, Costa Rica offers all the modern conveniences that discriminating international buyers expect and demand.

The community of Playa Flamingo is served by resorts, restaurants, nightclubs, casinos, shops, grocery stores, banks, pharmacies and beauty salons. It is located only 50 minutes from the International Airport at Liberia,

...fishing, golf, tennis, surfing, sailing, biking, scuba diving...whatever your pleasure, it's just minutes away!

and 15 minutes from the local airstrip in Tamarindo, which offers several flights daily to the nation's capital city of San José. Flamingo is surrounded by several championship world-class golf courses. A top-rated, fully accredited private school serves area residents from kindergarten through Grade 12.

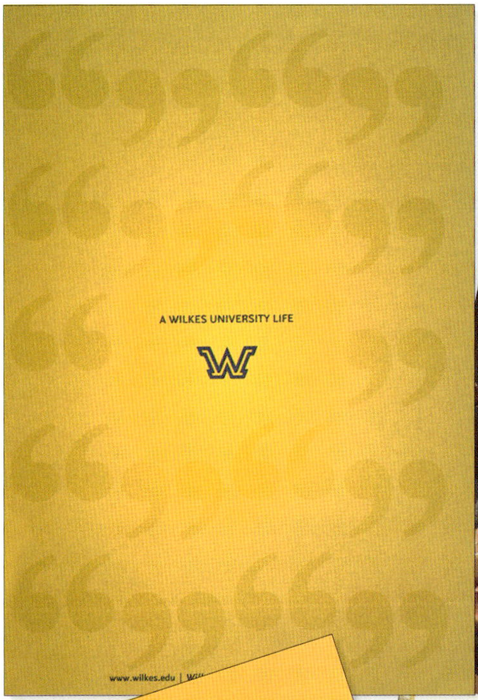

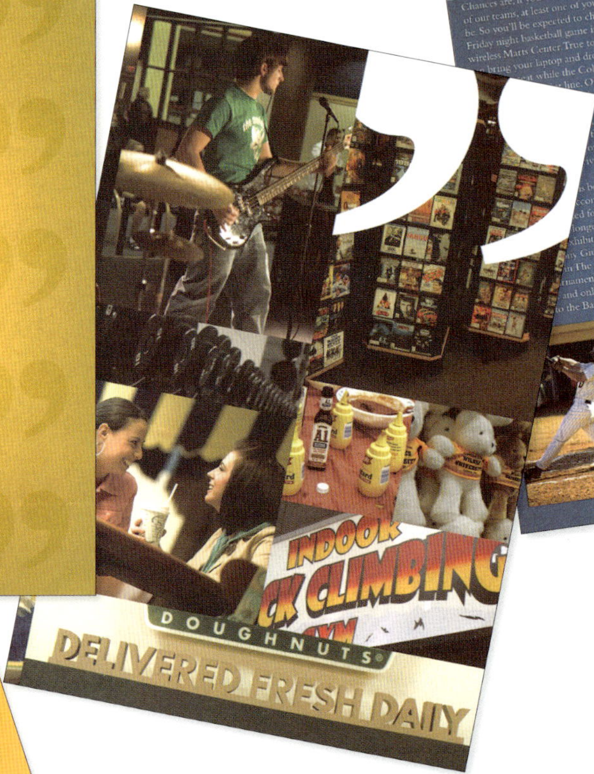

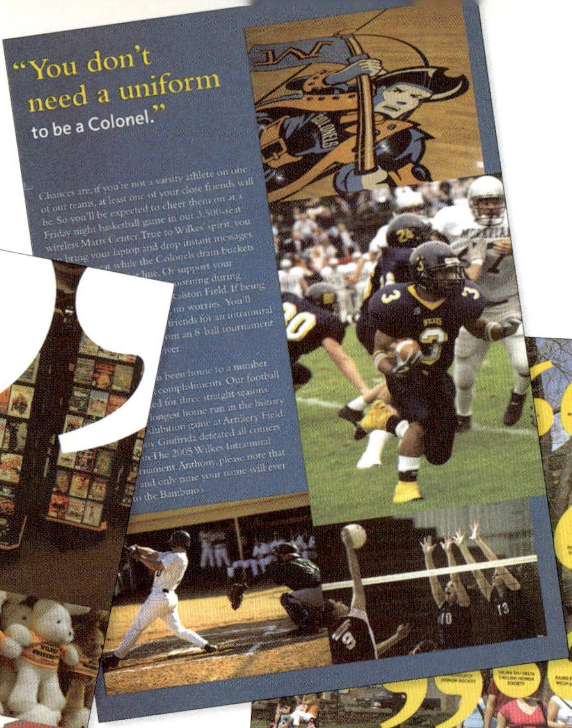

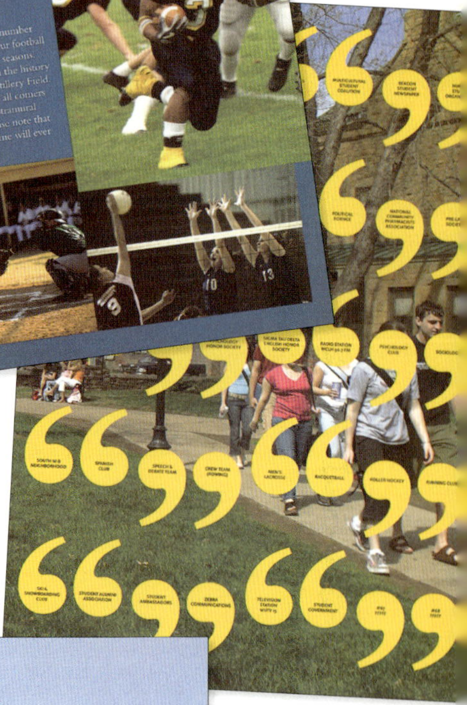

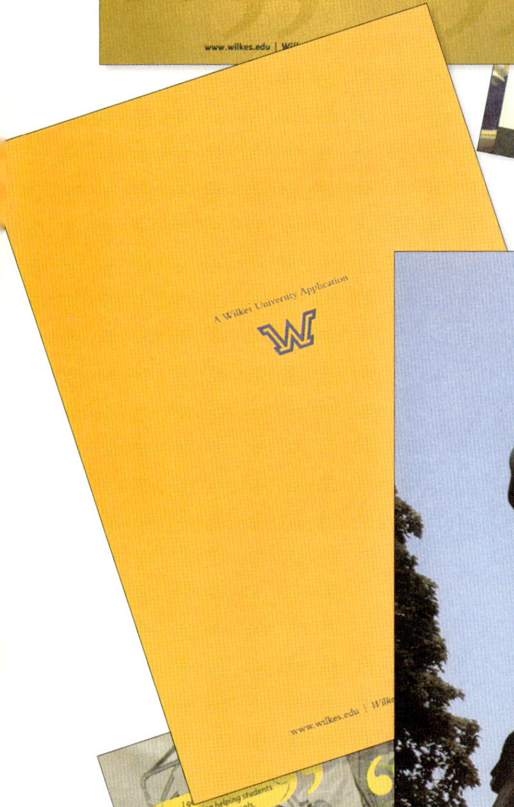

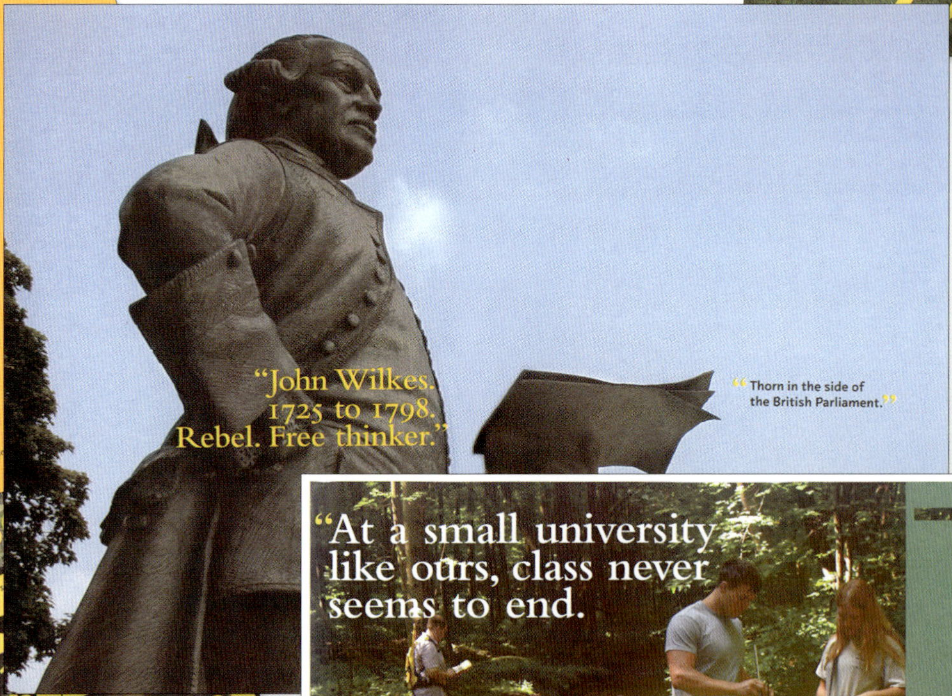

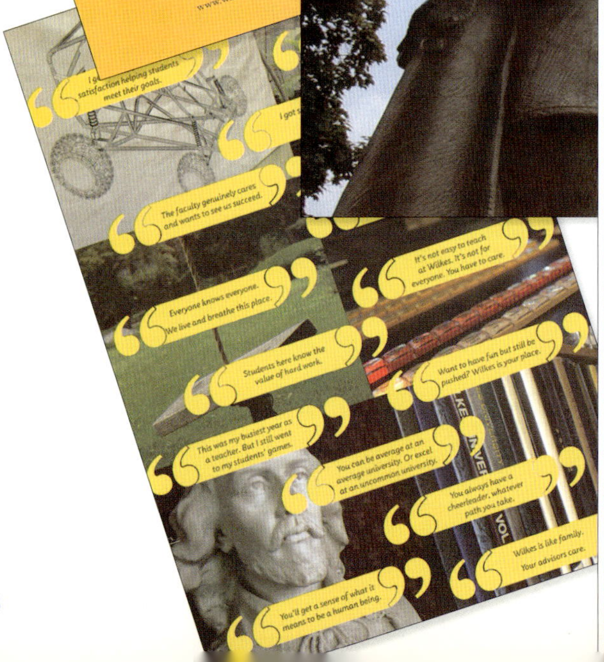

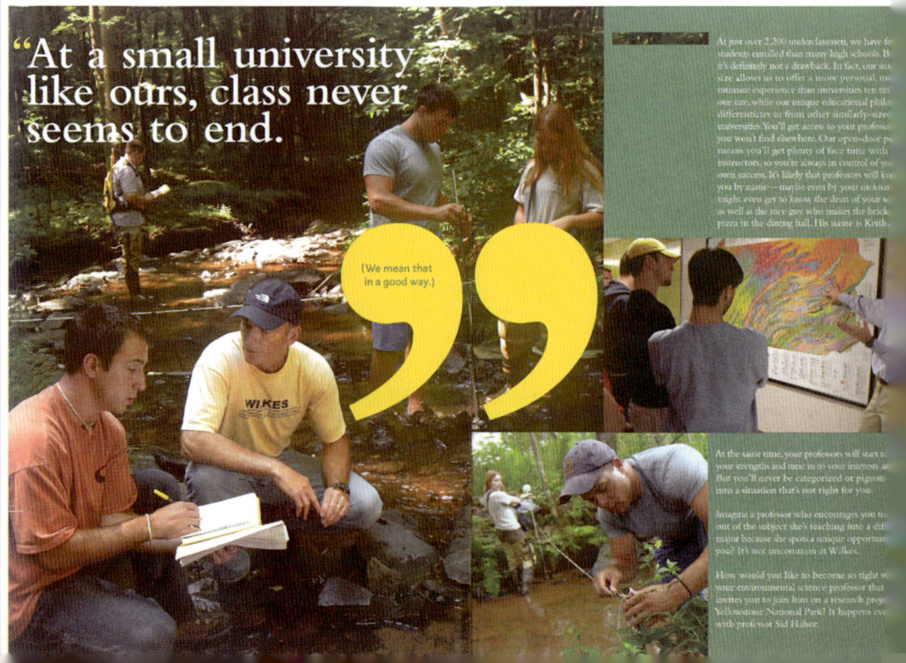

client
Wilkes University
design firm
160over90
designers
Darryl Cilli,
Jim Walls,
Adam Flanagan,
Giacomo Ciminello

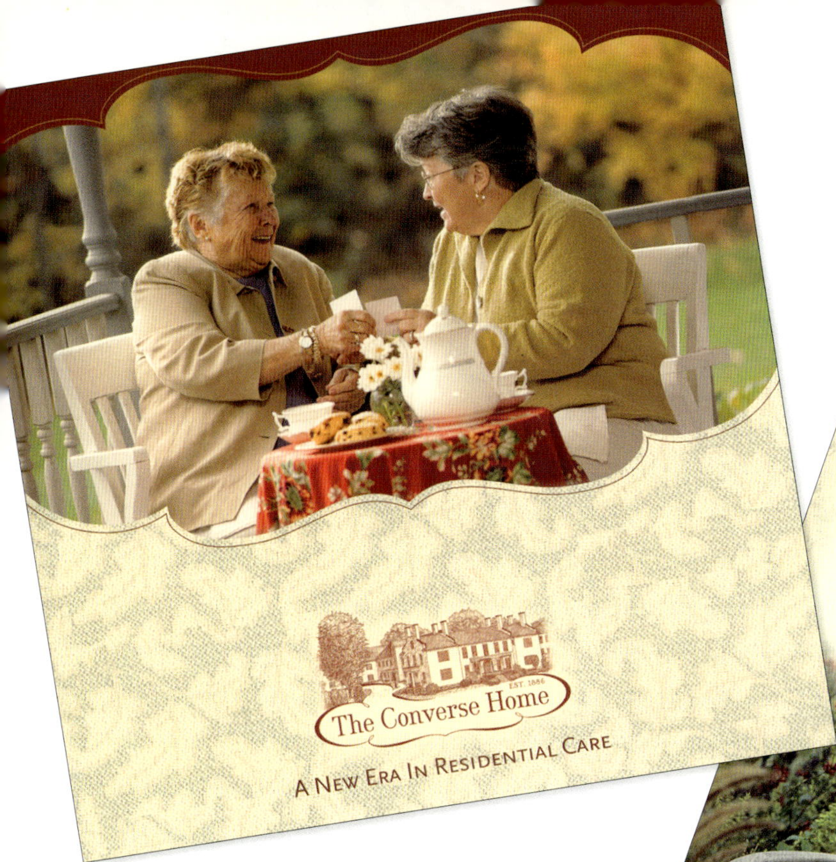

The Converse Home
EST. 1884

A NEW ERA IN RESIDENTIAL CARE

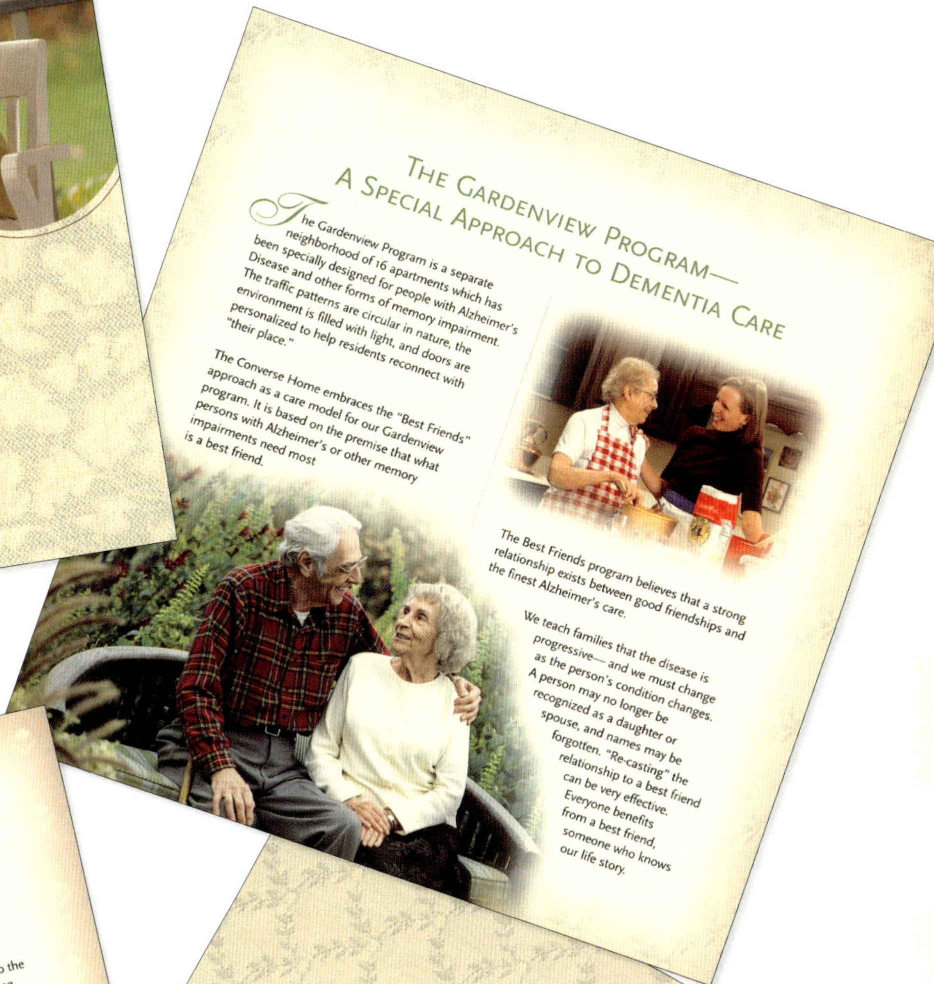

THE GARDENVIEW PROGRAM— A SPECIAL APPROACH TO DEMENTIA CARE

The Gardenview Program is a separate neighborhood of 16 apartments which has been specially designed for people with Alzheimer's Disease and other forms of memory impairment. The traffic patterns are circular in nature, the environment is filled with light, and doors are personalized to help residents reconnect with "their place."

The Converse Home embraces the "Best Friends" approach as a care model for our Gardenview program. It is based on the premise that what persons with Alzheimer's or other memory impairments need most is a best friend.

The Best Friends program believes that a strong relationship exists between good friendships and the finest Alzheimer's care.

We teach families that the disease is progressive— and we must change as the person's condition changes. A person may no longer be recognized as a daughter or spouse, and names may be forgotten. "Re-casting" the relationship to a best friend can be very effective. Everyone benefits from a best friend, someone who knows our life story.

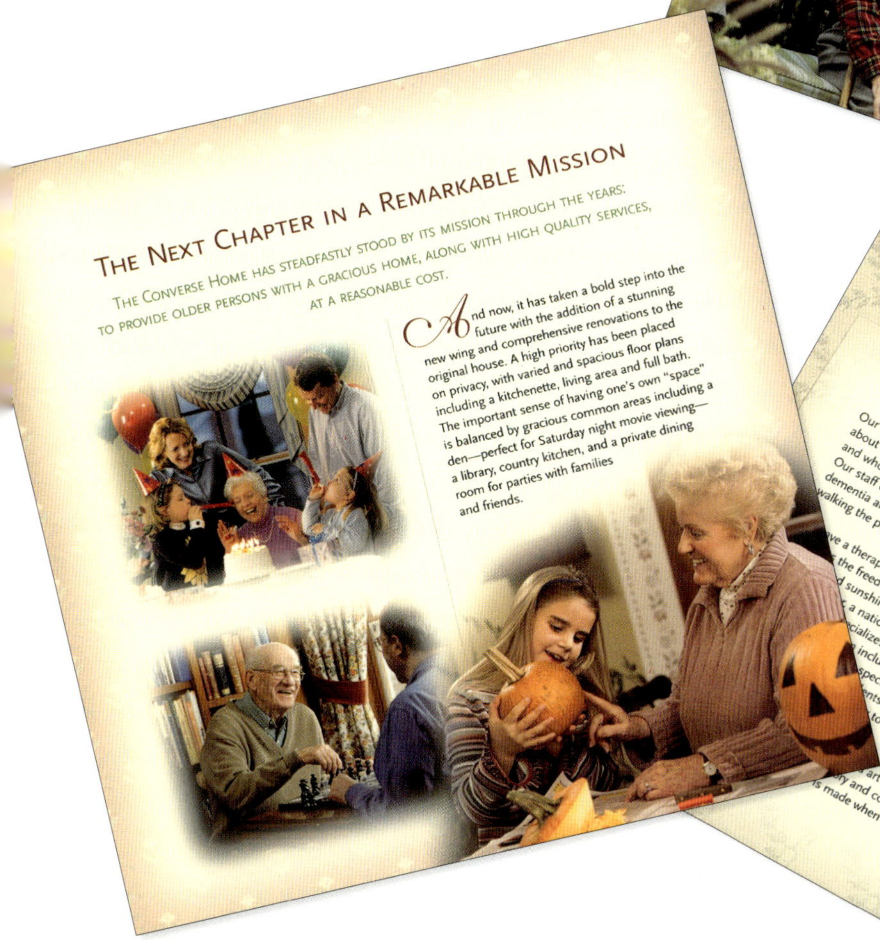

THE NEXT CHAPTER IN A REMARKABLE MISSION

THE CONVERSE HOME HAS STEADFASTLY STOOD BY ITS MISSION THROUGH THE YEARS: TO PROVIDE OLDER PERSONS WITH A GRACIOUS HOME, ALONG WITH HIGH QUALITY SERVICES, AT A REASONABLE COST.

And now, it has taken a bold step into the future with the addition of a stunning new wing and comprehensive renovations to the original house. A high priority has been placed on privacy, with varied and spacious floor plans including a kitchenette, living area and full bath. The important sense of having one's own "space" is balanced by gracious common areas including a den—perfect for Saturday night movie viewing—a library, country kitchen, and a private dining room for parties with families and friends.

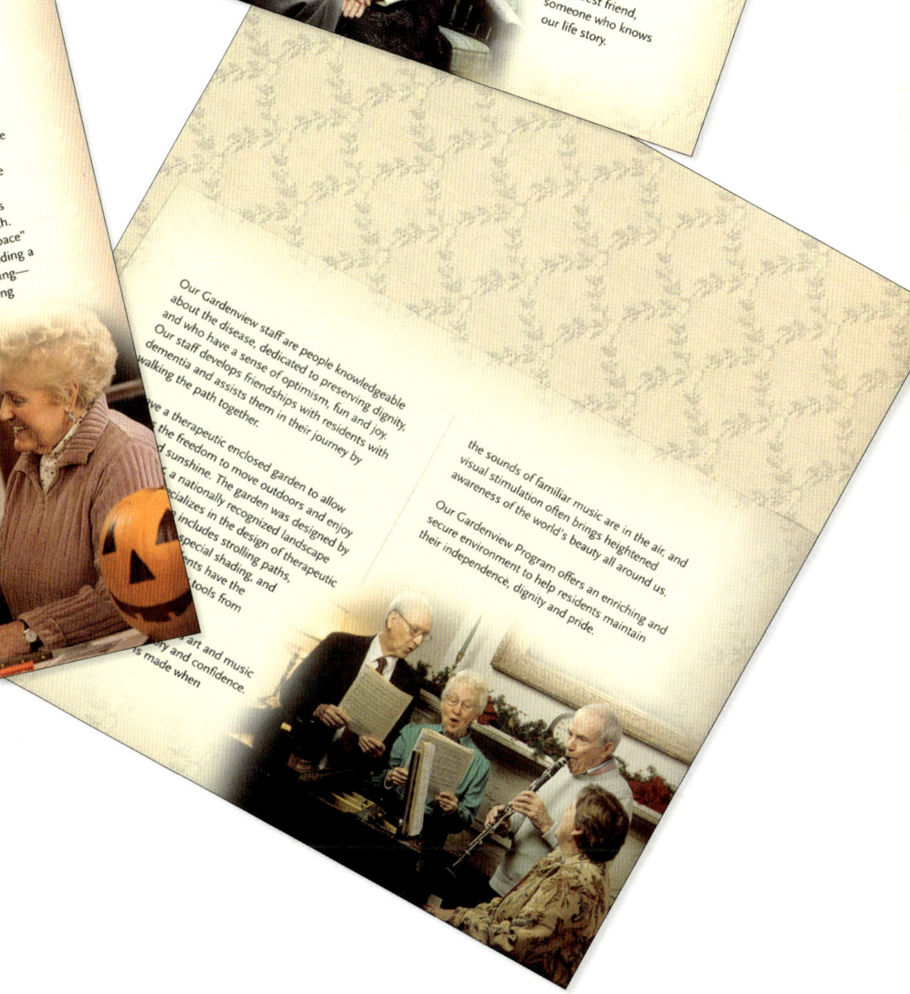

Our Gardenview staff are people knowledgeable about the disease, dedicated to preserving dignity, and who have a sense of optimism, fun and joy. Our staff develops friendships with residents with dementia and assists them in their journey by walking the path together.

the sounds of familiar music are in the air, and visual stimulation often brings heightened awareness of the world's beauty all around us.

Our Gardenview Program offers an enriching and secure environment to help residents maintain their independence, dignity and pride.

client
The Converse Home
design firm
Paul Kaza Associates
designer
Donda Thibault

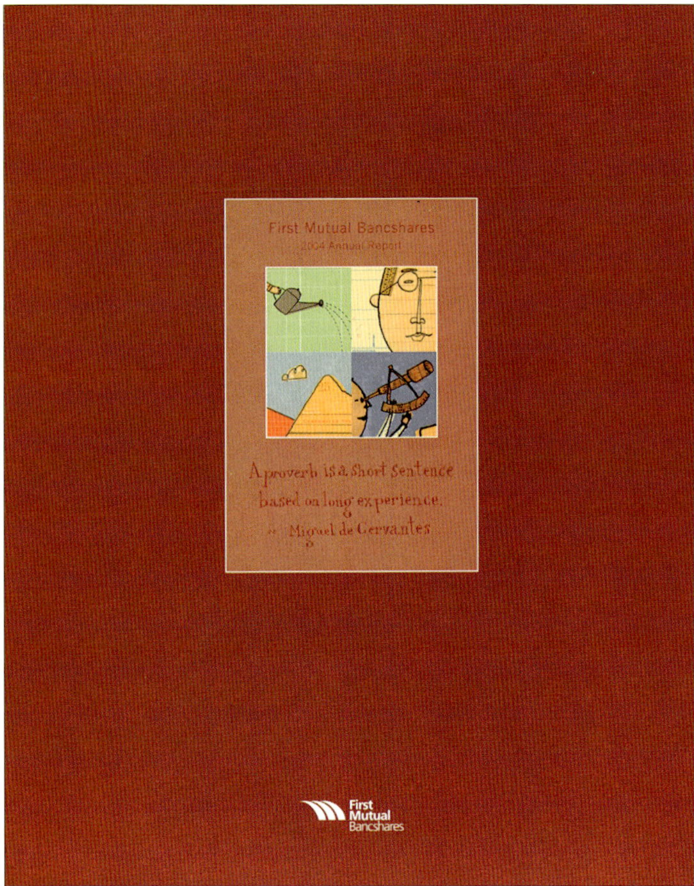

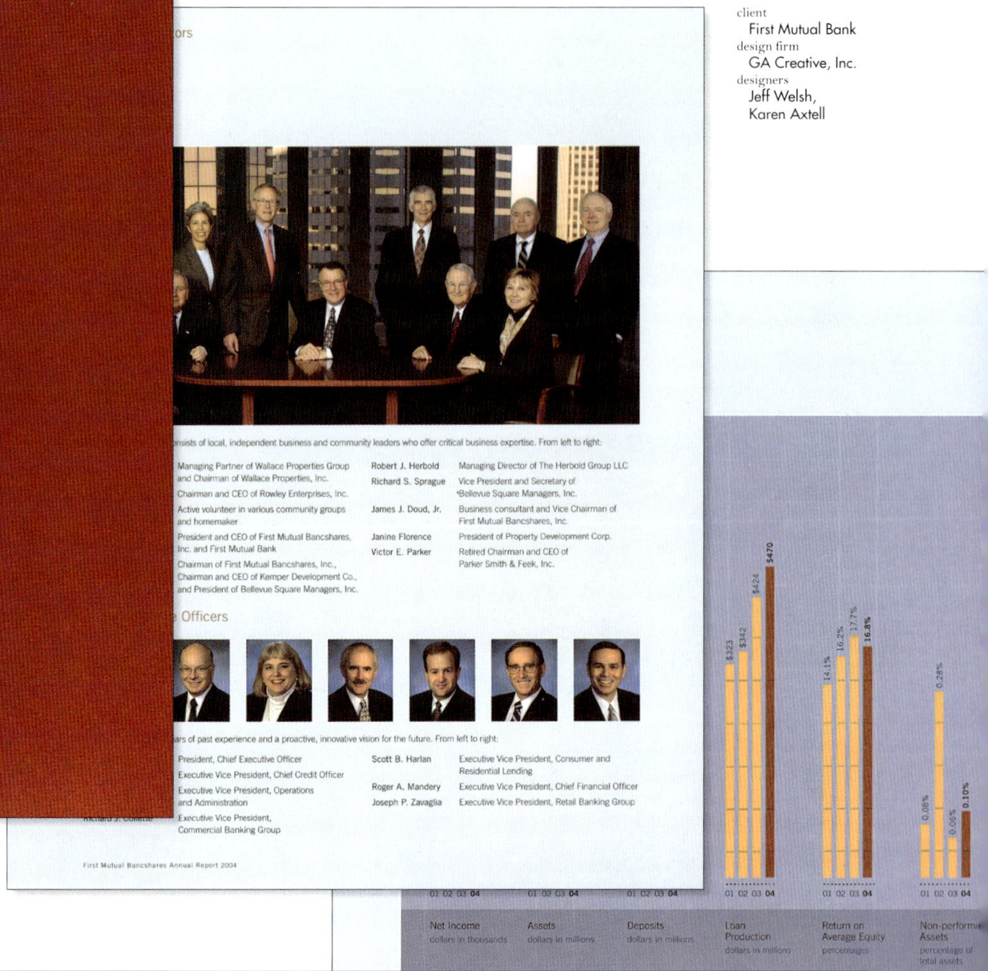

client
First Mutual Bank
design firm
GA Creative, Inc.
designers
Jeff Welsh,
Karen Axtell

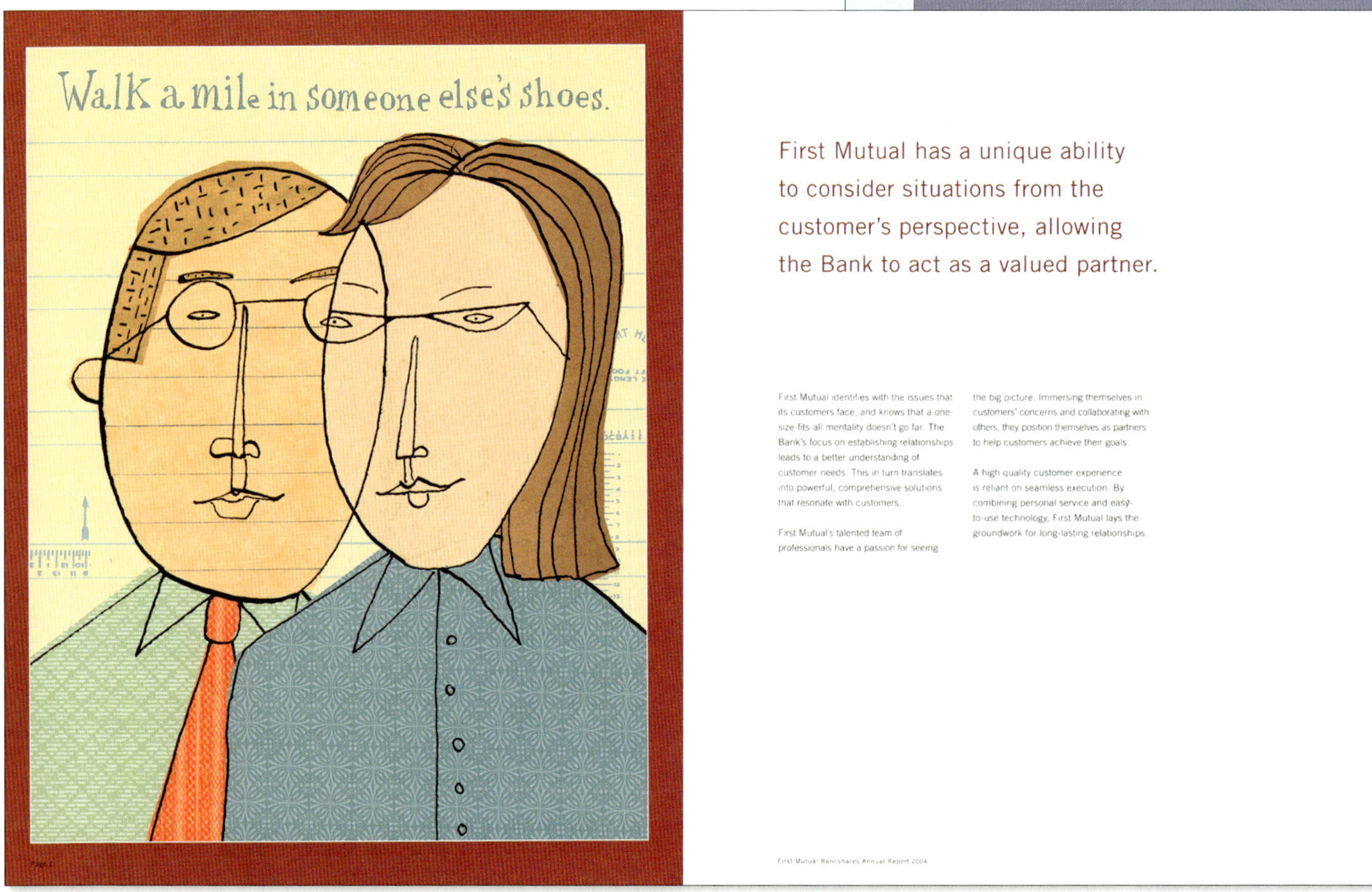

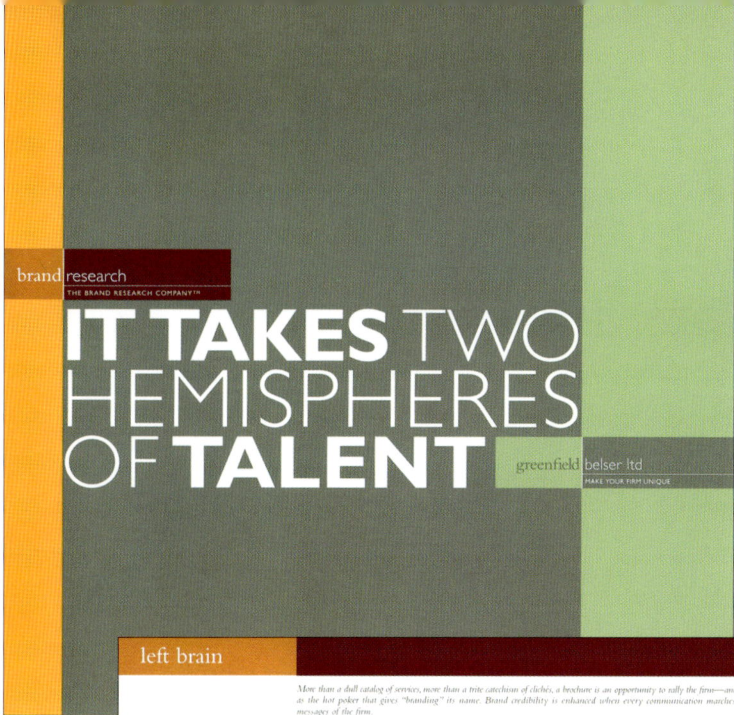

client
Greenfield/Belser Ltd.
design firm
Greenfield/Belser Ltd.
designers
Burkey Belser,
Siobhan Davis

left brain | unique | in print | right brain

More than a dull catalog of services, more than a trite catechism of clichés, a brochure is an opportunity to rally the firm—and make it as memorable as the hot poker that gives "branding" its name. Brand credibility is enhanced when every communication marches in step with the key messages of the firm.

no.1 CRITERIA OF CORPORATE BUYERS IS SPECIFIC EXPERTISE.
Marketing is all about telling stories. Be sure to include case studies rich with specifics and drama in your materials.

$50 BILLION
The amount spent on print advertising and collateral materials in 2004.
Although the Internet is the fastest-growing marketing medium, print material still accounts for half of all promotional expenditures because print is still the cheapest, most effective way of ensuring your message will land in the hands of interested buyers.

18%
PREDICTED ANNUAL GROWTH OF DIGITAL COLOR PRINTING THROUGH YEAR 2010.
The Holy Grail of marketing is to design customized, high-quality, printed sales materials as if they came off the press just for that client or prospect. On-demand brochures can be updated more frequently, targeting buyers more specifically.

92%
of C-level executives read professional services newsletters.
Some receive hundreds of newsletters each month. Only those that are short (four pages or less) and to the point are likely to be read. "Client Alerts" are preferred but make sure they arrive within 14 days of market shifts or regulatory changes or you can be certain your competition has beaten you to the punch.

No.1 and 92%: G/B and BRC proprietary research. 18%: Heidelberg CEO Bernhard Schreier. $50 billion: TAPPI and PIA.

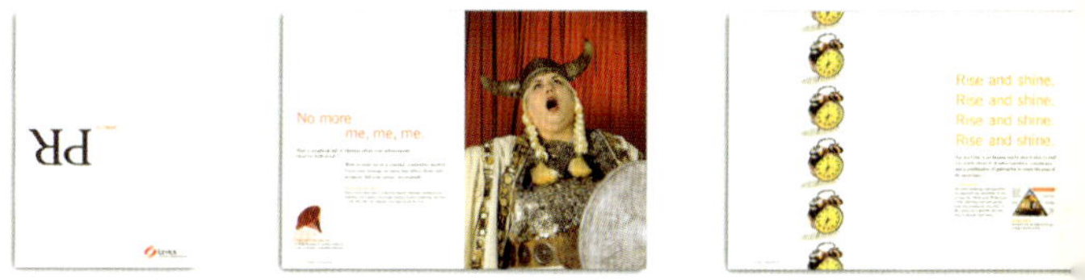

The cover declares, "PR is dead." **Levick Strategic Communications** replaces the image of "spinmeister" with a disciplined, contemporary approach to media relatio

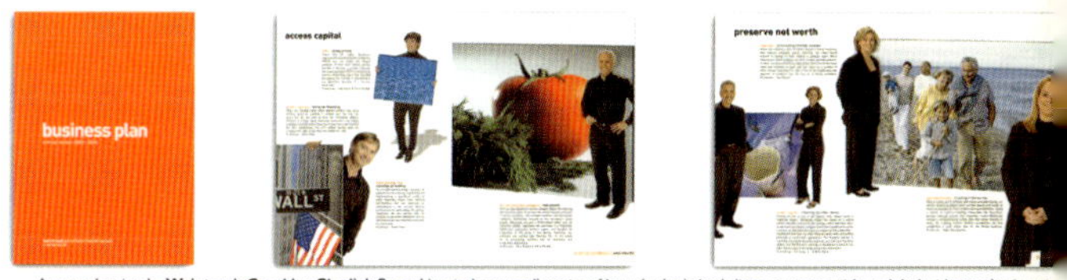

An annual review by **Weintraub Genshlea Chediak Sproul** lets its lawyers tell stories of how they've helped clients overcome risks and deal with complex issues.

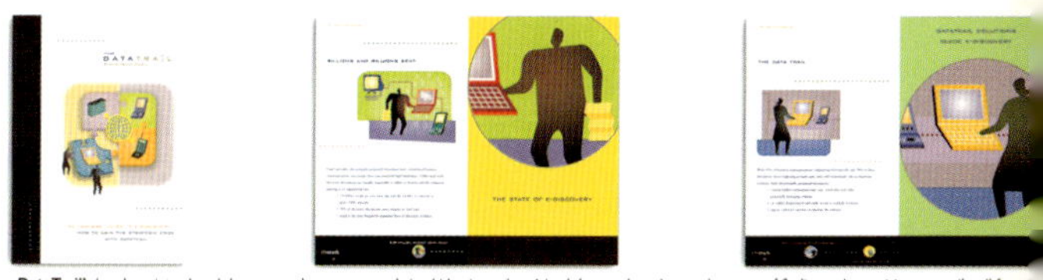

DataTrail's brochure introduced the company's new name and visual identity, and explained the poorly understood process of finding and organizing an email trail for tr

left brain | unique | in print | right brain

An ad can tell an interesting story, raise a pertinent question, offer a unique solution—or it can just make you smile. When an ad does all those things, we'll present it to you for approval.

1,600 Number of commercial messages Americans are exposed to every day.

0.5 Magazine readers spend less than half a second deciding whether to read an ad.
We live in a time of sensory overload. Give people a reason to pay attention to your ad, or they won't.

61% COLOR WORKS. ADS IN FULL COLOR ARE NOTICED 20 PERCENT MORE OFTEN THAN BLACK-AND-WHITE ADS, AND THEY ARE READ—AT LEAST HALFWAY THROUGH—61 PERCENT MORE OFTEN.

39% Size works. Full-page ads are noticed 39 percent more often than quarter-page ads.

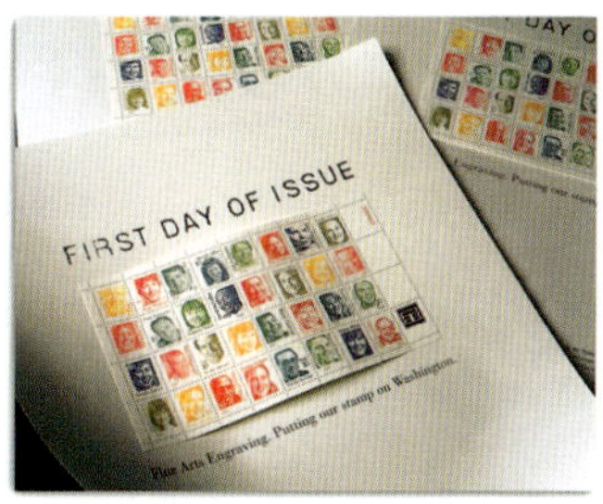

Fine Arts Engraving Company's employees became stamps in this engraving tour de force commemorating the opening of their Washington, D.C., plant.

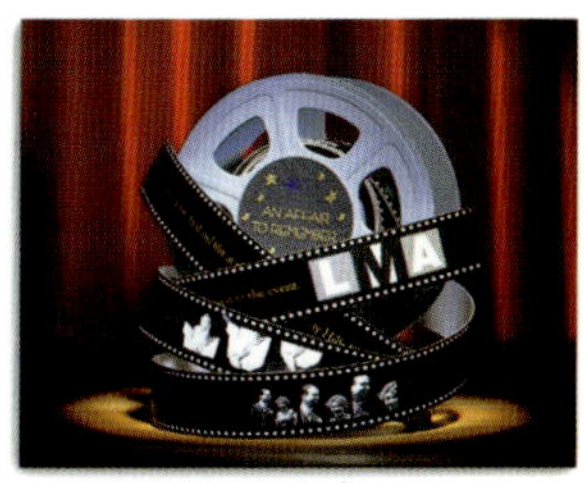

Invitation, packaged in a film can, to a **Legal Marketing Association** annual gala.

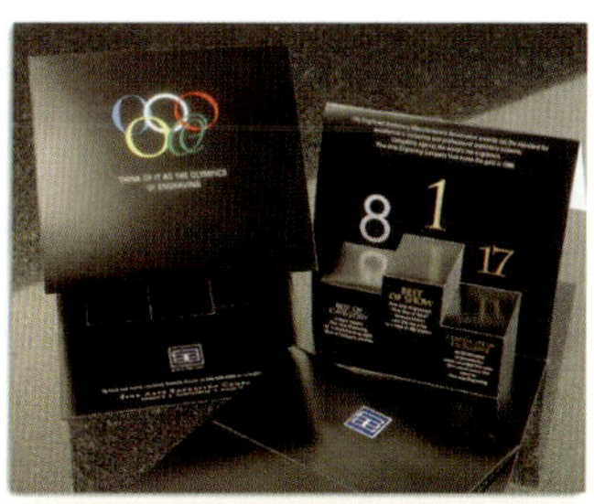

This direct-mail pop-up celebrates a sweep by **Fine Arts Engraving Company**

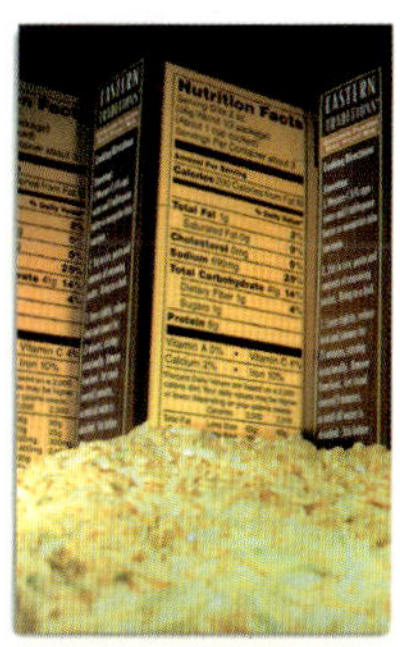

Nutrition Facts, created for the **FDA,** appears on

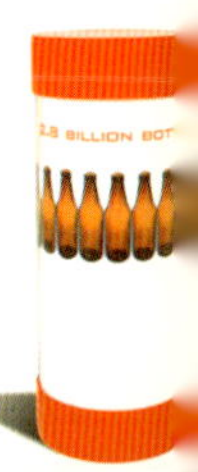

DataTrail sings of billi

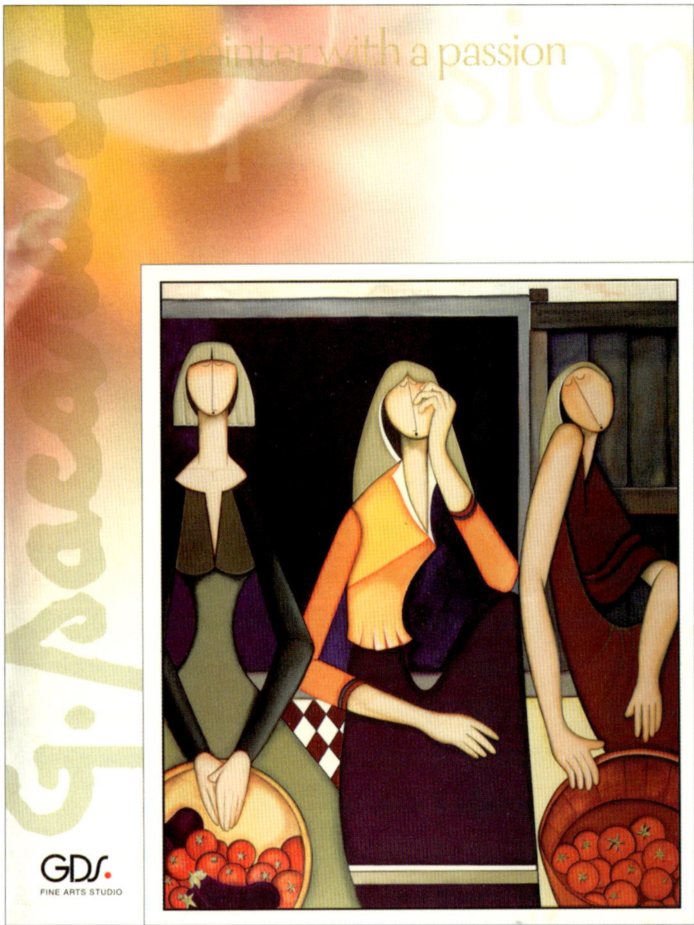

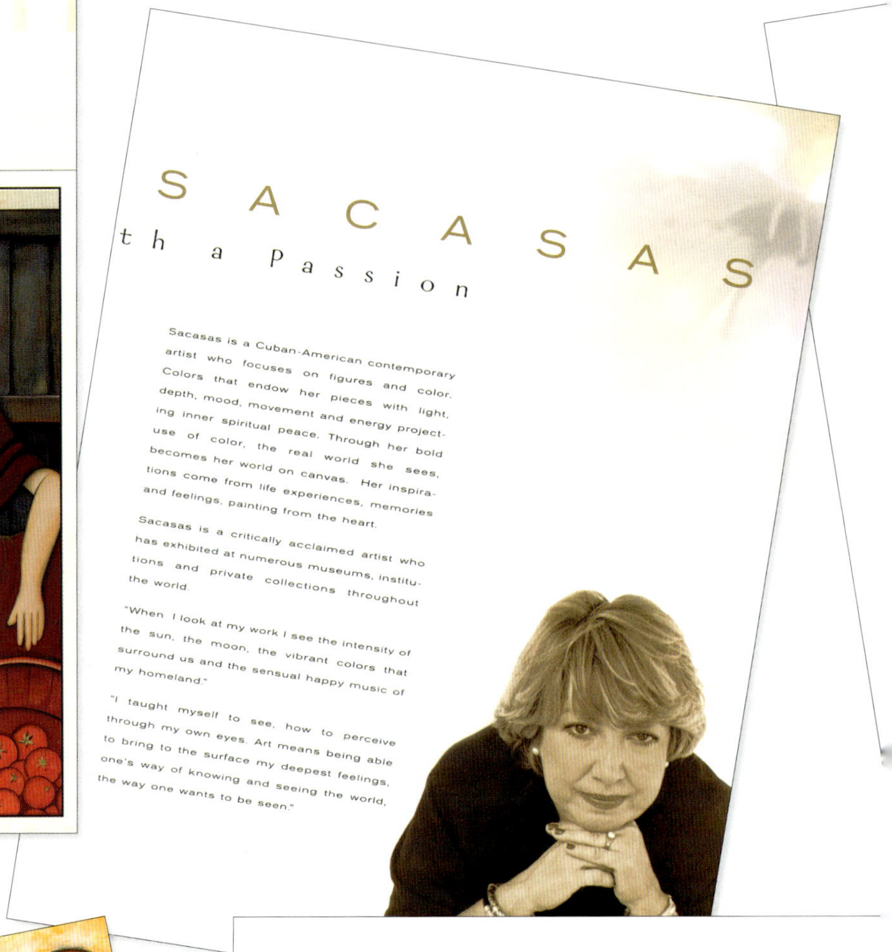

client
Gilda Sacasas
design firm
Original Impressions
designer
Frank Irias

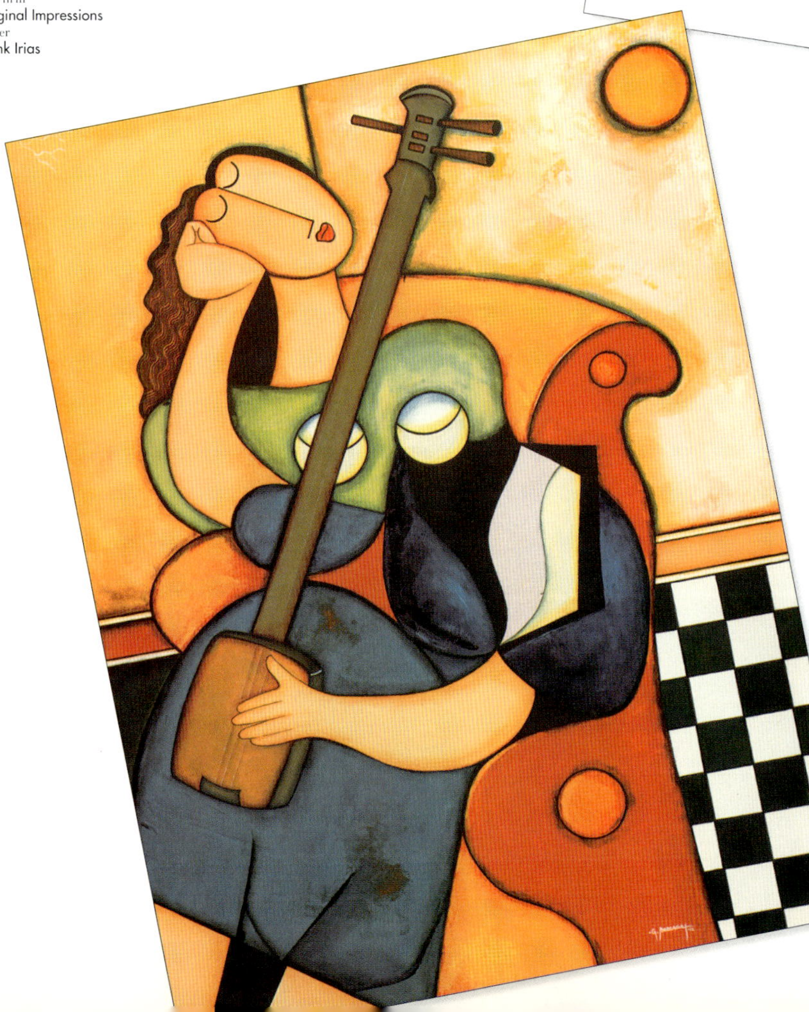

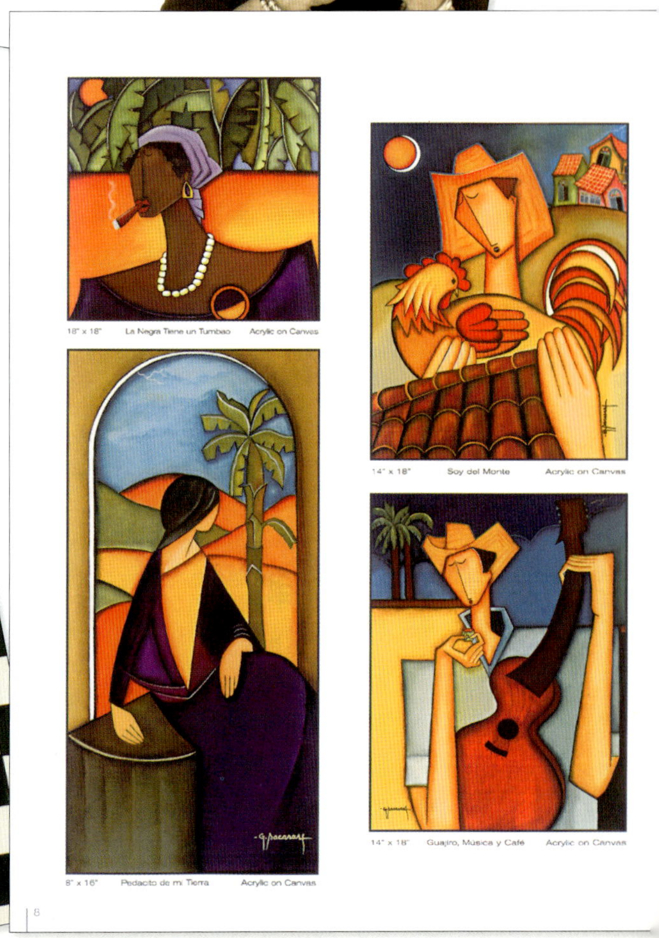

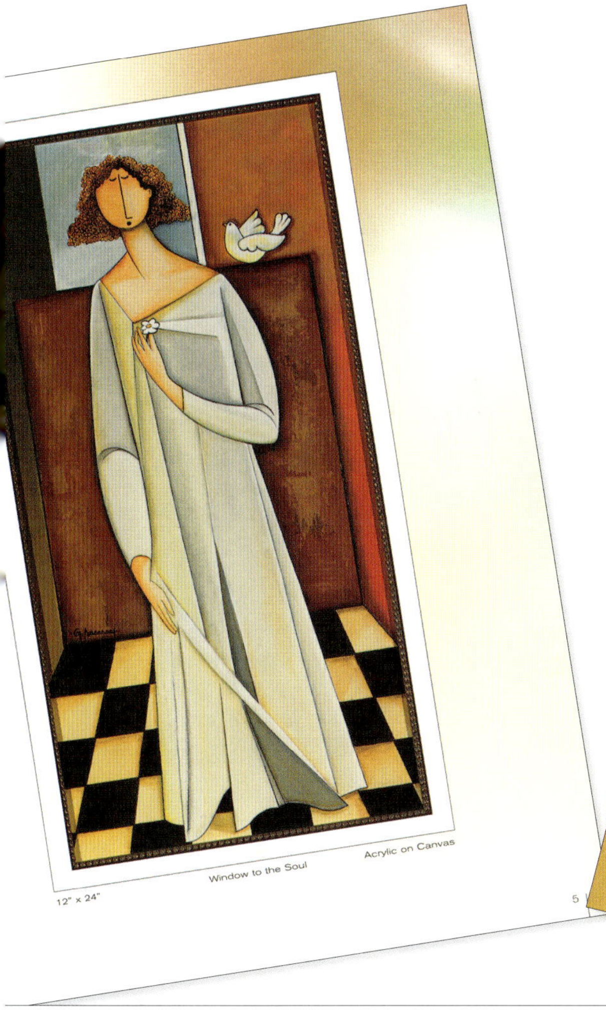
12" x 24"
Window to the Soul
Acrylic on Canvas
5

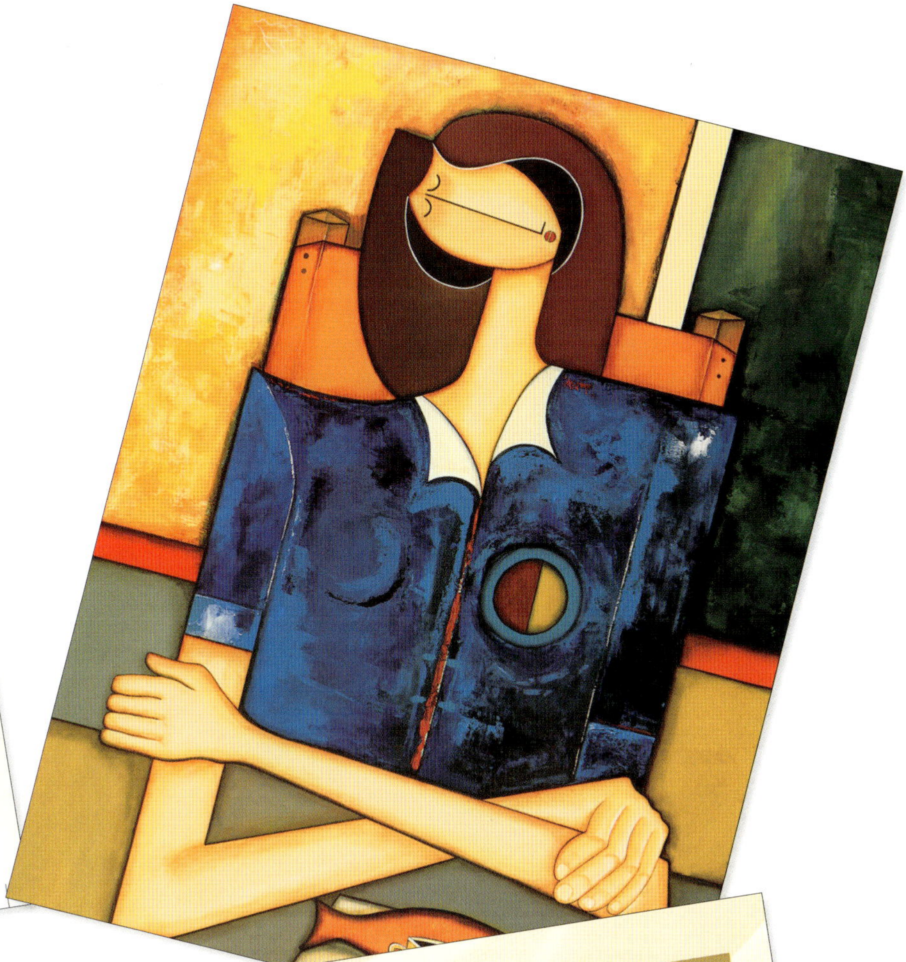

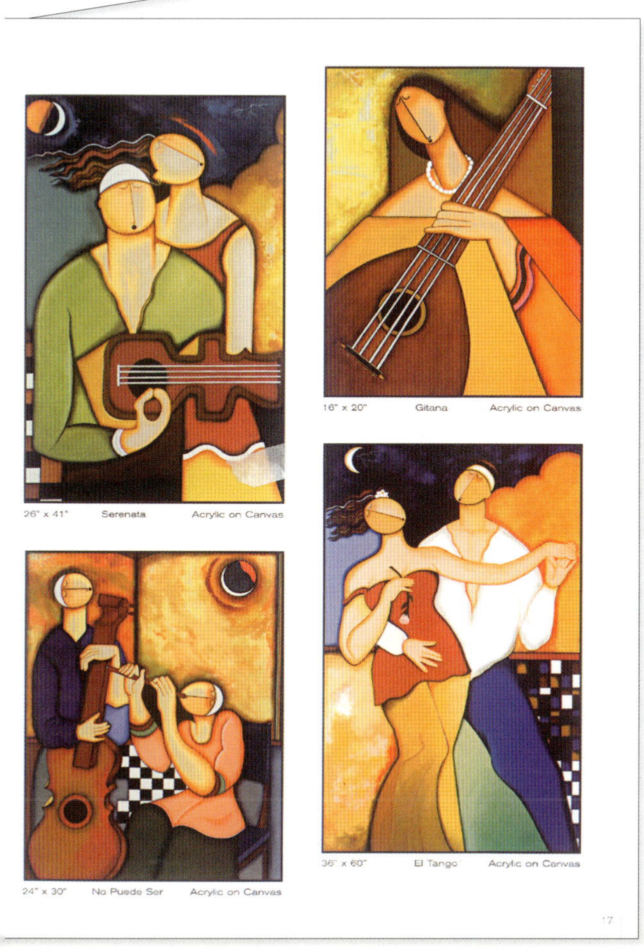
26" x 41"
Serenata
Acrylic on Canvas
16" x 20"
Gitana
Acrylic on Canvas
24" x 30"
No Puede Ser
Acrylic on Canvas
36" x 60"
El Tango
Acrylic on Canvas
17

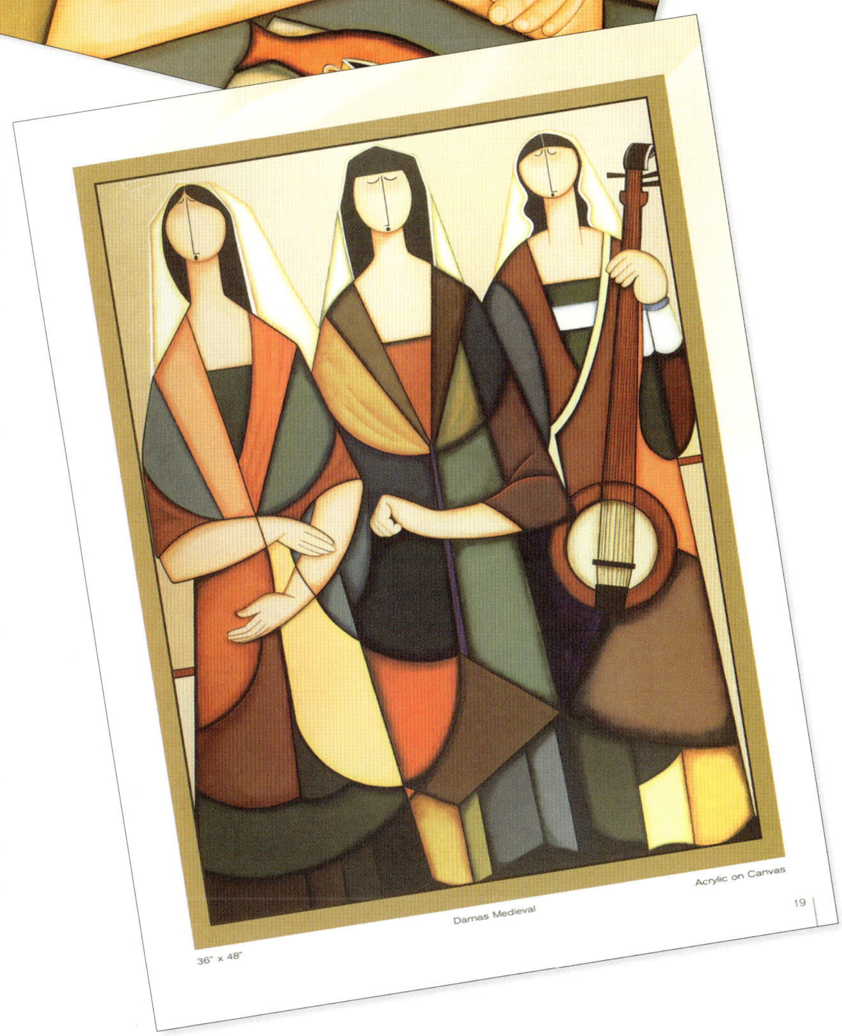
36" x 48"
Damas Medieval
Acrylic on Canvas
19

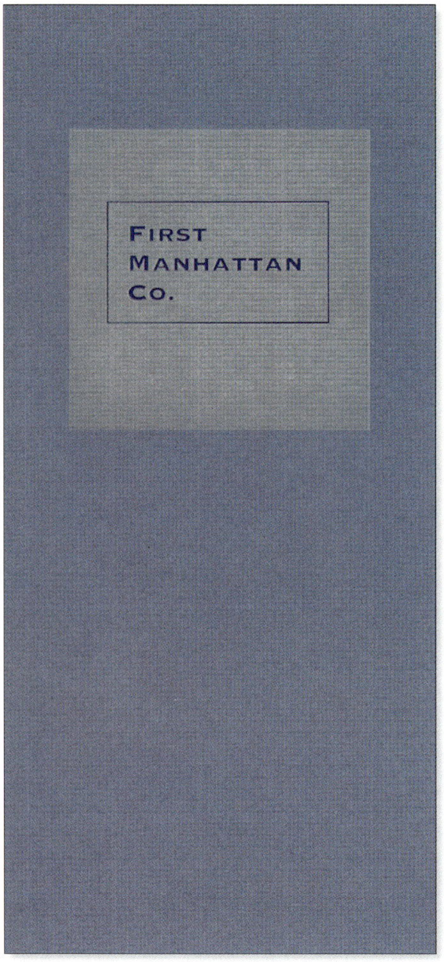

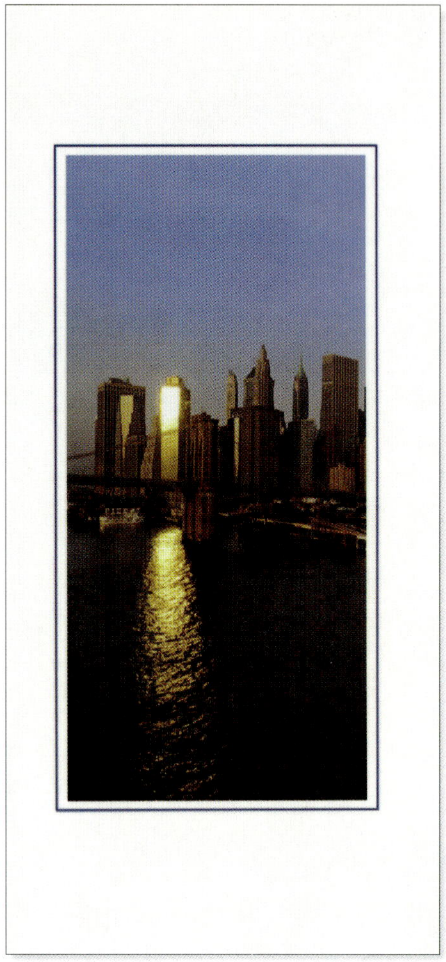

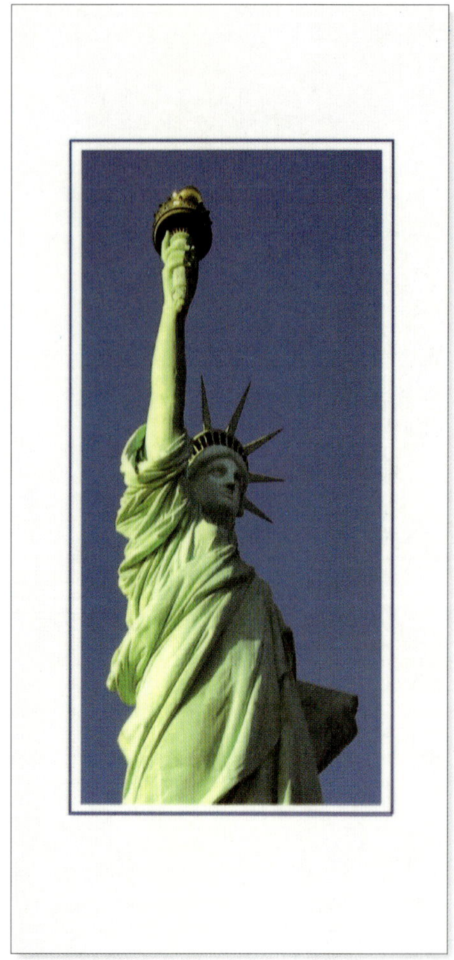

client
First Manhattan Co.
design firm
New IDEAS
designers
Patty O. Seger,
Deborah Denenberg

FIRST MANHATTAN CO.

We believe our hands-on research process is critical to our success in identifying attractive investment opportunities with acceptable levels of risk.

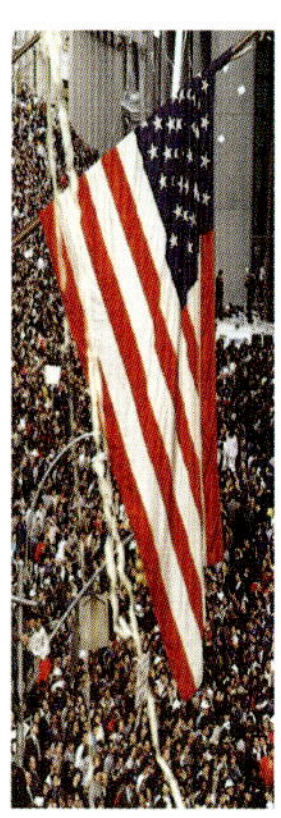

KEYS TO OUR SUCCESS

We believe in employing exceptional people and encouraging their development to the maximum level of their capabilities. The result has been a highly motivated team, providing important benefits for our clients, our employees, and our firm.

We strive to:

Conduct ourselves with integrity, fairness and the highest ethical standards.

Help preserve and increase the capital of our clients by

carefully helping them choose and achieve their investment goals,

thoroughly researching investment ideas focusing on long-term opportunities,

staying within our circle of competence.

Foster a work environment that respects the individual, encourages the free flow of ideas and rewards the contributions of all.

Promote our growth through the development of outstanding personnel.

Enjoy our work and our relationships with clients and associates.

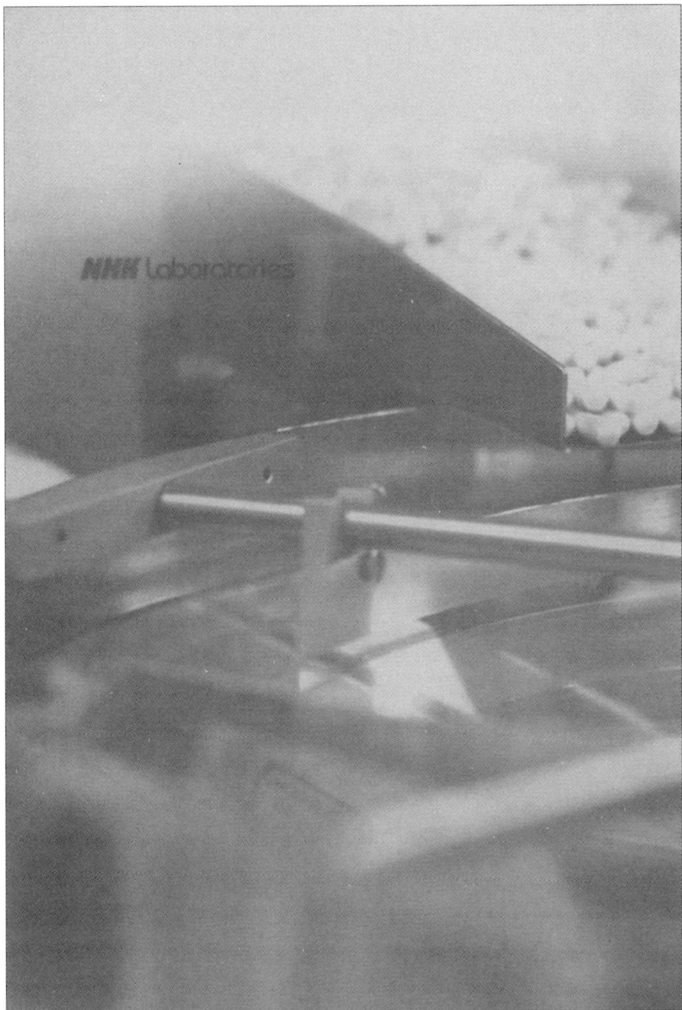

client
NHK Laboratories
design firm
IE Design + Communications
designers
Jane Kim,
Marcie Carson

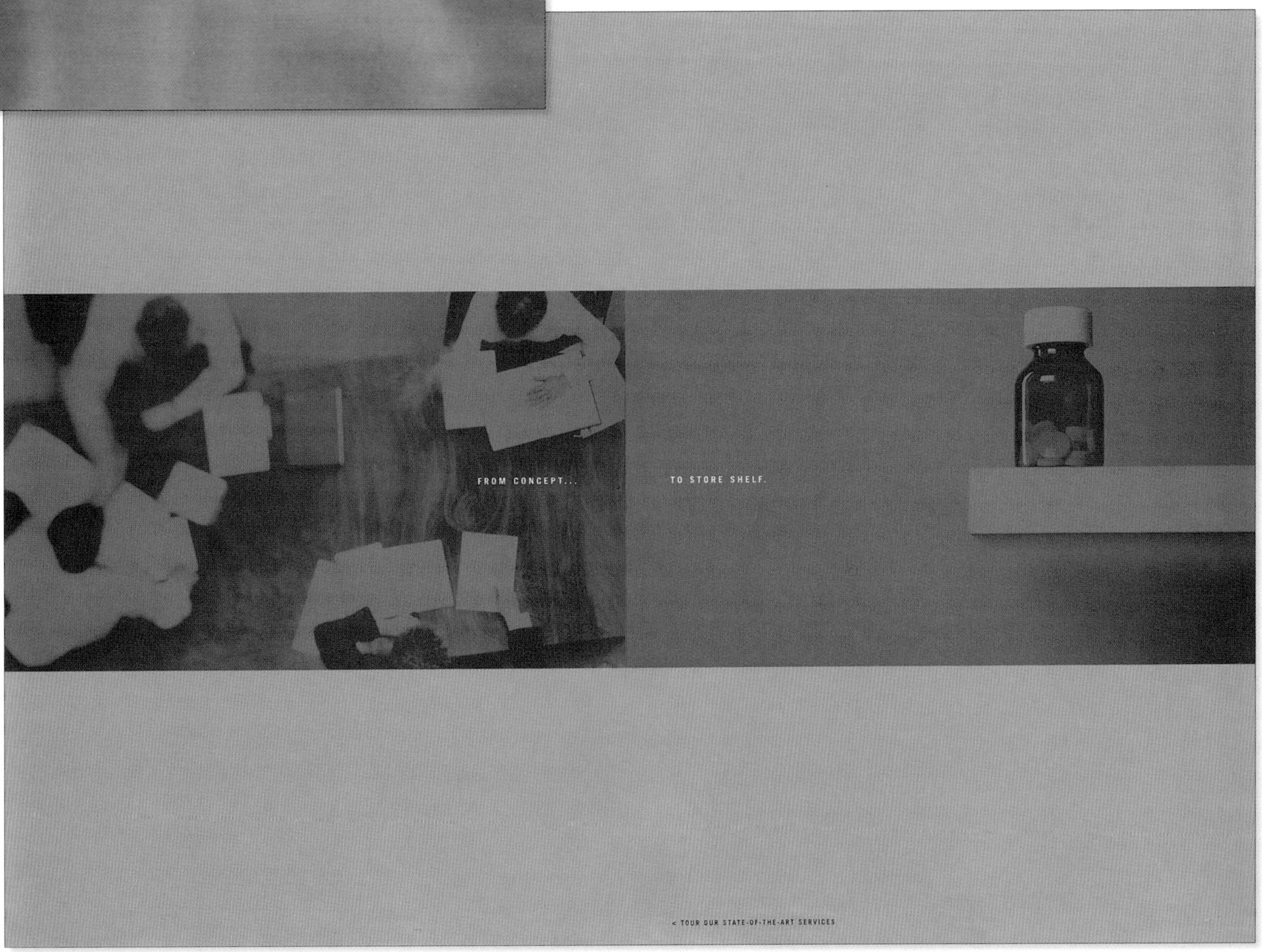

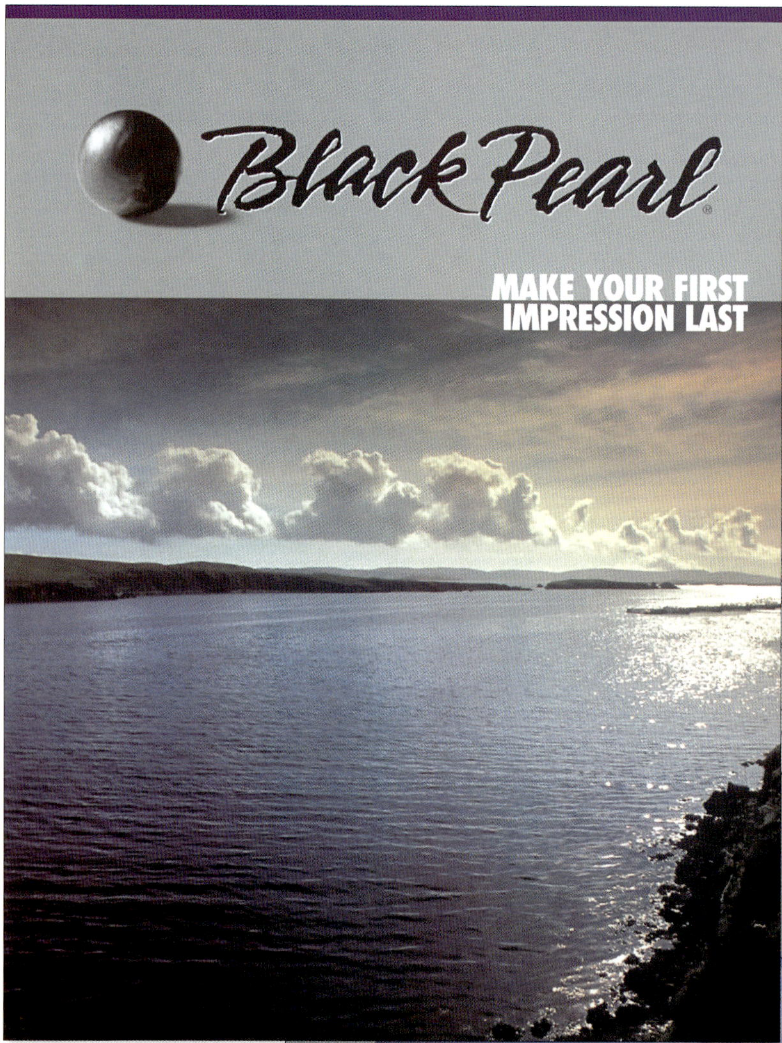

client
Martin International Corporation
design firm
Lorenz Advertising
designers
Arne Ratermanis,
Brian Lorenz

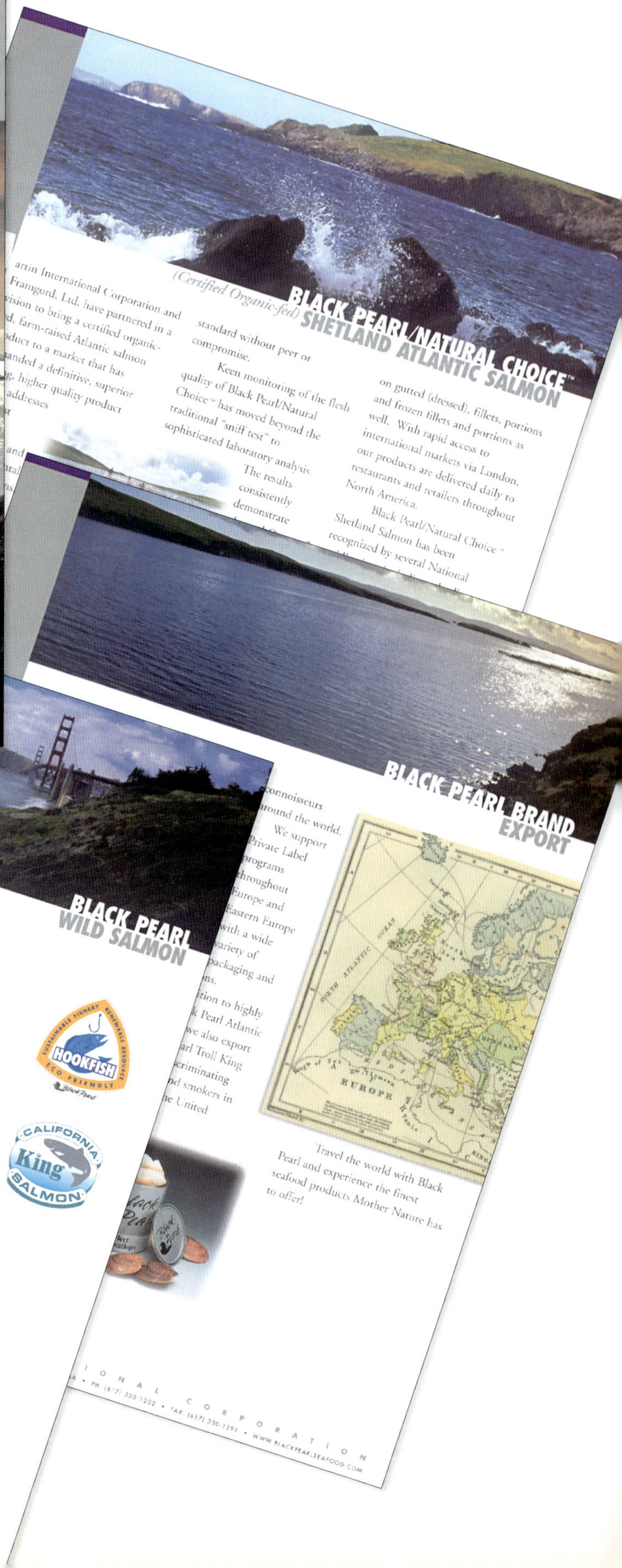

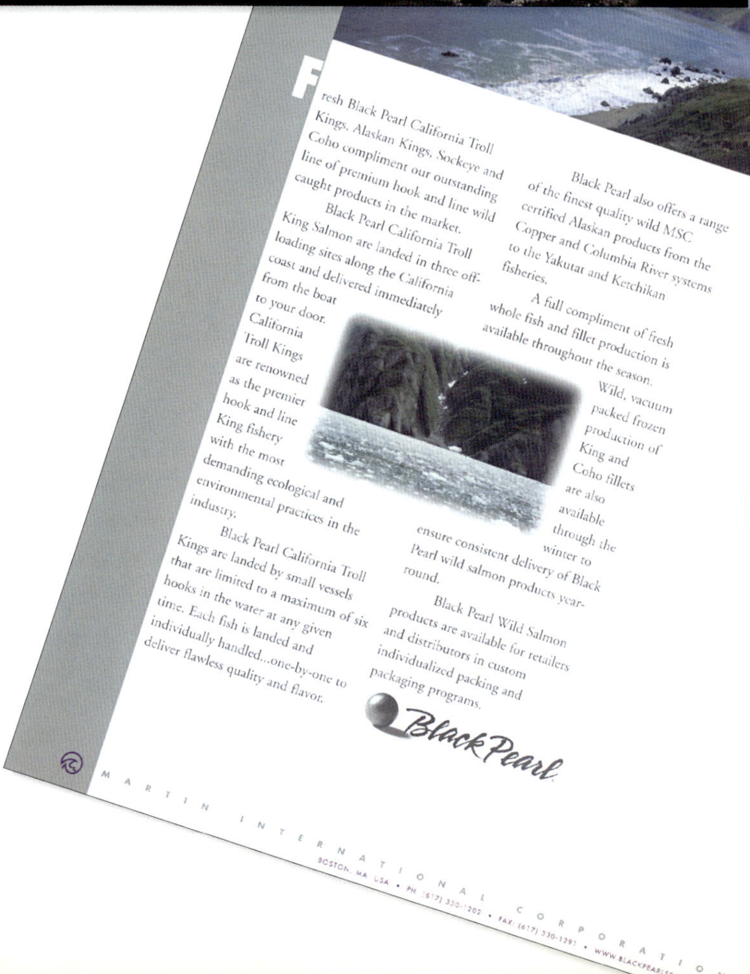

client
CW Brinkley
design firm
Sire Advertising
designers
Shawn Felty,
Jessica Varner

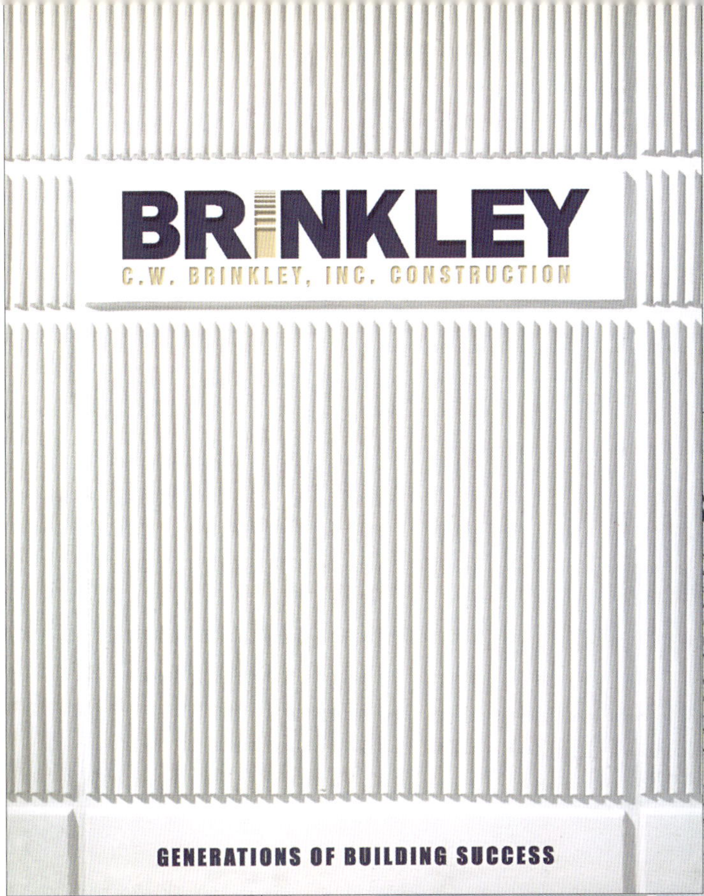

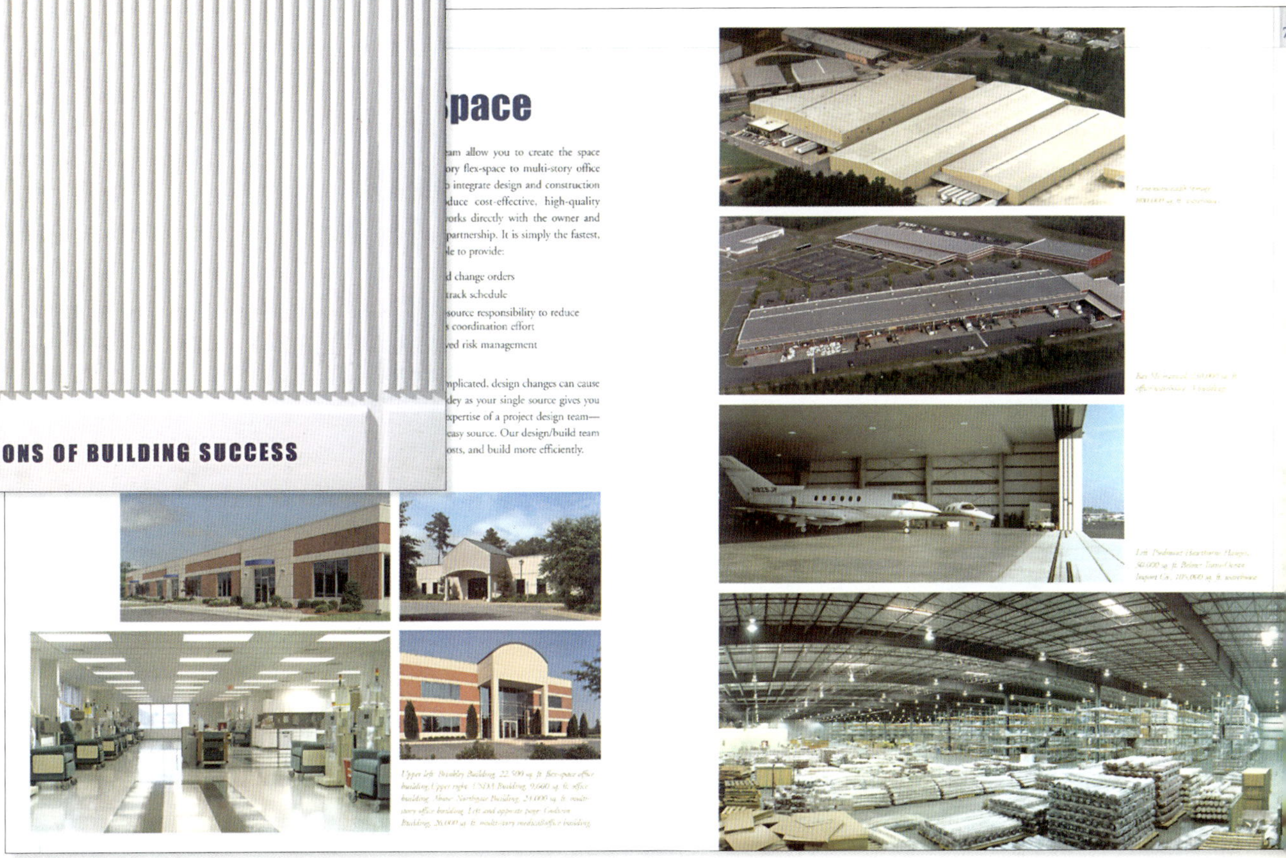

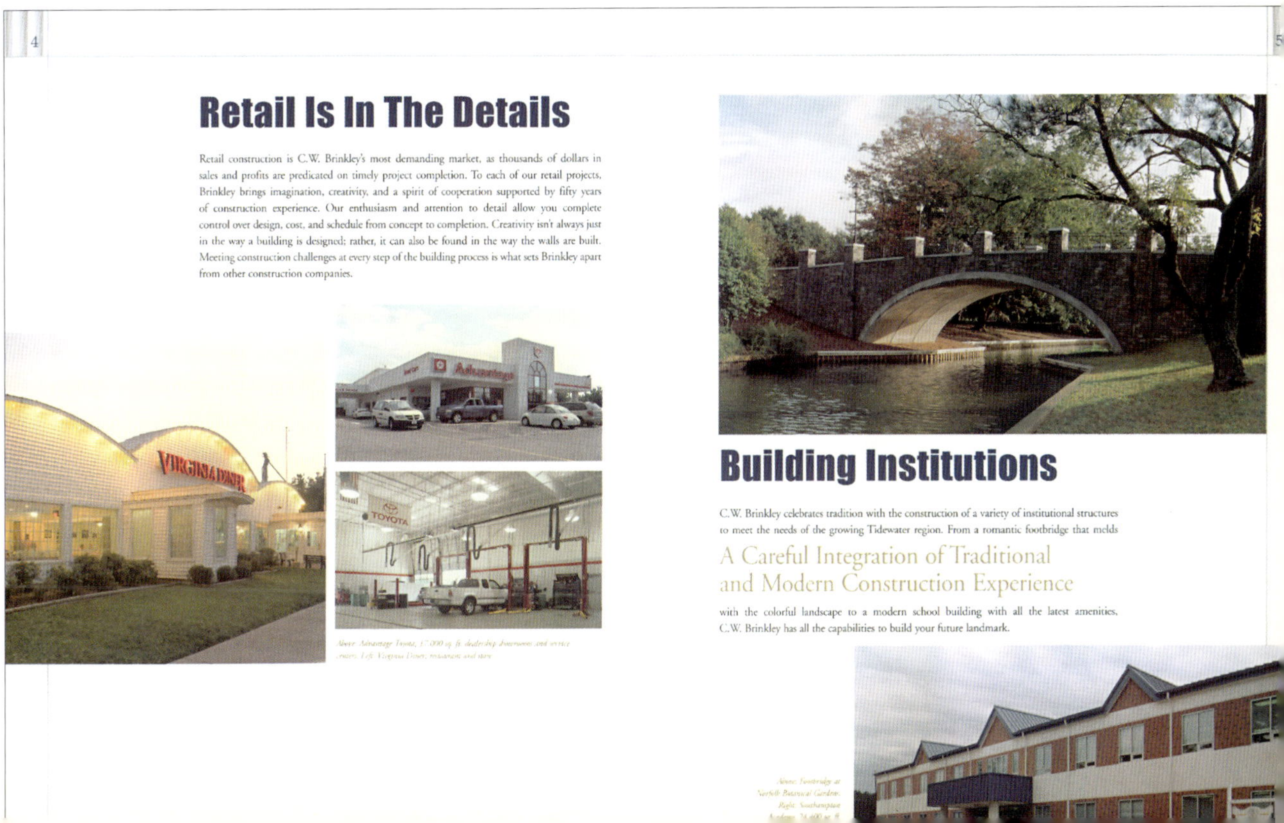

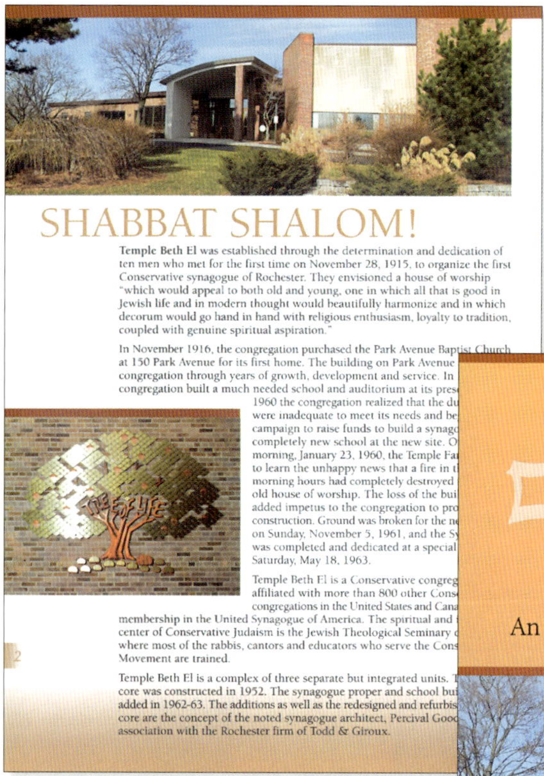

SHABBAT SHALOM!

Temple Beth El was established through the determination and dedication of ten men who met for the first time on November 28, 1915, to organize the first Conservative synagogue of Rochester. They envisioned a house of worship "which would appeal to both old and young, one in which all that is good in Jewish life and in modern thought would beautifully harmonize and in which decorum would go hand in hand with religious enthusiasm, loyalty to tradition, coupled with genuine spiritual aspiration."

In November 1916, the congregation purchased the Park Avenue Baptist Church at 150 Park Avenue for its first home. The building on Park Avenue congregation through years of growth, development and service. In congregation built a much needed school and auditorium at its pres 1960 the congregation realized that the du were inadequate to meet its needs and be campaign to raise funds to build a synago completely new school at the new site. O morning, January 23, 1960, the Temple Fa to learn the unhappy news that a fire in t morning hours had completely destroyed old house of worship. The loss of the bui added impetus to the congregation to pro construction. Ground was broken for the n on Sunday, November 5, 1961, and the S was completed and dedicated at a special Saturday, May 18, 1963.

Temple Beth El is a Conservative congreg affiliated with more than 800 other Cons congregations in the United States and Cana membership in the United Synagogue of America. The spiritual and center of Conservative Judaism is the Jewish Theological Seminary where most of the rabbis, cantors and educators who serve the Cons Movement are trained.

Temple Beth El is a complex of three separate but integrated units. T core was constructed in 1952. The synagogue proper and school bu added in 1962-63. The additions as well as the redesigned and refurbis core are the concept of the noted synagogue architect, Percival Good association with the Rochester firm of Todd & Giroux.

2

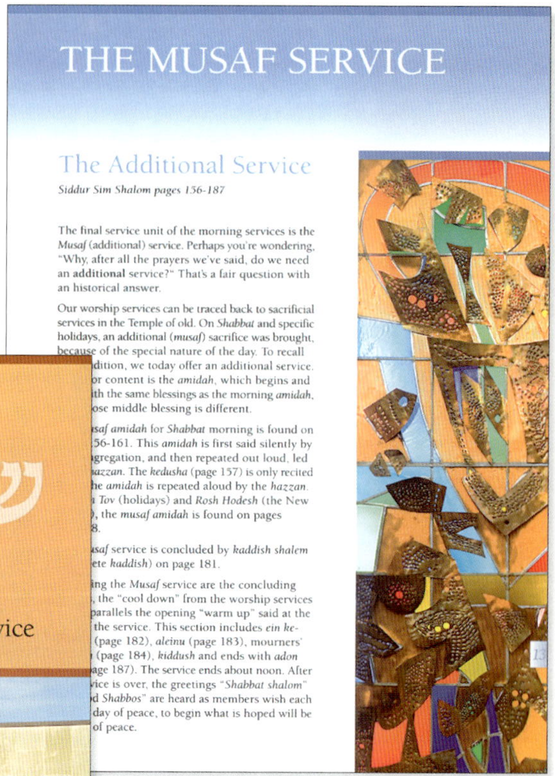

THE MUSAF SERVICE

The Additional Service

Siddur Sim Shalom pages 156-187

The final service unit of the morning services is the *Musaf* (additional) service. Perhaps you're wondering, "Why, after all the prayers we've said, do we need an **additional** service?" That's a fair question with an historical answer.

Our worship services can be traced back to sacrificial services in the Temple of old. On *Shabbat* and specific holidays, an additional (*musaf*) sacrifice was brought, because of the special nature of the day. To recall dition, we today offer an additional service. or content is the *amidah*, which begins and th the same blessings as the morning *amidah*, ose middle blessing is different.

saf amidah for *Shabbat* morning is found on 56-161. This *amidah* is first said silently by gregation, and then repeated out loud, led azzan. The *kedusha* (page 157) is only recited he *amidah* is repeated aloud by the *hazzan*. Tov (holidays) and *Rosh Hodesh* (the New), the *musaf amidah* is found on pages 8.

saf service is concluded by *kaddish shalem* ete *kaddish*) on page 181.

ing the *Musaf* service are the concluding , the "cool down" from the worship services parallels the opening "warm up" said at the the service. This section includes *ein ke-* (page 182), *aleinu* (page 183), mourners' (page 184), *kiddush* and ends with *adon* age 187). The service ends about noon. After ice is over, the greetings "*Shabbat shalom*" d *Shabbos*" are heard as members wish each day of peace, to begin what is hoped will be of peace.

13

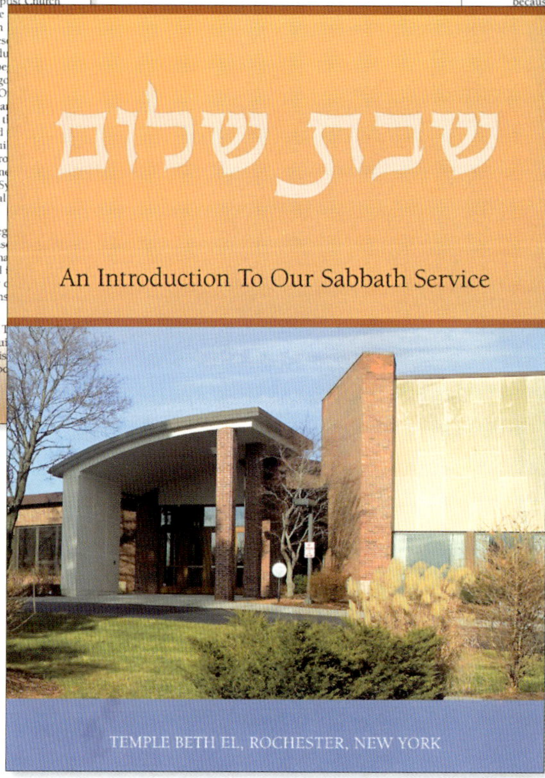

שבת שלום

An Introduction To Our Sabbath Service

TEMPLE BETH EL, ROCHESTER, NEW YORK

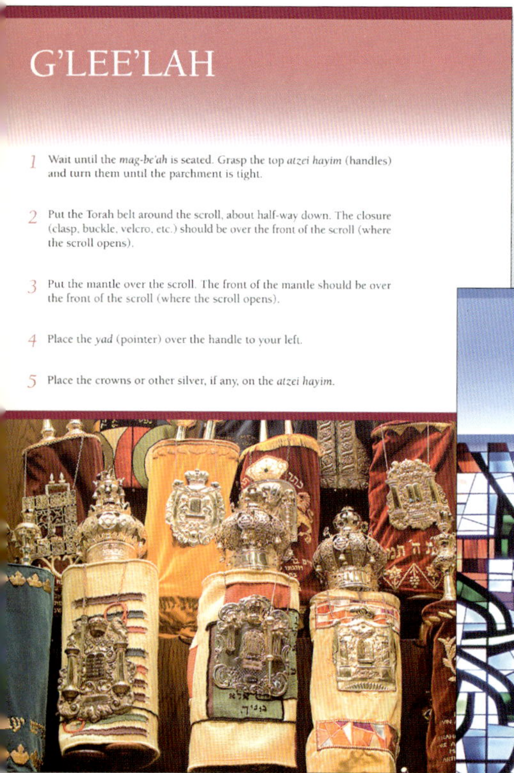

G'LEE'LAH

1 Wait until the *mag-be'ah* is seated. Grasp the top *atzei hayim* (handles) and turn them until the parchment is tight.

2 Put the Torah belt around the scroll, about half-way down. The closure (clasp, buckle, velcro, etc.) should be over the front of the scroll (where the scroll opens).

3 Put the mantle over the scroll. The front of the mantle should be over the front of the scroll (where the scroll opens).

4 Place the *yad* (pointer) over the handle to your left.

5 Place the crowns or other silver, if any, on the *atzei hayim*.

client
Temple Beth El
design firm
McElveney & Palozzi Design Group
designer
Lisa Gates

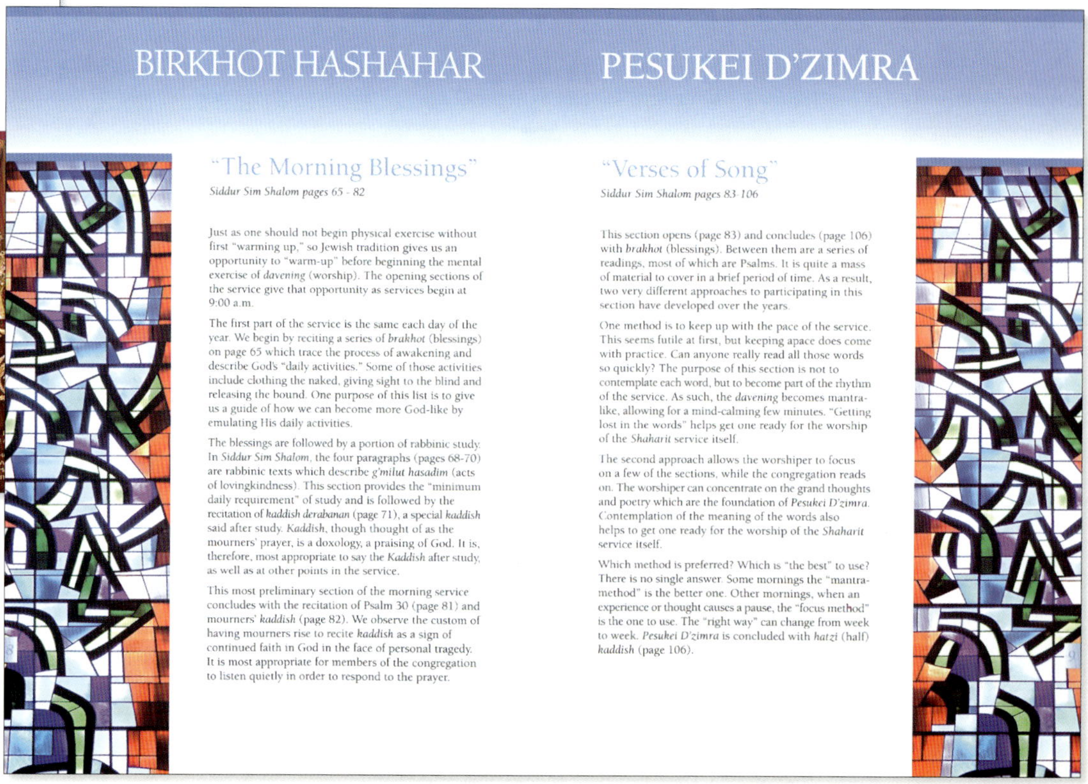

BIRKHOT HASHAHAR

"The Morning Blessings"

Siddur Sim Shalom pages 65 - 82

Just as one should not begin physical exercise without first "warming up," so Jewish tradition gives us an opportunity to "warm-up" before beginning the mental exercise of *davening* (worship). The opening sections of the service give that opportunity as services begin at 9:00 a.m.

The first part of the service is the same each day of the year. We begin by reciting a series of *brakhot* (blessings) on page 65 which trace the process of awakening and describe God's "daily activities." Some of those activities include clothing the naked, giving sight to the blind and releasing the bound. One purpose of this list is to give us a guide of how we can become more God-like by emulating His daily activities.

The blessings are followed by a portion of rabbinic study. In *Siddur Sim Shalom*, the four paragraphs (pages 68-70) are rabbinic texts which describe *g'milut hasadim* (acts of lovingkindness). This section provides the "minimum daily requirement" of study and is followed by the recitation of *kaddish derabanan* (page 71), a special *kaddish* said after study. *Kaddish*, though thought of as the mourners' prayer, is a doxology, a praising of God. It is, therefore, most appropriate to say the *Kaddish* after study, as well as at other points in the service.

This most preliminary section of the morning service concludes with the recitation of Psalm 30 (page 81) and mourners' *kaddish* (page 82). We observe the custom of having mourners rise to recite *kaddish* as a sign of continued faith in God in the face of personal tragedy. It is most appropriate for members of the congregation to listen quietly in order to respond to the prayer.

8

PESUKEI D'ZIMRA

"Verses of Song"

Siddur Sim Shalom pages 83-106

This section opens (page 83) and concludes (page 106) with *brakhot* (blessings). Between them are a series of readings, most of which are Psalms. It is quite a mass of material to cover in a brief period of time. As a result, two very different approaches to participating in this section have developed over the years.

One method is to keep up with the pace of the service. This seems futile at first, but keeping apace does come with practice. Can anyone really read all those words so quickly? The purpose of this section is not to contemplate each word, but to become part of the rhythm of the service. As such, the *davening* becomes mantra-like, allowing for a mind-calming few minutes. "Getting lost in the words" helps get one ready for the worship of the *Shaharit* service itself.

The second approach allows the worshiper to focus on a few of the sections, while the congregation reads on. The worshiper can concentrate on the grand thoughts and poetry which are the foundation of *Pesukei D'zimra*. Contemplation of the meaning of the words also helps to get one ready for the worship of the *Shaharit* service itself.

Which method is preferred? Which is "the best" to use? There is no single answer. Some mornings the "mantra-method" is the better one. Other mornings, when an experience or thought causes a pause, the "focus method" is the one to use. The "right way" can change from week to week. *Pesukei D'zimra* is concluded with *hatzi* (half) *kaddish* (page 106).

9

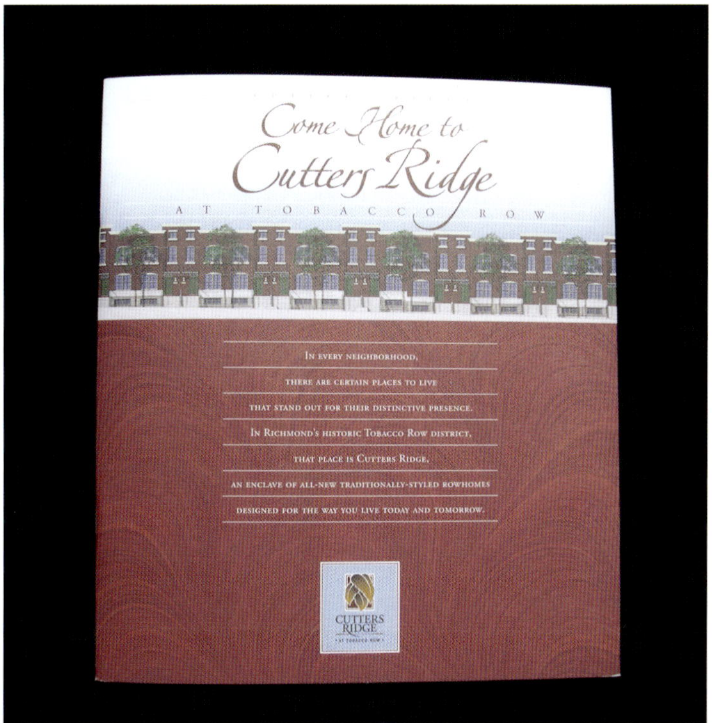

client
Forest City Washington
design firm
Herip Design Associates, Inc.
designers
Walter M. Herip,
Jen H. Crabtree,
John Menter

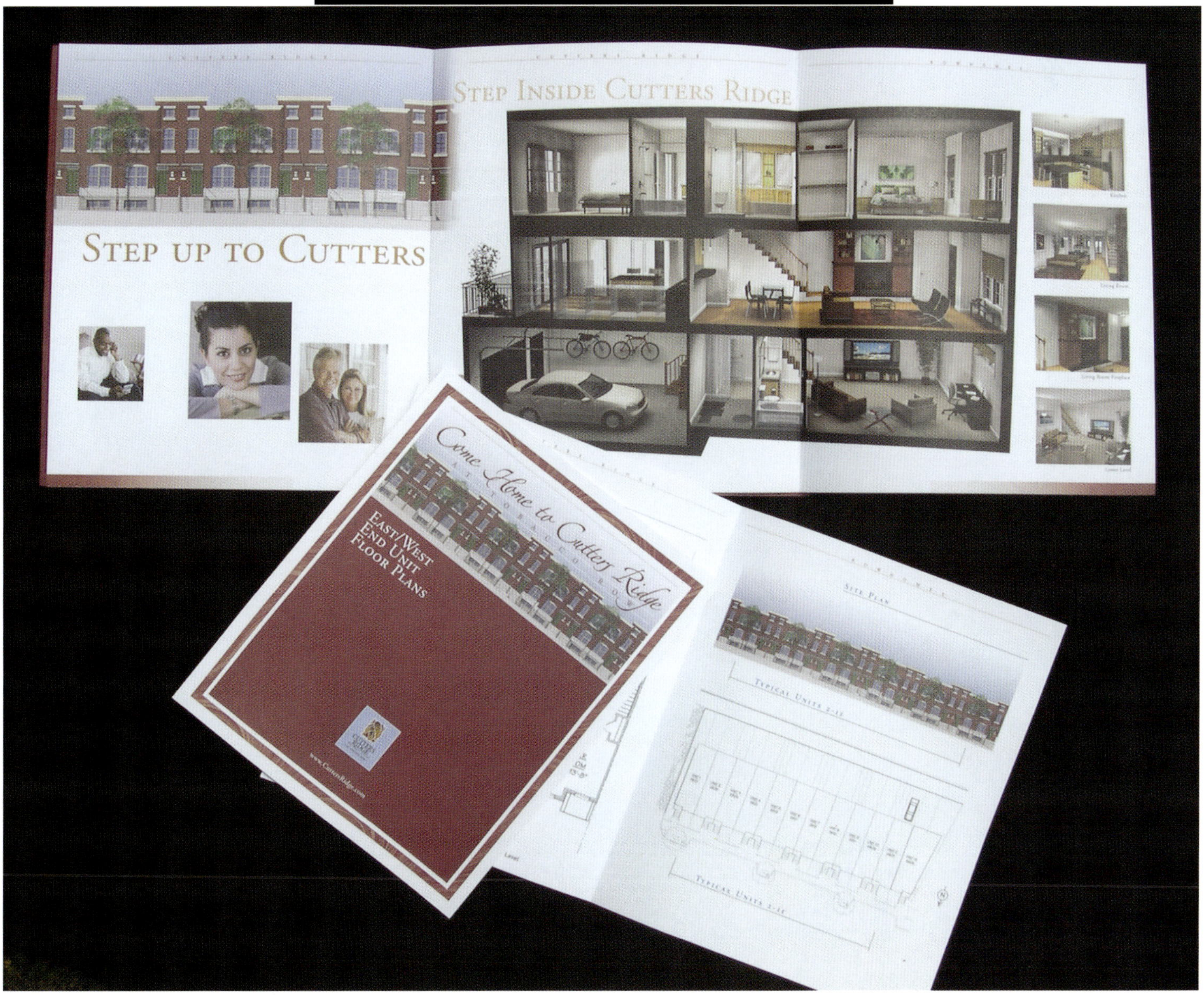

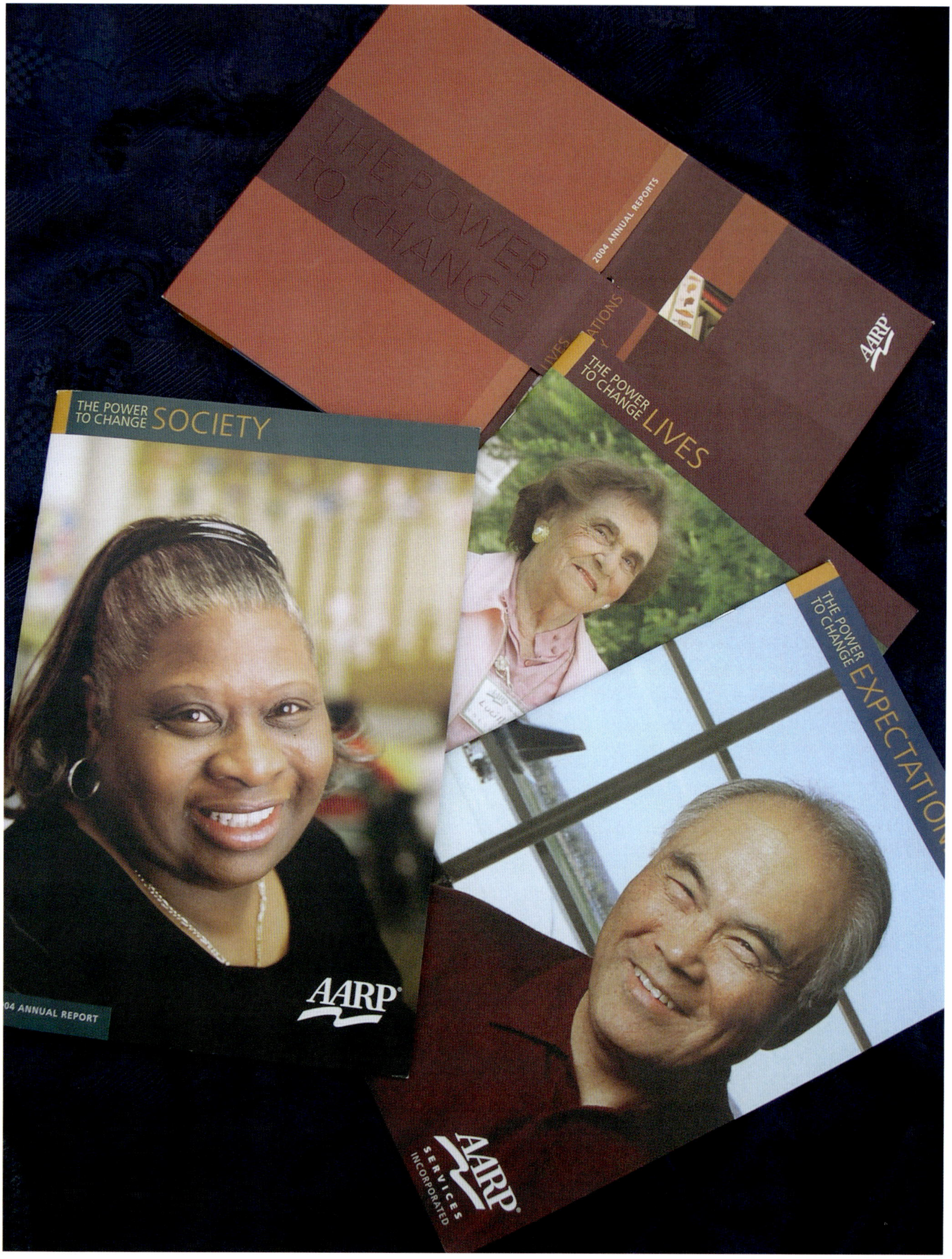

client
AARP
design firm
Grafik Marketing Communications
designers
Gregg Glaviano, Melissa Wilets, Judy Kirpich, Regina Esposito, Ivan Hooker, Heath Dwiggins

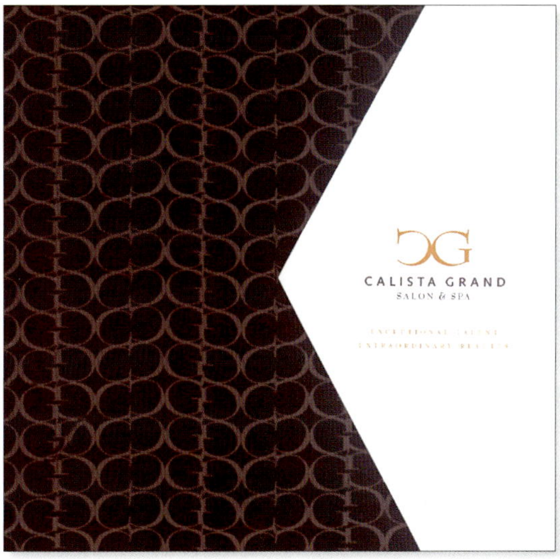

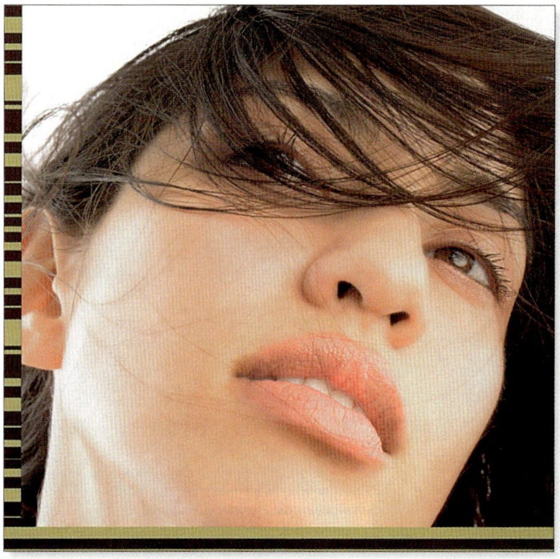

client
Calista Grand
design firm
Verve Marketing & Design
principal, creative director
Diane Lemonides
art director
Nancy Nguyen
designer
Katie McMullin

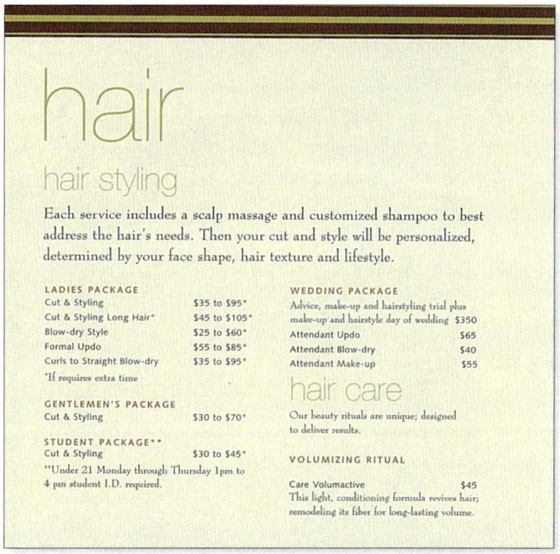

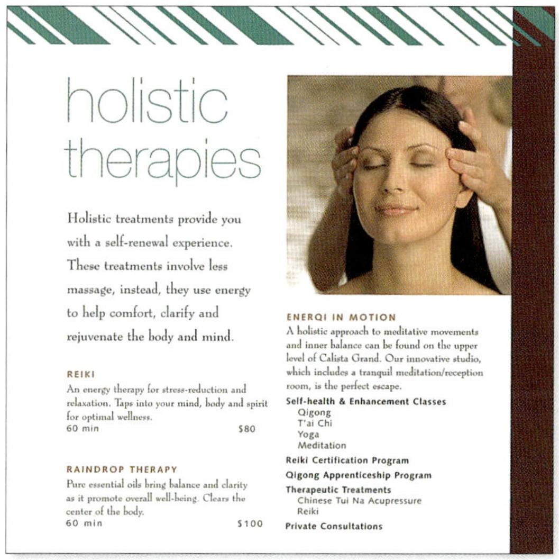

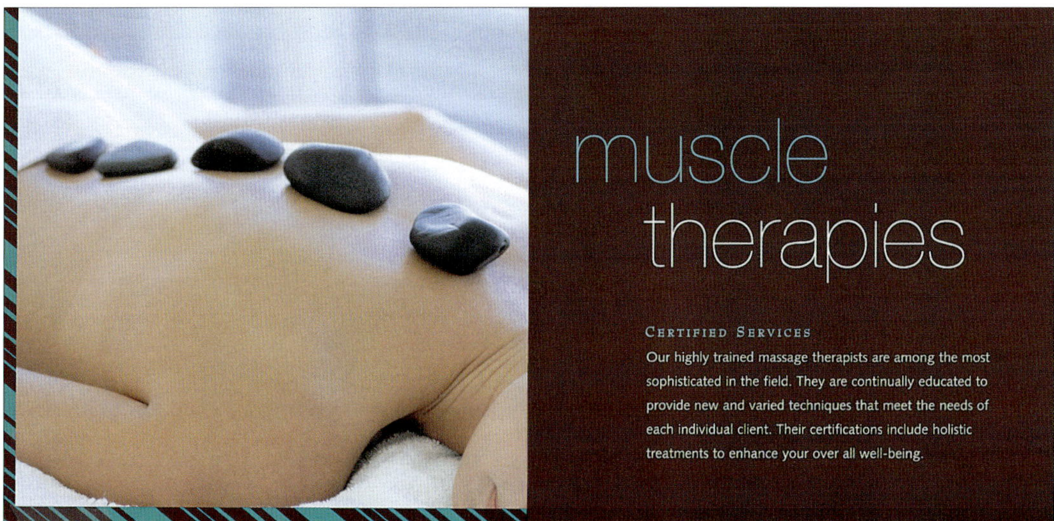

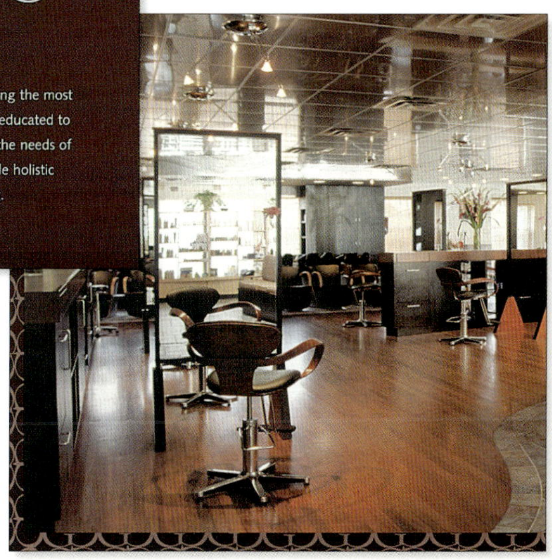

client
National Association of REALTORS

design firm
Crabtree + Company

designers
Susan Angrisani, Tamera Finn

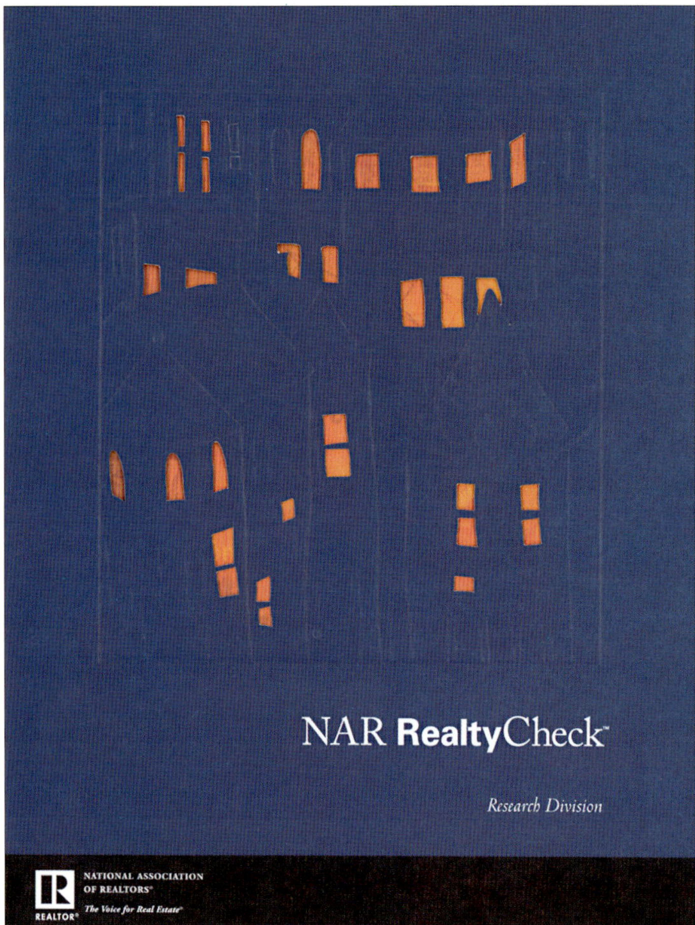

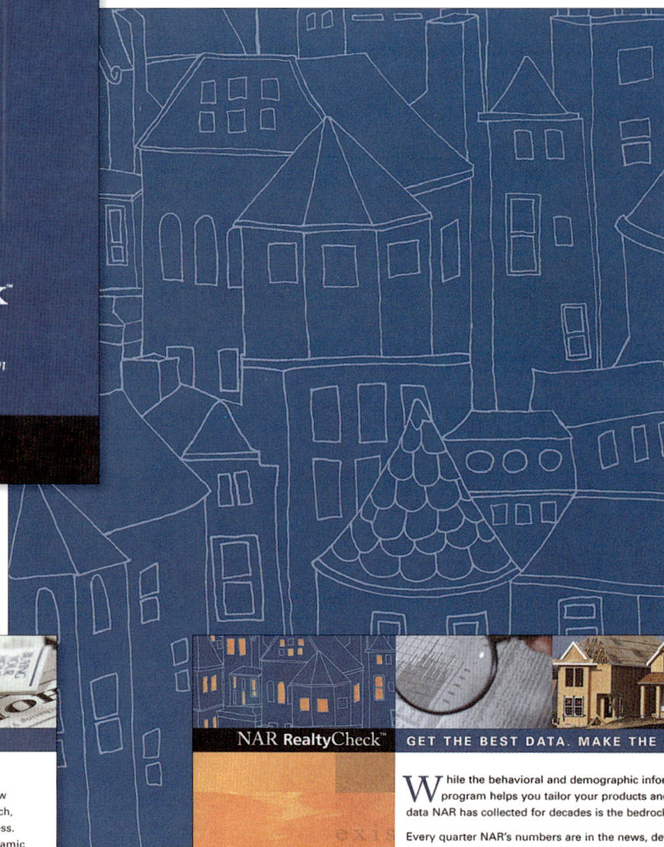

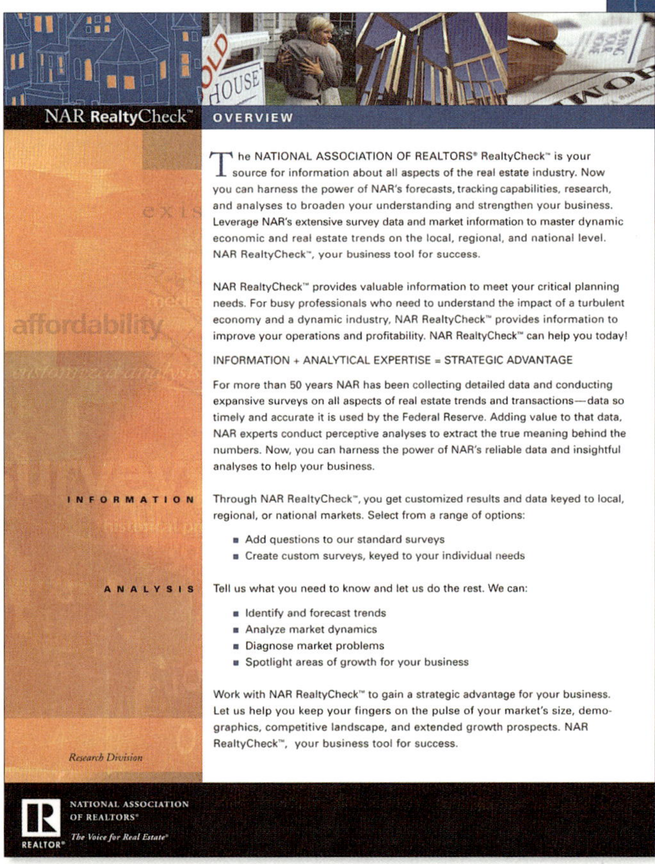

NAR RealtyCheck™ OVERVIEW

The NATIONAL ASSOCIATION OF REALTORS® RealtyCheck™ is your source for information about all aspects of the real estate industry. Now you can harness the power of NAR's forecasts, tracking capabilities, research, and analyses to broaden your understanding and strengthen your business. Leverage NAR's extensive survey data and market information to master dynamic economic and real estate trends on the local, regional, and national level. NAR RealtyCheck™, your business tool for success.

NAR RealtyCheck™ provides valuable information to meet your critical planning needs. For busy professionals who need to understand the impact of a turbulent economy and a dynamic industry, NAR RealtyCheck™ provides information to improve your operations and profitability. NAR RealtyCheck™ can help you today!

INFORMATION + ANALYTICAL EXPERTISE = STRATEGIC ADVANTAGE

For more than 50 years NAR has been collecting detailed data and conducting expansive surveys on all aspects of real estate trends and transactions—data so timely and accurate it is used by the Federal Reserve. Adding value to that data, NAR experts conduct perceptive analyses to extract the true meaning behind the numbers. Now, you can harness the power of NAR's reliable data and insightful analyses to help your business.

INFORMATION

Through NAR RealtyCheck™, you get customized results and data keyed to local, regional, or national markets. Select from a range of options:

- Add questions to our standard surveys
- Create custom surveys, keyed to your individual needs

ANALYSIS

Tell us what you need to know and let us do the rest. We can:

- Identify and forecast trends
- Analyze market dynamics
- Diagnose market problems
- Spotlight areas of growth for your business

Work with NAR RealtyCheck™ to gain a strategic advantage for your business. Let us help you keep your fingers on the pulse of your market's size, demographics, competitive landscape, and extended growth prospects. NAR RealtyCheck™, your business tool for success.

Research Division

NATIONAL ASSOCIATION OF REALTORS®
The Voice for Real Estate®
REALTOR®

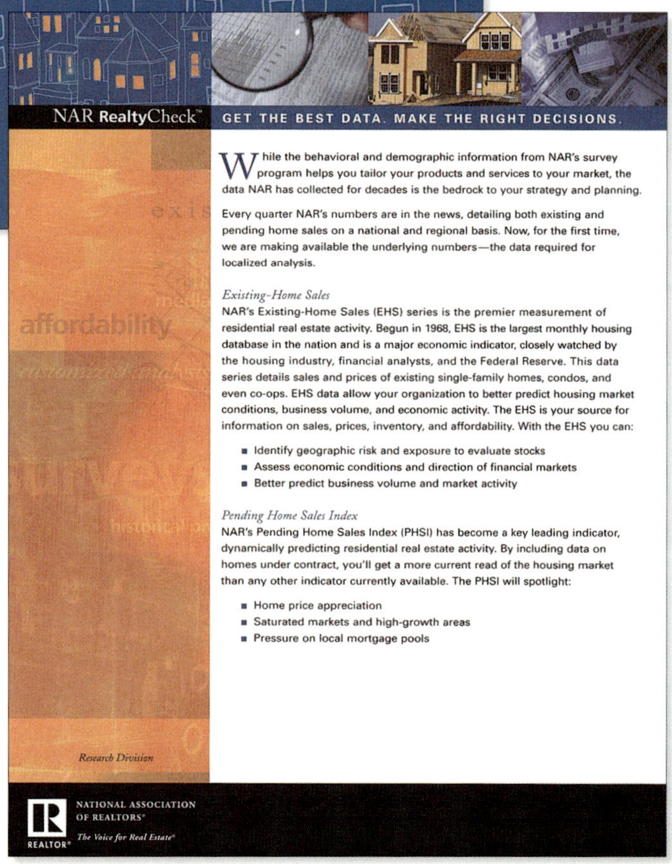

NAR RealtyCheck™ GET THE BEST DATA. MAKE THE RIGHT DECISIONS.

While the behavioral and demographic information from NAR's survey program helps you tailor your products and services to your market, the data NAR has collected for decades is the bedrock to your strategy and planning.

Every quarter NAR's numbers are in the news, detailing both existing and pending home sales on a national and regional basis. Now, for the first time, we are making available the underlying numbers—the data required for localized analysis.

Existing-Home Sales
NAR's Existing-Home Sales (EHS) series is the premier measurement of residential real estate activity. Begun in 1968, EHS is the largest monthly housing database in the nation and is a major economic indicator, closely watched by the housing industry, financial analysts, and the Federal Reserve. This data series details sales and prices of existing single-family homes, condos, and even co-ops. EHS data allow your organization to better predict housing market conditions, business volume, and economic activity. The EHS is your source for information on sales, prices, inventory, and affordability. With the EHS you can:

- Identify geographic risk and exposure to evaluate stocks
- Assess economic conditions and direction of financial markets
- Better predict business volume and market activity

Pending Home Sales Index
NAR's Pending Home Sales Index (PHSI) has become a key leading indicator, dynamically predicting residential real estate activity. By including data on homes under contract, you'll get a more current read of the housing market than any other indicator currently available. The PHSI will spotlight:

- Home price appreciation
- Saturated markets and high-growth areas
- Pressure on local mortgage pools

Research Division

NATIONAL ASSOCIATION OF REALTORS®
The Voice for Real Estate®
REALTOR®

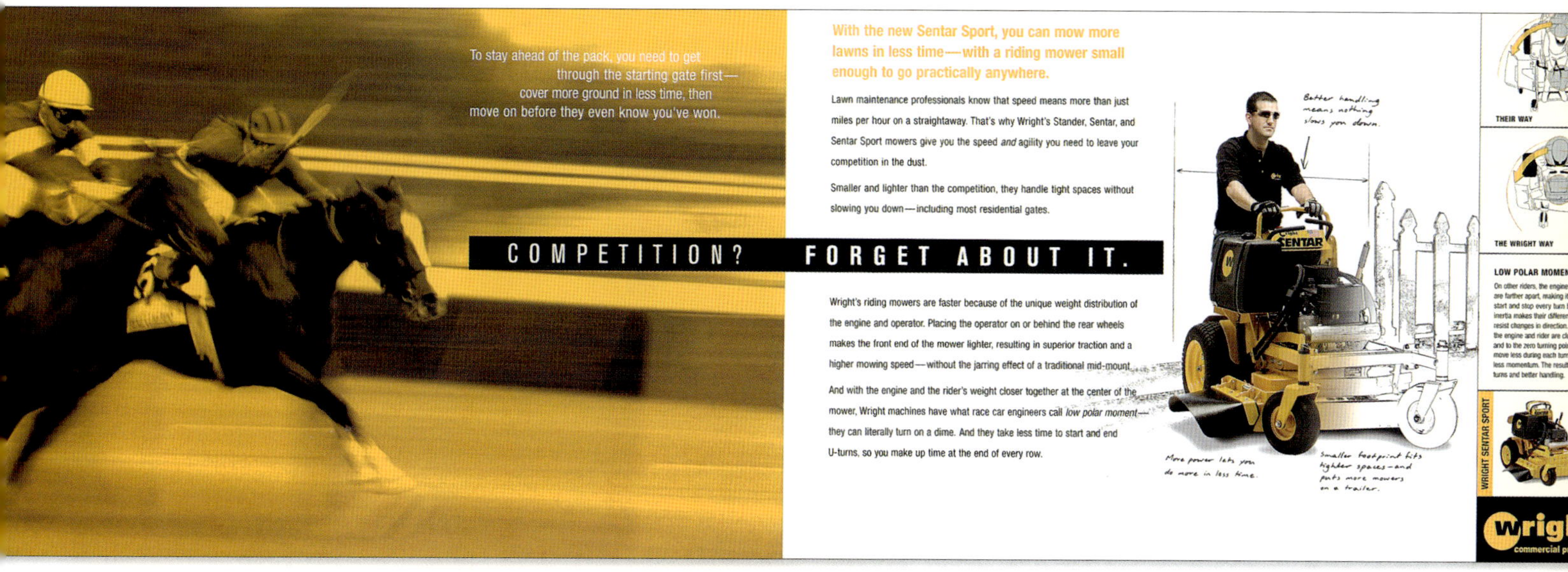

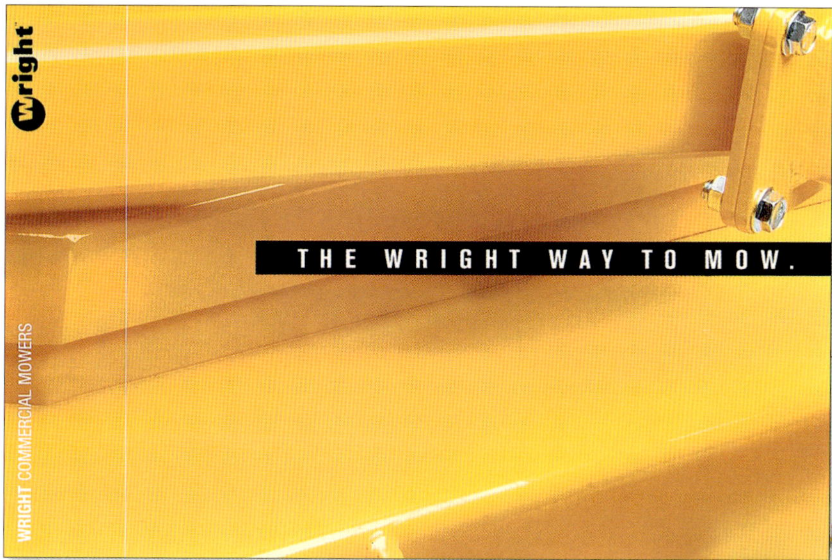

client
Wright Manufacturing
design firm
The Design Channel
designers
Jonathan Bruns,
David Franek,
Rachel Deutsch

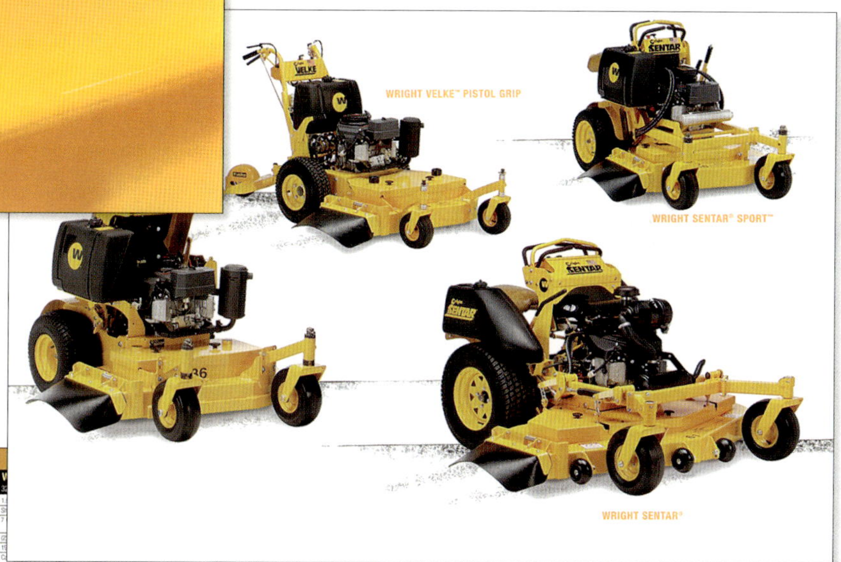

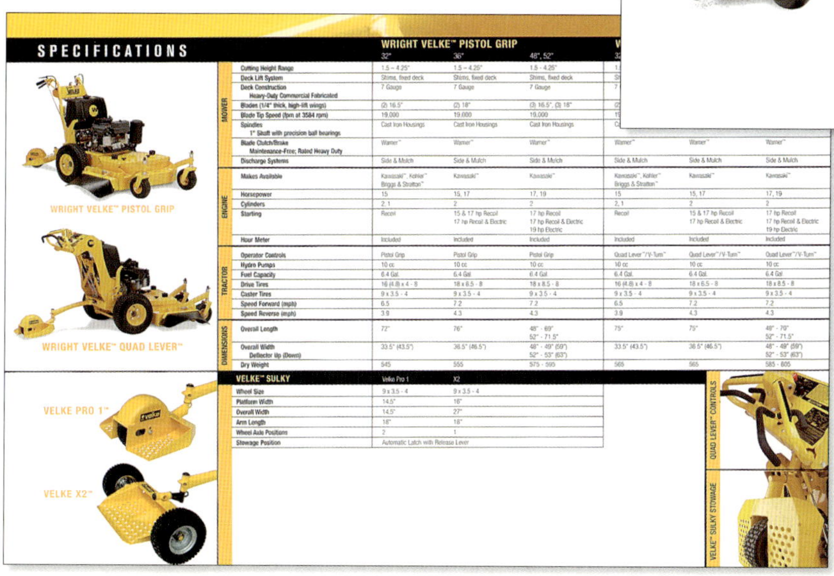

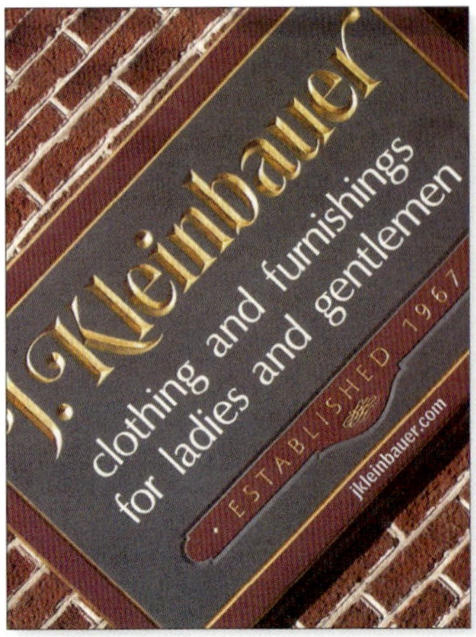

client
J. Kleinbauer
design firm
Sire Advertising
designers
Shawn Felty,
Jordan Chappell

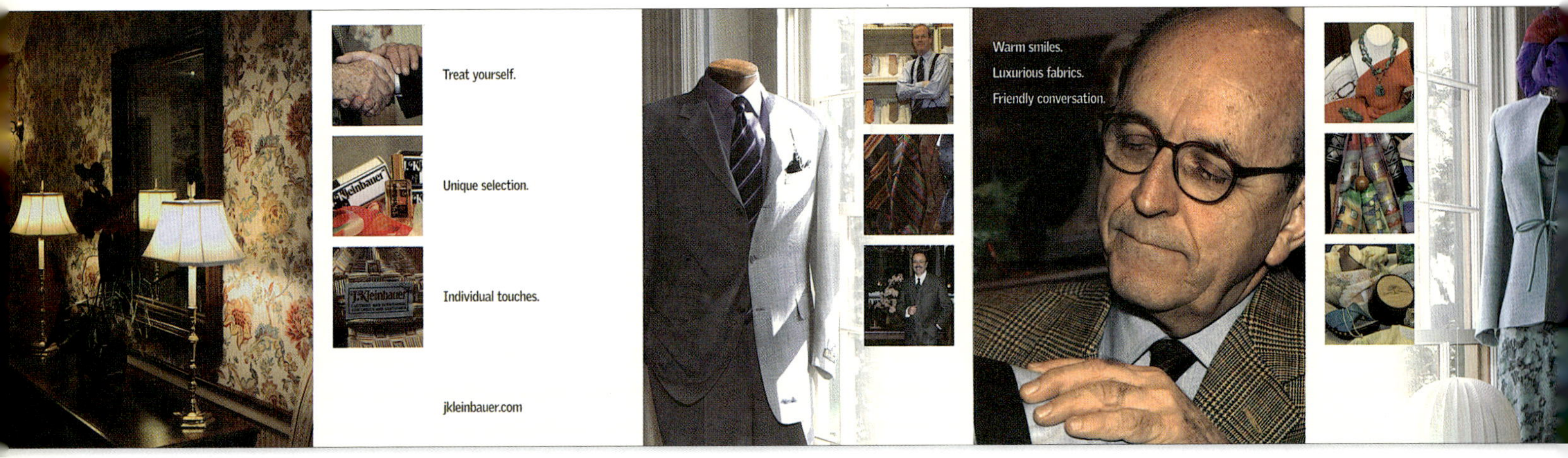

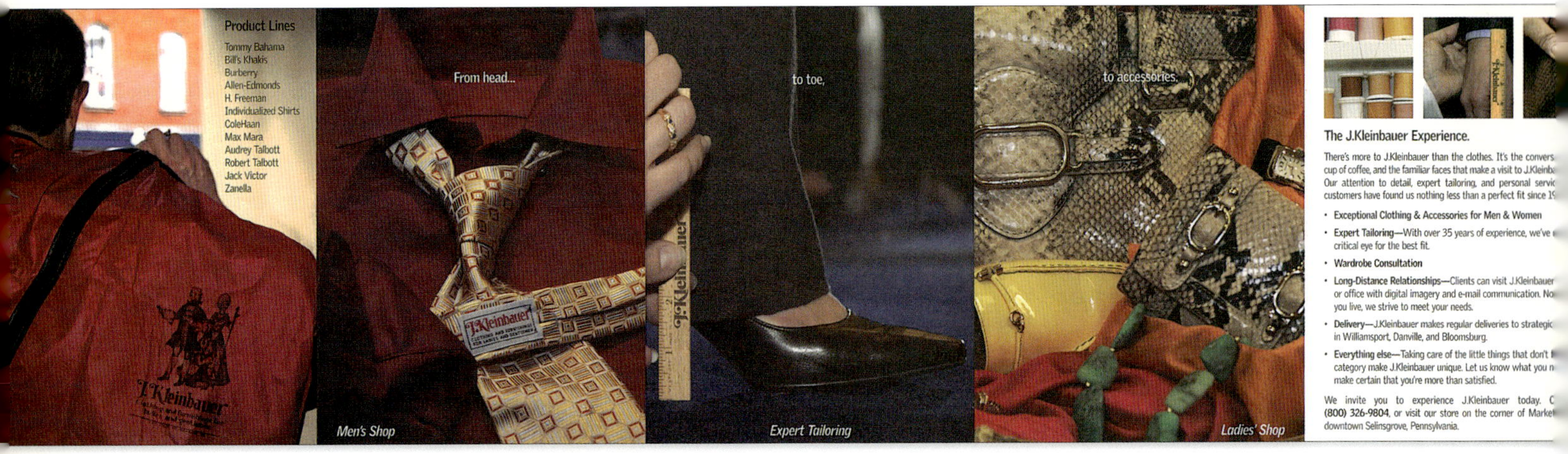

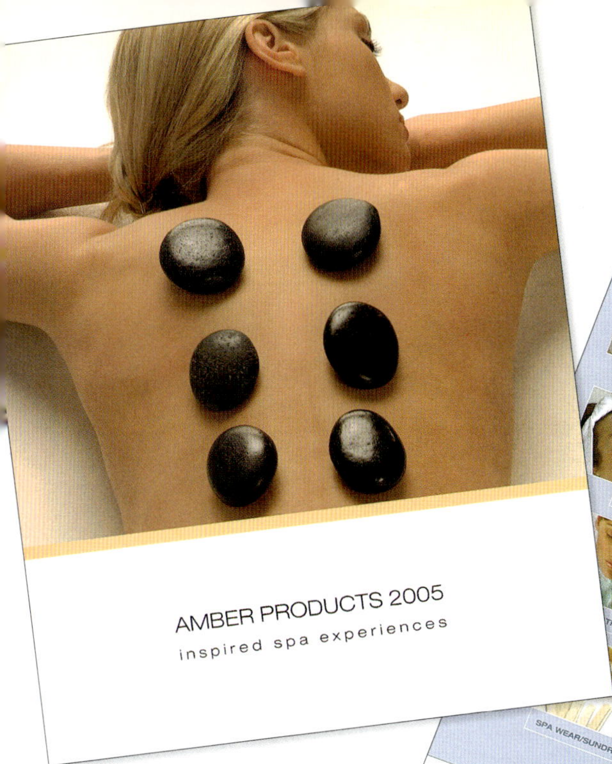

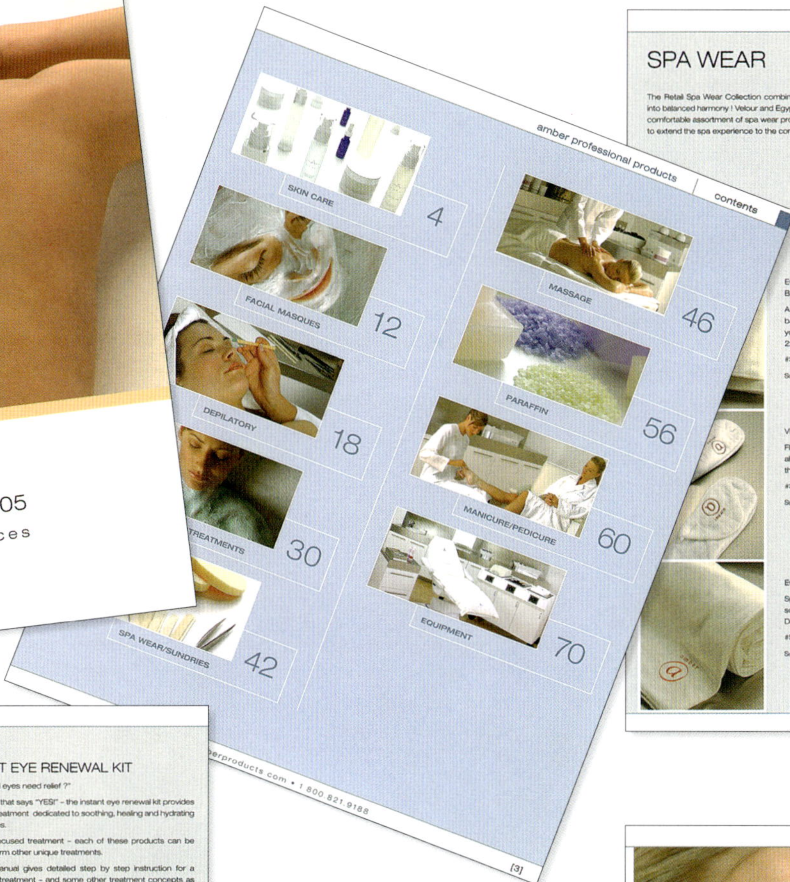

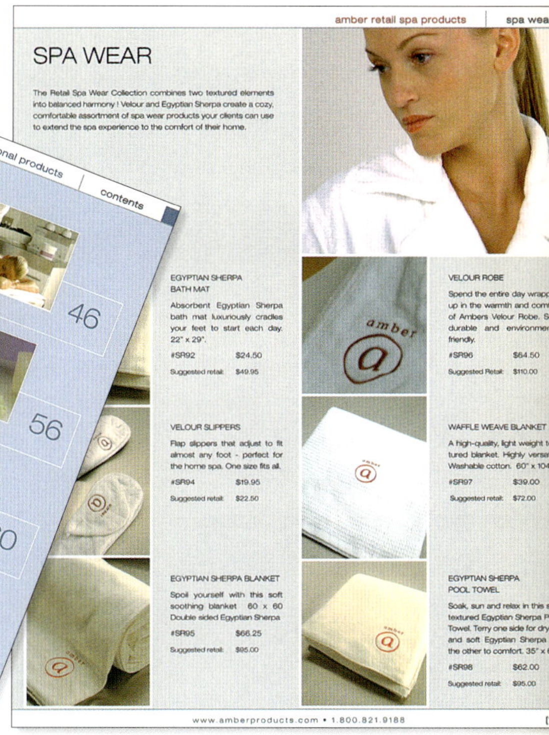

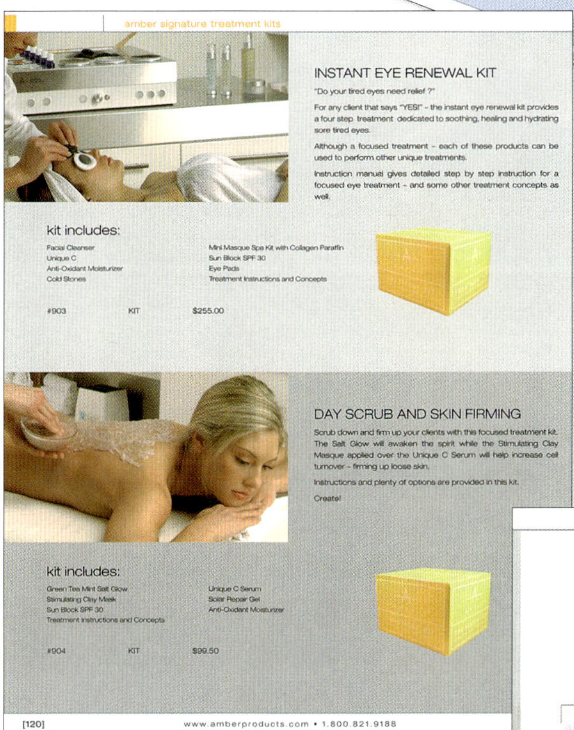

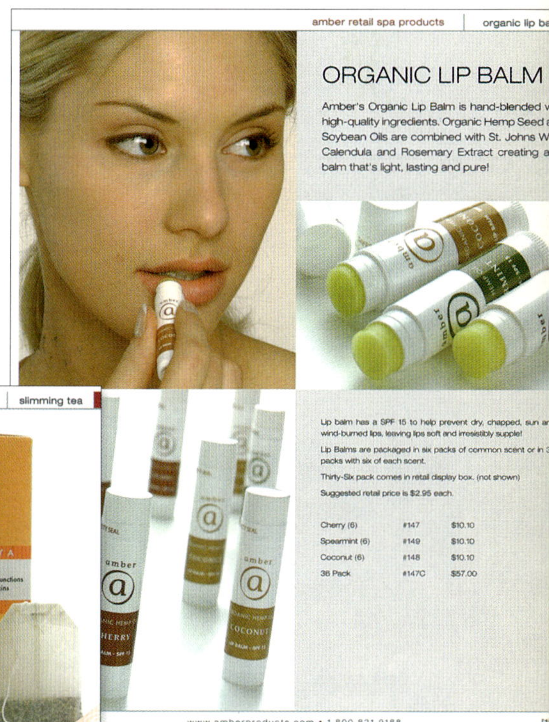

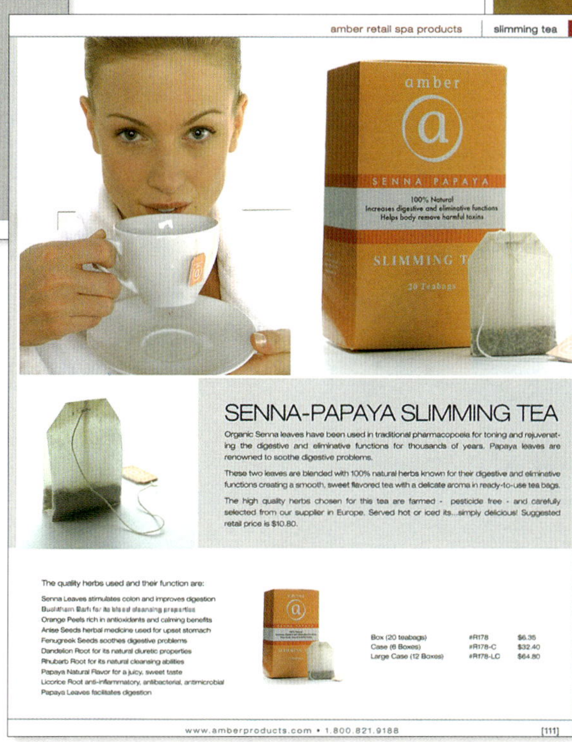

client
Amber Products Co.
design firm
Reinnov8 Design Group
designer
Richard A. Hooper

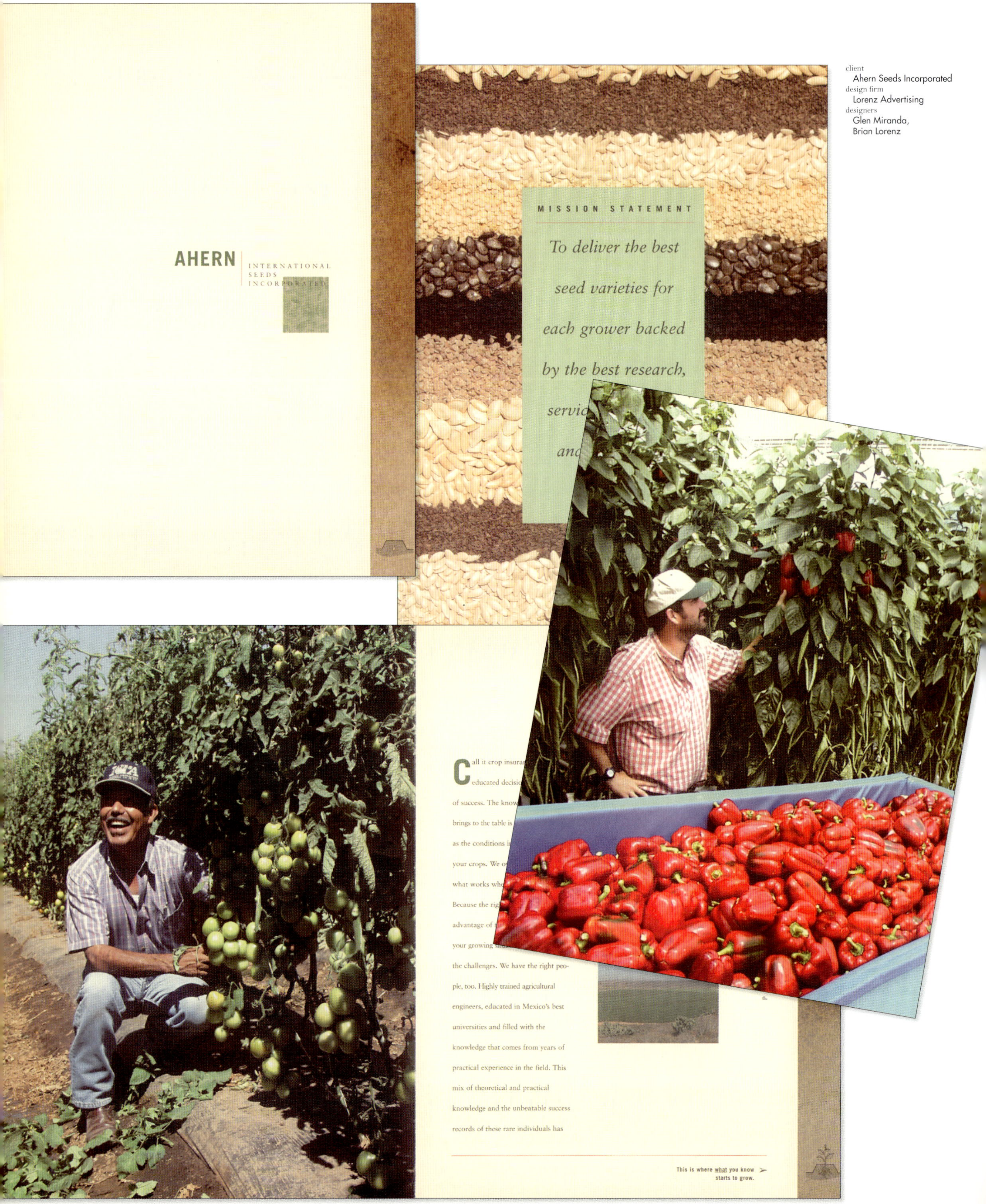

client
Ahern Seeds Incorporated
design firm
Lorenz Advertising
designers
Glen Miranda,
Brian Lorenz

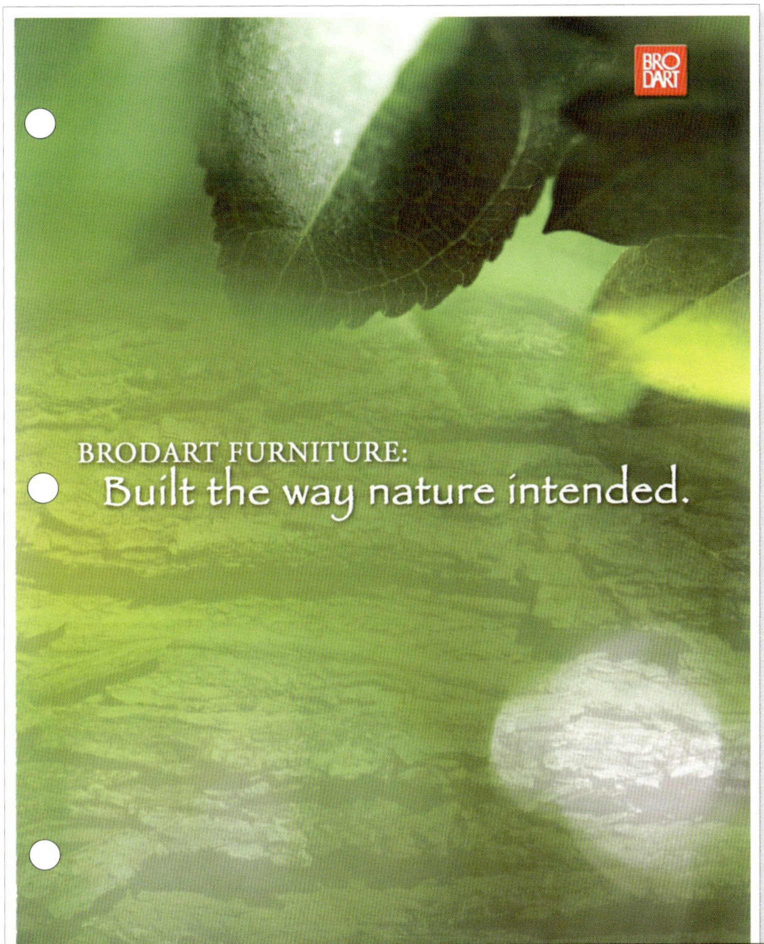

client
Brodart Furniture Company
design firm
Sire Advertising
designers
Shawn Felty,
Jessica Varner

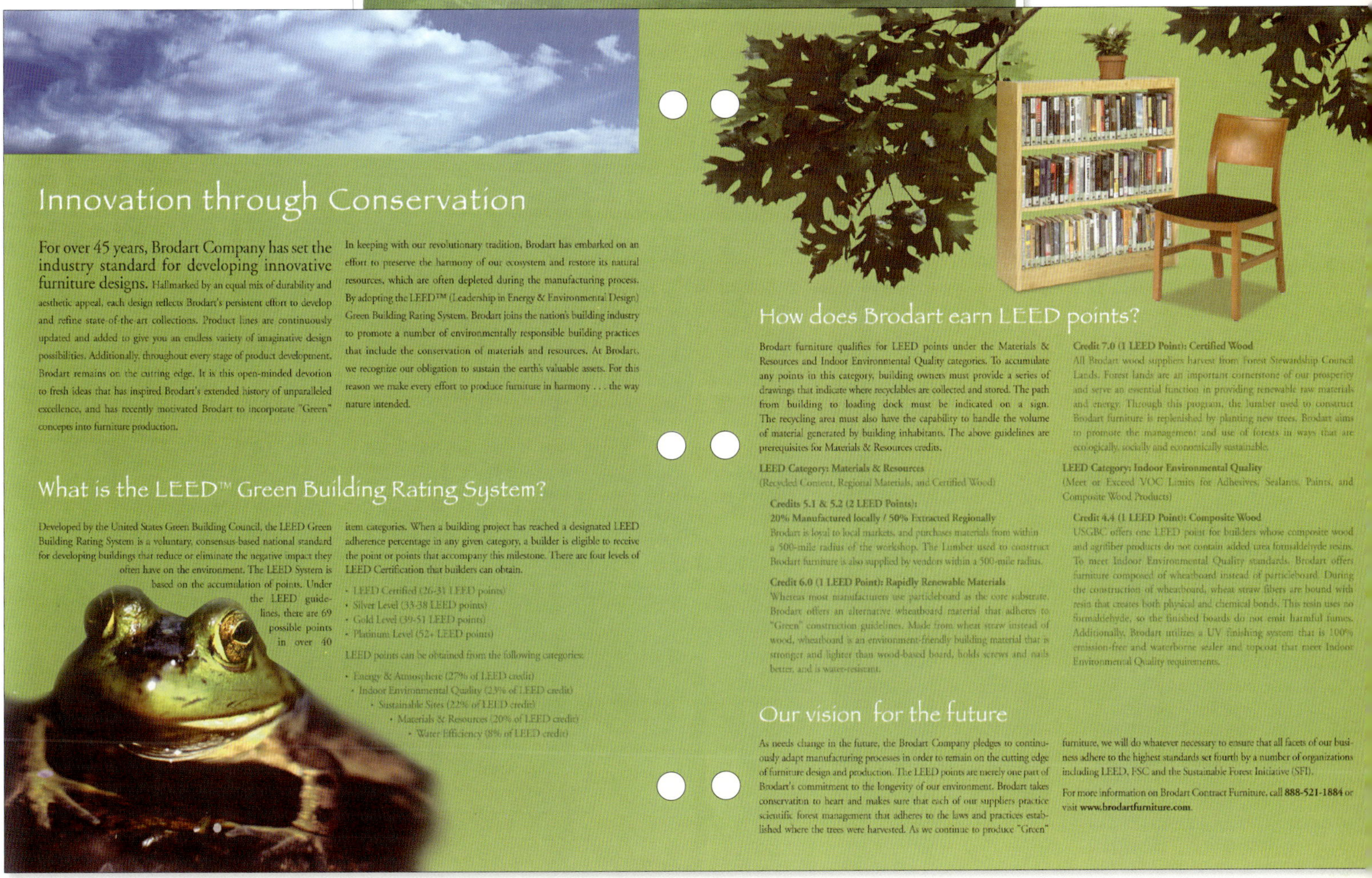

Innovation through Conservation

For over 45 years, Brodart Company has set the industry standard for developing innovative furniture designs. Hallmarked by an equal mix of durability and aesthetic appeal, each design reflects Brodart's persistent effort to develop and refine state-of-the-art collections. Product lines are continuously updated and added to give you an endless variety of imaginative design possibilities. Additionally, throughout every stage of product development, Brodart remains on the cutting edge. It is this open-minded devotion to fresh ideas that has inspired Brodart's extended history of unparalleled excellence, and has recently motivated Brodart to incorporate "Green" concepts into furniture production.

In keeping with our revolutionary tradition, Brodart has embarked on an effort to preserve the harmony of our ecosystem and restore its natural resources, which are often depleted during the manufacturing process. By adopting the LEED™ (Leadership in Energy & Environmental Design) Green Building Rating System, Brodart joins the nation's building industry to promote a number of environmentally responsible building practices that include the conservation of materials and resources. At Brodart, we recognize our obligation to sustain the earth's valuable assets. For this reason we make every effort to produce furniture in harmony . . . the way nature intended.

What is the LEED™ Green Building Rating System?

Developed by the United States Green Building Council, the LEED Green Building Rating System is a voluntary, consensus-based national standard for developing buildings that reduce or eliminate the negative impact they often have on the environment. The LEED System is based on the accumulation of points. Under the LEED guidelines, there are 69 possible points in over 40 item categories. When a building project has reached a designated LEED adherence percentage in any given category, a builder is eligible to receive the point or points that accompany this milestone. There are four levels of LEED Certification that builders can obtain.

- LEED Certified (26-31 LEED points)
- Silver Level (33-38 LEED points)
- Gold Level (39-51 LEED points)
- Platinum Level (52+ LEED points)

LEED points can be obtained from the following categories:

- Energy & Atmosphere (27% of LEED credit)
- Indoor Environmental Quality (23% of LEED credit)
- Sustainable Sites (22% of LEED credit)
- Materials & Resources (20% of LEED credit)
- Water Efficiency (8% of LEED credit)

How does Brodart earn LEED points?

Brodart furniture qualifies for LEED points under the Materials & Resources and Indoor Environmental Quality categories. To accumulate any points in this category, building owners must provide a series of drawings that indicate where recyclables are collected and stored. The path from building to loading dock must be indicated on a sign. The recycling area must also have the capability to handle the volume of material generated by building inhabitants. The above guidelines are prerequisites for Materials & Resources credits.

LEED Category: Materials & Resources
(Recycled Content, Regional Materials, and Certified Wood)

Credits 5.1 & 5.2 (2 LEED Points):
20% Manufactured locally / 50% Extracted Regionally
Brodart is loyal to local markets, and purchases materials from within a 500-mile radius of the workshop. The Lumber used to construct Brodart furniture is also supplied by vendors within a 500-mile radius.

Credit 6.0 (1 LEED Point): Rapidly Renewable Materials
Whereas most manufacturers use particleboard as the core substrate, Brodart offers an alternative wheatboard material that adheres to "Green" construction guidelines. Made from wheat straw instead of wood, wheatboard is an environment-friendly building material that is stronger and lighter than wood-based board, holds screws and nails better, and is water-resistant.

Credit 7.0 (1 LEED Point): Certified Wood
All Brodart wood suppliers harvest from Forest Stewardship Council Lands. Forest lands are an important cornerstone of our prosperity and serve an essential function in providing renewable raw materials and energy. Through this program, the lumber used to construct Brodart furniture is replenished by planting new trees. Brodart aims to promote the management and use of forests in ways that are ecologically, socially and economically sustainable.

LEED Category: Indoor Environmental Quality
(Meet or Exceed VOC Limits for Adhesives, Sealants, Paints, and Composite Wood Products)

Credit 4.4 (1 LEED Point): Composite Wood
USGBC offers one LEED point for builders whose composite wood and agrifiber products do not contain added urea formaldehyde resins. To meet Indoor Environmental Quality standards, Brodart offers furniture composed of wheatboard instead of particleboard. During the construction of wheatboard, wheat straw fibers are bound with resin that creates both physical and chemical bonds. This resin uses no formaldehyde, so the finished boards do not emit harmful fumes. Additionally, Brodart utilizes a UV finishing system that is 100% emission-free and waterborne sealer and topcoat that meet Indoor Environmental Quality requirements.

Our vision for the future

As needs change in the future, the Brodart Company pledges to continuously adapt manufacturing processes in order to remain on the cutting edge of furniture design and production. The LEED points are merely one part of Brodart's commitment to the longevity of our environment. Brodart takes conservation to heart and makes sure that each of our suppliers practice scientific forest management that adheres to the laws and practices established where the trees were harvested. As we continue to produce "Green" furniture, we will do whatever necessary to ensure that all facets of our business adhere to the highest standards set fourth by a number of organizations including LEED, FSC and the Sustainable Forest Initiative (SFI).

For more information on Brodart Contract Furniture, call **888-521-1884** or visit **www.brodartfurniture.com**.

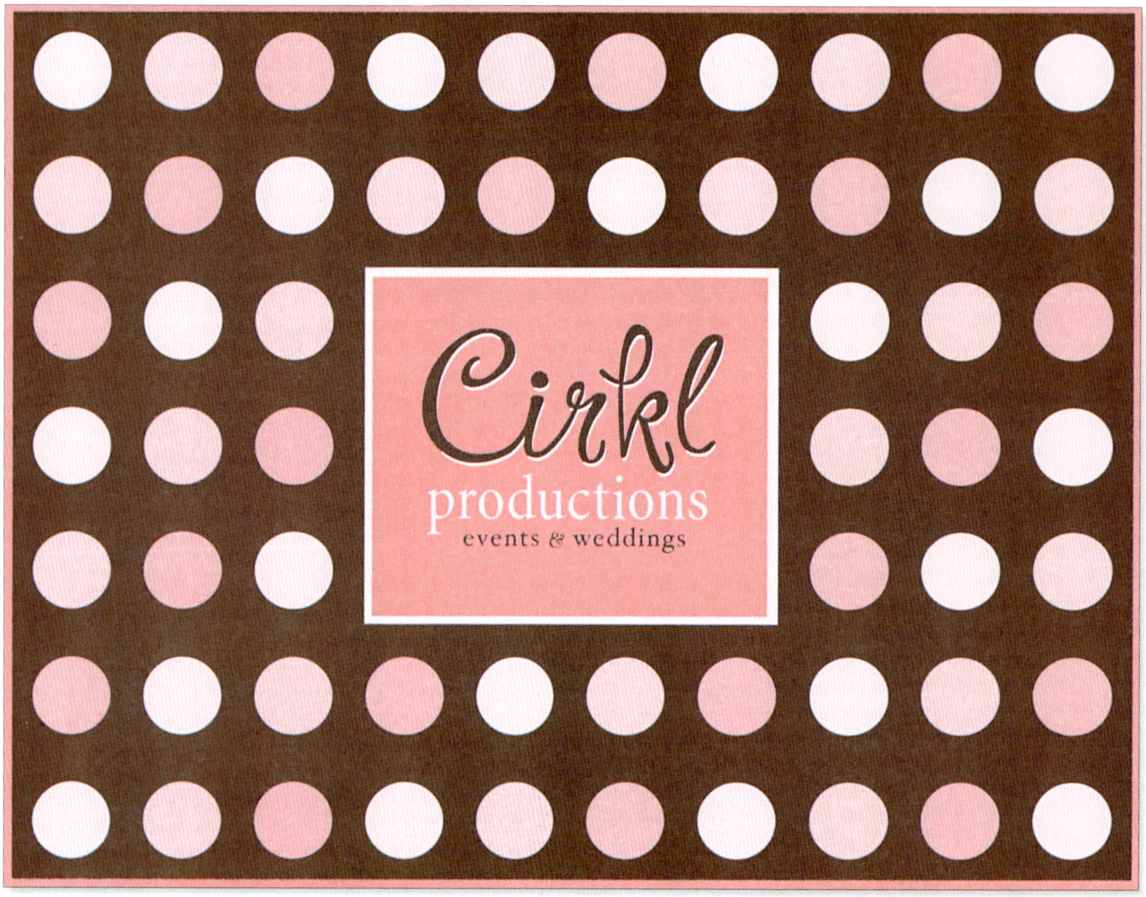

client
Cirkl Productions-Events & Weddings
design firm
Tristano Design
designer
Sara Tristano

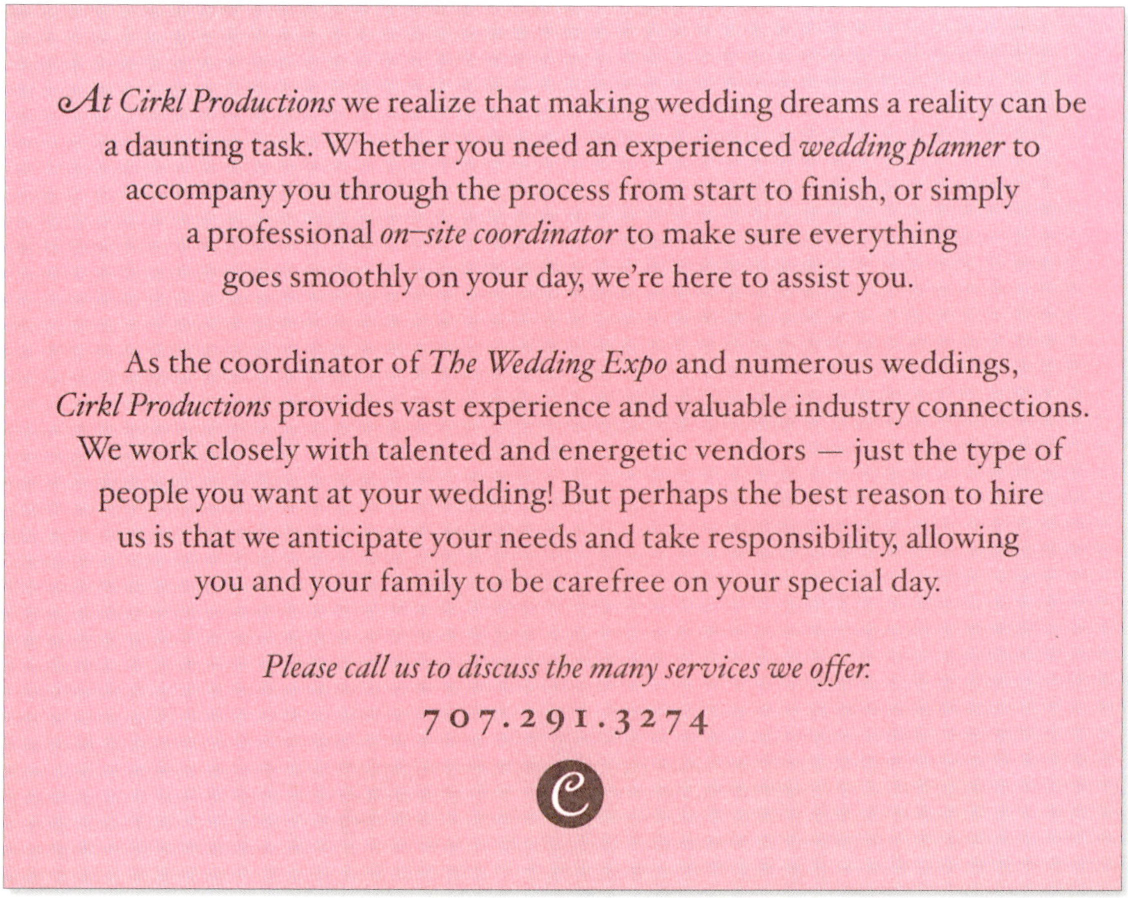

client
Cleo Design
design firm
Brand, ltd.
designer
Virginia Martino

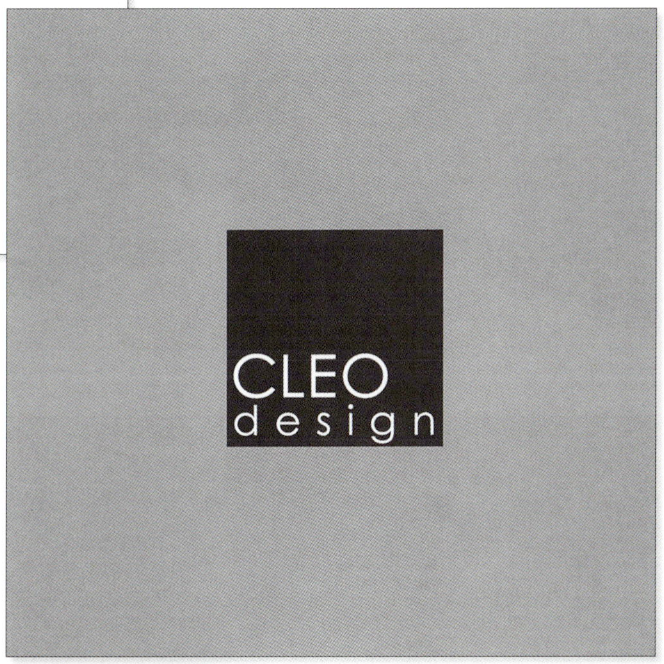

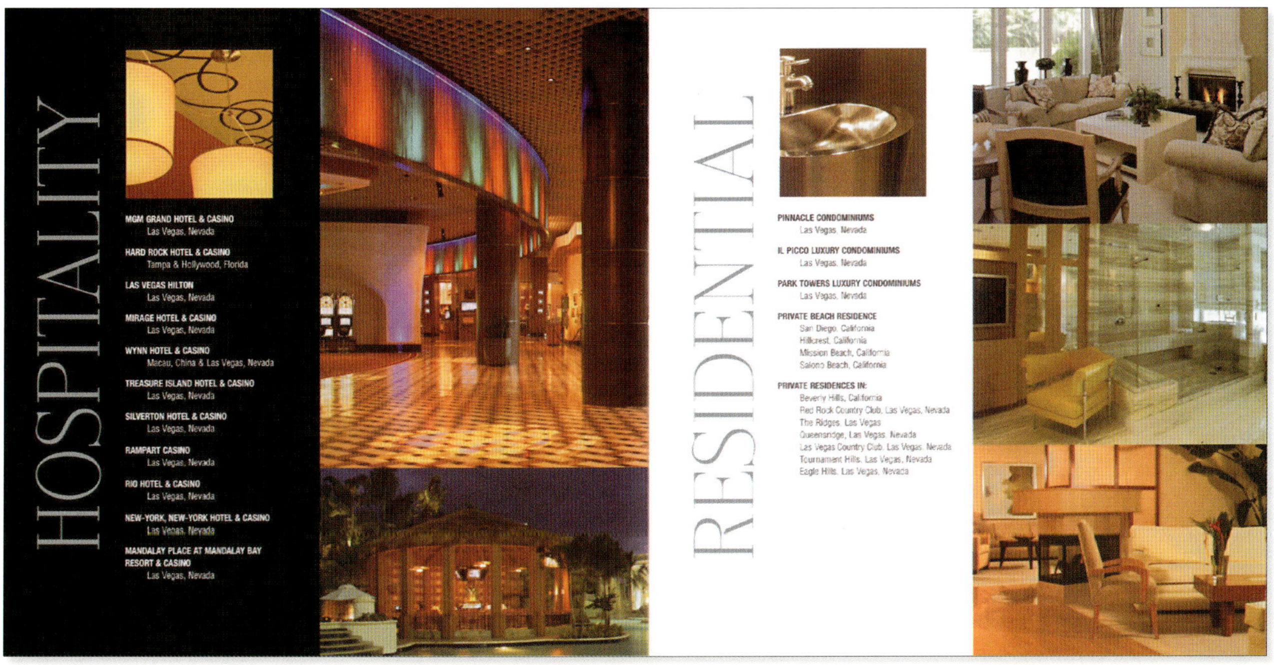

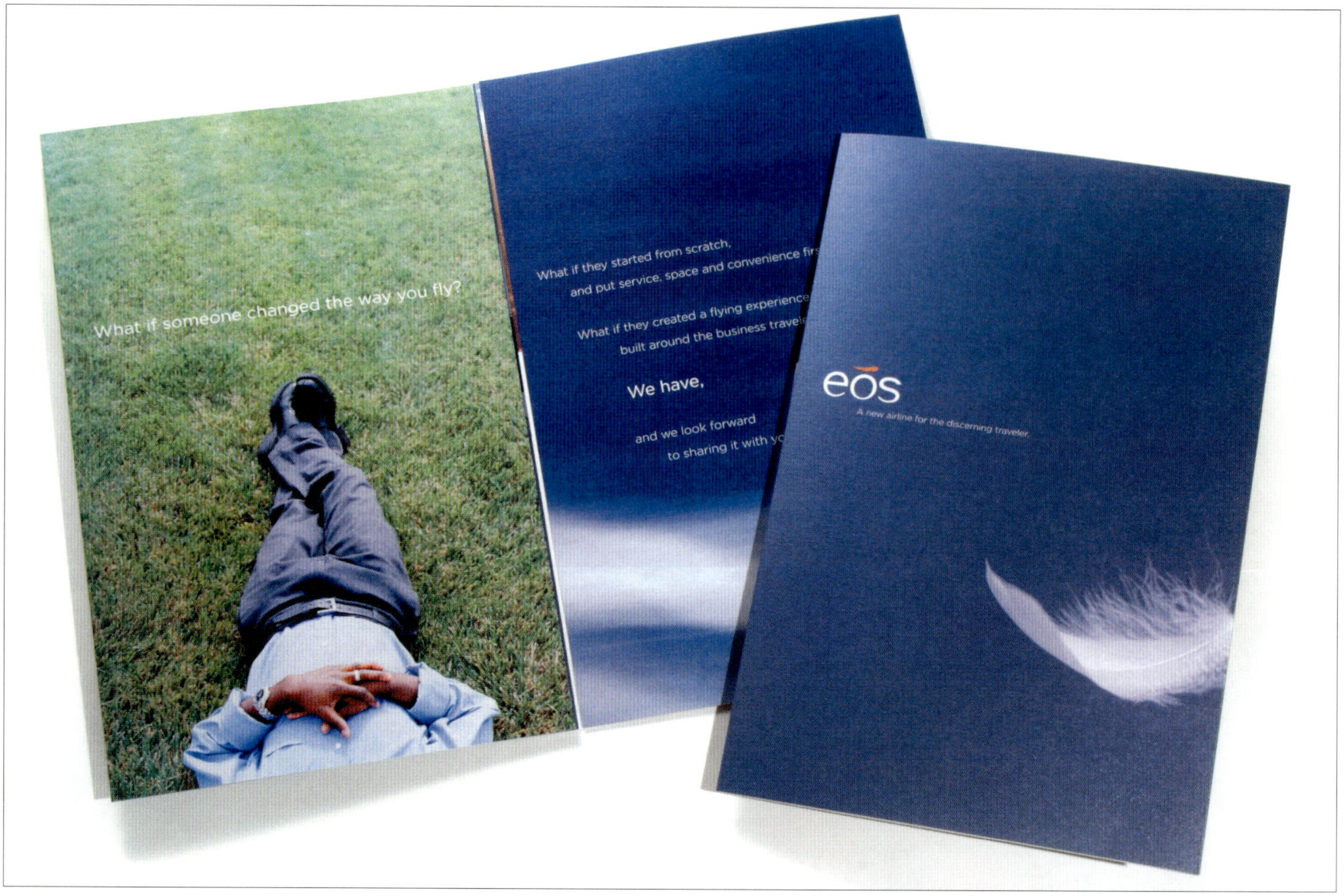

client
Eos Airlines
design firm
Hornall Anderson Design Works
designers
Jack Anderson, Mark Popich, David Bates, Andrew Wicklund, Leo Raymundo, Jacob Carter, Yuri Shvets

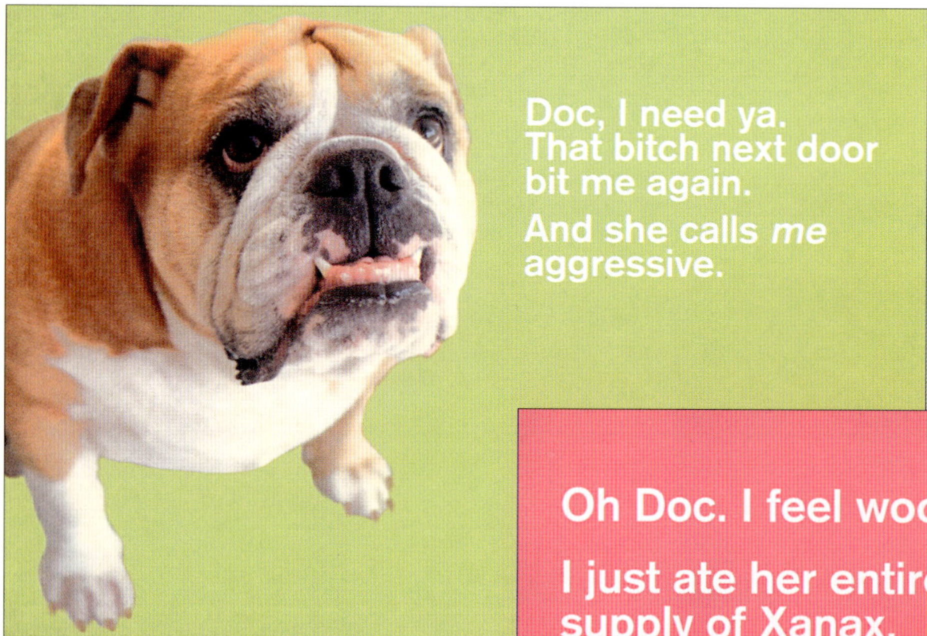

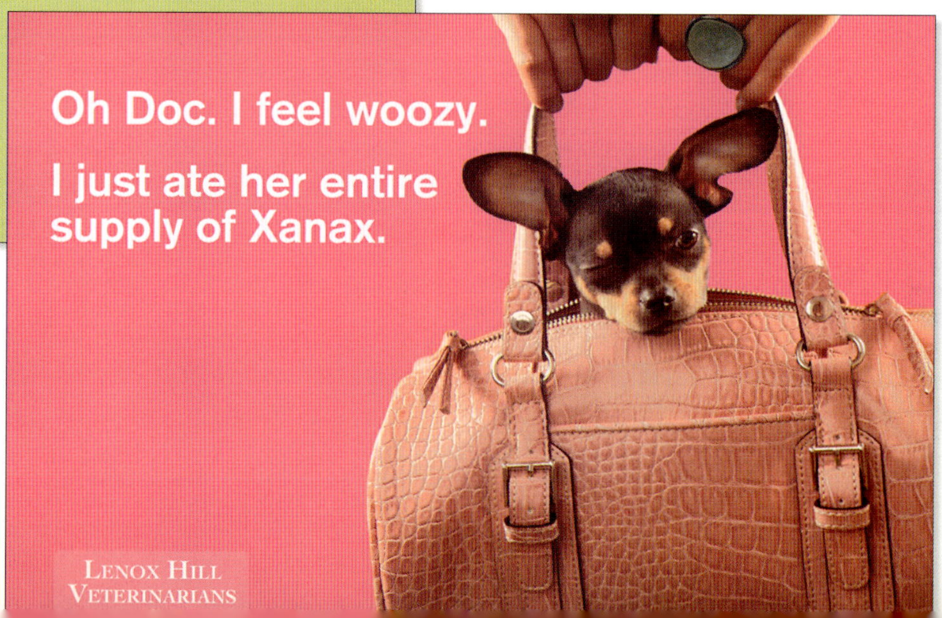

client
Lenox Hill Vets
design firm
Hotsauce
designer
Wyndy Wilder Sloan

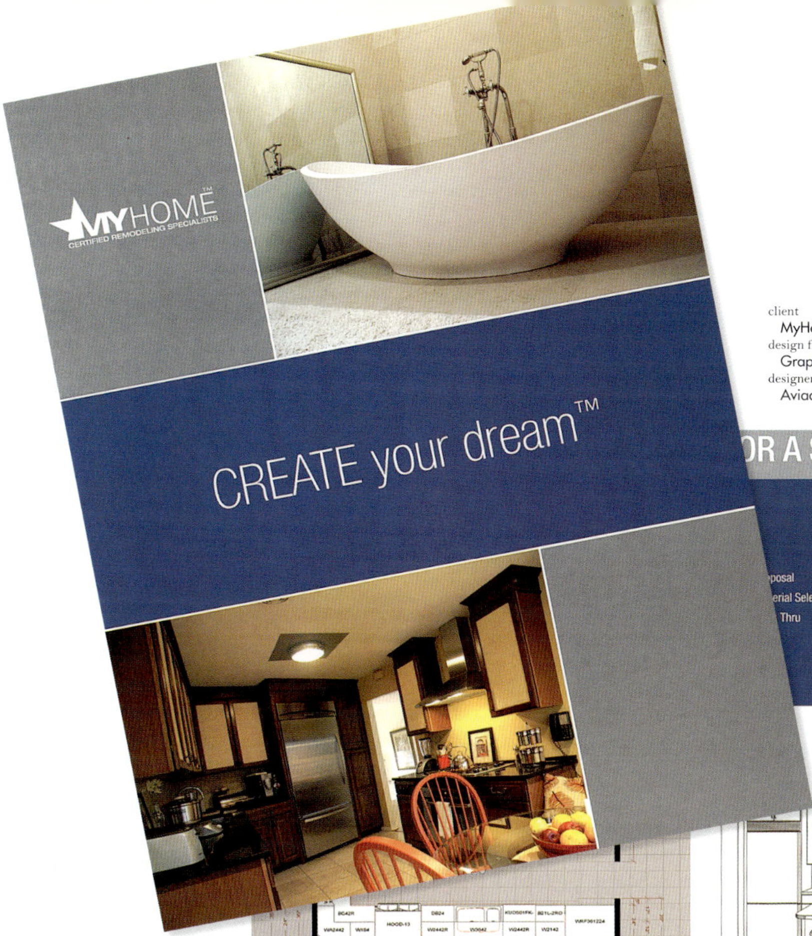

client
MyHome, LLC
design firm
Graphic Advances Inc.
designer
Aviad Stark

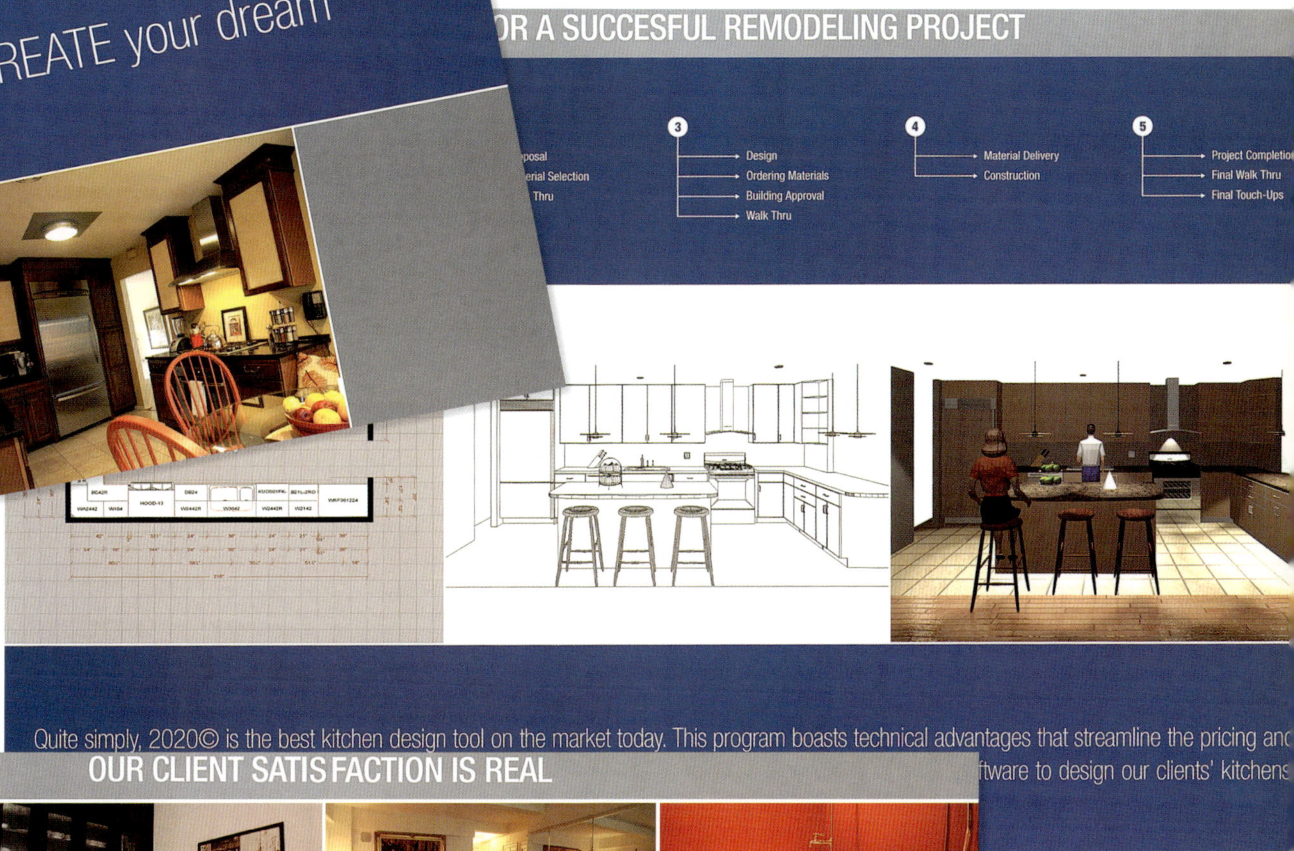

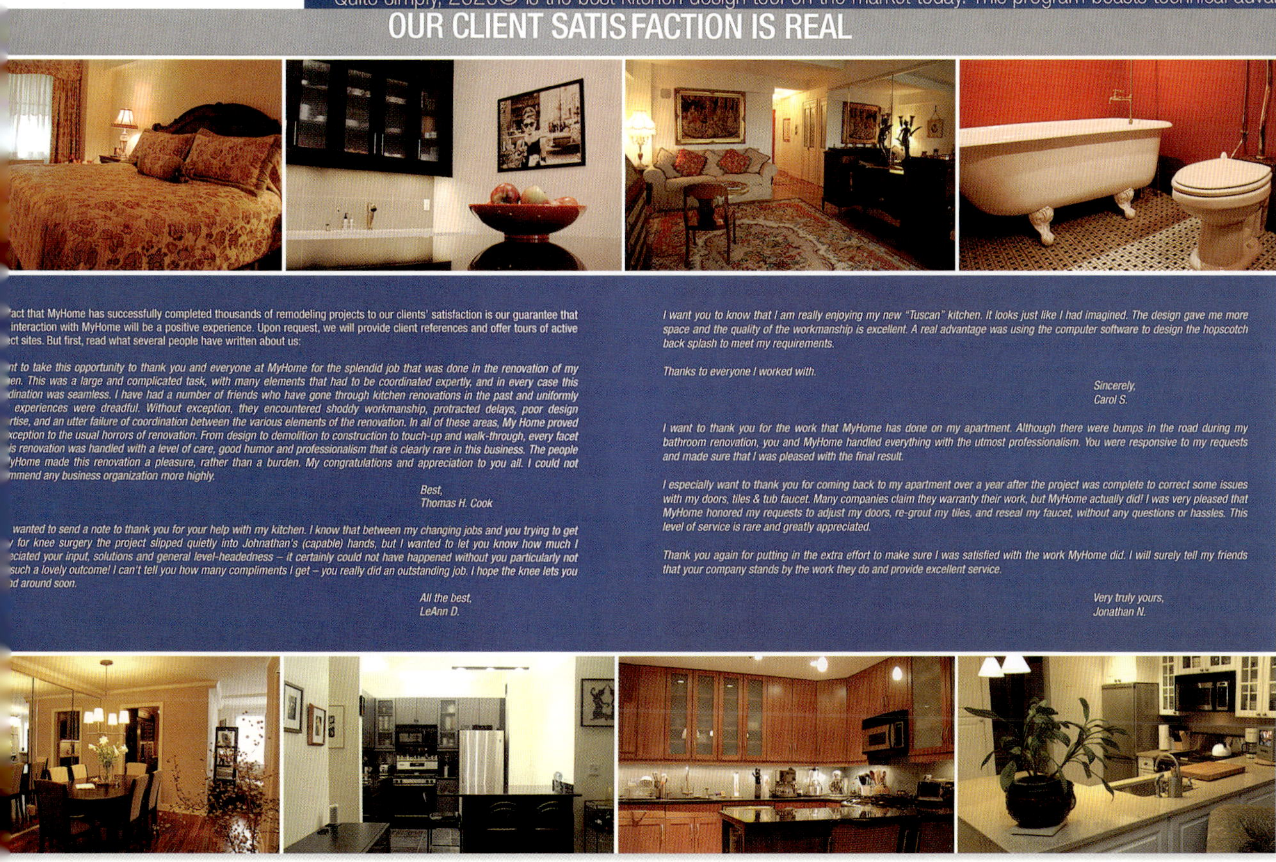

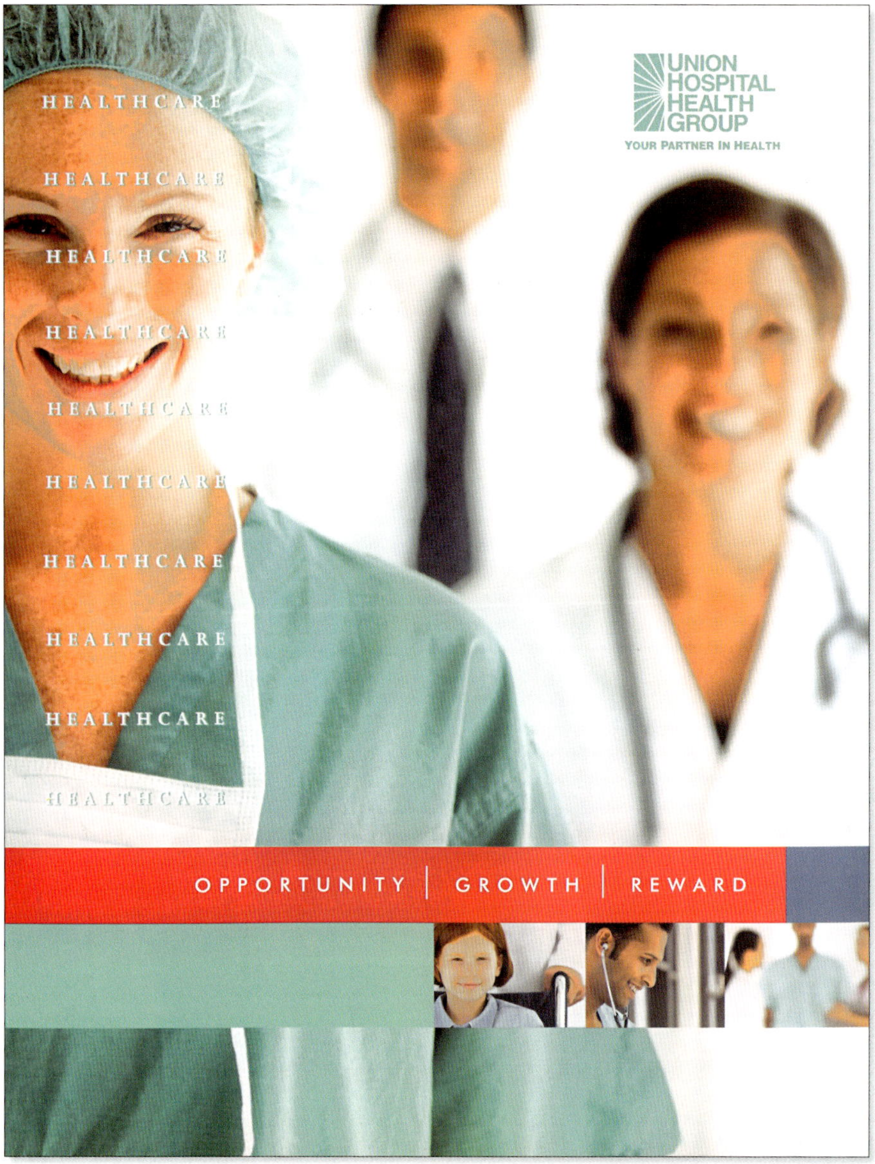

client
Union Hospital Health Group
design firm
Miller White, LLC
designer
Jenny Hoffeditz

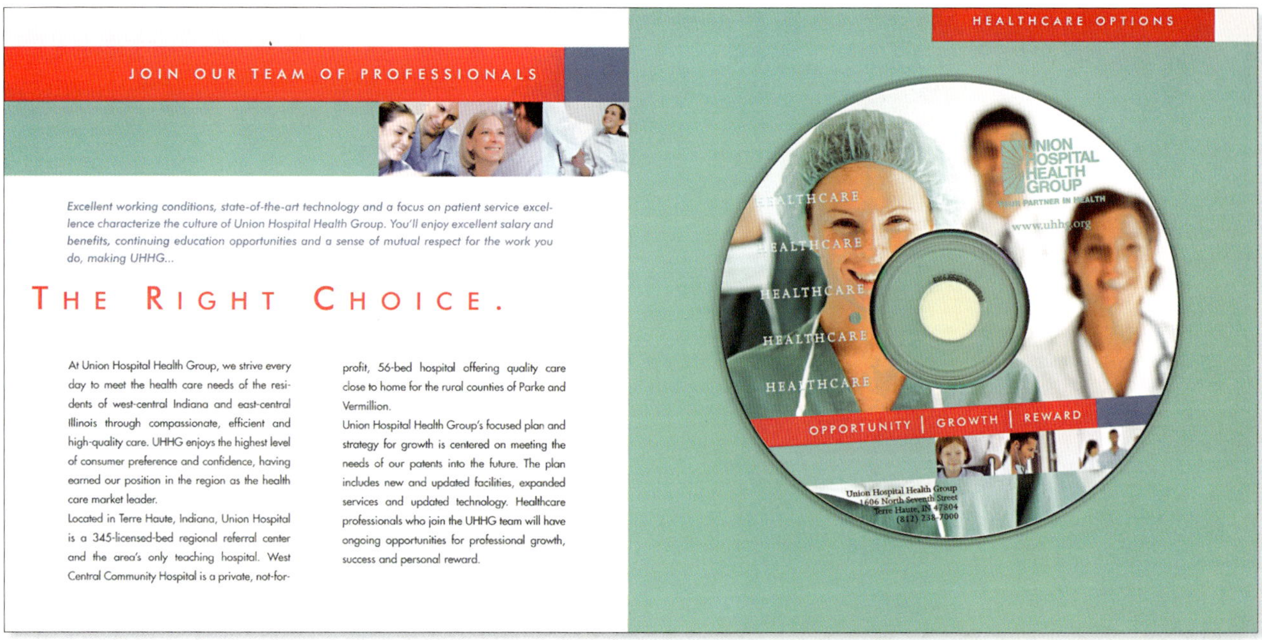

client
MMA Financial
design firm
Gill Fishman Associates
designer
Tammy Torrey

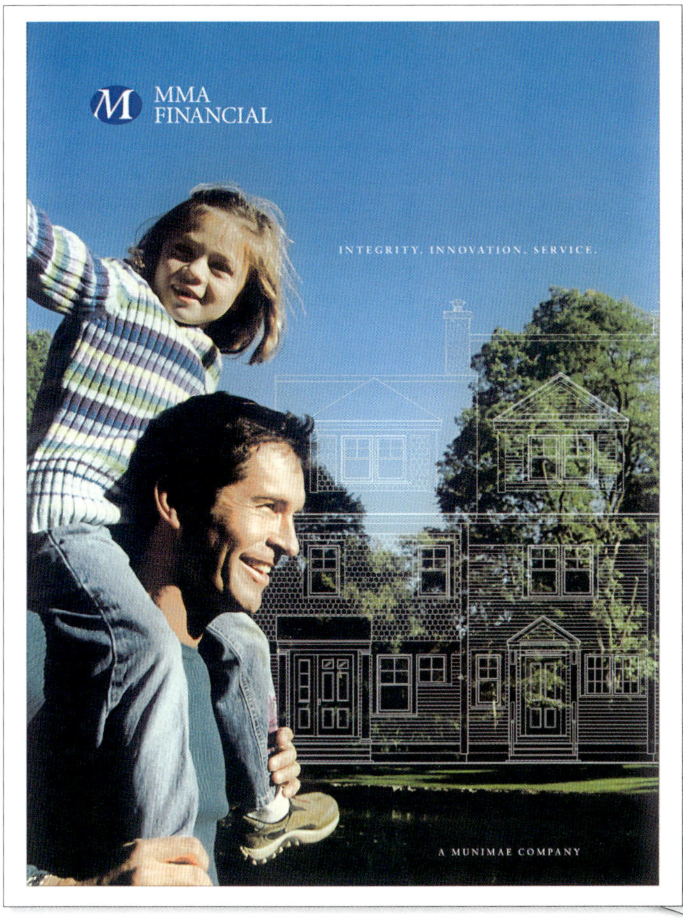

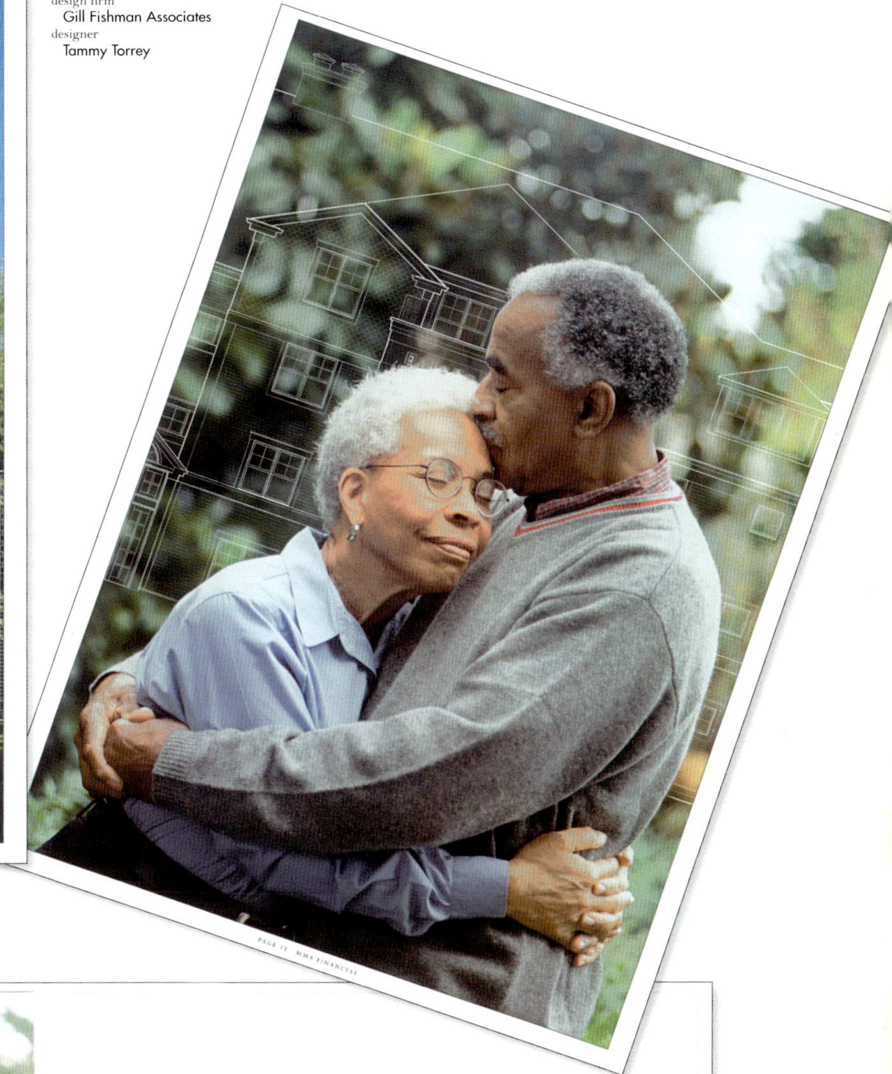

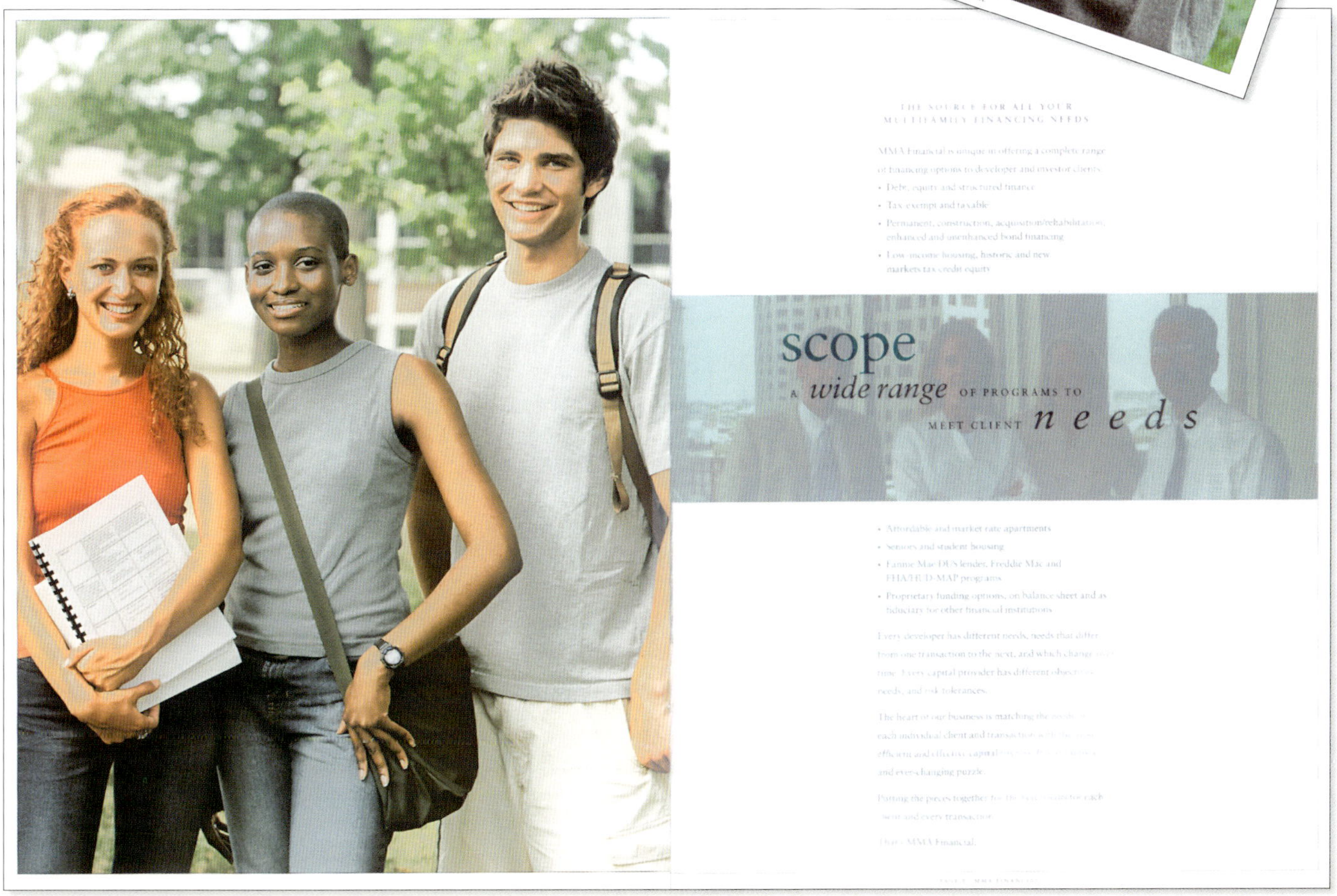

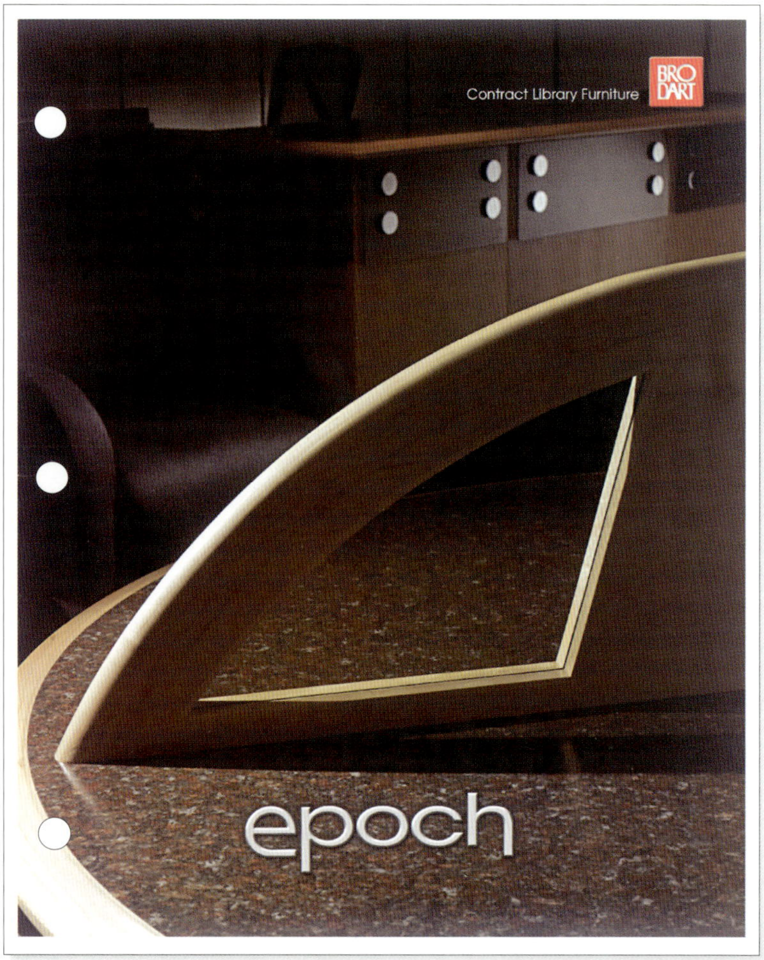

client
Brodart Furniture Company
design firm
Sire Advertising
designers
Shawn Felty,
Jordan Chappell

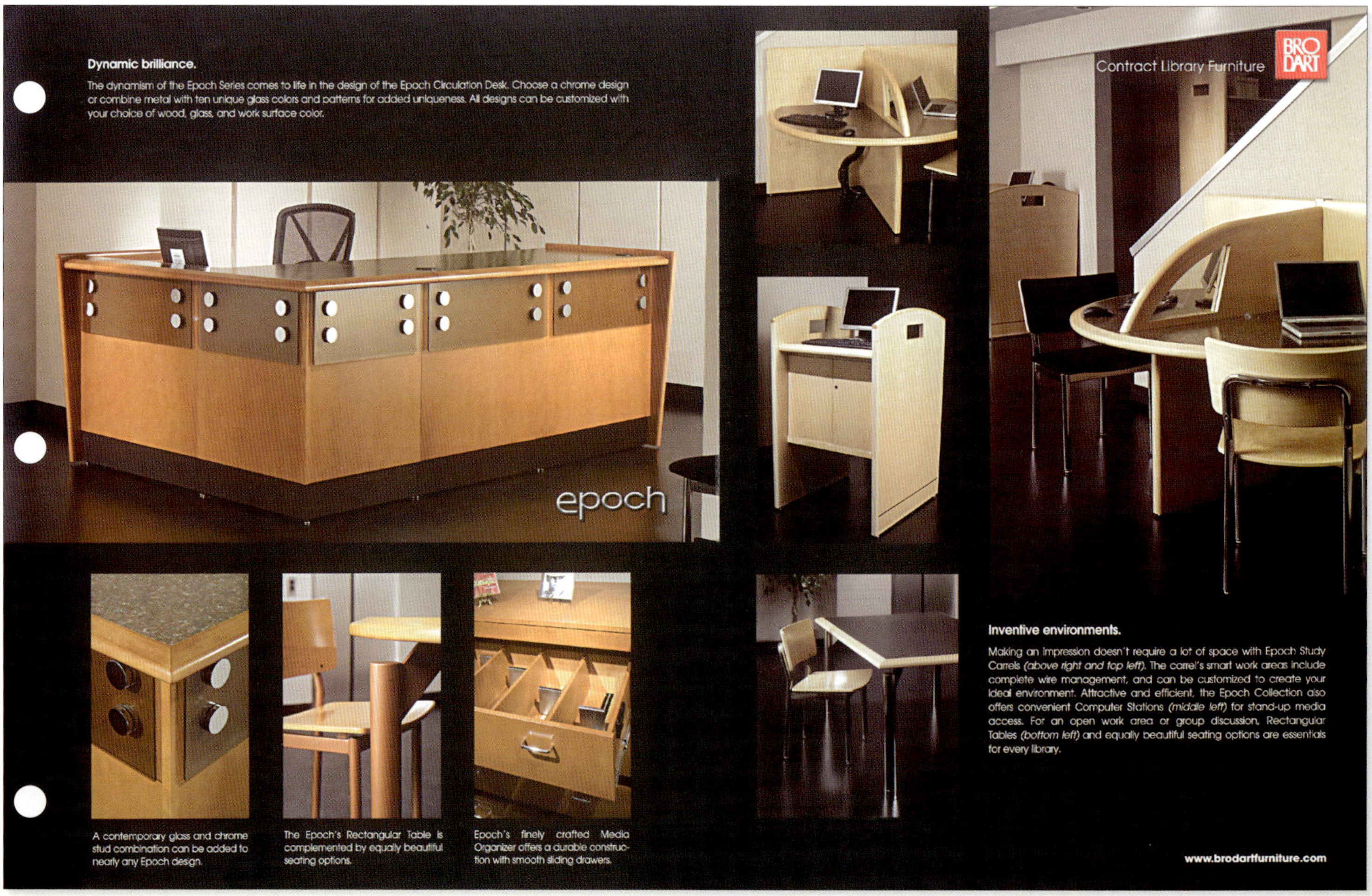

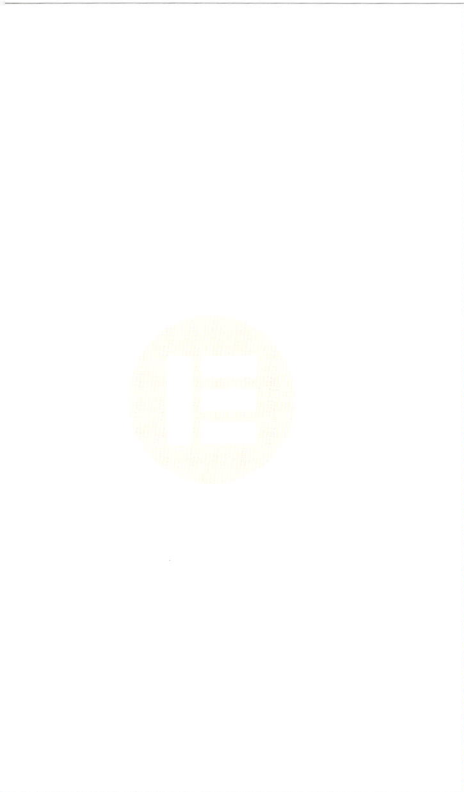

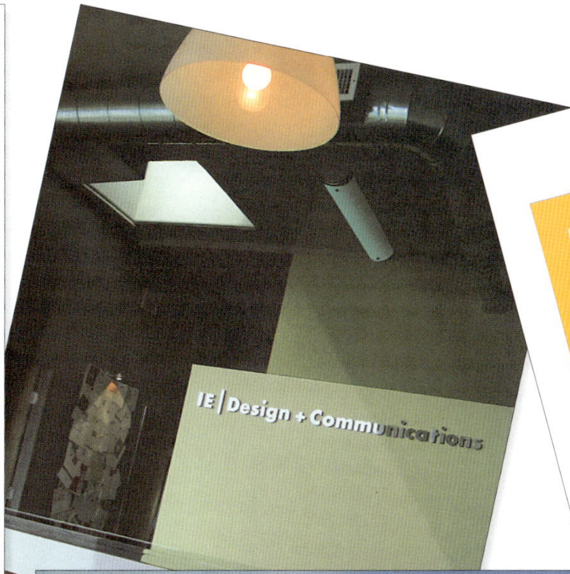

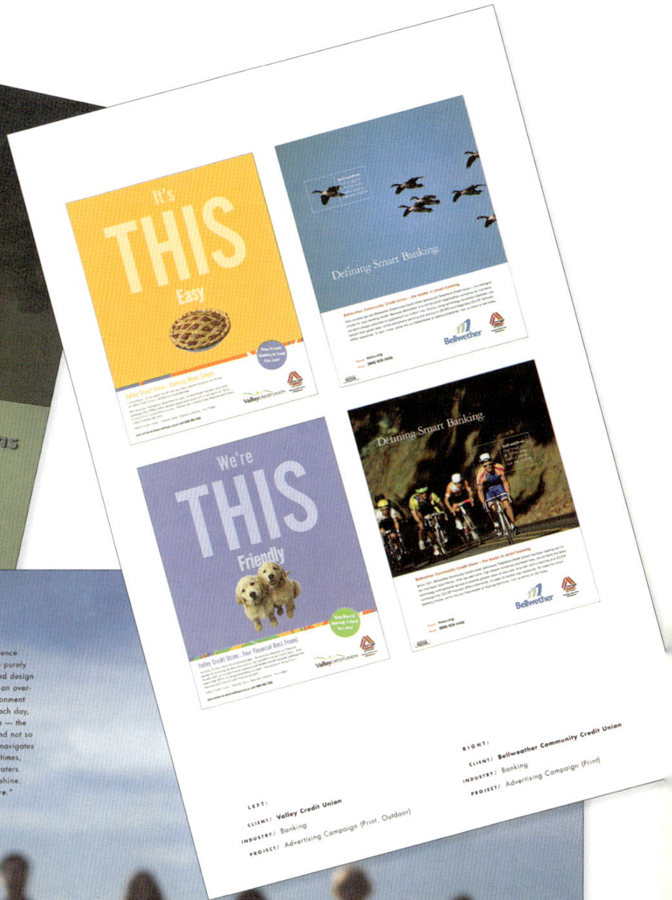

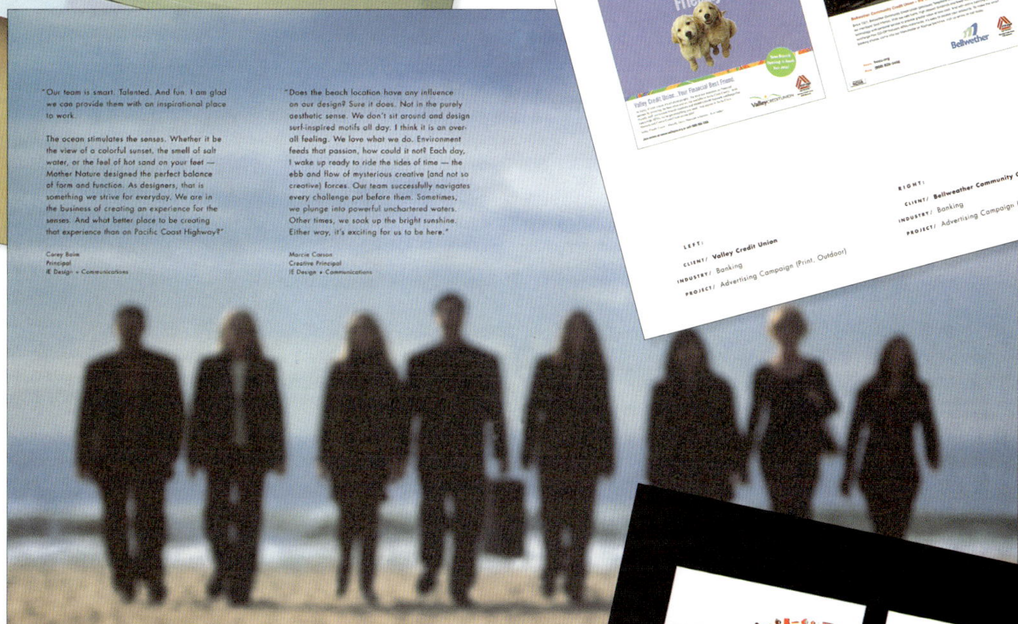

client
IE Design + Communications
design firm
IE Design + Communications
designer
Marcie Carson

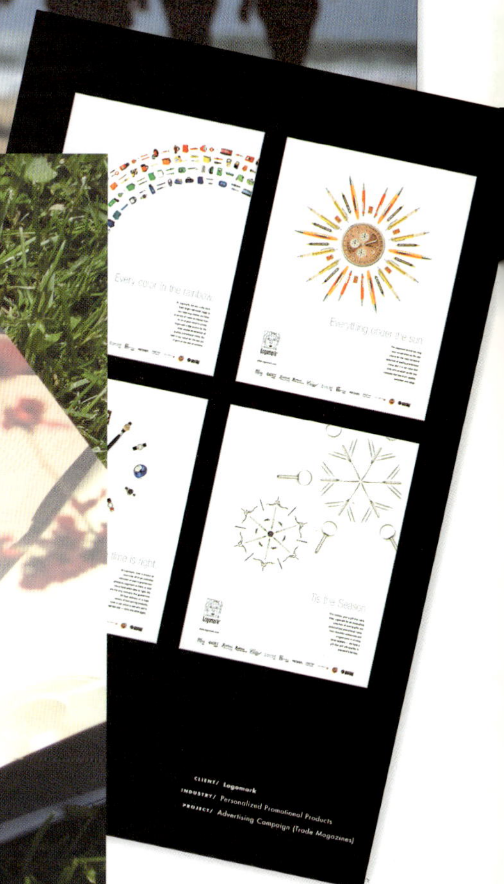

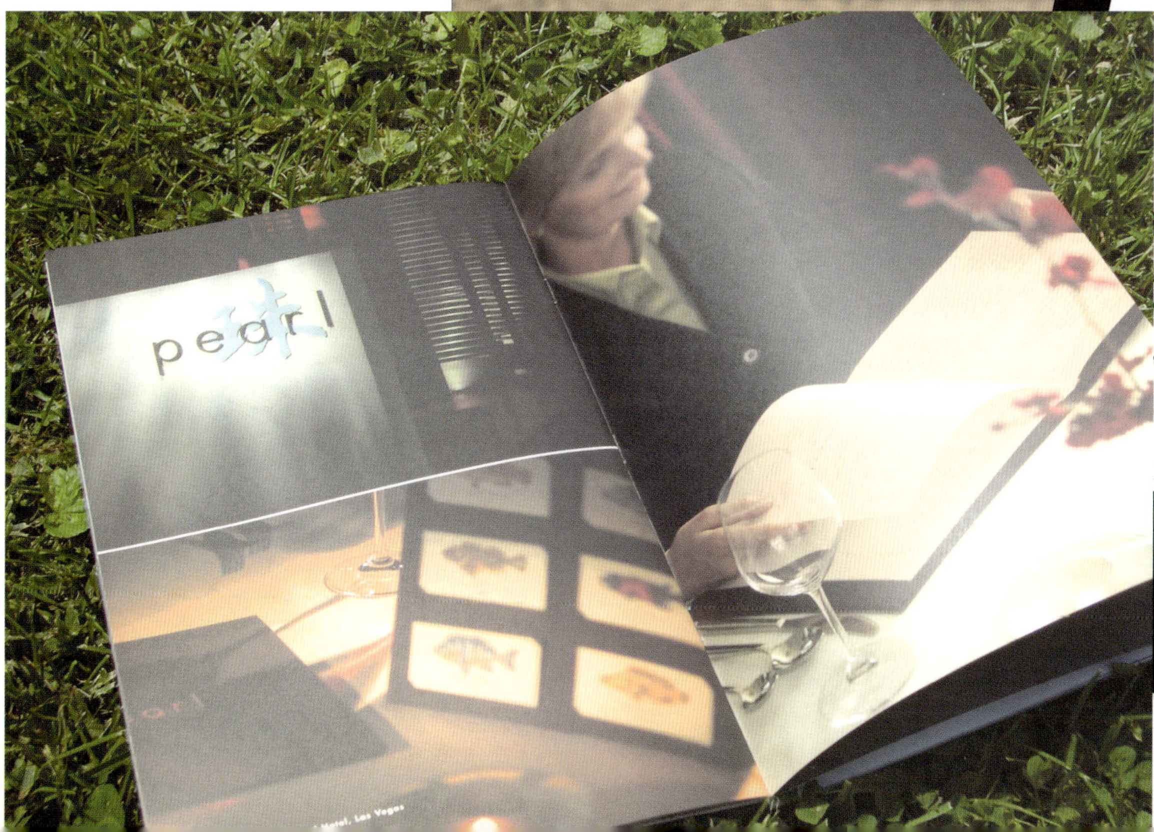

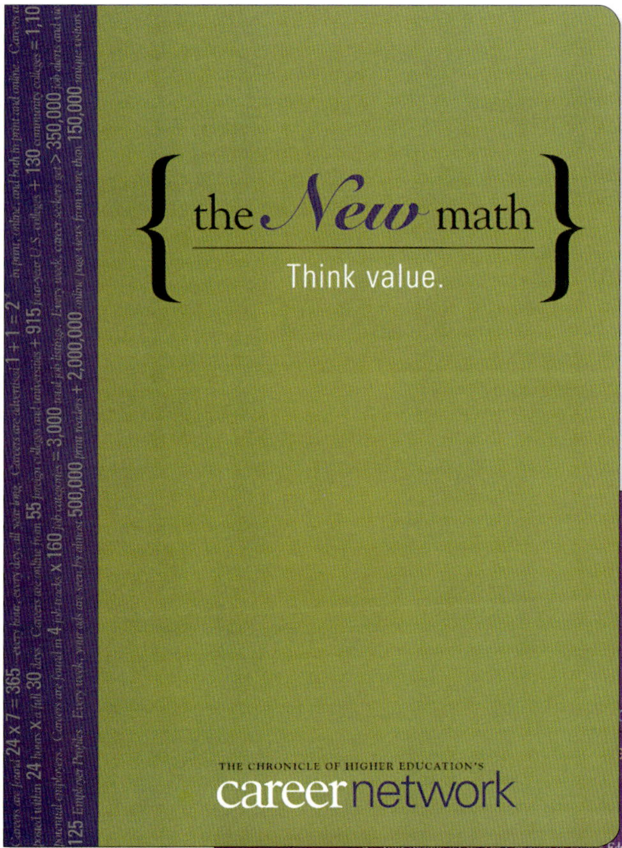

client
The Chronicle of Higher Education
design firm
Greenfield/Belser Ltd.
designers
Burkey Belser, Jill Sasser,
Siobhan Davis, Robyn McKenzie

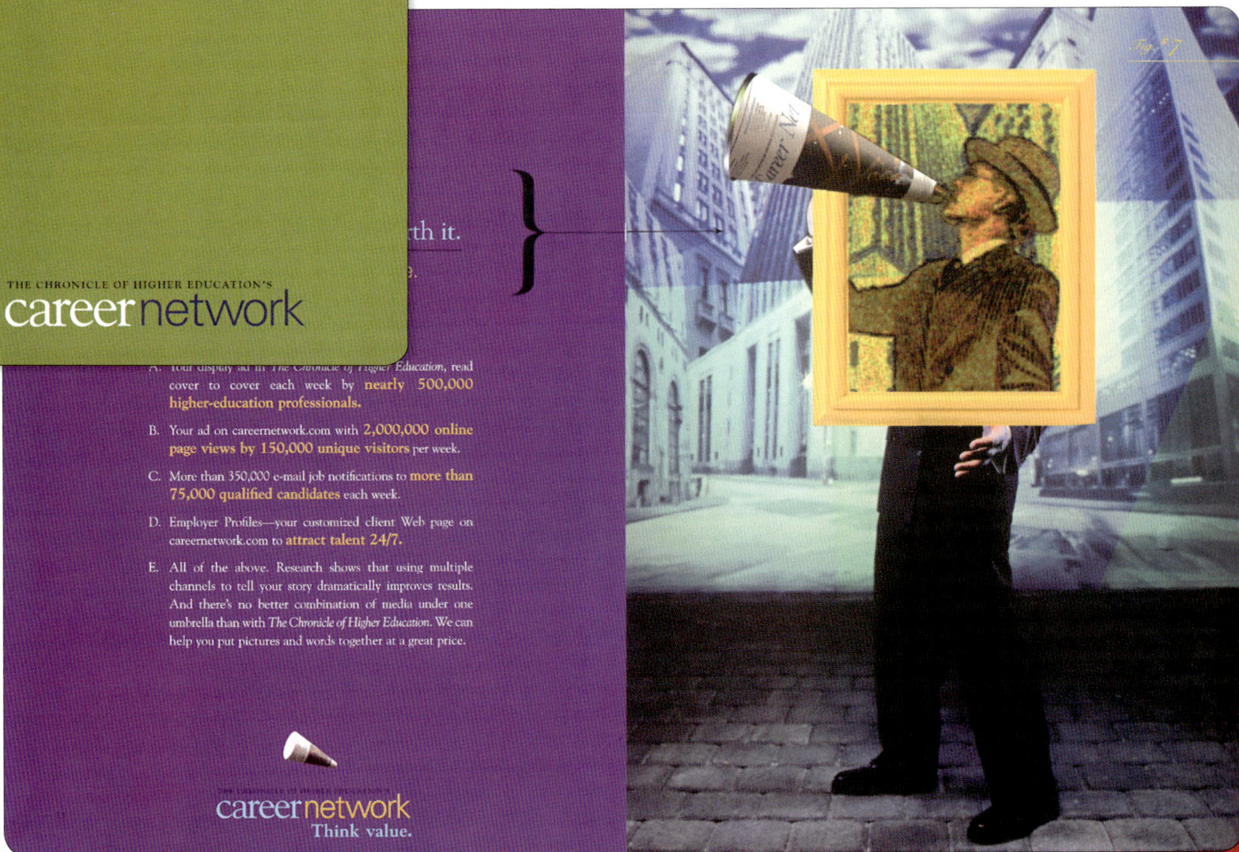

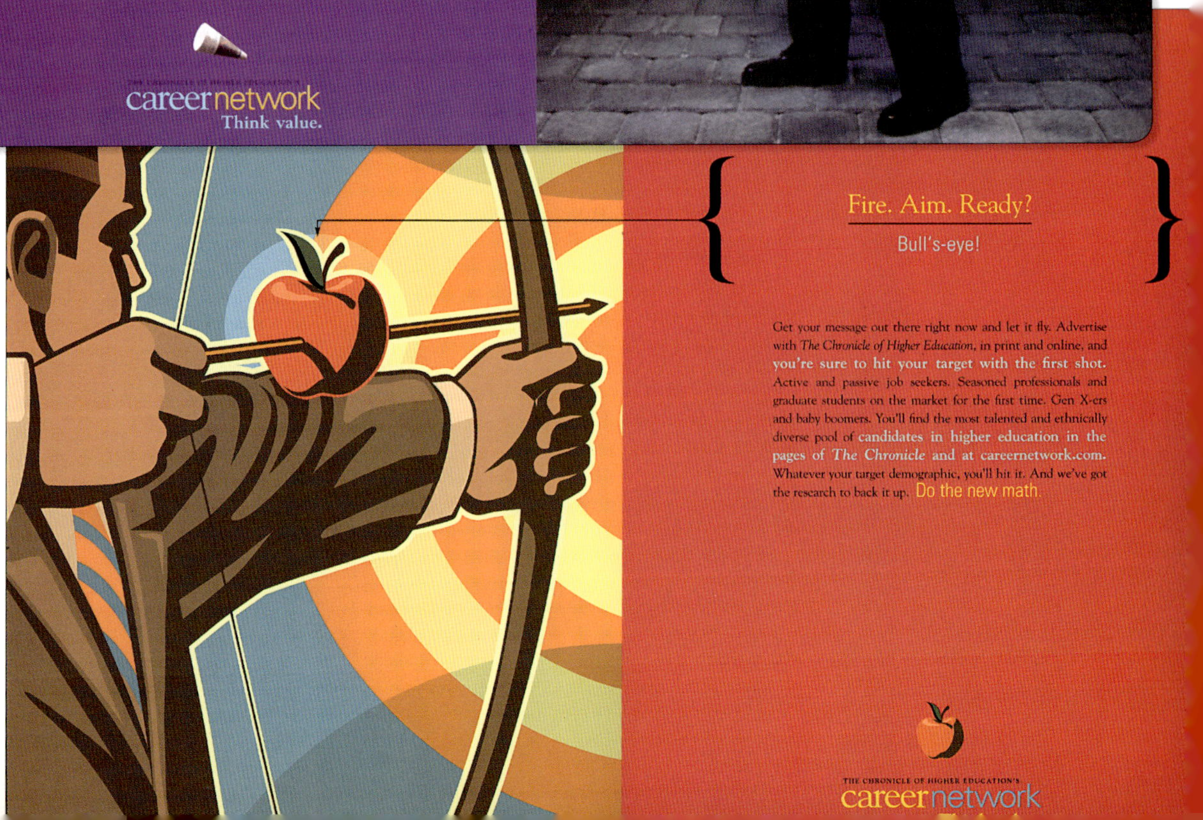

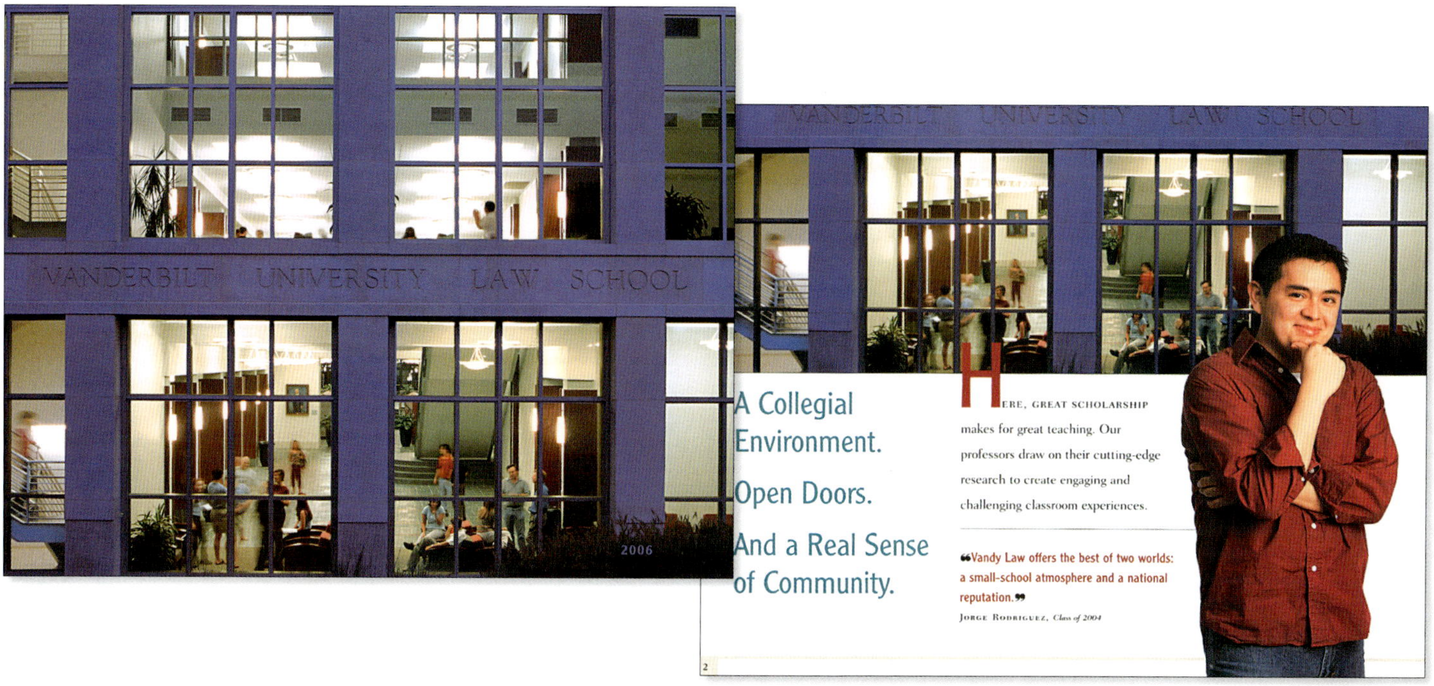

VANDERBILT UNIVERSITY LAW SCHOOL

2006

A Collegial Environment.

Open Doors.

And a Real Sense of Community.

Here, great scholarship makes for great teaching. Our professors draw on their cutting-edge research to create engaging and challenging classroom experiences.

"Vandy Law offers the best of two worlds: a small-school atmosphere and a national reputation."

Jorge Rodriguez, *Class of 2004*

2

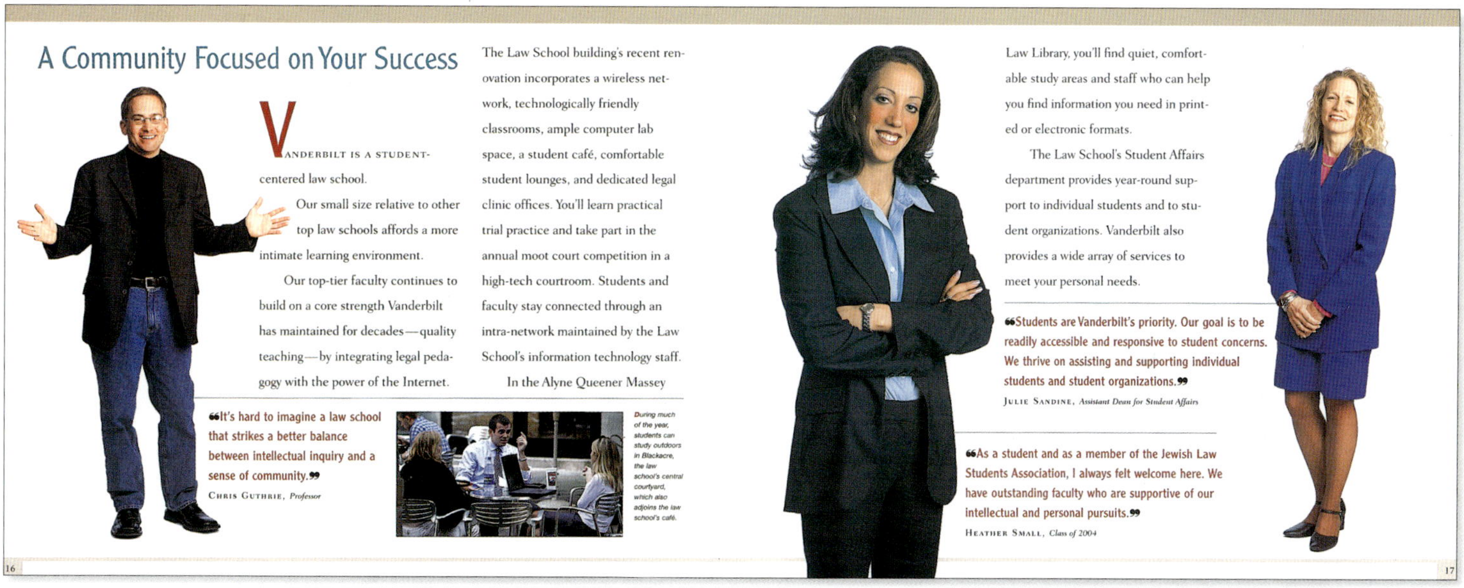

A Community Focused on Your Success

Vanderbilt is a student-centered law school.

Our small size relative to other top law schools affords a more intimate learning environment.

Our top-tier faculty continues to build on a core strength Vanderbilt has maintained for decades—quality teaching—by integrating legal pedagogy with the power of the Internet.

The Law School building's recent renovation incorporates a wireless network, technologically friendly classrooms, ample computer lab space, a student café, comfortable student lounges, and dedicated legal clinic offices. You'll learn practical trial practice and take part in the annual moot court competition in a high-tech courtroom. Students and faculty stay connected through an intra-network maintained by the Law School's information technology staff.

In the Alyne Queener Massey Law Library, you'll find quiet, comfortable study areas and staff who can help you find information you need in printed or electronic formats.

The Law School's Student Affairs department provides year-round support to individual students and to student organizations. Vanderbilt also provides a wide array of services to meet your personal needs.

"It's hard to imagine a law school that strikes a better balance between intellectual inquiry and a sense of community."

Chris Guthrie, *Professor*

During much of the year, students can study outdoors in Blackacre, the law school's central courtyard, which also adjoins the law school's café.

"Students are Vanderbilt's priority. Our goal is to be readily accessible and responsive to student concerns. We thrive on assisting and supporting individual students and student organizations."

Julie Sandine, *Assistant Dean for Student Affairs*

"As a student and as a member of the Jewish Law Students Association, I always felt welcome here. We have outstanding faculty who are supportive of our intellectual and personal pursuits."

Heather Small, *Class of 2004*

16 17

client
Vanderbilt University Law School
design firm
Ventress Design Group
designer
Tom Ventress

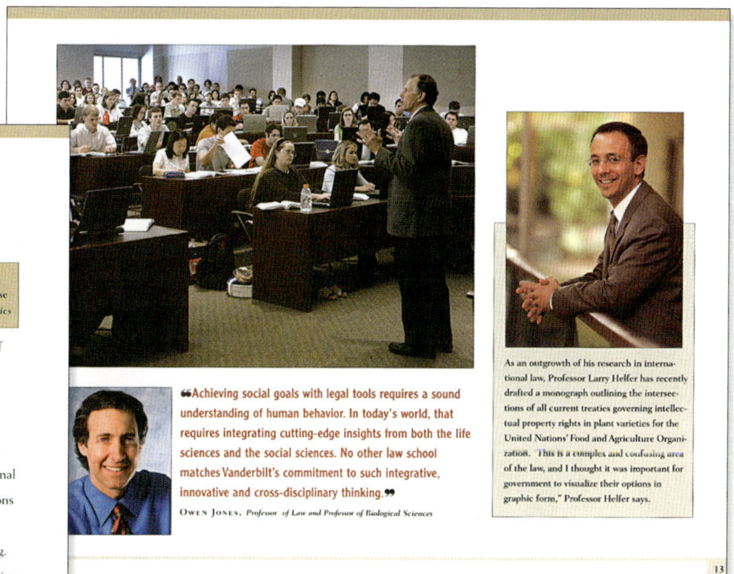

"Achieving social goals with legal tools requires a sound understanding of human behavior. In today's world, that requires integrating cutting-edge insights from both the life sciences and the social sciences. No other law school matches Vanderbilt's commitment to such integrative, innovative and cross-disciplinary thinking."

Owen Jones, *Professor of Law and Professor of Biological Sciences*

As an outgrowth of his research in international law, Professor Larry Helfer has recently drafted a monograph outlining the intersections of all current treaties governing intellectual property rights in plant varieties for the United Nations' Food and Agriculture Organization. "This is a complex and confusing area of the law, and I thought it was important for government to visualize their options in graphic form," Professor Helfer says.

13

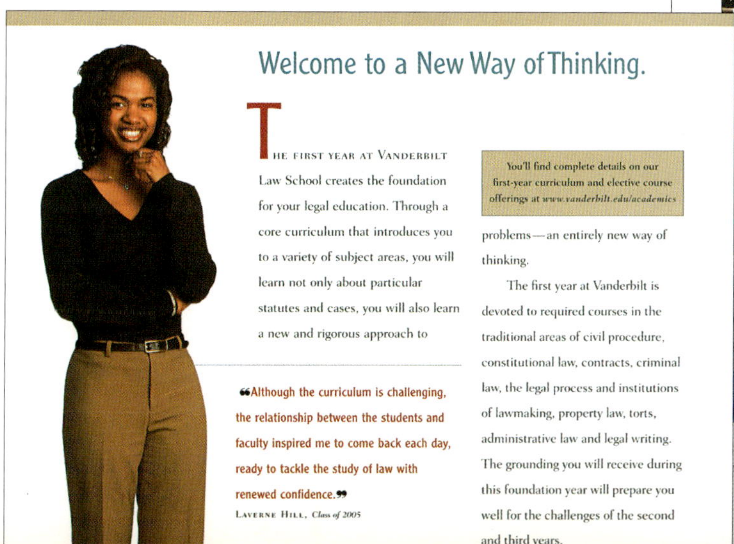

Welcome to a New Way of Thinking.

The first year at Vanderbilt Law School creates the foundation for your legal education. Through a core curriculum that introduces you to a variety of subject areas, you will learn not only about particular statutes and cases, you will also learn a new and rigorous approach to problems—an entirely new way of thinking.

You'll find complete details on our first-year curriculum and elective course offerings at *www.vanderbilt.edu/academics*

The first year at Vanderbilt is devoted to required courses in the traditional areas of civil procedure, constitutional law, contracts, criminal law, the legal process and institutions of lawmaking, property law, torts, administrative law and legal writing. The grounding you will receive during this foundation year will prepare you well for the challenges of the second and third years.

"Although the curriculum is challenging, the relationship between the students and faculty inspired me to come back each day, ready to tackle the study of law with renewed confidence."

Laverne Hill, *Class of 2005*

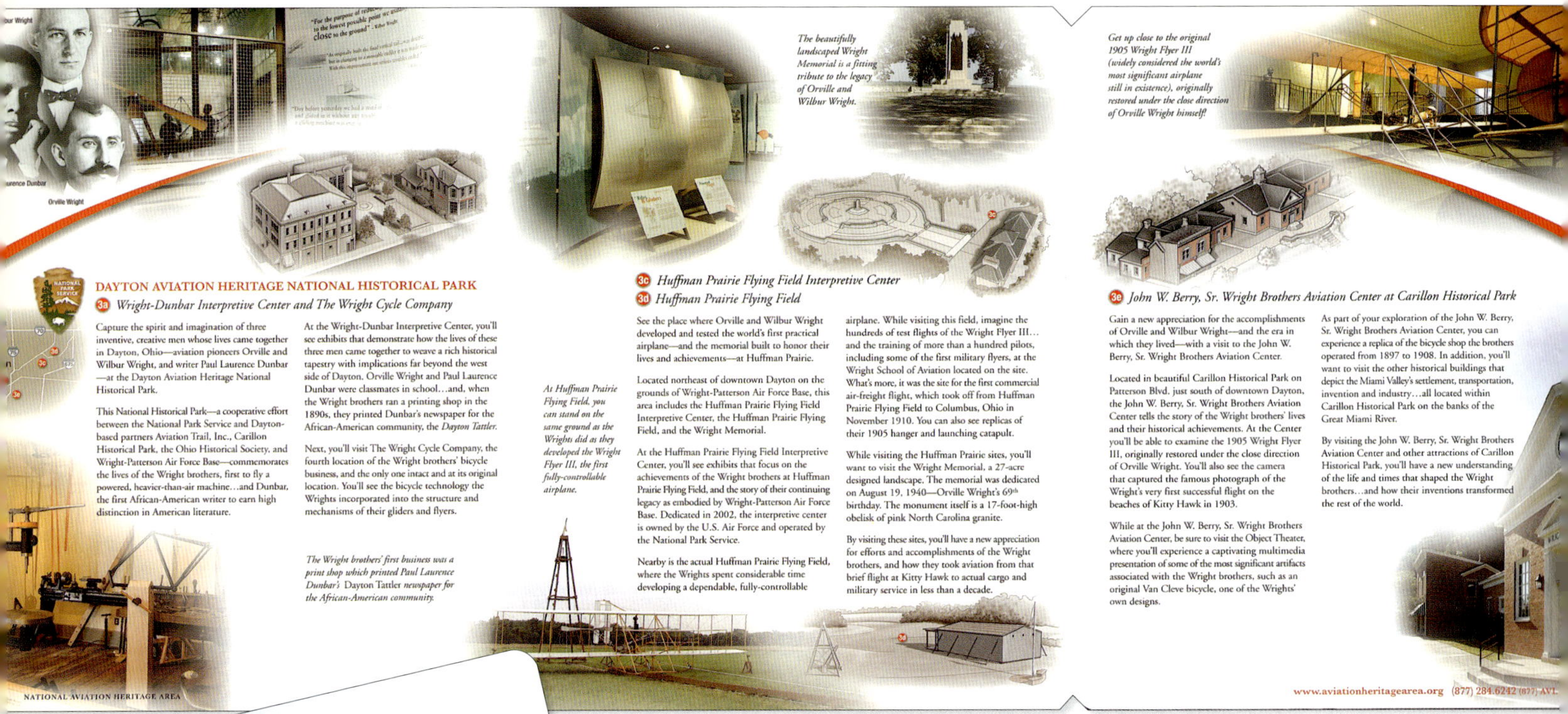

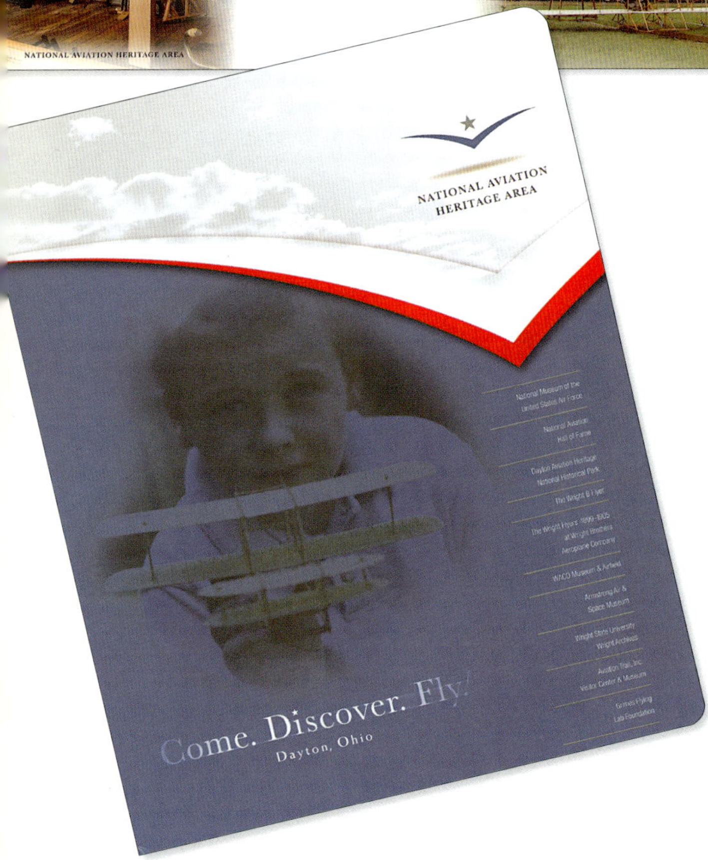

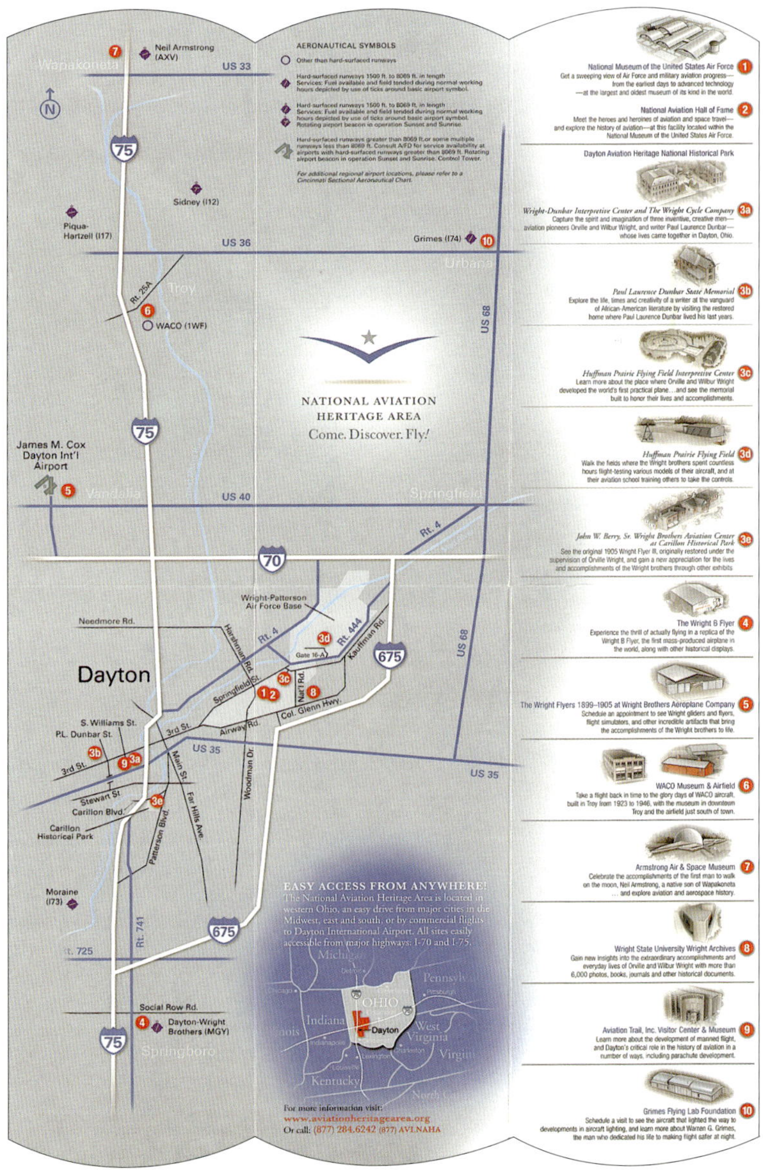

client
Aviation Heritage Foundation
design firm
VMA, Inc.
project manager
Kenneth Botts
account manager
Steve Goubeaux
creative director
Doug Knopp
production designer
Patrick Londergan
photographer
Dan Patterson

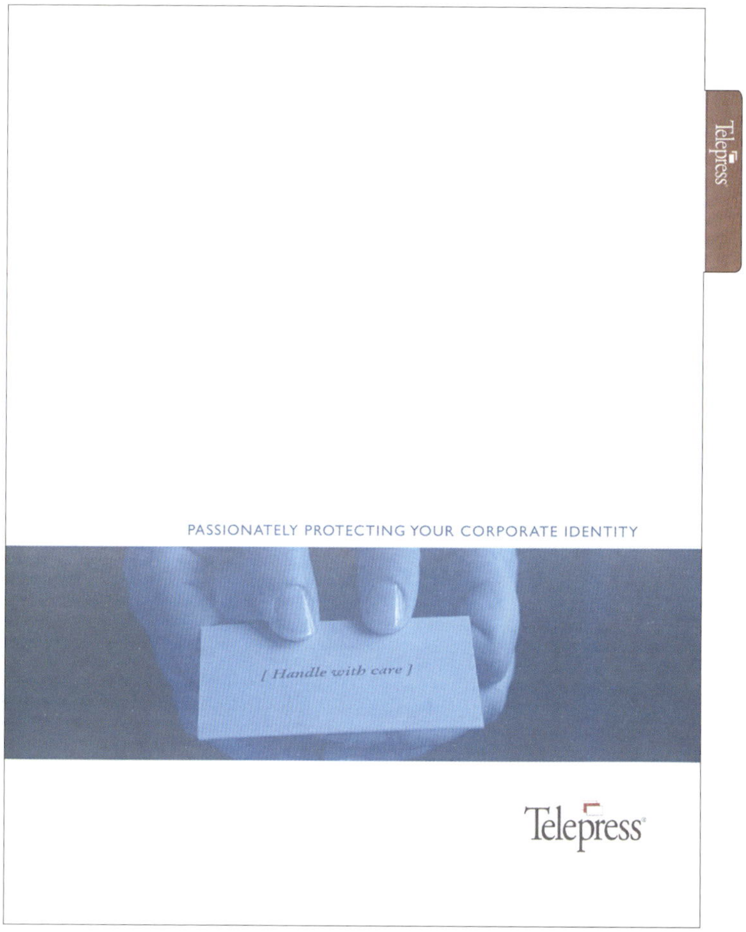

client
Telepress
design firm
Eben Design
designer
Dan Meehan

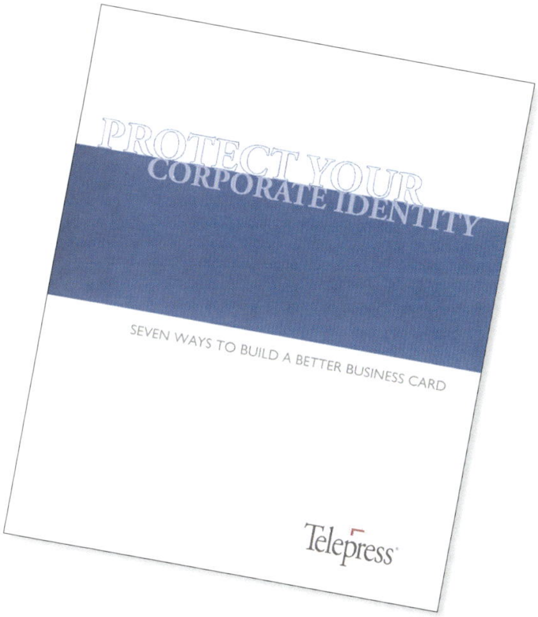

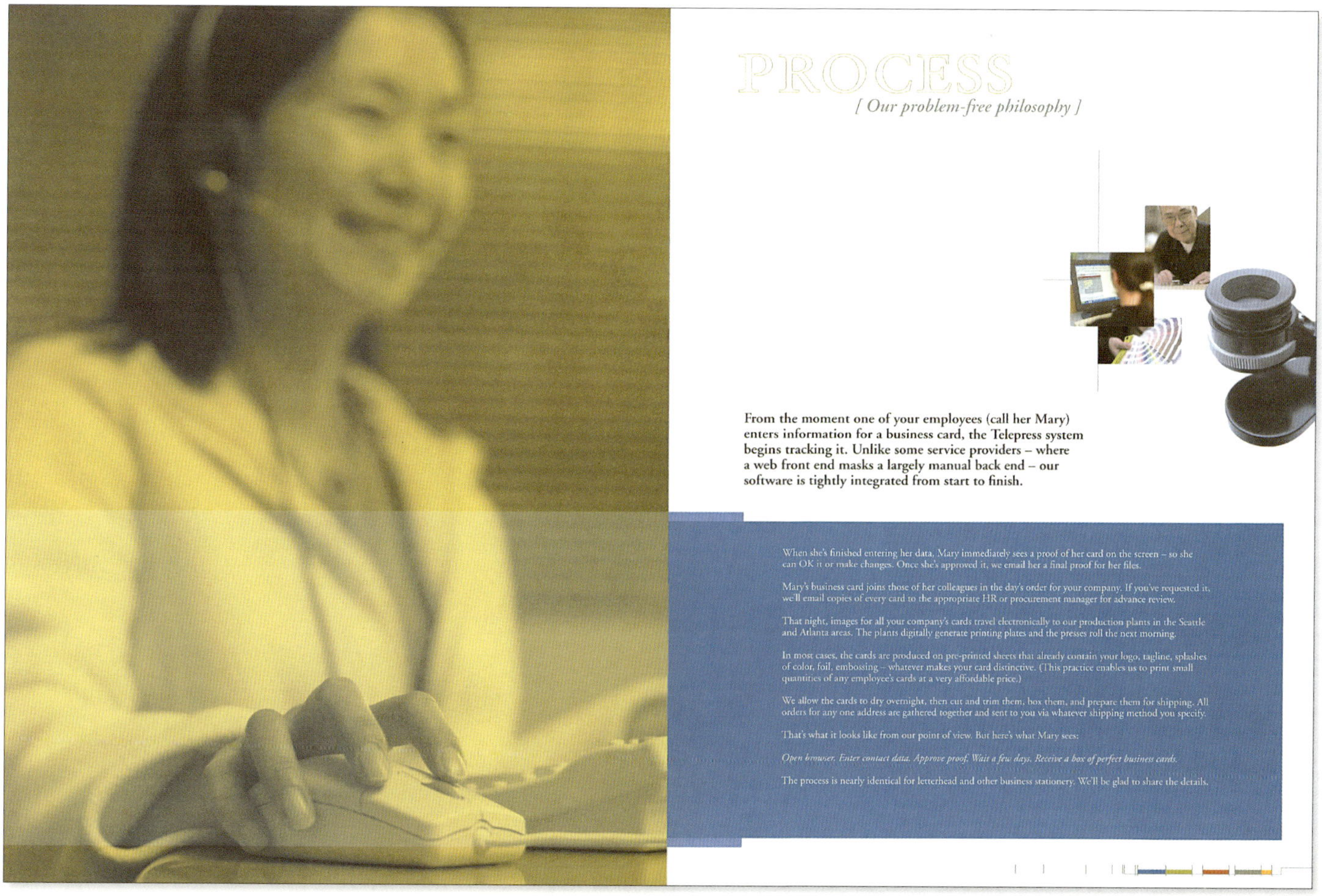

client
Kolter Communities
design firm
Gouthier Design

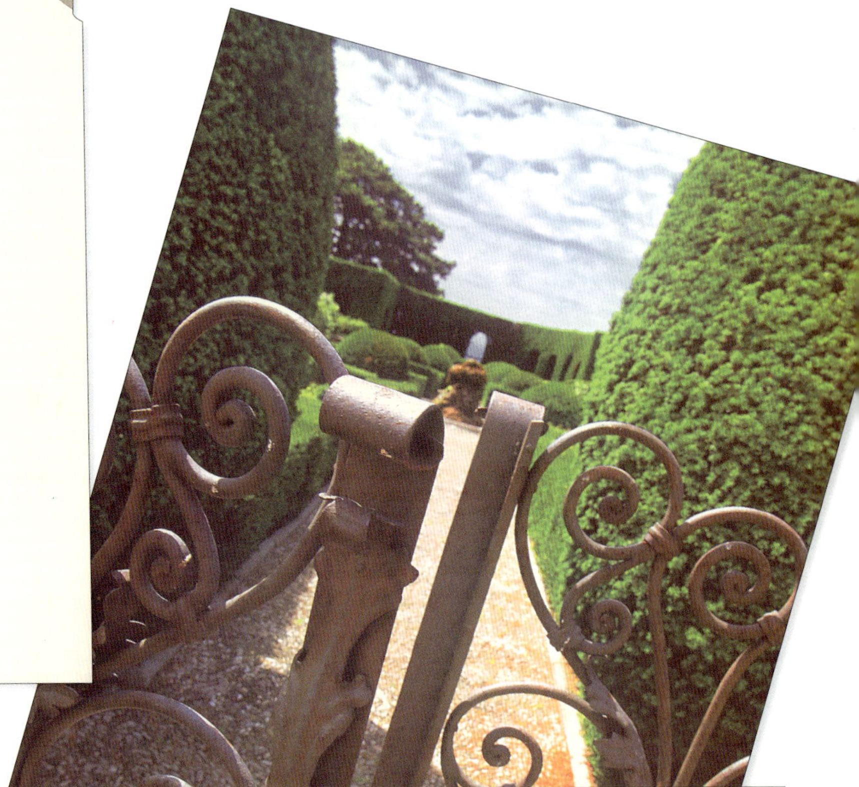

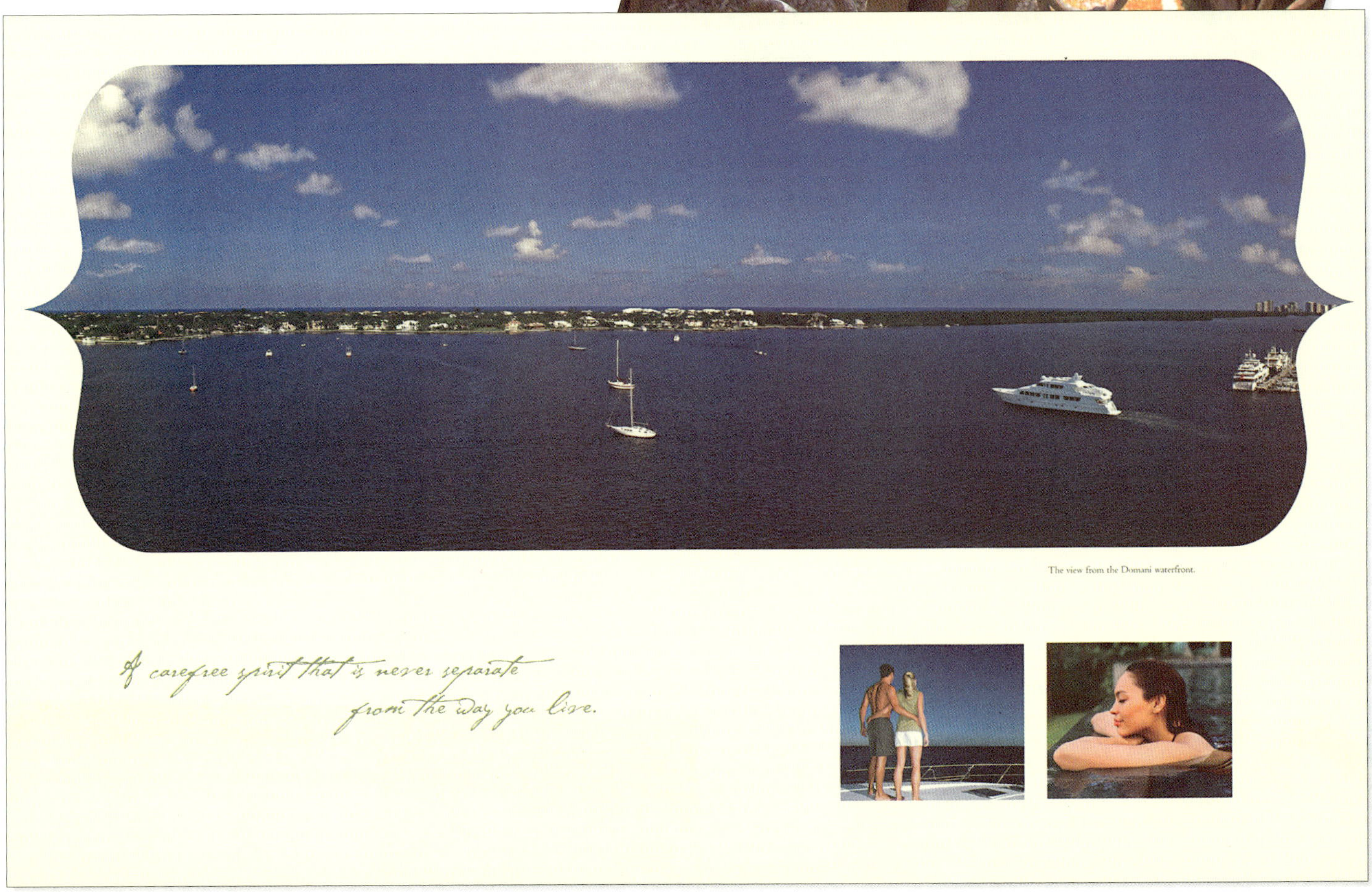

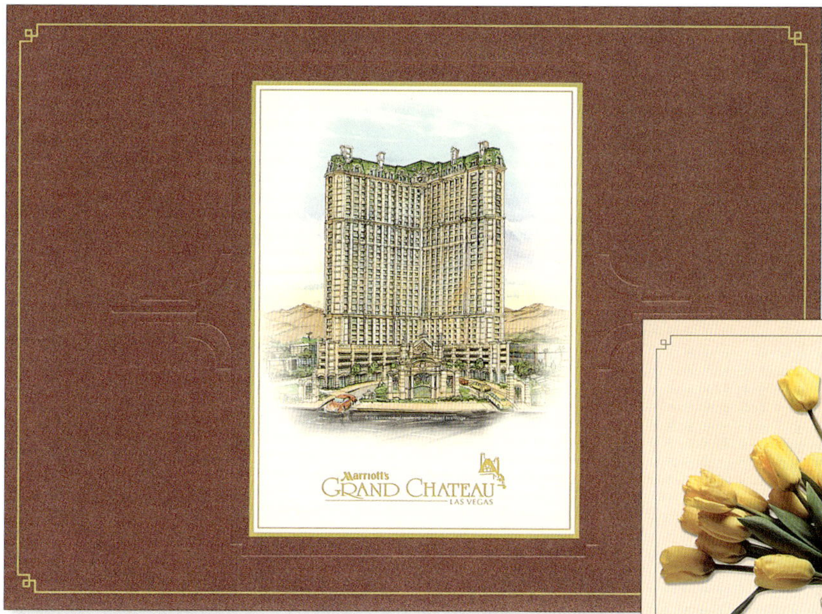

client
Marriott International, Inc.
design firm
CDI Studios
creative director
Victoria Hart
designer
Brian Felgar

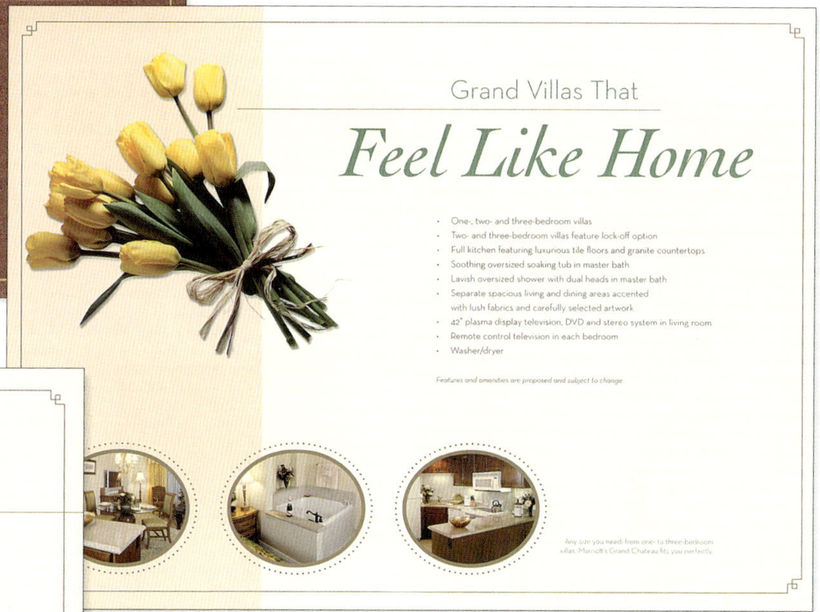

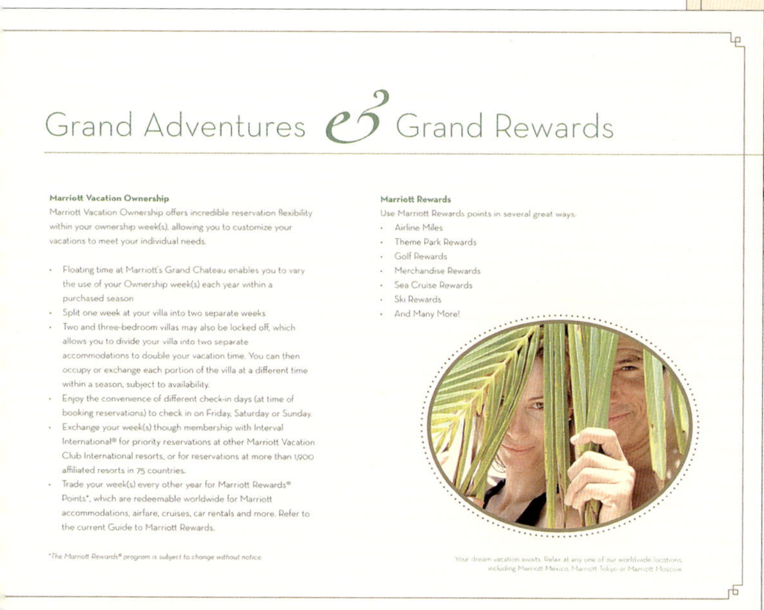

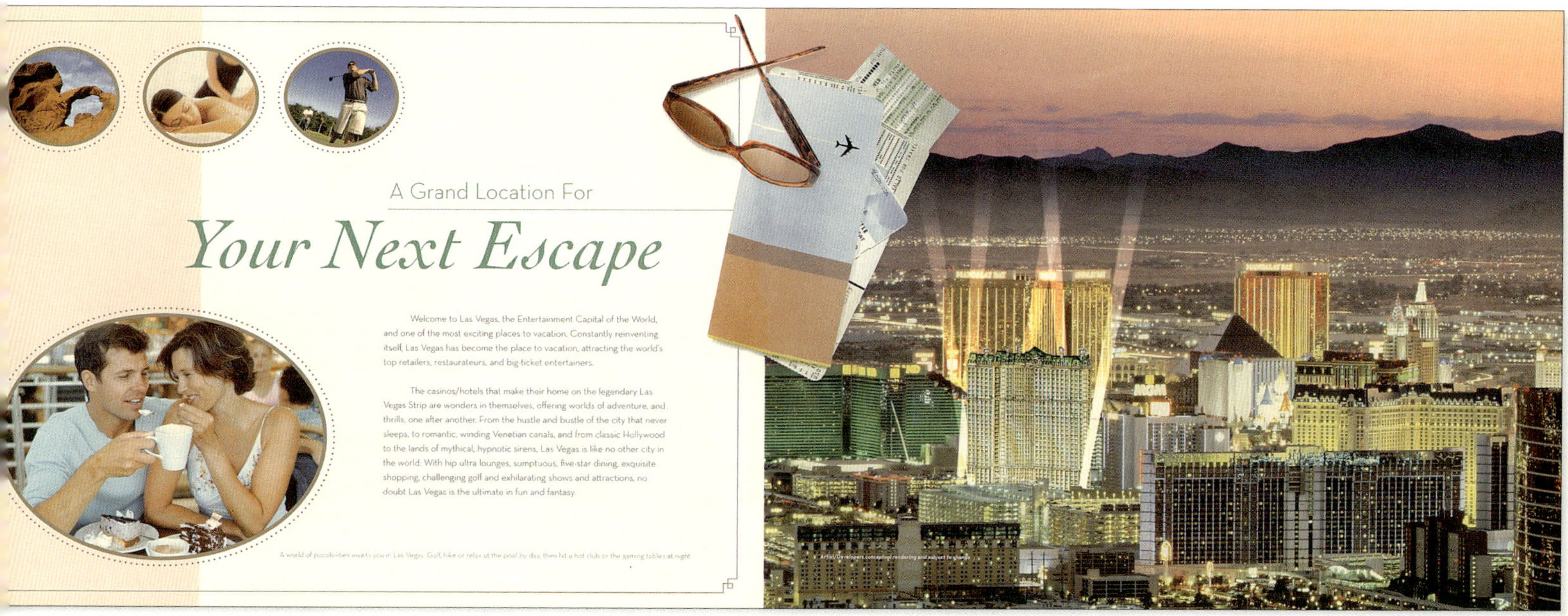

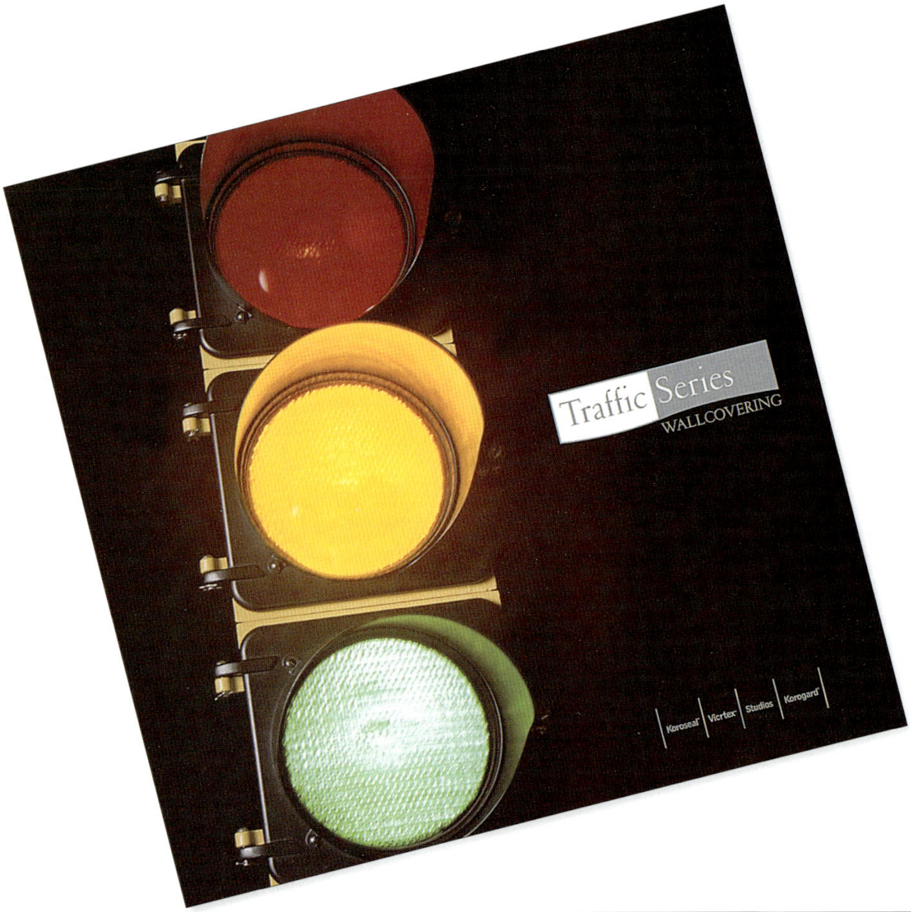

client
Koroseal Wall Protection Systems
design firm
Sire Advertising
designer
Shawn Felty

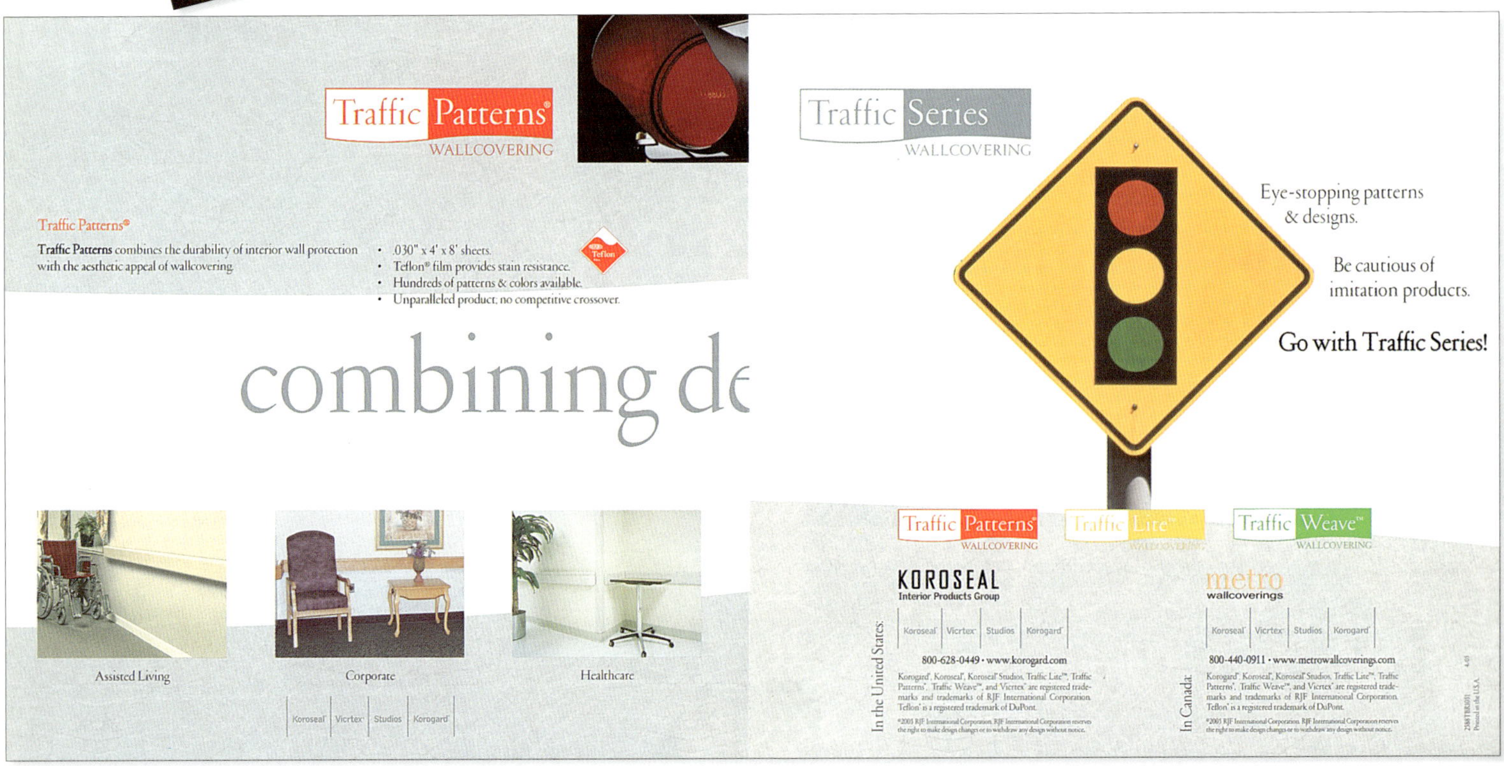

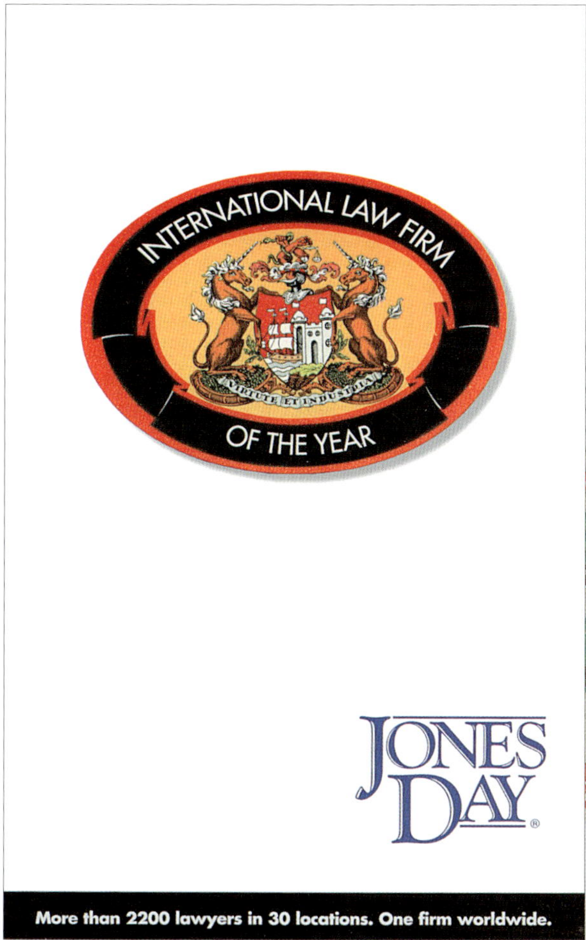

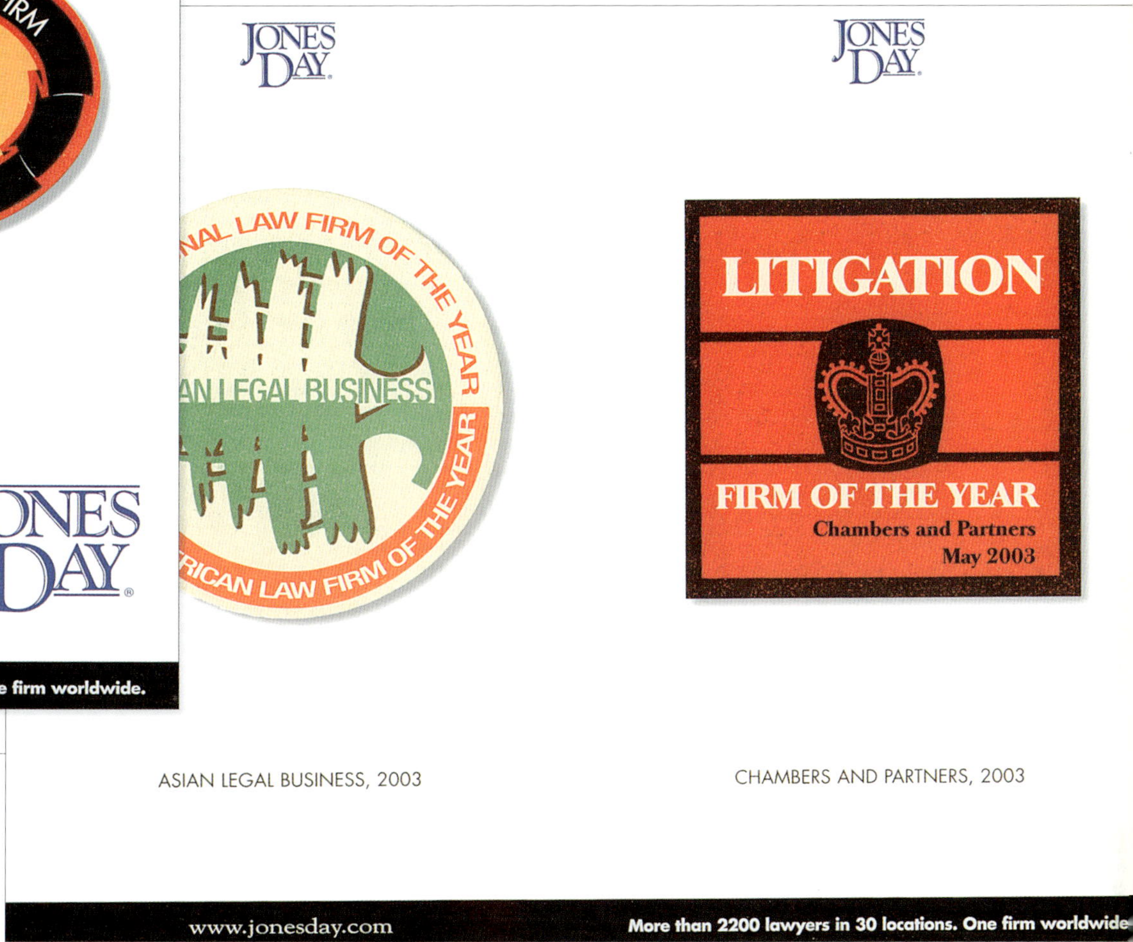

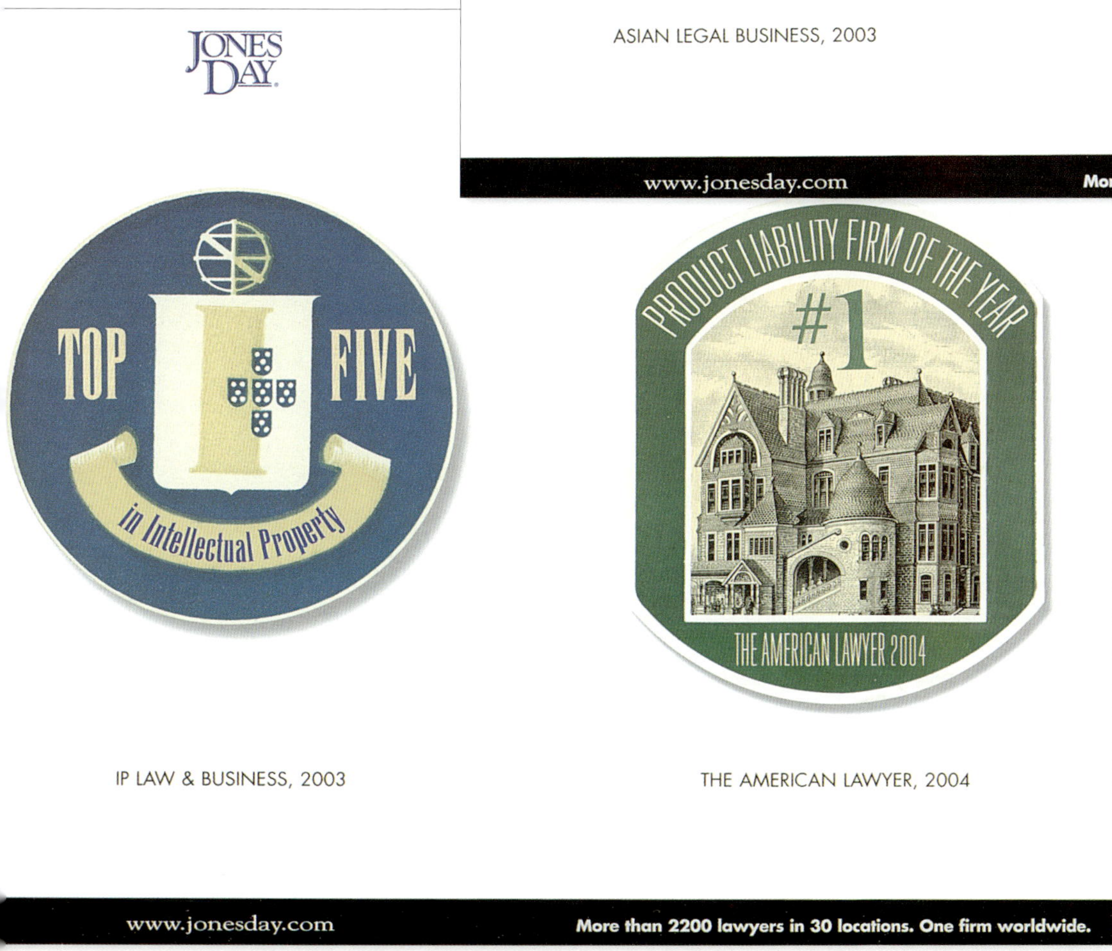

client
Jones Day
design firm
Greenfield/Belser Ltd.
designers
Burkey Belser,
Jonathan Bruns

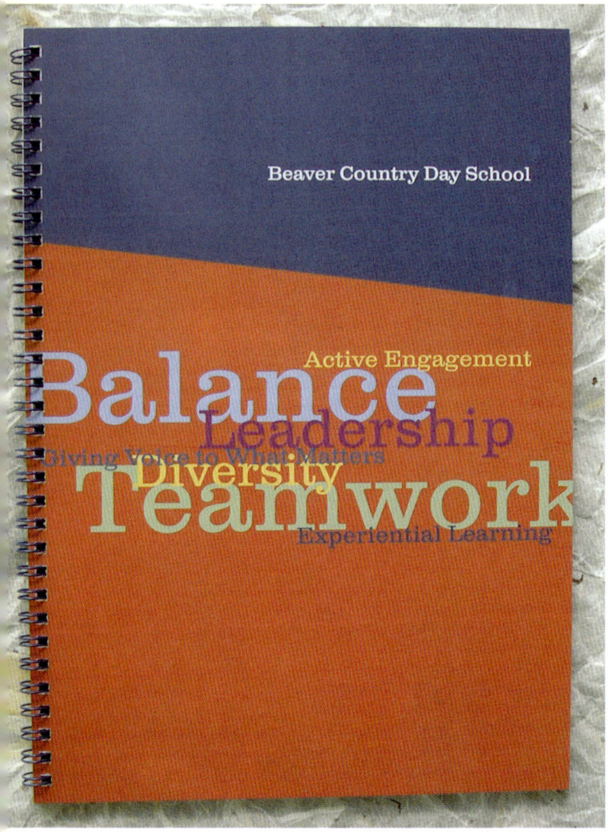

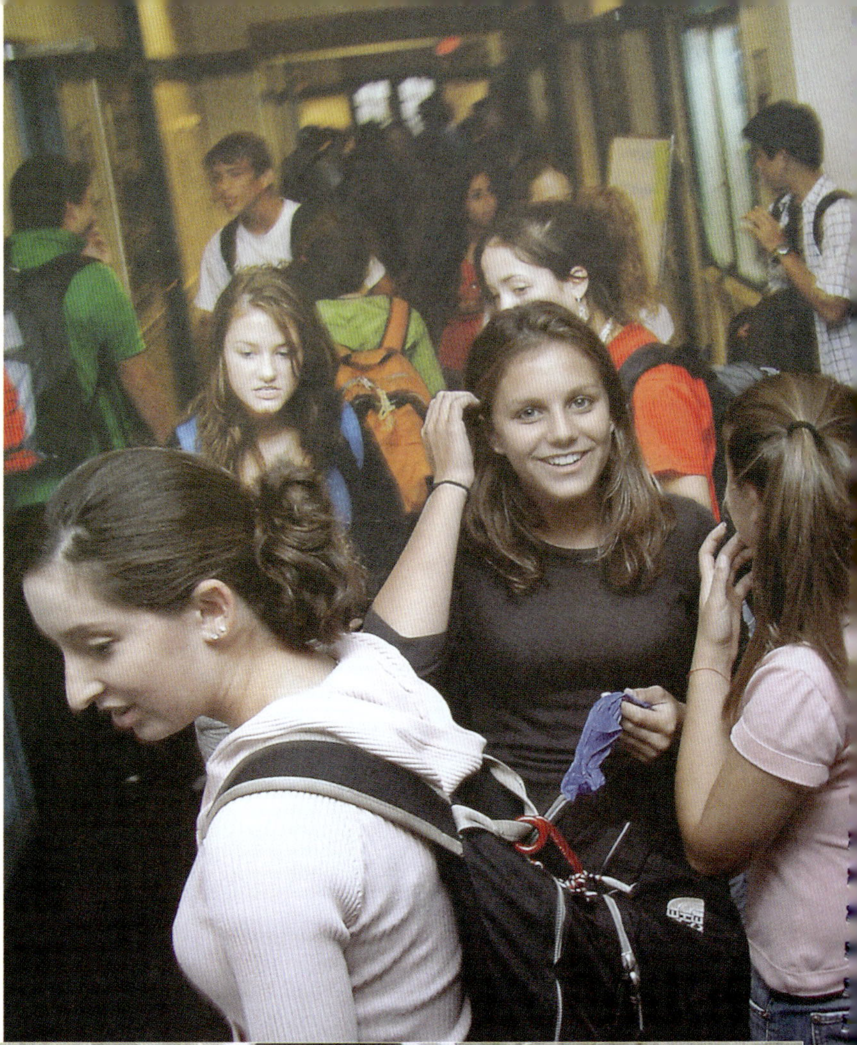

client
Beaver Country Day School
design firm
kor group
designer
Jim Gibson

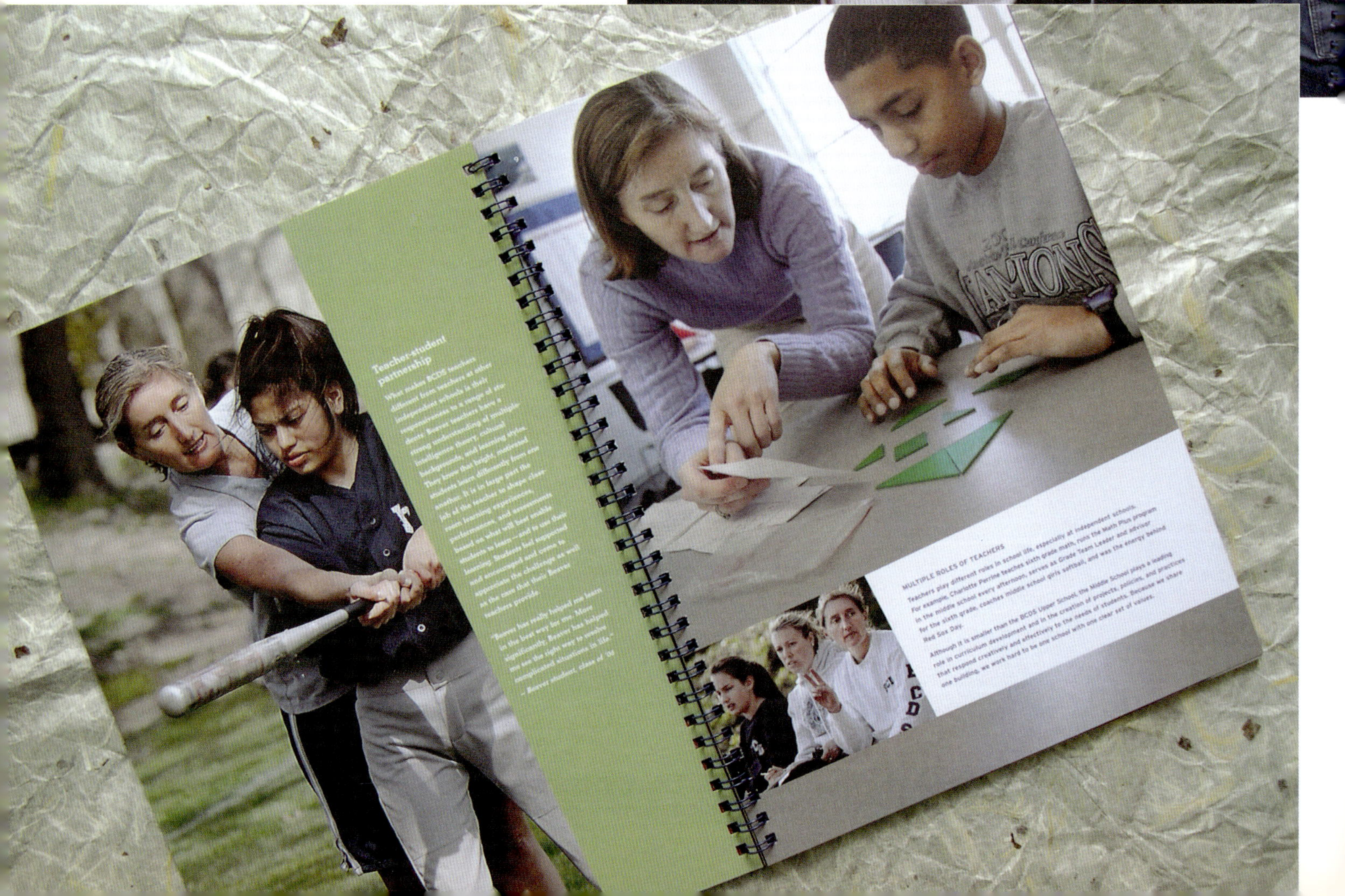

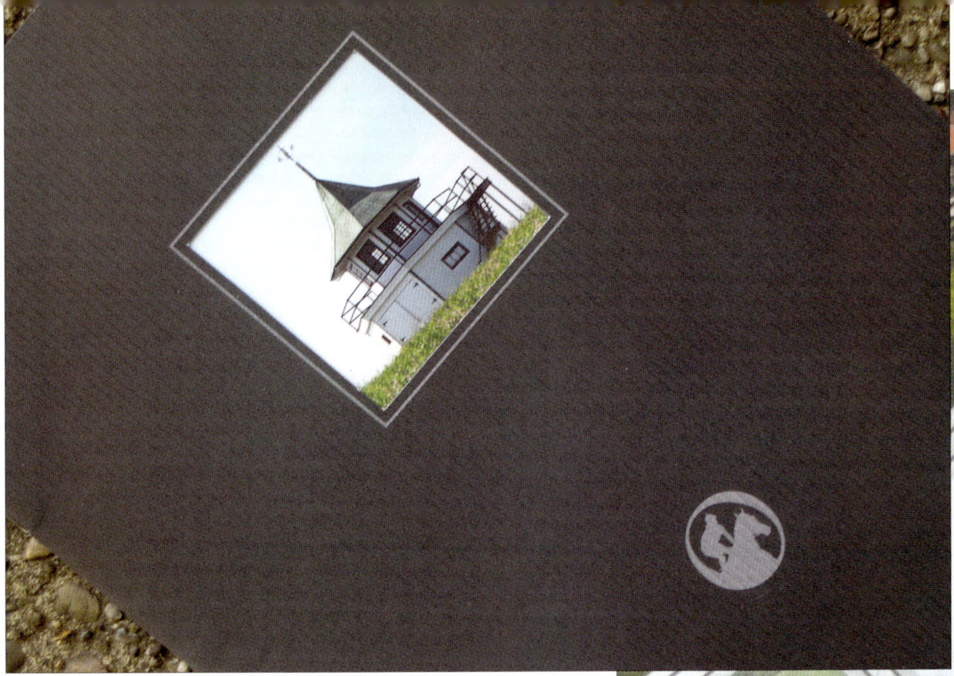

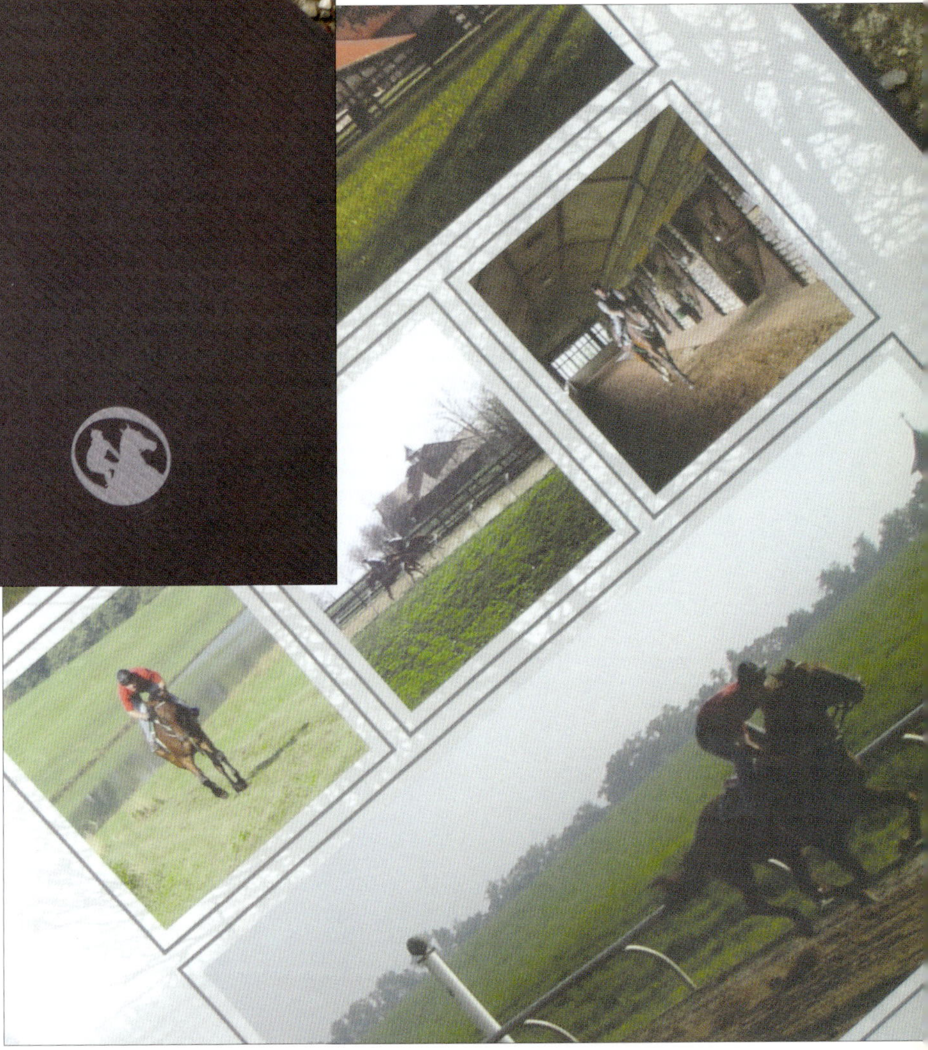

client
Stony Oak Farms
design firm
Annagram Studio and Design
art director, designer
Graham Allen

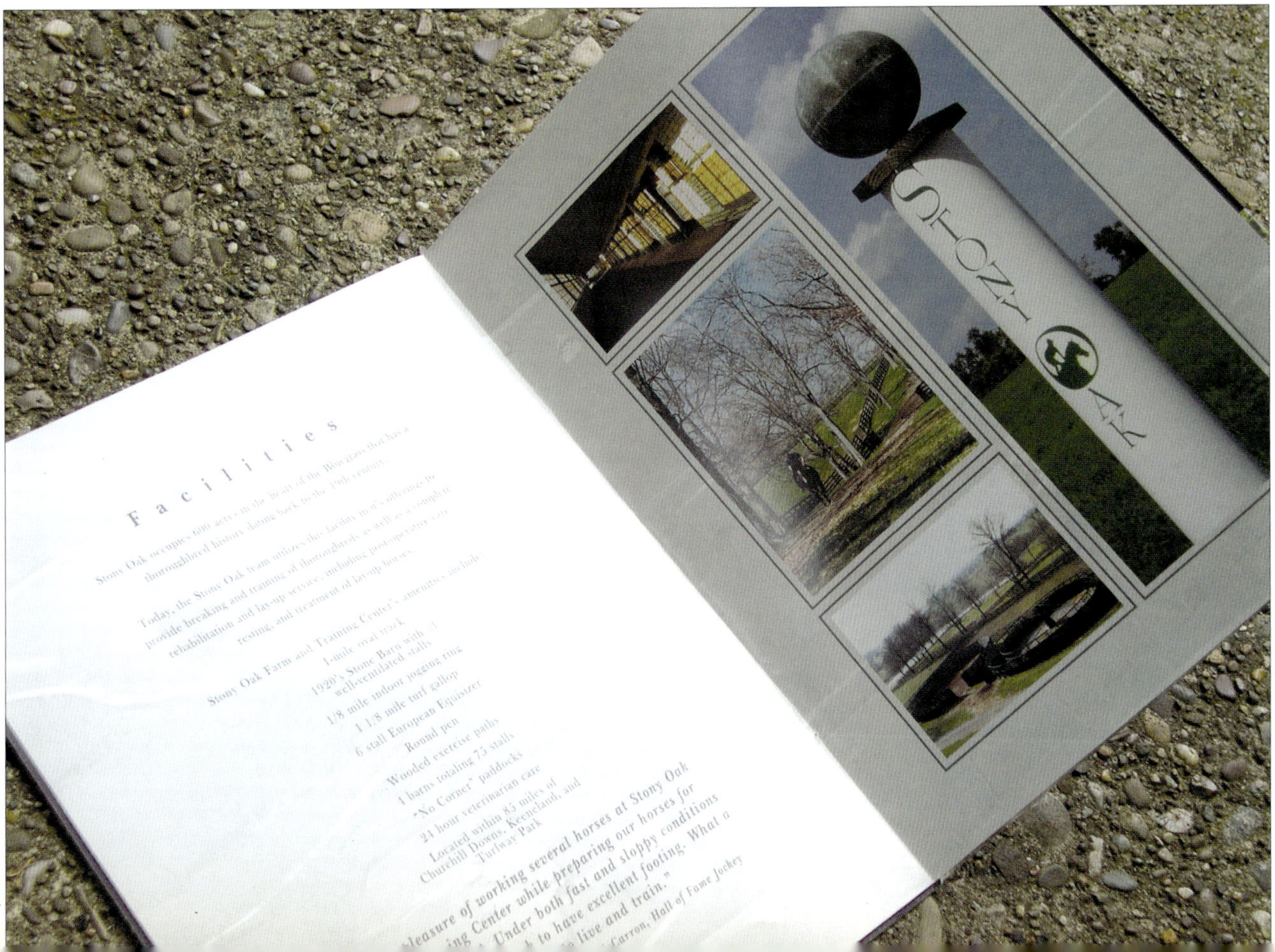

client
National Equity Fund
design firm
Namaro, Inc.
designers
Nadine Robbins,
Molly Ahearn

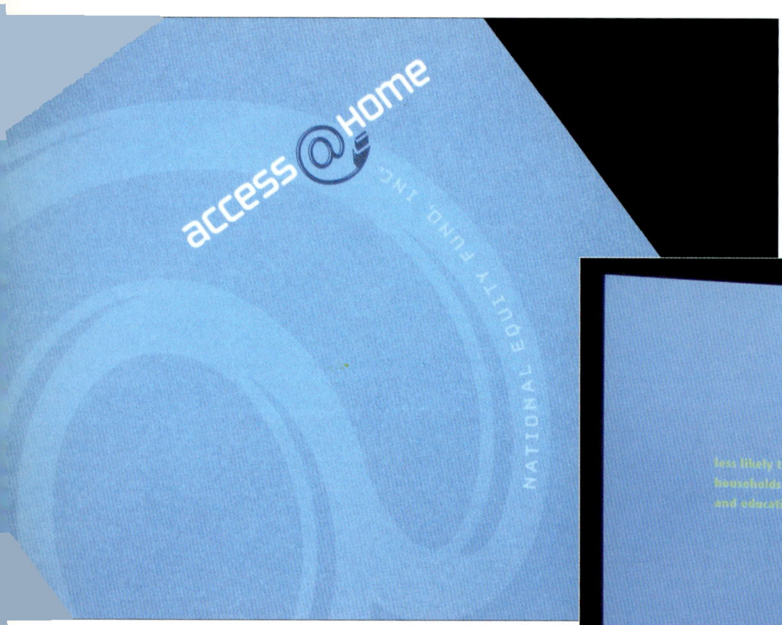

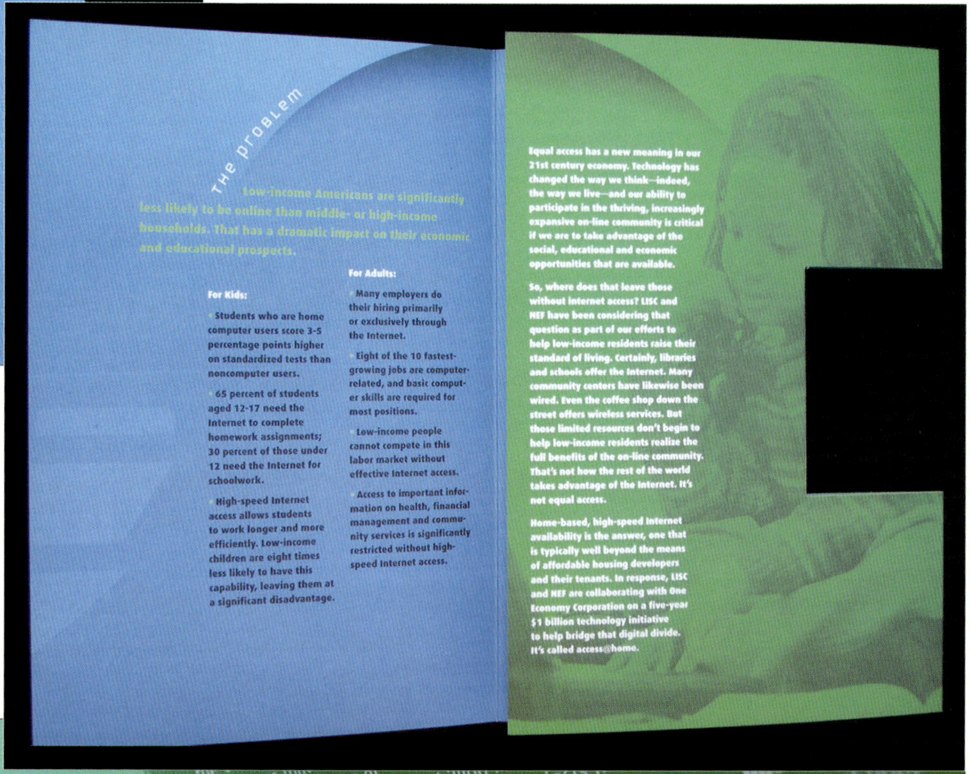

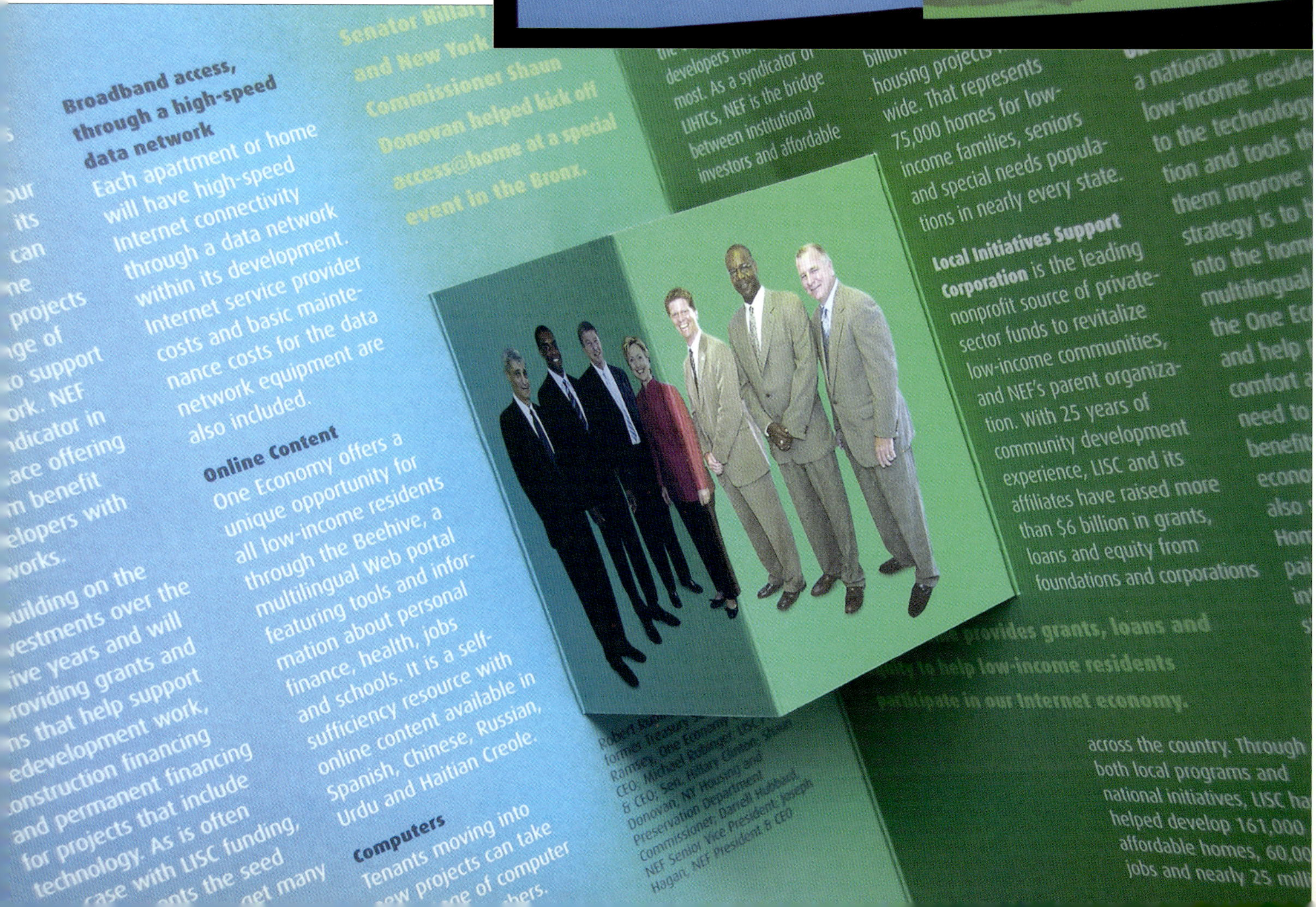

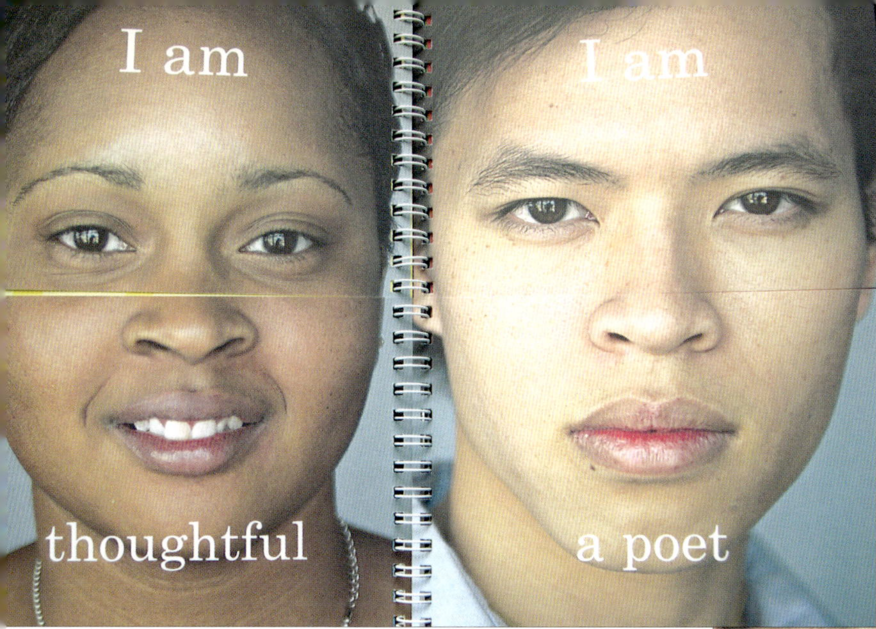

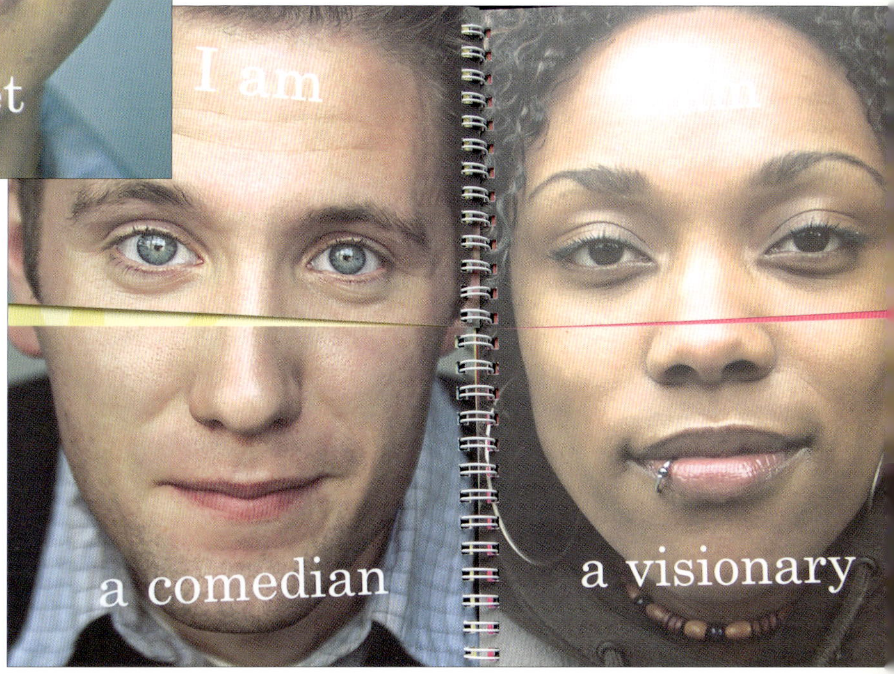

client
Emerson College
design firm
kor group
designer
James Grady
copywriter
Dorene Dzuiba

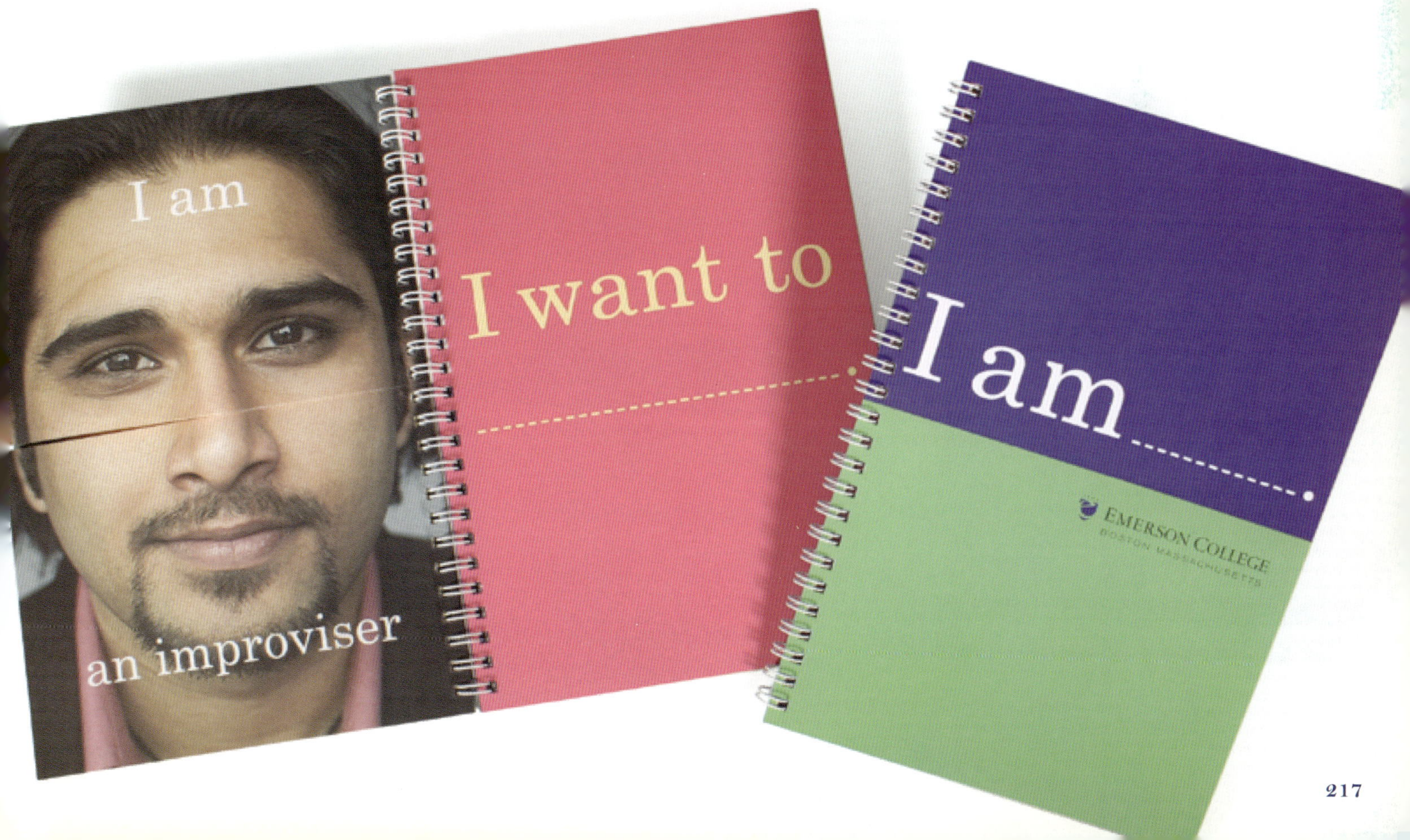

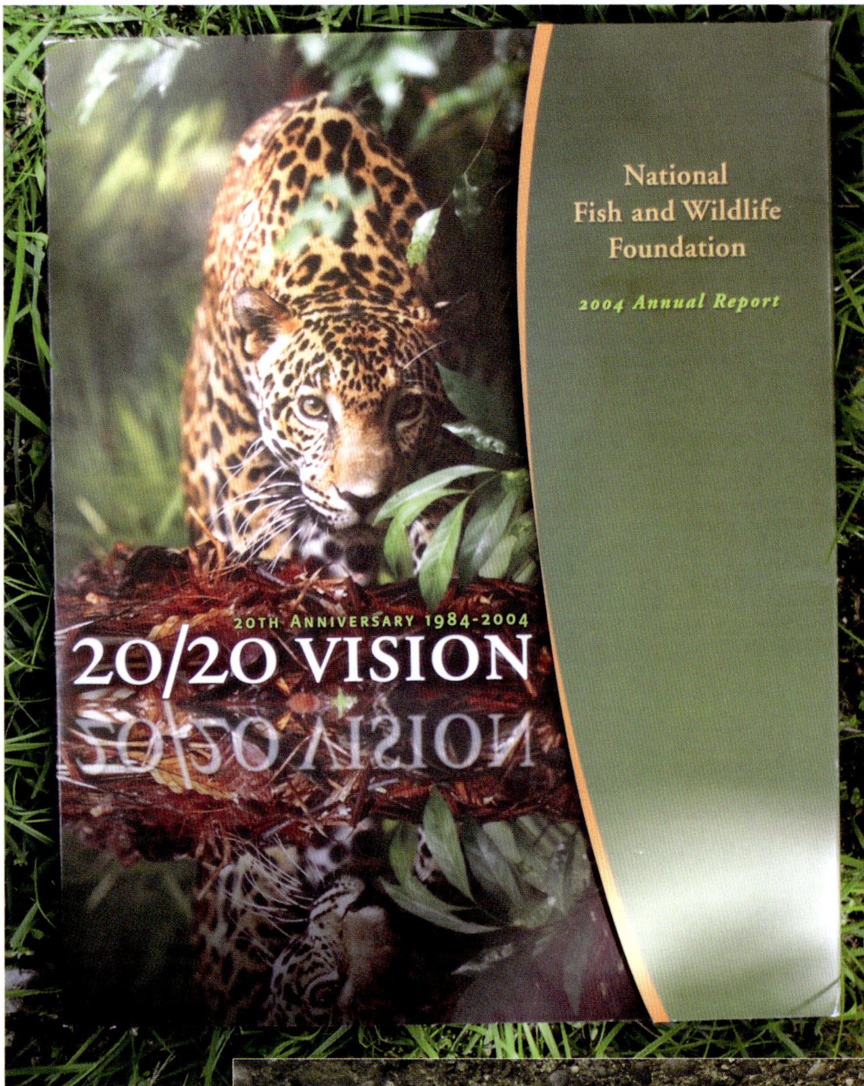

client
National Fish and Wildlife Foundation
design firm
Dever Designs
designers
Jeffrey Dever,
Kim Pollock

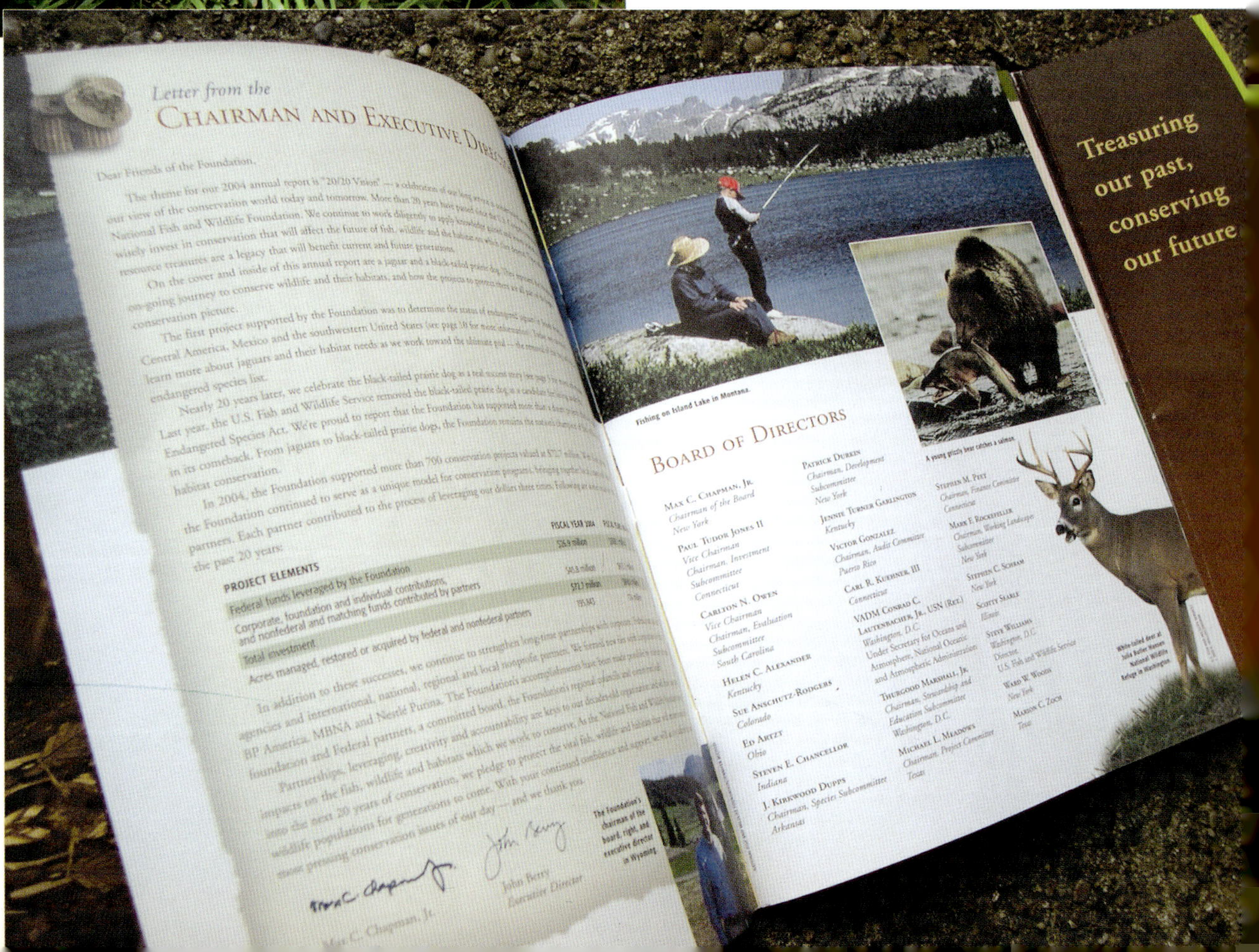

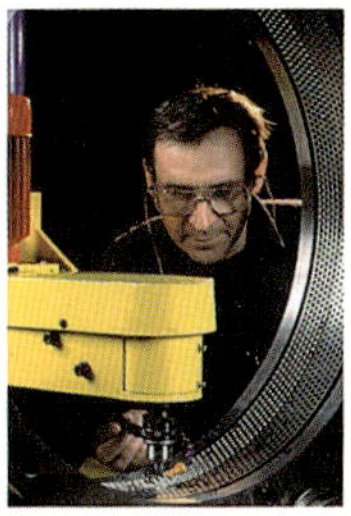

A WORK ETHIC TO ENVY

Pennsylvania workers are some of the most productive in the nation, and our region is especially known for its hard-working residents. We maintain and improve our workforce with customized job training programs and regional workforce assistance.

"We consider the work ethic of our region's residents to be a true competitive advantage."

-Denise B. Prince
Chief Operating Officer, Geisinger Ventures, Geisinger Health System

MAJOR INDUSTRY SECTORS IN CENTRAL PENNSYLVANIA

Diversified Manufacturing

- Plastics
- Metal Fabrication, Machinery & Equipment
- Food Processing
- Wood & Lumber Products

Logistics & Transportation

- Distribution & Warehousing
- Wholesale & Retail Trade

Services

- Educational
- Medical, Health Care & Social Services
- Information & Communication
- Building & Construction

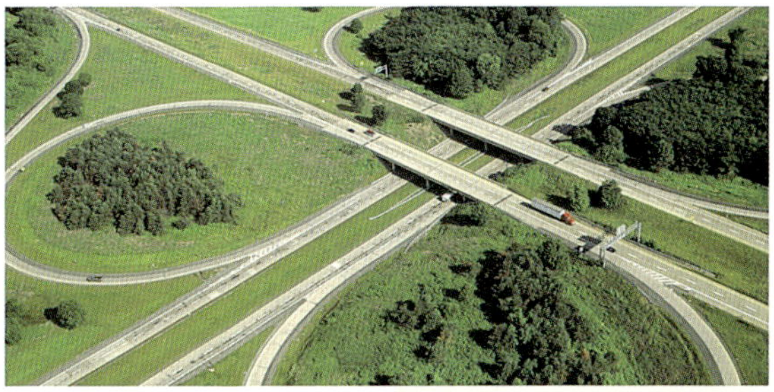

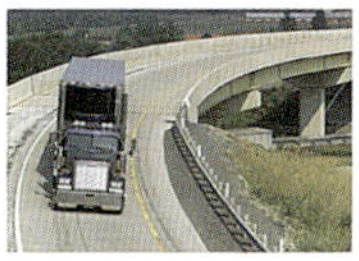

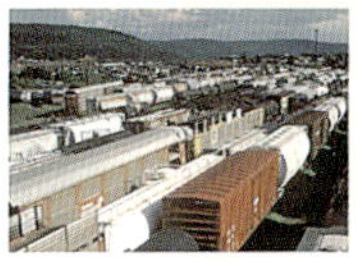

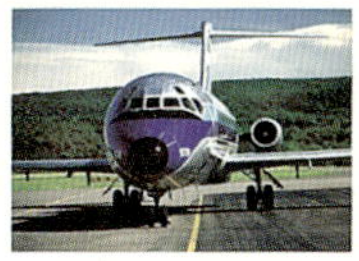

A CONVENIENT TRANSPORTATION INFRASTRUCTURE

With major highways like U.S. Interstate 80 crossing the region, major markets are never far from your new facility. In fact, companies in Central Pennsylvania have access to more than 40 percent of the U.S. and Canadian population and purchasing power.

Major Rail Providers

- Canadian Pacific Rail
- Norfolk Southern
- SEDA-Council of Governments Joint Rail Authority

Major Airports

- Harrisburg International Airport
- Wilkes-Barre/Scranton International Airport
- Williamsport Regional Airport
- University Park Airport, State College

Major Cities

DESTINATION	TIME	DISTANCE
Harrisburg	1:15	63
Baltimore	2:30	140
Philadelphia	2:30	165
New York City	2:45	175
Washington, D.C.	3:20	183
Pittsburgh	3:30	220
Richmond	5:00	287
Toronto	6:00	352
Boston	6:00	375
Detroit	6:45	450
Cincinnati	7:20	503
Chicago	9:15	627

(mapblast.com)

www.focuscentralpa.org 5

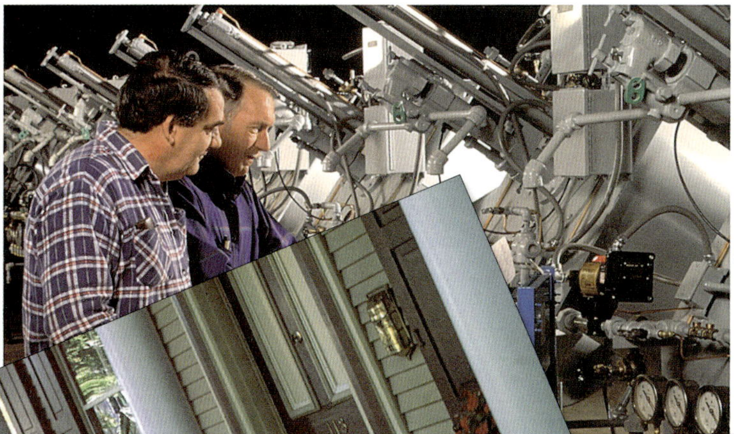

A RELAXED LIFESTYLE

There's a common trait among newcomers to Central Pennsylvania. It's that slight smile when driving past rich green landscapes, happy just to take it all in. And there are plenty of reasons to be happy; four beautiful seasons, relief from traffic congestion, and plenty of cultural and recreational activities.

HOUSING in Central Pennsylvania is affordable and full of variety. Our residents occupy everything from historic 19th century brick houses to quality new homes built by the region's skilled homebuilders. Many residents still don't hesitate to leave doors unlocked.

- Affordable and plentiful
- Low-crime neighborhoods
- Spacious countryside, convenient towns & cities
- A few hours to New York City, Philadelphia, Pittsburgh, Baltimore, Washington D.C.

HEALTHCARE in Central Pennsylvania is bolstered by well-rated hospitals like Evangelical Hospital, Geisinger Medical Center, and Susquehanna Health System.

- Well-rated hospitals
- Specialized healthcare institutions
- Healthy outdoor recreation
- Friendly personal care

CLIMATE can be an important factor in choosing a location. Central Pennsylvania residents enjoy four distinctly beautiful seasons, while remaining in a temperate zone just south of the harshest New England winters.

- Temperate zone
- Four distinct seasons

ENTERTAINMENT options in Central Pennsylvania can be as relaxing as a fishing trip, or as exciting as a roller coaster ride.

- Downtown shopping & dining
- Sporting events: Penn State University & more
- Admission-free amusement park: Knoebel's Grove
- Performing arts, museums, fairs, festivals
- Outdoor recreation: Susquehanna River, mountains
- Over 30 regional golf courses

www.focuscentralpa...

FOCUS

CENTRAL PENNSYLVANIA

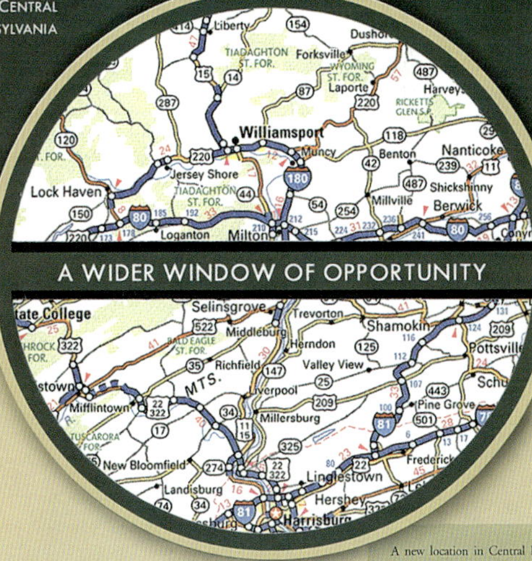

A WIDER WINDOW OF OPPORTUNITY

A new location in Central Pennsylvania means a wider window of opportunity, wide-open space for your facility, and a wide array of benefits for your business. Like highway infrastructure where ten miles is just ten minutes, loyal workers with outstanding work ethics, and quality low-crime living. It's all right here.

- State & Local Incentives
- Tax-FREE Keystone Opportunity Zones
- Capital Investment Programs
- Variety of Available Buildings
- Shovel-Ready Sites
- Easy Access to East Coast Regions
- FREE Confidential Assistance

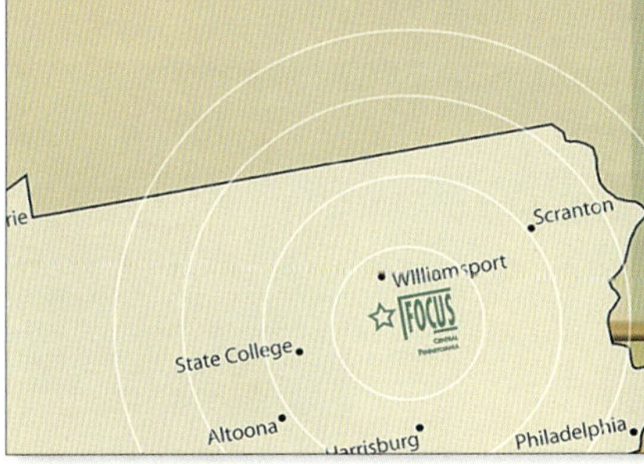

www.focuscentralpa.org

client
Focus Central Pennsylvania
design firm
Sire Advertising
designers
Shawn Felty,
Sumer Buttorff,
Jessica Varner

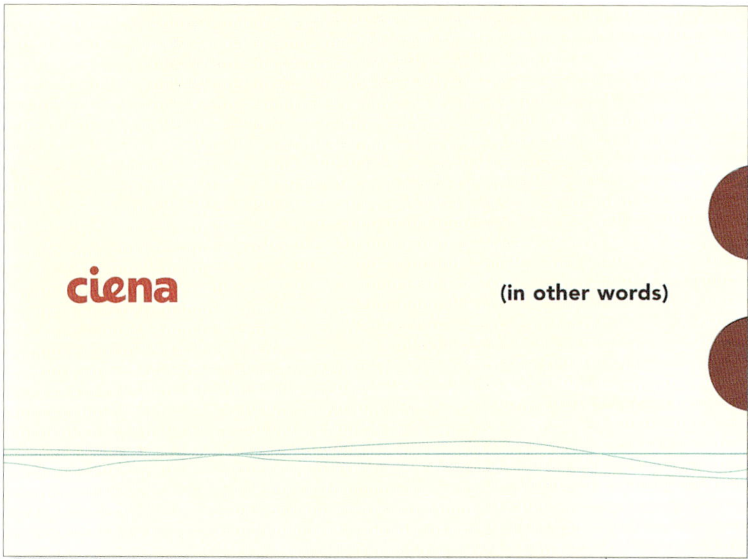

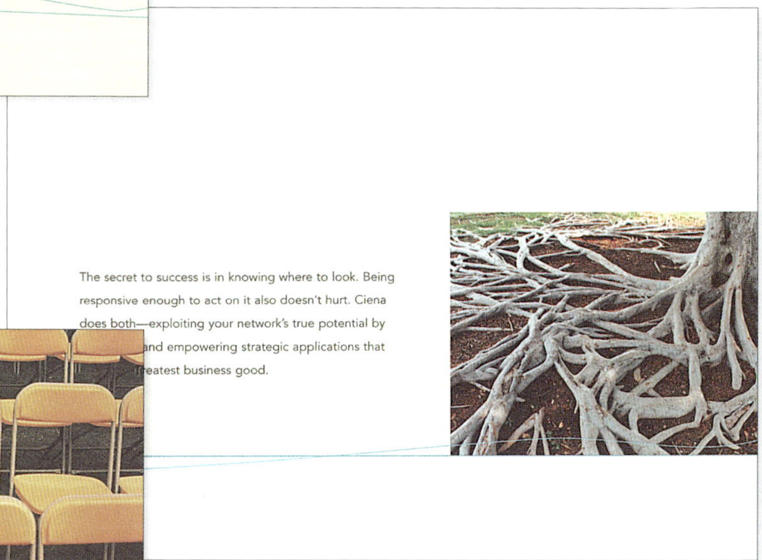

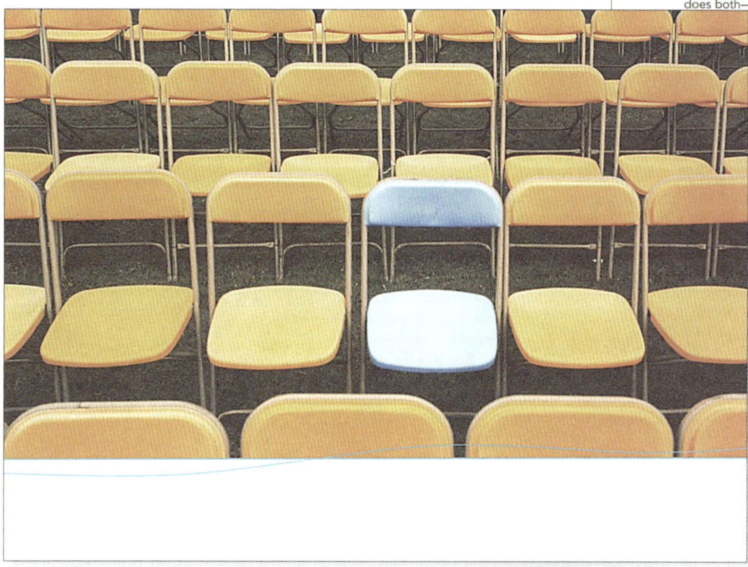

client
Ciena
design firm
Hornall Anderson Design Works
designers
Jack Anderson, Andy Davidhazy, Holly Craven, Sonja Max, Yuri Shvets, Andrew Wicklund, Kris Delaney

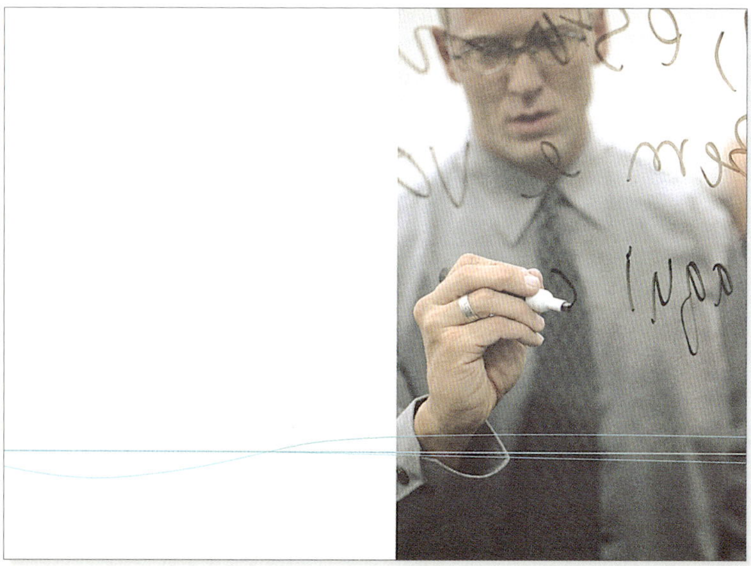

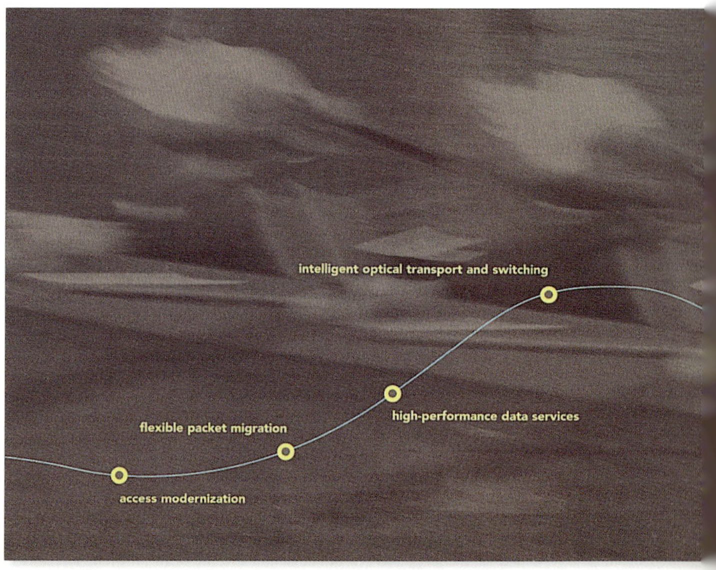

Trustworthy and Flexible

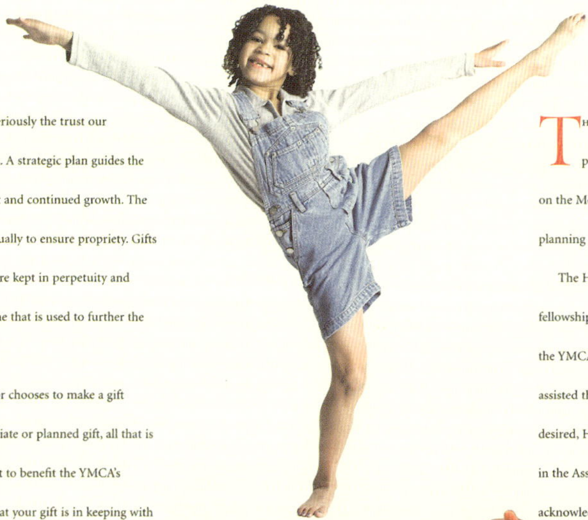

The YMCA takes seriously the trust our donors place in us. A strategic plan guides the Foundation's management and continued growth. The foundation is audited annually to ensure propriety. Gifts to the Endowment Fund are kept in perpetuity and invested to generate income that is used to further the work of the YMCA.

How a particular donor chooses to make a gift varies. Whether an immediate or planned gift, all that is necessary is a commitment to benefit the YMCA's Endowment. To be sure that your gift is in keeping with your estate and financial needs, the YMCA encourages donors to discuss contributions with their family legal and/or financial advisors.

Join the Heritage Circle

The Heritage Circle is a very special group of people who have chosen to have a lasting impact on the Montgomery YMCA by generously making or planning future gifts to the Foundation.

The Heritage Circle meets annually to enjoy the fellowship of new and old members, find inspiration in the YMCA's work, and to receive updates on programs assisted through the Endowment. Unless anonymity is desired, Heritage Circle members' names are published in the Association's annual report and are permanently acknowledged at a branch or association location.

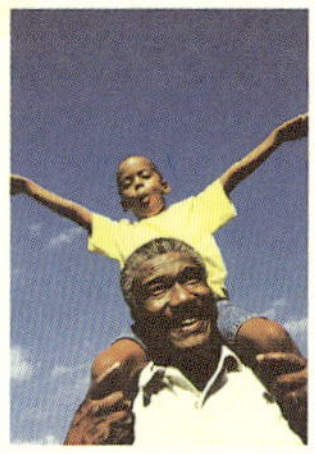

The YMCA strengthens lives, and with your help, the YMCA always will.

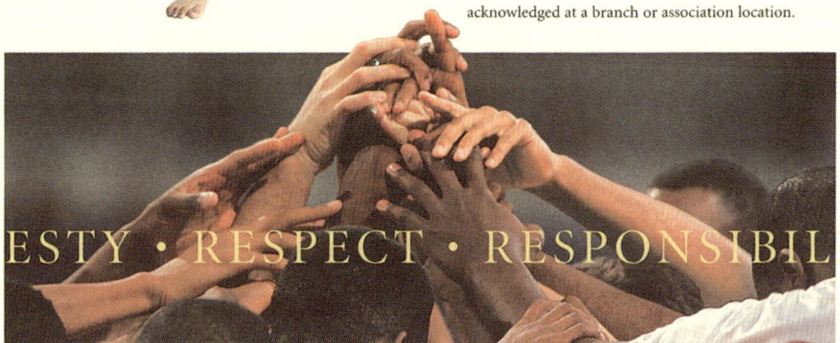

CARING • HONESTY • RESPECT • RESPONSIBILITY • FAITH

BUILD A BRIDGE FOR THE FUTURE

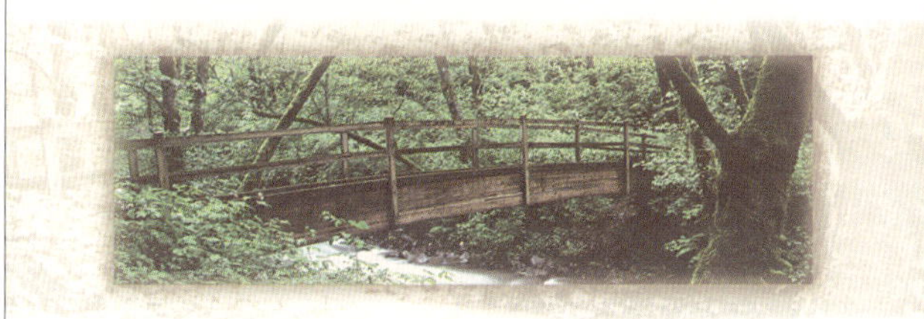

THE MONTGOMERY YMCA
WILLIAM C. CHANDLER
ENDOWMENT
FOUNDATION

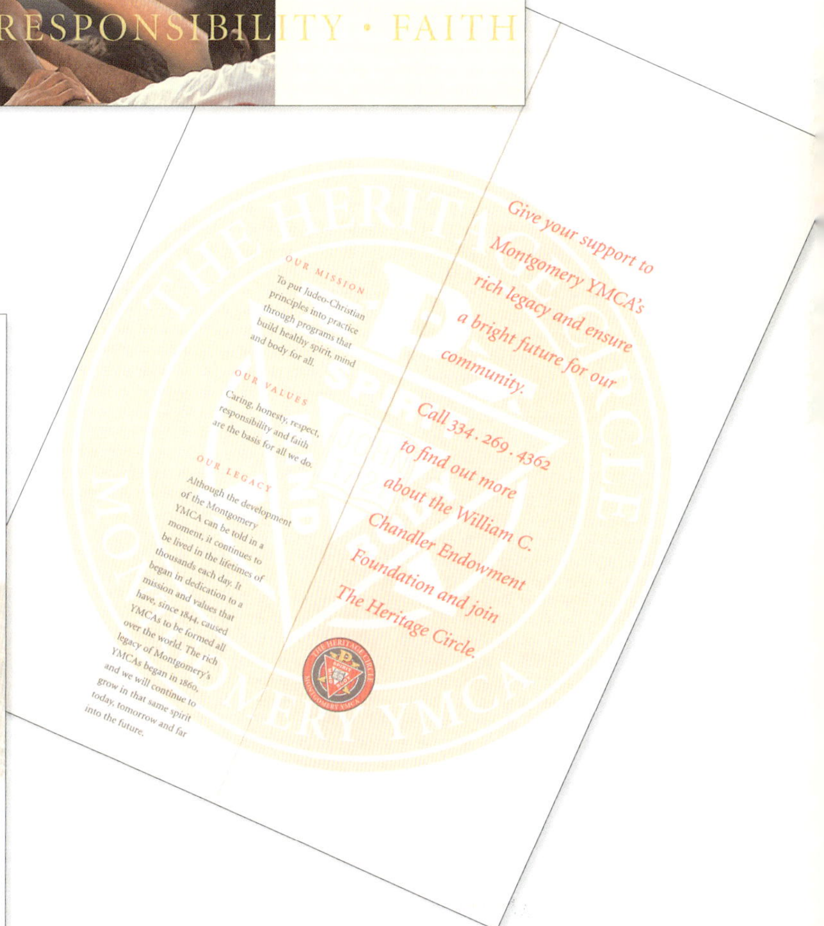

client
Montgomery YMCA
design firm
Ventress Design Group
designers
Tom Ventress,
Eric Ventress

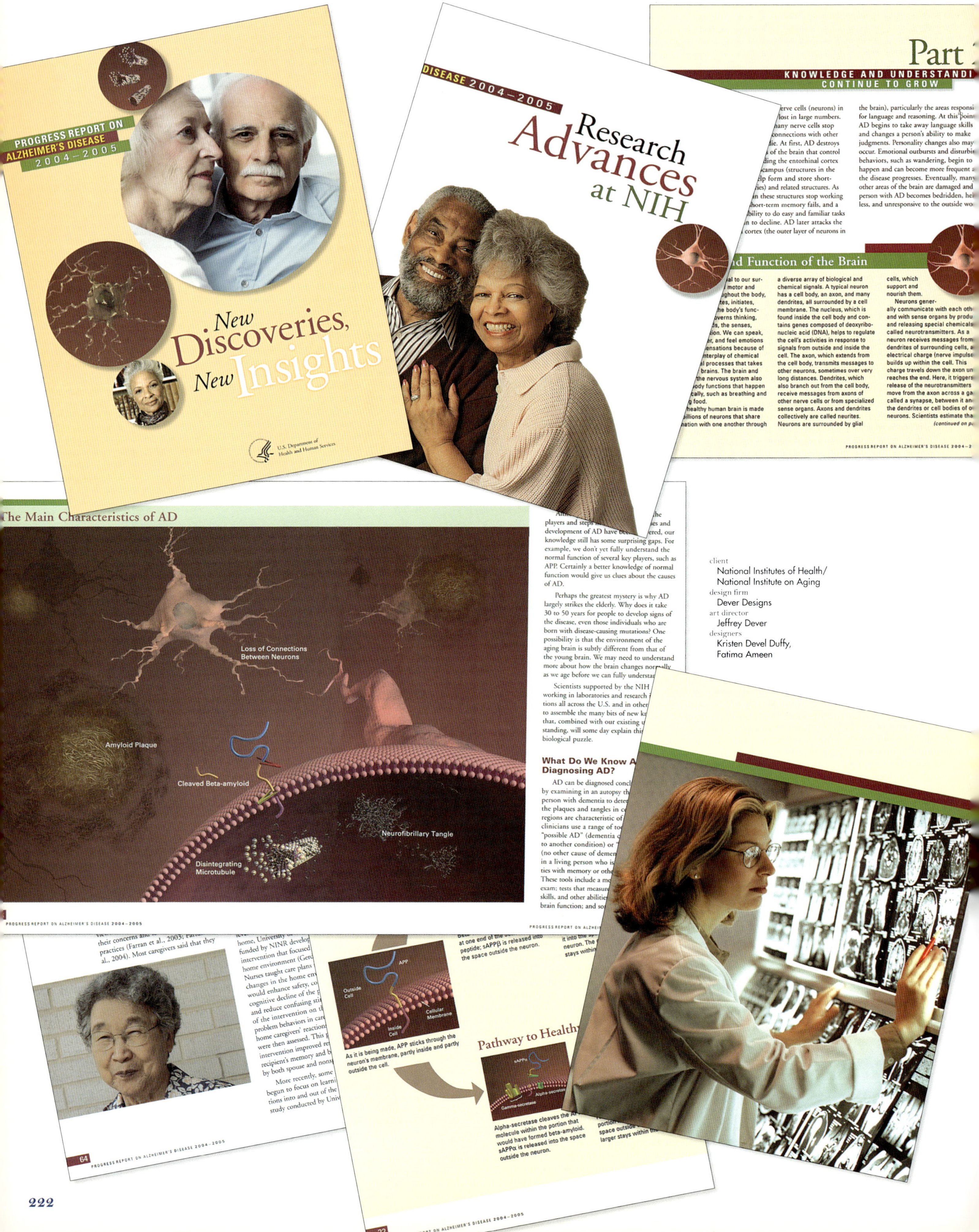

client
National Institutes of Health/
National Institute on Aging
design firm
Dever Designs
art director
Jeffrey Dever
designers
Kristen Devel Duffy,
Fatima Ameen

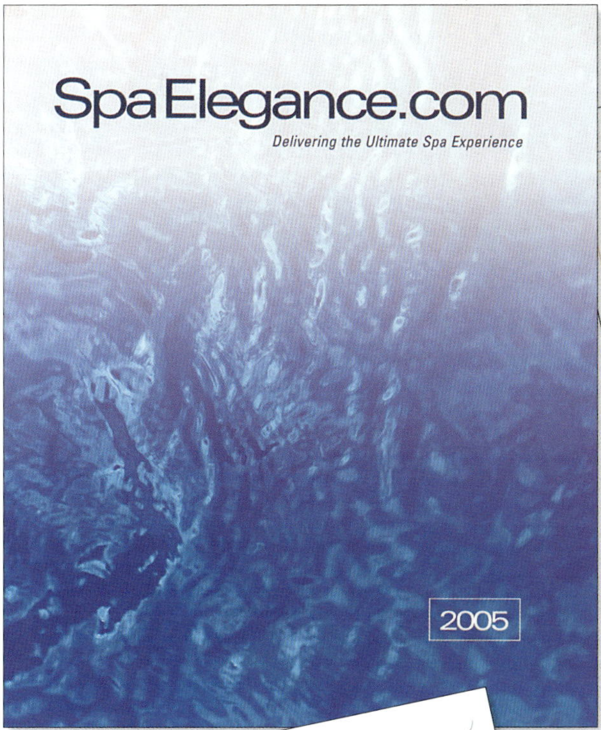

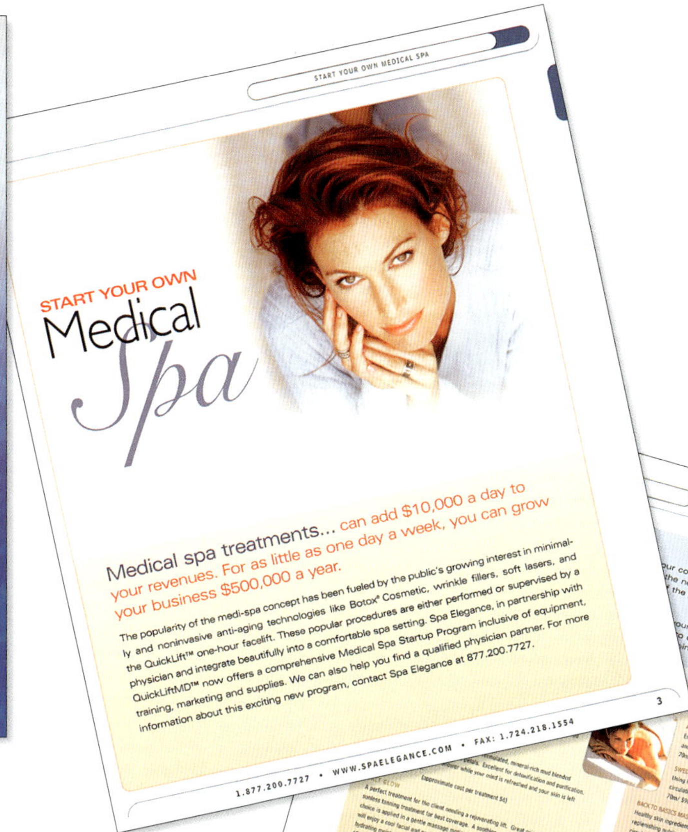

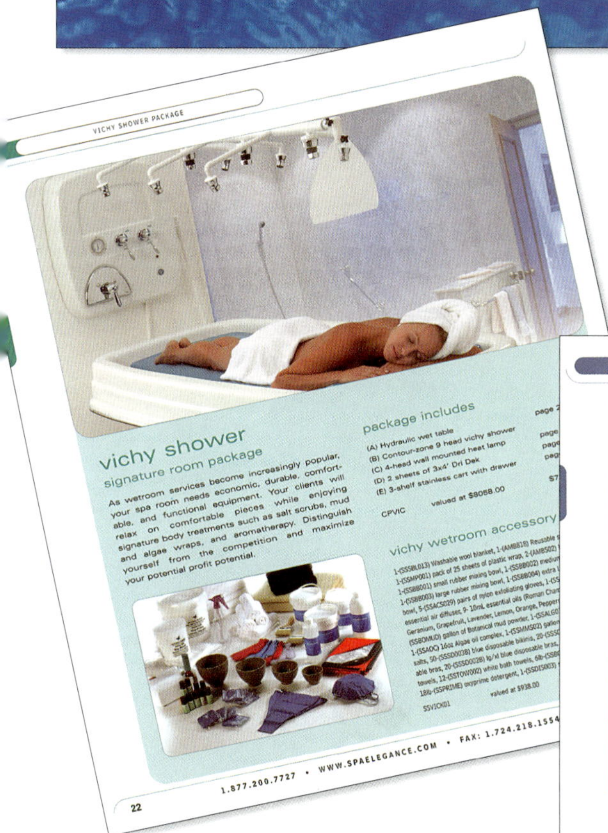

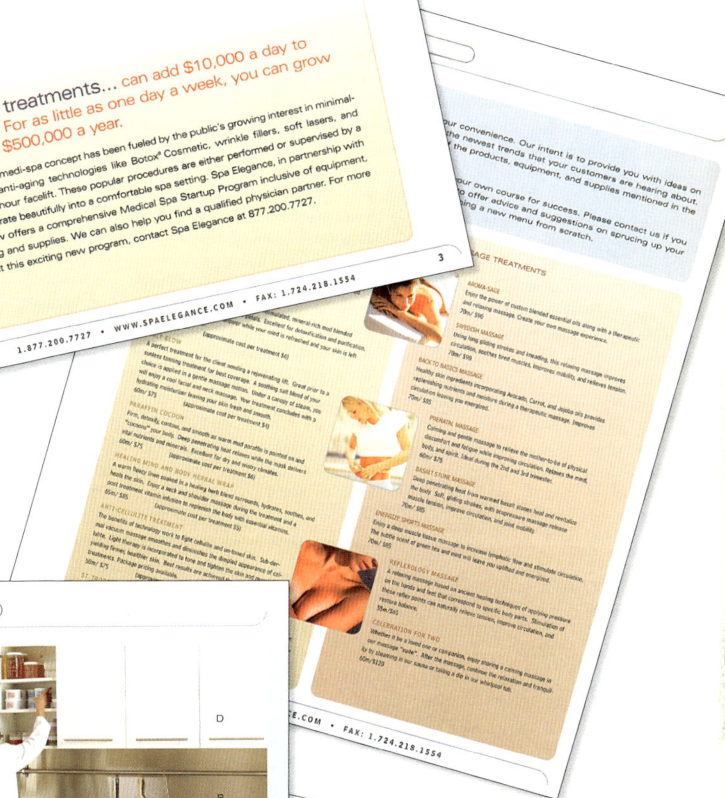

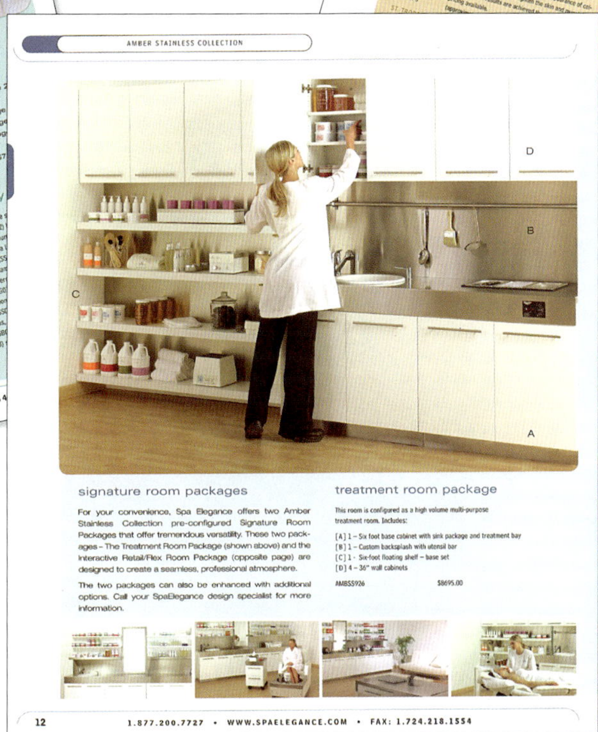

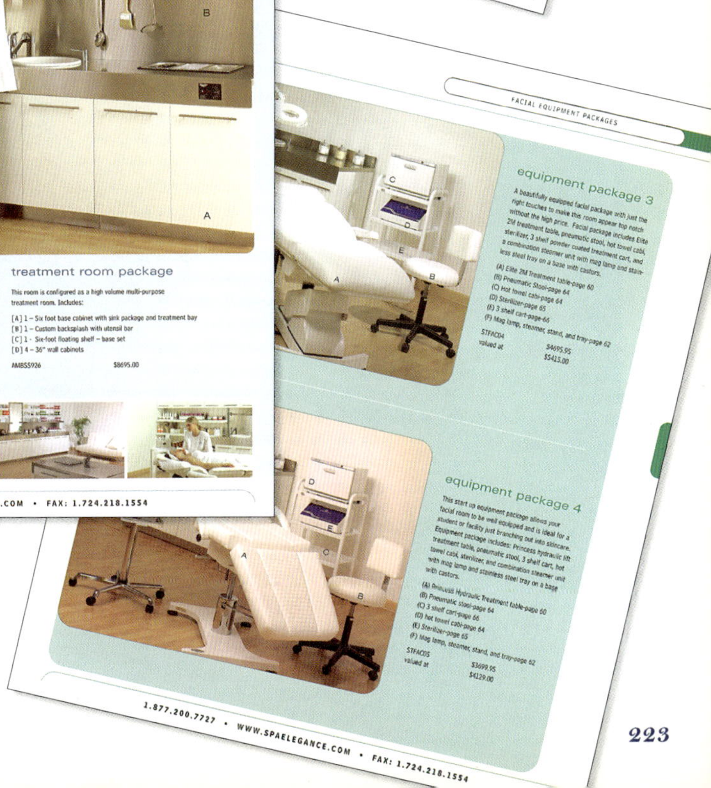

client
Spa Elegance
design firm
Reinnov8 Design Group
designer
Richard A. Hooper

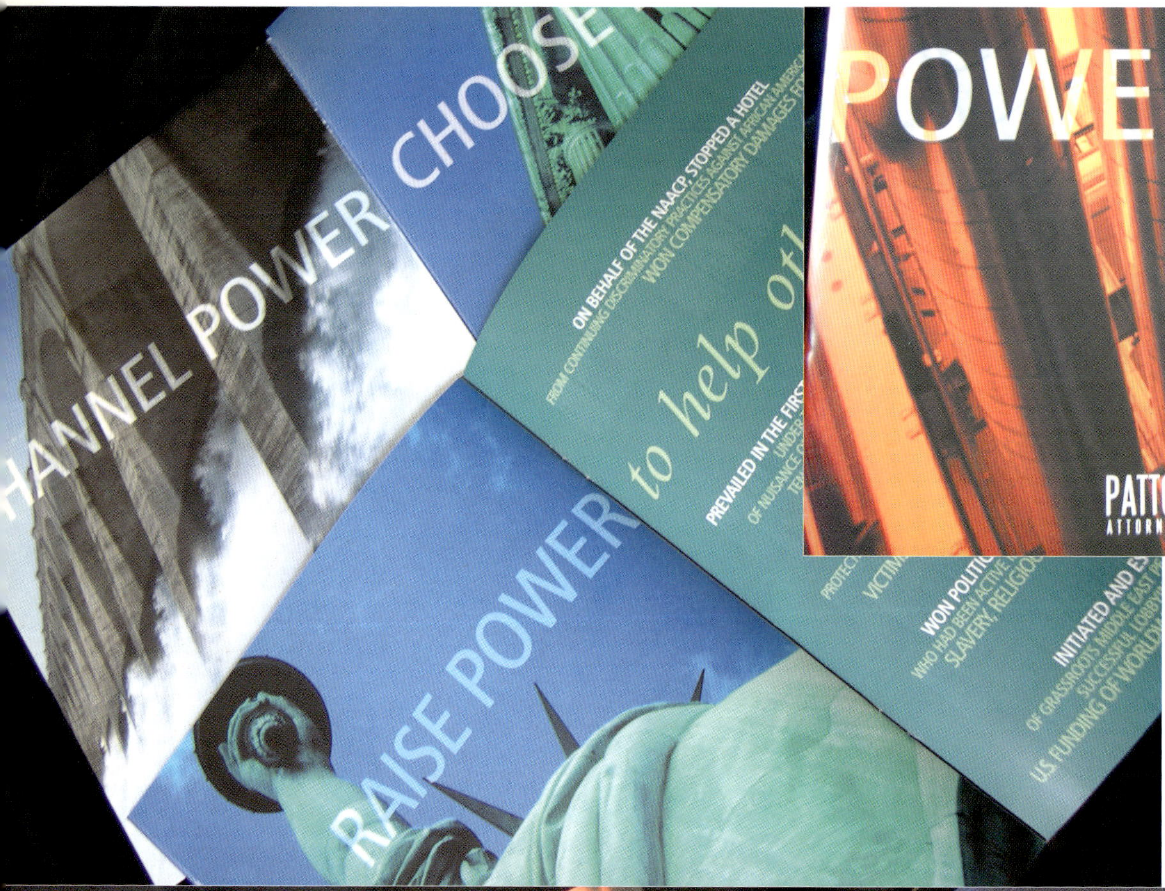

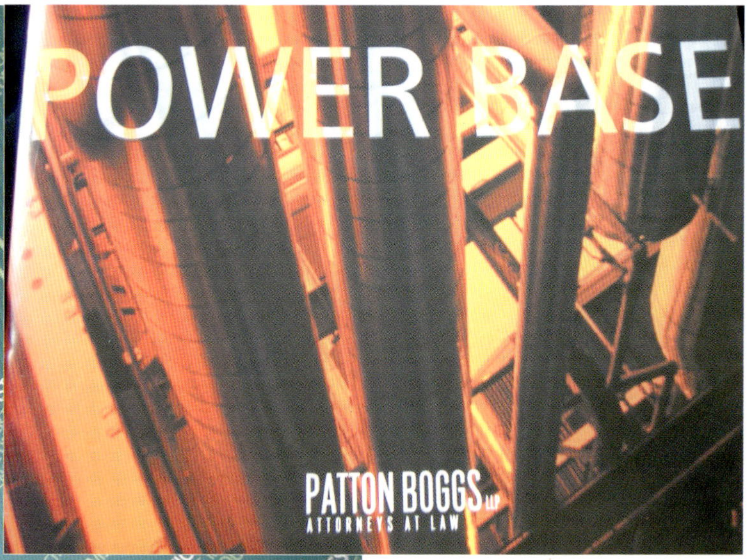

client
Patton Boggs LLP
design firm
Greenfield/Belser Ltd.
designers
Burkey Belser,
Jonathan Bruns

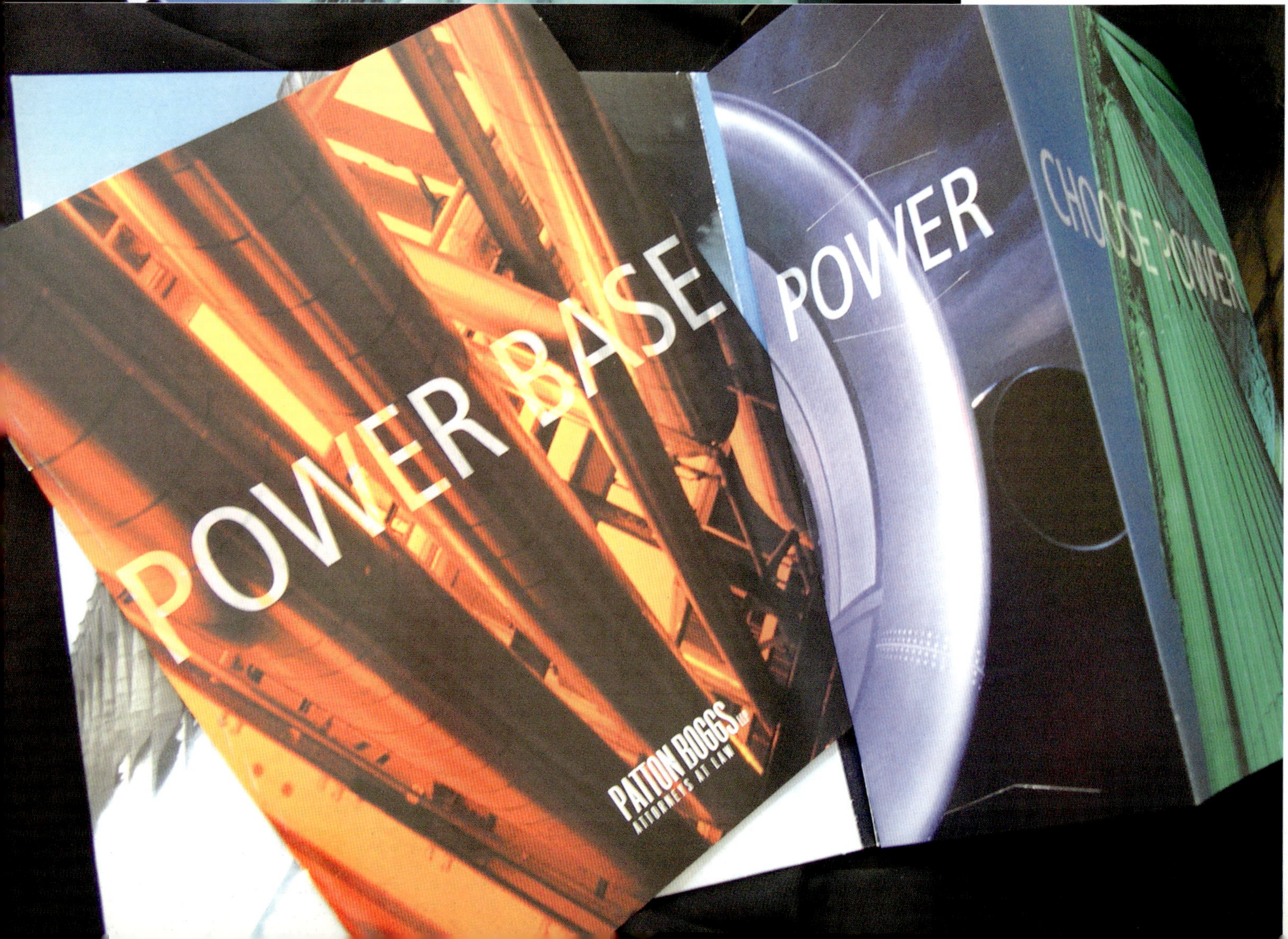

Trademark/Logo Design

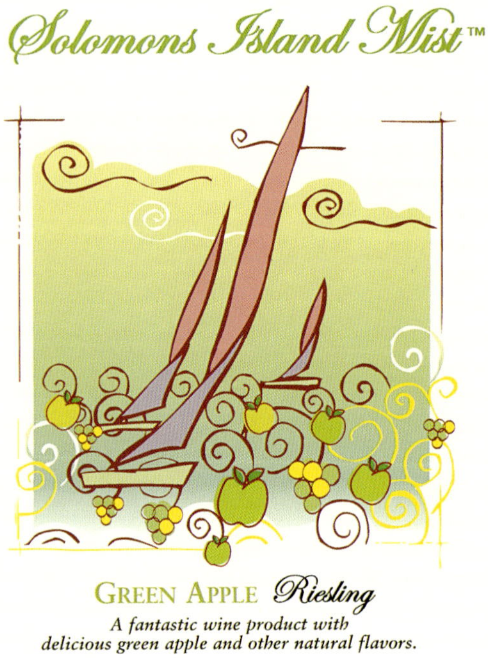

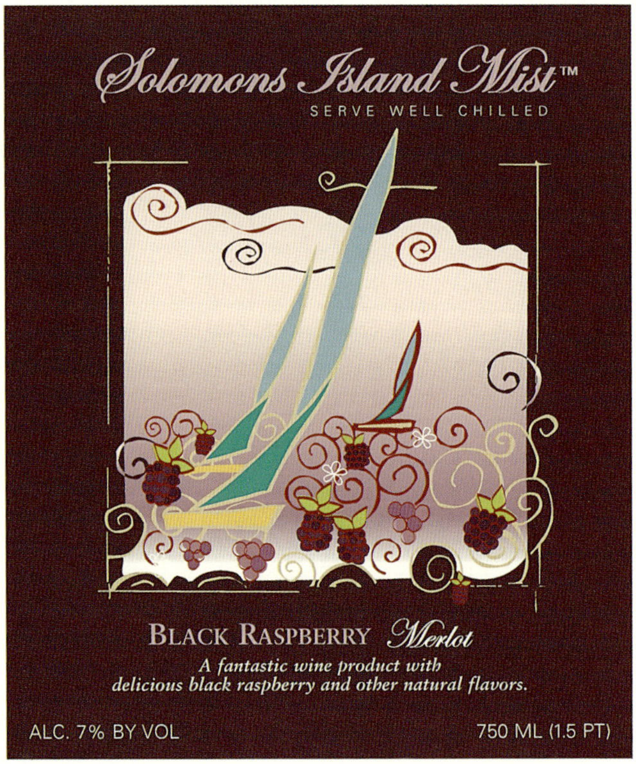

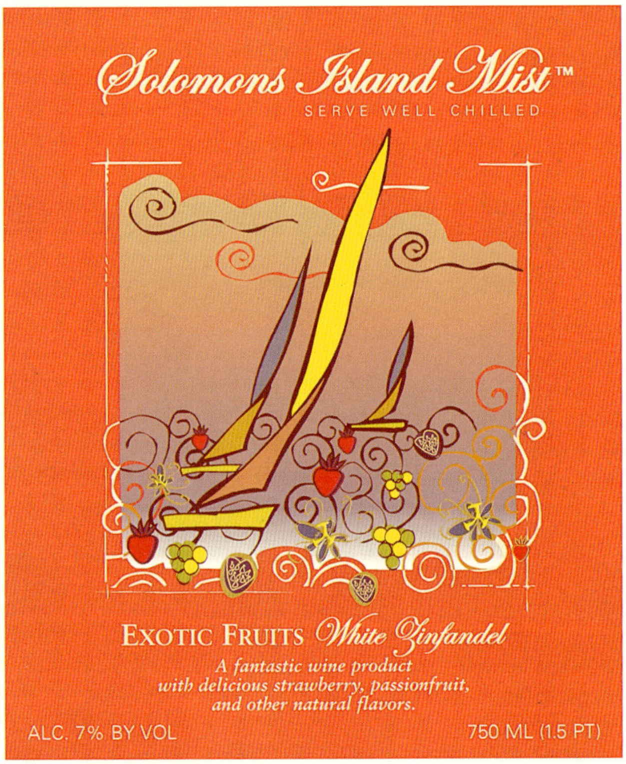

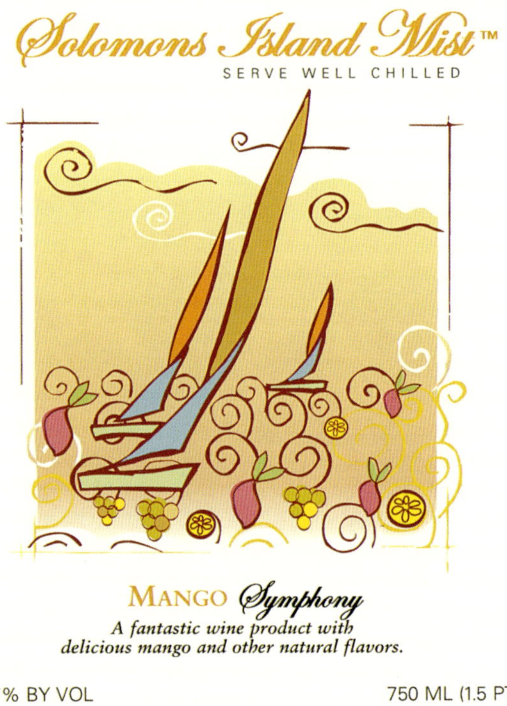

client
Solomons Island Winery
design firm
Crabtree + Company
designers
Susan Angrisani, Kiki Felix, Nisha Nair

client
Harvest Partners
design firm
Kiku Obata + Company
designer
Jim Redington

park
lane
DALLAS

client
Matisse Chocolatier
design firm
Words and Pictures
designer
Dave Gisler

matisse
chocolatier

client
Zoller Thomas
design firm
Walsh Design
designers
Miriam Lisco, Cathy Burnell

Zoller Thomas
clear stress ~ connect ~ create

inspired

client
InGEAR Corporation
design firm
InGEAR In-House Design Department
designer
So Yun Kim
product manager
Angela Jagla

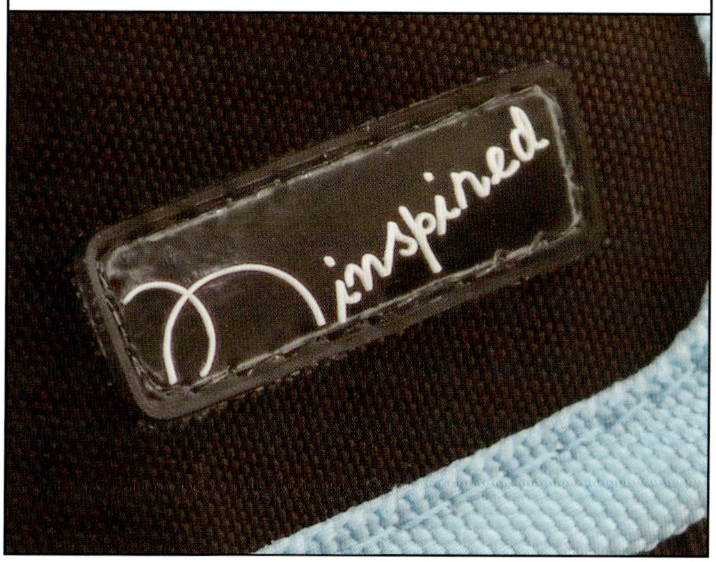

client
Oxford Obstetrics & Gynecology
design firm
Peg Faimon Design
designer
Peg Faimon

OXFORD
Obstetrics &
Gynecology

client
Splash, Ltd.
design firm
Kevin Hall Design
designer
Kevin Hall

client
Old Bay Billiards
design firm
The Wecker Group
designer
Robert Wecker

client
Animailers
design firm
Round 2 Communications
designer
John Welker

client
Gas Cylinder Technologies
design firm
Boyden & Youngblutt Advertising
designer
Todd Lemley

client
Maritime Landscape Design
design firm
Round 2 Communications
designer
Glen Villegas

client
Avpro
design firm
Round 2 Communications
designer
John Welker

client
Esterline Corporation
design firm
Perlman Company
designer
Robert Perlman

client
Oceanaeco
design firm
AF&A (Adam Filippo & Associates)
designers
Robert Adam,
Ralph James Russini,
Blair Good

client
RVSales.com
design firm
Hubbell Design Works
designer
Leighton Hubbell

client
R.A. Travel
design firm
3rd Edge Communications
designer
Frankie Gonzalez

client
You Send It, Inc.
design firm
Connie Hwang Design
designer
Connie Hwang

client
Gold Coast Rods
design firm
The Wecker Group
designer
Robert Wecker

client
Ooga Booga!, Inc.
design firm
Fifth Letter
designer
Elliot Strunk
illustrator
Jim Paillot

client
Rib Rack Restaurant
design firm
Catalyst Design, Inc.

client
Julie Anne's
design firm
CDI Studios
creative director
Victoria Hart
designer
Brian Felgar

client
Tonic
design firm
Sayles Graphic Design
designer
John Sayles

client
Forno Toscano
design firm
reduced fat
designer
John Bolster

client
Hot Sake Creative
design firm
A3 Design
designers
Alan Altman, Amanda Altman

client
Coffee Magazine
design firm
CDI Studios
creative director
Victoria Hart
designer
Brian Felgar

client
Simply Fresh
design firm
Mind's Eye Creative
designer
Stephen Brown

client
Red Stripe—An American Brasserie
design firm
Fresh Oil
designer
Nelson Couto

client
Frederick Festival of the Arts
design firm
Octavo Designs
designers
Sue Hough, Mark Burrier

client
Lydia Gardner—Clerk of the Circuit and County Courts, Orange County, Florida
design firm
Jowaisas Design
designer
Elizabeth Jowaisas

client
Eastlake Design District
design firm
Design Group West
designer
Jim Naegeli

client
Codign Software
design firm
Round 2 Communications
designer
Glen Villegas

client
Luxe Spa
design firm
Words and Pictures
designer
Dave Gisler

client
Virginia Hospital Center/Sumo Creative
design firm
Design Nut, LLC
creative director
Gabby Rojchin
designer
Brent Almond

client
Mead Westvaco
design firm
Smith Design
designer
Laura Markley

client
Ella Park
design firm
Eben Design
designers
Eben Design

client
Pure Source
design firm
3rd Edge Communications
designer
Melissa Medina Mackin

client
CBAA Soccer
design firm
Art 270, Inc.
designer
Sean Flanagan

client
SeliCor
design firm
bTaylor Design
designer
Brandon Taylor

client
4 Medica
design firm
Loomis Group
designer
Petra Andersson-Pardini

client
Metronome
design firm
Da Capo Design Company
designers
Chris LaValle, Lena C. Pleick

client
City of Port Angeles/
Capacity Provisioning, Inc.
design firm
Laurel Black Design, Inc.
designer
Laurel Black

client
The Maritime Aquarium at Norwalk
design firm
Tom Fowler, Inc.
designers
Thomas G. Fowler,
Elizabeth P. Ball

THE FIRST ANNUAL
Debonair Fish Affair
THE MARITIME AQUARIUM AT NORWALK

client
Red Nose Lighting
design firm
Sayles Graphic Design
designer
John Sayles

RED NOSE
LIGHTING

client
Fox Rehabilitation
design firm
160over90
designers
Darryl Cilli, Jim Walls,
Greg Klein, Stephen Penning

FOX
REHABILITATION

client
Alarm Watch
design firm
On Target Marketing
designer
Juan Medina

ALARMWATCH
ADVANCED CUSTOMER SECURITY

client
Shaggy Chic Pet Boutique
design firm
Fresh Oil
designer
Nelson Couto

Shaggy Chic
Pet Boutique

client
Roachsounds—Jeff Roach
design firm
Lewis—Nashville
designers
Clark Hook, Patrick Norris

client
Arent Fox
design firm
Greenfield/Belser Ltd.
designers
Burkey Belser, Tom Cameron

Arent Fox
ATTORNEYS AT LAW

client
Zombiecat Productions
design firm
angryporcupine*design
designer
Cheryl Roder-Quill

ZomBIECAT
productions

client
Sewickley Academy
design firm
Reinnov8 Design Group
designers
Richard A. Hooper,
Ken Nadeau

client
Pink & Yellow
design firm
CDI Studios
designers
Aaron Moses, Dan McElhattan III

Eagle View
GROUP, INC.

client
DCM—Doll Capital Management
design firm
Gee + Chung Design
designer
Earl Gee

YEAR OF
THE DOG

company
Jones Fish Hatcheries, Inc.
designer
Zack Pence

JONES FISH
HATCHERIES, INC.®

LOGIC™

IT JUST MAKES SENSE™

LOGIC™

IT JUST MAKES SENSE™

LOGIC™

IT JUST MAKES SENSE™

LOGIC™

IT JUST MAKES SENSE™

™

LOGIC™

IT JUST MAKES SENSE™

client
Logic Information Systems
design firm
Ecra Creative
designer
Jason Voiovich

client
Eos Airlines
design firm
Hornall Anderson Deesign Works
designers
Jack Anderson, Mark Popich,
David Bates, Andrew Wicklund,
Leo Raymundo, Jacob Carter,
Yuri Shvets

client
Dura Automotive Systems
design firm
Catalyst Design, Inc.

client
Friend Communications
design firm
Hubbell Design Works
designer
Leighton Hubbell

client
Taleo
design firm
Addis Group
designers
John Creson, Magdalena Hladka

client
Council for Advancement &
Support of Education
design firm
Design Nut, LLC
designer
Brent Almond

client
DynAccSys—eXtend Accounting
and Business Solutions
design firm
Fixation Marketing
designer
Bruce E. Morgan

client
Artisan Outdoor Lighting
design firm
Marcantel LeBlanc Brand Partnership
designers
Richard LeBlanc, Tom Marcantel

client
Briggs Inc.
design firm
Simon Graphics Ltd.
designer
Bob Simon

client
BrenWyn Fulfillment
design firm
The Wecker Group
designer
Robert Wecker

client
Apexos
design firm
ZGraphics, Ltd.
designers
Andy Matznick, Joe Zeller

client
Katrina Ferry
design firm
CDI Studios
designers
David Araujo,
Dan McElhattan III

client
Department B
design firm
Mortensen Design, Inc.
art director
Gordon Mortensen
designers
Gordon Mortensen,
Chris Rossi,
Patricia Margaret

client
Steiner & Associates
design firm
Kiku Obata + Company
designer
Rich Nelson

BAYSHORE

client
The Aledan Group
design firm
Original Impressions
designer
Lisa Cuervo

The Aledan Group
builders of quality homes

client
After 5
design firm
Rule 29
designer
Justin Ahrens

AFTER 5
COMPANIES

client
Blue Gin
design firm
Group T Design
designer
Tom Klinedinst

BLUEGIN

client
Basically Brazil, LLC
design firm
Very Memorable Design
designer
Michael Pinto

basically
BRAZ!L

client
Public Broadcasting Atlanta
design firm
Hired Gun Design
designer
Patrick Foster

ATLANTA FORUM NETWORK

client
Carnton Plantation
design firm
Lewis—Nashville
designer
Clark Hook

HISTORIC CARNTON PLANTATION

client
3-1/2 Flooring Co.
design firm
Pat Taylor
designer
Pat Taylor

client
Great Lakes Engineering
design firm
Ecra Creative
designer
Joseph Rodenwald

GREAT LAKES ENGINEERING

client
Greenberg Traurig
design firm
Brand, ltd.
designers
Michael Smith, Virginia Martino

GREENBERG TRAURIG ATTORNEYS AT LAW

client
J. Garner Photography
design firm
Eben Design
designer
Dan Meehan

j. garner photography

client
Greenspun Media Group
design firm
Greenspun Media Group
designer
Mami Awamura

lasvegas home&design

client
Marichal & Hernández Attorneys at Law
design firm
ID Group
designers
Mayra Maldonado, Abner Gutiérrez

Marichal & Hernández LLP
ATTORNEYS AT LAW

client
Marvin A. Williams Photography
design firm
Zero Gravity Design Group
designers
Zero Gravity Design Group

MARVIN A. WILLIAMS
PHOTOGRAPHY

client
Civitas Group
design firm
Kiku Obata + Company
designer
Rich Nelson

THE MERIDIAN
Premier City Living

client
Orchin Orthodontics
design firm
Greenfield/Belser Ltd.
designers
Burkey Belser, Maureen Meyer

ORCHIN
ORTHODONTICS

client
Dimitri Khazin
design firm
reduced fat
designer
John Bolster

oxygéne
FITNESS & SPA

client
R.T. Fisher & Associates
design firm
On Target Marketing
designer
Jesse Bloodworth

THE QUAD

client
Palomar Pomerado Health
design firm
Lorenz Advertising
designer
Arne Ratermanis

client
Farisi
design firm
Farisi
designers
Farisi/Saied

client
StepPrinting.com
design firm
Hubbell Design Works
designer
Leighton Hubbell

client
Universal Health Care Foundation of Connecticut
design firm
Fathom
designers
Anthony Acock, Bil Jenak

client
TN Contractors
design firm
Lewis—Nashville
designer
Clark Hook

client
Stranded
design firm
Jensen Design Associates, Inc.
designer
David Jensen

client
Theresa Kathryn
design firm
IE Design + Communications
designer
Kenny Goldstein

client
Stoltz
design firm
Kiku Obata + Company
designer
Joe Floresca

client
Shaser
design firm
Gill Fishman Associates
designer
Michael Persons

client
Vista Center for the Blind & Visually Impaired
design firm
Brand Engine
art directors
Yusuke Asaka, Eric Read
designers
Rebecca Escalera,
Meghan Zodrow, Casey Coyle

client
Wild Waterways Conservancy
design firm
Robert Meyers Design
designer
Robert Meyers

client
Window Rock Enterprises
design firm
Hubbell Design Works
designer
Leighton Hubbell

client
Mercy Hospital Foundation
design firm
Crowley Webb and Assoc.
designers
Kelly Gambino, Sarah Perrigo

Mercy Hospital Foundation

client
Fourth River Associates
design firm
Robert Meyers Design
designer
Robert Meyers

FOURTH RIVER ASSOCIATES

client
American Standard Companies
design firm
Ted DeCagna Graphic Design
designer
Ted DeCagna

LIFESTEPS IN MOTION

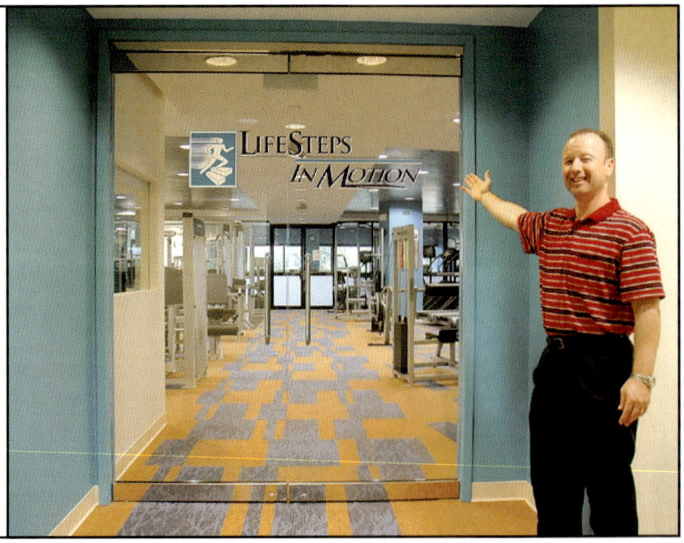

client
Praxis
design firm
Crowley Webb and Assoc.
designer
Katie Hazel

BREEZE STUDY

client
Wholesale Life Insurance Brokerage
design firm
Rule 29
designers
Justin Ahrens, Chad Nelson, Josh Jensen

WHOLESALELIFE™ INSURANCE BROKERAGE

client
Greater Washington Board of Trade
design firm
Fixation Marketing
designer
Randy Guseman

WELLNESS WORKS

client
SOCMA
design firm
Bremmer & Goris
designer
Nicole Hamam

ChemStewards℠
THE ROAD TO CONTINUOUS IMPROVEMENT

client
Springsoft
design firm
Pure Imagination
designer
Jacqueline Joyce

SPRINGsoft®
The clean water people

client
Unicentric
design firm
Robert Meyers Design
designer
Robert Meyers

unicentric

client
Septima Clark Public Charter School
design firm
Martin Randal Communications
designer
Eric Rotramel

SEPTIMA CLARK
KNOWLEDGE IS FREEDOM

client
Addition Technology
design firm
Crowley Webb and Assoc.
designer
Jeff Hopper

INTACS
FOUNDATION
for
KERATOCONUS

client
Berlin Productions
design firm
Berlin Productions
designer
Dylan Wood

BERLIN
PRODUCTIONS

client
Allconnect
design firm
Hornall Anderson Design Works
designers
Jack Anderson, James Tee,
Tiffany Place, Yuri Shvets,
Belinda Bowling, Sonja Max,
Stephanie Cooper

allconnect

client
Telematics Research Group
design firm
FigDesign
designer
David Fiegenschue

TRG
Telematics Research
Group Incorporated

client
Trinity Chiropractic
design firm
aijalon
designer
Lance Ford

TRINITY
CHIROPRACTIC

client
AirPlay Direct
design firm
bTaylor Design
designer
Brandon Taylor

AirPlay
DIRECT

client
Premier Financial Services
design firm
Daniels Design Inc.
designers
Larry Daniels, Kathie Rokita

Premier
Financial Services
Vintage and Exotic Motorcar Leasing

client
Market Research Dallas
design firm
FigDesign
designer
David Fiegenschue

client
StreamWorks Consulting
design firm
angryporcupine*design
designer
Cheryl Roder-Quill

client
CombineNet
design firm
Elias/Savion Advertising
designer
Ronnie Savion

client
Syniverse Technologies
design firm
Interbrand
creative director
Carlos Sanchez
designers
Carlyn Schlechter, Sam Ayling

client
CombineMed
design firm
Elias/Savion Advertising
designer
Ronnie Savion

client
Jay S. Volk
design firm
Reinnov8 Design Group
designers
Richard A. Hooper, Ken Nadeau

client
Accessa
design firm
Stahl Partners Inc.
designer
David Stahl

client
Titus Bicycles, Inc.
design firm
Hubbell Design Works for Damion Hickman Design
designer
Leighton Hubbell

client
Warren-Walker Green Valley Academy
design firm
Aquea Design
designer
Raymond Perez

client
Rockport
design firm
Rule 29
designer
Justin Ahrens

client
Rothschild, Inc.
design firm
Grizzell & Co.
designer
John H. Grizzell

client
Sunbury Broadcasting
design firm
MFDI
designer
Mark Fertig

client
Families Only/Sumo Creative
design firm
Design Nut, LLC
creative director
Gabby Rojchin
designer
Brent Almond

client
The Davidson Companies
design firm
Lorenc + Yoo Design
designer
Chung Youl Yoo

client
Democratic National Committee
design firm
Bremmer & Goris
designer
Li-Chou Mikilo

client
Duluth Festival Opera
design firm
HrupekDesign
designer
Michael Hrupek

client
Fyrestorm Inc.
design firm
Cintara
designer
Christopher Canote

client
MainStay Investments
design firm
NYLIM marketing
designers
Rene Teng, Dana Dunleavy

client
Martin James
design firm
Miller White, LLC
designer
Amanda Rose

client
Dura Automotive Systems
design firm
Catalyst Design, Inc.

client
M&T Bank
design firm
Crowley Webb and Assoc.
designers
Brian Grunert, Kevin Karn

client
All Hazards Planning Group
design firm
McDill Design
designer
Michael Dillon

client
Blue Heron Communications
design firm
The Design Channel
designers
Amanda Henderson, David Franek, Jonathan Bruns

client
Smithsonian Ornithology Division
design firm
Crabtree + Company
designers
Nisha Nair, Susan Angrisani

client
Lauth
design firm
Sommese Design
designers
Lanny Sommese, Kristin Sommese

client
Newmark Homes
design firm
Ecra Creative
designer
Joseph Rodenwald

client
Alliance Nursing
design firm
Eben Design
designer
Matthew Grimes

client
Pacific Coast National Bank
design firm
Design Group West
designer
Jim Naegeli

client
The HorseTV Channel
design firm
The HorseTV Channel
designers
Maureen Smullen, Ruben Esparza

client
Savidge Housing Group
design firm
Sire Advertising
designers
Shawn Felty, Bob Henninger

client
Mattamy Homes
design firm
A3 Design
designers
Alan Altman, Amanda Altman

client
Waters Less Traveled TV
design firm
Chevalier Advertising
designers
Eric Silvernail,
Robin Kizzar

client
Destiny USA
design firm
Interbrand
creative director
Carlos Sanchez
design director
Sandra Hill
designer
Beca Lee

client
Mazola
design firm
Axion Design Inc.

client
Kay Multimedia
design firm
Kay Multimedia
designers
Harvey Appelbaum, Christofer Nystrom

client
Horizon Group USA
design firm
Design Trends
designers
Tree Trapanese, David Un

client
ExecuChange
design firm
Hummingbird Creative Group
designer
Juli La Due

client
Unified Western Grocers
design firm
BrandSavvy Inc.
designer
Karl Peters

client
Monroe Station
design firm
Greenhaus
designers
Tracy Sabin,
Lisa Friedman,
Craig Fuller

client
SLO County Historical Museum
design firm
Pierre Rademaker Design
designers
Pierre Rademaker, Debbie Shibata

client
Epic Bancorp
design firm
Mortensen Design, Inc.
art director
Gordon Mortensen
designer
Patricia Margaret

client
Make the Grade
design firm
Pierre Rademaker Design
designers
Pierre Rademaker, Debbie Shibata

client
The College of Saint Rose Athletics Department
design firm
The Office of Public Relations
art director
Mark Hamilton
designer
Chris Parody

client
Consolidated Resorts, Inc.
design firm
Brand, ltd.
designer
Baub Mercurio

client
The Frazier Quarry
design firm
Grafix Dezine
designer
Oleg Yagolnikov

client
Sewickley Academy
design firm
Reinnov8 Design Group
designer
Richard A. Hooper

client
Miller Brewing Company
design firm
McDill Design
designer
Joel Harmeling

client
Susquehanna University
design firm
MFDI
designer
Mark Fertig

client
Founders Community Bank
design firm
Pierre Rademaker Design
designers
Pierre Rademaker, Debbie Shibata

client
Episcopal Community Services
design firm
The Bailey Group
designers
Dave Fiedler, Wendy Slavish

client
McCarthy's Chophouse
design firm
Bullet Communications, Inc.
designer
Tim Scott Kump

client
Los Angeles County Economic Development Corporation
design firm
Jerry Cowart Designers, Inc.
designer
Jerry Cowart

client
National Foundation for Affordable Housing
design firm
The Design Channel
designer
David Franek

client
Pine Creek Partners
design firm
Sightline Marketing

client
Hollywood Roosevelt Hotel
design firm
The Wecker Group
designer
Robert Wecker

client
Lake Country Cyclones
design firm
McDill Design
designer
Joel Harmeling

client
Picowave Technologies
design firm
Graphic Advance, Inc.
designer
Aviad Stark

client
Raising More Money
design firm
Walsh Design
designer
Miriam Lisco

The Joy of Fundraising

client
Pèpe International
design firm
The Wecker Group
designer
Robert Wecker

Pèpe
International

client
Bell Sound
design firm
Netherworld Productions
designers
Rodney Hom, Robby Jendrono

Bell Sound

client
KMart Corporation
design firm
InGEAR In-House Design Department
production manager
Heather Tvrdik
senior designer
Jeremy Swanson
designer
Brian Nillson

Swisstech

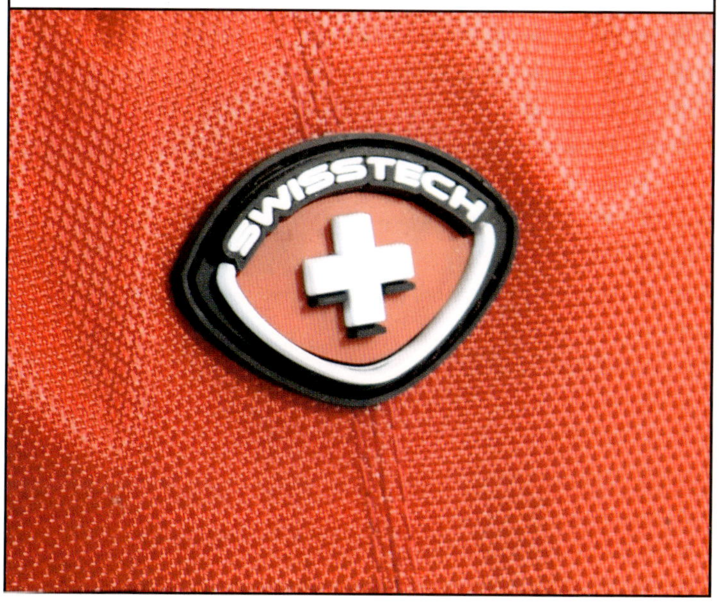

client
Uncommon Kneads
design firm
Paul Kaza Associates
designer
Carrisa Butler

Uncommon Kneads
Therapeutic Massage for Women

client
Southeast Missourian
design firm
Kiku Obata + Company
designers
Rich Nelson

client
Praxis
design firm
Crowley Webb and Assoc.
designer
Kathy Kastan

client
Redeemer's Chapel
design firm
Lewis—Nashville
designer
Clark Hook

client
Year-round Lawncare
design firm
Eye Integrated Communications
designers
Stanton Blakeslee, Brantley Barefoot

client
National Association of School Psychologists
design firm
Octavo Designs
designer
Sue Hough

client
Callawassie Golf Club
design firm
Nordyke Design
designer
John Nordyke

client
Stacee Gravel & Andrew Lawrence
design firm
Defteling Design
designer
Alex Wijnen

client
Stoltz
design firm
Kiku Obata + Company
designer
Amy Knopf

client
Consolidated Resorts, Inc.
design firm
Brand, ltd.
designer
Baub Mercurio

client
AMKC
design firm
Open Studio
designer
Shelly Fukushima

client
Benicia Historical Museum
design firm
Jeff Fisher LogoMotives
creative director
Sue Fisher
designer
Jeff Fisher

client
Monterey Church
design firm
The Wecker Group
designer
Robert Wecker

client
Scallions Restaurant
design firm
reduced fat
designer
John Bolster

client
The Tasty Taco
design firm
Never Boring Design Assoc.
designer
Katrina Furton

client
TKB Entertainment
design firm
Hubbell Design Works
designer
Leighton Hubbell

client
Schneider Custom Homes
design firm
aijalon
designer
Lance Ford

client
America Italiana
design firm
Cintara
designer
Rachelle Orosa

client
Livingston Court Theater Project
design firm
On Target Marketing
designers
Dusty Dahlgren, Jesse Bloodworth

client
EverythingBATH.com
design firm
Annagram Studio and Design
designer
Graham Allen

client
Blue Ribbon Blossoms
design firm
MFDI
designer
Mark Fertig

client
Furious Flower Poetry Center
design firm
Seran Design
designer
Sang Yoon

client
Consolidated Resorts, Inc.
design firm
Brand, ltd.
designers
Virginia Martino, John Dykema

client
Caffé Pazzesco
design firm
Klündt + Hosmer
designers
Judy Heggem-Davis, Darin Klündt

client
California WineWorks
design firm
Tom Fowler, Inc.
designer
Elizabeth P. Ball

client
Simply Fresh
design firm
Mind's Eye Creative
designer
Stephen Brown

client
SuccessArchitects
design firm
HrupekDesign
designers
Michael Hrupek

client
Artisan Wine Co.
design firm
McMillian Design
designer
William McMillian

client
Elite Repeat, Inc.
design firm
Da Capo Design Company
designers
Lena C. Pleick, Chris LaValle

client
Centex Homes
design firm
Hubbell Design Works for The Roxburgh Agency
designer
Leighton Hubbell

client
AquaZul
design firm
Sayles Graphic Design
designer
John Sayles

client
ka Architecture/General Growth Properties
design firm
Lorenc + Yoo Design
designers
Jisun An, David Park

client
Dr. Barry Frank
design firm
CDI Studios
designers
Aaron Moses, Dan McElhattan III

client
Nine-Ten Restaurant
design firm
Lorenz Advertising
designer
Arne Ratermanis

client
Alix Partners
design firm
Catalyst Design, Inc.

client
Avenidas Senior Center
design firm
Hausman Design
designer
Joan Hausman

client
Wentworth at Hidden Hills
design firm
HardBall Creative
designer
Andy Gosendi

client
Vineyard Lane
design firm
Daigle Design
art director
Candace Daigle
designer
Jessi Carpenter

client
Turrentine
design firm
Axion Design, Inc.

client
Forest City Washington
design firm
Herip Design Associates, Inc.
designers
Walter M. Herip,
Jen H. Crabtree

client
Schools International
design firm
Da Capo Design Company
designers
Lena C. Pleick, Chris LaValle

client
Eden's Honey Pecans
design firm
Taylor Design
designers
Suzanne Reusch, Daniel Taylor

client
Blue Diamond Growers
design firm
The Thompson Design Group
designers
The Thompson Design Group

client
Dorset Connects
design firm
Verve Marketing & Design
principal, creative director
Diane Lemonides
designer
Nancy Nguyen

client
Kip Flock
design firm
Sire Advertising
designers
Shawn Felty, Bob Henninger

client
intuition
design firm
Rokuroda Cornett
designers
Rick Cornett, Miki Rokuroda

client
Spaulding
design firm
Gill Fishman Associates
designer
Michael Persons

client
Turn
design firm
Addis Group
designer
John Creson

client
Giant Steps
design firm
Graphic Advance, Inc.
designer
Aviad Stark

client
IHRSA
design firm
T + T
designers
Theodore C. Alexander, Jr.,
Therese Alexander

client
Bernadette Johnson, Blaze Group
design firm
Indiblu Design
art director
Kimber Flynn

client
Pixie Maté
design firm
Brand Engine
art director
Will Burke
designer
Casey Coyle

client
Cabrini Mission
design firm
Interbrand
creative director
Carlos Sanchez
designers
Becca Lee, Katie Repine

client
Slo Maid Ice Cream
design firm
Pierre Rademaker Design
designers
Pierre Rademaker, Debbie Shibata

client
Seafarer Baking Company
design firm
Sabingrafik, Inc.
designer
Tracy Sabin

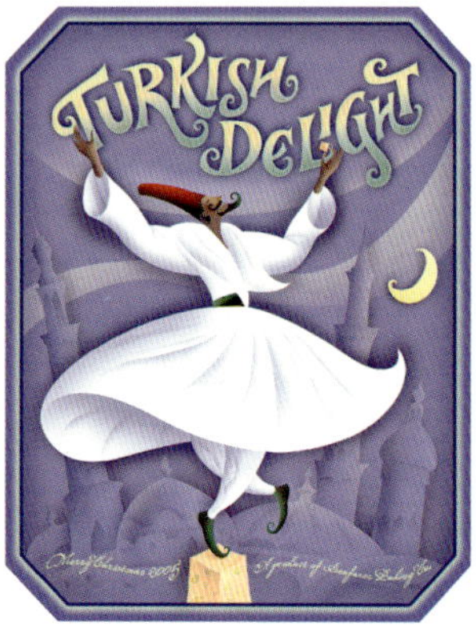

client
Monte Vista Chapel
design firm
Never Boring Design Associates
designer
Shawna Bayers

monte vista
CHAPEL

client
CyberAdvisors
design firm
HrupekDesign
designer
Michael Hrupek

CA CyberAdvisors

client
Sunset Radiology
design firm
Original Impressions
designer
Lisa Cuervo

SRI Sunset Radiology, Inc.

client
Standard Pacific Homes
design firm
Hubbell Design Works for
The Roxburgh Agency
designer
Leighton Hubbell

Lake@Walnut

client
IHS
design firm
Genesis Inc.
designer
Janet Johnson

IHS®
The Source
for Critical Information and Insight™

client
YFonGlobal
design firm
Hubbell Design Works for
The Woodbine Agency
designer
Leighton Hubbell

client
Donald Heiter Community Center
design firm
Sire Advertising
designers
Shawn Felty, Bob Henninger

client
Strategies 360
design firm
Walsh Design
designer
Miriam Lisco

client
Library Foundation of Buffalo
design firm
Crowley Webb and Assoc.
designer
Jeff Hopper

client
DigiScript
design firm
Ventress Design Group
designer
Tom Ventress

client
Fitness West
design firm
Laurel Black Design, Inc.
designer
Laurel Black

client
Beach House Supply Company
design firm
Acme Communications, Inc.
designer
Kiki Boucher

client
BLRB Architects
design firm
Hornall Anderson Design Works
designers
Daymon Bruck,
Yuri Shvets, Hillary Radbill

client
Leadership San Francisco
design firm
The Thompson Design Group
designers
The Thompson Design Group

client
Sterling Home Showcase
design firm
Never Boring Design Assoc.
designer
Katrina Furton

client
Downtown Entertainment
design firm
Mayhem Studios
designer
Calvin Lee

client
The Little Clinic
design firm
David ID
designer
Daniel Knol

client
Bike St. Louis
design firm
Kiku Obata + Company
designer
Troy Guzman

client
Literacy, Inc.
design firm
CorchiaWolinerRhoda
designers
Mintoo Kim,
Ellen Woliner,
Todd Rhoda

client
Greater Washington Sports Alliance
design firm
Fixation Marketing
designer
John Frantz

client
Benchmark Living
design firm
Gill Fishman Associates
designer
Michael Persons

client
ForSaleByOwner.com
design firm
Daniels Design Inc.
designers
Larry Daniels, Kathie Rokita

client
National Associations of Counties
design firm
Dever Designs
designer
Jeffrey Dever

client
Daily Item/Sunbury Broadcasting
design firm
MFDI
designer
Mark Fertig

BIG BOYS BIG TOYS

client
New Millennium
design firm
Lightspeed Commercial Arts
designer
Michael J. Hamers

Genesis ACCOUNTING™

RECOVER™

design firm
Ecra Creative
designers
Jason Voiovich,
Daniele Lanza

RECOVER CN™
WOUND CARE STRIPS FOR DOGS

RECOVER BD™
WOUND CARE STRIPS FOR BIRDS

client
Simulation Modeling Services
design firm
Bernard Design
designer
Brandon Taylor

client
Mues Design
design firm
Mues Design
designer
Nancy Mues-Thomas

client
Plantronics
design firm
Loomis Group
designer
Darin Greenwalt

client
Awnimation
design firm
Marcantel LeBlanc Brand Partnership
designers
Richard LeBlanc, Tom Marcantel

client
JaxLive 2005
design firm
HardBall Creative
designers
Andy Gosendi, Michael O'Connell

client
Inventive Productions
design firm
Walsh Design
designer
Miriam Lisco

client
Consolidated Resorts, Inc.
design firm
Brand, ltd.
designer
Baub Mercurio

SunShares™
A Consolidated Resorts Service
your recommendation is worth rewarding.

client
Vision Northwest
design firm
Woodson & Neuroth
designer
Michael Bossen

vision
Northwest

client
River Lights Chorus
design firm
Never Boring Design Associates
designer
Julie Orona

river lights
CHORUS

client
Center for Interactive Media Studies
design firm
Peg Faimon Design
designer
Peg Faimon

ai
armstrong
interactive

client
Balboa Park
design firm
Design Group West
designer
Jim Naegeli

BALBOA PARK
A Landscape of Art & Culture.

client
SBC (now AT&T)
design firm
Interbrand
creative director
Carlos Sanchez
design director
Craig Stout
designer
Loid Der

at&t

client
Praxis
design firm
Crowley Webb and Assoc.
designer
Kelly Gambino

client
Shooting Star
design firm
Never Boring Design Associates
designer
Julie Orona

client
American Institute of Architects Minnesota
design firm
Rubin Cordaro Design
designer
Jim Cordaro

client
Community Health Association of Spokane
design firm
Kländt Hosmer
designers
Henry Ortega, Darin Kländt

client
Mercomm, Inc.
design firm
Stan Gellman Graphic Design Inc.
designers
Bryan Wakeland, Barry Tilson

client
Dream Factory Community
design firm
Designing Words
creative director
Julianne Nardone

client
Connecticut Grand Opera & Orchestra
design firm
Tom Fowler, Inc.
art directors
Thomas G. Fowler, Elizabeth P. Ball
designers
Stephanie Goos Johnson, Thomas G. Fowler

A Masked Ball
masks to be provided

client
Mana Waere
design firm
Group T Design
designer
Tom Klinedinst

mana waere

client
Crown Flower Mart
design firm
Pat Taylor
designer
Pat Taylor

client
The Art Institute of Chicago
design firm
Liska + Associates
designer
Steve Liska

CH1CAGO
VISIONS

client
Zero Gravity Design Group
design firm
Zero Gravity Design Group
designers
Zero Gravity Design Group

zero gravity design group

client
Just Out Newsmagazine
design firm
Jeff Fisher LogoMotives
creative director
Marty Davis
designer
Jeff Fisher

just out

client
Pappas Properties
design firm
160over90
designers
Darryl Cilli, Greg Klein

client
Studio 718
design firm
Pierre Rademaker Design
designers
Pierre Rademaker, Anne Bussone

client
Cork Screw Wine Bar
design firm
A3 Design
designers
Alan Altman, Amanda Altman

client
Design Milieu
design firm
Design Nut, LLC
designer
Brent Almond

client
Blisscotti
design firm
Hornall Anderson Design Works
designers
Larry Anderson, Jack Anderson,
Holly Craven, Jay Hilburn, Chris Freed

client
Footlights
design firm
Hummingbird Creative Group
designer
Juli La Due

client
Outdoor Active Kids, Inc.
design firm
Berlin Productions
designers
Steven Klapow, Rick Berlin, Guillermo Hansz, Dylan Wood

client
Alliance Nursing
design firm
Eben Design
designer
Matthew Grimes

client
Friend Communications
design firm
Hubbell Design Works
designer
Leighton Hubbell

client
Greensleeve
design firm
Studio Signorella
designer
Michael Signorella

client
National Arbor Day Foundation
design firm
aijalon
designer
Lance Ford

client
Camellia Home Health & Hospice
design firm
Greenfield/Belser Ltd.
designers
Burkey Belser, Jonathan Bruns

client
Mighty Leaf Tea Company
design firm
Brand Engine
art director
Eric Read
designers
Meghan Zodrow, Kinkel Rowan

client
Healing Connections
design firm
Octavo Designs
designers
Mark Burrier, Sue Hough

client
Horizon Group Properties
design firm
Kiku Obata + Company
designer
Jim Redington

client
AgroPure
design firm
Rule 29
designers
Justin Ahrens, Kerri Liu

client
Dobbes Family Estate
design firm
Defteling Design
designer
Alex Wijnen

client
Schering-Plough Healthcare
design firm
Anthem Worldwide
designer
Walter Perlowski

client
Herrington Investment Solutions
design firm
Think Tank Designs
designers
Heath C. Meyette, Robin Lindblom

client
The Brave Heart Foundation
design firm
Outta My Mind Visual Communications
designer
Daniel Knol

client
Wedding Attendant
design firm
Marcantel LeBlanc Brand Partnership
designers
Richard LeBlanc, Tom Marcantel

client
NoBox Design
design firm
Jeff Fisher LogoMotives
creative director
Beverly Wells
designer
Jeff Fisher

client
Group Investment
design firm
Graphic Advance, Inc.
designer
Aviad Stark

client
Verve Marketing and Design
design firm
Verve Marketing and Design
principal, creative director
Diane Lemonides
designer
Nancy Nguyen

client
Women's Initiative Network
design firm
Indiblu
art director
Kimber Flynn

client
PrintPerfect
design firm
HrupekDesign
designer
Michael Hrupek

client
Room for Fun
design firm
aijalon
designer
Lance Ford

client
Sharp Advantage
design firm
Never Boring Design Associates
designer
Julie Orona

client
Hit Woman Productions
design firm
A3 Design
designers
Alan Altman, Amanda Altman

client
Toù Bagaille
design firm
Fresh Oil
designer
Dan Stebbings

client
Tosti Rosta
design firm
Axion Design Inc.

client
Hearts Bluff Music
design firm
Lewis—Nashville
designer
Clark Hook

client
Symposium on Stock Enhancement & Sea Ranching
design firm
Walsh Design
designer
Miriam Lisco

client
Fresno Dental Surgery Center
design firm
Never Boring Design Associates
designer
Julie Orona

client
Equus
design firm
Brand, ltd.
designers
Virginia Martino, Mark V. Martino

client
Professional Home Services
design firm
Ecra Creative
designer
Daniele Lanza

client
Providence Medford Medical Center
design firm
Kinesis
designer
Mark Mularz

client
Elizabeth Seton Pediatic Center
design firm
Interbrand
creative director
Carlos Sanchez
designers
Carlyn Schlechter, Beca Lee

client
Island Paradise Foods
design firm
Aquea Design
designers
Raymond Perez, Charon McFarland

client
Busy Bee Tailoring
design firm
Sayles Graphic Design
designer
John Sayles

DATASTRAIT™
Networks

client
DataStrait Networks
design firm
Ecra Creative
designers
Joseph Rodenwald,
Daniele Lanza, Jason Voiovich

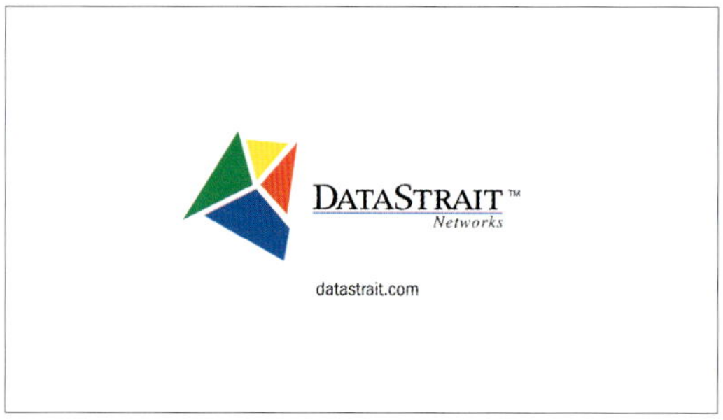

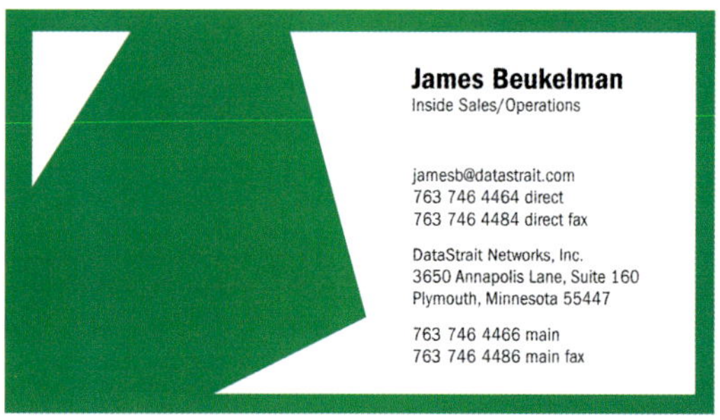

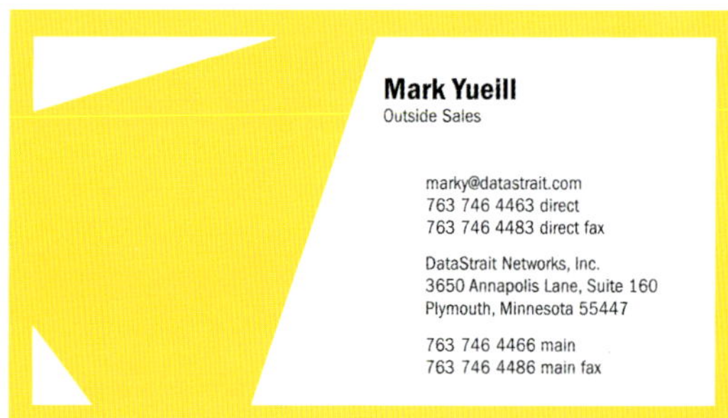

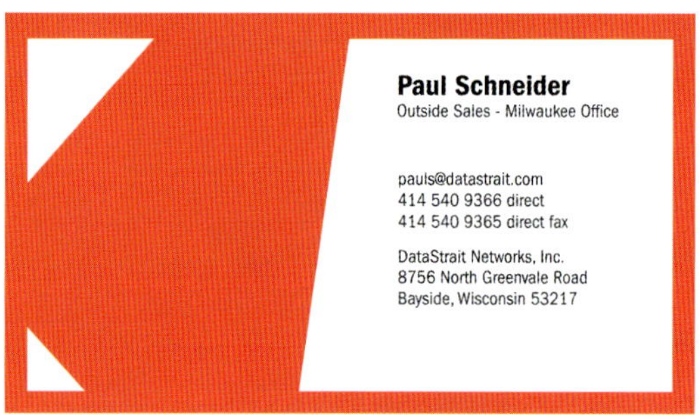

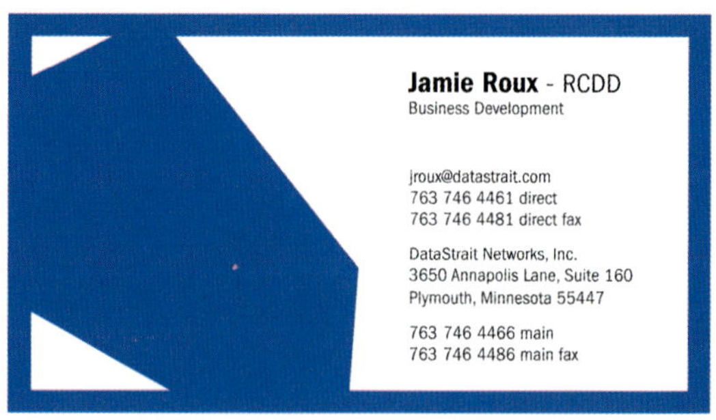

client
Fiducoldex-Proexport
design firm
VMA, Inc.
creative director
Doug Knopp
account manager
Steve Goubeaux
project manager
Kenneth Botts
graphic designer
Amritha Ward

Colombia®
is passion!

client
Kwik' Pak Fisheries
design firm
Walsh Design
designers
Miriam Lisco, Brian Erhart
illustrator
Jim Hays

KWIK'PAK
FISHERIES

client
ServiceMacs LLC
design firm
Tom Fowler, Inc.
designer
Elizabeth P. Ball

Service Macs LLC
Corporate Macintosh Solutions

client
Takoma Academy
design firm
Dever Designs
designer
Jeffrey Dever

Mime Music & Ministry
TA JAMAICA TOUR
2006

client
USA Arts of Minnesota
design firm
William Homan Design
designer
William Homan

ADA
15
YEARS STRONG
THEN, NOW &
BEYOND

client
InGEAR Corporation
design firm
InGEAR In-House Design Department
senior designer
Derek Crenshaw
product manager
Angela Jagla

client
Museum of the American Piano
design firm
Susan Meshberg Graphic Design
designer
Susan Meshberg
illustrator
Michele Kane

client
Frederick Festival of the Arts
design firm
Octavo Designs
designers
Sue Hough, Mark Burrier

client
American Merchant Services
design firm
Pernsteiner Creative Group, Inc.
designer
Todd Pernsteiner

client
KMart Corporation
design firm
InGEAR In-House Design Department
senior designer
Jeremy Swanson
designer
Brian Nillson
product manager
Heather Tvrdik

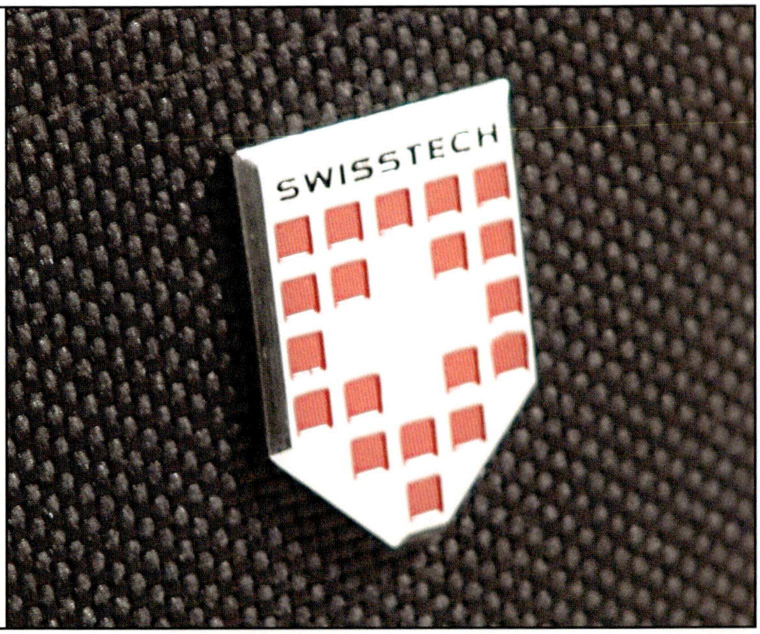

client
First Washington Mortgage
design firm
Group T Design
designer
Tom Klinedinst

client
Enviro-Air Solutions
design firm
Fifth Letter
designer
Elliot Strunk

client
Aviation Heritage Foundation
design firm
VMA, Inc.
creative director
Doug Knopp
account manager
Steve Goubeaux
project manager
Kenneth Botts
graphic designer
Amritha Ward

client
Brian Lake
design firm
CDI Studios
designer
Dan McElhattan III

client
BMI
design firm
Cintara
designer
Christopher Canote

client
Byrne Software Technologies, Inc.
design firm
Bright Rain Creative
designer
Matt Marino

client
Meeting Street
design firm
Im-aj Communications & Design, Inc.
designers
Jami Ouellette,
Lee Kosa, Katie Wetherby

Meeting Street
believing in the possibilities

client
Aromafloria
design firm
Liska + Associates
designer
Fernando Munoz

sensoryfusion

client
Zenprise, Inc.
design firm
Connie Hwang Design
designer
Connie Hwang

zenprise

client
MMG Worldwide
design firm
McMillian Design
designer
William McMillian

SPA
MINÉRALE

client
Legal Momentum
design firm
Interbrand
creative director
Carlos Sanchez
designers
Carlyn Schlechter, Beca Lee

LEGAL
momentum

client
Amber Products Co.
design firm
Reinnov8 Design Group
designers
Richard A. Hooper, Ken Nadeau

美 TAIO
THE BALANCE OF LIFE

client
The Inn at St. Johns
design firm
Catalyst Design, Inc.

client
Pro-Health
design firm
Duncan/Day Advertising
designer
Leigh Finney

client
Emtek Products, Inc.
design firm
Mayhem Studios
designer
Calvin Lee

client
Lithia Women's Care
design firm
Kinesis
designers
Sabrah Maple, Michelle Cheney

client
Lifestage Health
design firm
Crowley Webb and Assoc.
designer
Brian Grunert

client
Kelly Galloup
design firm
William Homan Design
designer
William Homan

client
Terry Barnhart Associates
design firm
Never Boring Design Associates
designer
Julie Orona

client
Play 54, LLC
design firm
Bright Rain Creative
designer
Matt Marino

client
Lee Sucharda, Jr.
design firm
Design North
designers
Gwen Granzow, Kristin Bochenek

client
Big Ear Advertising
design firm
aijalon
designer
Lance Ford

client
Rich Cleaners
design firm
Seran Design
designer
Sang Yoon

client
Triton Technical
design firm
Eben Design
designer
Matthew Grimes

client
Plaintiff Support Services
design firm
Crowley Webb and Assoc.
designers
David Buck, Kelly Gambino

client
Minnesota State University Moorhead
design firm
Allen Sheets Graphic Design
designer
Allen Sheets

client
Corporate Allocation Services
design firm
Lightspeed Commercial Arts
designer
Michael J. Hamers

client
Marcy Sagel + Associates
design firm
Round 2 Communications
designer
Zachary Nichols

client
Statesboro Arts Council
design firm
ARRDesign
designers
Angela Ryczkowski

client
CCM
design firm
Stephen Longo Design Assoc
designer
Stephen Longo

client
Braddy Investigative Group
design firm
Sire Advertising
designers
Shawn Felty & Jordan Chappell

client
Beztak Properties
design firm
Group 55 Marketing
designer
Jeannette Gutierrez

client
Helping Hands of Vegas Valley
design firm
Brand, ltd.
designers
Baub Mercurio,
Virginia Martino,
Mark V. Martino

client
Niagara Escarpment Resource Network
design firm
Foth & Van Dyke
designer
Daniel Green

client
Madhouse Cafe
design firm
Fresh Oil
designer
Nelson Couto

client
Mattamy Homes
design firm
A3 Design
designers
Alan Altman,
Amanda Altman

client
Cross Roads Church
design firm
Annagram Studio and Design
designer
Graham Allen

client
Lifespring Church
design firm
On Target Marketing
designer
Dusty Dahlgren

client
WeInterpret.net
design firm
Octavo Designs
designers
Mark Burrier, Sue Hough

client
Peabody College of Vanderbilt University
design firm
Ventress Design Group
designer
Tom Ventress

client
Wheelbarrow Creek Ranch
design firm
Catalyst Design, Inc.

client
Wise Kosher Natural Poultry, Inc.
design firm
Pure Design Co. LLC
designers
Dan Mishkind, Graeme Ritchie

client
Silverhook Coffee
design firm
IE Design + Communications
designer
Jane Kim

client
Sozo Healing Arts
design firm
Sire Advertising
designers
Shawn Felty, Bob Henninger

client
Splash, Ltd.
design firm
Kevin Hall Design
designer
Kevin Hall

client
Ser Humanos
design firm
Design Nut, LLC
designer
Brent Almond

client
Big Sky Development
design firm
Aquea Design
designers
Raymond Perez,
Kelly M. Enquist

client
Doc's Ski Haus
design firm
Annagram Studio and Design
designer
Graham Allen

client
Los Banos Redevelopment Agency
design firm
On Target Marketing
designer
Juan Medina

client
Manatí Medical Center
design firm
ID Group
designers
Jorge Colón,
Abner Gutiérrez

client
The Cataract Specialists
design firm
Randi Wolf Design
designer
Randi Wolf

client
Urban Visions
design firm
Hornall Anderson Design Works
designers
John Anicker,
Andrew Wicklund, Sonja Max

client
Edna Valley Market
design firm
Pierre Rademaker Design
designers
Pierre Rademaker, Debbie Shibata

client
SunTrust Bank
design firm
Siegel & Gale
creative director
Howard Belk
design director
Justin Peters
designer, illustrator
Bob Schroeder

client
Kings-Men Construction
design firm
Eben Design
designer
Matthew Grimes

client
Brent Lenthall
design firm
Lewis—Nashville
designer
Clark Hook

client
Timber Valley
design firm
Sayles Graphic Design
designer
John Sayles

client
Larson's Heavy Duty Skin Care
design firm
Think Tank Designs
designers
Heath C. Meyette, Robin Lindblom

client
The Timberworks Studio
design firm
Inklings Design + Associates
designers
J. Gruber, Stephen Smith

client
Cornerstone Productions
design firm
Fresh Oil
designer
Dan Stebbings

client
Woodmill Furniture Co.
design firm
On Target Marketing
designers
Dusty Dahlgren, Jesse Bloodworth

client
Foth & Van Dyke
design firm
Foth & Van Dyke
designer
Daniel Green

client
SMS Builders, Inc.
design firm
Chris Gorney Design
designer
Chris Gorney

client
Advance Auto
design firm
Daymon Worldwide Design
designers
Kyle Piper, Gig Wailgum

client
Davitt Design Build
design firm
Im-aj Communications & Design, Inc.
designers
Jami Ouellette, Leslie Emert

DAVITT
DESIGN BUILD

Crafted in every detail
DAVITT
DESIGN BUILD

client
The Inn at St. John's
design firm
Catalyst Design, Inc.

The Inn at St. John's
GOLF | RECEPTIONS | CONFERENCES

client
Albany Law School
design firm
GCF
designers
Domenica Genovese, Maureen Weiss

ALBANY LAW SCHOOL

client
Northern Illinois University
design firm
Andrew Byrom
designer
Andrew Byrom

Jack
olson
Gallery

client
Arc en Ciel Immobilier, Inc.
design firm
Da Capo Design Company
designers
Chris LaValle, Lena C. Pleick

Arc en Ciel
IMMOBILIER

client
Pinnacle Performance Institute
design firm
Marcantel LeBlanc Brand Partnership
designer
Richard LeBlanc

client
Franklin Road Academy
design firm
Ventress Design Group
designer
Tom Ventress

client
Emmanuel Baptist Church
design firm
aijalon
designer
Lance Ford

client
Bella Terra Developers & Homebuilders
design firm
Ecra Creative
designers
Daniele Lanza, Jason Voiovich

client
Pittsburgh Legal Administrators Association
design firm
Erisa Creative, LLC
designers
Erin May, Lisa Liptak

client
French Quarter Café
design firm
ARRDesign
designer
Angela Ryczkowski

client
Top 2 Bottom Professional Cleaning
design firm
Octavo Designs
designers
Sue Hough, Jack Sanger

client
National Development
design firm
Doerr Associates
designer
Joan Wilking

client
Lydia Gardner—Clerk of the Circuit and County Courts, Orange County, Florida
design firm
Jowaisas Design
designer
Elizabeth Jowaisas

client
Dry Cleaners Home Delivery
design firm
Ted DeCagna Graphic Design
designer
Ted DeCagna

client
BPM Financial Advisors
design firm
Ventress Design Group
designer
Tom Ventress

client
Art Lumiére
design firm
Pensaré Design Group
art director
Mary Ellen Vehlow
designer
Amy E. Billingham

client
Window Rock Enterprises
design firm
Hubbell Design Works
designer
Leighton Hubbell

client
National Equity Fund
design firm
Namaro Graphic Designs, Inc.
designers
Nadine Robbins, Wendy Macomber

client
Christian Heritage Children's Homes
design firm
aijalon
designer
Lance Ford

client
Oakland—A Communications Partner
design firm
Catalyst Design, Inc.

client
Mattamy Homes
design firm
A3 Design
designers
Alan Altman, Amanda Altman

client
zoomco
design firm
ZGraphics, Ltd.
designers
Andy Matznick, Joe Zeller

client
Southeast Student Film Festival
design firm
Mayhem Studios
designer
Calvin Lee

client
West Orange Arts Council
design firm
Stephen Longo Design Assoc.
designer
Stephen Longo

client
Keepman Roberts Productions
design firm
Keyword Design
designer
Judith Mayer

client
Art in Action
design firm
BrandSavvy Inc.
designer
Karl Peters

client
National Steinbeck Center
design firm
The Wecker Group
designer
Robert Wecker

client
Indiblu Design—Kimber Flynn
design firm
Indiblu Design
art director
Kimber Flynn

client
Brass Pacifica
design firm
Hubbell Design Works
designer
Leighton Hubbell

BRASS PACIFICA

client
Twisted Elegance Interactive
design firm
Jeff Fisher LogoMotives
creative director
Jason Holland
designer
Jeff Fisher

Twisted Elegance INTERACTIVE

client
Maverick Mosaics
design firm
Crabtree + Company
designers
Susan Angrisani,
Nisha Nail

MAVERICK MOSAICS

MAVERICK MOSAICS

Bonnie Fitzgerald
3401 Hickory Hills Drive
Oakton, VA 22124
Phone: 703.716.4890
www.maverickmosaics.com

client
Stora Enso North America
design firm
Gee + Chung Design
designer
Earl Gee

DESIGNER'S LUNCHEON

client
Orlando Chapter of the
Florida Public Relations Association
design firm
Jowaisas Design
designer
Elizabeth Jowaisas

the Art of PR
2005 IMAGE AWARDS

client
BestNotes.com
design firm
HardBall Creative
designers
Andy Gosendi, Michael O'Connell

client
The Converse Home
design firm
Paul Kaza Associates
designer
Donda Thibault

client
Round Peg Group
design firm
Crabtree + Company
designers
Susan Angrisani, Elena López

client
Sunoco Welcome America!
design firm
Munroe Creative Partners
designer
Mike Cavallaro

client
big BOING Toys
design firm
Axion Design Inc.

Student Work

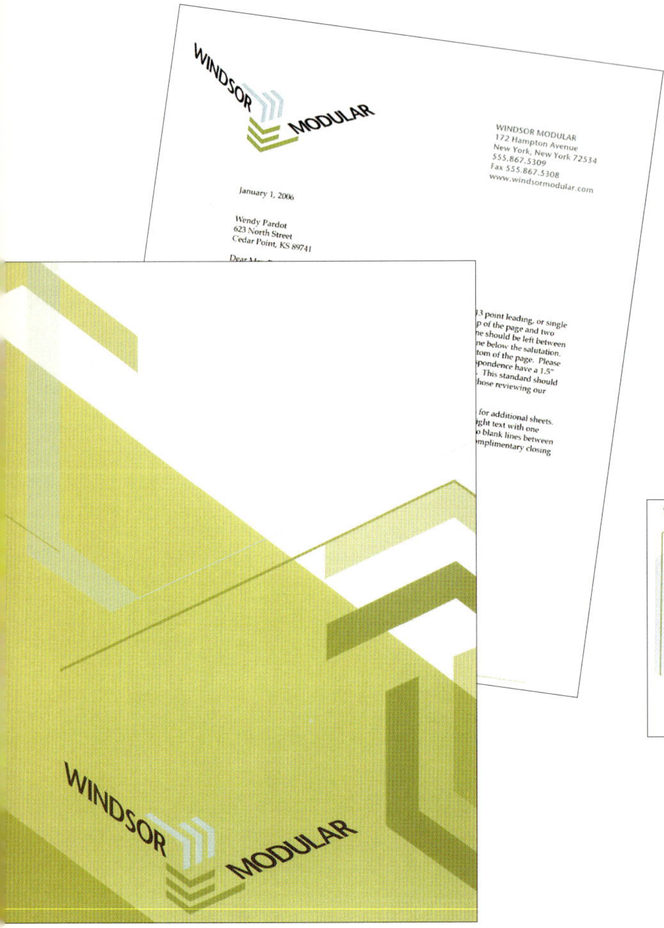

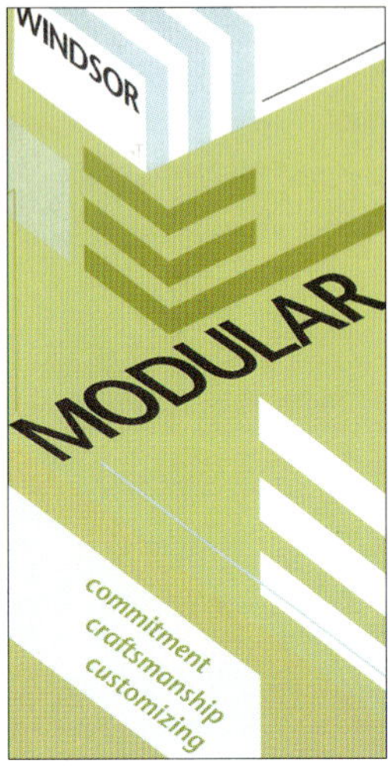

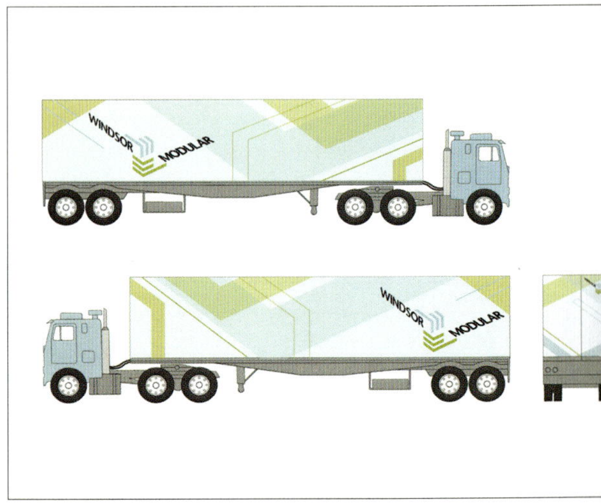

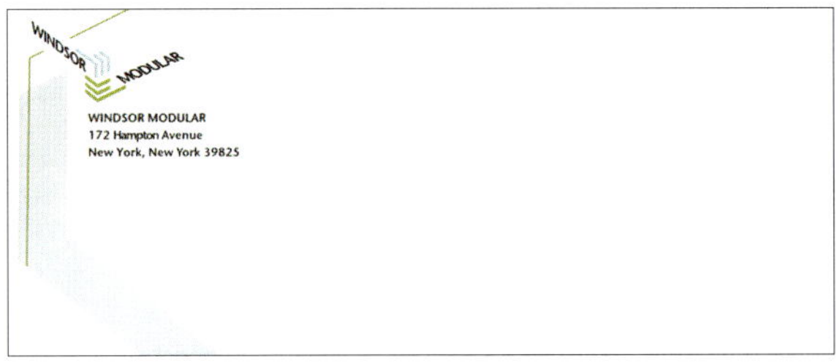

project
Windsor Modular
Complete Corporate Identity System
school
Iowa State University
designers
Brittni Heisterkamp,
Andrea Butson, Jessica Hibbs

project
Red Rock Station
Package Design
school
Susquehanna University
designer
Ann-Marie Reynolds

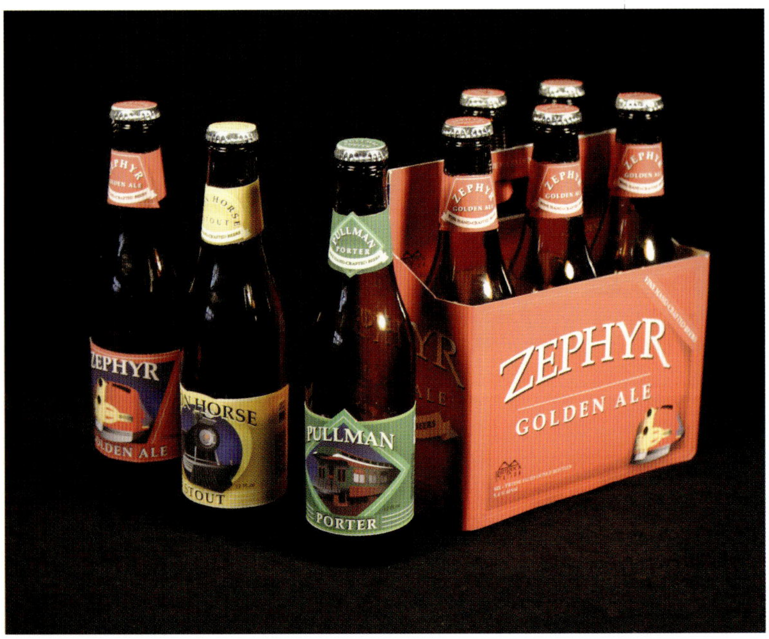

project
Jack's Guitars
Stationery Design
school
Susquehanna University
designer
Taylor Buckholz

project
Yee Haw Records
Trademark/Logo Design
school
Susquehanna University
designer
Taylor Buckholz

project
The Cigar Bar
Trademark/Logo Design
school
Susquehanna University
designer
Taylor Buckholz

project
Floyd's Full Service Station
Stationery Design
school
Texas Christian University
designer
Charlie Howlett

project
Smoky Mountain Chip Co.
Package Design
school
Susquehanna University
designer
Amanda Lenig

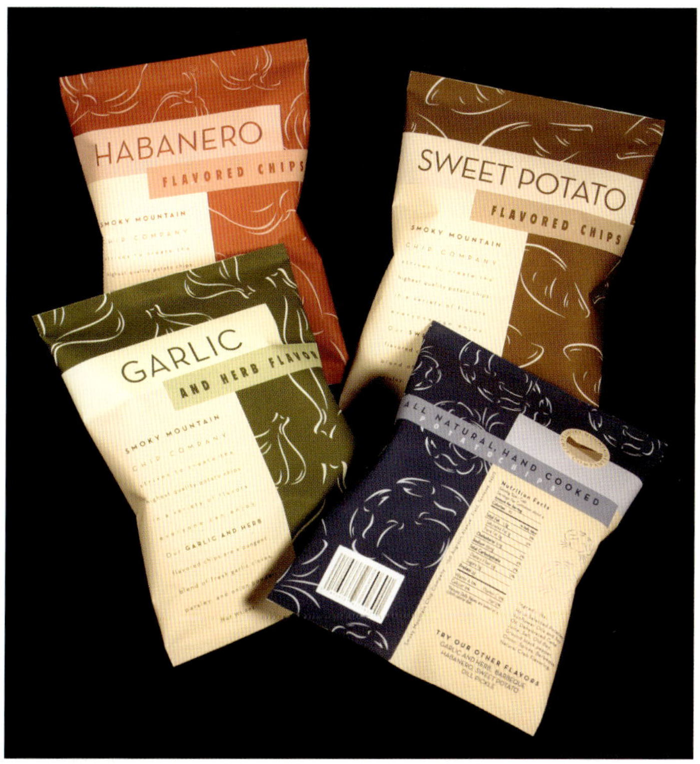

project
Coyote Grill
Trademark/Logo Design
school
Susquehanna University
designer
Katie Lesser

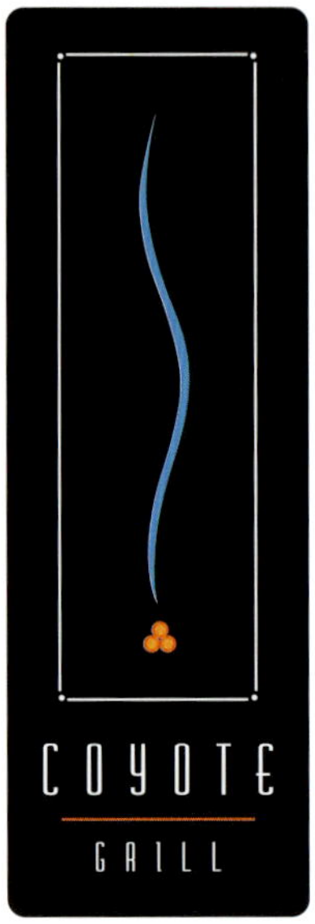

project
Paper Clip Communications
Trademark/Logo Design
school
Susquehanna University
designer
Taylor Buckholz

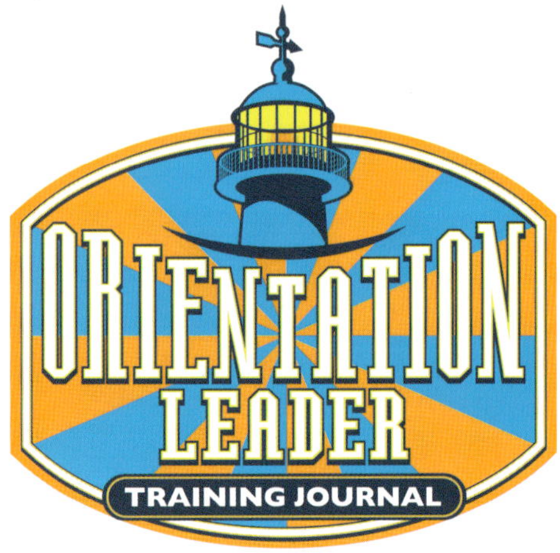

project
ProLine Pools
Stationery Design
school
Monmouth University
designer
Donald Campan, Jr.

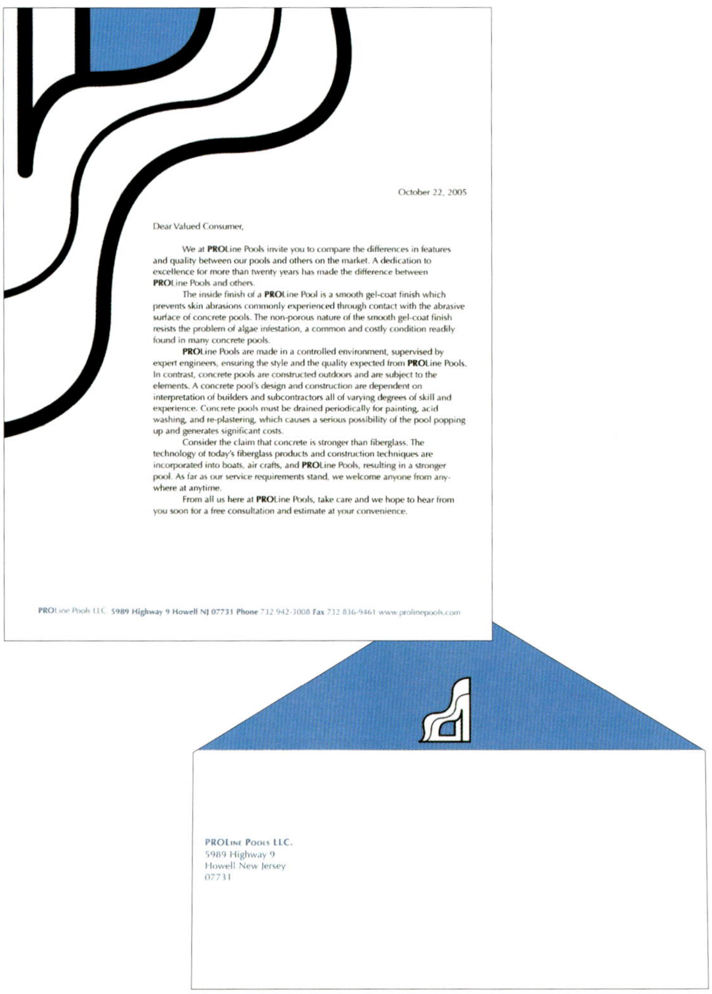

October 22, 2005

Dear Valued Consumer,

We at **PRO**Line Pools invite you to compare the differences in features and quality between our pools and others on the market. A dedication to excellence for more than twenty years has made the difference between **PRO**Line Pools and others.

The inside finish of a **PRO**Line Pool is a smooth gel-coat finish which prevents skin abrasions commonly experienced through contact with the abrasive surface of concrete pools. The non-porous nature of the smooth gel-coat finish resists the problem of algae infestation, a common and costly condition readily found in many concrete pools.

PROLine Pools are made in a controlled environment, supervised by expert engineers, ensuring the style and the quality expected from **PRO**Line Pools. In contrast, concrete pools are constructed outdoors and are subject to the elements. A concrete pool's design and construction are dependent on interpretation of builders and subcontractors all of varying degrees of skill and experience. Concrete pools must be drained periodically for painting, acid washing, and re-plastering, which causes a serious possibility of the pool popping up and generates significant costs.

Consider the claim that concrete is stronger than fiberglass. The technology of today's fiberglass products and construction techniques are incorporated into boats, air crafts, and **PRO**Line Pools, resulting in a stronger pool. As far as our service requirements stand, we welcome anyone from anywhere at anytime.

From all us here at **PRO**Line Pools, take care and we hope to hear from you soon for a free consultation and estimate at your convenience.

PROLine Pools LLC **5989 Highway 9 Howell NJ 07731 Phone** 732 942-3008 **Fax** 732 836-9461 www.prolinepools.com

project
Tahoe
Complete Corporate
IdentitySystems
school
Fresno State University
designer
Chris Jones

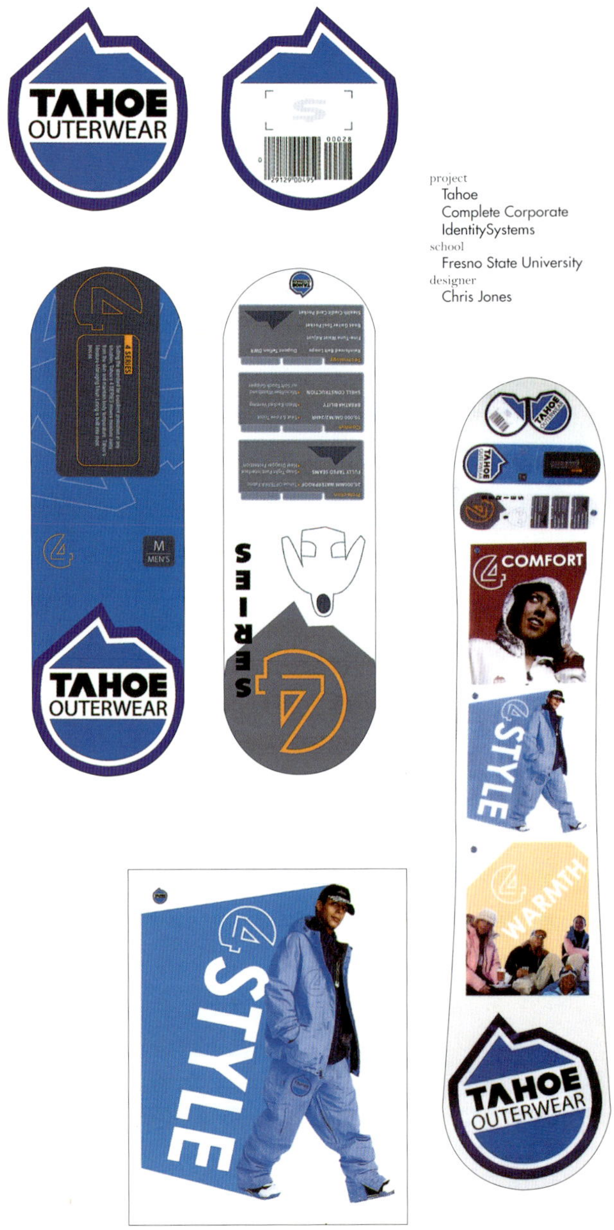

project
Changes Salon and Spa
Trademark/Logo Design
school
James Madison University
designer
Robin Smith

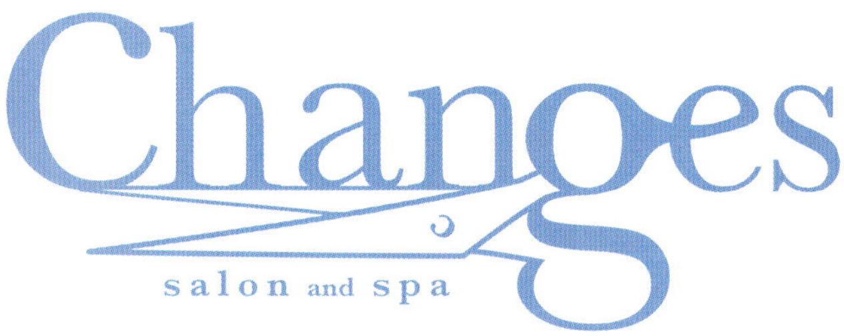

project
ProLine Pools
Trademark/Logo Design
school
Monmouth University
designer
Donald Campan, Jr.

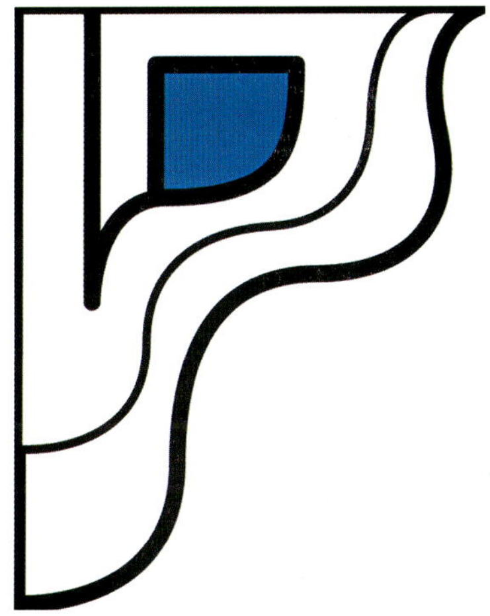

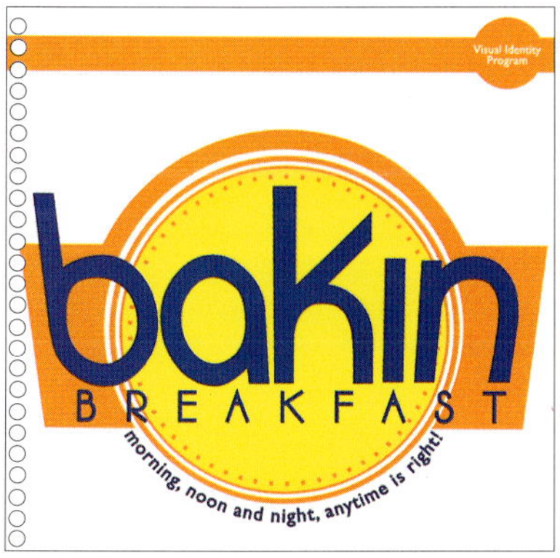

project
Bakin Breakfast
Corporate Identity Manuals
school
Iowa State University
designer
Jessica O'Brien

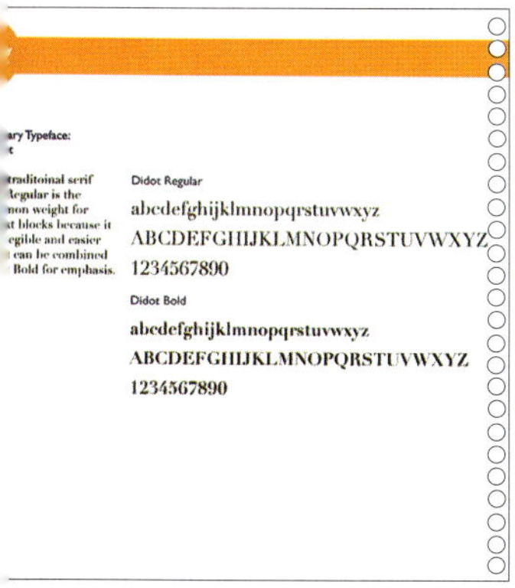

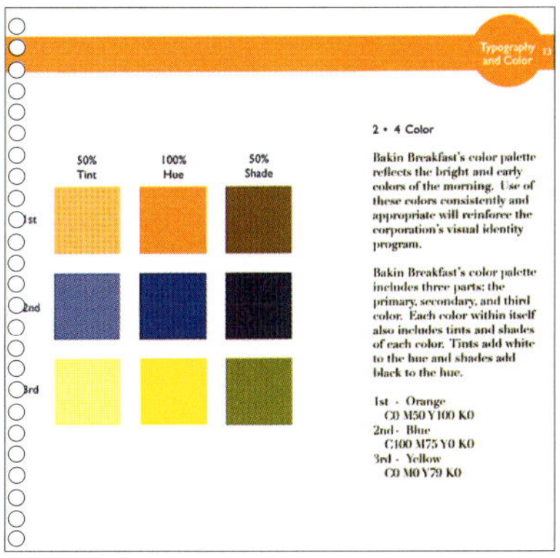

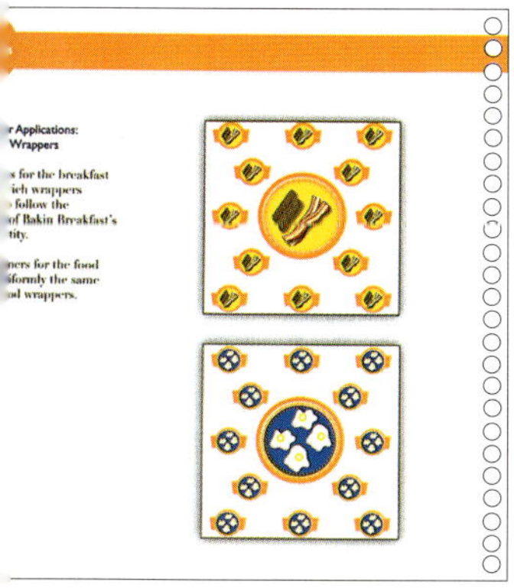

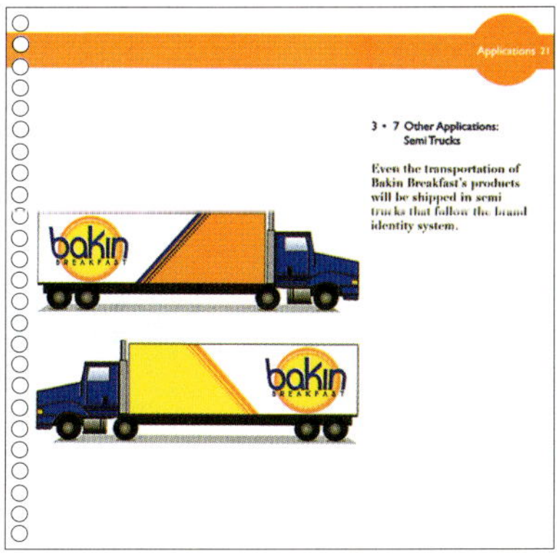

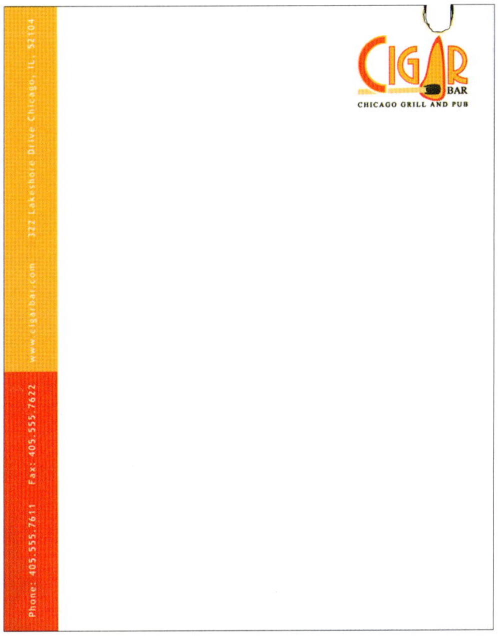

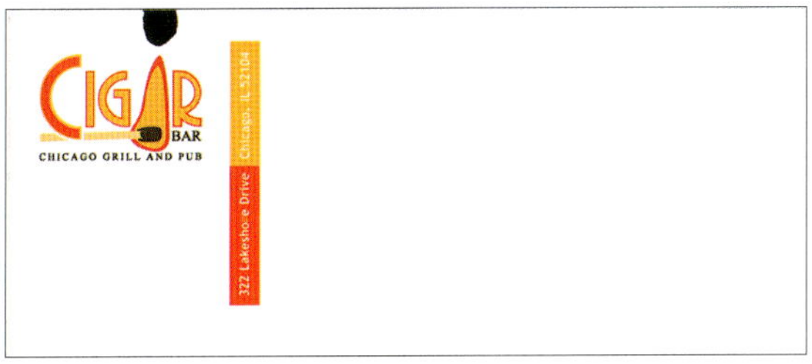

project
The Cigar Bar
Stationery Design
school
Susquehanna University
designer
Nick Stephenson

project
Black World Foundation
Trademark/Logo Design
school
Illinois State University
designer
Candice Waits

project
Julie Novak
Trademark/Logo Design
school
Towson University
designer
Julie Novak

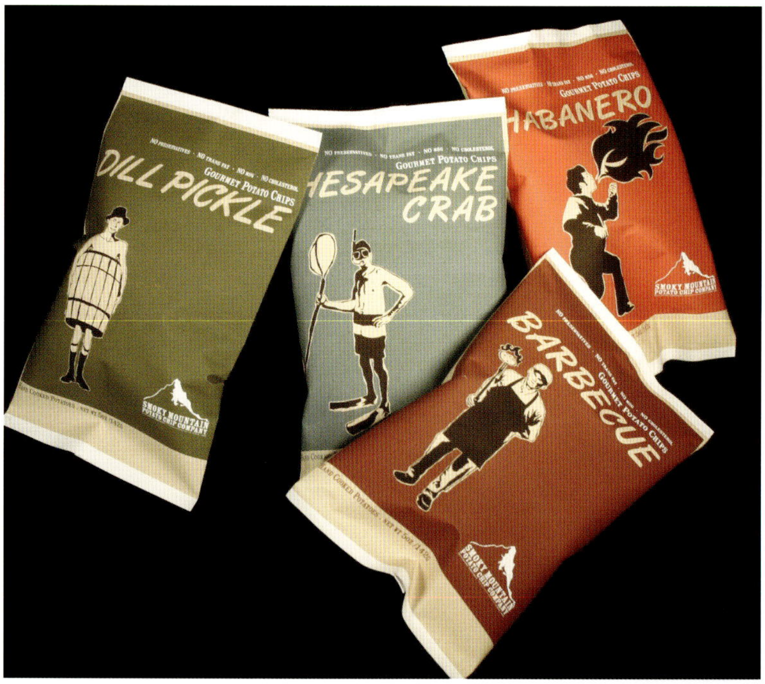

project
Smoky Mountain Chip Co.
Package Design
school
Susquehanna University
designer
Nick Stephenson

project
County College of Morris
Corporate Image Brochures
school
County College of Morris
designers
German Salazar,
Stephen Longo

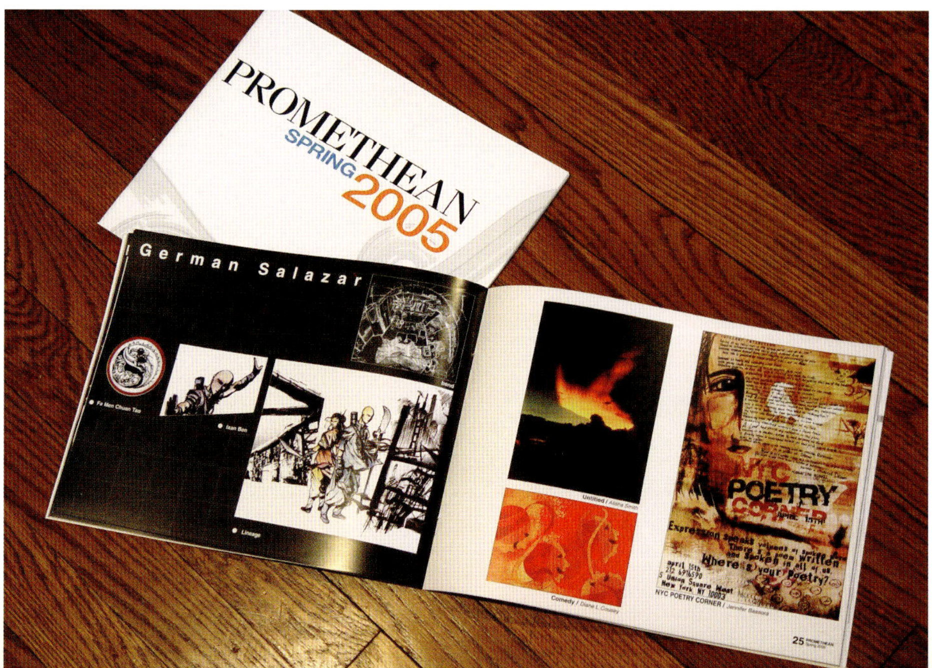

project
Kimberly Sotelo/Yoga Ananda
Trademark/Logo Design
school
Auburn University
designer
John Feldhouse

yoga ananda

project
Boogie Buds Inc.
Trademark/Logo Design
school
Iowa State University
designer
Brittni Heisterkamp

Boogie Buds

project
Office Angels
Stationery Design
school
Susquehanna University
designer
Amanda Lenig

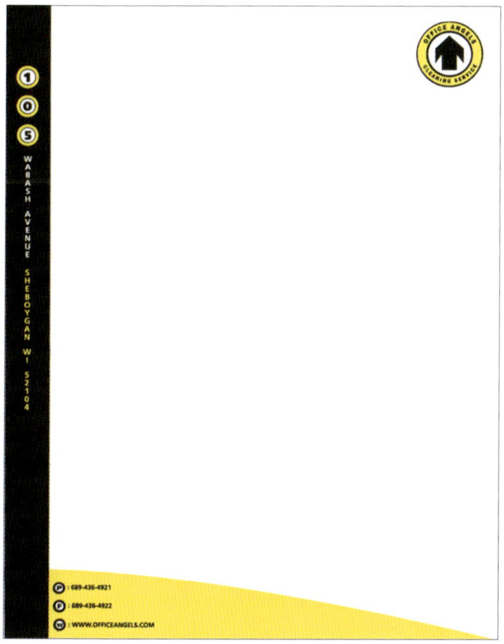

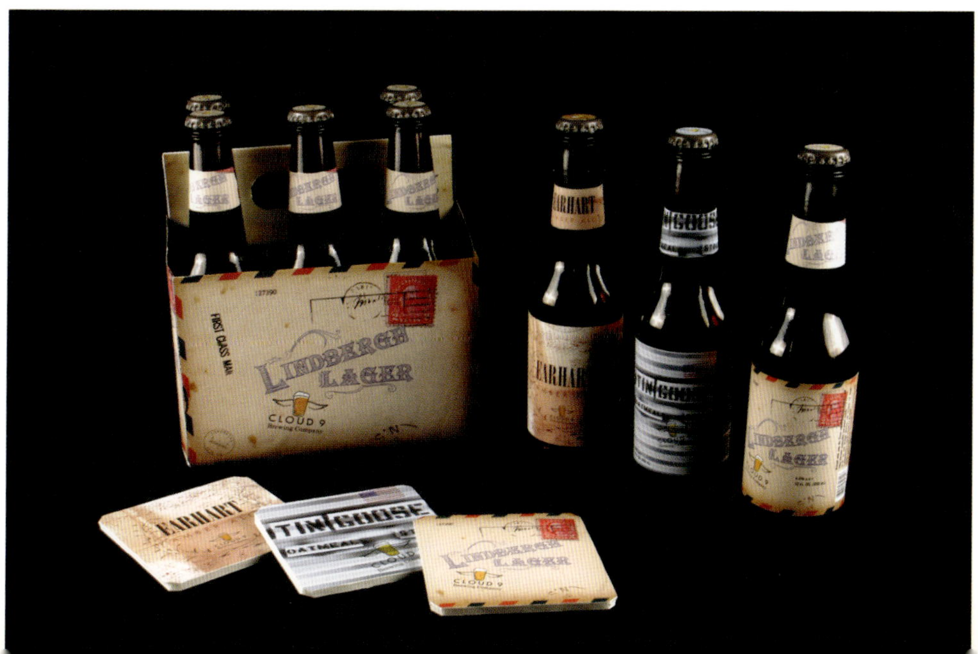

project
Cloud Nine Brewing Co.
Package Design
school
Susquehanna University
designer
Nick Stephenson

project
Roadrage Cafe
Trademark/Logo Design
school
Iowa State University
designer
Kelly Leaman

project
58 Dollar Productions
Trademark/Logo Design
school
Texas Christian University
designer
Nathan Sharp

project
PA Drug Free
Signage/Environmental Graphics
school
Harrisburg Area Community College
designer
Krzysztof Piatkowski

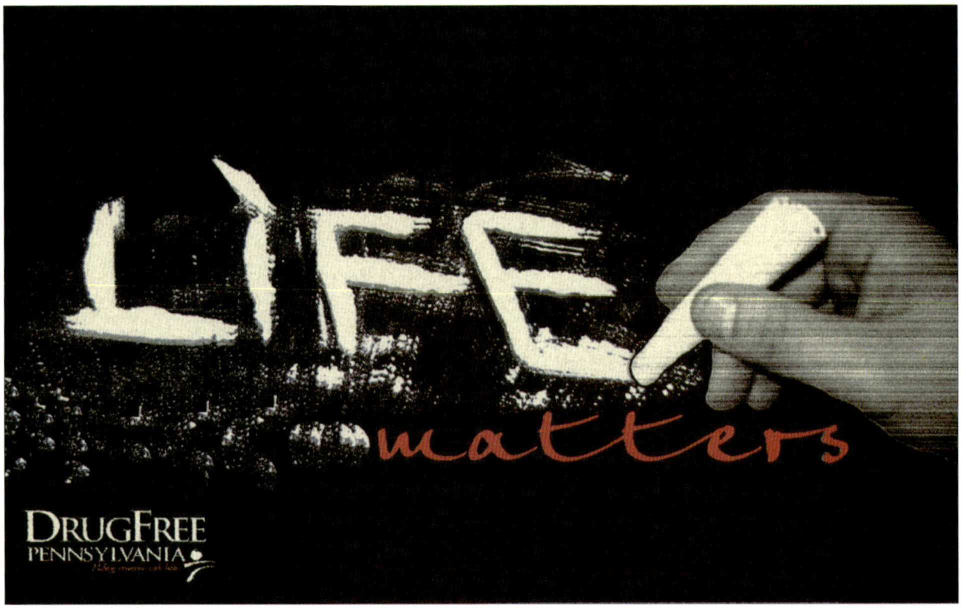

project
Red Rock Station
Package Design
school
Susquehanna University
designer
Cassandra Smolcic

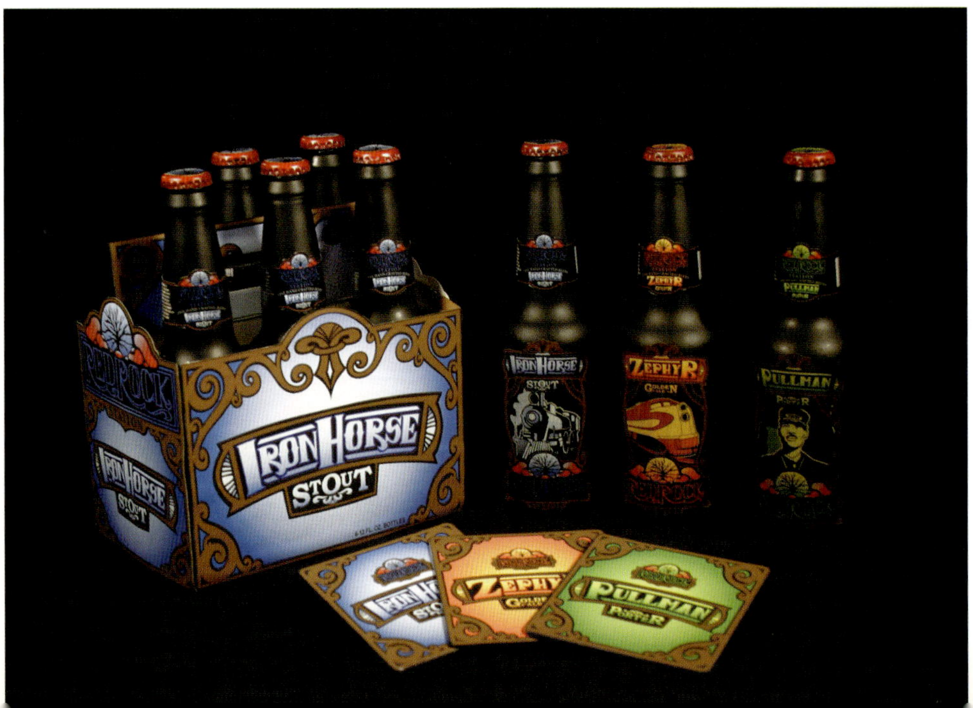

project
Tender Toes
Trademark/Logo Design
school
Iowa State University
designer
Jessica O'Brien

project
Bakin Breakfast
Complete Corporate Identity Programs
school
Iowa State University
designers
Jessica O'Brien,
Danielle Cain,
Mandy Oscarson

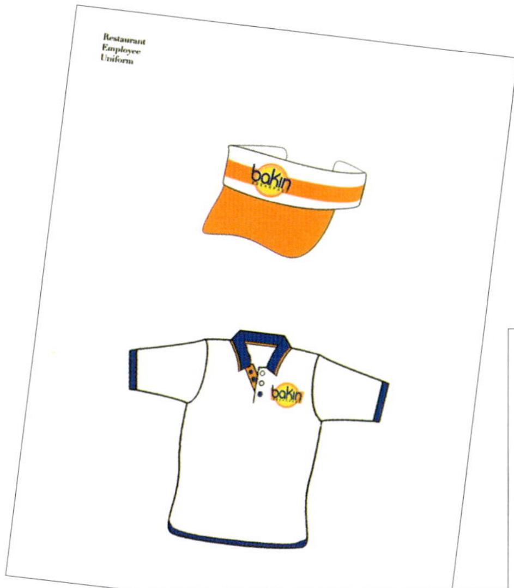

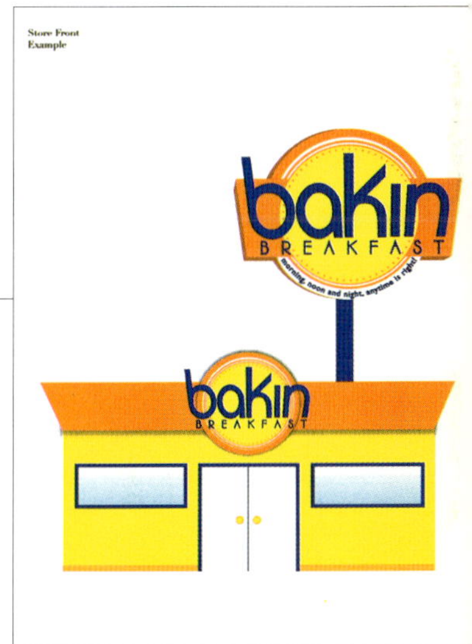

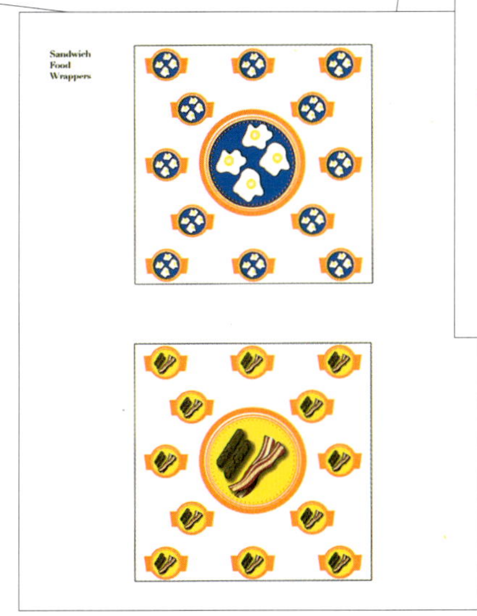

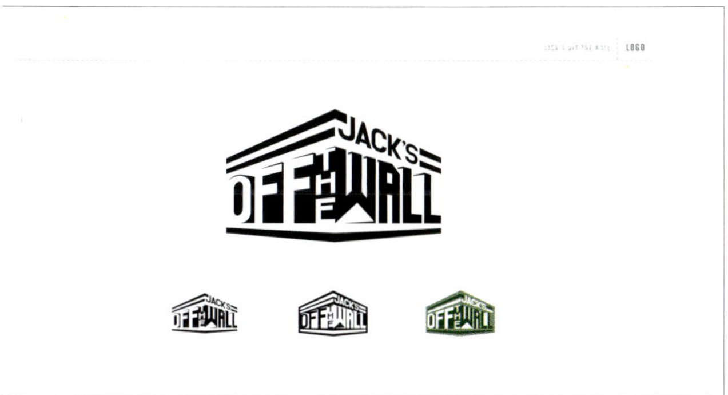

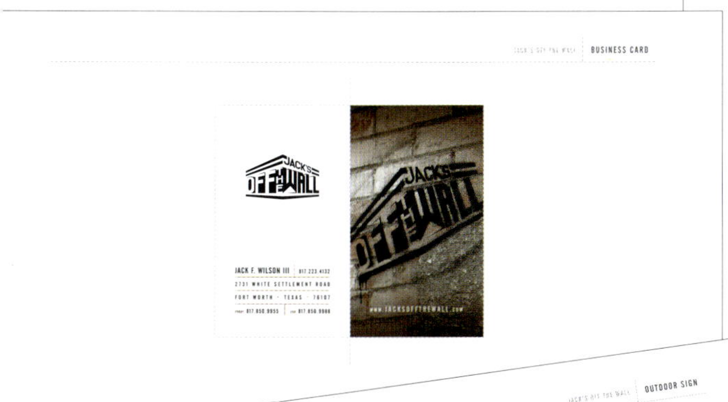

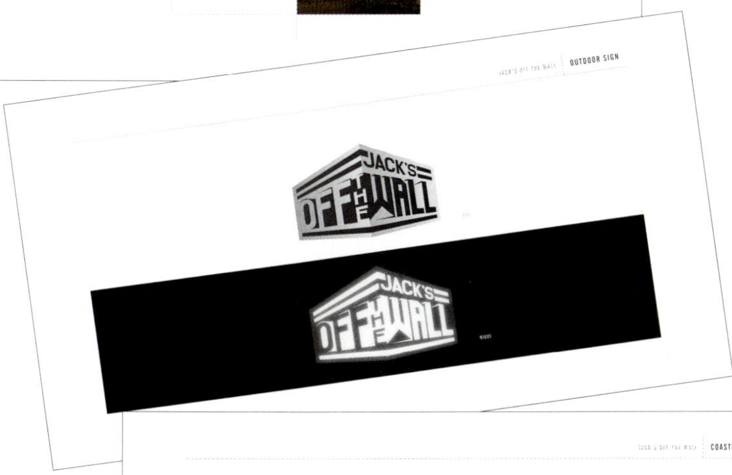

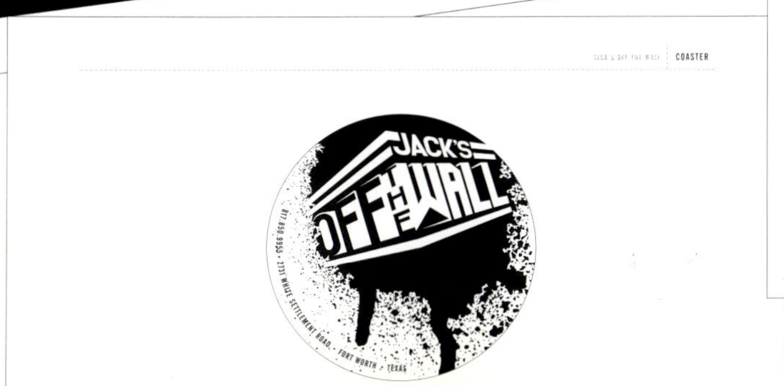

project
Jack's Off the Wall, Bar & Grill
Complete Corporate Identity Programs
school
Texas Christian University
designer
Charlie Howlett

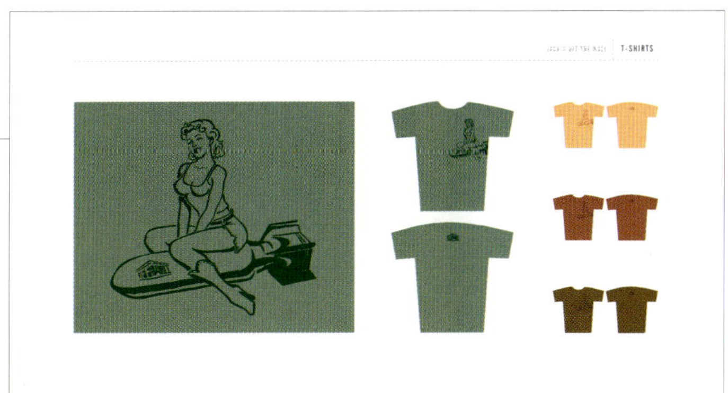

project
Jack's Off the Wall, Bar & Grill
Trademark/Logo Design
school
Texas Christian University
designer
Charlie Howlett

project
Cortech Architecture
Trademark/Logo Design
school
James Madison University
designer
Katherine Bundy

project
Time Pieces Inc.
Stationery Design
school
Monmouth University
designer
Danny Machado

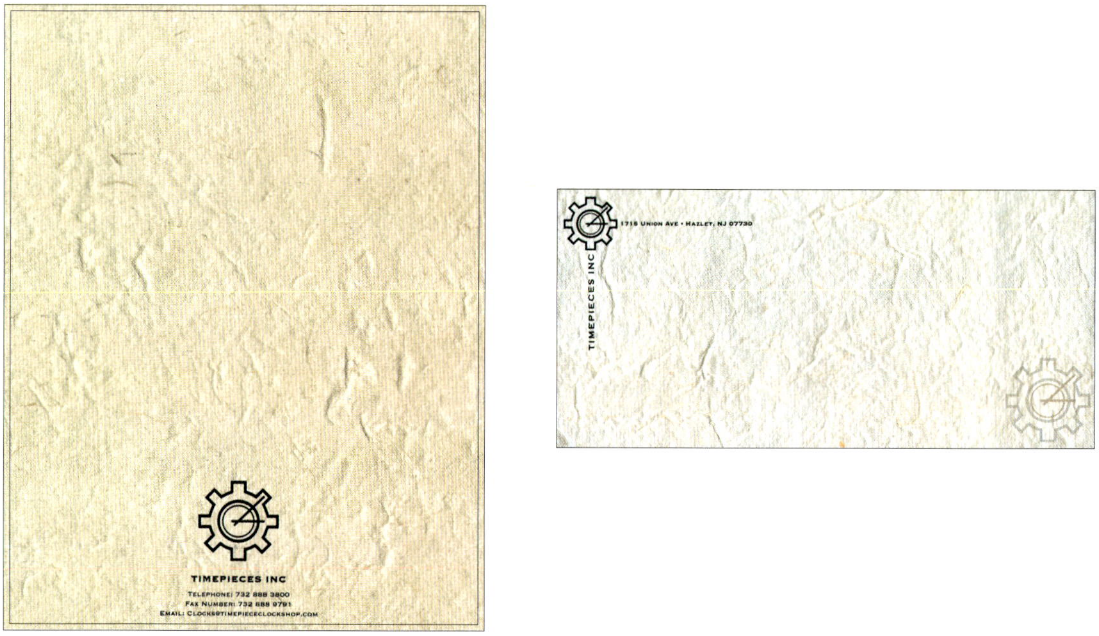

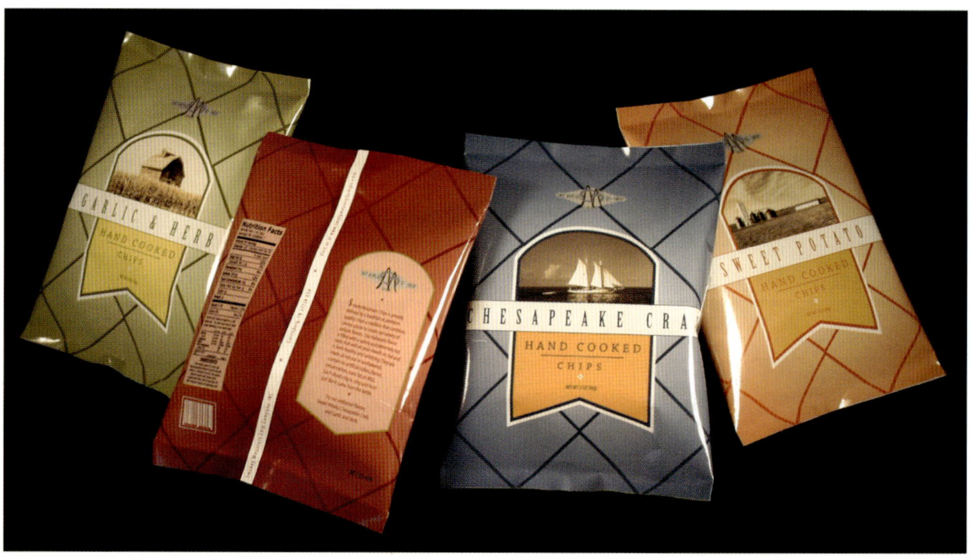

project
Smoky Mountain Chip Co.
Package Design
school
Susquehanna University
designer
Katie Lesser

Index